Lecture Notes in Computer Science 14672

FoLLI Publications on Logic, Language and Information

Subline of Lecture Notes in Computer Science

More information about this series at https://link.springer.com/bookseries/558

George Metcalfe · Thomas Studer ·
Ruy de Queiroz
Editors

Logic, Language, Information, and Computation

30th International Workshop, WoLLIC 2024
Bern, Switzerland, June 10–13, 2024
Proceedings

Springer

Editors
George Metcalfe
University of Bern
Bern, Switzerland

Thomas Studer
University of Bern
Bern, Switzerland

Ruy de Queiroz
Federal University of Pernambuco
Recife, Brazil

ISSN 0302-9743 ISSN 1611-3349 (electronic)
Lecture Notes in Computer Science
ISBN 978-3-031-62686-9 ISBN 978-3-031-62687-6 (eBook)
https://doi.org/10.1007/978-3-031-62687-6

This Springer imprint is published by the registered company Springer Nature Switzerland AG
The registered company address is: Gewerbestrasse 11, 6330 Cham, Switzerland

Preface

This volume contains the papers presented at the 30th Workshop on Logic, Language, Information and Computation (WoLLIC 2024) held June 10–13, 2024 at the Mathematical Institute and Institute of Computer Science, University of Bern, Switzerland. The WoLLIC series of workshops started in 1994 with the aim of fostering interdisciplinary research in pure and applied logic. The idea is to have a forum which is large enough in the number of possible interactions between logic and the sciences related to information and computation, and yet is small enough to allow for concrete and useful interaction among participants.

For WoLLIC 2024 there were 37 submissions. Each submission was single-blind reviewed by at least three program committee members or assigned subreviewers. The committee decided to accept 18 papers. This volume includes all the accepted papers, together with the abstracts of the invited speakers at WoLLIC 2024:

- Juan Aguilera (Vienna University of Technology)
- Maria Aloni (University of Amsterdam)
- Sam van Gool (Université Paris Cité)
- Dexter Kozen (Cornell University)
- Francesca Zaffora Blando (Carnegie Mellon University)

We would like to thank all people who contributed to making WoLLIC 2024 a success. We thank all invited speakers and the authors for their excellent contributions. We thank the Program Committee and all additional reviewers for the work they put into reviewing the submissions.

We would also like to thank the Steering Committee and Advisory Committee for their advice, and the Local Organizing Committee, especially Bettina Choffat and Borja Sierra Miranda, for their very welcome support. The submission and reviewing process was facilitated by the EasyChair system by Andrei Voronkov.

We gratefully acknowledge financial support for WoLLIC 2024 from the Swiss National Science Foundation (SNSF), the MOSAIC project (MSCA-RISE-2020), and the University of Bern. We also acknowledge the scientific sponsorship of the following organizations: Association for Symbolic Logic (ASL), European Association for Computer Science Logic (EACSL), Brazilian Logic Society (SBL), Interest Group in Pure and Applied Logics (IGPL), Association for Logic, Language and Information (FoLLI), and the European Association for Theoretical Computer Science (EATCS).

June 2024

George Metcalfe
Thomas Studer
Ruy de Queiroz

Organization

Program Committee Chairs

George Metcalfe	University of Bern, Switzerland
Thomas Studer	University of Bern, Switzerland

General Chair

Ruy de Queiroz	Universidade Federal de Pernambuco, Brazil

Steering Committee

Samson Abramsky	University College London, UK
Agata Ciabattoni	Vienna University of Technology, Austria
Anuj Dawar	University of Cambridge, UK
Juliette Kennedy	University of Helsinki, Finland
Ulrich Kohlenbach	Technische Universität Darmstadt, Germany
Daniel Leivant	Indiana University Bloomington, USA
Leonid Libkin	University of Edinburgh, UK
Lawrence Moss	Indiana University Bloomington, USA
Luke Ong	Oxford University, UK
Valeria de Paiva	Topos Institute/PUC-Rio, USA/Brazil
Elaine Pimentel	University College London, UK
Ruy de Queiroz	Universidade Federal de Pernambuco, Brazil
Alexandra Silva	Cornell University, USA
Renata Wassermann	Universidade de São Paulo, Brazil

Advisory Committee

Johan van Benthem	University of Amsterdam, Netherlands and Stanford University, USA
Joe Halpern	Cornell University, USA
Wilfrid Hodges	Queen Mary University of London, UK
Angus Macintyre	Oxford University, UK
Hiroakira Ono	Japan Advanced Institute of Science and Technology, Japan
Jouko Väänänen	University of Helsinki, Finland

Program Committee

Guillermo Badia	University of Queensland, Australia
Thomas Bolander	Danish Technical University, Denmark

Célia Borlido	University of Coimbra, Portugal
Sabine Broda	University of Porto, Portugal
Zoé Christoff	University of Groningen, Netherlands
Willem Conradie	University of the Witwatersrand, South Africa
Anupam Das	University of Birmingham, UK
Jacques Duparc	University of Lausanne, Switzerland
Federico Faroldi	University of Pavia, Italy
Chris Fermüller	Vienna University of Technology, Austria
Mário Florido	University of Porto, Portugal
Sujata Ghosh	Indian Statistical Institute, India
Nina Gierasimczuk	Danish Technical University, Denmark
Marianna Girlando	University of Amsterdam, Netherlands
Makoto Kanazawa	Hosei University, Japan
Fenrong Liu	Tsinghua University, China
Hugo Luiz Mariano	University of São Paulo, Brazil
George Metcalfe (Co-chair)	University of Bern, Switzerland
Cláudia Nalon	University of Brasilia, Brazil
Carles Noguera	University of Siena, Italy
Magdalena Ortiz	University of Umeå, Sweden
Aybüke Özgün	University of Amsterdam, Netherlands
Dusko Pavlovic	University of Hawaii, USA
Sylvain Pogodalla	INRIA Nancy, France
Revantha Ramanayake	University of Groningen, Netherlands
Luca Reggio	University College London, UK
Mehrnoosh Sadrzadeh	University College London, UK
Igor Sedlár	Czech Academy of Sciences, Czech Republic
Viorica Sofronie-Stokkermans	University of Koblenz, Germany
Thomas Studer (Co-chair)	University of Bern, Switzerland
Sara Ugolini	IIIA – CSIC Barcelona, Spain
Mladen Vukovic	University of Zagreb, Croatia
Fan Yang	Utrecht University, Netherlands
Richard Zach	University of Calgary, Canada

Additional Reviewers

Marco Abbadini
José Goudet Alvim
Maxime Amblard
Marija Boricic
Ivan Chajda
Dragan Doder
Armand Feuilleaubois
Marko Horvat
Tomáš Jakl
Andre Kornell
Clemens Kupke
Dazhu Li
Zhaohui Luo
António Machiavelo
Jérémie Marquès
Joseph McDonald
Brett McLean
Juan Meleiro

Luka Mikec
Tommaso Moraschini
Nelma Moreira
Paulo Oliva
Anantha Padmanabha
Charles Paperman
Shashank Pathak
Tin Perkov
Giuliano Rosella
Luigi Santocanale
Ana Luiza Tenório
Matteo Tesi
Patrick Uftring
Jialiang Yan
Zhiguang Zhao

Invited Talks

Model Theory of Gödel Logic

J. P. Aguilera

Vienna University of Technology, Vienna, Austria

Gödel logics are real-valued logics intermediate between intuitionistic logic and classical logic; they are one of the three fundamental fuzzy logics. Although heavily studied from the point of view of proof theory and computer science, its model theory is relatively unexplored and quite remarkable. Many classical theorems about first-order logic, such as the Löwenheim-Skolem theorem or the Compactness theorem fail for first-order Gödel logics in their usual formulation. However, they can be resurrected in weaker forms if one replaces the role of "infinity" in these theorems by "having very large cardinality."

Theorem 0.1. *Let ϕ be a first-order sentence. The following are equivalent:*

1. In real-valued Gödel logic, ϕ has a model of every infinite cardinality.
2. In real-valued Gödel logic, ϕ has a model of cardinality $\beth_\omega = \sup\{\aleph_0, 2^{\aleph_0}, 2^{2^{\aleph_0}}, \ldots\}$.
Moreover, the equivalence fails if one replaces $\beth_\omega$ by any smaller cardinality.

Theorem 0.2. *Let Γ be a set of sentences in first-order logic and let κ be the smallest ω_1-strongly compact cardinal. Suppose that every $\Gamma' \subset \Gamma$ of cardinality $<\kappa$ has a model in Gödel logic. Then, Γ has a model in Gödel logic.*
Moreover, this is not true if one replaces κ by a smaller cardinality.

While for classical logic one can replace $\beth_\omega$ and κ, respectively, by $\aleph_0$ in the two theorems above, this is no longer possible for Gödel logic. Note that ω_1-strongly compact cardinals are so large that they cannot be proved to exist within the Zermelo-Fraenkel axioms.

While these interactions between model theory and set theory are usually associated with logics much stronger than first-order logic, it is quite remarkable that they arise in the context of logics weaker than classical (finitary) first-order logic as well.

Model Theory of Gödel Logic

J. P. Aguilera

[illegible] University of Technology [illegible]

[illegible]

Nøthing is Logical

Maria Aloni

ILLC & Philosophy, University of Amsterdam
M.D.Aloni@uva.nl
https://www.marialoni.org

People often reason contrary to the prescriptions of classical logic. In the talk I will discuss cases of everyday deviations from classical logical-mathematical reasoning and propose that they are a consequence of a tendency in human cognition to disregard models which verify sentences by virtue of an empty witness set (*neglect-zero tendency*, [1]). I will then introduce a bilateral state-based modal logic (BSML) which formally represents the neglect-zero tendency and can be used to study its impact on reasoning and interpretation. The neglect-zero tendency is modelled in BSML by means of the non-emptyness atom, NE, from team semantics [3]. In team semantics, formulas are interpreted with respect to sets of points of evaluation (*teams*) rather than single points. In BSML, a team is identified with a set of possible worlds in a Kripke model and represents the information state of the relevant reasoner. After discussing some of the applications, I will compare BSML with related systems (truthmaker semantics, possibility semantics, and inquisitive semantics) via translations into Modal Information Logic [2].

References

1. Aloni, M.: Logic and conversation: the case of free choice. Semant. Pragmat. **15**(5), 1–60 (2022). https://doi.org/10.3765/sp.15.5
2. van Benthem, J.: Implicit and explicit stances in logic. J. Philos. Logic **48**, 571–601 (2019). https://doi.org/10.1007/s10992-018-9485-y
3. Yang, F., Väänänen, J.: Propositional team logics. Ann. Pure Appl. Logic **168**(7), 1406–1441 (2017). https://doi.org/10.1016/j.apal.2017.01.007

Probability and Nondeterminism with Multiset Semantics

Dexter Kozen

Cornell University, Ithaca, USA

Abstract. The combination of probability and nondeterminism in state-based systems is a notoriously challenging problem, mainly due to the known lack of a Beck distributive law between the powerset and probability monads. In this talk I will introduce a version of probabilistic Kleene algebra and a corresponding class of automata with nondeterminism formalized by multisets instead of powersets, based on the recently established Beck distributive law of probability over multisets by Jacobs. I will describe the operational and denotational semantics of automata and expressions and give a Kleene theorem in both directions.

(joint work with Shawn Ong and Stephanie Ma)

Theory and Practice of Uniform Interpolation

Sam van Gool

IRIF, Université Paris Cité, Paris, France

A formula I is called an *interpolant* of an entailment $A \vdash B$ if $A \vdash I$, $I \vdash B$, and I only uses propositional variables that appear in both A and B. The property that any entailment admits an interpolant is known as the (deductive) *interpolation property*, and holds for many logics, including classical and intuitionistic propositional logic.

An interpolant is called *right uniform* if it can be chosen independently from the formula on the right of the entailment. More precisely, I is a *right uniform interpolant* for a formula A with respect to a propositional variable p if I is p-free and the formula I is an interpolant for every p-free formula B such that $A \vdash B$. The concept of a *left uniform interpolant* is defined analogously. By an argument similar to the one for 'usual' interpolants, one obtains left and right uniform interpolants for any formula in classical propositional logic. In the case of *intuitionistic* propositional logic, a surprising theorem of A. Pitts [3] says that left and right uniform interpolants still exist, although they are more complicated to compute.

The aim of this talk is to survey a number of recent results related to uniform interpolation in propositional logics, involving its algebraic, topological, model-theoretic, and computational aspects. More specifically, I hope to explain: how uniform interpolation can be studied via adjunctions between congruence lattices [4]; how Pitts' theorem can be proved via an open mapping theorem for Esakia spaces [5]; how recent work on mechanization allows to compute uniform interpolants for various intuitionistic and modal logics [1, 2]. Throughout the talk, I will also point to some open problems that this work has led to.

References

1. Férée, H., van Gool, S.: Formalizing and computing propositional quantifiers. In: Proceedings of the 12th ACM SIGPLAN International Conference on Certified Programs and Proofs (CPP), pp. 148–158. Association for Computing Machinery (2023)
2. Férée, H., van der Giessen, I., van Gool, S., Shillito, I.: Mechanised uniform interpolation for modal logics K, GL, and iSL. In: International Joint Conference on Automated Reasoning (IJCAR) (2024, to appear)
3. Pitts, A.M.: On an interpretation of second order quantification in first order intuitionistic propositional logic. J. Symb. Log. **57**(1), 33–52 (1992)
4. van Gool, S., Metcalfe, G., Tsinakis, C.: Uniform interpolation and compact congruences. Ann. Pure Appl. Logic **168**(10),1927–1948 (2017)
5. van Gool, S., Reggio,L.: An open mapping theorem for finitely copresented Esakia spaces. Topology Appl. **240**, 69–77 (2018)

Pride and Probability

Francesca Zaffora Blando

Carnegie Mellon University, Pittsburgh, USA

Abstract. In both formal learning theory and modal approaches to belief revision, the phenomenon of convergence to the truth is often studied from a topological perspective. Ideally, we would like our beliefs, or the conjectures of our learning methods, to converge to the truth along every possible data stream (along every possible sequence of observations). However, there are inductive problems that are simply too difficult for this ideal to be attainable. And if convergence to the truth cannot occur everywhere, at least we would like it to happen along the vast majority of possible data streams. Topology provides a common framework for thinking about typicality, so achieving convergence to the truth along a topologically typical, or "large", collection of data streams is often taken to be the next best epistemic ideal.

Convergence to the truth is also fundamental to Bayesian epistemology. In this setting, however, convergence-to-the-truth results have a rather different flavor: they establish that, under mild assumptions, a Bayesian learner's beliefs are guaranteed to converge to the truth with probability one—where, crucially, the probability-one qualification is relative to the learner's subjective prior. So, Bayesian convergence-to-the-truth theorems are best understood as establishing that Bayesian learners enjoy a certain type of internal coherence: they cannot be skeptics about their own ability to be inductively successful in the long run.

The purpose of this talk is to clarify the extent to which these two perspectives on convergence to the truth, the probabilistic one and the topological one, are compatible with each other in the setting of Bayesian learning. This question is especially pressing because of a recent criticism of the Bayesian framework due to Gordon Belot, who argued that Bayesian convergence-to-the-truth results mandate a pernicious epistemic immodesty, in that Bayesian learners are forced to believe that they will be inductively successful even when they are guaranteed to face inductive failure on a co-meager (i.e., a topologically typical) collection of data streams.

My goal is to shed light on when Bayesian convergence to the truth occurs not only on a set of probability one, but also on a co-meager set of data streams. I will show that, by classifying the inductive problems faced by a Bayesian learner (the random variables that a Bayesian learner needs to successfully estimate) using the tools of descriptive set theory and computability theory, one can identify many natural classes of inductive problems for which convergence to the truth indeed happens on a co-meager set. Moreover, I will show that appealing to computability theory allows to offer a much more fine-grained analysis of the phenomenon of Bayesian convergence to the truth. In particular, we will see that the theories of algorithmic randomness and effective genericity can be used to single out specific co-meager sets of data streams along which successful learning provably occurs for several classes of effective inductive problems.

Contents

Strict-Tolerant Conditional Logics

Lin Chen and Xuefeng Wen(✉)

Institute of Logic and Cognition, Department of Philosophy, Sun Yat-sen University, Guangzhou, China
wxflogic@gmail.com

Abstract. We construct a conditional logic using selection models in a three-valued setting. When the selection function selects an empty set, the corresponding conditional is neither true nor false. The semantic consequence is defined as in Strict-Tolerant logic. The resulting logic validates Conditional Excluded Middle without assuming that a selection function always chooses a single world, reconciling Stalnaker and Lewis. We give a labelled sequent calculus for the logic and consider three extensions of it. It turns out two extensions are strongly connexive, hyperconnexive, superconnexive, and almost totally connexive.

Keywords: Conditional Excluded Middle · Strict-tolerant logic · Conditional logic · Connexive logic

1 Introduction

Possible worlds semantics with a structure of similarity between worlds initiated by Stalnaker [16] and Lewis [8] has become a standard tool of analysing conditionals. The similarity structure can be formalized in different ways. One way is using selection functions, which select for each world w and formula φ the closest φ-worlds to w. One key difference between Stalnaker and Lewis is that Stalnaker assumes that the closest world for each world and formula is unique, either a possible world, or an impossible world (the absurd world), whereas Lewis advocates that the closest worlds are not unique. If there is no such worlds, then it selects the empty set, which functions the same as Stalnaker's absurd world for conditionals. One consequence of the difference is that in Stalnaker's conditional logic, Conditional Excluded Middle (CEM), namely, $(\varphi > \psi) \vee (\varphi > \neg\psi)$ is valid, whereas in Lewis' conditional logics, it is invalid. This is expected: if the closest φ-world is unique, then at this world either ψ is true or its negation is true, or it is the absurd world, which makes $(\varphi > \psi) \vee (\varphi > \neg\psi)$ true. In contrary, if the closest φ-worlds are not unique, then it is possible that some of them are ψ-worlds and some are $\neg\psi$-worlds, which makes neither $\varphi > \psi$ nor $\varphi > \neg\psi$ true.

There are good reasons to give up Stalnaker's uniqueness assumption. In many cases, there are more than one closest worlds to a given world. For example, the closest worlds to the actual world in which Bizet and Verdi are compatriots could either be a world in which they are both French or a world in which

G. Metcalfe et al. (Eds.): WoLLIC 2024, LNCS 14672, pp. 1–17, 2024.
https://doi.org/10.1007/978-3-031-62687-6_1

they are both Italian. We cannot determine that one is closer than the other. Moreover, if we allow a selection function to select a set of worlds rather than a world, we can dispense with the absurd world, which is desirable.

On the other hand, CEM has been defended by more and more authors, including [7,14,17,21], among others. It is not only defended by scholars, but also supported by folk judgments [15]. One may wonder whether it is possible to keep both Lewis' set selection functions and Stalnaker's CEM. One motivation of this paper is to achieve this goal, so that we can reconcile Stalnaker and Lewis.

Our second motivation is to provide a natural semantics for strongly connexive logics, which are desirable but rare in the literature. *Connexive logics* are those logics of conditionals that validate the following theses, called Aristotle's thesis and Boethius' thesis, respectively.

AT $\neg(\varphi > \neg\varphi), \neg(\neg\varphi > \varphi)$
BT $(\varphi > \psi) > \neg(\varphi > \neg\psi), (\varphi > \neg\psi) > \neg(\varphi > \psi)$

Another way of expressing the ideas behind the two theses is using satisfiability instead of validity, which requires that

Unsat1 $\varphi > \neg\varphi$ is unsatisfiable, neither is $\neg\varphi > \varphi$
Unsat2 $\{\varphi > \psi, \varphi > \neg\psi\}$ is unsatisfiable

Logics not only validating AT and BT but also satisfying Unsat1 and Unsat2 are called *strongly connexive* [5].

Though both AT and BT are intuitive, they are not valid in classical logic, which makes it notoriously difficult to give natural semantics for connexive logics. Before Wansing's logic **C** [19], connexive logics are usually obtained by adding more constraints on the truth condition of standard material, strict (including intuitionistic), or relevant implication, which makes the semantics rather cumbersome and unbalanced between truth and falsity conditions. Wansing's logic **C**, based on strict implication, tweaks instead the falsity condition of conditionals, yielding a natural semantics for connexive logic. After Wansing's work, more and more connexive logics are provided (e.g. [6,12])[1]. However, strongly connexive logics are still rare in the literature. This may seem strange, as validity and satisfiability are dual notions: φ is valid iff $\neg\varphi$ is unsatisfiable. Unsat1 and Unsat2 just appear to be reformulations of AT and BT. But the duality only holds in two-valued settings. In many-valued logics, the duality does not hold anymore. As most (if not all) connexive logics are multiple-valued, it is nontrivial to obtain a strongly connexive logic, even if you have a connexive one.

The basic idea of achieving the above two goals is as follows. First, we extend Lewis's semantics for conditionals to a three-valued setting. Second, following Wansing's falsity tweaking strategy, we change the falsity condition of conditionals, to make the truth and falsity conditions of conditionals symmetric. Third, we put a precondition on both truth and falsity conditions of conditionals. If the precondition is not satisfied, the corresponding conditional is neither true nor false.

[1] See also a recent special issue of *Studia Logica* on connexive logic.

Finally, and probably most importantly, we adopt *st*-validity from strict-tolerant logics [3,13], which gives us both CEM without the uniqueness assumption and strongly connexive logics without changing the semantics. In fact, the logics are not only strongly connexive, but also hyperconnexive and superconnexive, and almost totally connexive, which are called for in the literature.[2]

The remaining part of the paper is organized as follows. Section 2 gives our semantics of conditionals, showing CEM is valid in the semantics. Section 3 proposes a labelled sequent calculus for the semantics and proves its soundness and completeness. Section 4 considers three extensions and proves their soundness and completeness. Section 5 discusses the properties of connexivity of the extensions. Section 6 concludes the paper and suggests some future work.

2 Semantics

Our language $\mathcal{L}$ is formed from a given set *At* of atomic formulas by standard Boolean connectives $\neg, \wedge, \vee$, and a binary connective $>$ for conditionals. Formulas without $>$ are called *Boolean.*

Definition 1 (Selection models). *A (three-valued) selection model is a tuple* $\mathfrak{M} = (W, f, V^+, V^-)$, *where*

- $W \neq \emptyset$ *consists of worlds,*
- $f : W \times \mathcal{L} \to \wp(W)$ *is a selection function, and*
- $V^+ : At \to \wp(W)$ *and* $V^- : At \to \wp(W)$ *are truth and falsity valuations, respectively, such that for all* $p \in At$, $V^+(p) \cap V^-(p) = \emptyset$

Following Lewis and pace Stalnaker, a selection function is defined as selecting a set of worlds instead of a world. It may selects an empty set, so that we can dispense with the absurd world introduced in Stalnaker's semantics. Here we do not impose any conditions on models, which will be considered in Sect. 4. We denote by stC the class of all selection models.

Definition 2 (Truth and falsity conditions). *Given a selection model* $\mathfrak{M} = (W, f, V^+, V^-)$, *the truth and falsity conditions of any formula* φ *at any* $w \in W$ *in* $\mathfrak{M}$ *is inductively defined as follows.*

- $\mathfrak{M}, w \Vdash p$ *iff* $w \in V^+(p)$
- $\mathfrak{M}, w \dashv\Vdash p$ *iff* $w \in V^-(p)$
- $\mathfrak{M}, w \Vdash \neg\varphi$ *iff* $\mathfrak{M}, w \dashv\Vdash \varphi$
- $\mathfrak{M}, w \dashv\Vdash \neg\varphi$ *iff* $\mathfrak{M}, w \Vdash \varphi$
- $\mathfrak{M}, w \Vdash \varphi \wedge \psi$ *iff* $\mathfrak{M}, w \Vdash \varphi$ *and* $\mathfrak{M}, w \Vdash \psi$
- $\mathfrak{M}, w \dashv\Vdash \varphi \wedge \psi$ *iff* $\mathfrak{M}, w \dashv\Vdash \varphi$ *or* $\mathfrak{M}, w \dashv\Vdash \psi$
- $\mathfrak{M}, w \Vdash \varphi \vee \psi$ *iff* $\mathfrak{M}, w \Vdash \varphi$ *or* $\mathfrak{M}, w \Vdash \psi$
- $\mathfrak{M}, w \dashv\Vdash \varphi \vee \psi$ *iff* $\mathfrak{M}, w \dashv\Vdash \varphi$ *and* $\mathfrak{M}, w \dashv\Vdash \psi$
- $\mathfrak{M}, w \Vdash \varphi > \psi$ *iff* $f(w, \varphi) \neq \emptyset$ *and if* $u \in f(w, \varphi)$, *then* $\mathfrak{M}, u \Vdash \psi$

[2] We'll explain the terminology in Sect. 5.

– $\mathfrak{M}, w \dashv\Vdash \varphi > \psi$ *iff* $f(w, \varphi) \neq \emptyset$ *and if* $u \in f(w, \varphi)$, *then* $\mathfrak{M}, u \dashv\Vdash \psi$

The set of worlds making φ true/false in $\mathfrak{M}$ is denoted by $[\![\varphi]\!]^+_{\mathfrak{M}}/[\![\varphi]\!]^-_{\mathfrak{M}}$, where the subscript $\mathfrak{M}$ is often omitted when no confusion occurs. We write $\mathfrak{M}, w \Vdash\vdash \Gamma$ if $\mathfrak{M}, w \Vdash\vdash \gamma$ for all $\gamma \in \Gamma$. Similarly for $\mathfrak{M}, w \dashv\Vdash \Gamma$. It is easily seen that a formula cannot be both true and false. More precisely, for all selection models $\mathfrak{M}$, for all $\varphi \in \mathcal{L}$, we have $[\![\varphi]\!]^+ \cap [\![\varphi]\!]^- = \emptyset$.

Compared to Lewis' semantics, we make three modifications. First, we generalize the two-valued setting to a three-valued one, allowing a formula to be neither true nor false (but not both true and false). For Boolean formulas, we adopt the truth and falsity conditions of strong Kleene logic, which is a most natural three-valued logic. Second, we tweak the falsity condition for conditionals to make it symmetric with their truth conditions. In Lewis' semantics, a conditional is false if it is not true and thus $\varphi > \psi$ is false if there is a closest φ-world making ψ false. In our semantics, $\varphi > \psi$ is false only if all closest φ-worlds make ψ false. In a three-valued setting, this modification is natural, as there is no reason to make the truth and falsity conditions asymmetric. From a three-valued point of view, Lewis' falsity condition for conditionals is actually a non-truth condition. Finally, we put a precondition, namely, $f(w, \varphi) \neq \emptyset$, on both truth and falsity conditions of conditionals, which is also a natural requirement. Though a contradiction entails everything, we seldom assert a conditional with a contradictory antecedent. It's weird to say "if Biden wins and Biden doesn't win, then...", whatever the consequent is. According to our semantics, such a conditional is neither true nor false.

Definition 3 (Validity). *Given a class of models* C, *we say that the inference from* Γ *to* Δ *is valid in* C, *denoted* $\Gamma \vDash_{\mathsf{C}} \Delta$, *if there is no* $\mathfrak{M}$ *in* C *and* w *in* $\mathfrak{M}$ *such that* $\mathfrak{M}, w \Vdash\vdash \Gamma$ *and* $\mathfrak{M}, w \dashv\Vdash \Delta$.

This notion of validity coincides with the standard truth-preserving one in two-valued settings. In a three-valued setting, however, it is the *st*-validity proposed in strict-tolerant logics, where a formula is called strictly true (s) if it true, and tolerantly true (t) if it is not false. For an inference to be *st*-valid, it does not require that the conclusion is strictly true whenever the premises are strictly true, which is the validity adopted in Kleene's three-valued logic **K3** (called *ss*-validity); it only requires that the conclusion is not false, namely tolerantly true, whenever the premises are strictly true, which is also different from the one adopted in Priests' three-valued logic **LP**, where an inference is valid if the conclusion is tolerantly true whenever the premises are tolerantly true (called *tt*-validity).[3] Surprisingly, unlike **K3** and **LP**, which are deemed as deviation from classical logic, the same truth and falsity conditions as **K3** (and **LP**) with *st*-validity yield the same logical consequence as in classical logic. Since we would like to keep classical logic as much as possible, we adopt *st*-validity instead of *ss*-validity or *tt*-validity.

[3] The third value has different meanings in **K3** and **LP**. In the former, it means neither true nor false. In the latter, it means both true and false. So tolerant truth in **LP** means either true or both true and false.

Another reason for adopting *st*-validity is that it is a reformulation of Strawson entailment [18, pp. 176–177], according to which an inference is valid if and only if the conclusion is true whenever the premises are true and all presuppositions involved in the statements of the inference are satisfied. If we assume that a statement is neither true nor false if its presuppositions are not satisfied, and a statement cannot be both true and false, then it turns out that Strawson entailment and *st*-validity coincide. For a conditional $\varphi > \psi$, we can regard $f(w, \varphi) \neq \emptyset$ as its presupposition. Even if atomic formulas are two-valued, a conditional could still be neither true nor false due to the unsatisfaction of its presupposition. Since Strawson entailment is a natural notion of validity for inferences of statements involving presuppositions, adopting it, or equivalently adopting *st*-validity, is also a natural choice for our purpose.

By adopting *st*-validity, we obtain both CEM and strongly connexive logics (considered in Sect. 5) for free. The validity of CEM in our semantics is expected. By *st*-validity, we only require that $(\varphi > \psi) \vee (\varphi > \neg\psi)$ is not false. The falsity of $(\varphi > \psi) \vee (\varphi > \neg\psi)$ requires both disjuncts to be false. By the tweaked falsity condition, this means the closest φ-worlds are both ψ-worlds and $\neg\psi$-words, which is only possible when the closest φ-worlds do not exist. But this contradicts our presupposition for a conditional to be true or false.

Proposition 1. $\vDash_{\mathsf{stC}} (\varphi > \psi) \vee (\varphi > \neg\psi)$.

3 A Labelled Sequent Calculus for stC

In this section, we introduce a labelled sequent calculus for $\vDash_{\mathsf{stC}}$. The labels are used to represent possible worlds. The calculus is adapted from those introduced for Lewis' conditional logics (SeqS/SeqS22) in [10,11].

Definition 4 (Labelled formulas). *Let $\mathcal{A}$ be a denumerable alphabet of labels, whose elements are denoted by $x, y, z, \ldots$. We define two kinds of labelled formulas.*

- *world formulas: denoted by $x : \varphi$, where $x \in \mathcal{A}$ and $\varphi \in \mathcal{L}$;*
- *transition formulas: denoted by $x \xrightarrow{\varphi} y$, where $x, y \in \mathcal{A}$ and $\varphi \in \mathcal{L}$.*

A world formula $x : \varphi$ is used to represent that φ is true or false in the world x. A transition formula $x \xrightarrow{\varphi} y$ is used to represent that $y \in f(x, \varphi)$.

Definition 5 (Truth and falsity conditions for labelled formulas). *Given a selection model $\mathfrak{M} = (W, f, V^+, V^-)$, a label alphabet $\mathcal{A}$, and a mapping $I : \mathcal{A} \to W$, the truth and falsity conditions of labelled formulas in $\mathfrak{M}$ under I are defined as follows.*

- $\mathfrak{M} \Vdash_I x : \varphi$ *iff* $I(x) \in [\![\varphi]\!]^+$
- $\mathfrak{M} \dashv\vert_I x : \varphi$ *iff* $I(x) \in [\![\varphi]\!]^-$
- $\mathfrak{M} \Vdash_I x \xrightarrow{\varphi} y$ *iff* $I(y) \in f(x, \varphi)$
- $\mathfrak{M} \dashv\vert_I x \xrightarrow{\varphi} y$ *iff* $I(y) \notin f(x, \varphi)$

We write $\mathfrak{M} \Vdash_I \Gamma$ *if* $\mathfrak{M} \Vdash_I \gamma$ *for all* $\gamma \in \Gamma$. *Similarly for* $\mathfrak{M} \dashv\!|_I \Gamma$.

Unlike world formulas, which might be neither true nor false, transition formulas are either true or false, because a world is either in a selected set or not.

Definition 6 (Labelled sequents, Pure sequents). *A labelled sequent is a pair* $\langle \Gamma, \Delta \rangle$, *denoted by* $\Gamma \Rightarrow \Delta$, *where* Γ *and* Δ *are sets of labelled formulas, called antecedents and consequents, respectively. A labelled sequent* $\Gamma \Rightarrow \Delta$ *is pure, if* Γ *and* Δ *are sets of world formulas. Otherwise, it is called impure.*

Definition 7 (Satisfiability and Validity of sequents)

- *A labelled sequent* $\Gamma \Rightarrow \Delta$ *is satisfied by* $\mathfrak{M} = (W, f, V^+, V^-)$, *if for all mappings* $I : \mathcal{A} \to W$, *it is not the case that both* $\mathfrak{M} \Vdash_I \Gamma$ *and* $\mathfrak{M} \dashv\!|_I \Delta$.
- *A labelled sequent is valid in* C, *if it is satisfied by all selection models in* C.

Sequents for multiple-valued logics usually have two readings: disjunctive reading and negated-conjunctive reading. In disjunctive reading, a two-sided sequent is satisfied by a model if either one of its antecedents is falsified or one of its consequents is satisfied. In negated-conjunctive reading, a two-sided sequent is satisfied if it is not the case that all the antecedents are satisfied and all the consequents are falsified. The two interpretation coincide in two-valued settings, but disparate in three or more valued settings. Here we adopt the negated-conjunctive reading to interpret sequents, because under this interpretation, a two-sided sequent system is enough for *st*-validity, whereas a three-sided sequent system is required if we adopt the disjunctive reading.[4]

For any set Γ of formulas, we write Γ^x for the corresponding set of labelled formulas labelled by x, namely, $\Gamma^x = \{x : \varphi \mid \varphi \in \Gamma\}$. The following lemma connects validity of inferences and labelled sequents, which is easily verified.

Lemma 1. *Let* C *be a class of models. Then* $\Gamma \vDash_{\mathsf{C}} \Delta$ *iff* $\Gamma^x \Rightarrow \Delta^x$ *is valid in* C.

Definition 8 (Syntactic consequence). *Given a labelled sequent calculus* $\mathbf{C}$, *we say that* Δ *is a syntactic consequence of* Γ *in* $\mathbf{C}$, *denoted* $\Gamma \vdash_{\mathbf{C}} \Delta$, *if* $\Gamma^x \Rightarrow \Delta^x$ *is provable in* $\mathbf{C}$.

The labelled sequent calculus **stC** consists of the axioms and rules in Table 1.

Example 1. We prove an instance of CEM in **stC**. Let $y \neq x$ and $p, q \in At$.

$$\dfrac{\dfrac{x \xrightarrow{p} y \Rightarrow x \xrightarrow{p} y \qquad \dfrac{x \xrightarrow{p} y, y : q \Rightarrow y : q}{x \xrightarrow{p} y \Rightarrow y : q, y : \neg q}\,(\neg\mathrm{R})}{\dfrac{x \xrightarrow{p} y \Rightarrow y : q, x : p > \neg q}{\Rightarrow x : p > q, x : p > \neg q}\,(>\mathrm{R}^-)}\,(>\mathrm{R}^+)}{\Rightarrow x : (p > q) \vee (p > \neg q)}\,(\vee\mathrm{R})$$

[4] For more on this, see [13].

Table 1. Axioms and rules of the sequent calculus **stC**

Axioms:

$\Gamma, x : p \Rightarrow \Delta, x : p \ (p \in At)$ $\qquad$ $\Gamma, x \xrightarrow{\varphi} y \Rightarrow \Delta, x \xrightarrow{\varphi} y$

Rules:

$$(\neg L)\ \frac{\Gamma \Rightarrow \Delta, x : \varphi}{\Gamma, x : \neg\varphi \Rightarrow \Delta} \qquad (\neg R)\ \frac{\Gamma, x : \varphi \Rightarrow \Delta}{\Gamma \Rightarrow \Delta, x : \neg\varphi}$$

$$(\wedge L)\ \frac{\Gamma, x : \varphi, x : \psi \Rightarrow \Delta}{\Gamma, x : \varphi \wedge \psi \Rightarrow \Delta} \qquad (\wedge R)\ \frac{\Gamma \Rightarrow \Delta, x : \varphi \qquad \Gamma \Rightarrow \Delta, x : \psi}{\Gamma \Rightarrow \Delta, x : \varphi \wedge \psi}$$

$$(\vee L)\ \frac{\Gamma, x : \varphi \Rightarrow \Delta \qquad \Gamma, x : \psi \Rightarrow \Delta}{\Gamma, x : \varphi \vee \psi \Rightarrow \Delta} \qquad (\vee R)\ \frac{\Gamma \Rightarrow \Delta, x : \varphi, x : \psi}{\Gamma \Rightarrow \Delta, x : \varphi \vee \psi}$$

$$(>L^+)\ \frac{\Gamma \Rightarrow \Delta, x \xrightarrow{\varphi} y \qquad \Gamma, y : \psi \Rightarrow \Delta}{\Gamma, x : \varphi > \psi \Rightarrow \Delta} \qquad (>L^-)\ \frac{\Gamma, x \xrightarrow{\varphi} y, y : \psi \Rightarrow \Delta}{\Gamma, x : \varphi > \psi \Rightarrow \Delta}\ (x \neq y, y \notin \Gamma, \Delta)$$

$$(>R^+)\ \frac{\Gamma \Rightarrow \Delta, x \xrightarrow{\varphi} y \qquad \Gamma \Rightarrow \Delta, y : \psi}{\Gamma \Rightarrow \Delta, x : \varphi > \psi} \qquad (>R^-)\ \frac{\Gamma, x \xrightarrow{\varphi} y \Rightarrow \Delta, y : \psi}{\Gamma \Rightarrow \Delta, x : \varphi > \psi}\ (x \neq y, y \notin \Gamma, \Delta)$$

A similar proof is given in the calculus SeqS22 [10], where their extensional rule for CEM is essentially our ($>$R$^+$). Note that in our semantics ($>$R$^+$) holds with no additional constraint on the selection models.

Theorem 1 (Soundness of stC). *If* $\Gamma \vdash_{\mathbf{stC}} \Delta$*, then* $\Gamma \vDash_{\mathsf{stC}} \Delta$*.*

We now turn to the completeness of **stC**. Essentially, completeness means that if a pure sequent is valid in stC then it is provable in **stC**. Following Ripley [13], we'll use the method of reduction trees. For any pure sequent, the reduction tree of it yields either a proof of it or a selection model that does not satisfy it. Firstly, we define the notions of subsequent, sequent union and reduction tree. Then we show how to construct a reduction tree in stages.

Definition 9 (Subsequents). *A sequent* $S = \Gamma \Rightarrow \Delta$ *is a subsequent of a sequent* $S' = \Gamma' \Rightarrow \Delta'$*, denoted* $S \sqsubseteq S'$*, if* $\Gamma \subseteq \Gamma'$ *and* $\Delta \subseteq \Delta'$*.*

Definition 10 (Sequent unions). *A sequent* $S = \Gamma \Rightarrow \Delta$ *is the sequent union of a set of sequents* $\{\Gamma_i \Rightarrow \Delta_i\}_{i \in I}$*, denoted* $S = \bigsqcup_{i \in I}\{\Gamma_i \Rightarrow \Delta_i\}$*, if* $\Gamma = \bigcup_{i \in I}\{\Gamma_i\}$ *and* $\Delta = \bigcup_{i \in I}\{\Delta_i\}$*.*

Definition 11 (Reduction trees). *A reduction tree of a pure sequent* $S_0 = \Gamma_0 \Rightarrow \Delta_0$ *is a tree which starts from a root sequent* S_0 *and is constructed in stages as specified below.*

Roughly, at each stage, we apply all applicable rules in reverse to each formula in the conclusion sequents by adding formulas. If the rule has two premises, the tree branches in two and if the rule has a single premise, we extend the tree unbranched. We ensure that every branch of the tree is ordered by the subsequent relation since we only add formulas at each stage. When the tip of any branch is an axiom, then the branch is *closed.* When a branch is closed, we stop extending it. A branch that's not closed is *open.* We repeat the procedure until either every branch is closed or there is an infinite open branch. If every branch has closed, then the tree itself is a proof of the sequent. If there is an infinite open branch $\mathcal{B}$, we construct a countermodel from $\mathcal{B}$.

To begin, we require a pure sequent $S_0 = \Gamma_0 \Rightarrow \Delta_0$, a set of labels which contains all the labels appearing in S_0 and is large enough for an application of each reduction rule for conditionals, and an enumeration of the labels.

Stage 0**:** Let $S_0 = \Gamma_0 \Rightarrow \Delta_0$ be the root of the tree.
Stage $n+1$**:** We proceed in substages and subsubstages.

1. Examine all branches after stage n, and do noting to the closed branch.
2. Then we extend the open branches. For each open branch, if a labelled formula A already occurred on the left/right-hand side of the sequents in that branch at stage n, and has not already been reduced during stage $n+1$, then reduce A as follows:
   - If A is a negation world formula $x : \neg\varphi$, then
     - if $x : \neg\varphi$ is on the left-hand side/right-hand side, extend the branch by copying its current tip and adding $x : \varphi$ to the right-hand side/left-hand side correspondingly.
   - If A is a conjunction world formulas $x : \varphi \wedge \psi$, then
     - if $x : \varphi \wedge \psi$ is on the left-hand side, extend the branch by copying its current tip and adding both $x : \varphi$ and $x : \psi$ to the left-hand side.
     - if $x : \varphi \wedge \psi$ is on the right-hand side, split the branch in two: extend the first by copying the current tip and adding $x : \varphi$ to the right-hand side; and extend the second by copying the current tip and adding $x : \psi$ to the right-hand side.
   - The case that A is a disjunction world formula $x : \varphi \vee \psi$ is similar to the case that A is a conjunction world formulas $x : \varphi \wedge \psi$, mutatis mutandis.
   - If A is a conditional world formula $x : \varphi > \psi$, then
     - if $x : \varphi > \psi$ is on the left-hand side, then
       * when $n+1$ is odd, extend the branch by copying the current tip and adding both $x \xrightarrow{\varphi} y$ and $y : \psi$ to the left-hand side, where y is the first label in the enumeration that does not occur anywhere in the current tip.
       * when $n+1$ is even, split the branch in two: extend the first by copying the current tip and adding $x \xrightarrow{\varphi} y$ to the right-hand side, and extend the second by copying the current tip and adding $y : \psi$ to the left-hand side, where y is the $\frac{n+1}{2}^{th}$ label in the enumeration.
     - if $x : \varphi > \psi$ is on the right-hand side, then
       * when $n+1$ is odd, extend the branch by copying the current tip and adding $x \xrightarrow{\varphi} y$ to the left-hand side and $y : \psi$ to the right-hand side, where y is the first label in the enumeration that does not occur anywhere in the current tip.

* when $n+1$ is even, split the branch in two: extend the first by copying the current tip and adding $x \xrightarrow{\varphi} y$ to the right-hand side, and extend the second by copying the current tip and adding $y : \psi$ to the right-hand side where y is the $\frac{n+1}{2}^{th}$ label in the enumeration.

- If A is a transition formula $x \xrightarrow{\varphi} y$, do nothing.

Repeat this procedure until every branch is closed, or until there is an infinite open branch.

Lemma 2. *Given a pure sequent $S_0 = \Gamma_0 \Rightarrow \Delta_0$, we have a reduction tree of S_0 built in the above stages. If every branch of the reduction tree is closed, then S_0 has a proof. Otherwise, there is a countermodel to S_0.*

Theorem 2 (Completeness of stC). *If $\Gamma \vDash_{\mathsf{stC}} \Delta$, then $\Gamma \vdash_{\mathbf{stC}} \Delta$.*

4 Extensions

In this section, we consider three extensions of **stC**, by imposing some natural conditions on models and adding inference rules in the calculus correspondingly.

4.1 ID

The following model condition is typical in conditional logic. It says that the closest-φ worlds are indeed the worlds making φ true.

(id) $\qquad f(w, \varphi) \subseteq [\![\varphi]\!]^+.$

We denote by stC1 the class of selection models satisfying (id). The condition is usually associated with the axiom $\varphi > \varphi$. Instead of adding this axiom, we give the proof system **stC1** for $\vDash_{\mathsf{stC1}}$ by adding the following rule (ID) to **stC**.

$$\text{(ID)}\ \frac{\Gamma, y : \varphi \Rightarrow \Delta}{\Gamma, x \xrightarrow{\varphi} y \Rightarrow \Delta}$$

With (ID), we can prove an instance of $\varphi > \varphi$ as follows.

Example 2. A proof of an instance of $\varphi > \varphi$ ($p \in At$).

$$\dfrac{\dfrac{y : p \Rightarrow y : p}{x \xrightarrow{p} y \Rightarrow y : p}\ \text{(ID)}}{\Rightarrow x : p > p}\ (>\text{R}^-)$$

Theorem 3 (Soundness of stC1). *If $\Gamma \vdash_{\mathbf{stC1}} \Delta$, then $\Gamma \vDash_{\mathsf{stC1}} \Delta$.*

As for completeness, we slightly modify the procedure for the reduction tree by adding backward applications of (ID). In the stages of extending infinite open branches, if A is a transition formula $x \xrightarrow{\varphi} y$ on the left-hand side, extend the branch by copying the current tip and adding $y : \varphi$ to the left-hand side instead of doing nothing.

When the reduction tree is closed, we have a proof for the root sequent in **stC1**. When there is an infinite open branch, we can construct a countermodel $\mathfrak{M} = (W, f, V^+, V^-)$ and a mapping I from that branch in the same way as shown in Lemma 2. It is not hard to see that the construction still makes sense and gives a real countermodel. However, this time we have that $x \xrightarrow{\varphi} y \in \Gamma_\omega$ implies $y : \varphi \in \Gamma_\omega$ because of the backward application of (ID) to each transition formula $x \xrightarrow{\varphi} y$. Note that via the construction of the countermodel, we have that $I(y) \in f(I(x), \varphi)$ implies $x \xrightarrow{\varphi} y \in \Gamma_\omega$, and $y : \varphi \in \Gamma_\omega$ implies $I(y) \in [\![\varphi]\!]^+$. Thus $I(y) \in f(I(x), \varphi)$ implies $I(y) \in [\![\varphi]\!]^+$, which means that $\mathfrak{M}$ satisfies (id).

By the method of reduction trees, a sequent is either provable with (ID) or has a countermodel with $f(w, \varphi) \subseteq [\![\varphi]\!]^+$, which gives us the completeness.

Theorem 4 (Completeness of stC1). *If $\Gamma \vDash_{\mathsf{stC1}} \Delta$, then $\Gamma \vdash_{\mathbf{stC1}} \Delta$.*

4.2 MP

In Lewis' conditional logics, another natural model condition says that if φ is true at w then w is a closest φ-world, which corresponds to modus ponens for $>$, namely, $\varphi, \varphi > \psi \vdash \psi$. As we are in a three-valued setting with *st*-validity, truth and falsity are no longer pairwise, which makes it difficult to obtain both soundness and completeness by imposing the model condition directly. The best we can do now is confining the condition to two-valued Boolean formulas.

(mp) $V^+(p) \cup V^-(p) = W$ for every $p \in At$ and $w \in [\![\varphi]\!]^+$ implies $w \in f(w, \varphi)$, where φ is Boolean.

We denote by stC2 the class of selection models satisfying (mp). Essentially, a selection model satisfying (mp) is a two-valued model and a Boolean formula is either true or false. A conditional, however, can still be neither true nor false due to the selection function.

The proof system **stC2** for $\vDash_{\mathsf{stC2}}$ is obtained by adding to **stC** the following rules (MP) and (CUT), where φ is Boolean.

$$\text{(MP)}\ \frac{\Gamma, x \xrightarrow{\varphi} x \Rightarrow \Delta}{\Gamma, x : \varphi \Rightarrow \Delta} \qquad \text{(CUT)}\ \frac{\Gamma, x : \varphi \Rightarrow \Delta \quad \Gamma \Rightarrow \Delta, x : \varphi}{\Gamma \Rightarrow \Delta}$$

Note that (CUT) is valid for Boolean world formula $x : \varphi$ in stC2 since a Boolean formula is either true or false in x. (CUT) for Boolean world formulas is required in giving the completeness of **stC2**:

Example 3. We prove an instance of (MP), where φ is Boolean and $q \in At$.

$$\dfrac{\dfrac{x \xrightarrow{\varphi} x \Rightarrow x \xrightarrow{\varphi} x, x : q}{x : \varphi \Rightarrow x \xrightarrow{\varphi} x, x : q} \text{(MP)} \qquad x : q, x : \varphi \Rightarrow x : q}{x : \varphi > q, x : \varphi \Rightarrow x : q} (>\mathrm{L}^+)$$

Theorem 5 (Soundness of stC2). *If $\Gamma \vdash_{\mathbf{stC2}} \Delta$, then $\Gamma \vDash_{\mathsf{stC2}} \Delta$.*

For completeness, we modify the procedure for the reduction tree by adding backward applications of (MP) and (CUT) for the Boolean. In the stages of extending infinite open branches, if A is a Boolean world formula on the left-hand side, we add $x \xrightarrow{\varphi} x$ to the left-hand side each time when we copy the current tip instead of simply copying the current tip. Then we need to allow (CUT) for Boolean world formulas. Firstly, we need an enumeration of the Boolean world formulas. We apply (CUT) for the Boolean in reverse at the end of each stage. Take the nth Boolean world formula in the enumeration, named A. For each open branch, split the branch in two: extend the first by copying the current tip and adding A to the left-hand side; and extend the second by copying the current tip and adding A to the right-hand side.

When the reduction tree is closed, we have a proof for the root sequent in **stC2**. When there is an infinite open branch, we can construct a countermodel $\mathfrak{M} = (W, f, V^+, V^-)$ and a mapping I from that branch in the same way as shown in Lemma 2. Note that each Boolean world formula occurs in S_ω and only occurs on one side. In particular, each atom occurs in Γ_ω or Δ_ω, but not simultaneously. Thus $V^+(p) \cup V^-(p) = W$ for every $p \in At$. Suppose $I(x) \in [\![\varphi]\!]^+$ and φ is Boolean. Then $x : \varphi \in \Gamma_\omega$. By the backward application of (MP), we have $x \xrightarrow{\varphi} x \in \Gamma_\omega$, whence $I(x) \in f(I(x), \varphi)$. So (mp) is satisfied by $\mathfrak{M}$. This gives the completeness of **stC2**.

Theorem 6 (Completeness of stC2). *If $\Gamma \vDash_{\mathsf{stC2}} \Delta$, then $\Gamma \vdash_{\mathbf{stC2}} \Delta$.*

4.3 ID+MP

We denote by stC3 the class of selection models satisfying both (id) and (mp). The proof system **stC3** for $\vDash_{\mathsf{stC3}}$ is obtained by adding to **stC** the rules (ID), (MP), and (CUT). By the proofs of soundness and completeness for **stC1** and **stC2**, we can obtain the soundness and completeness of **stC3** directly.

Theorem 7 (Soundness of stC3). *If $\Gamma \vdash_{\mathbf{stC3}} \Delta$, then $\Gamma \vDash_{\mathsf{stC3}} \Delta$.*

Theorem 8 (Completeness of stC3). *If $\Gamma \vDash_{\mathsf{stC3}} \Delta$, then $\Gamma \vdash_{\mathbf{stC3}} \Delta$.*

5 Connexivity

We show in this section that **stC1** and **stC3** are strongly connexive, hyperconnexive, and superconnexive. A connexive logic is *hyperconnexive*, if it validates cBT below; it is *superconnexive*, if it validates SA below.

cBT $\neg(\varphi > \neg\psi) > (\varphi > \psi), \neg(\varphi > \psi) > (\varphi > \neg\psi)$
SA $(\varphi > \neg\varphi) > \psi$

Fact 1. **stC1** *and* **stC3** *validate* AT *and* BT.

Fact 2. Unsat1 *and* Unsat2 *hold in* **stC1** *and* **stC3**.

Note that although validity of a formula in our semantics is defined by tolerant truth, we do not take tolerant truth to be the designated truth, as many connexive logics do (e.g., [1,2,9]). For an inference to be valid, we still suppose its premises to be (strictly) true to consider the truth of its conclusion. So satisfiability in our semantics is still defined by its possibility of being (strictly) true. That's why we can validate AT and BT and satisfy Unsat1 and Unsat2 simultaneously, which gives us strongly connexive logics.

Fact 3. **stC1** *and* **stC3** *validate* cBT.

Fact 4. **stC1** *and* **stC3** *validate* SA.

By the above facts, the following proposition is immediate.

Proposition 2. **stC1** *and* **stC3** *are strongly connexive, hyperconnexive, and superconnexive.*

Moreover, **stC1** and **stC3** are almost totally connexive. A strongly connexive logic is *totally connexive* [4], if the following conditions are satisfied. According to [20], there is still no totally connexive logic in the literature.

1. $\models \neg((\varphi > \psi) \wedge (\varphi > \neg\psi))$
2. $\models \neg((\varphi > \psi) \wedge (\neg\varphi > \psi))$
3. $\models \varphi \wedge \psi > \varphi, \models \varphi \wedge \psi > \psi$
4. $\models \varphi \wedge \varphi > \varphi, \models \varphi > \varphi \wedge \varphi$
5. $\not\models \varphi > (\psi > \varphi)$
6. $\not\models \varphi > (\neg\varphi > \psi)$
7. $\not\models \varphi > (\psi > \chi)$, where φ is a contingent and $\psi > \chi$ is a logical truth

Fact 5. **stC1** *and* **stC3** *satisfy all the conditions above except 2 and 7.*

6 Conclusion

We provide a new semantics for conditionals in the framework of three-valued selection models. By tweaking Lewis' falsity condition for conditionals, putting a precondition for both truth and falsity conditions of conditionals, and adopting *st*-validity from strict-tolerant logic, we validate conditional excluded middle without the uniqueness assumption for selection functions, reconciling Stalnaker and Lewis. Meanwhile, we obtain two logics in the semantics that are strongly connexive, hyperconnexive, superconnexive, and almost totally connexive. Labelled sequent calculus systems are also provided for the logics. We leave a detailed comparison to other conditional logics (including connexive logics) and strict-tolerant logics for future work.

Acknowledgments. This work was supported by National Social Science Foundation of China (Grant No. 22BZX129). We thank the anonymous referees for their helpful comments.

Appendix

Proof of. Proposition 1. Suppose there is $(\mathfrak{M}, w)$ such that $\mathfrak{M}, w \dashVert (\varphi > \psi) \vee (\varphi > \neg\psi)$. Then $\mathfrak{M}, w \dashVert \varphi > \psi$ and $\mathfrak{M}, w \dashVert \varphi > \neg\psi$, whence $f(w,\varphi) \neq \emptyset$, $f(w,\varphi) \subseteq [\![\psi]\!]^+$, and $f(w,\varphi) \subseteq [\![\neg\psi]\!]^+ = [\![\psi]\!]^-$. It follows that $f(w,\varphi) \subseteq [\![\psi]\!]^+ \cap [\![\psi]\!]^- = \emptyset$, contradiction. □

Proof of. Theorem 1. By Lemma 1, it suffices to show that if a labelled sequent is provable in **stC**, then it is valid in stC. It is easily verified that the axioms are valid, and the rules for Boolean connectives preserve validity. We show that (>L$^+$) and (>L$^-$) also preserve validity. The proof for (>R$^+$) and (>R$^-$) can be adapted from the proof for (>L$^+$) and (>L$^-$) correspondingly, mutatis mutandis.

- (>L$^+$) Suppose that (1) $\Gamma \Rightarrow \Delta, x \xrightarrow{\varphi} y$ and (2) $\Gamma, y : \psi \Rightarrow \Delta$ are valid, but (3) $\Gamma, x : \varphi > \psi \Rightarrow \Delta$ is not. Since (3) is not valid, there is a model $\mathfrak{M}$ and a mapping I such that: $\mathfrak{M} \Vdash_I \Gamma$, $\mathfrak{M} \dashVert_I \Delta$, and $\mathfrak{M} \Vdash_I x : \varphi > \psi$. Note that $\mathfrak{M} \Vdash_I x : \varphi > \psi$ means that $f(I(x),\varphi) \neq \emptyset$ and if $w \in f(I(x),\varphi)$, then $w \in [\![\psi]\!]^+$. By the validity of (1), it is not the case that $\mathfrak{M} \not\dashVert_I x \xrightarrow{\varphi} y$, whence $\mathfrak{M} \Vdash_I x \xrightarrow{\varphi} y$, i.e., $I(y) \in f(I(x),\varphi)$. So we have $\mathfrak{M} \Vdash_I \Gamma$, $\mathfrak{M} \dashVert_I \Delta$ and $I(y) \in [\![\psi]\!]^+$, contradicting the validity of (2).
- (>L$^-$) Suppose that (4) $\Gamma, x \xrightarrow{\varphi} y, x : \psi \Rightarrow \Delta$ is valid, but (3) is not. Since (3) is not valid, there is a model $\mathfrak{M}$ and a mapping I such that $\mathfrak{M} \Vdash_I \Gamma$, $\mathfrak{M} \dashVert_I \Delta$, and $\mathfrak{M} \Vdash_I x : \varphi > \psi$. Since $\mathfrak{M} \Vdash_I x : \varphi > \psi$, we have $f(I(x),\varphi) \neq \emptyset$ and if $w \in f(I(x),\varphi)$ then $w \in [\![\psi]\!]^+$. Take a world $u \in f(I(x),\varphi)$, and construct a new mapping I' by letting $I'(z) = I(z)$ if $z \neq y$ and $I'(y) = u$. Note that $x \neq y$ and y does not occurs in Γ, Δ. So we have $\mathfrak{M} \Vdash_{I'} \Gamma$, $\mathfrak{M} \dashVert_{I'} \Delta$, and $\mathfrak{M} \Vdash_{I'} x : \varphi > \psi$. Therefore $\mathfrak{M} \Vdash_{I'} \Gamma$, $\mathfrak{M} \dashVert_{I'} \Delta$, $I'(y) \in f(I'(x),\varphi)$ and $I'(y) \in [\![\psi]\!]^+$, contradicting the validity of (4). □

Proof of. Lemma 2. If every branch has closed, it can be verified that the reduction tree is a proof of the root sequent S_0, since the tree is constructed by backward application of the rules. So S_0 has a proof. If there is an infinite open branch $\mathcal{B}$, we can use the branch $\mathcal{B}$ to construct a countermodel to S_0.

First, we collect all of $\mathcal{B}$ into a single sequent $S_\omega = \Gamma_\omega \Rightarrow \Delta_\omega = \bigsqcup\{S \mid S \text{ is a sequent in } \mathcal{B}\}$. Note that, since the branch is ordered by the subsequent relation, any finite set of labelled formulas appearing in S_ω must have appeared in a sequent at some point on $\mathcal{B}$. Now we need to specify a selection model $\mathfrak{M} = (W, f, V^+, V^-)$ and a mapping $I : \mathcal{A} \to W$ to give a countermodel to S_0.

For the sake of simplification, we simply collect all the labels appearing in S_ω as the label alphabet $\mathcal{A}$ here, since then $\mathcal{A}$ has already contained all the labels in S_0 and is also large enough. Let $W = \mathcal{A}$ and I be the identity mapping. As for the selection function, let $f(x,\varphi) = \{y \mid x \xrightarrow{\varphi} y \in \Gamma_\omega\}$ for each $x \in W$ and $\varphi \in \mathcal{L}$. So far, we ensure that $x \xrightarrow{\varphi} y \in \Gamma_\omega$ iff $I(y) \in f(I(x), \varphi)$.

Then, we specify V^+ and V^-. For every $p \in At$, let $V^+(p) = \{x \mid x : p \in \Gamma_\omega\}$ and $V^-(p) = \{x \mid x : p \in \Delta_\omega\}$. The valuations make sense, since $x : p$ appears on at most one side in S_ω, otherwise there is a sequent in $\mathcal{B}$ which is an axiom and the branch would have closed. The valuations ensure that each atom in S_ω satisfies the corresponding truth or falsity conditions of the sequents in $\mathcal{B}$. Then we should verify the world formulas with higher complexity. In detail, if a world formula $x : \varphi$ appears in Γ_ω, then $I(x) \in [\![\varphi]\!]^+$; and if $x : \varphi$ appears in Δ_ω, then $I(x) \in [\![\varphi]\!]^-$.

The cases of Boolean connectives are as usual, which can be easily shown by using the rules we've used to extend $\mathcal{B}$. For example, if a conjunction world formula $x : \varphi \wedge \psi$ appears in Δ_ω, then either $x : \varphi \in \Delta_\omega$ or $x : \psi \in \Delta_\omega$. It's easy to see that we have $I(x) \in [\![\varphi \wedge \psi]\!]^-$ whether $I(x) \in [\![\varphi]\!]^-$ or $I(x) \in [\![\psi]\!]^-$, via the falsity condition.

If a conditional world formula $x : \varphi > \psi$ appears in Γ_ω, then we know that there is a label y different from x such that $x \xrightarrow{\varphi} y \in \Gamma_\omega$ and $y : \psi \in \Gamma_\omega$, since $x : \varphi > \psi$ has been reduced by the backward application of ($>$L$^-$), which extends the branch without splitting it. Thus $f(I(x), \varphi) \neq \emptyset$. Note that for each label y, either $x \xrightarrow{\varphi} y \in \Delta_\omega$ or $y : \psi \in \Gamma_\omega$, because in the procedure we have used each label to reduce $x : \varphi > \psi$ through backward applications of ($>$L$^+$). Suppose $I(y) \in f(I(x), \varphi)$, then $x \xrightarrow{\varphi} y \in \Gamma_\omega$. Thus we have $x \xrightarrow{\varphi} y \notin \Delta_\omega$, otherwise we have $x \xrightarrow{\varphi} y \in \Delta_\omega$ and $x \xrightarrow{\varphi} y \in \Gamma_\omega$, which means the branch would have closed. Therefore we have $y : \psi \in \Gamma_\omega$, whence $I(y) \in [\![\psi]\!]^+$ by the induction hypothesis. So we have $I(x) \in [\![\varphi > \psi]\!]^+$. The case when $x : \varphi > \psi$ appears in Δ_ω can be verified similarly.

Finally, since $S_0 \sqsubseteq S_\omega$, every world formula in Γ_0 satisfies the truth condition and every world formula in Δ_0 satisfies the falsity condition. Hence, the model is a countermodel to S_0. □

Proof of. Theorem 2. It suffices to show that if a pure sequent is valid in stC then it is provable in **stC**. By Lemma 2, for a pure sequent $\Gamma \Rightarrow \Delta$, either the sequent has a proof or it has a countermodel. If a pure sequent $\Gamma \Rightarrow \Delta$ is valid, then the sequent has no countermodel and therefore it has a proof. □

Proof of. Theorem 3. It suffices to show that (ID) preserves the validity for the selection models satisfying (id). Suppose (1) $\Gamma, y : \varphi \Rightarrow \Delta$ is valid, but (2) $\Gamma, x \xrightarrow{\varphi} y \Rightarrow \Delta$ is not. Since (2) is invalid, we have a model $\mathfrak{M}$ and a mapping I such that: $\mathfrak{M} \Vdash_I \Gamma$, $\mathfrak{M} \dashv\!\vert_I \Delta$, and $\mathfrak{M} \Vdash_I x \xrightarrow{\varphi} y$. Note that $\mathfrak{M}$ satisfies (id). Since $\mathfrak{M} \Vdash_I x \xrightarrow{\varphi} y$, we have $I(y) \in f(I(x), \varphi)$, whence $I(y) \in [\![\varphi]\!]^+$ by (id). Thus $\mathfrak{M} \Vdash_I \Gamma$, $\mathfrak{M} \dashv\!\vert_I \Delta$, and $\mathfrak{M} \Vdash_I y : \varphi$, contradicting the validity of (1). □

Proof of. Theorem 5. It suffices to show that (MP) preserves the validity for the selection models satisfying (mp). Suppose (1) $\Gamma, x \xrightarrow{\varphi} x \Rightarrow \Delta$ is valid, but (2) $\Gamma, x : \varphi \Rightarrow \Delta$ is not, where φ is Boolean. Since (2) is not valid, we have a model

$\mathfrak{M}$ and a mapping I such that: $\mathfrak{M} \Vdash_I \Gamma$, $\mathfrak{M} \dashv\!\Vert_I \Delta$, and $\mathfrak{M} \Vdash_I x : \varphi$. We have $I(x) \in [\![\varphi]\!]^+$, whence $I(x) \in f(I(x), \varphi)$ by (mp). Thus $\mathfrak{M} \Vdash_I \Gamma$, $\mathfrak{M} \dashv\!\Vert_I \Delta$, and $\mathfrak{M} \Vdash_I x \xrightarrow{\varphi} x$, contradicting the validity of (1). □

Proof of. Fact 1. For AT:

$$\dfrac{\dfrac{\dfrac{\dfrac{y : p \Rightarrow y : p}{x \xrightarrow{p} y \Rightarrow y : p}\,(\mathrm{ID})}{x \xrightarrow{p} y, y : \neg p \Rightarrow}\,(\neg \mathrm{L})}{x : p > \neg p \Rightarrow}\,(>\mathrm{L}^-)}{\Rightarrow x : \neg(p > \neg p)}\,(\neg \mathrm{R}) \qquad \dfrac{\dfrac{\dfrac{\dfrac{y : p \Rightarrow y : p}{y : p, y : \neg p \Rightarrow}\,(\neg \mathrm{L})}{x \xrightarrow{\neg p} y, y : p \Rightarrow}\,(\mathrm{ID})}{x : \neg p > p \Rightarrow}\,(>\mathrm{L}^-)}{\Rightarrow x : \neg(\neg p > p)}\,(\neg \mathrm{R})$$

For BT:

$$\dfrac{\dfrac{\dfrac{\dfrac{\dfrac{y \xrightarrow{p} z, z : \neg q \Rightarrow y \xrightarrow{p} z \qquad \dfrac{y \xrightarrow{p} z, z : q \Rightarrow z : q}{y \xrightarrow{p} z, z : q, z : \neg q \Rightarrow}\,(\neg \mathrm{L})}{y : p > q, y \xrightarrow{p} z, z : \neg q \Rightarrow}\,(>\mathrm{L}^+)}{y : p > q, y : p > \neg q \Rightarrow}\,(>\mathrm{L}^-)}{x \xrightarrow{p>q} y, y : p > \neg q \Rightarrow}\,(\mathrm{ID})}{x \xrightarrow{p>q} y \Rightarrow y : \neg(p > \neg q)}\,(\neg \mathrm{R})}{\Rightarrow x : (p > q) > \neg(p > \neg q)}\,(>\mathrm{R}^-)$$

The other form of BT can be prove similarly. □

Proof of. Fact 2. It suffices to show that Unsat 1 and Unsat2 hold in **stC1**. Let $\mathfrak{M} = (W, f, V^+, V^-)$ be a selection model satisfying (id). For Unsat1, suppose $\mathfrak{M}, w \Vdash \varphi > \neg\varphi$. Then $f(w, \varphi) \neq \emptyset$ and $f(w, \varphi) \subseteq [\![\neg\varphi]\!]^+ = [\![\varphi]\!]^-$. On the other hand, by (id), we have $f(w, \varphi) \subseteq [\![\varphi]\!]^+$. It follows that $f(w, \varphi) \subseteq [\![\varphi]\!]^- \cap [\![\varphi]\!]^+ = \emptyset$, contradiction. Similarly for $\neg\varphi > \varphi$.

For Unsat2: suppose $\mathfrak{M}, w \Vdash \varphi > \psi$, then $\emptyset \neq f(w, \varphi) \subseteq [\![\psi]\!]^+$. Thus $\emptyset \neq f(w, \varphi) \nsubseteq [\![\psi]\!]^- = [\![\neg\psi]\!]^+$, which means $\mathfrak{M}, w \nVdash \varphi > \neg\psi$. □

Proof of. Fact 3. An instance of one form of cBT is proved in **stC1** as follows.

$$\dfrac{\dfrac{\dfrac{\dfrac{\dfrac{y \xrightarrow{p} z \Rightarrow y \xrightarrow{p} z, z : \neg q \qquad \dfrac{y \xrightarrow{p} z, z : q \Rightarrow z : q}{y \xrightarrow{p} z \Rightarrow z : q, z : \neg q}\,(\neg \mathrm{R})}{y \xrightarrow{p} z \Rightarrow y : p > q, z : \neg q}\,(>\mathrm{R}^+)}{\Rightarrow y : p > q, y : p > \neg q}\,(>\mathrm{R}^-)}{y : \neg(p > \neg q) \Rightarrow y : p > q}\,(\neg \mathrm{L})}{x \xrightarrow{\neg(p>\neg q)} y \Rightarrow y : p > q}\,(\mathrm{ID})}{\Rightarrow x : \neg(p > \neg q) > (p > q)}\,(>\mathrm{R}^-)$$

The other form of cBT can be proved similarly. □

Proof of. Fact 4. We prove an instance of SA in **stC1**.

$$\dfrac{\dfrac{\dfrac{\dfrac{\dfrac{z : p \Rightarrow y : q, z : p}{z : p, z : \neg p \Rightarrow y : q}\,(\neg\mathrm{L})}{y \xrightarrow{p} z, z : \neg p \Rightarrow y : q}\,(\mathrm{ID})}{y : p > \neg p \Rightarrow y : q}\,(>\mathrm{L}^-)}{x \xrightarrow{p > \neg p} y \Rightarrow y : q}\,(\mathrm{ID})}{\Rightarrow x : (p > \neg p) > q}\,(>\mathrm{R}^-)$$

Proof of. Fact 5. For validity, we give a proof in **stC1**. For invalidity, we give a counterexample in **stC3**.

For 1, we have

$$\dfrac{\dfrac{\dfrac{\dfrac{x \xrightarrow{p} y, y : \neg q \Rightarrow x \xrightarrow{p} y \qquad \dfrac{x \xrightarrow{p} y, y : q \Rightarrow y : q}{x \xrightarrow{p} y, y : q, y : \neg q \Rightarrow}\,(\neg\mathrm{L})}{x : p > q, x \xrightarrow{p} y, x : \neg q \Rightarrow}\,(>\mathrm{L}^+)}{x : p > q, x : p > \neg q \Rightarrow}\,(>\mathrm{L}^-)}{x : (p > q) \wedge (p > \neg q) \Rightarrow}\,(\wedge\mathrm{L})}{\Rightarrow x : \neg((p > q) \wedge (p > \neg q))}\,(\neg\mathrm{R})$$

Clause 2 does not hold. Here is a countermodel. Let $\mathfrak{M} = (W, f, V^+, V^-)$ be a selection model, where $W = \{w, u\}$, $f(w, p) = \{w\}$, $f(w, \neg p) = \{u\}$, $V^+(p) = \{w\}$, $V^-(p) = \{u\}$, $V^+(q) = W$, $V^-(q) = \emptyset$. Note that $\mathfrak{M}$ satisfies (id) and (mp). Then $\emptyset \neq f(w, p) \subseteq [\![q]\!]^+$ and $\emptyset \neq f(w, \neg p) \subseteq [\![q]\!]^+$. Thus we have that $\mathfrak{M}, w \Vdash p > q$ and $\mathfrak{M}, w \Vdash \neg p > q$, hence $\mathfrak{M}, w \Vdash (p > q) \wedge (\neg p > q)$, i.e., $\mathfrak{M}, w \dashv\!\vert\, \neg((p > q) \wedge (\neg p > q))$.

Clause 3 and 4 are obvious. We leave the verification to the reader.

For 5, let $\mathfrak{M} = (W, f, V^+, V^-)$ be a selection model, where $W = \{w, u\}$, $f(w, p) = \{w\}$, $f(w, q) = \{u\}$, $V^+(p) = \{w\}$, $V^-(p) = \{u\}$, $V^+(q) = \{u\}$, $V^-(q) = \{w\}$. Note that $\mathfrak{M}$ satisfies (id) and (mp). Then it can be verified that $\mathfrak{M}, w \dashv\!\vert\, p > (q > p)$.

For 6, let $\mathfrak{M} = (W, f, V^+, V^-)$ be a selection model, where $W = \{w, u\}$, $f(w, p) = \{w\}$, $f(w, \neg p) = \{u\}$, $V^+(p) = \{w\}$, $V^-(p) = \{u\}$, $V^+(q) = \emptyset$, $V^-(q) = W$. Note that $\mathfrak{M}$ satisfy (id) and (mp). Then it can be verified that $\mathfrak{M}, w \dashv\!\vert\, p > (\neg p > q)$.

Clause 7 does not hold. To invalidate $\varphi > (\psi > \chi)$, we need to find a world w such that all the closest φ-worlds (which cannot be empty) falsify $\psi > \chi$, which is impossible since $\psi > \chi$ is a logical truth. □

References

1. Angell, R.B.: A propositional logic with subjunctive conditionals. J. Symbolic Logic **27**(3), 327–343 (1962)
2. Cantwell, J.: The logic of conditional negation. Notre Dame J. Formal Logic **49**(3), 245–260 (2008)
3. Cobreros, P., Egré, P., Ripley, D., van Rooij, R.: Tolerant, classical, strict. J. Philos. Log. **41**(2), 347–385 (2012)

4. Estrada-González, L., Ramírez-Cámara, E.: A comparison of connexive logics. IfColog J. Logics Their Appl. **3**(3), 341–355 (2016)
5. Kapsner, A.: Strong connexivity. Thought J. Philosophy **1**(2), 141–145 (2012)
6. Kapsner, A., Omori, H.: Counterfactuals in Nelson logic. In: Baltag, A., Seligman, J., Yamada, T. (eds.) LORI 2017. LNCS, vol. 10455, pp. 497–511. Springer, Heidelberg (2017). https://doi.org/10.1007/978-3-662-55665-8_34
7. Klinedinst, N.: Quantified conditionals and conditional excluded middle. J. Semant. **28**(1), 149–170 (2011)
8. Lewis, D.: Counterfactuals. Harvard University Press (1973)
9. McCall, S.: Connexive implication. J. Symbolic Logic **31**(3), 415–433 (1966)
10. Olivetti, N., Panic, N., Pozzato, G.L.: Labelled sequent calculi for conditional logics: conditional excluded middle and conditional modus ponens finally together. In: Dovier, A., Montanari, A., Orlandini, A. (eds.) AIxIA 2022 – Advances in Artificial Intelligence, pp. 345–357. Springer, Cham (2023). https://doi.org/10.1007/978-3-031-27181-6_24
11. Olivetti, N., Pozzato, G.L., Schwind, C.B.: A sequent calculus and a theorem prover for standard conditional logics. ACM Trans. Comput. Logic **8**(4), 22–es (2007)
12. Omori, H.: From paraconsistent logic to dialetheic logic. In: Andreas, H., Verdée, P. (eds.) Logical Studies of Paraconsistent Reasoning in Science and Mathematics. TL, vol. 45, pp. 111–134. Springer, Cham (2016). https://doi.org/10.1007/978-3-319-40220-8_8
13. Ripley, D.: Conservatively extending classical logic with transparent truth. Rev. Symbolic Logic **5**(2), 354–378 (2012)
14. Santorio, P.: Path semantics for indicative conditionals. Mind **131**(521), 59–98 (2022)
15. Shaffer, M.J., Beebe, J.: Folk judgments about conditional excluded middle. In: Aberdein, A., Inglis, M. (eds.) Advances in Experimental Philosophy of Logic and Mathematics, pp. 251–276. Bloomsbury Academic (2019)
16. Stalnaker, R.: A theory of conditionals. In: Rescher, N. (ed.) Studies in Logical Theory, pp. 98–112. Basil Blackwell Publishers (1968)
17. Stalnaker, R.C.: A defense of conditional excluded middle. In: Harper, W.L., Stalnaker, R., Pearce, G. (eds.) IFS: Conditionals, Belief, Decision, Chance and Time. The University of Western Ontario Series in Philosophy of Science, pp. 87–104. Springer, Dordrecht (1981). https://doi.org/10.1007/978-94-009-9117-0_4
18. Strawson, P.F.: Introduction to Logical Theory. Introduction to Logical Theory, Wiley, Oxford, England (1952)
19. Wansing, H.: Connexive modal logic. In: Schmidt, R., Pratt-Hartmann, I., Reynolds, M., Wansing, H. (eds.) Advances in Modal Logic, vol. 5, pp. 367–383. CSLI Publications (2005)
20. Wansing, H., Omori, H.: Connexive logic, connexivity, and connexivism: remarks on terminology. Studia Logica **112**, 1–35 (2023)
21. Williams, J.R.G.: Defending conditional excluded middle. Noûs **44**(4), 650–668 (2010)

A Linear Proof Language for Second-Order Intuitionistic Linear Logic

Alejandro Díaz-Caro[1,2,3], Gilles Dowek[4], Malena Ivnisky[2,3,5](✉), and Octavio Malherbe[6]

[1] DCyT, Universidad Nacional de Quilmes, Bernal, PBA, Argentina
[2] FCEyN, DC, Universidad de Buenos Aires, Buenos Aires, Argentina
malenaivnisky@gmail.com
[3] ICC, Universidad de Buenos Aires-CONICET, Buenos Aires, Argentina
[4] Inria, LMF, ENS Paris-Saclay, Gif-sur-Yvette, France
[5] PEDECIBA, Universidad de la República–MEC, Montevideo, Uruguay
[6] IMERL, FIng, Universidad de la República, Montevideo, Uruguay

Abstract. We present a polymorphic linear lambda-calculus as a proof language for second-order intuitionistic linear logic. The calculus includes addition and scalar multiplication, enabling the proof of a linearity result at the syntactic level.

Keywords: Proof theory · Lambda calculus · Linear logic · Polymorphism

1 Introduction

Linear Logic [19] is named as such because it is modelled by vector spaces and linear maps, and more generally by monoidal categories [5,6,17,22]. These types of categories also include the so-called Cartesian categories, generating a formal place of interaction between purely algebraic structures and purely logical structures, i.e. between algebraic operations and the exponential connective "!". In the strictly linear fragment (without !), functions between two propositions are linear functions. However, expressing this linearity within the proof-term language itself is challenging. Properties such as $f(u+v) = f(u) + f(v)$ and $f(a \cdot u) = a \cdot f(u)$, for some scalar a, require operations like addition and scalar multiplication, which are typically absent in the proof language.

In [12], this challenge has been addressed. The Intuitionistic Multiplicative Additive Linear Logic is considered and extended with addition and scalar multiplication within the proof-terms. The resulting calculus, the $\mathcal{L}^{\mathcal{S}}$-calculus, does not alter the provability of formulas but allows us to express linear properties. It has been proved that any proof-term $t\ (u \mathbin{\boldsymbol{+}} v)$, where t is a proof-term of $A \multimap B$

Supported by PICT 2021-I-A-00090 and 2019-1272, PIP 11220200100368CO, the French-Argentinian IRP SINFIN, and CSIC-UdelaR I+D-22520220100073UD.

G. Metcalfe et al. (Eds.): WoLLIC 2024, LNCS 14672, pp. 18–35, 2024.
https://doi.org/10.1007/978-3-031-62687-6_2

and u and v are proof-terms of A, is extensionally equivalent to the proof-term $t\ u \boldsymbol{+} t\ v$. Similarly, $t\ (a \bullet u)$ is equivalent to $a \bullet t\ u$.

This extension involves changing the proof-term $\star$ of proposition $\mathtt{1}$ into a family of proof-terms $a.\star$, one for each scalar a in a given fixed semiring $\mathcal{S}$:

$$\frac{}{\vdash a.\star : \mathtt{1}}\ \mathtt{1}_i(a)$$

The following two deduction rules have also been added:

$$\frac{\Gamma \vdash t : A \quad \Gamma \vdash u : A}{\Gamma \vdash t \boldsymbol{+} u : A}\ \text{sum} \qquad\qquad \frac{\Gamma \vdash t : A}{\Gamma \vdash a \bullet t : A}\ \text{prod}(a)$$

Incorporating these rules requires adding commuting rules to preserve cut-elimination. Indeed, the new rules may appear between an introduction and an elimination of some connective. For example, consider the following derivation.

$$\frac{\dfrac{\dfrac{\Gamma \vdash A \quad \Gamma \vdash B}{\Gamma \vdash A \,\&\, B}\ \&_i}{\Gamma \vdash A \,\&\, B}\ \text{prod}(a) \qquad \Gamma, A \vdash C}{\Gamma \vdash C}\ \&_{e1}$$

To achieve cut-elimination, we must commute the rule prod(a) either with the introduction or with the elimination, as follows:

$$\frac{\dfrac{\dfrac{\Gamma \vdash A}{\Gamma \vdash A}\ \text{prod}(a) \quad \dfrac{\Gamma \vdash B}{\Gamma \vdash B}\ \text{prod}(a)}{\Gamma \vdash A \,\&\, B}\ \&_i \qquad \Gamma, A \vdash C}{\Gamma \vdash C}\ \&_{e1} \qquad \frac{\dfrac{\dfrac{\Gamma \vdash A \quad \Gamma \vdash B}{\Gamma \vdash A \,\&\, B}\ \&_i \qquad \Gamma, A \vdash C}{\Gamma \vdash C}\ \&_{e1}}{\Gamma \vdash C}\ \text{prod}(a)$$

Both of these are reducible. We refer to the sum and prod(a) rules as *interstitial rules*, as they can appear in the interstice between an introduction and an elimination. We choose to commute these rules with the introductions as much as possible. This means we introduce the following commutation rule $a \bullet \langle t, u\rangle \longrightarrow \langle a \bullet t, a \bullet u\rangle$ instead of the alternative rule $\delta^1_\&(a \bullet t, x^A.u) \longrightarrow a \bullet \delta^1_\&(t, x^A.u)$. This choice provides a better introduction property: A closed irreducible proof-term of a proposition $A \,\&\, B$ is a pair.

In this new paper, we extend the proof system to second-order intuitionistic linear logic, adding the exponential connective and a universal quantifier. We prove that the linearity result still holds for second order. This is an intermediate step in a long-term research towards the definition of second-order categorical semantics in linear categories, building on the work of [20] and extending the semantics defined in [15]. The midterm objective is to define a second-order linear model in which quantum computing can be encoded.

The initial development of the proof language $\mathcal{L}^{\mathcal{S}}$ [12], paved the way for the development of the second-order version presented in this paper. While our primary focus is on introducing a minimal extension to the proof language within the realm of second-order intuitionistic linear logic, our work draws inspiration from various domains, particularly quantum programming languages. These languages were trailblazers in merging programming constructs with algebraic operations, such as addition and scalar multiplication.

QML [1] introduced the concept of superposition of terms through the if° constructor, allowing the representation of linear combinations $a.u + b.v$ by the expression $\mathsf{if}^\circ\ a.|0\rangle + b.|1\rangle$ $\mathsf{then}\ u\ \mathsf{else}\ v$. The linearity (and even unitarity) properties of QML were established through a translation to quantum circuits.

The ZX calculus [9], a graphical language based on a categorical model, lacks direct syntax for addition or scalar multiplication but defines a framework where such constructs can be interpreted. This language is extended by the Many Worlds Calculus [8] which allows for linear combinations of diagrams.

The algebraic lambda-calculus [24] and Lineal [4] exhibit syntax similarities with $\mathcal{L}^{\mathcal{S}}$-calculus. However, the algebraic lambda-calculus lacks a proof of linearity in its simple intuitionistic type system. In contrast, Lineal enforces linearity without a dedicated type system, relying on explicit definitions like $f(u + v) = f(u) + f(v)$ and $f(a.u) = a.f(u)$. Several type systems have been proposed for Lineal [2,3,13,14,16], including some polymorphic ones. However, none of these systems are related to linear logic, and their purpose is not to prove linearity, as we do, but rather to enforce it.

Our contributions are as follows:

- We extend the $\mathcal{L}^{\mathcal{S}}$-calculus to Church-style second-order intuitionistic linear logic, resulting in the $\mathcal{L}^{\mathcal{S}}_2$-calculus (Sect. 2).
- We prove its correctness (Sect. 3), namely, Subject Reduction (Theorem 3.1), Confluence (Theorem 3.2), Strong Normalisation (Theorem 3.12), and the Introduction Property (Theorem 3.13). In particular, the proof of strong normalisation involves applying two techniques due to Girard: ultra-reduction and reducibility candidates.
- Since it is an extension, the encodings for vectors (Sect. 4.1) and matrices (Sect. 4.2), already present in the $\mathcal{L}^{\mathcal{S}}$-calculus are still valid. We provide detailed explanations of these encodings for self-containment. Since we have polymorphism and the exponential connective, we also show an example of an iterator in the $\mathcal{L}^{\mathcal{S}}_2$-calculus (Sect. 4.3).
- Finally, we prove that the linearity result is also valid for the second order without exponentials (Sect. 5).

Due to space limitations, a version of this paper with all the omitted proofs has been uploaded to `arXiv:2310.08517`.

2 The $\mathcal{L}^{\mathcal{S}}_2$-Calculus

The $\mathcal{L}^{\mathcal{S}}_2$-logic is the second-order intuitionistic linear logic (we follow the presentation of F_{DILL} [20], extended with the additive linear connectives).

$$A = X \mid \mathtt{1} \mid A \multimap A \mid A \otimes A \mid \top \mid \mathtt{0} \mid A \,\&\, A \mid A \oplus A \mid !A \mid \forall X.A$$

The α-equivalence relation and the free and bound variables of a proposition are defined as usual, we write as $\mathsf{FV}(A)$ the set of free variables of A. Propositions are defined modulo α-equivalence. A proposition is closed if it contains no free variables. We write $(B/X)A$ for the substitution of B for X in A.

Let $\mathcal{S}$ be a semiring of *scalars*, for instance $\{\star\}$, $\mathbb{N}$, $\mathbb{Q}$, $\mathbb{R}$, or $\mathbb{C}$. The proof-terms of the $\mathcal{L}_2^{\mathcal{S}}$-calculus are given in Fig. 1, where a is a scalar in $\mathcal{S}$.

	Introductions	Eliminations	Connective
$t = x \mid t \mathbin{+} u \mid a \bullet t$			
	$\mid a.\star$	$\mid \delta_{\mathtt{1}}(t, u)$	$(\mathtt{1})$
	$\mid \lambda x^A.t$	$\mid t\ u$	$(\multimap)$
	$\mid t \otimes u$	$\mid \delta_{\otimes}(t, x^A y^B.u)$	$(\otimes)$
	$\mid \langle\rangle$		$(\top)$
		$\mid \delta_{\mathtt{0}}(t)$	$(\mathtt{0})$
	$\mid \langle t, u\rangle$	$\mid \delta^1_{\&}(t, x^A.u) \mid \delta^2_{\&}(t, x^B.u)$	$(\&)$
	$\mid inl(t) \mid inr(t)$	$\mid \delta_{\oplus}(t, x^A.u, y^B.v)$	$(\oplus)$
	$\mid !t$	$\mid \delta_!(t, x^A.u)$	$(!)$
	$\mid \Lambda X.t$	$\mid t\ A$	$(\forall)$

Fig. 1. The proof-terms of the $\mathcal{L}_2^{\mathcal{S}}$-calculus.

The α-equivalence relation and the free and bound variables of a proof-term are defined as usual, we write as $\mathsf{fv}(t)$ the set of free variables of t. Proof-terms are defined modulo α-equivalence. A proof-term is closed if it contains no free variables. We write $(u/x)t$ for the substitution of u for x in t and if $\mathsf{fv}(t) \subseteq \{x\}$, we also use the notation $t\{u\}$, when there is at most one free variable in t.

A judgement has the form $\Xi; \Gamma \vdash t : A$, where Ξ is the non-linear context and Γ the linear one. The deduction rules are those of Fig. 2. These rules are exactly the deduction rules of second-order intuitionistic linear natural deduction, with proof-terms, with two differences: the interstitial rules and the scalars (see Sect. 1).

The reduction rules are those of Fig. 3. As usual, the reduction relation is written $\longrightarrow$, its inverse $\longleftarrow$, its reflexive-transitive closure $\longrightarrow^*$, the reflexive-transitive closure of its inverse ${}^*\!\longleftarrow$, and its reflexive-symmetric-transitive closure $\equiv$. The first nine rules correspond to the reduction of cuts on the connectives $\mathtt{1}$, $\multimap$, $\otimes$, $\&$, $\oplus$, $!$, and $\forall$. The sixteen others enable us to commute the interstitial rules sum and prod(a) with the introduction rules of the connectives $\mathtt{1}$, $\multimap$, $\top$, $\&$, $!$, and $\forall$, and with the elimination rule of the connectives $\otimes$ and $\oplus$. For instance, the rule $\langle t, u\rangle \mathbin{+} \langle v, w\rangle \longrightarrow \langle t \mathbin{+} v, u \mathbin{+} w\rangle$ pushes the symbol $\mathbin{+}$ inside the pair. The zero-ary commutation rules add and multiply the scalars: $a.\star \mathbin{+} b.\star \longrightarrow (a + b).\star$, $a \bullet b.\star \longrightarrow (a \times b).\star$.

3 Correctness

We now prove the subject reduction, confluence, strong normalisation, and introduction properties of the $\mathcal{L}^{\mathcal{S}}_{2}$-calculus.

The subject reduction property is not completely trivial. As noted in the introduction, we commute the sum rule with the introductions *as much as possible*. It is not possible in the case of the connectives $\otimes$ and $\oplus$, since it would break subject reduction. For example, the rule $(t \otimes u) \boldsymbol{+} (v \otimes w) \longrightarrow (t \boldsymbol{+} v) \otimes (u \boldsymbol{+} w)$ would not be valid, as we have $\varnothing; x^A, y^A \vdash (x \otimes y) \boldsymbol{+} (y \otimes x) : A \otimes A$ but $\varnothing; x^A, y^A \nvdash (x \boldsymbol{+} y) \otimes (y \boldsymbol{+} x) : A \otimes A$, since the rule $\otimes_i$ is multiplicative.

$$\frac{}{\Xi; x^A \vdash x : A}\ \text{lin-ax} \qquad \frac{}{\Xi, x^A; \varnothing \vdash x : A}\ \text{ax} \qquad \frac{\Xi;\Gamma \vdash t : A \quad \Xi;\Gamma \vdash u : A}{\Xi;\Gamma \vdash t \boldsymbol{+} u : A}\ \text{sum}$$

$$\frac{\Xi;\Gamma \vdash t : A}{\Xi;\Gamma \vdash a \bullet t : A}\ \text{prod}(a) \qquad \frac{}{\Xi;\varnothing \vdash a.\star : \mathtt{1}}\ \mathtt{1}_i(a) \qquad \frac{\Xi;\Gamma \vdash t : \mathtt{1} \quad \Xi;\Delta \vdash u : A}{\Xi;\Gamma,\Delta \vdash \delta_{\mathtt{1}}(t,u) : A}\ \mathtt{1}_e$$

$$\frac{\Xi;\Gamma, x^A \vdash t : B}{\Xi;\Gamma \vdash \lambda x^A.t : A \multimap B}\ \multimap_i \qquad \frac{\Xi;\Gamma \vdash t : A \multimap B \quad \Xi;\Delta \vdash u : A}{\Xi;\Gamma,\Delta \vdash t\ u : B}\ \multimap_e$$

$$\frac{\Xi;\Gamma \vdash t : A \quad \Xi;\Delta \vdash u : B}{\Xi;\Gamma,\Delta \vdash t \otimes u : A \otimes B}\ \otimes_i \qquad \frac{\Xi;\Gamma \vdash t : A \otimes B \quad \Xi;\Delta, x : A, y : B \vdash u : C}{\Xi;\Gamma,\Delta \vdash \delta_{\otimes}(t, x^A y^B.u) : C}\ \otimes_e$$

$$\frac{}{\Xi;\Gamma \vdash \langle\rangle : \top}\ \top_i \qquad \frac{\Xi;\Gamma \vdash t : \mathtt{0}}{\Xi;\Gamma,\Delta \vdash \delta_{\mathtt{0}}(t) : C}\ \mathtt{0}_e \qquad \frac{\Xi;\Gamma \vdash t : A \quad \Xi;\Gamma \vdash u : B}{\Xi;\Gamma \vdash \langle t, u\rangle : A \mathbin{\&} B}\ \&_i$$

$$\frac{\Xi;\Gamma \vdash t : A \mathbin{\&} B \quad \Xi;\Delta, x^A \vdash u : C}{\Xi;\Gamma,\Delta \vdash \delta^1_{\&}(t, x^A.u) : C}\ \&_{e1} \qquad \frac{\Xi;\Gamma \vdash t : A \mathbin{\&} B \quad \Xi;\Delta, x^B \vdash u : C}{\Xi;\Gamma,\Delta \vdash \delta^2_{\&}(t, x^B.u) : C}\ \&_{e2}$$

$$\frac{\Xi;\Gamma \vdash t : A}{\Xi;\Gamma \vdash \mathit{inl}(t) : A \oplus B}\ \oplus_{i1} \qquad \frac{\Xi;\Gamma \vdash t : B}{\Xi;\Gamma \vdash \mathit{inr}(t) : A \oplus B}\ \oplus_{i2}$$

$$\frac{\Xi;\Gamma \vdash t : A \oplus B \quad \Xi;\Delta, x^A \vdash u : C \quad \Xi;\Delta, y^B \vdash v : C}{\Xi;\Gamma,\Delta \vdash \delta_{\oplus}(t, x^A.u, y^B.v) : C}\ \oplus_e$$

$$\frac{\Xi;\varnothing \vdash t : A}{\Xi;\varnothing \vdash\ !t : !A}\ !_i \qquad \frac{\Xi;\Gamma \vdash t : !A \quad \Xi, x^A;\Delta \vdash u : B}{\Xi;\Gamma,\Delta \vdash \delta_{!}(t, x^A.u) : B}\ !_e$$

$$\frac{\Xi;\Gamma \vdash t : A \quad X \notin \mathsf{FV}(\Xi,\Gamma)}{\Xi;\Gamma \vdash \Lambda X.t : \forall X.A}\ \forall_i \qquad \frac{\Xi;\Gamma \vdash t : \forall X.B}{\Xi;\Gamma \vdash t\ A : (A/X)B}\ \forall_e$$

Fig. 2. The deduction rules of the $\mathcal{L}^{\mathcal{S}}_{2}$-calculus.

Theorem 3.1 (Subject reduction). *If $\Xi;\Gamma \vdash t : A$ and $t \longrightarrow u$, then $\Xi;\Gamma \vdash u : A$.* □

Theorem 3.2 (Confluence). *The $\mathcal{L}^{\mathcal{S}}_{2}$-calculus is confluent.*

Proof. The reduction system of Fig. 3 applied to well-formed proof-terms is left linear and has no critical pairs. By [21, Theorem 6.8], it is confluent. □

We now prove that all reduction sequences are finite. To handle the symbols $\boldsymbol{+}$ and $\bullet$ and the associated reduction rules, we prove the strong normalisation of an extended reduction system, in the spirit of Girard's ultra-reduction[1] [18], whose strong normalisation obviously implies that of the rules of Fig. 3.

$$
\begin{array}{rlrl}
\delta_1(a.\star, t) & \longrightarrow a \bullet t & \delta_\oplus(\mathit{inl}(t), x^A.v, y^B.w) & \longrightarrow (t/x)v \\
(\lambda x^A.t)\ u & \longrightarrow (u/x)t & \delta_\oplus(\mathit{inr}(u), x^A.v, y^B.w) & \longrightarrow (u/y)w \\
\delta_\otimes(u \otimes v, x^A y^B.w) & \longrightarrow (u/x, v/y)w & \delta_!(!t, x^A.u) & \longrightarrow (t/x)u \\
\delta^i_\&(\langle t_1, t_2\rangle, x^A.v) & \longrightarrow (t_i/x)v & (\Lambda X.t)\ A & \longrightarrow (A/X)t \\
\hline
a.\star \boldsymbol{+} b.\star & \longrightarrow (a+b).\star & \langle t, u\rangle \boldsymbol{+} \langle v, w\rangle & \longrightarrow \langle t \boldsymbol{+} v, u \boldsymbol{+} w\rangle \\
(\lambda x^A.t) \boldsymbol{+} (\lambda x^A.u) & \longrightarrow \lambda x^A.(t \boldsymbol{+} u) & \delta_\oplus(t \boldsymbol{+} u, x^A.v, y^B.w) & \longrightarrow \\
\delta_\otimes(t \boldsymbol{+} u, x^A y^B.v) & \longrightarrow & \multicolumn{2}{r}{\delta_\oplus(t, x^A.v, y^B.w) \boldsymbol{+} \delta_\oplus(u, x^A.v, y^B.w)} \\
\multicolumn{2}{r}{\delta_\otimes(t, x^A y^B.v) \boldsymbol{+} \delta_\otimes(u, x^A y^B.v)} & !t \boldsymbol{+} !u & \longrightarrow !(t \boldsymbol{+} u) \\
\langle\rangle \boldsymbol{+} \langle\rangle & \longrightarrow \langle\rangle & (\Lambda X.t) \boldsymbol{+} (\Lambda X.u) & \longrightarrow \Lambda X.(t \boldsymbol{+} u) \\
\hline
a \bullet b.\star & \longrightarrow (a \times b).\star & a \bullet \langle t, u\rangle & \longrightarrow \langle a \bullet t, a \bullet u\rangle \\
a \bullet \lambda x^A.t & \longrightarrow \lambda x^A.a \bullet t & \delta_\oplus(a \bullet t, x^A.v, y^B.w) & \longrightarrow a \bullet \delta_\oplus(t, x^A.v, y^B.w) \\
\delta_\otimes(a \bullet t, x^A y^B.v) & \longrightarrow a \bullet \delta_\otimes(t, x^A y^B.v) & a \bullet !t & \longrightarrow !(a \bullet t) \\
a \bullet \langle\rangle & \longrightarrow \langle\rangle & a \bullet \Lambda X.t & \longrightarrow \Lambda X.a \bullet t
\end{array}
$$

Fig. 3. The reduction rules of the $\mathcal{L}^S_2$-calculus.

Definition 3.3 (Ultra-reduction). *Ultra-reduction is defined with the rules of Fig. 3, plus the rules*

$$t \boldsymbol{+} u \longrightarrow t \qquad\qquad t \boldsymbol{+} u \longrightarrow u \qquad\qquad a \bullet t \longrightarrow t$$

Our proof is an extension from the proof of the $\mathcal{L}^S$-calculus [12] and that of System F, using the methods introduced by Tait [23] for Gödel's System T and generalised to System F by Girard [18].

Definition 3.4. SN *is the set of strongly normalising proof-terms and* $Red(t)$ *is the set of one-step reducts of* t. *That is,* $\mathsf{SN} = \{t \mid t \text{ strongly normalises}\}$ *and* $Red(t) = \{u \mid t \longrightarrow u\}$.

Definition 3.5 (Reducibility candidates). *A set of proof-terms* E *is a reducibility candidate if and only if the following conditions are satisfied.*

(CR1) $E \subseteq \mathsf{SN}$.

[1] Ultra-reduction is used, in particular, in the adequacy of the connectives $\boldsymbol{+}$ and $\bullet$.

(CR2) If $t \in E$ and $t \longrightarrow t'$, then $t' \in E$.
(CR3) If t is not an introduction and $Red(t) \subseteq E$, then $t \in E$.
(CR4) If $t \in E$, then for every X and A, $(A/X)t \in E$.

Definition 3.6. *Let E, F be sets of proof-terms. We define the following sets.*

$$
\begin{aligned}
E \mathbin{\hat{\multimap}} F &= \{t \in \mathsf{SN} \mid \textit{if } t \longrightarrow^* \lambda x^A.u, \textit{ then for every } v \in E, (v/x)u \in F\}\\
E \mathbin{\hat{\otimes}} F &= \{t \in \mathsf{SN} \mid \textit{if } t \longrightarrow^* u \otimes v, \textit{ then } u \in E \textit{ and } v \in F\}\\
E \mathbin{\hat{\&}} F &= \{t \in \mathsf{SN} \mid \textit{if } t \longrightarrow^* \langle u, v\rangle, \textit{ then } u \in E \textit{ and } v \in F\}\\
E \mathbin{\hat{\oplus}} F &= \{t \in \mathsf{SN} \mid \textit{if } t \longrightarrow^* \textit{inl}(u), \textit{ then} u \in E \textit{ and if } t \longrightarrow^* \textit{inr}(v), \textit{ then } v \in F\}\\
\hat{!} E &= \{t \in \mathsf{SN} \mid \textit{if } t \longrightarrow^* !u, \textit{ then } u \in E\}
\end{aligned}
$$

The set of all reducibility candidates is called $\mathcal{R}$. A valuation ρ is a map from proposition variables to $\mathcal{R}$.

Definition 3.7. *For any proposition A and valuation ρ, the set of proof-terms $[\![A]\!]_\rho$ is defined as follows:*

$$
\begin{aligned}
[\![X]\!]_\rho &= \rho(X) & [\![\top]\!]_\rho = [\![\mathsf{0}]\!]_\rho &= \mathsf{SN}\\
[\![\mathsf{1}]\!]_\rho &= \mathsf{SN} & [\![A \,\&\, B]\!]_\rho &= [\![A]\!]_\rho \mathbin{\hat{\&}} [\![B]\!]_\rho\\
[\![A \multimap B]\!]_\rho &= [\![A]\!]_\rho \mathbin{\hat{\multimap}} [\![B]\!]_\rho & [\![A \oplus B]\!]_\rho &= [\![A]\!]_\rho \mathbin{\hat{\oplus}} [\![B]\!]_\rho\\
[\![A \otimes B]\!]_\rho &= [\![A]\!]_\rho \mathbin{\hat{\otimes}} [\![B]\!]_\rho & [\![!A]\!]_\rho &= \hat{!}[\![A]\!]_\rho\\
[\![\forall X.A]\!]_\rho &= \{t \in \mathsf{SN} \mid \textit{if } t \longrightarrow^* \Lambda X.u, \textit{ then for every } E \in \mathcal{R}\\
&\qquad \textit{and every proposition } B, (B/X)u \in [\![A]\!]_{\rho, E/X}\}
\end{aligned}
$$

Remark 3.8. The set $[\![A]\!]_\rho$ is defined by induction on the structure of A. Thus, in the case of $\forall$, it cannot directly relate the reducibility candidate E with $[\![B]\!]_\rho$; otherwise, the definition would be circular, particularly when $B = \forall X.A$. This is why Girard proposed the reducibility candidates initially [18] and why there are universal quantifications for both E and B in this definition.

Lemma 3.9. *For any proposition A and valuation ρ, $[\![A]\!]_\rho \in \mathcal{R}$.* □

Lemma 3.10 (Variables). *For any proposition A and any valuation ρ, the set $[\![A]\!]_\rho$ contains all the proof-term variables.*

Proof. By Lemma 3.9, $[\![A]\!]_\rho \in \mathcal{R}$. Since $Red(x)$ is empty, by CR3, $x \in [\![A]\!]_\rho$. □

Theorem 3.11 (Adequacy). *If $\Xi; \Gamma \vdash t : A$, then for any ρ and σ such that for each $x^B \in \Xi \cup \Gamma$, $\sigma(x) \in [\![B]\!]_\rho$, we have $\sigma t \in [\![A]\!]_\rho$.*

Proof. By induction on t. If t is a variable, then, by the definition of σ, $\sigma t \in [\![A]\!]_\rho$. For the other proof-term constructors, we use the adequacy lemmas provided in Appendix A, for example if $t = u\ B$, where u is a proof-term of $\forall X.C$, then, by induction hypothesis, $\sigma u \in [\![\forall X.C]\!]_\rho$. Hence, by Lemma A.8, $\sigma u\ B \in [\![(B/X)C]\!]_\rho$, that is $\sigma t \in [\![A]\!]_\rho$. □

Corollary 3.12 (Strong normalisation). *If* $\Xi; \Gamma \vdash t : A$, *then,* $t \in \mathsf{SN}$.

Proof. By Lemma 3.10, for each $x^B \in \Xi \cup \Gamma$, $x^B \in [\![B]\!]_\rho$. Then, by Theorem 3.11, $t = \mathsf{id}(t) \in [\![A]\!]_\rho$. Hence, by Lemma 3.9, $t \in \mathsf{SN}$. □

Theorem 3.13 (Introduction). *Let* t *be a closed irreducible proof-term of* A.

- *The proposition* A *is not* X.
- *If* A *is* $\mathtt{1}$, *then* t *has the form* $a.\star$.
- *If* A *has the form* $B \multimap C$, *then* t *has the form* $\lambda x^B.u$.
- *If* A *has the form* $B \otimes C$, *then* t *has the form* $u \otimes v$, $u \boldsymbol{+} v$, *or* $a \bullet u$.
- *If* A *is* $\top$, *then* t *is* $\langle\rangle$.
- *The proposition* A *is not* $\mathtt{0}$.
- *If* A *has the form* $B \,\&\, C$, *then* t *has the form* $\langle u, v\rangle$.
- *If* A *has the form* $B \oplus C$, *then* t *has the form* $\mathit{inl}(u)$, $\mathit{inr}(u)$, $u \boldsymbol{+} v$, *or* $a \bullet u$.
- *If* A *has the form* $!B$, *then* t *has the form* $!u$.
- *If* A *has the form* $\forall X.B$, *then* t *has the form* $\Lambda X.u$. □

4 Encodings

In this section, we present the encodings for vectors (Sect. 4.1) and matrices (Sect. 4.2), which were initially introduced in [12] and are replicated here for self-containment. Additionally, we provide one example that uses polymorphism for iteration as an illustration (Sect. 4.3).

Since $\mathcal{S}$ is a semiring, we work with semimodules. However, to help intuition, the reader may think of $\mathcal{S}$ as a field, obtaining a vector space instead.

4.1 Vectors

As there is one rule $\mathtt{1}_i$ for each scalar a, there is one closed irreducible proof-term $a.\star$ for each scalar a. Thus, the closed irreducible proof-terms $a.\star$ of $\mathtt{1}$ are in one-to-one correspondence with the elements of $\mathcal{S}$. Therefore, the proof-terms $\langle a.\star, b.\star\rangle$ of $\mathtt{1} \,\&\, \mathtt{1}$ are in one-to-one correspondence with the elements of $\mathcal{S}^2$, the proof-terms $\langle\langle a.\star, b.\star\rangle, c.\star\rangle$ of $(\mathtt{1} \,\&\, \mathtt{1}) \,\&\, \mathtt{1}$, and also the proof-terms $\langle a.\star, \langle b.\star, c.\star\rangle\rangle$ of $\mathtt{1} \,\&\, (\mathtt{1} \,\&\, \mathtt{1})$, are in one-to-one correspondence with the elements of $\mathcal{S}^3$, etc.

Definition 4.1 (The set $\mathcal{V}$). *The set* $\mathcal{V}$ *is inductively defined as follows:* $\mathtt{1} \in \mathcal{V}$, *and if* A *and* B *are in* $\mathcal{V}$, *then so is* $A \,\&\, B$.

We now show that if $A \in \mathcal{V}$, then the set of closed irreducible proof-terms of A has a structure of $\mathcal{S}$-semimodule.

Definition 4.2 (Zero vector). *If* $A \in \mathcal{V}$, *we define the proof-term* 0_A *of* A *by induction on* A. *If* $A = \mathtt{1}$, *then* $0_A = 0.\star$. *If* $A = A_1 \,\&\, A_2$, *then* $0_A = \langle 0_{A_1}, 0_{A_2}\rangle$.

Lemma 4.3 ($\mathcal{S}$-semimodule structure [12, Lemma 3.4]). *If* $A \in \mathcal{V}$ *and* t, t_1, t_2, *and* t_3 *are closed proof-terms of* A, *then*

1. $(t_1 \mathbin{\boldsymbol{+}} t_2) \mathbin{\boldsymbol{+}} t_3 \equiv t_1 \mathbin{\boldsymbol{+}} (t_2 \mathbin{\boldsymbol{+}} t_3)$
2. $t_1 \mathbin{\boldsymbol{+}} t_2 \equiv t_2 \mathbin{\boldsymbol{+}} t_1$
3. $t \mathbin{\boldsymbol{+}} 0_A \equiv t$
4. $a \bullet b \bullet t \equiv (a \times b) \bullet t$
5. $1 \bullet t \equiv t$
6. $a \bullet (t_1 \mathbin{\boldsymbol{+}} t_2) \equiv a \bullet t_1 \mathbin{\boldsymbol{+}} a \bullet t_2$
7. $(a + b) \bullet t \equiv a \bullet t \mathbin{\boldsymbol{+}} b \bullet t$ □

Definition 4.4 (Dimension of a proposition in $\mathcal{V}$). *To each proposition $A \in \mathcal{V}$, we associate a positive natural number $d(A)$, which is the number of occurrences of the symbol $\mathtt{1}$ in A: $d(\mathtt{1}) = 1$ and $d(B \,\&\, C) = d(B) + d(C)$.*

If $A \in \mathcal{V}$ and $d(A) = n$, then the closed irreducible proof-terms of A and the vectors of $\mathcal{S}^n$ are in one-to-one correspondence.

Definition 4.5 (One-to-one correspondence). *Let $A \in \mathcal{V}$ with $d(A) = n$. To each closed irreducible proof-term t of A, we associate a vector $\underline{t}$ of $\mathcal{S}^n$ as follows:*

If $A = \mathtt{1}$, then $t = a.\star$. We let $\underline{t} = (\,a\,)$.

If $A = A_1 \,\&\, A_2$, then $t = \langle u, v\rangle$. We let $\underline{t}$ be the vector with two blocks $\underline{u}$ and $\underline{v}$: $\underline{t} = \left(\begin{smallmatrix}\underline{u}\\ \underline{v}\end{smallmatrix}\right)$.

To each vector $\mathbf{u}$ of $\mathcal{S}^n$, we associate a closed irreducible proof-term $\overline{\mathbf{u}}^A$ of A as follows:

If $n = 1$, then $\mathbf{u} = (\,a\,)$. We let $\overline{\mathbf{u}}^A = a.\star$.

If $n > 1$, then $A = A_1 \,\&\, A_2$, let n_1 and n_2 be the dimensions of A_1 and A_2. Let $\mathbf{u}_1$ and $\mathbf{u}_2$ be the two blocks of $\mathbf{u}$ of n_1 and n_2 lines, so $\mathbf{u} = \left(\begin{smallmatrix}\mathbf{u}_1\\ \mathbf{u}_2\end{smallmatrix}\right)$. We let $\overline{\mathbf{u}}^A = \langle \overline{\mathbf{u}_1}^{A_1}, \overline{\mathbf{u}_2}^{A_2}\rangle$.

We extend the definition of $\underline{t}$ to any closed proof-term of A, $\underline{t}$ is by definition $\underline{t'}$ where t' is the irreducible form of t.

The next theorem shows that the symbol $\boldsymbol{+}$ expresses the sum of vectors and the symbol $\bullet$, the product of a vector by a scalar.

Theorem 4.6 (Sum and scalar product of vectors [12, Lemmas 3.7 and 3.8]). *Let $A \in \mathcal{V}$, u and v two closed proof-terms of A, and $a \in \mathcal{S}$ a scalar. Then, $\underline{u \mathbin{\boldsymbol{+}} v} = \underline{u} + \underline{v}$ and $\underline{a \bullet u} = a\underline{u}$.* □

4.2 Matrices

We now want to prove that if $A, B \in \mathcal{V}$ with $d(A) = m$ and $d(B) = n$, and F is a linear function from $\mathcal{S}^m$ to $\mathcal{S}^n$, then there exists a closed proof-term f of $A \multimap B$ such that, for all vectors $\mathbf{u} \in \mathcal{S}^m$, $\underline{f\ \overline{\mathbf{u}}^A} = F(\mathbf{u})$. This can equivalently be formulated as the fact that if M is a matrix with m columns and n lines, then there exists a closed proof-term f of $A \multimap B$ such that for all vectors $\mathbf{u} \in \mathcal{S}^m$, $\underline{f\ \overline{\mathbf{u}}^A} = M\mathbf{u}$.

A similar theorem has been proved also in [11] for a non-linear calculus.

Theorem 4.7 (Matrices [12, Theorem 3.10]). *Let $A, B \in \mathcal{V}$ with $d(A) = m$ and $d(B) = n$ and let M be a matrix with m columns and n lines, then there exists a closed proof-term t of $A \multimap B$ such that, for all vectors $\mathbf{u} \in \mathcal{S}^m$, $\underline{t\ \overline{\mathbf{u}}^A} = M\mathbf{u}$.* □

Example 4.8 (Matrices with two columns and two lines). The matrix $\left(\begin{smallmatrix} a & c \\ b & d \end{smallmatrix}\right)$ is expressed as the proof-term $t = \lambda x^{1\&1}.\delta^1_{\&}(x, y^1.\delta_1(y, \langle a.\star, b.\star\rangle)) + \delta^2_{\&}(x, z^1.\delta_1(z, \langle c.\star, d.\star\rangle))$. Then, $t\ \langle e.\star, f.\star\rangle \longrightarrow^* \langle (a\times e+c\times f).\star, (b\times e+d\times f).\star\rangle$.

4.3 Matrix Iterator

The polymorphic extension included in the $\mathcal{L}^{\mathcal{S}}_2$-calculus allows us to encode, for example, natural numbers in a usual way [19, Chapter 5].

$$\mathsf{Nat} = \forall X.X \multimap !(X \multimap X) \multimap X \qquad \mathsf{zero} = \Lambda X.\lambda x^X.\lambda f^{!(X\multimap X)}.\delta_!(f, f'^{X\multimap X}.x)$$
$$\mathsf{succ} = \lambda n^{\mathsf{Nat}}.\Lambda X.\lambda x^X.\lambda f^{!(X\multimap X)}.\delta_!(f, f'^{X\multimap X}.f'(n\ X\ x\ (!f')))$$

We can express the application n times of a square matrix over a vector as follows, where $A \in \mathcal{V}$ with $d(A) = m$.

$$\mathsf{Miter} = \lambda n^{\mathsf{Nat}}.\lambda m^{!(A\multimap A)}.\lambda v^A.n\ A\ v\ m$$

Let M be a square matrix with m columns and lines, and t be the closed proof-term of $A \multimap A$ representing such a matrix. For any vector $\mathbf{u} \in \mathcal{S}^m$ we have $\underline{\mathsf{Miter}\ \hat{n}\ !t\ \overline{\mathbf{u}}^A} = M^n\mathbf{u}$ where $\hat{n}$ is the encoding of $n \in \mathbb{N}$.

5 Linearity

In this section, we prove the converse to Theorem 4.7, that is, that if $A, B \in \mathcal{V}$, then each closed proof-term t of $A \multimap B$ expresses a linear function.

This result is trivially false when we consider the exponential connective. For example, the proof-term $f = \lambda x^{!1}.\delta_!(x, y^1.2.\star)$ of proposition $!1 \multimap 1$ represents the constant function 2, which is not linear. Indeed,

$$f\ (!(a.\star) + !(b.\star)) \longrightarrow^* 2.\star \neq 4.\star \ {}^*\!\!\longleftarrow (f\ !a.\star) + (f\ !b.\star)$$

Hence, this section refers to the $\mathcal{L}^{\mathcal{S}^-}_2$-calculus, which is the $\mathcal{L}^{\mathcal{S}}_2$-calculus without !. That is, we remove the propositions $!A$ and the proof-terms $!t$ and $\delta_!(t, x^A.u)$ from the syntax (cf. Sect. 2), together with their three corresponding reduction rules (cf. Fig. 3). Additionally, we remove the deduction rules ax, $!_i$, and $!_e$ (cf. Fig. 2). With these changes, all interesting judgements have the shape $\varnothing; \Gamma \vdash t : A$; thus, we simply write $\Gamma \vdash t : A$ instead.

Note that the $\forall$ connective is meaningful only when a specific subproof-term is employed more than once. Within the linear deduction system, this can happen in two scenarios: (1) In the multiplicative case, applying the ! constructor to the subproof-term becomes necessary for a valid proof-term. (2) Conversely, in the additive case, the subproof-term can be utilised multiple times without requiring the ! constructor. Hence, the polymorphic construction retains significance even in the absence of the exponential connective.

This section extends the proof for the $\mathcal{L}^{\mathcal{S}}$-calculus [12], adding the polymorphic cases. For self-containment, we include all the definitions.

We want to prove that for any closed proof-term t of $A \multimap B$, if u_1 and u_2 are closed proof-terms of A, then

$$t\ (u_1 + u_2) \equiv t\ u_1 + t\ u_2 \qquad \text{and} \qquad t\ (a \bullet u_1) \equiv a \bullet t\ u_1 \tag{1}$$

The property, however, is not true in general. Consider, for example, $t = \lambda x^{\mathtt{1}}.\lambda y^{\mathtt{1}\multimap\mathtt{1}}.y\ x$ and we have

$$t\ (1.\star + 2.\star) \longrightarrow^* \lambda y^{\mathtt{1}\multimap\mathtt{1}}.y\ 3.\star \not\equiv \lambda y^{\mathtt{1}\multimap\mathtt{1}}.(y\ 1.\star) + (y\ 2.\star)\ {}^*\!\longleftarrow (t\ 1.\star) + (t\ 2.\star)$$

Nevertheless, although the proof-terms $\lambda y^{\mathtt{1}\multimap\mathtt{1}}.y\ 3.\star$ and $\lambda y^{\mathtt{1}\multimap\mathtt{1}}.(y\ 1.\star) + (y\ 2.\star)$ are not equivalent, if we apply them to the identity $\lambda z^{\mathtt{1}}.z$, then both proof-terms $(\lambda y^{\mathtt{1}\multimap\mathtt{1}}.y\ 3.\star)\ \lambda z^{\mathtt{1}}.z$ and $(\lambda y^{\mathtt{1}\multimap\mathtt{1}}.(y\ 1.\star) + (y\ 2.\star))\ \lambda z^{\mathtt{1}}.z$ reduce to $3.\star$. This leads us to introduce a notion of observational equivalence.

Definition 5.1 (Observational equivalence). *Two proof-terms t_1 and t_2 of a proposition B are* observationally equivalent, *$t_1 \sim t_2$, if for all propositions C in $\mathcal{V}$ and for all proof-terms c such that $x^B \vdash c : C$, we have $c\{t_1\} \equiv c\{t_2\}$.*

We shall prove (Corollary 5.6) that for all proof-terms t of proposition $A \multimap B$ and for all closed proof-terms u_1 and u_2 of A, we have $t\ (u_1 + u_2) \sim t\ u_1 + t\ u_2$ and $t\ (a \bullet u_1) \sim a \bullet t\ u_1$. However, a proof of this property by induction on t does not go through and to prove it, we first prove Theorem 5.5, expressing that for all proof-terms t of $A \multimap B$, with $B \in \mathcal{V}$, and closed proof-terms u_1 and u_2 of A, we have the property (1).

We define the following measure which is non-increasing along reduction (see Lemma B.2), over which we will make the induction to prove the linearity theorem (Theorem 5.5).

Definition 5.2 (Measure of a proof-term). *We define the measure μ as follows:*

$$\begin{aligned}
\mu(x) &= 0 & \mu(t + u) &= 1 + \max(\mu(t), \mu(u))\\
\mu(a \bullet t) &= 1 + \mu(t) & \mu(a.\star) &= 1\\
\mu(\delta_{\mathtt{1}}(t, u)) &= 1 + \mu(t) + \mu(u) & \mu(\lambda x^A.t) &= 1 + \mu(t)\\
\mu(t\ u) &= 1 + \mu(t) + \mu(u) & \mu(t \otimes u) &= 1 + \mu(t) + \mu(u)\\
\mu(\delta_{\otimes}(t, x^A y^B.u)) &= 1 + \mu(t) + \mu(u) & \mu(\langle\rangle) &= 1\\
\mu(\delta_{\top}(t)) &= 1 + \mu(t) & \mu(\langle t, u\rangle) &= 1 + \max(\mu(t), \mu(u))\\
\mu(\delta^1_{\&}(t, y^A.u)) &= 1 + \mu(t) + \mu(u) & \mu(\delta^2_{\&}(t, y^A.u)) &= 1 + \mu(t) + \mu(u)\\
\mu(\mathit{inl}(t)) &= 1 + \mu(t) & \mu(\mathit{inr}(t)) &= 1 + \mu(t)
\end{aligned}$$
$$\mu(\delta_{\oplus}(t, y^A.u, z^B.v)) = 1 + \mu(t) + \max(\mu(u), \mu(v))$$
$$\mu(\Lambda X.t) = 1 + \mu(t) \qquad \mu(t\ A) = 1 + \mu(t)$$

Any proof-term in the linear fragment of the $\mathcal{L}_2^{\mathcal{S}^-}$-calculus can be decomposed into a sequence of elimination rules, forming an elimination context, and a proof-term u that is either a variable, an introduction, a sum, or a product.

Definition 5.3 (Elimination context). *An elimination context is a proof-term with a single free variable, written* _, *that is a proof-term in the language*

$$K = \_ \mid \delta_1(K, u) \mid K\ u \mid \delta_\otimes(K, x^A y^B.v) \mid \delta_0(K)$$
$$\mid \delta^1_\&(K, x^A.r) \mid \delta^2_\&(K, x^B.r) \mid \delta_\oplus(K, x^A.r, y^B.s) \mid K\ A$$

where u is a closed proof-term, $\mathsf{fv}(v) = \{x, y\}$, $\mathsf{fv}(r) \subseteq \{x\}$, *and* $\mathsf{fv}(s) \subseteq \{y\}$.

Lemma 5.4 (Decomposition of a proof-term). *In the $\mathcal{L}^{\mathcal{S}^-}_2$-calculus, if t is an irreducible proof-term such that $x^C \vdash t : A$, then there exist an elimination context K, a proof-term u, and a proposition B, such that $\_^B \vdash K : A$, $x^C \vdash u : B$, u is either the variable x, an introduction, a sum, or a product, and $t = K\{u\}$.*

Proof. See Appendix B. □

We now have the tools to prove the linearity theorem. We first prove (Theorem 5.5) that for any proof-term t of $B \in \mathcal{V}$ such that $x^A \vdash t : B$, we have the property (1). Then, Corollary 5.6 generalises the proof-term for any B stating the observational equivalence. Finally, Corollary 5.7 is just a reformulation of it, in terms of linear functions.

Theorem 5.5 (Linearity). *In the $\mathcal{L}^{\mathcal{S}^-}_2$-calculus, if A is a proposition, B is proposition of $\mathcal{V}$, t is a proof-term such that $x^A \vdash t : B$ and u_1 and u_2 are two closed proof-terms of A, then $t\{u_1 + u_2\} \equiv t\{u_1\} + t\{u_2\}$ and $t\{a \bullet u_1\} \equiv a \bullet t\{u_1\}$.*

Proof (Sketch, see Appendix B*).* Without loss of generality, we can assume that t is irreducible. We proceed by induction on $\mu(t)$, using Lemma 5.4, to decompose the proof-term t into $K\{t'\}$ where t' is either the variable x, an introduction, a sum, or a product. Then, we analyse case by case. □

We can now generalise the linearity result, as explained at the beginning of the section, by using the observational equivalence $\sim$.

Corollary 5.6 ([12, Corollary 4.11]). *In the $\mathcal{L}^{\mathcal{S}^-}_2$-calculus, if A and B are any propositions, t a proof-term such that $x^A \vdash t : B$, and u_1 and u_2 two closed proof-terms of A, then $t\{u_1 + u_2\} \sim t\{u_1\} + t\{u_2\}$ and $t\{a \bullet u_1\} \sim a \bullet t\{u_1\}$.*

Proof. See Appendix B. □

Finally, the next corollary is the converse of Theorem 4.7.

Corollary 5.7. *In the $\mathcal{L}^{\mathcal{S}^-}_2$-calculus, let $A, B \in \mathcal{V}$, such that $d(A) = m$ and $d(B) = n$, and t be a closed proof-term of $A \multimap B$. Then the function F from $\mathcal{S}^m$ to $\mathcal{S}^n$, defined as $F(\mathbf{u}) = \underline{t\ \overline{\mathbf{u}}^A}$ is linear.*

Proof. Using Corollary 5.7 and Theorem 4.6, we have

$$\begin{aligned} F(\mathbf{u}+\mathbf{v}) &= \underline{t\ \overline{\mathbf{u}+\mathbf{v}}^A} = \underline{t\ (\overline{\mathbf{u}}^A + \overline{\mathbf{v}}^A)} = \underline{t\ \overline{\mathbf{u}}^A + t\ \overline{\mathbf{v}}^A} \\ &= \underline{t\ \overline{\mathbf{u}}^A} + \underline{t\ \overline{\mathbf{v}}^A} = F(\mathbf{u}) + F(\mathbf{v}) \\ F(a\mathbf{u}) &= \underline{t\ \overline{a\mathbf{u}}^A} = \underline{t\ (a \bullet \overline{\mathbf{u}}^A)} = \underline{a \bullet t\ \overline{\mathbf{u}}^A} = a\underline{t\ \overline{\mathbf{u}}^A} = aF(\mathbf{u}) \end{aligned}$$

□

6 Conclusion

In this paper, we have presented the $\mathcal{L}_2^{\mathcal{S}}$-calculus, an extension of the $\mathcal{L}^{\mathcal{S}}$-calculus with second-order polymorphism and the exponential connective, allowing non-linear functions and making it a more expressive language. We have proved all its correctness properties, including algebraic linearity for the linear fragment.

The $\mathcal{L}^{\mathcal{S}}$-calculus was originally introduced as a core language for quantum computing. Its ability to represent matrices and vectors makes it suitable for expressing quantum programs when taking $\mathcal{S} = \mathbb{C}$. Moreover, by taking $\mathcal{S} = \mathbb{R}^+$, one can consider a probabilistic language, and by taking $\mathcal{S} = \{\star\}$, a linear extension of the parallel lambda calculus [7].

To consider this calculus as a proper quantum language, we would need not only to ensure algebraic linearity but also to ensure unitarity, using techniques such as those in [14]. Also, the language $\mathcal{L}^{\mathcal{S}}$ can be extended with a non-deterministic connective $\odot$ [11], from which a quantum measurement operator can be encoded. We did not add such a connective to our presentation, to stay in a pure linear logic setting, however, the extension is straightforward. Another future work is to extend the categorical model of the $\mathcal{L}\odot^{\mathcal{S}}$-calculus given in [15]. To accommodate the $\mathcal{L}_2^{\mathcal{S}}$-calculus, we would need to use hyperdoctrines [10], following the approach of [20], a direction we are willing to pursue.

A Proof of Section 3

Lemma A.1. *For any A, B, and valuation ρ, $[\![(B/X)A]\!]_\rho = [\![A]\!]_{\rho,[\![B]\!]_\rho/X}$.*

Proof. The proof follows by induction on A. □

In Lemmas A.3 to A.8, we prove the adequacy of each proof-term constructor. We only provide those that differ from their non-polymorphic counterpart [12].

If t is a strongly normalising proof-term, we write $|t|$ for the maximum length of a reduction sequence issued from t.

Lemma A.2 (Normalisation of sums and products). *If t and u strongly normalise, then so do $t + u$ and $a \bullet t$.*

Proof. We prove that all the one-step reducts of $t + u$ strongly normalise, by induction first on $|t|+|u|$ and then on the size of t. If the reduction takes place in t or in u we apply the induction hypothesis. Otherwise, the reduction occurs at the root, and the only new rule to consider is either $(\Lambda X.t') + (\Lambda X.u') \longrightarrow \Lambda X.(t' + u')$ or $!t' + !u' \longrightarrow !(t' + u')$. In both cases by induction hypothesis, the proof-term $t' + u'$ strongly normalises, thus so do the proof-terms $\Lambda X.(t' + u')$, and $!(t' + u')$.

The case of $a \bullet t$ is similar. □

Lemma A.3 (Adequacy of +). *For every valuation ρ, if $\Xi; \Gamma \vdash t_1 : A$, $\Xi; \Gamma \vdash t_2 : A$, $t_1 \in [\![A]\!]_\rho$ and $t_2 \in [\![A]\!]_\rho$, then $t_1 + t_2 \in [\![A]\!]_\rho$.*

Proof. By induction on A. The proof-terms t_1 and t_2 strongly normalise. Thus, by Lemma A.2, the proof-term $t_1 + t_2$ strongly normalises. Furthermore:

- If the proposition A has the form X, then $t_1, t_2 \in \rho(X) \in \mathcal{R}$. Using CR3, we need to prove that each of the one step reducts of $t_1 + t_2$ is in $\rho(X)$. Since $t_1, t_2 \in \rho(X)$, we have that $t_1, t_2 \in \mathsf{SN}$. We proceed by induction on $|t_1| + |t_2|$.

  - If $t_1 \longrightarrow t_1'$, then $t_1 + t_2 \longrightarrow t_1' + t_2$. By CR2, $t_1' \in \rho(X)$. Since $|t_1'| < |t_1|$, by the induction hypothesis $t_1' + t_2 \in \rho(X)$.
  - If $t_2 \longrightarrow t_2'$, then $t_1 + t_2 \longrightarrow t_1 + t_2'$. By CR2, $t_2' \in \rho(X)$. Since $|t_2'| < |t_2|$, by the induction hypothesis $t_1 + t_2' \in \rho(X)$.
  - By ultra-reduction, we have that $t_1 + t_2 \longrightarrow t_1$. By hypothesis, $t_1 \in \rho(X)$.
  - By ultra-reduction, we have that $t_1 + t_2 \longrightarrow t_2$. By hypothesis, $t_2 \in \rho(X)$.
  - There are no more cases since t_1 and t_2 are proof-terms of X.

- If the proposition A has the form $!B$, and $t_1 + t_2 \longrightarrow^* !v$ then $t_1 \longrightarrow^* !u_1$, $t_2 \longrightarrow^* !u_2$, $u_1 + u_2 \longrightarrow^* v$, or $t_1 \longrightarrow^* !v$, or $t_2 \longrightarrow^* !v$. In the first case, as t_1 and t_2 are in $[\![A]\!]_\rho$, u_1 and u_2 are in $[\![B]\!]_\rho$. By induction hypothesis, $u_1 + u_2 \in [\![B]\!]_\rho$, and by CR2, $v \in [\![B]\!]_\rho$. In the second and the third, as t_1 and t_2 are in $[\![A]\!]_\rho$, $v \in [\![B]\!]_\rho$.
- If the proposition A has the form $\forall X.B$, and $t_1 + t_2 \longrightarrow^* \Lambda X.v$ then either $t_1 \longrightarrow^* \Lambda X.u_1$, $t_2 \longrightarrow^* \Lambda X.u_2$ and $u_1 + u_2 \longrightarrow^* v$, or $t_1 \longrightarrow^* \Lambda X.v$, or $t_2 \longrightarrow^* \Lambda X.v$. Let $E \in \mathcal{R}$ and C be a proposition. In the first case, as $t_1, t_2 \in [\![\forall X.B]\!]_\rho$, $(C/X)u_1, (C/X)u_2 \in [\![B]\!]_{\rho,E/X}$. By the induction hypothesis, $(C/X)u_1 + (C/X)u_2 = (C/X)(u_1 + u_2) \in [\![B]\!]_{\rho,E/X}$. By CR2, since $(C/X)(u_1 + u_2) \longrightarrow^* (C/X)v$, $(C/X)v \in [\![B]\!]_{\rho,E/X}$. In the second and third cases, as $t_1, t_2 \in [\![\forall X.B]\!]_\rho$, $(C/X)v \in [\![B]\!]_{\rho,E/X}$.
- The remaining cases are already treated in [12]. □

Lemma A.4 (Adequacy of $\bullet$). *For every valuation ρ, if $\Xi; \Gamma \vdash t : A$ and $t \in [\![A]\!]_\rho$, then $a \bullet t \in [\![A]\!]_\rho$.*

Proof. By induction on A. The proof-term t strongly normalises. Thus, by Lemma A.2, the proof-term $a \bullet t$ strongly normalises. Furthermore:

- If the proposition A has the form X, then $t \in \rho(X) \in \mathcal{R}$. Using CR3, we need to prove that each of the one step reducts of $a \bullet t$ is in $\rho(X)$. Since $t \in \rho(X)$, we have that $t \in \mathsf{SN}$. We proceed by induction on $|t|$.

  - If $t \longrightarrow t'$, $a \bullet t \longrightarrow a \bullet t'$. By CR2, $t' \in \rho(X)$. Since $|t'| < |t|$, by the induction hypothesis, $a \bullet t' \in \rho(X)$.
  - By ultra-reduction, we have that $a \bullet t \longrightarrow t$. By hypothesis, $t \in \rho(X)$.
  - There are no more cases since t_1 and t_2 are proof-terms of X.

- If the proposition A has the form $!B$, and $a \bullet t \longrightarrow^* !v$ then $t \longrightarrow^* !u$ and $a \bullet u \longrightarrow^* v$, or $t \longrightarrow^* !v$. In the first case, as t is in $[\![A]\!]_\rho$, u is in $[\![B]\!]_\rho$. By induction hypothesis, $a \bullet u \in [\![B]\!]_\rho$ and by CR2, $v \in [\![B]\!]_\rho$. In the second, as t is in $[\![A]\!]_\rho$, $v \in [\![B]\!]_\rho$.

- If the proposition A has the form $\forall X.B$, and $a \bullet t \longrightarrow^* \Lambda X.v$ then either $t \longrightarrow^* \Lambda X.u$ and $a \bullet u \longrightarrow^* v$, or $t \longrightarrow^* \Lambda X.v$. Let $E \in \mathcal{R}$ and C be a proposition. In the first case, as $t \in [\![\forall X.B]\!]_\rho$, $(C/X)u \in [\![B]\!]_{\rho,E/X}$. By the induction hypothesis, $a \bullet (C/X)u = (C/X)(a \bullet u) \in [\![B]\!]_{\rho,E/X}$. By CR2, since $(C/X)(a \bullet u) \longrightarrow^* (C/X)v$, $(C/X)v \in [\![B]\!]_{\rho,E/X}$. In the second case, as $t \in [\![\forall X.B]\!]_\rho$, $(C/X)v \in [\![B]\!]_{\rho,E/X}$.
- The remaining cases are already treated in [12]. □

Lemma A.5 (Adequacy of !). *For every valuation ρ, if $t \in [\![A]\!]_\rho$, then $!t \in [\![!A]\!]_\rho$.*

Proof. The proof-term t strongly normalises. Consider a reduction sequence issued from $!t$. This sequence can only reduce t, hence it is finite. Thus, $!t$ strongly normalises. Furthermore, if $!t \longrightarrow^* !t'$, then $t \longrightarrow^* t'$. By CR2, $t' \in [\![A]\!]_\rho$. □

Lemma A.6 (Adequacy of Λ). *If $t \in [\![A]\!]_{\rho,E/X}$ for every $E \in \mathcal{R}$, then $\Lambda X.t \in [\![\forall X.A]\!]_\rho$.*

Proof. Let B be a proposition, and $F \in \mathcal{R}$. By Lemma 3.9, $[\![A]\!]_{\rho,F/X} \in \mathcal{R}$. Then, $t \in \mathsf{SN}$, and $\Lambda X.t \in \mathsf{SN}$. By CR4, $(B/X)t \in [\![A]\!]_{\rho,F/X}$. □

Lemma A.7 (Adequacy of $\delta_!$). *For every valuation ρ, if $t_1 \in [\![!A]\!]_\rho$ and, for all u in $[\![A]\!]_\rho$, $(u/x)t_2 \in [\![B]\!]_\rho$, then $\delta_!(t_1, x^C.t_2) \in [\![B]\!]_\rho$.*

Proof. By Lemma 3.10, $x \in [\![A]\!]_\rho$ thus $t_2 = (x/x)t_2 \in [\![B]\!]_\rho$. Hence, t_1 and t_2 strongly normalise. We prove, by induction on $|t_1|+|t_2|$, that $\delta_!(t_1, x^C.t_2) \in [\![B]\!]_\rho$. Using CR3, we only need to prove that every of its one step reducts is in $[\![B]\!]_\rho$. If the reduction takes place in t_1 or t_2, then we apply CR2 and the induction hypothesis.

Otherwise, the proof-term t_1 has the form $!u$ and the reduct is $(u/x)t_2$. As $!u \in [\![!A]\!]_\rho$, we have $u \in [\![A]\!]_\rho$. Hence, $(u/x)t_2 \in [\![B]\!]_\rho$. □

Lemma A.8 (Adequacy of proposition application). *If $t \in [\![\forall X.A]\!]_\rho$, then $t\ B \in [\![(B/X)A]\!]_\rho$.*

Proof. Since $t \in [\![\forall X.A]\!]_\rho$, $t \in \mathsf{SN}$, therefore $t\ B \in \mathsf{SN}$. By Lemma A.1, it suffices to show that $t\ B \in [\![A]\!]_{\rho,[\![B]\!]_\rho/X}$. We proceed by induction on $|t|$. Using CR3, we need to prove that each of its one step reducts is in $[\![A]\!]_{\rho,[\![B]\!]_\rho/X}$.

- If $t = \Lambda X.u$, then $t\ B \longrightarrow (B/X)u$. Since $t \in [\![\forall X.A]\!]_\rho$, then $(B/X)u \in [\![A]\!]_{\rho,[\![B]\!]_\rho/X}$.
- If $|t| = 0$ and $t \neq \Lambda X.u$, then $Red(t\ B)$ is empty.
- If $|t| > 0$, let $t \longrightarrow t'$. Then, $t\ B \longrightarrow t'\ B$. By CR2, $t' \in [\![\forall X.A]\!]_\rho$. Since $|t'| < |t|$, by the induction hypothesis $t'\ B \in [\![\forall X.A]\!]_\rho$. □

B Proof of Section 5

Due to space limitations[2], we only present the new cases with respect to [12].

Lemma B.1. *If $\Gamma, x^A \vdash t : B$ and $\Delta \vdash u : A$ then $\mu((u/x)t) \leq \mu(t) + \mu(u)$.*

Proof. By induction on t. The new cases are the following.

- If $t = \Lambda X.t_1$, then $B = \forall X.C$, $\Gamma, x^A \vdash t_1 : C$ and $X \notin \mathsf{FV}(\Gamma, A)$. Using the induction hypothesis, we get $\mu((u/x)t) = 1 + \mu((u/x)t_1) \leq 1 + \mu(t_1) + \mu(u) = \mu(t) + \mu(u)$.
- If $t = t_1\ C$, then $B = (C/X)D$ and $\Gamma, x^A \vdash t_1 : D$. Using the induction hypothesis, we get $\mu((u/x)t) = 1 + \mu((u/x)t_1) \leq 1 + \mu(t_1) + \mu(u) = \mu(t) + \mu(u)$. □

As a corollary, we get a similar measure preservation theorem for reduction.

Lemma B.2. *If $\Gamma \vdash t : A$ and $t \longrightarrow u$, then $\mu(t) \geq \mu(u)$.*

Proof. By induction on t. The context cases are trivial because the functions used to define $\mu(t)$ in function of μ of the subproof-terms of t are monotone. We check the rules one by one, using Lemma B.1. The new cases are the following.

- $\mu((\Lambda X.t)\ B) = 2 + \mu(t) > \mu(t) = \mu((B/X)t)$
- $\mu((\Lambda X.t) + (\Lambda X.u)) = 1 + \max(1 + \mu(t), 1 + \mu(u)) = 2 + \max(\mu(t), \mu(u))$ $= \mu(\Lambda X.(t + u))$
- $\mu(a \bullet \Lambda X.t) = 2 + \mu(t) = \mu(\Lambda X.a \bullet t)$ □

In the case of elimination contexts, Lemma B.1 can be strengthened.

Lemma B.3. $\mu(K\{t\}) = \mu(K) + \mu(t)$

Proof. By induction on K. The only new case is the case $K = K_1\ A$. Then $K\{t\} = K_1\{t\}\ A$. We have, by induction hypothesis, $\mu(K\{t\}) = 1 + \mu(K_1\{t\}) = 1 + \mu(K_1) + \mu(t) = \mu(K) + \mu(t)$. □

Proof of Lemma 5.4. By induction on t. The only new case is the case $t = t_1\ D$, then by the inversion property $A = (D/X)E$ and $x^C \vdash t_1 : \forall X.E$. By induction hypothesis, there exist K_1, u_1 and B_1 such that $\_^{B_1} \vdash K_1 : \forall X.E$, $x^C \vdash u_1 : B_1$, and $t_1 = K_1\{u_1\}$. We take $u = u_1$, $K = K_1\ D$, and $B = B_1$. We have $\_^B \vdash K : A$, $x^C \vdash u : B$, and $K\{u\} = K_1\{u_1\}\ D = t$. □

A final lemma shows that we can always decompose an elimination context K different from $\_$ into a smaller elimination context K_1 and a last elimination rule K_2. This is similar to the fact that we can always decompose a non-empty list into a smaller list and its last element.

[2] Limited to 5 pages of appendix and references.

Lemma B.4 (Decomposition of an elimination context). *If K is an elimination context such that $\_^A \vdash K : B$ and $K \neq \_$, then K has the form $K_1\{K_2\}$ and K_2 is an elimination of the top symbol of A.*

Proof. As K is not $\_$, it has the form $K = L_1\{L_2\}$. If $L_2 = \_$, we take $K_1 = \_$, $K_2 = L_1$ and, as the proof-term is well-typed, K_2 must be an elimination of the top symbol of A. Otherwise, by induction hypothesis, L_2 has the form $L_2 = K_1'\{K_2'\}$, and K_2' is an elimination of the top symbol of A. Hence, $K = L_1\{K_1'\{K_2'\}\}$. We take $K_1 = L_1\{K_1'\}$, $K_2 = K_2'$. □

Proof of Theorem 5.5. Without loss of generality, we can assume that t is irreducible. We proceed by induction on $\mu(t)$.

Using Lemma 5.4, the proof-term t can be decomposed as $K\{t'\}$ where t' is either the variable x, an introduction, a sum, or a product. The only new case is in the case of t' being the variable x, in which we need to prove $K\{u_1 + u_2\} \equiv K\{u_1\} + K\{u_2\}$ and $K\{a \bullet u_1\} \equiv a \bullet K\{u_1\}$.

By Lemma B.4, K has the form $K_1\{K_2\}$ and K_2 is an elimination of the top symbol of A. We have to consider the various cases for K_2. There is only one new case, which is the case $K = K_1\{\_\ C\}$, then u_1 and u_2 are closed proof-terms of $\forall X.D$, thus $u_1 \longrightarrow^* \Lambda X.u_1'$ and $u_2 \longrightarrow^* \Lambda X.u_2'$. Using the induction hypothesis with the proof-term K_1 ($\mu(K_1) < \mu(K) = \mu(t)$), we get

$K\{u_1 + u_2\} \longrightarrow^* K_1\{(\Lambda X.u_1' + \Lambda X.u_2')\ C\} \longrightarrow^* K_1\{(C/X)u_1' + (C/X)u_2'\} = (C/X)K_1\{u_1' + u_2'\} \equiv (C/X)(K_1\{u_1'\} + K_1\{u_2'\}) = K_1\{(C/X)u_1'\} + K_1\{(C/X)u_2'\}\ {}^*\!\longleftarrow K_1\{(\Lambda X.u_1')\ C\} + K_1\{(\Lambda X.u_2')\ C\}\ {}^*\!\longleftarrow K\{u_1\} + K\{u_2\}$.

And $K\{a \bullet u_1\} \longrightarrow^* K_1\{(a \bullet \Lambda X.u_1')\ C\} \longrightarrow^* K_1\{a \bullet (C/X)u_1'\} = (C/X)K_1\{a \bullet u_1'\} \equiv (C/X)(a \bullet K_1\{u_1'\}) = a \bullet K_1\{(C/X)u_1'\}\ {}^*\!\longleftarrow a \bullet K_1\{(\Lambda X.u_1')\ C\}\ {}^*\!\longleftarrow a \bullet K\{u_1\}$. □

Proof of Corollary 5.6. Let $C \in \mathcal{V}$ and c be a proof-term such that $y^B \vdash c : C$. Then applying Theorem 5.5 to the proof-term $c\{t\}$ we get $c\{t\{u_1 + u_2\}\} \equiv c\{t\{u_1\}\} + c\{t\{u_2\}\}$ and $c\{t\{a \bullet u_1\}\} \equiv a \bullet c\{t\{u_1\}\}$, and applying it again to the proof-term c we get $c\{t\{u_1\} + t\{u_2\}\} \equiv c\{t\{u_1\}\} + c\{t\{u_2\}\}$ and $c\{a \bullet t\{u_1\}\} \equiv a \bullet c\{t\{u_1\}\}$.

Thus, $c\{t\{u_1 + u_2\}\} \equiv c\{t\{u_1\} + t\{u_2\}\}$ and $c\{t\{a \bullet u_1\}\} \equiv c\{a \bullet t\{u_1\}\}$, that is $t\{u_1 + u_2\} \sim t\{u_1\} + t\{u_2\}$ and $t\{a \bullet u_1\} \sim a \bullet t\{u_1\}$. □

References

1. Altenkirch, T., Grattage, J.: A functional quantum programming language. In: Proceedings of LICS 2005, pp. 249–258 (2005)
2. Arrighi, P., Díaz-Caro, A.: A system F accounting for scalars. Log. Methods Comput. Sci. **8**(1:11) (2012)
3. Arrighi, P., Díaz-Caro, A., Valiron, B.: The vectorial lambda-calculus. Inf. Comput. **254**(1), 105–139 (2017)
4. Arrighi, P., Dowek, G.: Lineal: a linear-algebraic lambda-calculus. Log. Methods Comput. Sci. **13**(1) (2017)

5. Barr, M.: $*$-Autonomous categories and linear logic. Math. Struct. Comput. Sci. **1**(2) (1991)
6. Bénabou, J.: Catégories avec multiplication. Comptes Rendus des Séances de l'Académie des Sciences **256**, 1887–1890 (1963)
7. Boudol, G.: Lambda-calculi for (strict) parallel functions. Inf. Comput. **108**(1), 51–127 (1994)
8. Chardonnet, K.: Towards a Curry-Howard correspondence for quantum computation. Ph.D. thesis, Université Paris-Saclay (2023)
9. Coecke, B., Kissinger, A.: Picturing Quantum Processes: A First Course in Quantum Theory and Diagrammatic Reasoning. Cambridge University Press (2017)
10. Crole, R.L.: Categories for Types. Cambridge University Press (1993)
11. Díaz-Caro, A., Dowek, G.: A new connective in natural deduction, and its application to quantum computing. Theoret. Comput. Sci. **957**, 113840 (2023)
12. Díaz-Caro, A., Dowek, G.: A linear linear lambda-calculus. Math. Struct. Comput. Sci. (2024, to appear)
13. Díaz-Caro, A., Dowek, G., Rinaldi, J.: Two linearities for quantum computing in the lambda calculus. Biosystems **186**, 104012 (2019)
14. Díaz-Caro, A., Guillermo, M., Miquel, A., Valiron, B.: Realizability in the unitary sphere. In: Proceedings of LICS 2019, pp. 1–13 (2019)
15. Díaz-Caro, A., Malherbe, O.: The sup connective in IMALL: a categorical semantics. Draft at arXiv:2205.02142 (2024)
16. Díaz-Caro, A., Petit, B.: Linearity in the non-deterministic call-by-value setting. In: Ong, L., de Queiroz, R. (eds.) WoLLIC 2012. LNCS, vol. 7456, pp. 216–231. Springer, Heidelberg (2012). https://doi.org/10.1007/978-3-642-32621-9_16
17. Eilenberg, S., Kelly, G.M.: Closed categories. In: Eilenberg, S., Harrison, D.K., MacLane, S., Röhrl, H. (eds.) Proceedings of the Conference on Categorical Algebra, pp. 421–562. Springer, Heidelberg (1966). https://doi.org/10.1007/978-3-642-99902-4_22
18. Girard, J.-Y.: Interprétation fonctionnelle et élimination des coupures dans l'arithmétique d'ordre supérieure. Ph.D. thesis, Université Paris Diderot, France (1972)
19. Girard, J.-Y.: Linear logic. Theoret. Comput. Sci. **50**, 1–102 (1987)
20. Maneggia, P.: Models of linear polymorphism. Ph.D. thesis, The University of Birmingham, UK (2004)
21. Mayr, R., Nipkow, T.: Higher-order rewrite systems and their confluence. Theoret. Comput. Sci. **192**(1), 3–29 (1998)
22. Seely, R.: Linear logic, $*$-autonomous categories and cofree coalgebras. In: Gray, J.W., Scedrov, A. (eds.) Categories in Computer Science and Logic, Contemporary Mathematics. American Mathematical Society (1989)
23. Tait, W.W.: Intensional interpretations of functionals of finite type I. J. Symbolic Logic **32**(2), 198–212 (1967)
24. Vaux, L.: The algebraic lambda calculus. Math. Struct. Comput. Sci. **19**(5), 1029–1059 (2009)

A Logic of Isolation

Can Başkent[1], David Gilbert[2(✉)], and Giorgio Venturi[3]

[1] Department of Computer Science, Middlesex University, London, UK
c.baskent@mdx.ac.uk
[2] Department of Philosophy, University of British Columbia, Vancouver, Canada
dave.gilbert@ubc.ca
[3] Dipartimento di Civiltá e Forme del Sapere, University of Pisa, Pisa, Italy
giorgio.venturi@unipi.it

Abstract. In the vein of recent work that provides non-normal modal interpretations of various topological operators, this paper proposes a modal logic for a spatial isolation operator. Focussing initially on neighborhood systems, we prove several characterization results, demonstrating the adequacy of the interpretation and highlighting certain semantic insensitivities that result from the relative expressive weakness of the isolation operator. We then transition to the topological setting, proving a result for discrete spaces.

Keywords: Topological Semantics · Neighborhood Systems · Isolation

1 Introduction

Topological interpretations provided some of the earliest semantics for modal logics (e.g., [7,12,13]). These early interpretations focused on $\Diamond$ as topological closure. Subsequent work demonstrated that $\Diamond$ can also be interpreted as the derivative[1] ([1,3,7,10]). More recently, it has been shown that other topological operators—including border and boundary operators—can provide fruitful interpretations of various, usually non-normal, modal operators ([11]).

This paper attempts to continue this more recent line of inquiry by proposing a modal logic for isolated points. When $\mathcal{X} = \langle X, \tau \rangle$ is a topological space and $S \subseteq X$, x is an *isolated point* of S if there is an open neighborhood U of x such that $U \cap S = \{x\}$. We demonstrate that the $[i]$ operator introduced in [6] (where it is intended to model a notion of factive ignorance) can be spatially interpreted as an isolated points operator.

In §2, the basic syntax, axiomatic system and relational semantics are introduced briefly. Due to the relative lack of algebraic structure of the isolated points operator, instead of immediately focussing on topologies, we begin, in §3, by considering neighborhood systems.[2] As neighborhood systems are a generalization

[1] The *derivative* of a set S, $d(S)$, is the set of *limit points* of S.

[2] Some authors use the term *neighborhood system* to refer only to those families of neighborhoods that give rise to a topological space. Our usage will be more liberal, allowing any set equipped with a neighborhood function to qualify.

G. Metcalfe et al. (Eds.): WoLLIC 2024, LNCS 14672, pp. 36–46, 2024.
https://doi.org/10.1007/978-3-031-62687-6_3

of topologies, we similarly generalize the concept of an isolated point, showing that this notion can be logically captured by $[i]$. Finally, in §4, we transition to considering topological spaces, discrete spaces in particular, before concluding in §5.

2 Syntax, Proof System, and Relational Semantics

Take *Prop* to be a countably infinite set of propositional variables. The set *Form* of well-formed formulas of the language $\mathcal{L}^i$ is recursively defined:

$$\alpha ::= p \mid \neg\alpha \mid \alpha \wedge \alpha \mid [i]\alpha$$

for $p \in Prop$.

2.1 Axiom System

The basic axiomatic proof system, $\mathbf{S^i}$, as defined in [4] (where it is referred to as $\mathbf{L^i}$), is as follows:

Definition 1 (Proof System $\mathbf{S^i}$).

(Taut) All instances of propositional tautologies
(A1) $[i]\varphi \rightarrow \varphi$
(A2) $([i]\varphi \wedge [i]\psi) \rightarrow [i](\varphi \vee \psi)$
(MP) From $\vdash \varphi$ *and* $\vdash \varphi \rightarrow \psi$ *infer* $\vdash \psi$
(R1) From $\vdash \varphi \rightarrow \psi$ *infer* $\vdash \varphi \rightarrow ([i]\psi \rightarrow [i]\varphi)$

Our notions of *derivation*, *theorem*, and *consistency* are the usual ones.

Proposition 1. *The following are all theorems of* $\mathbf{S^i}$*:*

a. $([i]\varphi \wedge [i]\psi) \rightarrow [i](\varphi \wedge \psi)$
b. $[i](\varphi \vee \psi) \rightarrow ([i]\varphi \vee [i]\psi)$
c. $[i]\varphi \rightarrow [i][i]\varphi$

In addition, the rule allowing $\vdash [i]\varphi \leftrightarrow [i]\psi$ *from* $\vdash \varphi \leftrightarrow \psi$ *is derivable.*

2.2 Relational Semantics

Using relational semantics, satisfaction for $[i]$-formulas is defined as follows:

$$M, w \models [i]\varphi \text{ iff } (M, w \models \varphi \text{ and } \forall w' \neq w(wRw' \text{ implies } M, w' \not\models \varphi))$$

Theorem 1 ([4]). $\mathbf{S^i}$ *is sound and strongly complete with respect to the class of all relational frames.*

3 Neighborhood Semantics for S^{i}

As mentioned above, the ultimate goal of this paper is to make strides toward a topological interpretation of $[i]$. In particular, we suggest interpreting $[i]$ as an isolated points operator. Recall the definition of an isolated point in a topological space:

Definition 2 (Isolated Point). *Let $\mathcal{X} = \langle X, \tau\rangle$ be a topological space and $S \subseteq X$. x is an* isolated point *of S if there is an open neighborhood U of x such that $U \cap S = \{x\}$.*

Instead of beginning immediately with a purely topological semantics, we start by providing a more general semantic account in terms of neighborhood systems (we follow [2,9], for instance, in the treatment of neighborhood semantics).

Definition 3 (Neighborhood Frame). *A* neighborhood frame *is a pair $\langle X, N\rangle$ such that $X \neq \emptyset$ and $N : X \to \wp(\wp(X))$. A* neighborhood model *is a pair $\langle F, V\rangle$, where F is a neighborhood frame and $V : Prop \to \wp(X)$ is a valuation function.*

Generalizing the above definition of an isolated point to the context of neighborhood systems, where less mathematical structure is insisted upon, one can say that x is an isolated point of S if there is a neighborhood U of x, i.e., $U \in N(x)$, such that $U \cap S = \{x\}$. We can formalize this intuition in the definition of satisfaction for formulas in $\mathcal{L}^i$ with respect to neighborhood models. Given a model M and a formula α, the *truth set* of α in M, denoted $[\![\alpha]\!]^M$ is defined via recursion:

$$\begin{array}{ll}
[\![p]\!]^M & := V(p)\\
[\![\neg\varphi]\!]^M & := X \setminus [\![\varphi]\!]^M = ([\![\varphi]\!]^M)^c\\
[\![\varphi \wedge \psi]\!]^M & := [\![\varphi]\!]^M \cap [\![\psi]\!]^M\\
[\![[i]\varphi]\!]^M & := \{x : \exists U \in N(x) \text{ s.t. } U \cap [\![\varphi]\!]^M = \{x\}\}
\end{array}$$

When no ambiguity can arise, the M superscript will be omitted. A formula is *valid* in a class of frames when it is true at all points in all models based on frames in the class. A set of formulas is *satisfiable* in a class of frames when there is a state in a model based on a frame in the class at which all the elements are true.

3.1 Semantic Insensitivities

In the context of relational frames and the semantics given in §2, $\mathcal{L}^i$ is *reflexive-insensitive.* That is, the satisfaction of $\mathcal{L}^i$-formulas in a model $M = \langle W, R, V\rangle$ is not affected when arbitrary elements from id_W are either added to, or removed from, R. In the neighborhood context, there are similar insensitivities.

In particular, because the definition of $[\![\cdot]\!]$ utilizes only sets of each $N(x)$ that contain x, the addition or removal of sets that do not contain x will be immaterial.

For a given neighborhood frame $\langle X, N \rangle$, consider the set

$$S_x := \{Y \in \wp(X) : x \notin Y\}$$

for each $x \in X$. (Here, we are following the notation of [5], which was concerned with neighborhood semantics for a different logic that was also insensitive to reflexivity in the relational setting.)

Then, given a neighborhood frame $F = \langle X, N \rangle$, construct the frames $F = \langle X, N^+ \rangle$ and $F = \langle X, N^- \rangle$, where N^+ and N^- are defined as follows for all $x \in X$:

$$N^+(x) := N(x) \cup S_x$$

$$N^-(x) := N(x) \setminus S_x$$

When M is a neighborhood model, M^+ (M^-) is that model identical to M, but with N^+ (N^-) replacing N.

Proposition 2. *Let M be a neighborhood model. Then M, M^+, and M^- (as well as the intermediate models) are all pointwise equivalent. That is,*

$$[\![\alpha]\!]^{M^-} = [\![\alpha]\!]^M = [\![\alpha]\!]^{M^+}$$

for all $\alpha \in Form$.

However, in the current setting there are additional sensitivities that one can utilize.

Definition 4 (Supplemented Neighborhood System). *A neighborhood frame is* supplemented *when its neighborhood function is closed under supersets: for every x, if $Y \subseteq N(x)$ and $Y \subseteq Z$, then $Z \subseteq N(x)$.*

Given a neighborhood frame, $F = \langle X, N \rangle$, let $F^s = \langle X, N^s \rangle$ be the supplementation *of F when, for all $x \in X$:*

$$N^s(x) = \{Y \subseteq \wp(X) : \exists U \subseteq Y \text{ s.t. } U \in N(x)\}$$

For a model $M = \langle F, V \rangle$, let $M^s = \langle F^s, V \rangle$.

Remark 1. Let M be a model and M^s its supplementation. Then it is not necessarily the case that

$$[\![\alpha]\!]^M = [\![\alpha]\!]^{M^s}$$

The countermodels demonstrating this observation make use of supplementing some $N(x)$ containing at least one set from S_x and thereby adding sets to $N(x)$ not in S_x. (For instance, consider some state x such that $N(x) = \{\emptyset\}$. Then for no φ will it be the case that $x \in [\![\varphi]\!]^M$. However, since $\{x\} \in N^s(x)$, $x \in [\![\varphi]\!]^{M^s}$ for every φ such that $x \in [\![\varphi]\!]^{M^s}$. This is discussed further in §4, below.)

However, if no such sets are present in any $N(x)$ (for instance, as in neighborhood filters in topological spaces), then supplementation will not affect satisfaction.

Definition 5 (Anchored Neighborhood System). *A neighborhood function (and, hence, the resulting system) is* anchored *when, for every point $x \in X$,*

$$\forall U \in N(x)(x \in U)$$

(Note that we do not force $N(x) \neq \emptyset$ in order to be anchored.)

Proposition 3. *Let M be an anchored neighborhood model. Then*

$$[\![\alpha]\!]^M = [\![\alpha]\!]^{M^s}$$

Proof. Induction on α. We omit all but the modal case.

If $x \in [\![[i]\varphi]\!]^M$, then there is some $U \in N(x)$ s.t. $U \cap [\![\varphi]\!]^M = \{x\}$. Since $U \in N^s(x)$ and $[\![\varphi]\!]^M = [\![\varphi]\!]^{M^s}$, by the induction hypothesis, $x \in [\![[i]\varphi]\!]^{M^s}$.

In the other direction, if $x \in [\![[i]\varphi]\!]^{M^s}$, there is a $U \in N^s(x)$ s.t. $U \cap [\![\varphi]\!]^{M^s} = \{x\}$. Thus, there must have been some $U_1 \in N(x)$ s.t. $U_1 \subseteq U$. But, since N is anchored, $x \in U_1$, and so $U_1 \cap [\![\varphi]\!]^{M^s} = \{x\}$. By the induction hypothesis, $[\![\varphi]\!]^{M^s} = [\![\varphi]\!]^M$, so $U_1 \cap [\![\varphi]\!]^M = \{x\}$. Hence, $x \in [\![[i]\varphi]\!]^M$.

In particular, Proposition 3 guarantees that

$$[\![\alpha]\!]^{M^{-s}} = [\![\alpha]\!]^M$$

So every model will be pointwise equivalent to some supplemented model.

3.2 Soundness and Completeness

Using standard methods, characterization results for $\mathbf{S^i}$, with respect to the given neighborhood semantics, are readily obtained. A logic is said to be *sound* with respect to a class of frames when all theorems of the logic are valid in the class. A logic is *complete* with respect to a class of frames when every consistent formula is satisfiable in the class. A logic is *strongly complete* with respect to a class when every consistent set of formulas is satisfiable in the class.

A neighborhood frame $\langle X, N\rangle$ is said to be *closed under intersections* when, for every $x \in X$, if $U \in N(x)$ and $V \in N(x)$, then $U \cap V \in N(x)$.

Theorem 2 (Soundness). *$\mathbf{S^i}$ is sound with respect to the class of neighborhood frames that are closed under intersections.*

Proof. The proof is standard, and proceeds by showing that all axioms are valid and rules preserve validity. We include only the cases unique to $\mathbf{S^i}$.

$[i]\varphi \to \varphi$: Assume $x \in [\![[i]\varphi]\!]$. Then $\exists U \in N(x)$ s.t. $U \cap [\![\varphi]\!] = \{x\}$, so $x \in [\![\varphi]\!]$.

$([i]\varphi \wedge [i]\psi) \rightarrow [i](\varphi \vee \psi)$: Assume $x \in [\![[i]\varphi]\!]$ and $x \in [\![[i]\psi]\!]$. Then $\exists U_1 \in N(x)$ s.t. $U_1 \cap [\![\varphi]\!] = \{x\}$ and $\exists U_2 \in N(x)$ s.t. $U_2 \cap [\![\psi]\!] = \{x\}$. Since N is closed under intersections, $U_1 \cap U_2 \in N(x)$. But $(U_1 \cap U_2) \cap [\![\varphi \vee \psi]\!] = \{x\}$, so $x \in [\![[i](\varphi \vee \psi)]\!]$.

From $\vdash \varphi \rightarrow \psi$ infer $\vdash \varphi \rightarrow ([i]\psi \rightarrow [i]\varphi)$: Assume the validity of $\varphi \rightarrow \psi$. Then $[\![\varphi]\!] \subseteq [\![\psi]\!]$ in all models. Assume, further, $x \in [\![\varphi]\!]$. If $x \in [\![[i]\psi]\!]$, then $U \cap [\![\psi]\!] = \{x\}$, for some $U \in N(x)$. Since $[\![\varphi]\!] \subseteq [\![\psi]\!]$, $U \setminus \{x\} \subseteq X \setminus [\![\psi]\!] \subseteq X \setminus [\![\varphi]\!]$. Hence, $U \cap [\![\varphi]\!] = \{x\}$, so $x \in [\![[i]\varphi]\!]$.

Theorem 3 (Completeness). $\mathbf{S^i}$ *is strongly complete with respect to the class of neighborhood frames that are anchored and closed under intersections.*

Proof. We give a canonical model construction. (The argument for completeness given the canonical model is standard.) Given the set of maximal $\mathbf{S^i}$-consistent sets, $\Sigma_{\mathbf{S^i}}$, define

$$|\alpha| = \{x \in \Sigma_{\mathbf{S^i}} : \alpha \in x\}$$

Construct the canonical model $M^{\mathbf{S^i}} = \langle X^{\mathbf{S^i}}, N^{\mathbf{S^i}}, V^{\mathbf{S^i}} \rangle$ as follows:

- $X^{\mathbf{S^i}} := \Sigma_{\mathbf{S^i}}$
- for each $x \in X^{\mathbf{S^i}}$, $N(x) := \{|\neg\varphi| \cup \{x\} : [i]\varphi \in x\}$
- for each $p \in \mathit{Prop}$, $V^{\mathbf{S^i}}(p) = |p|$

(The derivable rule mentioned in Proposition 1 ensures that N is well-defined.) A straightforward induction then demonstrates that, for all $\alpha \in \mathit{Form}$,

$$[\![\alpha]\!]^{\mathbf{S^i}} = |\alpha|$$

The only non-trivial case is that of the modality. (In what follows, we omit all $\mathbf{S^i}$ superscipts.)

If $x \in |[i]\varphi|$, then, by definition, $|\neg\varphi| \cup \{x\} = (X \setminus |\varphi|) \cup \{x\} \in N(x)$. By the induction hypothesis, $|\varphi| = [\![\varphi]\!]$, so $(X \setminus [\![\varphi]\!]) \cup \{x\} \in N(x)$. Since $x \in |[i]\varphi \rightarrow \varphi|$, $x \in |\varphi| = [\![\varphi]\!]$. Finally, $((X \setminus [\![\varphi]\!]) \cup \{x\}) \cap [\![\varphi]\!] = \{x\}$, so $x \in [\![[i]\varphi]\!]$.

If $x \in [\![[i]\varphi]\!]$, then there is some $U \in N(x)$ such that $U \cap [\![\varphi]\!] = \{x\}$ (hence, $x \in [\![\varphi]\!] = |\varphi|$, by the induction hypothesis). By construction, $U = |\neg\psi| \cup \{x\}$ for some ψ such that $x \in |[i]\psi|$ (and $x \in |\psi|$). But then $|\neg\psi| \subseteq |\neg\varphi|$, and so $|\varphi| \subseteq |\psi|$, meaning that $\vdash \varphi \rightarrow \psi$. Therefore, $\vdash \varphi \rightarrow ([i]\psi \rightarrow [i]\varphi)$. Since $x \in |\varphi|$, $x \in |[i]\psi \rightarrow [i]\varphi|$. And, because $x \in |[i]\psi|$, $x \in |[i]\varphi|$.

Lastly, the model is both closed under intersections and anchored. Anchoring is by construction.

For closure under intersections, assume that $U_1, U_2 \in N(x)$. Then, $U_1 = |\neg\varphi_1| \cup \{x\}$ and $U_2 = |\neg\varphi_2| \cup \{x\}$ with $x \in |[i]\varphi_1|$ and $x \in |[i]\varphi_2|$. Since x is a maximal $\mathbf{S^i}$-consistent set, $x \in |[i]\varphi_1 \wedge [i]\varphi_2|$, and so $x \in |[i](\varphi_1 \vee \varphi_2)|$. By construction, $|\neg(\varphi_1 \vee \varphi_2)| \cup \{x\} \in N(x)$. But $|\neg(\varphi_1 \vee \varphi_2)| = |\neg\varphi_1| \cap |\neg\varphi_2|$, and $U_1 \cap U_2 = (|\neg\varphi_1| \cap |\neg\varphi_2|) \cup \{x\}$, so $U_1 \cap U_2 \in N(x)$.

Corollary 1. $\mathbf{S^i}$ *is strongly complete with respect to the class of neighborhood frames that are anchored, closed under intersections, and supplemented.*

Proof. Since $M^{\mathbf{S^i}}$ is anchored, it is pointwise equivalent to its supplementation, from Proposition 3.

In addition, making use of the standard conversion between relational frames and augmented neighborhood structures, a completeness theorem can also be obtained with respect to the class of all augmented neighborhood frames.

Definition 6 (Augmented Neighborhood System). *A neighborhood function (and, hence, the resulting system) is* augmented *when, for every point* $x \in X$, $N(x)$ *is supplemented and* $\bigcap N(x) \in N(x)$.

Lemma 1. *For every relational model, there is a pointwise equivalent neighborhood model that is augmented.*

Proof. Let $M = \langle W, R, V\rangle$ be an arbitrary relational model. Define the function $N_R : W \to \wp(\wp(W))$ as

$$N_R(w) := \{X : R(w) \subseteq X\}$$

where $R(w) = \{y \in W : wRy\}$. Let $M^N = \langle W, N_R, V\rangle$. Note that N_R is augmented.

For all wffs α,

$$M, w \models \alpha \text{ iff } w \in [\![\alpha]\!]^{M^N}$$

This is, again, an induction on α and only the modal case will be discussed.

Assume $M, w \models [i]\varphi$. Then $M, w \models \varphi$ and $\forall z \neq w$, wRz implies $M, z \not\models \varphi$. Hence, $w \in [\![\varphi]\!]$ (from the induction hypothesis) and $R(w) \setminus \{w\} \subseteq W \setminus [\![\varphi]\!]$. Since N_R is augmented, $R(w) \cup \{w\} \in N_R$, and $(R(w) \cup \{w\}) \cap [\![\varphi]\!] = \{w\}$, so $w \in [\![[i]\varphi]\!]$.

Assume now that $M, w \not\models [i]\varphi$. Then either $M, w \not\models \varphi$ or, for some $z \neq w$ s.t. wRz, $M, z \models \varphi$.

If $M, w \not\models \varphi$ then, by the induction hypothesis, $w \notin [\![\varphi]\!]$, and so $w \notin [\![[i]\varphi]\!]$.

Otherwise, assume that $M, w \models \varphi$ and $M, z \models \varphi$ for some $z \neq w$ s.t. wRz. Then $\{z\} \subseteq R(w)$ and $\{w, z\} \subseteq [\![\varphi]\!]$. Therefore, $\{z\} \subseteq U \cap [\![\varphi]\!]$ for all $U \in N_R(w)$, so $w \notin [\![[i]\varphi]\!]$.

Clearly, if the original model was reflexive, then the resulting augmented model is anchored.

Lemma 2. *For every augmented neighborhood model, there exists a pointwise equivalent relational model.*

Proof. Let $M = \langle X, N, V\rangle$ be an arbitrary augmented neighborhood model. Define the relational model $M^R = \langle X, R_N, V\rangle$ such that xR_Ny iff $y \in \bigcap N(x)$. Then, for all wffs α,

$$x \in [\![\alpha]\!]^M \text{ iff } M^R, x \models \alpha$$

Induction on α.

Assume $x \in [\![[i]\varphi]\!]$. Then there is a $U \in N(x)$ such that $U \cap [\![\varphi]\!] = \{x\}$. Hence, from the induction hypothesis, $M^R, x \models \varphi$. Moreover, $\bigcap N(x) \subseteq U$, so $\bigcap N(x) \setminus \{x\} \subseteq X \setminus [\![\varphi]\!]$. Therefore, for any $y \neq x$ such that $y \in \bigcap N(x)$, $y \in X \setminus [\![\varphi]\!]$, so $M^R, y \not\models \varphi$, by the induction hypothesis. Hence, $M^R, x \models [i]\varphi$.

In the other direction, if $M^R, x \models [i]\varphi$, then $M^R, x \models \varphi$ and $\forall y \neq x$, xR_Ny implies $M, y \not\models \varphi$. By the induction hypothesis, $x \in [\![\varphi]\!]$ and $\forall y \neq x$, if xR_Ny, then $y \notin [\![\varphi]\!]$. But xR_Ny iff $y \in \bigcap N(x)$. Hence, $\bigcap N(x) \setminus \{x\} \subseteq X \setminus [\![\varphi]\!]$. Let $U = \bigcap N(x) \cup \{x\}$. Then $U \in N(x)$, since $N(x)$ is supplemented. Moreover, $U \cap [\![\varphi]\!] = \{x\}$, so $x \in [\![[i]\varphi]\!]$.

If the original neighborhood system was anchored, then the resulting relational model is reflexive.

Corollary 2. $\mathbf{S^i}$ *is sound and (strongly) complete with respect to the class of all augmented neighborhood frames and all anchored, augmented neighborhood frames.*

Proof. For the anchored, augmented neighborhood frames, strong completeness follows from taking the reflexive closure of the canonical model used in the proof of Theorem 1 (as defined in [4]) along with Lemma 1.

4 Discrete Neighborhood Systems

Definition 7. *A neighborhood system is* discrete *when* $\{x\} \in N(x)$, *for every* $x \in X$.

Consider the following axiom schema:

$$\varphi \leftrightarrow [i]\varphi \tag{Disc}$$

Call **SDisc** the system obtained by adding (Disc) to $\mathbf{S}^i$.

In the presence of (Disc), no other modal axioms are necessary and neither is the rule (R1).

Proposition 4. **SDisc** *can be axiomatized by the following:*

(Taut) All instances of propositional tautologies
(Disc) $\varphi \leftrightarrow [i]\varphi$
(MP) From $\vdash \varphi$ *and* $\vdash \varphi \to \psi$ *infer* $\vdash \psi$

Proposition 5. **SDisc** *is valid on a relational frame* F *if and only if, for each* w, *if* wRz, *then* $w = z$.

Corollary 3. **SDisc** *is sound with respect to the class of relational frames in which, for each* w*, if* wRz*, then* $w = z$*.*

Theorem 4. **SDisc** *is strongly complete with respect to the class of relational frames in which, for each* w*, if* wRz*, then* $w = z$*.*

Proof. This is easily seen by inspecting the canonical model for $\mathbf{S^i}$—as given in [4]—and observing that $[i]\top$ is an element of each maximal consistent set and will, therefore, have an empty accessibility relation.

In terms of neighborhood systems, a characterization result for **SDisc** is also straightforward.

Theorem 5. **SDisc** *is sound and strongly complete with respect to the class of discrete neighborhood systems. (Hence, due to the semantic insensitivities noted above, also with respect to anchored, discrete, supplemented neighborhood systems.)*

Proof. Soundness is immediate.

For completeness, one need only look at the canonical model construction in the proof of Theorem 3 and observe that, in the presence of (Disc), $[i]\top \in x$, for every $x \in X^{\mathbf{SDisc}}$. Hence, $|\bot| \cup \{x\} = \{x\} \in N(x)$.

4.1 Discrete Topologies

We can conclude the main section of the paper by (finally) transitioning to topologies proper.

Recall that a topo-model is a pair $M = \langle \mathcal{X}, V\rangle$ where $\mathcal{X} = \langle X, \tau\rangle$ is a topological space and $V : Prop \to \wp(X)$ is a valuation function. A formula φ is true in M when it is true at every $x \in \mathcal{X}$. φ is valid in $\mathcal{X}$ when it is true in every M based on $\mathcal{X}$. φ is valid in a class of topological spaces when φ is valid in every member of the class.

Satisfaction at points in a topo-model is defined as usual, with the clause for $[i]$ resembling closely the one given for neighborhood systems, but with reference to the topology τ rather than the neighborhood function N:

$$[\![[i]\varphi]\!] := \{x : \exists U \in \tau \text{ s.t. } U \cap [\![\varphi]\!] = \{x\}\}$$

With the semantics so defined, $\mathbf{S^i}$ is sound with respect to the class of all topo-models (the proof is fundamentally the same as that of Theorem 2). Moreover, **SDisc** is sound with respect to the class of all discrete topological spaces, since all singletons are open.

The results above, concerning discrete neighborhood spaces, can be transferred over to the topological setting to render a completeness result for **SDisc** as well.

Definition 8 (Neighborhood Topology). *A neighborhood function N is a* neighborhood topology *when the following conditions are met:*

a. If $S \in N(x)$, then $x \in S$;
b. each $N(x)$ is closed under supersets;
c. each $N(x)$ is closed under intersections;
d. for each $S \in N(x)$, there is a $T \subseteq S$ such that $T \in N(x)$ and, for each $y \in T$, $S \in N(y)$.

Moreover, given a neighborhood topology over a set X, the pair $\langle X, \tau \rangle$ is a topological space when[3]

$$U \in \tau \text{ iff } \forall x \in U, U \in N(x)$$

Theorem 6. **SDisc** *is complete with respect to the class of all discrete topological spaces.*

Proof. Consider $M^{\mathbf{SDisc}}$, the canonical neighborhood model for **SDisc** (referred to in Theorem 5). The model is anchored and discrete. Let M^S be the supplementation of $M^{\mathbf{SDisc}}$. The frame of M^S is then a neighborhood topology. Consider the resulting topological space $\langle X, \tau \rangle$. Since, for each x, $\{x\} \in N(x)$, the topology is discrete. Let $M_{\mathcal{X}}$ be the topo-model obtained by adding V, the valuation function from M^S, to $\mathcal{X}$. A straighforward induction proves that M^S and $M_{\mathcal{X}}$ are pointwise equivalent.

5 Conclusion and Future Work

Thus far we have tried to argue that there is a plausible interpretation of $[i]$ as an isolated points operator in a variety of neighborhood systems, including those that correspond to discrete topologies. Immediately, there is the question of whether or not there exist intermediate logics (between $\mathbf{S^i}$ and **SDisc**) that characterize interesting classes of either neighborhood systems or topologies. It is not immediately obvious what such logics look like, or if any even exist.

It might be slightly more promising to examine extensions of $\mathbf{S^i}$ with only neighborhood systems in mind. For example, one can consider adding to $\mathbf{S^i}$ the axiom $\neg[i]\top$. Relationally, this has the effect of forcing all worlds to be non-reflexively serial (that is, for each x, there is a $y \neq x$ such that xRy). It is easy to see that, in neighborhood systems, this axiom forces a lack of discreteness (hence, the resulting logic is not an intermediate logic, but inconsistent with **SDisc**), and that it is sound and strongly complete with respect to the class of all neighborhood systems in which $\{x\} \notin N(x)$.[4]

We leave these questions for future work.

[3] See, for instance, [8].

[4] In the canonical model, the only way $\{x\}$ could be added to $N(x)$ is if there is a formula φ such that $[\![\neg\varphi]\!] \cup \{x\} = \{x\}$. This can only occur if either $[\![\neg\varphi]\!] = \emptyset$, which is ruled out by the new axiom, or if $[\![\neg\varphi]\!] = \{x\}$, but this is impossible because no formulas uniquely identify a maximal consistent set.

Acknowledgements. CB's work on this paper was supported by a London Mathematical Society Computer Science Scheme 7 grant [grant number SC7-2022-05]. We would like to thank three anonymous referees for helpful comments and feedback.

References

1. Bezhanishvili, G., Esakia, L., Gabelaia, D.: Some results on modal axiomatization and definability for topological spaces. Stud. Logica. **81**(3), 325–355 (2005)
2. Chellas, B.: Modal Logic: an Introduction. Cambridge University Press (1980)
3. Esakia, L.: Intuitionistic logic and modality via topology. Ann. Pure Appl. Logic **127**(1), 155–170 (2004)
4. Gilbert, D., Kubyshkina, E., Petrolo, M., Venturi, G.: Logics of ignorance and being wrong. Logic J. IGPL **30**(5), 870–885 (2021)
5. Gilbert, D., Venturi, G.: Neighborhood semantics for logics of unknown truths and false beliefs. Australas. J. Log. **14**(1), 246–267 (2017)
6. Kubyshkina, E., Petrolo, M.: A logic for factive ignorance. Synthese **198**, 5917–5928 (2021)
7. McKinsey, J.C.C., Tarski, A.: The algebra of topology. Ann. Math. **45**(1), 141–191 (1944)
8. Mendelson, B.: Introduction to Topology, 3d edn. Allyn and Bacon, Boston (1974)
9. Pacuit, E.: Neighborhood Semantics for Modal Logic. Springer, Cham, Switzerland (2017)
10. Shehtman, V.: Derived sets in Euclidean spaces and modal logic. Technical report, The University of Amsterdam (1990)
11. Steinsvold, C.: A note on logics of ignorance and borders. Notre Dame J. Formal Logic **49**(4), 385–392 (2008)
12. Tang, T.-C.: Algebraic postulates and a geometric interpretation for the Lewis calculus of strict implication. Bull. (new series) Am. Math. Society **44**(10), 737–744 (1938)
13. Tarski, A.: Der Aussagenkalkül und die Topologie. Fundam. Math. **31**, 103–134 (1938)

A Simple Loopcheck for Intuitionistic K

Marianna Girlando[1(✉)], Roman Kuznets[2], Sonia Marin[3], Marianela Morales[4], and Lutz Straßburger[5]

[1] University of Amsterdam, Amsterdam, Netherlands
[2] TU Wien, Vienna, Austria
[3] University of Birmingham, Birmingham, UK
[4] IMDEA Software Institute, Madrid, Spain
[5] INRIA Saclay, Palaiseau, France

Abstract. In this paper, we present an algorithm for establishing decidability and finite model property of intuitionistic modal logic IK. These two results have been previously established independently by proof theoretic and model theoretic techniques respectively. Our algorithm, by contrast, enables us to establish both properties at the same time and simplifies previous approaches. It implements root-first proof search in a labelled sequent calculus that employs two binary relations: one corresponding to the modal accessibility relation and the other to the preorder relation of intuitionistic models. As a result, all the rules become invertible, hence semantic completeness could be established directly by extracting a (possibly infinite) countermodel from a failed proof attempt. To obtain the finite model property, we rather introduce a simple loopcheck ensuring that root-first proof search always terminates. The resulting finite countermodel displays a layered structure akin to that of intuitionistic first-order models.

Keywords: Intuitionistic modal logic · Labelled sequent calculus · Decidability · Root-first proof search · Finite model property

1 Introduction

The search for intuitionistic variants of classical modal logics originated from several different research traditions. In particular, computer scientists defined intuitionistic modal systems which could model reasoning on partial information in a concurrent setting [14], or which extended the Curry–Howard correspondence to the modal language [1], leading to varied ways of combining intuitionistic and modal behaviors [6]. For pure logicians, the preferred intuitionistic variant of modal logic is typically what came to be known as *intuitionistic modal logic* IK, originally axiomatized by Fischer Servi as some adequately chosen subset of K-validities [3]. She calls it a *reasonable intuitionistic analog* of classical modal K

M. Girlando—Funded by Horizon 2021, Marie Skłodowska-Curie grant CYDER (101064105).
R. Kuznets—Funded by the FWF ByzDEL project (P33600).

G. Metcalfe et al. (Eds.): WoLLIC 2024, LNCS 14672, pp. 47–63, 2024.
https://doi.org/10.1007/978-3-031-62687-6_4

as it can be understood as a bimodal logic by directly extending the Gödel translation of intuitionistic propositional logic IPL into modal logic S4 to a product with K. In terms of semantics [2], IK also corresponds to combining the relational models of classical modal logic K, which use branching to represent modal operators, with those for IPL, which use branching to strengthen the implication.

Simpson [13] also observed the *naturalness* of this way of defining intuitionistic modal logic for its ability to translate into intuitionistic first-order logic via the *standard translation*, thus facilitating the design of proof systems in labelled natural deduction and sequent calculus formalisms. In his Ph.D. thesis, Simpson studied modal logic IK in detail and provided two distinct methods to prove its decidability. The first, non-constructive method adapts a standard model-theoretic argument by filtration. The finite model property (FMP) for IK is established by constructing a finite quotient of the canonical model. Together with Fisher Servi's finite axiomatization, the FMP then yields decidability. The second, constructive method is based on Simpson's labelled sequent calculus. The validity of a formula is determined by using a proof-search strategy supplied with a termination measure that guarantees the formula is invalid whenever the proof search is terminated with failure. Both methods are quite involved. The first one relies on heavy semantic machinery to provide finite countermodels for invalid formulas without computing proofs for valid ones. Conversely, when the proof search in the second method does not yield a proof, it terminates on a partial derivation which does not provide a method of constructing a countermodel, finite or infinite. Since Simpson's calculus employs non invertible rules, a countermodel cannot be immediately "read off" from a failed branch.

In this work we introduce a novel algorithm which implements terminating proof search for IK, constructively producing either a proof or a countermodel for the formula at the root. By building *one* proof search tree we check for validity of a formula and, in case of failure, the same object allows to construct a suitable finite countermodel. To this end, we extend Simpson's labelled sequents, which use a single relational symbol for the modalities, to *fully labelled sequents* that also add a symbol for the intuitionistic preorder relation [9]. This strategy, which represents an alternative to Gentzen's *one formula on the right* methodology, allows us to impose the intuitionistic discipline to the calculus, similarly to [11] for IPL and [8] for intuitionistic epistemic logics. It has the consequence of rendering all rules invertible, meaning that backtracking in root-first proof search is not needed anymore. Yet, as in Simpson's proof, one still needs to know when to terminate proof search. In [11], the proof-search algorithm for IPL applies most rules eagerly except for the right implication, for which a loopcheck needs to be employed. If a loop is detected in a proof, proof search stops and a finite countermodel can be generated by reproducing the loop in the model.

By moving from (singly) labelled to fully labelled sequents, we similarly recover invertibility of all rules and a backtracking-free proof search. On the other hand, devising a criterion to terminate proof search is not as straightforward since we also need to account for the modal part of the relational structure. In previous work [4,10], we relied on several intricate loopchecks to ensure termination in the case where both the intuitionistic and modal relations are transitive and require separate loopchecks. By contrast, in the case of IK, the modal search terminates with no need for loops, making it possible to separate the modal search from the intuitionistic one in a modular way. In this work, we introduce the concept of *shrinking* which turns out to be the missing piece to recover the termination of proof search for IK as a simple extension of the one for IPL in [11].

In summary, via this simple loopcheck, we obtain a proof-search algorithm that, starting from a given formula, either gives a correct proof or a suitable finite countermodel. This provides an alternative simpler constructive proof of decidability and the finite model property of IK.

The paper is organized as follows. In Sect. 2, we lay out preliminaries for the syntax and semantics of intuitionistic modal logic. In Sect. 3, we present the proof system $\mathsf{labIK^s}$, a fully labelled sequent calculus based on sets rather than multisets to streamline proof search. In Sect. 4, we describe the strong connection between fully labelled sequents and birelational models that we then exploit in Sect. 5 to deduce properties of the proof-search algorithm. We close with conclusions and future directions in Sect. 6. For the sake of brevity, all the proofs can be found in the Appendix, together with some additional examples.

2 Preliminaries

The formulas of our language, denoted by $A, B, C, \ldots$ are constructed from a countable set $\mathcal{A}$ of atomic propositions, denoted by $a, b, c, \ldots$ through the grammar $A ::= \bot \mid a \mid (A \wedge A) \mid (A \vee A) \mid (A \supset A) \mid \Box A \mid \Diamond A$. An axiomatization of intuitionistic modal logic IK is obtained by adding to an axiomatization of intuitionistic propositional logic IPL the following axioms:

$$\mathsf{k}_1 : \Box(A \supset B) \supset (\Box A \supset \Box B) \qquad \mathsf{k}_3 : \Diamond(A \vee B) \supset (\Diamond A \vee \Diamond B) \qquad \mathsf{k}_5 : \Diamond\bot \supset \bot$$
$$\mathsf{k}_2 : \Box(A \supset B) \supset (\Diamond A \supset \Diamond B) \qquad \mathsf{k}_4 : (\Diamond A \supset \Box B) \supset \Box(A \supset B)$$

A formula is a theorem of IK iff it is derivable from the axioms via the rules of *modus ponens* (infer B from A and $A \supset B$) and *necessitation* (infer $\Box A$ from A).

Let us now recall the *birelational models* [2,12] for intuitionistic modal logics, which combine the Kripke semantics for IPL and for classical modal logics.

Definition 2.1. A ***birelational frame*** $\mathcal{F}$ is a triple $\langle W, R, \leq \rangle$ of a nonempty set W of ***worlds*** equipped with an ***accessibility relation*** R and a preorder $\leq$ (i.e., a reflexive and transitive relation) satisfying the conditions of *forward confluence* fc and *backward confluence* bc:

fc For all $x, y, z \in W$, if $x \leq z$ and xRy, there exists $u \in W$ with zRu and $y \leq u$.
bc For all $x, y, z \in W$, if xRy and $y \leq z$, there exists $u \in W$ with $x \leq u$ and uRz.

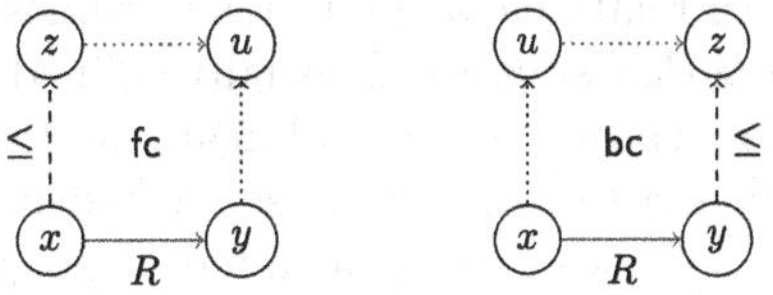

Definition 2.2. A ***birelational model*** $\mathcal{M}$ is a quadruple $\langle W, R, \leq, V\rangle$ where $\langle W, R, \leq\rangle$ is a birelational frame and $V: W \to 2^{\mathcal{A}}$ a ***valuation function***, i.e., a function mapping each world w to the subset of propositional atoms that are true at w, additionally subject to ***monotonicity***: if $w \leq w'$, then $V(w) \subseteq V(w')$. We write $\mathcal{M}, w \Vdash a$ iff $a \in V(w)$ and we recursively extend relation $\Vdash$ to compound formulas as follows:

$$\begin{array}{lll}
\mathcal{M}, w \nVdash \bot & & \\
\mathcal{M}, w \Vdash A \wedge B & \text{iff} & \mathcal{M}, w \Vdash A \text{ and } \mathcal{M}, w \Vdash B; \\
\mathcal{M}, w \Vdash A \vee B & \text{iff} & \mathcal{M}, w \Vdash A \text{ or } \mathcal{M}, w \Vdash B; \\
\mathcal{M}, w \Vdash A \supset B & \text{iff} & \text{for all } w' \text{ with } w \leq w', \text{if } \mathcal{M}, w' \Vdash A, \text{ then } \mathcal{M}, w' \Vdash B; \\
\mathcal{M}, w \Vdash \Box A & \text{iff} & \text{for all } w' \text{ and } u \text{ with } w \leq w' \text{and } w'Ru, \text{ we have } \mathcal{M}, u \Vdash A; \\
\mathcal{M}, w \Vdash \Diamond A & \text{iff} & \text{there exists } u \text{ such that } wRu \text{ and } \mathcal{M}, u \Vdash A.
\end{array}$$

Monotonicity of the valuation V extends to the relation $\Vdash$ by induction on the complexity of formulas.

Proposition 2.3 (Monotonicity). *For any formula A and for any $w, w' \in W$, if $w \leq w'$ and $\mathcal{M}, w \Vdash A$, then $\mathcal{M}, w' \Vdash A$.*

Definition 2.4 (Validity). Formula A is ***valid in a model*** $\mathcal{M} = \langle W, R, \leq, V\rangle$ iff $\mathcal{M}, w \Vdash A$ for all $w \in W$. Formula A is ***valid in a frame*** $\mathcal{F} = \langle W, R, \leq\rangle$ iff it is valid in $\langle W, R, \leq, V\rangle$ for all valuations V.

The correspondence between syntax and semantics for IK is as follows:

Theorem 2.5 ([3,12]). *A formula A is a theorem of* IK *if and only if A is valid in every birelational frame $\langle W, R, \leq\rangle$.*

From now on, we shall say that a formula is IK-***valid***, or just ***valid***, if it is valid in every birelational frame $\langle W, R, \leq\rangle$.

3 Labelled Sequent Calculus labIK^{s}

We now present the fully labelled sequent sequent calculus labIK^{s} for IK that is used in our decision algorithm. It is an equivalent formulation (together with some notational variations) of the sequent calculus for IK presented in [9].

To define a labelled proof system, we first enrich the language of IK by a countable set of ***labels***, denoted by x, y, z, *etc.* Then, we define ***relational atoms*** as expression xRy or $x \leq y$ where x and y are labels, and ***labelled formulas*** as pairs $x{:}A$ of a label x and a formula A. The labelled calculus introduced by Simpson in [13] employs only one kind of relational atoms, xRy. We here follow the fully labelled approach from [9], which instead employs relational atoms in correspondence to both relations of birelational frames.

In the literature, a ***labelled sequent*** is usually defined as a triple $\mathcal{R}, \Gamma \Longrightarrow \Delta$ where $\mathcal{R}$ is a set of relational atoms and Γ and Δ are multisets (or sets) of labelled formulas respectively, all written as comma-separated lists. To simplify subsequent definitions and proofs, we employ a different notation for our sequents.

$$\text{id}\ \frac{}{\mathcal{G}, x{:}a^\bullet, x{:}a^\circ} \qquad \bot^\bullet\ \frac{}{\mathcal{G}, x{:}\bot^\bullet}$$

$$\wedge^\bullet\ \frac{\mathcal{G}, x{:}A \wedge B^\bullet, x{:}A^\bullet, x{:}B^\bullet}{\mathcal{G}, x{:}A \wedge B^\bullet} \qquad \wedge^\circ\ \frac{\mathcal{G}, x{:}A \wedge B^\circ, x{:}A^\circ \quad \mathcal{G}, x{:}A \wedge B^\circ, x{:}B^\circ}{\mathcal{G}, x{:}A \wedge B^\circ}$$

$$\vee^\bullet\ \frac{\mathcal{G}, x{:}A \vee B^\bullet, x{:}A^\bullet \quad \mathcal{G}, x{:}A \vee B^\bullet, x{:}B^\bullet}{\mathcal{G}, x{:}A \vee B^\bullet} \qquad \vee^\circ\ \frac{\mathcal{G}, x{:}A \vee B^\circ, x{:}A^\circ, x{:}B^\circ}{\mathcal{G}, x{:}A \vee B^\circ}$$

$$\supset^\bullet\ \frac{\mathcal{G}, x{:}A \supset B^\bullet, x{:}A^\circ \quad \mathcal{G}, x{:}A \supset B^\bullet, x{:}B^\bullet}{\mathcal{G}, x{:}A \supset B^\bullet} \qquad \supset^\circ\ \frac{\mathcal{G}, x{\leq}z, z{:}A^\bullet, x{:}A \supset B^\circ, z{:}B^\circ}{\mathcal{G}, x{:}A \supset B^\circ}\ z \text{ fresh}$$

$$\Box^\bullet\ \frac{\mathcal{G}, xRy, x{:}\Box A^\bullet, y{:}A^\bullet}{\mathcal{G}, xRy, x{:}\Box A^\bullet} \qquad \Box^\circ\ \frac{\mathcal{G}, x{\leq}u, uRz, x{:}\Box A^\circ, z{:}A^\circ}{\mathcal{G}, x{:}\Box A^\circ}\ u, z \text{ fresh}$$

$$\Diamond^\bullet\ \frac{\mathcal{G}, xRy, x{:}\Diamond A^\bullet, y{:}A^\bullet}{\mathcal{G}, x{:}\Diamond A^\bullet}\ y \text{ fresh} \qquad \Diamond^\circ\ \frac{\mathcal{G}, xRy, x{:}\Diamond A^\circ, y{:}A^\circ}{\mathcal{G}, xRy, x{:}\Diamond A^\circ}$$

$$\text{mon}^\bullet\ \frac{\mathcal{G}, x{\leq}y, x{:}A^\bullet, y{:}A^\bullet}{\mathcal{G}, x{\leq}y, x{:}A^\bullet} \qquad \text{weak}\ \frac{\mathcal{G}}{\mathcal{G}, \mathcal{G}'} \qquad \leq_{\text{rf}}\ \frac{\mathcal{G}, x{\leq}x}{\mathcal{G}} \qquad \leq_{\text{tr}}\ \frac{\mathcal{G}, x{\leq}y, y{\leq}z, x{\leq}z}{\mathcal{G}, x{\leq}y, y{\leq}z,}$$

$$\text{fc}\ \frac{\mathcal{G}, xRy, x{\leq}z, y{\leq}u, zRu}{\mathcal{G}, xRy, x{\leq}z}\ u \text{ fresh} \qquad \text{bc}\ \frac{\mathcal{G}, xRy, y{\leq}z, x{\leq}u, uRz}{\mathcal{G}, xRy, y{\leq}z}\ u \text{ fresh}$$

Fig. 1. System $\mathsf{labIK}^{\mathsf{s}}$

First, we assign a polarity to each labelled formula: $^\bullet$ (input) or $^\circ$ (output). Then, we define a ***polarized labelled sequent*** $\mathcal{G}$ as a *set* of relational atoms and labelled formulas with polarities, with $\mathcal{G}, \mathcal{G}'$ meaning $\mathcal{G} \cup \mathcal{G}'$ and $\mathcal{G}, F$ standing for $\mathcal{G} \cup \{F\}$, for F being a relational atom or a labelled formula. In the following, we simply write ***sequent*** to mean *polarized labelled sequent.*

Example 3.1. $\mathcal{G} = x{\leq}y, yRz, yRu, x{:}a \wedge b^\bullet, y{:}c^\circ, z{:}\Box a^\circ$ is such a sequent.

Intuitively, the polarities play the role of the sequent arrow $\Longrightarrow$, allowing us to identify the left- and right-hand side of a sequent. The input formulas, or $^\bullet$-formulas, are those that would occur in the antecedent of a labelled sequent, and the output formulas, or $^\circ$-formulas, are those occurring in the succedent.[1] Thus, every sequent can be translated into a labelled sequent, and vice versa.

Example 3.2. Sequent $\mathcal{G}$ from Example 3.1 corresponds to the labelled sequent $x{\leq}y, yRz, yRu, x{:}a \wedge b \Longrightarrow y{:}c, z{:}\Box a$.

The rules of $\mathsf{labIK}^{\mathsf{s}}$ are displayed in Fig. 1.[2] The rules in the upper part of the Figure are ***logical rules***, and those in the lower part of the figure are ***structural***

[1] We do not assign polarities to relational atoms because, as in the case of standard labelled sequents, they only occur in the antecedent.

[2] The superscript s stands for *sets*, as our calculus works on sets, unlike the original labIK [9] that works on multisets.

rules. Observe that, since sequents are defined as sets, contraction is embedded into the system. We have chosen a cumulative version of the rules, with the principal formula repeated in the premise(s), as this will become useful in the definition of the proof-search algorithm. Finally, thanks to the presence of $\mathsf{mon}^\bullet$, an explicit structural rule for monotonicity, rules id, $\supset^\bullet$, and $\Box^\bullet$ are formulated as in the classical case.

Definition 3.3. A ***derivation tree*** (or ***derivation*** for short) over a set S of inference rules is a tree whose nodes are labeled with sequents and such that a node labeled with $\mathcal{G}$ is the parent of nodes labeled with $\mathcal{G}_1, \ldots, \mathcal{G}_k$, where $k \geq 0$, iff $\mathsf{r}\dfrac{\mathcal{G}_1 \quad \ldots \quad \mathcal{G}_k}{\mathcal{G}}$ is an instance of inference rule $\mathsf{r} \in \mathsf{S}$. A ***proof*** is a derivation where each leaf is the conclusion of id or $\bot^\bullet$.

An example of a proof in $\mathsf{labIK^s}$ can be found in the Appendix. A rule r is ***admissible*** iff, whenever there are proofs of its premise(s), there is a proof of its conclusion. Rule r is ***derivable*** whenever there is a derivation of its conclusion whose leaves consist of its premise(s). Rule r is ***invertible*** iff, whenever there is a proof of its conclusion, then there are proofs of all its premises. All the rules of $\mathsf{labIK^s}$ are invertible, and the proof closely follows the proof in [9].

To prove soundness and completeness of $\mathsf{labIK^s}$, we show how to translate every proof in $\mathsf{labIK^s}$ into a proof in labIK and back. System labIK is the fully labelled sequent calculus for IK introduced in [9], which employs labelled sequents $\mathcal{R}, \Gamma \Longrightarrow \Delta$ as discussed above in their multiset formulation. The rules of labIK are the same as the rules of $\mathsf{labIK^s}$, except that they are not cumulative, rules weak and $\mathsf{mon}^\bullet$ are admissible, and rules id, $\supset^\bullet$, and $\Box^\bullet$ are formulated as follows (employing our notation):

$$\mathsf{id}\,\frac{}{\mathcal{G}, x{\leq}y, x{:}a^\bullet, y{:}a^\circ}$$

$$\supset^\bullet \frac{\mathcal{G}, x{\leq}y, x{:}A \supset B^\bullet, y{:}A^\circ \quad \mathcal{G}, y{:}B^\bullet}{\mathcal{G}, x{\leq}y, x{:}A \supset B^\bullet} \qquad \Box^\bullet \frac{\mathcal{G}, x{\leq}y, yRz, x{:}\Box A^\bullet, z{:}A^\bullet}{\mathcal{G}, x{\leq}y, yRz, x{:}\Box A^\bullet}$$

Using admissibility of the structural rules (including contraction) in labIK and through trivial translations of $\mathsf{labIK^s}$ sequents into labIK labelled sequents and vice versa, it is easy to show that the two proof systems are equivalent. From this, we immediately obtain soundness and completeness of $\mathsf{labIK^s}$.

Theorem 3.4. *A formula A is a theorem of IK iff for every x, the sequent $x{:}A^\circ$ has a proof in $\mathsf{labIK^s}$.*

4 Models from Sequents

A fully labelled sequent contains sufficient information to extract a birelational model. This will be useful when proving completeness, as we will be able to immediately construct a (counter)model from a leaf of a failed proof-search tree.

Notation 4.1. Let $\mathcal{G}$ be a sequent. We write $\ell(\mathcal{G})$ for the set of labels occurring in $\mathcal{G}$. On this set we define two binary relations $R_{\mathcal{G}}$ and $\leq_{\mathcal{G}}$ as follows: $xR_{\mathcal{G}}y$ iff $xRy \in \mathcal{G}$ and $x\leq_{\mathcal{G}}y$ iff $x\leq y \in \mathcal{G}$.

Definition 4.2 (Model of a sequent). Let $\mathcal{G}$ be a sequent. We define the ***model*** $\mathcal{M}_{\mathcal{G}}$ ***of*** $\mathcal{G}$ to be the quadruple $\mathcal{M}_{\mathcal{G}} = \langle \ell(\mathcal{G}), R_{\mathcal{G}}, \leq_{\mathcal{G}}, V\rangle$ where $V\colon \ell(\mathcal{G}) \to 2^{\mathcal{A}}$ is such that for all atoms $a \in \mathcal{A}$ we have $a \in V(w)$ iff $w{:}a^{\bullet} \in \mathcal{G}$.

This model will be a proper birelational model, provided that the sequent satisfies a number of properties. Intuitively, we want all the rules of $\mathsf{labIK^s}$ to have been exhaustively but non-redundantly applied to the sequent. We shall express these requirements with the notion of a *happy sequent* below.

Definition 4.3 (Happy labelled formula). Let $\mathcal{G}$ be a sequent. We say that a formula $x{:}A^{\bullet} \in \mathcal{G}$ (resp. $x{:}A^{\circ} \in \mathcal{G}$) is ***happy*** iff the following conditions hold:

- $x{:}a^{\bullet} \in \mathcal{G}$ is always happy;
- $x{:}a^{\circ} \in \mathcal{G}$ is happy iff $x{:}a^{\bullet} \notin \mathcal{G}$;
- $x{:}\bot^{\bullet} \in \mathcal{G}$ is never happy;
- $x{:}\bot^{\circ} \in \mathcal{G}$ is always happy;
- $x{:}A \wedge B^{\bullet} \in \mathcal{G}$ is happy iff $x{:}A^{\bullet} \in \mathcal{G}$ and $x{:}B^{\bullet} \in \mathcal{G}$;
- $x{:}A \wedge B^{\circ} \in \mathcal{G}$ is happy iff $x{:}A^{\circ} \in \mathcal{G}$ or $x{:}B^{\circ} \in \mathcal{G}$;
- $x{:}A \vee B^{\bullet} \in \mathcal{G}$ is happy iff $x{:}A^{\bullet} \in \mathcal{G}$ or $x{:}B^{\bullet} \in \mathcal{G}$;
- $x{:}A \vee B^{\circ} \in \mathcal{G}$ is happy iff $x{:}A^{\circ} \in \mathcal{G}$ and $x{:}B^{\circ} \in \mathcal{G}$;
- $x{:}A \supset B^{\bullet} \in \mathcal{G}$ is happy iff $x{:}A^{\circ} \in \mathcal{G}$ or $x{:}B^{\bullet} \in \mathcal{G}$;
- $x{:}A \supset B^{\circ} \in \mathcal{G}$ is happy iff $y{:}A^{\bullet} \in \mathcal{G}$ and $y{:}B^{\circ} \in \mathcal{G}$ for some y with $x\leq_{\mathcal{G}}y$;
- $x{:}\Box A^{\bullet} \in \mathcal{G}$ is happy iff $z{:}A^{\bullet} \in \mathcal{G}$ for all z with $xR_{\mathcal{G}}z$;
- $x{:}\Box A^{\circ} \in \mathcal{G}$ is happy iff $z{:}A^{\circ} \in \mathcal{G}$ for some y, z s.t. $x\leq_{\mathcal{G}}y$ and $yR_{\mathcal{G}}z$;
- $x{:}\Diamond A^{\bullet} \in \mathcal{G}$ is happy iff $y{:}A^{\bullet} \in \mathcal{G}$ for some y with $xR_{\mathcal{G}}y$;
- $x{:}\Diamond A^{\circ} \in \mathcal{G}$ is happy iff $y{:}A^{\circ} \in \mathcal{G}$ for all y s.t. $xR_{\mathcal{G}}y$.

Otherwise, the formula is ***unhappy***.

Definition 4.4 (Happy label). A label x occurring in a sequent $\mathcal{G}$ is ***happy*** iff all formulas occurring at x in $\mathcal{G}$ are happy.

Definition 4.5 (Structurally happy sequent). A sequent $\mathcal{G}$ is ***structurally happy*** iff the following holds:

($\mathsf{mon}^{\bullet}$) if $x\leq_{\mathcal{G}}y$ and $x{:}C^{\bullet} \in \mathcal{G}$, then $y{:}C^{\bullet} \in \mathcal{G}$;
(fc) if $xR_{\mathcal{G}}y$ and $x\leq_{\mathcal{G}}z$, then there is u such that $y\leq_{\mathcal{G}}u$ and $zR_{\mathcal{G}}u$;
(bc) if $xR_{\mathcal{G}}y$ and $y\leq_{\mathcal{G}}z$, then there is u such that $x\leq_{\mathcal{G}}u$ and $uR_{\mathcal{G}}z$;
($\leq$tr) if $x\leq_{\mathcal{G}}y$ and $y\leq_{\mathcal{G}}z$, then $x\leq_{\mathcal{G}}z$;
($\leq$rf) $x\leq_{\mathcal{G}}x$ for all x occurring in $\mathcal{G}$;

$$\begin{aligned}\mathcal{R} &= 1{\leq}1, 2{\leq}2, 3{\leq}3, 4{\leq}4, 5{\leq}5, 6{\leq}6,\\ &\quad 1{\leq}2, 2{\leq}5, 3{\leq}4, 1{\leq}5, 2R3, 5R4, 4R6\\ \mathcal{G}^{\circ} &= 1{:}\Box(c \vee (\Diamond d \supset e))^{\circ}, 3{:}c \vee (\Diamond d \supset e)^{\circ},\\ &\quad 3{:}c^{\circ}, 3{:}\Diamond d \supset e^{\circ}, 4{:}e^{\circ}\\ \mathcal{G} &= \mathcal{R}, 1{:}a \vee b^{\bullet}, 2{:}a \vee b^{\bullet}, 5{:}a \vee b^{\bullet},\\ &\quad 1{:}a^{\bullet}, 2{:}a^{\bullet}, 5{:}a^{\bullet}, 4{:}\Diamond d^{\bullet}, 6{:}d^{\bullet}, \mathcal{G}^{\circ}\end{aligned}$$

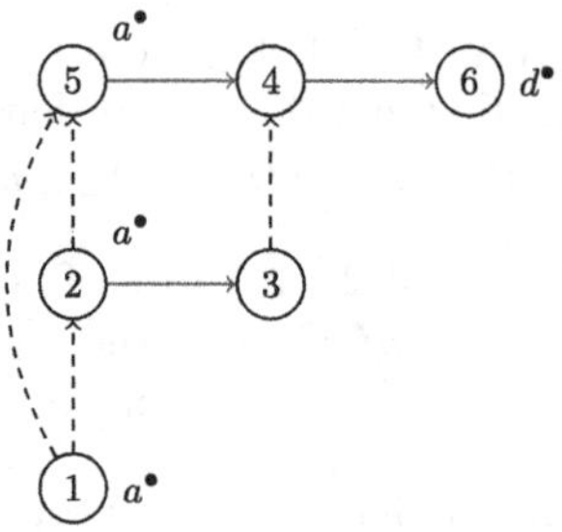

Fig. 2. Model $\mathcal{M}_{\mathcal{G}}$ of sequent $\mathcal{G}$. The nodes represent the worlds of the model, the dashed arrows represent the $\leq$-relation, and the solid arrow represent the R-relation. For simplicity, we do not represent the reflexive $\leq$-edges of $\mathcal{M}_{\mathcal{G}}$.

Definition 4.6 (Happy sequent). A sequent $\mathcal{G}$ is ***happy*** iff it is structurally happy and all labels in the sequent are happy.

We can now show that the model of a happy sequent is a birelational model. Moreover, all input formulas are satisfied in the model, and all output formulas are falsified in the model.

Theorem 4.7. *For a happy sequent $\mathcal{G}$, its model $\mathcal{M}_{\mathcal{G}} = \langle \ell(\mathcal{G}), R_{\mathcal{G}}, \leq_{\mathcal{G}}, V\rangle$ is a birelational model satisfying the following: i) if $x{:}A^{\bullet} \in \mathcal{G}$, then $\mathcal{M}_{\mathcal{G}}, x \Vdash A$; and ii) if $x{:}A^{\circ} \in \mathcal{G}$, then $\mathcal{M}_{\mathcal{G}}, x \nVdash A$.*

Example 4.8. Take the model $\mathcal{M}_{\mathcal{G}}$ of $\mathcal{G}$ represented in Fig. 2. It holds that, e.g., $\mathcal{M}_{\mathcal{G}}, 4 \Vdash \Diamond d$ and $\mathcal{M}_{\mathcal{G}}, 1 \nVdash \Box(c \vee (\Diamond d \supset e))$.

In what follows, we will often make use of the notion of axiomatic sequent.

Definition 4.9 (Axiomatic sequent). A sequent $\mathcal{G}$ is ***axiomatic*** iff there is a label x such that either $x{:}a^{\bullet} \in \mathcal{G}$ and $x{:}a^{\circ} \in \mathcal{G}$ for some a, or $x{:}\bot^{\bullet} \in \mathcal{G}$. Otherwise, $\mathcal{G}$ is called ***non-axiomatic***.

Remark 4.10. An axiomatic sequent $\mathcal{G}$ is never happy, because either $x{:}a^{\circ} \in \mathcal{G}$ or $x{:}\bot^{\bullet} \in \mathcal{G}$ is unhappy.

5 The Proof-Search Algorithm

We shall here define an algorithmic procedure that performs proof search in $\mathsf{labIK^s}$, with the aim of obtaining either a set of axiomatic sequents, from which a $\mathsf{labIK^s}$ derivation can be easily constructed, or a happy sequent, from which a (counter)model can be extracted (also a sequent that can be easily transformed into a happy sequent will suffice for this purpose). Our algorithm relies on the fact that the sequents created by the algorithm are all ***layered*** (provided the endsequent contains only one label), where each layer can be thought of as a classical K-model.

Definition 5.1 (Layer). For a sequent $\mathcal{G}$, we define the relation $R_{\mathcal{G}}^{\leftrightarrow}$ to be the transitive and reflexive closure of $R_{\mathcal{G}} \cup R_{\mathcal{G}}^{-1}$. Since this is an equivalence relation, we can define a ***layer*** L in $\mathcal{G}$ to be an equivalence class of $R_{\mathcal{G}}^{\leftrightarrow}$. A layer L is ***happy*** if all labels $x \in L$ are happy.

Definition 5.2 (Layered sequent). We say that a sequent $\mathcal{G}$ is ***layered*** iff for any labels x, x', y, and y' occurring in $\mathcal{G}$:

1. if $xR_{\mathcal{G}}^{\leftrightarrow}y$ for $x \neq y$, then $x \not\leq_{\mathcal{G}} y$ and $y \not\leq_{\mathcal{G}} x$; and
2. if $xR_{\mathcal{G}}^{\leftrightarrow}y$, $x'R_{\mathcal{G}}^{\leftrightarrow}y'$, and $x \leq_{\mathcal{G}} x'$ for $x \neq x'$, then $y' \not\leq_{\mathcal{G}} y$.

For layers L_1 and L_2, we define $L_1 \leq L_2$ whenever there are labels $x \in L_1$ and $y \in L_2$ such that $x \leq_{\mathcal{G}} y$. We write $L_1 < L_2$ iff $L_1 \leq L_2$ and $L_1 \neq L_2$.

Proposition 5.3. *For a layered structurally saturated sequent $\mathcal{G}$, relation $\leq$ is an order relation on its layers.*

The main observation to make is that all logical rules of $\mathsf{labIK^s}$, except for $\supset^\circ$ and $\Box^\circ$, only work locally on a layer, whereas $\supset^\circ$ and $\Box^\circ$ create a new layer. As in classical K, where proof search terminates without any particular loopcheck, we can exhaustively apply the rules $\wedge^\bullet, \wedge^\circ, \vee^\bullet, \vee^\circ, \supset^\bullet, \Box^\bullet, \Diamond^\bullet$, and $\Diamond^\circ$. This process is called ***saturation*** and motivates the following definition:

Definition 5.4. (Almost happy). A label x in a sequent $\mathcal{G}$ is ***almost happy*** iff all formulas occurring at x are happy except, possibly, those of the shapes $\bot^\bullet$, a°, $A \supset B^\circ$, and $\Box A^\circ$. A layer L (resp. sequent $\mathcal{G}$) is ***almost happy*** iff all labels in L (resp. $\mathcal{G}$) are almost happy.

Definition 5.5. (Saturation). A ***saturation tree*** is a derivation tree $\mathcal{T}$ over the rule set $\{\wedge^\bullet, \wedge^\circ, \vee^\bullet, \vee^\circ, \supset^\bullet, \Box^\bullet, \Diamond^\bullet, \Diamond^\circ\}$, whose leaves are almost happy. If $\mathcal{G}$ is the root of $\mathcal{T}$, then the set of its leaves form a ***saturation*** of $\mathcal{G}$.

With this, we can define a *macro rule*

$$\mathsf{sat}\ \frac{\mathcal{G}_1 \quad \ldots \quad \mathcal{G}_n}{\mathcal{G}}\ \text{where } \{\mathcal{G}_1, \ldots, \mathcal{G}_n\} \text{ is a saturation of } \mathcal{G} \tag{1}$$

and immediately obtain the following:

Proposition 5.6. *The* sat*-rule is derivable in* $\mathsf{labIK^s}$.

Remark 5.7. The saturation of a sequent is in general not uniquely defined since sequents can differ up to a renaming of labels. However, we can fix a strategy and naming scheme for fresh labels when applying the inference rules $\wedge^\bullet, \wedge^\circ, \vee^\bullet, \vee^\circ, \supset^\bullet, \Box^\bullet, \Diamond^\bullet, \Diamond^\circ$, so that without loss of generality, we can for the context of this paper speak of *the* saturation of a sequent $\mathcal{G}$, and denote it by $\lceil \mathcal{G} \rceil$.

The rules $\supset^\circ$ and $\Box^\circ$ create a new layer, and our algorithm immediately completes the layer, making the sequent structurally happy, by applying the structural rules of $\mathsf{labIK^s}$. To make this formal, we introduce the notion of ***lifting***.

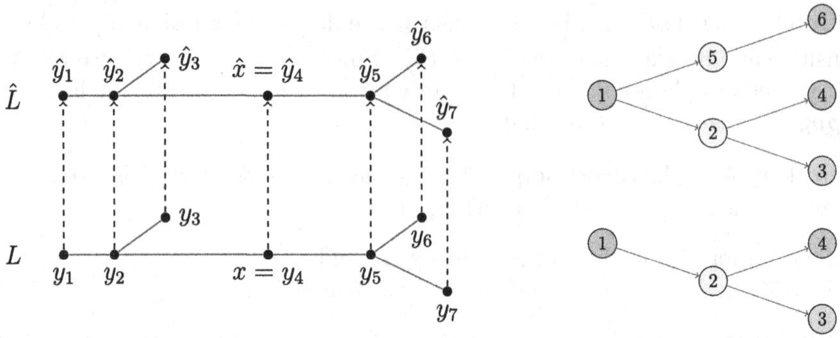

Fig. 3. *Left*: Lifting of the layer L. *Right*: An example of shrinking, for $2 \sim 5$, $4 \sim 6$.

Construction 5.8 (Lifting). Let $\mathcal{G}$ be an almost happy sequent, and let L be a layer in $\mathcal{G}$. Then $L = \{y_1, \dots, y_l\}$ for some $l \geq 1$. Let us assume $x \in L$. Now let $\hat{L}$ be a set of fresh labels $\{\hat{y}_1, \dots, \hat{y}_l\}$. We define $\mathcal{G}{\uparrow}^x$ to be the sequent containing for every $i = 1 \dots l$:

1. relational atom $\hat{y}_i {\leq} \hat{y}_i$;
2. for every label w occurring in $\mathcal{G}$: the relational atom $w {\leq} \hat{y}_i$ whenever $w {\leq}_{\mathcal{G}} y_i$;
3. for every $i' = 1 \dots l$: the relational atom $\hat{y}_i R \hat{y}_{i'}$ whenever $y_i R_{\mathcal{G}} y_{i'}$,
4. for every formula C: the labelled formula $\hat{y}_i{:}C^\bullet$ whenever $y_i{:}C^\bullet \in \mathcal{G}$.

In other words, $\mathcal{G}{\uparrow}^x$ contains a copy of L, without the $\circ$-formulas, that would be put on top of L if $\mathcal{G}{\uparrow}^x$ was added to $\mathcal{G}$, so that $\mathcal{G} \cup \mathcal{G}{\uparrow}^x$ would be structurally happy. Now assume there is some unhappy formula $x{:}F^\circ \in \mathcal{G}$, for $F = A \supset B$ or $F = \Box B$, and $x \in L$. Then $x = y_j$ for some $j = 1 \dots l$. We let $\hat{x} = \hat{y}_j$, and we define the ***lifting*** $\mathcal{G}{\uparrow}^{x:F^\circ}$ as follows:

- If $F = A \supset B$, then $\mathcal{G}{\uparrow}^{x:A\supset B^\circ} = \mathcal{G}{\uparrow}^x \cup \{\hat{x}{:}A^\bullet, \hat{x}{:}B^\circ\}$.
- If $F = \Box B$, then $\mathcal{G}{\uparrow}^{x:\Box B^\circ} = \mathcal{G}{\uparrow}^x \cup \{\hat{x}Rz, z{\leq}z, z{:}B^\circ\}$ for some fresh label z.

We can now define a second macro rule, denoted lift:

$$\mathsf{lift}\,\frac{\mathcal{G} \cup \mathcal{G}{\uparrow}^{x:F^\circ}}{\mathcal{G}} \quad \text{where } F \in \{A \supset B, \Box B\} \text{ and } x{:}F^\circ \text{ is unhappy in } \mathcal{G}. \tag{2}$$

The idea behind lifting a layer is depicted on the left in Fig. 3. Any application of the lift rule to a formula $x{:}F^\circ \in \mathcal{G}$ can be simulated by the rules of $\mathsf{labIK^s}$: it suffices to apply to $\mathcal{G}$ one instance of rule $\supset^\circ$ or $\Box^\circ$ (depending on the shape of F), followed by possibly multiple applications of rules fc, bc, ${\leq}$rf, ${\leq}$tr and mon$^\bullet$. Thus, the following holds:

Proposition 5.9 *The* lift*-rule is derivable in* $\mathsf{labIK^s}$.

One might assume that it is enough to simply repeat saturation and lifting until we see a repetition of a layer. This is indeed the basic idea of what the algorithm is doing. And when $\supset^\circ$ is the only layer creating rule, this is enough, as it would corresponds to the standard loopcheck for proof search in IPL [11]. However, the $\Box^\circ$ rule makes layers grow, and a possible repetition is not visible at the moment of the layer creation, but possibly only several steps later. A simple example is shown in Fig. 5. For this reason we need another operation that we call ***shrinking***.

Definition 5.10 (Equivalent labels and simulation). Let $\mathcal{G}$ be a sequent and let $x, y \in \ell(\mathcal{G})$. We say that x and y are ***equivalent***, denoted as $x \sim y$, iff for all formulas A, we have $x{:}A^\bullet \in \mathcal{G}$ iff $y{:}A^\bullet \in \mathcal{G}$ and also $x{:}A^\circ \in \mathcal{G}$ iff $y{:}A^\circ \in \mathcal{G}$. A ***simulation*** xSy of y by x is a relation $S \subseteq \ell(\mathcal{G}) \times \ell(\mathcal{G})$ such that whenever xSy, we have $x \sim y$ and, for any y' such that $yR_\mathcal{G}y'$, there is x' such that $xR_\mathcal{G}x'$ and $x'Sy'$.

In the following, we write $\mathcal{G}[y/x]$ for the sequent obtained by uniformly substituting x for y in $\mathcal{G}$.

Definition 5.11 (Shrinking). Let $\mathcal{G}$ be a sequent. Two labels $x, y \in \ell(\mathcal{G})$ are ***siblings***, denoted as $x|y$, if there is a label $z \in \ell(\mathcal{G})$ with $zR_\mathcal{G}x$ and $zR_\mathcal{G}y$. A label $y \in \ell(\mathcal{G})$ is ***redundant*** if there is a sibling x of y with xSy for some simulation S. A sequent $\mathcal{G}$ is ***shrunk*** iff there are no redundant labels in $\ell(\mathcal{G})$. A ***shrinking tree*** is a derivation tree $\mathcal{T}$ over the inference rule

$$\mathsf{shrk}\,\frac{\mathcal{G}[y/x]}{\mathcal{G}}\ \text{where } x|y \text{ and } xSy \text{ for some simulation } S \tag{3}$$

whose leaf[3] is a shrunk sequent. If $\mathcal{G}$ is the conclusion of $\mathcal{T}$, then the leaf of $\mathcal{T}$ is called a ***shrinking*** of $\mathcal{G}$.

Example 5.12. To illustrate the above definition, on the top right of Fig. 3 is displayed a sequent with only one layer. Colours indicate equivalence of labels, so we assume that $2 \sim 5$ and $4 \sim 6$. Moreover, it holds that $2|5$. Thus, the sequent can be shrunk by uniformly substituting first label 2 for label 5 and then 4 for 6. The result is displayed in the lower part of the figure.

Remark 5.13. As with saturation, also the shrinking of a sequent $\mathcal{G}$ is not uniquely defined because of possible label renamings. But as before, we can impose a strategy on the order of the applications of the shrk-rule when computing the shrinking, so that we can speak of *the* shrinking of $\mathcal{G}$ and denote it by $\lfloor \mathcal{G} \rfloor$.

Combining Remarks 5.7 and 5.13, we can define the ***shrink-saturation*** of a sequent $\mathcal{G}$ as follows

$$\llbracket \mathcal{G} \rrbracket = \{ \lfloor \mathcal{H} \rfloor \mid \mathcal{H} \in \lceil \mathcal{G} \rceil \} \tag{4}$$

i.e., for computing it, we first compute the saturation of $\mathcal{G}$, and then compute the shrinking of each sequent in the saturation.

[3] There is exactly one leaf since the shrk-rule has one premise.

0. Given a formula F, let $\mathcal{G}_0 = r{\leq}r, r{:}F^\circ$ and let $\mathfrak{G}_0 = \llbracket \mathcal{G}_0 \rrbracket$.
1. If all sequents in $\mathfrak{G}_i$ are axiomatic, then terminate.
   → The formula F is provable and we can give a proof of $r{:}F^\circ$ in $\mathsf{labIK^s}$.
2. Otherwise, pick a non-axiomatic sequent $\mathcal{G}_i \in \mathfrak{G}_i$.
   (a) If there is an allowed formula $x{:}F^\circ \in \mathcal{G}_i$, then compute the lifting $\mathcal{G}_i{\uparrow}^{x:F^\circ}$, let $\mathfrak{G}_{i+1} = (\mathfrak{G}_i \setminus \{\mathcal{G}_i\}) \cup \llbracket \mathcal{G}_i + \mathcal{G}_i{\uparrow}^{x:F^\circ} \rrbracket$, and go to Step 1.
   (b) Otherwise, if $\mathcal{G}_i$ does not contain any allowed formulas, then terminate.
   → The formula F is not provable, and $\mathcal{G}_i$ defines a countermodel.

Fig. 4. Proof-search algorithm

We are now ready to formally define our loopcheck, which is essentially checking whether we see a repetition of a layer. In that case we stop applying $\supset^\circ$ and $\Box^\circ$ and do not create new layers.

Definition 5.14 (Equivalent layers). Let $\mathcal{G}$ be a sequent and let L_1 and L_2 be layers in $\mathcal{G}$. We say that L_1 and L_2 are ***equivalent***, denoted as $L_1 \sim L_2$, if there is a bijection $f\colon L_1 \to L_2$ such that for all $x, y \in L_1$ we have $x \sim f(x)$ and $xR_{\mathcal{G}}y$ iff $f(x)R_{\mathcal{G}}f(y)$.

Definition 5.15 (Allowed formula). Let $\mathcal{G}$ be a saturated sequent with an unhappy formula $x{:}A \supset B^\circ$ (or $x{:}\Box A^\circ$), and let L be the layer of x. We say that the formula $x{:}A \supset B^\circ$ (resp. $x{:}\Box A^\circ$) is ***allowed*** iff: there is no layer $L' < L$ with $L' \sim L$, and all layers $L' < L$ are happy.

We can now put all the pieces together in our proof search algorithm, which is given in Fig. 4, and which has the following properties:

Theorem 5.16. *The algorithm given in Fig. 4 always terminates.*

Theorem 5.17. *If the algorithm shown in Fig. 4 terminates in Step 1, then the formula F is a theorem of* IK.

Theorem 5.18. *If the algorithm shown in Fig. 4 terminates in Step 2b, then there is a finite model in which the formula F is not valid.*

Corollary 5.19. *The logic* IK *is decidable and has the FMP.*

6 Conclusions and Future Work

We have presented a proof-search algorithm to decide validity of IK formulas, essentially implementing proof search within $\mathsf{labIK^s}$, a fully labelled calculus for IK. When compared to Simpson's model-theoretic and proof-theoretic techniques to establish decidability of IK, our algorithm has the advantage of producing either a proof or a countermodel for a formula through the same construction. Moreover, since a finite countermodel is extracted from a finite proof search branch, we are able to establish in one go both decidability and the

FMP for IK. Thanks to invertibility of all the rules of $\mathsf{labIK}^{\mathsf{s}}$, backtracking is not necessary and the countermodel construction is immediate, in contrast to [7].

In future work, we plan to study the complexity of our decision procedure. Specifically, we are interested in bounding the size of the countermodels generated by the algorithm, which at the moment we estimate as non-elementary. We conjecture that smaller countermodels could be found by refining the steps of our algorithm. Moreover, we plan to further extend our algorithm to other logics in the intuitionistic modal family. Finally, we intend to create a theorem prover implementing our algorithm, by analogy with [5].

A Proofs

Proof (of Theorem 4.7*).* The worlds W of $\mathcal{M}_{\mathcal{G}}$ are the labels of the sequent. Conditions fc and bc, as well as transitivity and reflexivity of $\leq_{\mathcal{G}}$, and monotonicity of V all follow by construction due to structural happiness. Thus, $\mathcal{M}_{\mathcal{G}}$ is a birelational model. It only remains to show the two properties about forcing, which we prove by mutual induction on the size of A, proceeding by case analysis on the main connective of A:

- $x{:}\bot^\bullet \in \mathcal{G}$: it is not possible for a happy sequent.
- $x{:}\bot^\circ \in \mathcal{G}$: we have $\mathcal{M}_{\mathcal{G}}, x \not\Vdash \bot$ by definition.
- $x{:}a^\bullet \in \mathcal{G}$: by Definition 4.2, $\mathcal{M}_{\mathcal{G}}, x \Vdash a$.
- $x{:}a^\circ \in \mathcal{G}$: it is not the case that $x{:}a^\bullet \in \mathcal{G}$ by happiness of x, hence, $\mathcal{M}_{\mathcal{G}}, x \not\Vdash a$ by Definition 4.2.
- $x{:}B \wedge C^\bullet \in \mathcal{G}$: by happiness of x, both $x{:}B^\bullet \in \mathcal{G}$ and $x{:}C^\bullet \in \mathcal{G}$. Then $\mathcal{M}_{\mathcal{G}}, x \Vdash B$ and $\mathcal{M}_{\mathcal{G}}, x \Vdash C$ by IH. Therefore, $\mathcal{M}_{\mathcal{G}}, x \Vdash B \wedge C$.
- $x{:}B \wedge C^\circ \in \mathcal{G}$: by happiness of x, either $x{:}B^\circ \in \mathcal{G}$ or $x{:}C^\circ \in \mathcal{G}$. Then either $\mathcal{M}_{\mathcal{G}}, x \not\Vdash B$ or $\mathcal{M}_{\mathcal{G}}, x \not\Vdash C$ by IH. Therefore, $\mathcal{M}_{\mathcal{G}}, x \not\Vdash B \wedge C$.
- Cases for $x{:}B \vee C^\bullet \in \mathcal{G}$ and $x{:}B \vee C^\circ \in \mathcal{G}$ are analogous.
- $x{:}B \supset C^\bullet \in \mathcal{G}$: consider any y with $x \leq_{\mathcal{G}} y$. By $(\mathsf{mon}^\bullet)$-structural saturation, $y{:}B \supset C^\bullet \in \mathcal{G}$. By happiness of y, either $y{:}B^\circ \in \mathcal{G}$ or $y{:}C^\bullet \in \mathcal{G}$. By IH, either $\mathcal{M}_{\mathcal{G}}, y \not\Vdash B$ or $\mathcal{M}_{\mathcal{G}}, y \Vdash C$. Thus, $\mathcal{M}_{\mathcal{G}}, y \Vdash B$ implies $\mathcal{M}_{\mathcal{G}}, y \Vdash C$ for all y with $x \leq_{\mathcal{G}} y$. Therefore, $\mathcal{M}_{\mathcal{G}}, x \Vdash B \supset C$.
- $x{:}B \supset C^\circ \in \mathcal{G}$: by happiness of x, there is a world y such that $x \leq_{\mathcal{G}} y$, $y{:}B^\bullet \in \mathcal{G}$, and $y{:}C^\circ \in \mathcal{G}$. By IH, $\mathcal{M}_{\mathcal{G}}, y \Vdash B$ and $\mathcal{M}_{\mathcal{G}}, y \not\Vdash C$. Therefore, $\mathcal{M}_{\mathcal{G}}, x \not\Vdash B \supset C$.
- $x{:}\Diamond B^\bullet \in \mathcal{G}$: by happiness of x, there is a world y such that $x R_{\mathcal{G}} y$ and $y{:}B^\bullet \in \mathcal{G}$. By IH, we have $\mathcal{M}_{\mathcal{G}}, y \Vdash B$ and, therefore, $\mathcal{M}_{\mathcal{G}}, x \Vdash \Diamond B$.
- $x{:}\Diamond B^\circ \in \mathcal{G}$: by happiness of x, we have $y{:}B^\circ \in \mathcal{G}$ for all worlds y such that $x R_{\mathcal{G}} y$. Thus, by IH, $\mathcal{M}_{\mathcal{G}}, y \not\Vdash B$ whenever $x R_{\mathcal{G}} y$. Therefore, $\mathcal{M}_{\mathcal{G}}, x \not\Vdash \Diamond B$.
- $x{:}\Box B^\bullet \in \mathcal{G}$: consider arbitrary y and z with $x \leq_{\mathcal{G}} y$ and $y R_{\mathcal{G}} z$. By $(\mathsf{mon}^\bullet)$-structural saturation, $y{:}\Box B^\bullet \in \mathcal{G}$. By happiness of y, we have $z{:}B^\bullet \in \mathcal{G}$. Thus, by IH, $\mathcal{M}_{\mathcal{G}}, z \Vdash B$ whenever $x \leq_{\mathcal{G}} y$ and $y R_{\mathcal{G}} z$. Therefore, $\mathcal{M}_{\mathcal{G}}, x \Vdash \Box B$.
- $x{:}\Box B^\circ \in \mathcal{G}$: by happiness of x, there exist y and z such that $x \leq_{\mathcal{G}} y$, $y R_{\mathcal{G}} z$, and $z{:}B^\circ \in \mathcal{G}$. By IH, $\mathcal{M}_{\mathcal{G}}, z \not\Vdash B$. Therefore, $\mathcal{M}_{\mathcal{G}}, x \not\Vdash \Box B$. □

Proof (of Theorem 5.16*).* First, all formulas that occur in a sequent must be subformulas of F. This means that the number of equivalence classes of the label equivalence relation $\sim$ is finite. Next, observe that the algorithm only produces layered sequents, and the labels of each layer in a sequent $\mathcal{G}$ form a tree defined by the $R_{\mathcal{G}}$-relation. These trees have the following properties:

(i) Their depth is bounded by the maximal modal depth of F. Whenever a new node is created or a formula moves from a parent to a child, one modality is removed (this happens in the rules $\Diamond^{\bullet}, \Diamond^{\circ}, \Box^{\bullet}$, and $\Box^{\circ}$).
(ii) The number of children that a node can have is also bounded, because for every given depth, the number of different trees with that depth that do not simulate each other is also finite. Note that the only rules that create new branches are $\Diamond^{\bullet}$ and $\Box^{\circ}$, where $\Diamond^{\bullet}$ is only applied when there is no child with the corresponding subformula, and $\Box^{\circ}$ is only applied after the shrinking operation.

These two properties ensure that the number of layer equivalence classes (Definition 5.14) is finite. Since the layers in the sequent form a tree with respect to the layer ordering $\leq$, we must eventually see a repetition along each branch of that tree. This triggers our loopcheck, i.e., there are no allowed formulas left. □

Proof (of Theorem 5.17*).* We are going to show that whenever the algorithm terminates in Step 1, then we can produce a proof of the formula F in $\mathsf{lablK^s}$. By inspecting the algorithm in Fig. 4, we can observe that the set $\mathfrak{S}$ that is computed at each round is in fact the set of leaves of a derivation tree with root $\mathcal{G}_0$, over the rules sat, shrk, and lift.

We have already observed (Propositions 5.6 and 5.9) that the rules sat and lift are derivable in $\mathsf{lablK^s}$. Furthermore, every instance of the shrk-rule is an instance of the weak with an augmentation of the premise by additional relational atoms. We are now going to show that these additional relational atoms are never used in the derivation by other rule instances. Therefore, all instances of shrk can be replaced by weak, and we obtain a derivation in $\mathsf{lablK^s}$ of the sequent $\mathcal{G}_0$, from which we can get $r{:}F^{\circ}$, as required by Theorem 3.4.

The first observation to make is that in every sequent $\mathcal{G}$ that the algorithm visits, the relation $R_{\mathcal{G}}$ defines a tree-structure on each layer. Assume now we have an instance of the shrk-rule with conclusion $\mathcal{G}$ and premise $\mathcal{G}' = \mathcal{G}[y/x]$, eliminating all occurrences of the label y. Then all labels u with $yR_{\mathcal{G}}u$ are redundant in $\mathcal{G}'$, by using the same simulation S as for y in $\mathcal{G}$. Thus, whenever the shrinking removes a label y, it also removes the whole R-subtree rooted at that label. Therefore, a shrinking never introduces additional R-relational atoms.

The next observation to make is that the shrk-rule only removes labels that are in a layer that is maximal with respect to the layer ordering $\leq$. The reason is that the only way to create new layers is via the lift-rule, and that only happens if the layers below that new layer are already shrunk. Therefore, a shrinking only introduces additional relational atoms of the form $v{\leq}w$, where w is in a layer that is maximal and almost happy.

The only inference rule in $\mathsf{labIK^s}$ that uses $\leq$-relational atoms to move formulas into another label is the $\mathsf{mon}^\bullet$-rule that is employed in the lifting. But there it only uses the freshly created $\leq$-relational atoms for the new layer. Hence, the additional relational atoms are never used, and we can replace all shrk-instances by weak. □

Proof (of Theorem 5.18*).* Assume the algorithm in Fig. 4 terminates in Step 2b, i.e., there is an almost happy sequent $\mathcal{G}_i$ with no allowed formulas. That means that whenever there is an unhappy formula, it is of shape $x{:}A \supset B^\circ$ or $x{:}\Box A^\circ$, and x is in a layer L, such that (i) L is maximal with respect to $\leq$, and (ii) there is a layer L' with $L' \sim L$ and $L' < L$.

We have (i) because if a formula is not allowed, then there is no other allowed formula in the same layer, and we have (ii) because otherwise the unhappy $x{:}A \supset B^\circ$ or $x{:}\Box A^\circ$ would be allowed.

We can now take the bijection $f\colon L \to L'$ that makes L and L' equivalent and define $\mathcal{G}_i'$ to be the sequent obtained from $\mathcal{G}_i$ by adding the relational atom $v{\leq}f(v)$ for every $v \in L$. This makes every unhappy $x{:}A \supset B^\circ$ or $x{:}\Box A^\circ$ with $x \in L$ happy, and does not affect happiness of other formulas in the sequent.

We can repeat this for all layers that contain unhappy formulas, yielding eventually a happy sequent, to which we can apply Theorem 4.7. □

B Examples

Example B.1. We report a proof of sequent $1{:}(\Diamond p \supset \Box q) \supset \Box(p \supset q)^\circ$. For reasons of space, we avoid repeating the principal formulas in the premise(s) of the rules, and we abbreviate with $\mathcal{R}$ the sequent $1{\leq}2, 2R3, 3{\leq}4, 2{\leq}5, 5R4, 1{\leq}5$.

$$
\supset^\circ\dfrac{\Box^\circ\dfrac{\supset^\circ\dfrac{\mathsf{bc}\dfrac{\leq\mathsf{tr}\dfrac{\mathsf{mon}^\bullet\dfrac{\dfrac{\Diamond^\circ\dfrac{\mathsf{id}\dfrac{}{\mathcal{R}, 4{:}p^\bullet, 4{:}p^\circ, 4{:}q^\circ}}{\mathcal{R}, 4{:}p^\bullet, 5{:}\Diamond p^\circ, 4{:}q^\circ} \qquad \Box^\bullet\dfrac{\mathsf{id}\dfrac{}{\mathcal{R}, 4{:}p^\bullet, 4{:}q^\bullet, 4{:}q^\circ}}{\mathcal{R}, 4{:}p^\bullet, 5{:}\Box q^\bullet, 4{:}q^\circ}}{1{\leq}2, 2R3, 3{\leq}4, 2{\leq}5, 5R4, 1{\leq}5, 4{:}p^\bullet, 5{:}\Diamond p \supset \Box q^\bullet, 4{:}q^\circ}}{1{\leq}2, 2R3, 3{\leq}4, 2{\leq}5, 5R4, 1{\leq}5, 4{:}p^\bullet, 1{:}\Diamond p \supset \Box q^\bullet, 4{:}q^\circ}}{1{\leq}2, 2R3, 3{\leq}4, 2{\leq}5, 5R4, 4{:}p^\bullet, 1{:}\Diamond \supset \Box q^\bullet, 4{:}q^\circ}}{1{\leq}2, 2R3, 3{\leq}4, 4{:}p^\bullet, 1{:}\Diamond p \supset \Box q^\bullet, 4{:}q^\circ}}{1{\leq}2, 2R3, 1{:}\Diamond p \supset \Box q^\bullet, 3{:}p \supset q^\circ}}{1{:}\Diamond p \supset \Box q^\bullet, 1{:}\Box(p \supset q)^\circ}}{1{:}(\Diamond p \supset \Box q) \supset \Box(p \supset q)^\circ}
$$

Example B.2. Let us consider the formula $A = ((a \supset \Box b) \supset \bot) \supset \bot$. To check whether the formula is valid in IK, we apply the procedure described in Sect. 5, by taking $\mathcal{G}_0 = r{\leq}r, r{:}A^\circ$. On the right of Fig. 5 is displayed one of the sequents $\mathcal{G}_i$ produced by the algorithm, where $\mathcal{H} = (a \supset \Box b) \supset \bot^\bullet, a \supset \Box b^\circ$. Observe that $\mathcal{G}_i$ is layered, and that all the layers $L_0 - L_5$ are happy, while layer L_6 is almost happy: formula $10{:}\Box b^\circ$ is not happy. Moreover, the sequent can be shrunk:

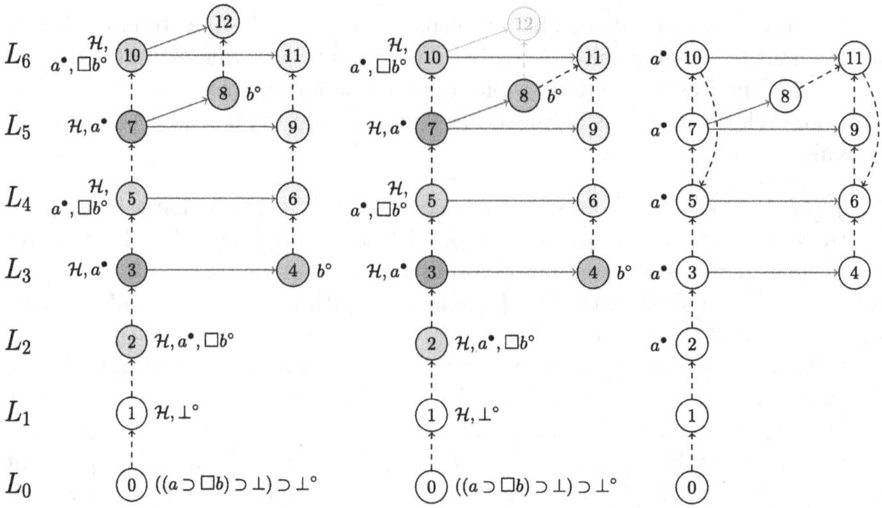

Fig. 5. *Left*: Graphical representation of a sequent $\mathcal{G}$ produced by the algorithm, where $\mathcal{H} = (a \supset \Box b) \supset \bot^\bullet, a \supset \Box b^\circ$. *Middle*: The result of shrinking $\mathcal{G}$. *Right*: The countermodel produced according to the procedure described in the proof of Theorem 5.18.

again, we use colours to indicate label equivalence, and it holds that $11 \sim 12$, and furthermore that $11|12$. In the middle of the Figure is represented the result applying shrinking to $\mathcal{G}_i$. After the shrinking, it holds that layer L_6 and layer L_4 are equivalent. Thus, the unhappy formula $10{:}\Box b^\circ$ is not allowed and, since there are no allowed formulas, the algorithm terminates. At this point, using the construction described above, we make formula $10{:}\Box b^\circ$ happy by adding the relational atoms $10 \leq 5$ and $11 \leq 6$ to the sequent. The result is represented on the left-hand side of Fig. 5. It is easy to check that this sequent is happy, and thus defines a countermodel for A.

References

1. Bellin, G., de Paiva, V., Ritter, E.: Extended Curry–Howard correspondence for a basic constructive modal logic. In: Areces, C., de Rijke, M. (eds.) Workshop Proceedings of Methods for Modalities, vol. 2 (2001)
2. Fischer Servi, G.: Semantics for a class of intuitionistic modal calculi. In: Dalla Chiara, M.L. (ed.) Italian Studies in the Philosophy of Science, Boston Studies in the Philosophy of Science, vol. 47, pp. 59–72. D. Reidel Publishing Company (1980). https://doi.org/10.1007/978-94-009-8937-5_5
3. Fischer Servi, G.: Axiomatizations for some intuitionistic modal logics. Rendiconti del Seminario Matematico, Università e Politecnico di Torino **42**(3), 179–194 (1984)
4. Girlando, M., Kuznets, R., Marin, S., Morales, M., Straßburger, L.: Intuitionistic S4 is decidable. In: 2023 38th Annual ACM/IEEE Symposium on Logic in Computer Science (LICS), 26–29 June 2023, Boston, USA. IEEE (2023). https://doi.org/10.1109/LICS56636.2023.10175684

5. Girlando, M., Straßburger, L.: MOIN: a nested sequent theorem prover for intuitionistic modal logics (system description). In: Peltier, N., Sofronie-Stokkermans, V. (eds.) IJCAR 2020. LNCS (LNAI), vol. 12167, pp. 398–407. Springer, Cham (2020). https://doi.org/10.1007/978-3-030-51054-1_25
6. Kavvos, G.A.: The many worlds of modal λ-calculi: I. Curry–Howard for necessity, possibility and time. Eprint 1605.08106, arXiv (2016). https://doi.org/10.48550/arXiv.1605.08106
7. Kuznets, R., Straßburger, L.: Maehara-style modal nested calculi. Arch. Math. Logic **58**(3–4), 359–385 (2019). https://doi.org/10.1007/s00153-018-0636-1
8. Maffezioli, P., Naibo, A., Negri, S.: The Church-Fitch knowability paradox in the light of structural proof theory. Synthese **190**(14), 2677–2716 (2013). https://doi.org/10.1007/s11229-012-0061-7
9. Marin, S., Morales, M., Straßburger, L.: A fully labelled proof system for intuitionistic modal logics. J. Log. Comput. **31**(3), 998–1022 (2021). https://doi.org/10.1093/logcom/exab020
10. Morales, M.: Unusual proof systems for modal logics with applications to decision problems. Ph.D. thesis, Polytechnic Institute of Paris, Palaiseau, France (2023). https://theses.hal.science/tel-04546959. Prepared at École polytechnique
11. Negri, S.: Proofs and countermodels in non-classical logics. Log. Univers. **8**(1), 25–60 (2014). https://doi.org/10.1007/s11787-014-0097-1
12. Plotkin, G., Stirling, C.: A framework for intuitionistic modal logics. In: Halpern, J.Y. (ed.) Theoretical Aspects of Reasoning About Knowledge: Proceedings of the 1986 Conference, pp. 399–406. Morgan Kaufmann (1986). https://dl.acm.org/doi/10.5555/1029786.1029823
13. Simpson, A.K.: The proof theory and semantics of intuitionistic modal logic. Ph.D. thesis, University of Edinburgh, Edinburgh, Scotland, UK (1994). http://hdl.handle.net/1842/407
14. Wijesekera, D.: Constructive modal logics I. Ann. Pure Appl. Logic **50**(3), 271–301 (1990). https://doi.org/10.1016/0168-0072(90)90059-B

A Compositional Theory of Krivine's Classical Realisability

Daichi Hayashi[1(✉)] and Graham E. Leigh[2(✉)]

[1] Department of Philosophy and Ethics, Hokkaido University, Sapporo, Japan
d-hayashi@eis.hokudai.ac.jp

[2] Department of Philosophy, Linguistics and Theory of Science, University of Gothenburg, Göteborg, Sweden
graham.leigh@gu.se

Abstract. This paper presents a formal theory of Krivine's classical realisability interpretation for first-order Peano arithmetic (PA). To formulate the theory as an extension of PA, we first modify Krivine's original definition to the form of number realisability, similar to Kleene's intuitionistic realisability for Heyting arithmetic. By axiomatising our realisability with additional predicate symbols, we obtain a first-order theory CR which can formally realise every theorem of PA. Although CR itself is conservative over PA, adding a type of reflection principle that roughly states that "realisability implies truth" results in CR being essentially equivalent to the Tarskian theory CT of typed compositional truth, which is known to be proof-theoretically stronger than PA. We also prove that a weaker reflection principle which preserves the distinction between realisability and truth is sufficient for CR to achieve the same strength as CT.

Keywords: Classical realisability · Axiomatic theory of truth · Typed truth predicate · Proof-theoretic strength

1 Introduction

Tarski [22] presented a truth definition for a formal language by distinguishing the object language from the metalanguage. Although Tarski preferred a model-theoretic definition of truth, many researchers have also performed axiomatic studies to examine the logical and ontological principles underpinning a formal the conception of truth. As a typical example of such attempts, the language $\mathcal{L}$ of classical first-order Peano arithmetic (PA) is frequently selected as the object language, to which a fresh unary predicate $\mathrm{T}(x)$ for truth is added. The compositional truth theory CT (see Definition 1) is a natural axiomatisation of Tarski's truth definition for $\mathcal{L}$, defined as an extension of PA by a finite list of axioms concerning T. Various hierarchical or self-referential definitions of truth and their axiomatisations have been proposed [7–9,11,18,19]; however, most follow Tarski's paradigm, at least partially.

G. Metcalfe et al. (Eds.): WoLLIC 2024, LNCS 14672, pp. 64–79, 2024.
https://doi.org/10.1007/978-3-031-62687-6_5

As another semantic framework for classical theories, Krivine formulated classical realisability [14–16], which is a classical version of Kleene's intuitionistic realisability [12]. In the following, we briefly explain Krivine's classical realisability. There are two kinds of syntactic expressions, *terms* t, which represent programs, and *stacks* π, which represent evaluation contexts. A *process* $t \star \pi$ is a pair of a term t and a stack π. In addition, we fix a set $\perp\!\!\!\perp$ (*pole*) of processes that is closed under several evaluation rules for processes. Then, for each sentence A, the set $|A|_{\perp\!\!\!\perp}$ (*realisers*) of terms and the set $\|A\|_{\perp\!\!\!\perp}$ (*refuters*) of stacks are defined inductively such that $t \star \pi \in \perp\!\!\!\perp$ for any $t \in |A|_{\perp\!\!\!\perp}$ and $\pi \in \|A\|_{\perp\!\!\!\perp}$. Here, a term t *universally realises* A if $t \in |A|_{\perp\!\!\!\perp}$ for every pole $\perp\!\!\!\perp$. Then, Krivine proved that each theorem of second-order arithmetic is universally realisable.[1] In particular, we can take the empty set $\emptyset$ as a pole, and it is easy to show that if $|A|_\emptyset$ is not empty, then A is true in the standard model $\mathbb{N}$ of arithmetic. In summary, Krivine's (universal) realisability implies truth in $\mathbb{N}$; thus, Tarskian truth can be positioned in Krivine's general framework.

The purpose of this paper is to axiomatise a formal theory CR for Krivine's classical realisability in a similar manner to CT for Tarski's truth definition. To clarify the relationship with CT, we formulate CR over PA. As clarified in the above explanation of Krivine's realisability, we require additional vocabularies for a pole $\perp\!\!\!\perp$ and the relations $t \in |A|_{\perp\!\!\!\perp}$ and $\pi \in \|A\|_{\perp\!\!\!\perp}$. With the help of Gödel-numbering, they can be expressed by a unary predicate $x \in \perp\!\!\!\perp$ and binary predicates $x\mathrm{T}y$ and $x\mathrm{F}y$, respectively. Although Krivine's realisability uses λ-terms to express terms, stacks, and processes, we define realisers and refuters as natural numbers, similar to Kleene's number realisability. Since our base theory is PA, this modification can simplify the formulation of CR substantially (Sect. 2.1).

The remainder of this paper is organised as follows. In Sect. 2 we define classical number realisability as a combination of Krivine's classical realisability and Kleene's intuitionistic number realisability. By formalising our realisability, we obtain a first-order theory CR of compositional realisability (Definition 4). In Sect. 3, we observe that our classical number realisability can realise every theorem of PA, which is formalisable in CR (Theorem 1). Then, in Sect. 4, we study the proof-theoretic strength of CR. First, CR is shown to be conservative over PA (Proposition 3). Then, we formulate a kind of reflection principle under which CR essentially amounts to CT (Proposition 4). We also consider a weaker reflection principle that is sound with respect to any pole, and we prove that the principle can make CR as strong as CT (Theorem 2). Finally, potential future work is discussed in Sect. 5.

1.1 Conventions and Notations

We introduce abbreviations for common formal concepts concerning coding and recursive functions. We denote by $\mathcal{L}$ the first-order language of PA. The logical symbols of $\mathcal{L}$ are $\rightarrow$, $\forall$ and $=$. The non-logical symbols are a constant symbol $\underline{0}$

[1] Moreover, Krivine's classical realisability can be given to other strong theories, such as Zermelo–Fraenkel set theory [14].

and the function symbols for all primitive recursive functions. In particular, $\mathcal{L}$ has the successor function $x+1$, with which we can define *numerals* $\underline{0}, \underline{1}, \underline{2}, \ldots$. Thus, we identify natural numbers with the corresponding numeral. We also employ the false equation $0 = 1$ as the propositional constant $\bot$ for contradiction, and then the other logical symbols are defined in a standard manner, e.g., $\neg A = A \to \bot$.

The primitive recursive pairing function is denoted $\langle \cdot, \cdot \rangle$ with projection functions $(\cdot)_0$ and $(\cdot)_1$ satisfying $(\langle x, y\rangle)_0 = x$ and $(\langle x, y\rangle)_1 = y$. Sequences are treated as iterated pairing: $\langle x_0, x_1, \ldots, x_k\rangle := \langle x_0, \langle x_1, \ldots, x_k\rangle\rangle$. Based on these constructors, each finite extension of $\mathcal{L}$ is associated a fixed Gödel coding (denoted $\ulcorner e \urcorner$ where e is a finite string of symbols of the extended language) for which the basic syntactic constructions are primitive recursive. In particular, $\mathcal{L}$ contains a binary function symbol *sub* representing the mapping $\ulcorner A(x)\urcorner, n \mapsto \ulcorner A(\underline{n})\urcorner$ in the case that x is the only free variable of $A(x)$, and binary function symbols $\dot{=}$, $\dot{\to}$ and $\dot{\forall}$ representing, respectively, the operations $\ulcorner s\urcorner, \ulcorner t\urcorner \mapsto \ulcorner s = t\urcorner$, $\ulcorner A\urcorner, \ulcorner B\urcorner \mapsto \ulcorner A \to B\urcorner$ and $\ulcorner x\urcorner, \ulcorner A\urcorner \mapsto \ulcorner \forall x A\urcorner$. These operations will sometimes be omitted and we write $\ulcorner s = t\urcorner$ and $\ulcorner A \to B\urcorner$ for $\dot{=}(\ulcorner s\urcorner, \ulcorner t\urcorner)$ and $\dot{\to}(\ulcorner A\urcorner, \ulcorner B\urcorner)$, etc.

We introduce a number of abbreviations for $\mathcal{L}$-expressions corresponding to common properties or operations on Gödel codes. The property of being the code of a variable is expressed by the formula $\mathit{Var}(x)$, $\mathit{ClTerm}(x)$ denotes the formula expressing that x is a code of a *closed* $\mathcal{L}$-term, and for a fixed extension $\mathcal{L}'$ of $\mathcal{L}$, $\mathit{Sent}_{\mathcal{L}'}(x)$ expresses that x is the code of a sentence. The concepts above are primitive recursively definable meaning that the representing $\mathcal{L}$-formula is simply an equation between $\mathcal{L}$-terms. Given a formula $A(x)$ with at most x is free, $\ulcorner A(\dot{x})\urcorner$ abbreviates the term $\mathit{sub}(\ulcorner A(x)\urcorner, x)$ expressing the code of the formula $A(\underline{n})$ where n is the value of x. For sequences $\boldsymbol{x}$ of variables, $\ulcorner A(\dot{\boldsymbol{x}})\urcorner$ is defined similarly.

Quantification over codes is associated similar abbreviations:

- $\forall \ulcorner A\urcorner \in \mathit{Sent}_{\mathcal{L}'}.\ B(\ulcorner A\urcorner)$ abbreviates $\forall x(\mathit{Sent}_{\mathcal{L}'}(x) \to B(x))$.
- $\forall \ulcorner s\urcorner.\ B(\ulcorner s\urcorner)$ abbreviates $\forall x(\mathit{ClTerm}(x) \to B(x))$.
- $\forall \ulcorner A_v\urcorner \in \mathit{Sent}_{\mathcal{L}'}.\ B(v, \ulcorner A\urcorner)$ abbr. $\forall x \forall v(\mathit{Var}(v) \wedge \mathit{Sent}_{\mathcal{L}'}(\dot{\forall} v x) \to B(v, x))$, namely quantification relative to codes of formulas with at most one distinguished variable free.

Partial recursive functions can be expressed in $\mathcal{L}$ via the Kleene 'T predicate' method. The ternary relation $x \cdot y \simeq z$ expresses that the result of evaluating the x-th partial recursive function on input y terminates with output z. Note that this relation has a Σ^0_1 definition in PA as a formula $\exists w(T(x, y, w) \wedge (w)_0 = z)$ where T is primitive recursive. It will be notationally convenient to use $x \cdot y$ in place of a *term* (with the obvious interpretation) though use of this abbreviation will be constrained to contexts in which potential for confusion is minimal.

With the above ternary relation we can express the property of two closed terms having equal value, via a Σ^0_1-formula $\mathit{Eq}(y, z)$. That is, $\mathit{Eq}(y, z)$ expresses that y and z are codes of closed $\mathcal{L}$-terms s and t respectively such that $s = t$ is a true equation.

1.2 Classical Compositional Truth

Tarskian truth for $\mathcal{L}$ is characterised inductively in the standard manner:

- A closed equation $s = t$ is true iff s and t denote the same value in $\mathbb{N}$;
- $A \rightarrow B$ is true iff if A is true, then B is true;
- $\forall x A(x)$ is true iff $A(s)$ is true for all closed terms s.

Quantification over $\mathcal{L}$-sentences and the operations on syntax implicit in the above clauses can be expressed via a Gödel-numbering. Thus, employing a unary (truth) predicate T, a formal system CT can be defined corresponding, in a straightforward manner, to the Tarskian truth clauses.

Definition 1 (CT). *For a unary predicate* T, *let* $\mathcal{L}_\mathrm{T} = \mathcal{L} \cup \{\mathrm{T}\}$. *The* $\mathcal{L}_\mathrm{T}$*-theory* CT *(compositional truth) consists of* PA *formulated for the language* $\mathcal{L}_\mathrm{T}$ *plus the following three axioms.*

$(\mathsf{CT}_=)$ $\forall \ulcorner s \urcorner, \ulcorner t \urcorner (\mathrm{T}(s \mathbin{\dot{=}} t) \leftrightarrow Eq(s,t))$.
$(\mathsf{CT}_\rightarrow)$ $\forall \ulcorner A \urcorner, \ulcorner B \urcorner \in Sent_{\mathcal{L}} (\mathrm{T} \ulcorner A \mathbin{\dot{\rightarrow}} B \urcorner \leftrightarrow (\mathrm{T} \ulcorner A \urcorner \rightarrow \mathrm{T} \ulcorner B \urcorner))$.
$(\mathsf{CT}_\forall)$ $\forall \ulcorner A_v \urcorner \in Sent_{\mathcal{L}} (\mathrm{T} \ulcorner \dot{\forall} v A \urcorner \leftrightarrow \forall x \mathrm{T} \ulcorner A(\dot{x}) \urcorner)$.

Two consequences of the above axioms are of particular relevance. The first is the observation that CT staisfies Tarski's Convention T [22, pp. 187–188] for formulas in $\mathcal{L}$:

Lemma 1. *The Tarski-biconditional is derivable in* CT *for every formula of* $\mathcal{L}$. *That is, for each formula* $A(x_1, \ldots, x_k)$ *of* $\mathcal{L}$ *in which only the distinguished variables occur free, we have*

$$\mathsf{CT} \vdash \forall x_1, \ldots, x_k (\mathrm{T} \ulcorner A(\dot{x}_1, \ldots, \dot{x}_k) \urcorner \leftrightarrow A(x_1, \ldots, x_k)).$$

Second is the 'term regularity principle' stating that the truth value of each formula depends only on the value of terms and not their 'structure'. Let *subt* be a primitive recursive function function such that $subt \colon \ulcorner A(x) \urcorner, \ulcorner x \urcorner, \ulcorner s \urcorner \mapsto \ulcorner A(s) \urcorner$ for each formula A, variable x and term s.

Lemma 2. *Provable in* CT *is the term regularity principle:*

$$\forall \ulcorner s \urcorner \forall \ulcorner t \urcorner \forall \ulcorner A_v \urcorner \in Sent_{\mathcal{L}}.\ Eq(\ulcorner s \urcorner, \ulcorner t \urcorner) \rightarrow (\mathrm{T} \ulcorner A(s) \urcorner \rightarrow \mathrm{T} \ulcorner A(t) \urcorner)$$

where the term $\ulcorner A(s) \urcorner$ *is shorthand for* $subt(\ulcorner A \urcorner, v, \ulcorner s \urcorner)$, *and* $\ulcorner A(t) \urcorner$ *likewise.*

2 Classical Realisability

We present a classical number realisability interpretation for PA and the corresponding axiomatic theory CR.

2.1 Classical Number Realisability

We introduce a realisability interpretation for PA based on Krivine's classical realisability. For our setting we require several modifications from Krivine's original definition. The first modification is about realisers. In Krivine's formulation, realisers are essentially lambda terms (cf. [20]). As we seek to formalise realisability over PA, it is natural to assume that realisers are natural numbers, similar to Kleene's number realisability for the intuitionistic arithmetic [12].

Second, we must define the realisability and refutability conditions explicitly for equality. In the language of second-order arithmetic, the equality $a = b$ between a and b is definable by Leibniz equality $\forall X(a \in X \to b \in X)$, which in Krivine's definition, determines the realisability and refutability conditions of the equation uniquely. For a first-order language, equality is a primitive logical symbol and it is a matter of choice what constitutes a refutation of a closed equation. In some sense, we take the most naive approach motivated by Kleene and Krivine's choices: a true equation is refuted by every element of the pole $\perp\!\!\!\perp \subseteq \mathbb{N}$ and a false equation by every natural number. Although a natural question, we do not delve into the possibility of other definitions.

The third modification involves the interpretation of the first-order universal quantifier $\forall x$. In Krivine's definition, it is interpreted *uniformly*, i.e., a term t realises a universal sentence $\forall x A$ when t realises every instance $A(n)$. This definition is sufficient for the interpretation of second-order arithmetic because the set of natural numbers $\mathbb{N}$ is definable so the axiom of induction does not need to be realised explicitly. In contrast, in case of the first-order arithmetic, realisers of induction must be presented and the uniform interpretation is not ideal for this purpose. As an alternative, we use Kleene's interpretation, where a realiser of a universal sentence $\forall x A$ is, in essence, the code of a recursive function that maps each natural number n to a realiser of $A(n)$. The modifier 'in essence' above is merely because it is the notion of 'refuter' (not 'realiser') which is primitive. The relation between the two in the case of quantifiers is qualified in Lemma 3.

In light of the above remarks, we introduce the following definitions.

Definition 2. *A* ***pole*** $\perp\!\!\!\perp$ *is a subset of* $\mathbb{N}$ *such that it is conversely closed under computation: for all* $e, m, n \in \mathbb{N}$, *if* $e \cdot m \simeq n$ *and* $n \in \perp\!\!\!\perp$, *then* $\langle e, m\rangle \in \perp\!\!\!\perp$.

Note that the empty set $\emptyset$ and natural numbers $\mathbb{N}$ trivially satisfy the above condition; thus, they are poles.

Given a pole $\perp\!\!\!\perp$ and $\mathcal{L}$-sentence A, we define sets $\|A\|_{\perp\!\!\!\perp}, |A|_{\perp\!\!\!\perp} \subseteq \mathbb{N}$ of, respectively, *refutations* (or a counter-proofs) and *realisations* (or proofs) of A. The sets are defined such that every pair $\langle n, m\rangle \in |A|_{\perp\!\!\!\perp} \times \|A\|_{\perp\!\!\!\perp}$ of a realisation and refutation is an element of the pole $\perp\!\!\!\perp$. Thus, $\perp\!\!\!\perp$ can be seen as the set of contradictions.

Definition 3. *Fix a pole* $\perp\!\!\!\perp$. *For each* $\mathcal{L}$*-sentence* A, *the sets* $|A|_{\perp\!\!\!\perp}, \|A\|_{\perp\!\!\!\perp} \subseteq \mathbb{N}$ *are defined as follows. The set* $|A|_{\perp\!\!\!\perp}$ *is defined directly from* $\|A\|_{\perp\!\!\!\perp}$:

$$|A|_{\perp\!\!\!\perp} = \{n \in \mathbb{N} \mid \forall m \in \|A\|_{\perp\!\!\!\perp}.\ \langle n, m\rangle \in \perp\!\!\!\perp\}.$$

The set $\|A\|_{\perp\!\!\!\perp}$ *is defined inductively:*

- $\|s = t\|_{\perp\!\!\!\perp} = \begin{cases} \mathbb{N}, & \textit{if } \mathbb{N} \not\models s = t, \\ \perp\!\!\!\perp, & \textit{otherwise.} \end{cases}$
- $\|A \to B\|_{\perp\!\!\!\perp} = \{n \mid (n)_0 \in |A|_{\perp\!\!\!\perp} \textit{ and } (n)_1 \in \|B\|_{\perp\!\!\!\perp}\}$.
- $\|\forall x A\|_{\perp\!\!\!\perp} = \{n \mid (n)_1 \in \|A(\underline{(n)_0})\|_{\perp\!\!\!\perp}\}$.

The motivation for the definitions of $\|A\|_{\perp\!\!\!\perp}$ and $|A|_{\perp\!\!\!\perp}$ should be clear. A false equation is refuted by every number whereas a true equation is refuted only by 'contradictions', i.e., elements of the pole. A refutation of $A \to B$ is a pair $\langle m, n\rangle$ for which m realises A and n refutes B. A refutation of $\forall x A$ is a pair $\langle m, n\rangle$ such that n refutes $A(\underline{m})$. Finally, a realiser of A is a number n that contradicts all refutations of A, i.e., $\langle n, m\rangle \in \perp\!\!\!\perp$ for every $m \in \|A\|_{\perp\!\!\!\perp}$. In particular, the closure condition on poles implies that every partial recursive function $\|A\|_{\perp\!\!\!\perp} \to \perp\!\!\!\perp$ is a realiser of A: if for every $n \in \|A\|_{\perp\!\!\!\perp}$, $e \cdot n$ is defined and an element of $\perp\!\!\!\perp$ then, by definition, $\langle e, n\rangle \in \perp\!\!\!\perp$ for every $n \in \|A\|_{\perp\!\!\!\perp}$. It is also clear that every realiser of A induces a canonical partial recursive function mapping $\|A\|_{\perp\!\!\!\perp}$ to $\perp\!\!\!\perp$.

2.2 Compositional Theory for Realisability

A corollary of Tarski's undefinability of truth, the language of PA is insufficient to express classical realisability fully without expanding the non-logical vocabulary. Let $\mathcal{L}_R$ extend $\mathcal{L}$ by three new predicate symbols:

- a unary predicate $\perp\!\!\!\perp$ for a pole (written $x \in \perp\!\!\!\perp$);
- a binary predicate F for refutation (written $x\mathrm{F}y$);
- a binary predicate T for realisation (written $x\mathrm{T}y$).[2]

Definition 4 (Compositional Realisability). *The $\mathcal{L}_R$-theory* CR *extends* PA *formulated over $\mathcal{L}_R$ by the universal closures of the following axioms:*

($\mathsf{Ax}_{\perp\!\!\!\perp}$) $\forall x, y, z(x \cdot y \simeq z \to (z \in \perp\!\!\!\perp \to \langle x, y\rangle \in \perp\!\!\!\perp))$
(Ax_{T}) $\forall \ulcorner A \urcorner \in Sent_{\mathcal{L}} \forall a(a\mathrm{T}\ulcorner A\urcorner \leftrightarrow \forall b(b\mathrm{F}\ulcorner A\urcorner \to \langle a, b\rangle \in \perp\!\!\!\perp))$
($\mathsf{CR}_=$) $\forall \ulcorner s\urcorner, \ulcorner t\urcorner \forall a(a\mathrm{F}\ulcorner s = t\urcorner \leftrightarrow (Eq(\ulcorner s\urcorner, \ulcorner t\urcorner) \to a \in \perp\!\!\!\perp))$
($\mathsf{CR}_\to$) $\forall \ulcorner A\urcorner, \ulcorner B\urcorner \in Sent_{\mathcal{L}} \forall a(a\mathrm{F}\ulcorner A \to B\urcorner \leftrightarrow ((a)_0\mathrm{T}\ulcorner A\urcorner \wedge (a)_1\mathrm{F}\ulcorner B\urcorner))$
($\mathsf{CR}_\forall$) $\forall \ulcorner A_v\urcorner \in Sent_{\mathcal{L}} \forall a(a\mathrm{F}\ulcorner \forall v A\urcorner \leftrightarrow (a)_1\mathrm{F}(sub(\ulcorner A\urcorner, (a)_0)))$

Remark 1. The universal closure of the axiom ($\mathsf{CR}_=$) is equivalent to the conjunction of the following:

($\mathsf{CR}_{=1}$) $\forall \ulcorner s\urcorner \forall \ulcorner t\urcorner(\neg Eq(\ulcorner s\urcorner, \ulcorner t\urcorner) \to \forall a.\ a\mathrm{F}\ulcorner s = t\urcorner)$;
($\mathsf{CR}_{=2}$) $\forall \ulcorner s\urcorner \forall \ulcorner t\urcorner(Eq(\ulcorner s\urcorner, \ulcorner t\urcorner) \to \forall a(a\mathrm{F}\ulcorner s = t\urcorner \leftrightarrow a \in \perp\!\!\!\perp))$.

A straightforward formal induction in CR verifies the term regularity principle for refutations (cf. Lemma 2).

Proposition 1. *Refutations are provably invariant under term values:*

$$\forall \ulcorner s\urcorner \forall \ulcorner t\urcorner \forall \ulcorner A_v\urcorner \in Sent_{\mathcal{L}}.\ Eq(\ulcorner s\urcorner, \ulcorner t\urcorner) \to \forall x(x\mathrm{F}\ulcorner A(s)\urcorner \to x\mathrm{F}\ulcorner A(t)\urcorner).$$

[2] Although T is definable by F and $\perp\!\!\!\perp$, we introduce T as a primitive to simplify the notation.

We provide a model of CR based on classical number realisability. First, the interpretation of the vocabularies of $\mathcal{L}$ is naturally given by the standard model $\mathbb{N}$ of arithmetic. Second, we fix any pole $\perp\!\!\!\perp \subseteq \mathbb{N}$ for the interpretation of the predicate $x \in \perp\!\!\!\perp$. The sets $\mathbb{T}_{\perp\!\!\!\perp}, \mathbb{F}_{\perp\!\!\!\perp} \subseteq \mathbb{N} \times \mathbb{N}$ (for the interpretations of $x\mathrm{T}y$ and $x\mathrm{F}y$, respectively) are defined by the sets $|A|_{\perp\!\!\!\perp}$ and $\|A\|_{\perp\!\!\!\perp}$ in Definition 3:

$$\mathbb{T}_{\perp\!\!\!\perp} := \{(n,m) \in \mathbb{N}^2 \mid m \text{ is a code of an } \mathcal{L}\text{-sentence } A \text{ and } n \in |A|_{\perp\!\!\!\perp}\},$$
$$\mathbb{F}_{\perp\!\!\!\perp} := \{(n,m) \in \mathbb{N}^2 \mid m \text{ is a code of an } \mathcal{L}\text{-sentence } A \text{ and } n \in \|A\|_{\perp\!\!\!\perp}\}.$$

Then, the following is clear.

Proposition 2. *Let* $\mathbb{N}$ *be the standard model of* $\mathcal{L}$ *and take any* $\mathcal{L}_R$*-sentence* A*. If* $\mathsf{CR} \vdash A$*, then the* $\mathcal{L}_R$*-model* $\langle \mathbb{N}, \perp\!\!\!\perp, \mathbb{T}_{\perp\!\!\!\perp}, \mathbb{F}_{\perp\!\!\!\perp}\rangle$ *satisfies* A*.*

3 Formalised Realisation of Peano Arithmetic

We demonstrate that the theory of classical number realisability realises every theorem of PA. In particular, we observe that this is formalisable in CR. For that purpose, the following lemmas are useful.

Lemma 3. *There exists numbers* i, u *and* s *such that*

1. $\mathsf{CR} \vdash \forall \ulcorner A \urcorner, \ulcorner B \urcorner \in Sent_{\mathcal{L}} \forall a, b (a\mathrm{T}\ulcorner A \to B \urcorner \wedge b\mathrm{T}\ulcorner A \urcorner \to (\mathsf{i} \cdot \langle a, b\rangle)\mathrm{T}\ulcorner B \urcorner)$.
2. $\mathsf{CR} \vdash \forall \ulcorner A_x \urcorner \in Sent_{\mathcal{L}}.\ (\forall x. (a \cdot x)\mathrm{T}\ulcorner A(\dot{x})\urcorner) \to (\mathsf{u} \cdot a)\mathrm{T}\ulcorner \forall x A \urcorner$.
3. $\mathsf{CR} \vdash \forall \ulcorner A_x \urcorner \in Sent_{\mathcal{L}} \forall a (a\mathrm{T}\ulcorner \forall x A \urcorner \to \forall y (\mathsf{s} \cdot \langle a, y\rangle)\mathrm{T}\ulcorner A(\dot{y})\urcorner)$.

The meaning of these functions should be clear, i.e., i computes a realiser of B from those for $A \to B$ and A, and u expresses that if there exists a procedure that computes every instance $A(n)$, then $\forall x A$ is realised. Conversely, s computes a realiser of $A(n)$ for each n.

Proof. 1. Let i be such that $\mathsf{i} \cdot \langle a, b\rangle \simeq \lambda x.\langle a, b, x\rangle$. To show that i is the required one, we take any $\mathcal{L}$-sentence $A \to B$ and assume $a\mathrm{T}\ulcorner A \to B\urcorner$ and $b\mathrm{T}\ulcorner A\urcorner$. Then, we must show $(\mathsf{i} \cdot \langle a, b\rangle)\mathrm{T}\ulcorner B\urcorner$. By the axiom ($\mathsf{Ax}_{\mathrm{T}}$), taking any c such that $c\mathrm{F}\ulcorner B\urcorner$, we prove $\langle \mathsf{i} \cdot \langle a, b\rangle, c\rangle \in \perp\!\!\!\perp$. As $(\mathsf{i} \cdot \langle a, b\rangle) \cdot c \simeq \langle a, b, c\rangle$, it is sufficient by the axiom ($\mathsf{Ax}_{\perp\!\!\!\perp}$) to show that $\langle a, b, c\rangle$ is in $\perp\!\!\!\perp$. From the assumptions $b\mathrm{T}\ulcorner A\urcorner$ and $c\mathrm{F}\ulcorner B\urcorner$, as well as the axiom ($\mathsf{Ax}_{\mathrm{T}}$), we obtain $\langle b, c\rangle\mathrm{F}\ulcorner A \to B\urcorner$. Thus, ($\mathsf{Ax}_{\mathrm{T}}$) yields that $\langle a, b, c\rangle = \langle a, \langle b, c\rangle\rangle \in \perp\!\!\!\perp$.
2. Let u be such that $\mathsf{u} \cdot a \simeq \lambda x.\langle a \cdot (x)_0, (x)_1\rangle$. To prove that this u is the required one, we take any a and any $\mathcal{L}$-sentence $\forall x A$. Then, under the assumption that a is total and $\forall x. (a \cdot x)\mathrm{T}\ulcorner A(\dot{x})\urcorner$ holds, we must show $(\mathsf{u} \cdot a)\mathrm{T}\ulcorner \forall x A\urcorner$. By the axiom ($\mathsf{Ax}_{\mathrm{T}}$), taking any b such that $b\mathrm{F}\ulcorner \forall x A\urcorner$, we prove $\langle \mathsf{u} \cdot a, b\rangle \in \perp\!\!\!\perp$. As $(\mathsf{u} \cdot a) \cdot b \simeq \langle a \cdot (b)_0, (b)_1\rangle$, it is sufficient by the axiom ($\mathsf{Ax}_{\perp\!\!\!\perp}$) to show the latter is in $\perp\!\!\!\perp$. From the assumption, we obtain the formula $(a \cdot (b)_0)\mathrm{T}\ulcorner A((\dot{b})_0)\urcorner$. In addition, by the axiom ($\mathsf{CR}_\forall$), we have $(b)_1\mathrm{F}\ulcorner A((\dot{b})_0)\urcorner$. Thus, the axiom ($\mathsf{Ax}_{\mathrm{T}}$) implies $\langle a \cdot (b)_0, (b)_1\rangle \in \perp\!\!\!\perp$.

3. Let s be such that $\mathsf{s} \cdot \langle a, b \rangle \simeq \lambda c.\langle a, b, c \rangle$, and we show that this function is a required one. Thus, taking any $\ulcorner \forall x A(x) \urcorner \in Sent_{\mathcal{L}}$ and any a, b, c, we assume $a\mathrm{T}\ulcorner \forall x A \urcorner$ and $c\mathrm{F}\ulcorner A(\dot{b}) \urcorner$. Then, by the axiom ($\mathsf{CR}_\forall$), we obtain $\langle b, c \rangle \mathrm{F} \ulcorner \forall x A \urcorner$. Thus, it follows that $\langle a, b, c \rangle \in \perp\!\!\!\perp$ by the axiom (Ax_T). Therefore, the axiom ($\mathsf{Ax}_{\perp\!\!\!\perp}$) implies that $\langle \mathsf{s} \cdot \langle a, b \rangle, c \rangle \in \perp\!\!\!\perp$. Here, the c is arbitrary; thus, we obtain $(\mathsf{s} \cdot \langle a, b \rangle)\mathrm{T}\ulcorner A(\dot{b}) \urcorner$ again by (Ax_T). □

Lemma 4. *There are numbers* k_π *and* $\mathsf{k}_{\perp\!\!\!\perp}$ *such that*

1. $\mathsf{CR} \vdash \forall \ulcorner A \urcorner, \ulcorner B \urcorner \in Sent_{\mathcal{L}}.\ \forall a (a\mathrm{F}\ulcorner A \urcorner \to (\mathsf{k}_\pi \cdot a)\mathrm{T}\ulcorner A \to B \urcorner)$.
2. $\mathsf{CR} \vdash \forall a (a \in \perp\!\!\!\perp \to \forall \ulcorner A \urcorner \in Sent_{\mathcal{L}}.\ (\mathsf{k}_{\perp\!\!\!\perp} \cdot a)\mathrm{T}\ulcorner A \urcorner)$.

Proof. 1. Let $\mathsf{k}_\pi := \lambda a.\lambda b.\langle (b)_0, a \rangle$. We prove that this k_π is the required number. By taking any a and any $\mathcal{L}$-sentence $A \to B$, we assume $a\mathrm{F}\ulcorner A \urcorner$. To demonstrate that $(\mathsf{k}_\pi \cdot a)\mathrm{T}\ulcorner A \to B \urcorner$, we take any b such that $b\mathrm{F}\ulcorner A \to B \urcorner$, and then we must prove $\langle \mathsf{k}_\pi \cdot a, b \rangle \in \perp\!\!\!\perp$. By the supposition $b\mathrm{F}\ulcorner A \to B \urcorner$ and the axiom ($\mathsf{CT}_\to$), it follows that $(b)_0\mathrm{T}\ulcorner A \urcorner$. Thus, we obtain $(\mathsf{k}_\pi \cdot a) \cdot b \simeq \langle (b)_0, a \rangle \in \perp\!\!\!\perp$, which implies $\langle \mathsf{k}_\pi \cdot a, b \rangle \in \perp\!\!\!\perp$ by the axiom ($\mathsf{Ax}_{\perp\!\!\!\perp}$).
2. Assuming $a \in \perp\!\!\!\perp$, we define a number $\mathsf{k}_{\perp\!\!\!\perp} := \lambda a.\lambda b.a$. To show $(\mathsf{k}_{\perp\!\!\!\perp} \cdot a)\mathrm{T}\ulcorner A \urcorner$, we take any b such that $b\mathrm{F}\ulcorner A \urcorner$. Then, $(\mathsf{k}_{\perp\!\!\!\perp} \cdot a) \cdot b \simeq a \in \perp\!\!\!\perp$; thus, the axiom ($\mathsf{Ax}_{\perp\!\!\!\perp}$) implies $\langle \mathsf{k}_{\perp\!\!\!\perp} \cdot a, b \rangle \in \perp\!\!\!\perp$. Therefore, $(\mathsf{k}_{\perp\!\!\!\perp} \cdot a)\mathrm{T}\ulcorner A \urcorner$ holds by the axiom (Ax_T). □

Note that the above k_π is the CPS translation of *call with current continuation* (cf. [10, 15]). Using k_π, we can define a realiser for Peirce's law. In Krivine's formulation, Peirce's law is realised by the constant symbol cc. Thus, our formulation is more similar to Oliva and Streicher's formulation of classical realisability [20] in that these constants are definable, i.e., they are not introduced as primitive symbols.

With the above preparations, we can now show the formalised realisability of PA.

Theorem 1. *We assume that* PA *is formulated in the language* $\mathcal{L}$. *For each* $\mathcal{L}$-*sentence* A, *if* $\mathsf{PA} \vdash A$, *then there exists a closed term* s *such that* $\mathsf{CR} \vdash s\mathrm{T}\ulcorner A \urcorner$. *Moreover, this claim is formally expressible in* CR, *i.e., we can find a number* k_{PA} *such that:*

$$\mathsf{CR} \vdash \forall x \forall \ulcorner A \urcorner \in Sent_{\mathcal{L}}.\ Bew_{\mathsf{PA}}(x, \ulcorner A \urcorner) \to (\mathsf{k}_{\mathsf{PA}} \cdot x)\mathrm{T}\ulcorner A \urcorner,$$

where $Bew_{\mathsf{PA}}(x, y)$ *is a canonical provability predicate for* PA *expressing means that* x *is a code of the proof of a sentence* y.

Proof. The proof is by induction on the length of the derivation of A in PA. Here, we divide the cases by the last axiom or rule.

Peirce's law. Assume that $A = ((B \to C) \to B) \to B$. According to Lemmas 3 and 4, we define a term s as follows:

$$s = \lambda b.\langle \mathsf{i} \cdot \langle (b)_0, \mathsf{k}_\pi \cdot (b)_1 \rangle, (b)_1 \rangle.$$

We show that $s\mathrm{T}\ulcorner((B \to C) \to B) \to B\urcorner$. Thus, taking any b satisfying $b\mathrm{F}\ulcorner((B \to C) \to B) \to B\urcorner$, we prove $\langle s, b\rangle \in \perp\!\!\!\perp$. By the axiom ($\mathsf{Ax}_{\perp\!\!\!\perp}$), it is sufficient to show $\langle \mathsf{i} \cdot \langle (b)_0, \mathsf{k}_\pi \cdot (b)_1\rangle, (b)_1\rangle \in \perp\!\!\!\perp$. From the axiom ($\mathsf{CR}_\to$), we obtain $(b)_0\mathrm{T}\ulcorner(B \to C) \to B\urcorner$ and $(b)_1\mathrm{F}\ulcorner B\urcorner$. Thus, by Lemma 4, we obtain $(\mathsf{k}_\pi \cdot (b)_1)\mathrm{T}\ulcorner B \to C\urcorner$, which implies that $(\mathsf{i} \cdot \langle (b)_0, \mathsf{k}_\pi \cdot (b)_1\rangle)\mathrm{T}\ulcorner B\urcorner$ by Lemma 3. Thus, by the axiom (Ax_T), we can derive the required formula $\langle \mathsf{i} \cdot \langle (b)_0, (\mathsf{k}_\pi \cdot (b)_1)\rangle, (b)_1\rangle \in \perp\!\!\!\perp$.

Induction schema. Assume $A = B(0) \to (\forall x(B(x) \to B(x+1)) \to \forall x B(x))$. We take any $b\mathrm{F}\ulcorner B(0) \to (\forall x(B(x) \to B(x+1)) \to \forall x B(x))\urcorner$. Then, we obtain the following:

- $(b)_0\mathrm{T}\ulcorner B(0)\urcorner$;
- $((b)_1)_0\mathrm{T}\ulcorner\forall x(B(x) \to B(x+1))\urcorner$;
- $((b)_1)_1\mathrm{F}\ulcorner\forall x(B(x))\urcorner$.

By the recursion theorem, choose a number k such that

1. $(\mathsf{k} \cdot b) \cdot 0 \simeq (b)_0$
2. $(\mathsf{k} \cdot b) \cdot (n+1) \simeq \mathsf{i} \cdot \langle \mathsf{s} \cdot \langle ((b)_1)_0, n\rangle, (\mathsf{k} \cdot b) \cdot n\rangle$ for each n.

Then, we obtain $\forall x. ((\mathsf{k} \cdot b) \cdot x)\mathrm{T}\ulcorner B(\dot{x})\urcorner$; thus, Lemma 3 yields the formula $\langle \mathsf{u} \cdot (\mathsf{k} \cdot b), ((b)_1)_1\rangle \in \perp\!\!\!\perp$. Therefore, for the term $s := \lambda b.\langle \mathsf{u} \cdot (\mathsf{k} \cdot b), ((b)_1)_1\rangle$, we have $\langle s, b\rangle \in \perp\!\!\!\perp$ by the axiom ($\mathsf{Ax}_{\perp\!\!\!\perp}$), and thus $s\mathrm{T}\ulcorner A\urcorner$ follows.

Note that the other cases are treated in a similar manner. □

4 Proof-Theoretic Strength of Compositional Realisability

In Sect. 3, we observed that CR is expressively strong enough to formalise the classical number realisability. In the following, we turn to the proof-theoretic strength of CR and its relationship with CT. First, we show the conservativity of CR over PA.

Proposition 3. CR *is conservative over* PA.

Proof. We define a translation $\mathcal{T}\colon \mathcal{L}_R \to \mathcal{L}$ such that the vocabularies of $\mathcal{L}$ are unchanged, and then we show the following:

$$\text{for } \mathcal{L}_R\text{-formula } A, \text{ if } \mathsf{CR} \vdash A, \text{ then } \mathsf{PA} \vdash \mathcal{T}(A).$$

If $A \in \mathcal{L}$, we have $\mathcal{T}(A) = A$; thus, the conservativity follows.

The translation $\mathcal{T}$ is defined as follows:

- $\mathcal{T}(s = t) = s = t$;
- $\mathcal{T}(s \in \perp\!\!\!\perp) = \mathcal{T}(s\mathrm{F}t) = \mathcal{T}(s\mathrm{T}t) = (0 = 0)$;
- $\mathcal{T}$ commutes with the logical symbols.

Roughly speaking, each pair is contradictory, and each sentence is realised and refuted by every number under this interpretation. Therefore, we can easily see that the translation of each axiom of CR is derivable in PA. □

4.1 Compositional Realisability as Compositional Truth

Although CR itself is proof-theoretically weak, here, we show that some assumption on the pole provides CR with the same strength as CT.

Lemma 5. *Let* $\perp\!\!\!\perp = \emptyset$ *denote the sentence* $\neg\exists x(x \in \perp\!\!\!\perp)$*, and let* $\mathsf{CR}^{\emptyset}$ *be* CR *augmented with* $\perp\!\!\!\perp = \emptyset$*. Then,* $\mathsf{CR}^{\emptyset}$ *can define the truth prediate of* CT *as, e.g., the predicate* $0\mathrm{T}x$*. In other words,* $\mathsf{CR}^{\emptyset}$ *derives the following:*

$(\mathsf{CT}_=)'$ $\forall \ulcorner s \urcorner, \ulcorner t \urcorner(\underline{0}\mathrm{T}\ulcorner s = t\urcorner \leftrightarrow Eq(\ulcorner s\urcorner, \ulcorner t\urcorner))$
$(\mathsf{CT}_\to)'$ $\forall \ulcorner A\urcorner, \ulcorner B\urcorner \in Sent_{\mathcal{L}}\,(\underline{0}\mathrm{T}\ulcorner A \to B\urcorner \leftrightarrow (\underline{0}\mathrm{T}\ulcorner A\urcorner \to \underline{0}\mathrm{T}\ulcorner B\urcorner))$
$(\mathsf{CT}_\forall)'$ $\forall \ulcorner A_x\urcorner \in Sent_{\mathcal{L}}(\underline{0}\mathrm{T}\ulcorner\forall x A\urcorner \leftrightarrow \forall x\, 0\mathrm{T}\ulcorner A(\dot{x})\urcorner$.

Therefore, every $\mathcal{L}$*-theorem of* CT *is derivable in* $\mathsf{CR}^{\emptyset}$*.*

Proof. By $\perp\!\!\!\perp = \emptyset$ and the axiom (Ax_T), we easily obtain the following:

$$0\mathrm{T}\ulcorner A\urcorner \leftrightarrow \forall b(\neg b\mathrm{F}\ulcorner A\urcorner).$$

With this, we can derive the formulas $(\mathsf{CT}_=)'$, $(\mathsf{CT}_\to)'$, and $(\mathsf{CT}_\forall)'$.

$(\mathsf{CT}_=)'$ In $\mathsf{CR}^{\emptyset}$, we deduce as follows.

$$\begin{aligned} 0\mathrm{T}\ulcorner s = t\urcorner &\Leftrightarrow \forall b(\neg b\mathrm{F}\ulcorner s = t\urcorner) && \text{by } (\mathsf{Ax}_\mathrm{T}) \text{ and } \perp\!\!\!\perp = \emptyset \\ &\Rightarrow Eq(s,t) && \text{by } (\mathsf{CR}_{=1}) \\ &\Rightarrow \forall b(\neg b\mathrm{F}\ulcorner s = t\urcorner) && \text{by } (\mathsf{CR}_{=2}) \text{ and } \perp\!\!\!\perp = \emptyset \end{aligned}$$

$(\mathsf{CT}_\forall)'$

$$\begin{aligned} 0\mathrm{T}\ulcorner\forall x A\urcorner &\Leftrightarrow \forall b\,\neg b\mathrm{F}\ulcorner\forall x A\urcorner && \text{by } (\mathsf{Ax}_\mathrm{T}) \text{ and } \perp\!\!\!\perp = \emptyset \\ &\Leftrightarrow \forall b\,\neg((b)_1\mathrm{F}(sub(\ulcorner A\urcorner, (b)_0))) && \text{by } (\mathsf{CR}_\forall) \\ &\Leftrightarrow \forall x\forall y\,\neg(y\mathrm{F}\ulcorner A(\dot{x})\urcorner) && \\ &\Leftrightarrow \forall x\, 0\mathrm{T}\ulcorner A(\dot{x})\urcorner && \text{by } (\mathsf{Ax}_\mathrm{T}) \text{ and } \perp\!\!\!\perp = \emptyset \end{aligned}$$

The other cases are similar. □

Thus, the assumption $\perp\!\!\!\perp = \emptyset$ reduces truth to realisability. Next, we give another characterisation of this assumption using a kind of reflection principle stating that realisability is subsumed by truth.

Lemma 6. *Over* CR*, the following are equivalent.*

1. *The reflection schema:* $\exists x(x\mathrm{T}\ulcorner A\urcorner) \to A$ *for every* $\mathcal{L}$*-sentence* A*.*
2. *The axiom:* $\perp\!\!\!\perp = \emptyset$*.*

Proof. (1) ⇒ (2): Assume for a contradiction that $a \in \perp\!\!\!\perp$ for some a. Then, $\mathsf{k}_{\perp\!\!\!\perp} \cdot a$ verifies every $\mathcal{L}$-sentence by Lemma 4. Thus, the schema (1) implies every sentence, a contradiction. Therefore, the axiom (2):$\perp\!\!\!\perp = \emptyset$ follows.

(2) $\Rightarrow$ (1): As shown in Lemma 5, CR with $\perp\!\!\!\perp = \emptyset$ can define the truth predicate of CT as $0\mathrm{T}x$. Thus, similar to Lemma 1, we obtain $0\mathrm{T}\ulcorner A \urcorner \to A$ for every $\mathcal{L}$-sentence A. Therefore, we also have schema (1). □

Proposition 4. *The theories* $\mathsf{CR}^{\emptyset}$, CR *with the reflection schema, and* CT *have exactly the same* $\mathcal{L}$*-consequences.*

Proof. In Lemma 5, we observed that CT is interpretable in $\mathsf{CR}^{\emptyset}$; thus, it is interpretable in CR with the reflection schema (Lemma 6).

For the converse direction, we note that the model construction of CR in Proposition 2 is also applicable to $\mathsf{CR}^{\emptyset}$ and is formalisable in the theory ACA, the second-order system for arithmetical comprehension, which has the same $\mathcal{L}$-consequences as CT (for the proof, see, e.g., [11]). □

4.2 Compositional Realisability with the Reflection Rule

Although $\mathsf{CR}^{\emptyset}$ (or equivalently CR with the reflection schema) and CT have the same proof-theoretic strength, $\mathsf{CR}^{\emptyset}$ is satisfied only when the pole $\perp\!\!\!\perp$ is empty. Thus, our next goal is to find a principle that is compatible with any choice of the pole. Here, our suggestion is to weaken the reflection schema to the rule form.

Definition 5 (CR^{+})**.** *The* $\mathcal{L}_R$*-theory* CR^{+} *is the extension of* CR *with the reflection rule:*

$$\frac{s\mathrm{T}\ulcorner A \urcorner}{A}$$

for every closed term s *and* $\mathcal{L}$*-sentence* A*.*

Proposition 5. *Let* A *be any* $\mathcal{L}_R$*-sentence and assume that* $\mathsf{CR}^{+} \vdash A$*. Then, for any pole* $\perp\!\!\!\perp$*, we have* $\langle \mathbb{N}, \perp\!\!\!\perp, \mathbb{T}_{\perp\!\!\!\perp}, \mathbb{F}_{\perp\!\!\!\perp} \rangle \models A$*.*

Proof. The proof is by induction on the derivation of A. Since the other cases are already contained in the proof of Proposition 2, it is sufficient to consider the case of the reflection rule. Therefore, we assume that an $\mathcal{L}$-sentence A is derived by the reflection rule from $s\mathrm{T}\ulcorner A \urcorner$ for some closed term s. By the induction hypothesis, it follows that $\langle \mathbb{N}, \perp\!\!\!\perp, \mathbb{T}_{\perp\!\!\!\perp}, \mathbb{F}_{\perp\!\!\!\perp} \rangle \models s\mathrm{T}\ulcorner A \urcorner$ for any pole $\perp\!\!\!\perp$. Thus, particularly for the empty pole $\perp\!\!\!\perp = \emptyset$, we obtain $\langle \mathbb{N}, \emptyset, \mathbb{T}_{\perp\!\!\!\perp}, \mathbb{F}_{\perp\!\!\!\perp} \rangle \models A$ by Proposition 2 and Lemma 6. As A is an $\mathcal{L}$-sentence, we also have $\langle \mathbb{N}, \perp\!\!\!\perp, \mathbb{T}_{\perp\!\!\!\perp}, \mathbb{F}_{\perp\!\!\!\perp} \rangle \models A$ for any pole $\perp\!\!\!\perp$. □

In the remainder of this paper, we prove that CR^{+} has the same proof-theoretic strength as CT and $\mathsf{CR}^{\emptyset}$. The upper bound of CR^{+} is obvious: Lemma 6 and Proposition 5 establish that CR^{+} is a *proper* subtheory of $\mathsf{CR}^{\emptyset}$. The lower-bound argument is more difficult because CR^{+} is not expressively rich enough to interpret CT. Instead we can proceed directly through a well-ordering proof for CR^{+} by showing that the principle of transfinite induction for $\mathcal{L}$-formulas is provable for each ordinal below $\varepsilon_{\varepsilon_0}$. The argument is, essentially, just the extraction of the computational content of the standard well-ordering proof for CT (for the detailed proof, see Appendix A).

As a result, we can determine the proof-theoretic strength of CR^+.

Theorem 2. CR^+ *has exactly the same* $\mathcal{L}$*-theorems as* CT *and* $\mathsf{CR}^\emptyset$.

5 Future Work

In this paper, we have axiomatised Krivine's classical realisability in a similar manner to the formalisation of Tarskian hierarchical truth. Given that various self-referential approaches to truth have been developed [7,9,13,19], it is natural to consider self-referential generalisations of classical realisability. One desideratum for such a self-referential system can be found in the formal realisability of Heyting arithmetic (HA). Kleene's realisability relation "n realises A" can be expressed by some arithmetical sentence $n\mathrm{r}A$. Then, HA is known to be *self-realisable* in the sense that for any arithmetical sentence A, if $\mathsf{HA} \vdash A$, then $\mathsf{HA} \vdash n\mathrm{r}A$ for some numeral n (cf. [23, Theorem 4.10]). If an analogous property for classical realisability is defined, the question is whether there exists a well-motivated self-realisable system S. When S contains the additional vocabularies $x \in \perp\!\!\!\perp$, $x\mathrm{T}y$, and $x\mathrm{F}y$ of $\mathcal{L}_R$, we must define their own realisability and refutability conditions, and this is where considerations on self-referentiality for classical realisability are required.

Another direction of future work is the formalisation of alternative interpretations for classical theories. Alternative realisability interpretations for PA and its extensions are presented in, e.g., [1–6]. It is also reasonable to consider the axiomatisation of intuitionistic realisability interpretations over Heyting arithmetic.

Acknowledgments. We would like to thank the anonymous referees for their helpful comments on an earlier version of the paper. The first author was partially supported by Graduate Grant Program of Graduate School of Humanities and Human Sciences, Hokkaido University. The second author was supported by the Knut and Alice Wallenberg Foundation [2025.0199].

A Well-Ordering Proof in Compositional Realisability

Here, we determine the proof-theoretic strength of CR^+. However, in contrast to $\mathsf{CR}^\emptyset$, CR^+ is not sufficiently expressively strong to relatively interpret CT. Thus, we provide a well-ordering proof of CR^+, from which we can conclude that CR^+ derives the same $\mathcal{L}$-consequences as both CT and $\mathsf{CR}^\emptyset$.

For this purpose, we require an ordinal notation system OT for predicative ordinal numbers. We use several facts about OT (for the proof, see, e.g., [21]). A formula $x \in OT$ is defined as meaning that x is a representation of an ordinal number in OT. Let α, β, and γ range over the ordinal numbers in OT. Thus, $\forall \alpha A(\alpha)$ abbreviates $\forall x(x \in OT \to A(x))$. By the standard method, we can define relations and operations on OT. Let $<$ be the less-than relation, 0 is zero as the ordinal number, $\alpha \in Suc$ means that α is a successor ordinal, $\alpha \in Lim$ says that α is a limit ordinal, $+$ is the ordinal addition, φxy is the Veblen function, and the binary primitive recursive function $[\alpha]_x$ returns the x-th element of the fundamental sequence for α. For these symbols, the following notations and facts are used in this paper:

- Let $\omega^\alpha := \varphi 0\alpha$ and $1 := \omega^0$.
- $[\omega^\alpha]_n = \begin{cases} \omega^{\alpha-1} \times n & \text{if } \alpha \in Suc, \\ \omega^{[\alpha]_n} & \text{if } \alpha \in Lim. \end{cases}$
- Let $\omega_n(\alpha) := \begin{cases} \alpha & \text{if } n = 0, \\ \omega^{\omega_{n-1}(\alpha)} & \text{if } n > 0. \end{cases}$
- Let $\varepsilon_\alpha := \varphi 1\alpha$. This paper uses ordinals only up to $\varepsilon_{\varepsilon_0}$.
- $[\varepsilon_\alpha]_n = \begin{cases} \omega_n(1) & \text{if } \alpha = 0, \\ \omega_n(\varepsilon_{\alpha-1}+1) & \text{if } \alpha \in Suc, \\ \varepsilon_{[\alpha]_n} & \text{if } \alpha \in Lim. \end{cases}$

The T-free consequences of CT can be expressed using some transfinite induction schema. For an $\mathcal{L}$-formula $A(x)$ and an ordinal α, we define the formula $\mathsf{TI}(A,\alpha) = \mathsf{Prog}\lambda x A(x) \to A(\alpha)$, where $\mathsf{Prog}\lambda x A(x) = \forall\alpha(\forall\beta < \alpha(A(\beta)) \to A(\alpha))$. Then, we define the schema: $\mathsf{TI}(\alpha) = \{\mathsf{TI}(A,\beta) \mid A \text{ is an } \mathcal{L}\text{-formula}\}$. In addition, let $\mathsf{TI}(<\alpha) := \bigcup_{\beta<\alpha} \mathsf{TI}(\beta)$. Finally, let the $\mathcal{L}$-theory $\mathsf{PA} + \mathsf{TI}(<\alpha)$ be the extension of PA with the schema $\mathsf{TI}(<\alpha)$.

The following is well-known (see, e.g., [11, Theorem 8.35]):

Theorem 3. *The theory* CT *derives the same* $\mathcal{L}$*-formulae as* $\mathsf{PA} + \mathsf{TI}(<\varepsilon_{\varepsilon_0})$.

According to this fact, it is sufficient to show that the schema $\mathsf{TI}(<\varepsilon_{\varepsilon_0})$ is derivable in CR^+. To this end, in Lemma 9, we prove that each instance of $\mathsf{TI}(<\varepsilon_{\varepsilon_0})$ is realisable in CR. Then, CR^+ can derive $\mathsf{TI}(<\varepsilon_{\varepsilon_0})$ itself according to the reflection rule.

The proof is essentially based on the standard well-ordering proof of CT (cf. [17, Lemma 3.11]). So, we briefly sketch the outline of the proof in CT. Let $I_0(\alpha) = \forall\ulcorner A\urcorner \in Sent_{\mathcal{L}}.\ \mathrm{T}\ulcorner\mathsf{TI}(A,\dot\alpha)\urcorner$, which expresses the schema $\mathsf{TI}(\alpha)$ as a single statement. In PA, we can derive the schemata $\mathsf{TI}(0)$, $\mathsf{TI}(\alpha+1)$ from $\mathsf{TI}(\alpha)$, and $\mathsf{TI}(\omega^\alpha)$ from $\mathsf{TI}(\alpha)$, respectively (e.g., see [21, Section 7.4]). By formalising these results, CT can derive $I_0(\varepsilon_0)$. Furthermore, by generalising this argument in CT, we can derive $I_0(\varepsilon_\alpha) \to I_0(\varepsilon_{\alpha+1})$. In addition, CT derives $\alpha \in Lim \to \{[\forall\beta < \alpha I_0(\varepsilon_\beta)] \to I_0(\varepsilon_\alpha)\}$. These facts together mean that $I_0(\varepsilon_x)$ is progressive, i.e., $\mathsf{CT} \vdash \mathsf{Prog}\lambda x I_0(\varepsilon_x)$. Since CT can derive the transfinite induction for $I_0(\varepsilon_x)$ up to ε_0, the schema $\mathsf{TI}(<\varepsilon_{\varepsilon_0})$ is obtained in CT, as required. To emulate this proof within CR, we must extract the computational content of the proof. For example, it is necessary to explicitly give a partial recursive function that computes a realiser of $\mathsf{TI}(\alpha+1)$ from that of $\mathsf{TI}(\alpha)$.

We define $I_0(e,\alpha) = \forall\ulcorner A\urcorner \in Sent_{\mathcal{L}}.\ (e \cdot \ulcorner A\urcorner)\mathrm{T}\ulcorner\mathsf{TI}(A,\dot\alpha)\urcorner$, which means that e computes a realiser of the transfinite induction $\mathsf{TI}(A,\alpha)$ for each $\mathcal{L}$-sentence A.

Lemma 7. *1. There exists a number* k_0 *such that:*

$$\mathsf{CR} \vdash I_0(\mathsf{k}_0, 0).$$

2. There exists a number k_{suc} *such that:*

$$\mathsf{CR} \vdash I_0(e, \alpha) \to I_0(\mathsf{k}_{suc} \cdot \langle e, \alpha \rangle, \alpha + 1).$$

3. There exists a number k_ω *such that:*

$$\mathsf{CR} \vdash I_0(e, \alpha) \to I_0(\mathsf{k}_\omega \cdot \langle e, \alpha \rangle, \omega^\alpha).$$

4. There exists a number k_{lim} *such that:*

$$\mathsf{CR} \vdash \alpha \in Lim \to [\forall n I_0(e \cdot n, [\alpha]_n) \to I_0(\mathsf{k}_{lim} \cdot \langle e, \alpha \rangle, \alpha)].$$

Note that k_0 realises the schema $\mathsf{TI}(0)$; k_{suc} realises $\mathsf{TI}(\alpha+1)$ from $\mathsf{TI}(\alpha)$; k_ω realises $\mathsf{TI}(\omega^\alpha)$ from $\mathsf{TI}(\alpha)$; k_{lim} realises $\mathsf{TI}(\alpha)$ for a limit ordinal α if each $\mathsf{TI}([\alpha]_n)$ is realised.

Proof. 1. For every $\mathcal{L}$-formula A, we can primitive recursively find a proof of $\mathsf{TI}(A, 0)\urcorner)$ in PA. Thus, by Theorem 1, there exists a required k_0.

2. In PA, we can primitive recursively find a proof of $\forall\alpha(\mathsf{TI}(A,\alpha) \to \mathsf{TI}(A, \alpha+1))$ for each $\mathcal{L}$-formula A. Thus, by Theorem 1, there exists a number k such that $\mathsf{CR} \vdash ((\mathsf{k} \cdot \alpha) \cdot \ulcorner A \urcorner) \mathrm{T} \ulcorner \mathsf{TI}(A, \alpha) \to \mathsf{TI}(A, \alpha+1)\urcorner$. For this k, we define k_{suc} to be such that for any $\mathcal{L}$-sentence A,

$$(\mathsf{k}_{suc} \cdot \langle e, \alpha \rangle) \cdot \ulcorner A \urcorner \simeq \mathsf{i} \cdot \langle (\mathsf{k} \cdot \alpha) \cdot \ulcorner A \urcorner, e \cdot \ulcorner A \urcorner \rangle.$$

Then, if e satisfies $I_0(e, \alpha)$, we have $((\mathsf{k}_{suc} \cdot \langle e, \alpha \rangle) \cdot \ulcorner A \urcorner) \mathrm{T} \ulcorner \mathsf{TI}(A, \dot{\alpha}+1)\urcorner$, as required.

3. For every $\mathcal{L}$-formula A, there exists an $\mathcal{L}$-formula A' such that we can primitive recursively find a proof of $\forall\alpha(\mathsf{TI}(A', \alpha) \to \mathsf{TI}(A, \omega^\alpha))$ in PA. Thus, similar to the proof of the item 2, there is a required function k_ω.

4. We assume $\forall n I_0(e \cdot n, [\alpha]_n)$. From this e, we can primitive recursively define $\mathsf{k}^\dagger$ such that:

$$\forall \ulcorner A \urcorner \in Sent_{\mathcal{L}}.\ ((\mathsf{k}^\dagger \cdot \langle e, \alpha \rangle) \cdot \ulcorner A \urcorner) \mathrm{T} \ulcorner \forall \beta < \dot{\alpha} \mathsf{TI}(A, \beta)\urcorner.$$

In addition, for each $\mathcal{L}$-formula A, we obtain $\forall\beta < \alpha \mathsf{TI}(A, \beta) \to \mathsf{TI}(A, \alpha)$ in PA; thus, according to Theorem 1, we take a number $\mathsf{k}^\ddagger$ such that:

$$((\mathsf{k}^\ddagger \cdot \alpha) \cdot \ulcorner A \urcorner) \mathrm{T} \ulcorner \forall \beta < \dot{\alpha} \mathsf{TI}(A, \beta) \to \mathsf{TI}(A, \dot{\alpha})\urcorner.$$

Now, we define k_{lim} such that:

$$(\mathsf{k}_{lim} \cdot \langle e, \alpha \rangle) \cdot \ulcorner A \urcorner \simeq \mathsf{i} \cdot \langle (\mathsf{k}^\ddagger \cdot \alpha) \cdot \ulcorner A \urcorner, (\mathsf{k}^\dagger \cdot \langle e, \alpha \rangle) \cdot \ulcorner A \urcorner \rangle.$$

We then obtain $((\mathsf{k}_{lim} \cdot \langle e, \alpha \rangle) \cdot \ulcorner A \urcorner) \mathrm{T} \ulcorner \mathsf{TI}(A, \dot{\alpha})\urcorner$, as required. □

The following lemma shows the progressiveness of the epsilon function.

Lemma 8. *1. There exists a number* $\mathsf{k}_{\varepsilon\_0}$ *such that:*

$$\mathsf{CR} \vdash I_0(\mathsf{k}_{\varepsilon\_0}, \varepsilon_0).$$

2. There exists a number $\mathsf{k}_{\varepsilon\_suc}$ *such that:*

$$\mathsf{CR} \vdash I_0(e, \varepsilon_\alpha) \to I_0(\mathsf{k}_{\varepsilon\_suc} \cdot \langle e, \alpha \rangle, \varepsilon_{\alpha+1}).$$

3. There exists a number k_ε *such that:*

$$\mathsf{CR} \vdash \mathsf{Prog}\lambda\alpha I_0(\mathsf{k}_\varepsilon \cdot \alpha, \varepsilon_\alpha).$$

Proof. 1. We define a number k as follows:

$$\begin{cases} \mathsf{k} \cdot 0 :\simeq \mathsf{k}_{suc} \cdot \langle \mathsf{k}_0, 0 \rangle, \\ \mathsf{k} \cdot (n+1) :\simeq \mathsf{k}_\omega \cdot \langle \mathsf{k} \cdot n, [\varepsilon_0]_n \rangle \quad \text{for each } n. \end{cases}$$

Then, we clearly have $\mathsf{CR} \vdash \forall n (I_0(\mathsf{k} \cdot n, [\varepsilon_0]_n)$, hence by item 4 in Lemma 7, the number $\mathsf{k}_{\varepsilon\_0} := \mathsf{k}_{lim} \cdot \langle \mathsf{k}, \varepsilon_0 \rangle$ is the required one.

2. The proof is nearly the same as that of item 1.
3. For an ordinal α and a number e, let $e[\alpha]$ be such that $e[\alpha] \cdot n :\simeq e \cdot [\alpha]_n$. Here, k_ε is defined as follows:

$$\begin{cases} \mathsf{k}_\varepsilon \cdot 0 :\simeq \mathsf{k}_{\varepsilon\_0} \\ \mathsf{k}_\varepsilon \cdot (\alpha+1) :\simeq \mathsf{k}_{\varepsilon\_suc} \cdot \langle \mathsf{k}_\varepsilon \cdot \alpha, \alpha \rangle \\ \mathsf{k}_\varepsilon \cdot \alpha :\simeq \mathsf{k}_{lim} \cdot \langle \mathsf{k}_\varepsilon[\alpha], \varepsilon_\alpha \rangle \quad \text{for } \alpha \in Lim. \end{cases}$$

Then, to show the claim, we take any α and assume $\forall \beta < \alpha I_0(\mathsf{k}_\varepsilon \cdot \beta, \varepsilon_\beta)$.

- If $\alpha = 0$, then the conclusion $I_0(\mathsf{k}_\varepsilon \cdot \alpha, \varepsilon_\alpha)$ is clear by item 1.
- If $\alpha \in Suc$, then by the assumption, we obtain $I_0(\mathsf{k}_\varepsilon \cdot (\alpha-1), \varepsilon_{\alpha-1})$; thus, we obtain the conclusion by item 2.
- If $\alpha \in Lim$, then we obtain $I_0(\mathsf{k}_\varepsilon[\alpha] \cdot n, \varepsilon_{[\alpha]_n})$ for each n. Here, since $[\varepsilon_\alpha]_n = \varepsilon_{[\alpha]_n}$, Lemma 7 implies that $I_0(\mathsf{k}_{lim} \cdot \langle \mathsf{k}_\varepsilon[\alpha], \varepsilon_\alpha \rangle, \varepsilon_\alpha \rangle$; thus, it follows that $I_0(\mathsf{k}_\varepsilon \cdot \alpha, \varepsilon_\alpha)$. □

Lemma 9. *For each $\mathcal{L}$-formula A and for each ordinal number $\alpha < \varepsilon_{\varepsilon_0}$, we can find a term s such that* $\mathsf{CR} \vdash s\mathrm{T}\ulcorner \mathsf{TI}(\alpha, A) \urcorner$.

Proof. We fix any ordinal $\alpha < \varepsilon_{\varepsilon_0}$, and then there exists an ordinal $\beta < \varepsilon_0$ such that $\alpha \leq \varepsilon_\beta < \varepsilon_{\varepsilon_0}$. Thus, by taking any $\mathcal{L}$-formula A, it is sufficient to prove $((\mathsf{k}_\varepsilon \cdot \beta) \cdot \ulcorner A \urcorner)\mathrm{T}\ulcorner \mathsf{TI}(\varepsilon_\beta, A)\urcorner$ because we can primitive recursively find a required term s from the term $(\mathsf{k}_\varepsilon \cdot \beta) \cdot \ulcorner A \urcorner$.

Since PA derives any transfinite induction for $\beta < \varepsilon_0$, we have $\mathsf{TI}(\beta, I_0(\mathsf{k}_\varepsilon \cdot x, \varepsilon_x))$. Therefore, according to item 3 in Lemma 8, we have $I_0(\mathsf{k}_\varepsilon \cdot \beta, \varepsilon_\beta)$. Thus, it follows that $((\mathsf{k}_\varepsilon \cdot \beta) \cdot \ulcorner A \urcorner)\mathrm{T}\ulcorner \mathsf{TI}(\varepsilon_\beta, A)\urcorner$, as desired. □

By Lemma 9 and the reflection rule, CR^+ yields the formula $\mathsf{TI}(\alpha, A)$ for each $\mathcal{L}$-formula A and $\alpha < \varepsilon_{\varepsilon_0}$. Thus, CR^+ derives every theorem of $\mathsf{PA} + \mathsf{TI}(< \varepsilon_{\varepsilon_0})$. Therefore, according to Proposition 4 and Theorem 3, the proof of Theorem 2 is completed.

References

1. Aschieri, F.: Learning, realizability and games in classical arithmetic. arXiv preprint arXiv:1012.4992 (2010)
2. Aschieri, F.: Interactive realizability for classical peano arithmetic with skolem axioms. In: Computer Science Logic 2012 (2012)
3. Avigad, J.: A realizability interpretation for classical arithmetic. In: Logic Colloquium, vol. 98, pp. 57–90 (2000)
4. Berger, U., Oliva, P.: Modified bar recursion and classical dependent choice. In: Logic Colloquium, vol. 1, pp. 89–107 (2005)
5. Blot, V.: Typed realizability for first-order classical analysis. Log. Methods Comput. Sci. **11** (2015)
6. Blot, V.: Realizability for Peano arithmetic with winning conditions in HON games. Ann. Pure Appl. Logic **168**(2), 254–277 (2017)
7. Cantini, A.: A theory of formal truth arithmetically equivalent to ID_1. J. Symb. Logic **55**(1), 244–259 (1990)
8. Feferman, S.: Reflecting on incompleteness. J. Symb. Logic **56**(1), 1–49 (1991)
9. Friedman, H., Sheard, M.: An axiomatic approach to self-referential truth. Ann. Pure Appl. Logic **33**, 1–21 (1987)
10. Griffin, T.G.: A formulae-as-type notion of control. In: Proceedings of the 17th ACM SIGPLAN-SIGACT Symposium on Principles of Programming Languages, pp. 47–58 (1989)
11. Halbach, V.: Axiomatic Theories of Truth, 2nd edn. Cambridge University Press, Cambridge (2014)
12. Kleene, S.C.: On the interpretation of intuitionistic number theory. J. Symb. Logic **10**(4), 109–124 (1945)
13. Kripke, S.: Outline of a theory of truth. J. Philos. **72**(19), 690–716 (1976)
14. Krivine, J.L.: Typed lambda-calculus in classical Zermelo-Fraenkel set theory. Arch. Math. Logic **40**(3), 189–205 (2001)
15. Krivine, J.L.: Dependent choice, 'quote' and the clock. Theoret. Comput. Sci. **308**(1–3), 259–276 (2003)
16. Krivine, J.L.: Realizability in classical logic. Panoramas et synthèses **27**, 197–229 (2009)
17. Leigh, G.E.: Reflecting on truth. IfCoLog J. Log. Appl. **3**(4), 557–594 (2016)
18. Leigh, G.E., Rathjen, M.: An ordinal analysis for theories of self-referential truth. Arch. Math. Logic **49**(2), 213–247 (2010)
19. Leitgeb, H.: What truth depends on. J. Philos. Log. **34**, 155–192 (2005)
20. Oliva, P., Streicher, T.: On Krivine's realizability interpretation of classical second-order arithmetic. Fund. Inform. **84**(2), 207–220 (2008)
21. Pohlers, W.: Proof Theory: The First Step into Impredicativity. Springer, Heidelberg (2008). https://doi.org/10.1007/978-3-540-69319-2
22. Tarski, A.: The concept of truth in formalized languages. In: Tarski, A. (ed.) Logic, Semantics, Metamathematics, 2nd edn, pp. 152–278. Hackett, Indianapolis (1983)
23. Troelstra, A., van Dalen, D.: Constructivism in Mathematics: An Introduction, vol. 1. Elsevier, Amsterdam (1988)

Intersection Types via Finite-Set Declarations

Fairouz Kamareddine(✉) and Joe Wells

Heriot-Watt University, Edinburgh, UK
{f.d.kamareddine,joe.wells}@hw.ac.uk

Abstract. The λ-cube is a famous pure type system (PTS) cube of eight powerful explicit type systems that include the simple, polymorphic and dependent type theories. The λ-cube only types Strongly Normalising (SN) terms but not all of them. It is well known that even the most powerful system of the λ-cube can only type the same pure untyped λ-terms that are typable by the higher-order polymorphic implicitly typed λ-calculus F_ω, and that there is an untyped λ-term $\dot{U}$ that is SN but is not typable in F_ω or the λ-cube. Hence, neither system can type all the SN terms it expresses. In this paper, we present the f-cube, an extension of the λ-cube with finite-set declarations (FSDs) like $y\bar{\in}\{C_1, \cdots, C_n\} : B$ which means that y is of type B and can only be one of $C_1, \cdots, C_n$. The novelty of our FSDs is that they allow to represent intersection types as Π-types. We show how to translate and type the term $\dot{U}$ in the f-cube using an encoding of intersection types based on FSDs. Notably, our translation works without needing anything like the usual troublesome intersection-introduction rule that proves a pure untyped λ-term M has an intersection type $\Phi_1 \cap \cdots \cap \Phi_k$ using k independent subderivations. As such, our approach is useful for language implementers who want the power of intersection types without the pain of the intersection-introduction rule.

Keywords: Intersection Types · Typability · Strong Normalisation

1 The Troublesome Intersection-Introduction Rule

Type theory was first developed by Bertrand Russell to avoid the contradictions in Frege's work. Since, type theory was adapted and used by Ramsey, Hilbert/Ackermann and Church and later exploded into powerful exciting formalisms that played a substantial role in the development of programming languages and theorem provers, and in the verification of software. As advocated by Russell, type theory remains to this day a powerful tool at avoiding loops/contradictions and at characterising strong normalization (SN). There are 2 styles of typing: *explicit* (à la Church) as in $\lambda x : T.x$ and *implicit* (à la Curry) as in $\lambda x : x$. We call the latter *untyped.* A type assignment engine needs to work harder to assign a type to an untyped term than to an explicitly typed one.

Intersection types were independently invented near the end of the 1970s by Coppo and Dezani [7] and Pottinger [12] with aims such as the analysis of normalization properties, which requires a very precise analysis (see also [4,10,14]).

G. Metcalfe et al. (Eds.): WoLLIC 2024, LNCS 14672, pp. 80–92, 2024.
https://doi.org/10.1007/978-3-031-62687-6_6

Aiming to make use of this precision, the members of the Church Project worked on a compiler that used intersection types not only to support the usual kind of type polymorphism but also to represent a precise polyvariant flow analysis that was used to enable optimizing representation transformations [20]. Among the many challenges that were faced, a major difficulty was the intersection-introduction typing rule, which made it complicated to do local optimizations (an essential task for a compiler) while at the same time retaining type information and the ability to verify it. The intersection-introduction rule usually looks like this:

$$\frac{E \vdash M : \sigma \qquad E \vdash M : \tau}{E \vdash M : \sigma \cap \tau} \quad (\cap\text{-Intro})$$

The proof terms are the same for both premises and the conclusion! No syntax is introduced. A system with this rule does not fit into the proofs-as-terms (PAT, a.k.a. propositions-as-types and Curry/Howard) correspondence, because it has proof terms that do not encode deductions. This trouble is related to the fact that the $\cap$ type constructor is not a truth-functional propositional connective, but rather one that depends on the proofs of the propositions it connects sharing some specific key structural details but not all details [19].

There is an immediate puzzle in how to make a type-annotated variant of the system. The usual strategy fails immediately, e.g.:

$$\frac{E \vdash (\lambda x : \sigma.x) : \sigma \to \sigma \qquad E \vdash (\lambda x : \tau.x) : \tau \to \tau}{E \vdash (\lambda x : \boxed{???}.x) : (\sigma \to \sigma) \cap (\tau \to \tau)}$$

Where $\boxed{???}$ appears, what should be written? A compiler using intersection types must have some way of organizing the type information of the separate typing subderivations for the same program points, because a transformation at a program point must simultaneously deal with all of the separate subderivations. It would be nice if this was principled rather than *ad hoc.*

The various solutions to this problem each have their own strengths and weaknesses. The most basic strategy is to accept the usual style of ($\cap$-Intro), and not try to have proof terms that contain type annotations [8,11]. This is fine if the plan is to discard much or most type information early in compilation, but is unhelpful if checkable type-correctness is to be maintained through program transformations.

Another strategy is to have proof terms whose structure makes multiple copies of subprograms typed with the ($\cap$-Intro) rule [20]. This means that proof terms can not be merely annotated versions of the λ-terms being typed, because the branching structure of the proof terms can not be the same as that of the λ-terms. Our experience is that this makes local program transformations complicated and awkward if checkable type-correctness is to be maintained. Another option is to limit the possible typings and the set of typable terms, and accept not having the full power of intersection types [6]. However, this causes difficulty when the purpose of using intersection types is to support arbitrarily precise program analyses, and also when program transformations go outside of the restricted set of typings that are supported.

These issues led us to search for ways to get the power of intersection types without the usual multiple-premise-style (∩-Intro) rule ([21] gives an overview of earlier solutions). Some solutions do manage to merge the premises of the (∩-Intro) rule into just one premise, but do not provide proof terms containing type information for variable bindings or any other easy-to-manipulate representation of typing derivations [5,13].

2 Finite-Set Declarations and Encoding ∩-Types

Pure type systems (PTSs) were independently given in [2] and [16] and have been used to reason simultaneously about families of type systems and logics. The well known λ-cube of 8 specific PTS's [1] captured the core essence of polymorphic, dependent and Calculus of Constructions (CoC) systems. PTSs were extended with *definitions* [3,15] in order to better represent mathematics and computation. In addition to old $x : A$ declarations, these definitions allow declarations of the form $x =_d D : A$ which declare x to be A and to have type B. Of course extra typing rules are added to type the new terms with definitions.

While analysing the troublesome (∩-Intro) rule, we noted that definitions can be generalised to represent intersection types. This article is the result of this observation. We present the new syntax which extends the λ-cube with finite set declarations that generalise definitions to support intersection types without the troublesome (∩-Intro) rule. Instead of definitions $\lambda x =_d D : A.B$, the new syntax adds finite-set declarations (FSDs) $\lambda x \bar{\in} \{D_1, D_2, \cdots, D_n\} : A.B$ where $n \geq 1$. This latter term is a function like $\lambda x : A.B$ that also requires its argument x to exhibit at most the behaviors of $D_1, \cdots, D_n$.

We show that FSDs give the power of intersection types by translating an intersection type $\Phi_1 \cap \cdots \cap \Phi_k$ to a Π-term of the form:

$$\Pi z \bar{\in} \{P_{1,k}, \cdots, P_{k,k}\} : *_k.z\Phi_1 \cdots \Phi_k$$

where $*_k$ abbreviates $\underbrace{* \to \cdots \to * \to *}_{k \text{ arrows}}$ and $P_{i,k} = (\lambda x_1 : *. \cdots .\lambda x_k : *.x_i)$ picks the i-th of k arguments. So, if $z = P_{i,k}$, then $z\Phi_1 \cdots \Phi_k = \Phi_i$. Notably, our translation from intersection types works without anything in the translation result like the usual (∩-Intro) rule that proves a pure untyped λ-term M has an intersection type $\Phi_1 \cap \cdots \cap \Phi_k$ using k independent subderivations. In PTS style, these "subderivations" are done simultaneously because in the scope of the declaration $z \bar{\in} \{P_{1,k}, \cdots, P_{k,k}\} : *_k$, the type $z(A_1 \to B_1) \cdots (A_k \to B_k)$ can be converted to the equal type $(zA_1 \cdots A_k) \to (zB_1 \cdots B_k)$.

Existing methods for getting rid of the (∩-Intro) rule which support some kind of type equivalence [21] differ from our method in that our type equivalence is a consequence of the FSDs restriction on z, which is added to a system supporting Π-types, including those usually referred to as "higher-order polymorphic types" and "dependent types". Thus, FSDs might be a good way to add the power of intersection types to languages like Coq, Agda, and Idris. By supporting the full power of intersection types, FSDs might also help represent results of arbitrarily precise program analyses (e.g., a polyvariant flow analysis) in language implementations that have Π-types in their internal representation.

FSDs can do more than support a translation of intersection types. FSDs can represent a "definition" by a β-redex where the abstraction has a FSD with only one term in the restriction. The point of using a definition like $(\lambda x \overline{\in}\{D\} : C.B)D$ instead of a β-redex like $(\lambda x : C.B)D$ is that in the former, x is D can be used to help justify type-correctness of B, which might otherwise require replacing many instances of x by D. Although using an FSD instead of a traditional definition requires forming the abstraction $\lambda x \overline{\in}\{D\} : C.B$ and its type, and hence an additional type formation rule, it is worth noting that, adding support for FSDs to suitable systems does not require huge changes. This is the case since although not always prominently stated in theory papers, in practice, proof assistants support definitions in the formal systems of their implementations.

Section 3 introduces into the λ-cube with the new feature of finite-set declarations. Section 4 presents examples that demonstrate how the new syntax can be used to simulate intersection types and shows how a term of Urzyczyn which is untypable in the λ-cube can be typed in the f-cube.

Let $\mathbb{N}_1 = \mathbb{N} \setminus \{0\}$ be the positive natural numbers. Given $i, j \in \mathbb{Z}$, define $i..j = \{k \in \mathbb{Z} \mid i \leq k \leq j\}$ and $[i..j) = i..(j-1)$. Write $|S|$ for the size of set S.

As usual, the composition $X \circ Y$ is $\{(y, x) \mid \exists z.(y, z) \in Y \text{ and } (z, x) \in X\}$. Given $n \in \mathbb{N}_1$, let X^n be such that $X^1 = X$ and $X^{i+1} = X \circ (X^i)$ for $i \in \mathbb{N}_1$.

3 Extending the Syntax of the λ-cube

The new syntax has declarations of the form $x\rho : A$, meaning that the variable x has type A and x also obeys restriction $\rho = \overline{\in}\{A_1, \cdots, A_k\}$ for $k \in \mathbb{N}$. When $k = 0$, then $x\overline{\in}\{\} : A$ is the usual (unrestricted) declaration $x : A$ of the λ-cube. When $k \in \mathbb{N}_1$, we get the new restricted finite-set declaration (FSD) $x\rho : B$ which only permits x to be one of the A_i's. These FSDs are the innovation of the f-cube.

Definition 1 (Syntax). *Figures 1 and 2 use the usual pseudo-grammar notation to define the sets of syntactic entities. Many of these entities are clear from the usual type-free/typed λ-calculus. In the λ-cube we have the sorts $*$ and $\square$, the rules $\boldsymbol{R} \in$* RuleSet, *and the declarations δ and contexts Δ. In the extended cube however, the declarations are a generalised version of those of the λ-cube and a declaration δ may not only be of the usual form $x : A$ (which we also write as $x\diamond : A$ and states that x is of type A) but may also be of the form $x\overline{\in}\{A_1, \cdots, A_i\} : A$ which states that x is declared as any of the A_js (for $j \in 1..i$) and is of type A. We call declarations of the form $x\overline{\in}\{A_1, \cdots, A_i\} : A$, where $i \neq 0$ restricted declarations and these belong to* RDeclaration.

Expressions of the f-cube and the pure λ-calculus are given respectively by Term *and* LTerm. *Figure 1 defines default set ranges for metavariables.* Variable *is used as the set of what we call names. There are two name classes:* Variable* *marked with sort $*$ and* Variable$^\square$ *marked with sort $\square$. For embedding reasons, it is usual to take the type free λ-calculus variables* LVariable *to be* Variable*. *So, x^**

$$
\begin{array}{rl}
a, b, \quad i, \ldots, n, \quad q, r & \in \mathbb{N} \\
\varsigma & \in \mathsf{Sort} \quad ::= * \mid \square \\
a^{\varsigma}, \ldots, z^{\varsigma} & \in \mathsf{Variable}^{\varsigma} \\
f, g, h, \quad q, \ldots, z & \in \mathsf{Variable} \;= \mathsf{Variable}^{*} \cup \mathsf{Variable}^{\square} \\
\dot{a}, \cdots, \dot{h}, \quad \dot{k}, \cdots, \dot{z} & \in \mathsf{LVariable} = \mathsf{Variable}^{*} \\
\dot{A}, \cdots, \dot{Z} & \in \mathsf{LTerm} \quad ::= \dot{x} \mid \lambda \dot{x}.\dot{M} \mid \dot{M}\dot{N} \quad \textit{(type-free } \lambda\textit{terms)}
\end{array}
$$

Fig. 1. Metavariable declarations and type free terms.

and $\dot{x}$ *range over* Variable* = LVariable *whereas* $x^{\square}$ *ranges over* Variable$^{\square}$. *If no confusion occurs, we simply write* x *to range over* Variable = Variable* ∪ Variable$^{\square}$. *Let* Syntax *be the uniton of all the sets of syntactic entities that we define in Figs. 1 and 2. Let* χ *range over* Syntax. *We assume the usual assumptions of binding,* α*-conversion and the Barendregt variable renaming. We take* α*-convertible expressions to denote the same syntactic entities, e.g., even if* $\dot{x} \neq \dot{y}$, *it nonetheless holds that* $\lambda\dot{x}.\dot{x} = \lambda\dot{y}.\dot{y}$. *As usual, let* $\mathsf{FV}(\chi)$ *be the collection of all variables in* χ. *We say* χ *is closed iff* $\mathsf{FV}(\chi) = \{\}$. *We assume the usual substitution in the* λ*calculus where the capture of free variables must be avoided.*

$$
\begin{array}{rll}
\pi & \in \mathsf{Binder} & ::= \lambda \mid \Pi \\
\rho & \in \mathsf{Restriction} & ::= \bar{\in}\{A_1, \ldots, A_i\} \quad \text{where } i \in \mathbb{N} \\
\delta & \in \mathsf{Declaration} & ::= x\,\rho : A \\
\Delta & \in \mathsf{Context} & ::= \varepsilon \mid \delta_1, \ldots, \delta_i \quad \text{where } i \in \mathbb{N}_1 \\
\gamma & \in \mathsf{RDeclaration} & ::= x\,\rho \quad \text{where } \rho \neq \diamond \\
\Gamma & \in \mathsf{RContext} & ::= \varepsilon \mid \gamma_1, \ldots, \gamma_i \quad \text{where } i \in \mathbb{N}_1 \\
A, \ldots, H, \quad J, \quad L, \ldots, W & \in \mathsf{Term} & ::= \varsigma \mid x \mid \pi\delta.\,A \mid A\,B \\
& \mathsf{Rule} & ::= (\varsigma, \varsigma') \\
\boldsymbol{R} & \in \mathsf{RuleSet} & ::= \{X \subseteq \mathsf{Rule} \mid (*, *) \in X\}
\end{array}
$$

- Define the null restriction $\diamond = \bar{\in}\{\}$ and write $x\diamond : A$ as the usual declaration $x : A$.
- Define the restriction declarations of Δ by: $\mathsf{rdec}(x\diamond : A, \Delta) = \mathsf{rdec}(\Delta)$; $\mathsf{rdec}(\varepsilon) = \varepsilon$; and $\mathsf{rdec}(x\,\bar{\in}\{A_1, \ldots, A_k\} : A, \Delta) = x\,\bar{\in}\{A_1, \ldots, A_k\}, \mathsf{rdec}(\Delta)$.
- For the λ-cube, Restriction = $\{\diamond\}$; RDeclaration = $\varnothing$ and $\mathsf{rdec}(\Delta) = \varepsilon$.
- Define the variables of a δ or γ by: $\mathsf{vars}\,(x\rho : A) = \mathsf{vars}\,(x\rho) = \{x\}$ and define $\mathsf{vars}\,(\varepsilon) = \{\}$; $\quad \mathsf{vars}\,(\delta, \Delta) = \mathsf{var}(\delta) \cup \mathsf{vars}\,(\Delta)$; $\quad \mathsf{vars}\,(\gamma, \Gamma) = \mathsf{var}(\gamma) \cup \mathsf{vars}\,(\Gamma)$.
- Define $\sharp(B)$, the degree of B where $\sharp \in \mathsf{Term} \to 0..3$ by: $\sharp(\square) = 3$, $\sharp(*) = 2$, $\sharp(x^{\varsigma}) = \sharp(\varsigma) - 2$, and $\sharp(\pi\delta.\,A) = \sharp(A\,B) = \sharp(A)$.
- Define rsort and tsort by:
  - If $\sharp(B) = 0$ then $\mathsf{rsort}(B) = *$ and if $\sharp(B) = 1$ then $\mathsf{rsort}(B) = \square$.
  - If $\sharp(B) = 1$ then $\mathsf{tsort}(B) = *$ and if $\sharp(B) = 2$ then $\mathsf{tsort}(B) = \square$.

Fig. 2. λ- and f-cube systems syntax definitions.

Definition 2 (Rewriting). *We use the usual notion of* compatibility *of a relation on syntactic entities. Let* $\underline{\beta}$ *and* β *be the smallest compatible relations where:*

$$(\lambda x.\, \dot{M})\dot{N}\ \underline{\beta}\ \dot{M}[x := \dot{N}]$$
$$(\lambda x\, \rho : A.\, B)\, C\ \beta\ B[x := C]$$

For $r \in \{\underline{\beta}, \beta\}$, *let* $\to_r$, $\twoheadrightarrow_r$, *and* $=_r$ *be defined as usual:* $(\to_r) = (r)$; *and* $\twoheadrightarrow_r$ *is the smallest transitive relation containing* r *that is reflexive on* Syntax; *and* $=_r$ *is the smallest transitive symmetric relation containing* $\twoheadrightarrow_r$.

The following theorem shows that our rewriting rules are confluent.

Theorem 1 (Confluence for β). *If* $\chi_1 \twoheadrightarrow_\beta \chi_2$ *and* $\chi_1 \twoheadrightarrow_\beta \chi_3$ *then there exists* $\chi_4 \in$ Syntax *such that* $\chi_2 \twoheadrightarrow_\beta \chi_4$ *and* $\chi_3 \twoheadrightarrow_\beta \chi_4$.

Proof. First, translate Syntax and β into a higher-order rewriting (HOR) framework, e.g., van Oostrom's framework [18]. It is then straightforward to show that β is *orthogonal.* It follows by a standard HOR result that β is *confluent.* ⊠

Definition 3 (Normal Forms). *A syntactic entity* χ is a normal form, *written* $\mathsf{isnf}(\chi)$, *iff there is no* χ' *such that* $\chi \to_r \chi'$ *for* $r \in \{\underline{\beta}, \beta\}$. *The* normal form of χ, *written* $\mathsf{nf}(\chi)$, *is the unique syntactic entity* χ' *such that* $\chi \twoheadrightarrow_r \chi'$ *for* $r \in \{\underline{\beta}, \beta\}$ *and* $\mathsf{isnf}(\chi')$. *(Note that* $\mathsf{nf}(\chi)$ *might be undefined, e.g., consider* $\chi = B\,B \in$ Term *where* $B = \lambda x \diamond : y.\, x\, x$, *has no normal form (and is also not type-correct).) A syntactic entity* χ *is strongly normalizing, written* $\mathsf{SN}(\chi)$, *iff there is no infinite* r*-rewriting sequence starting at* χ *for* $r \in \{\underline{\beta}, \beta\}$.

Each of the λ-cube and the f-cube has 8 type systems each defined by a set $\boldsymbol{R}$ which contains type formation rules which the (Π) and (λ) rules use to regulate the allowed abstractions. Figure 3 gives the 8 systems defined by these $\boldsymbol{R}$s. E.g., $\widehat{\lambda C}$ uses all combinations (ς, ς') where $\varsigma \in \{*, \square\}$.

$\widehat{\lambda\to}$	$(*,*)$			
$\widehat{\lambda 2}$	$(*,*)$	$(\square,*)$		
$\widehat{\lambda P}$	$(*,*)$		$(*,\square)$	
$\widehat{\lambda P2}$	$(*,*)$	$(\square,*)$	$(*,\square)$	
$\widehat{\lambda\underline{\omega}}$	$(*,*)$			$(\square,\square)$
$\widehat{\lambda\omega}$	$(*,*)$	$(\square,*)$		$(\square,\square)$
$\widehat{\lambda P\underline{\omega}}$	$(*,*)$		$(*,\square)$	$(\square,\square)$
$\widehat{\lambda C}$	$(*,*)$	$(\square,*)$	$(*,\square)$	$(\square,\square)$

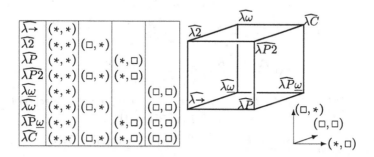

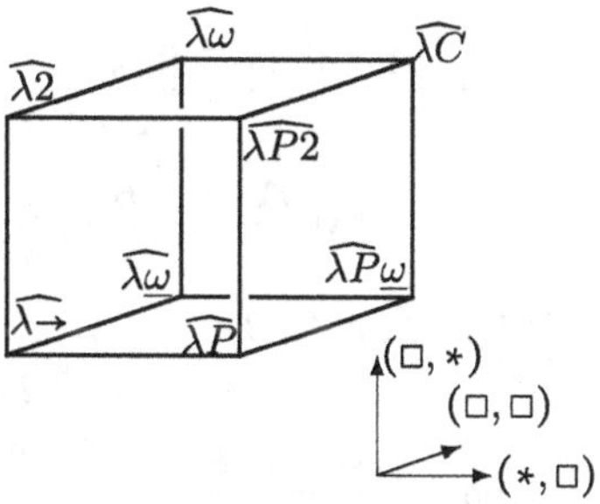

Fig. 3. The rule sets for the λ-cube and f-cube

Definition 4 (Typing Rules and Judgements and Type Systems). *The typing rules for the* λ- *and f-cubes are given in Fig. 5. If* $\Delta \vdash^{\boldsymbol{R}} A : B$ *then:*

- *In type system* $\lambda^{\boldsymbol{R}}$ *and in context* Δ *the term* A *has* type B.
- Δ, A, *and* B *are* $\lambda^{\boldsymbol{R}}$-legal *(or simply legal) and* A *and* B *are* Δ*-terms.*
- A *has sort* ς *if also* $\Delta \vdash^{\boldsymbol{R}} B : \varsigma$ *holds (in this case, note that* $\mathsf{sort}(A) = \varsigma$*).*

$$\text{(ref)}\ \frac{i \in 1..n; \qquad B =_\beta A_i}{\varepsilon \Vdash B \overline{\in}\{A_1, \cdots, A_n\}}$$

$$\text{(ctR)}\ \frac{x \notin \mathsf{vars}(\Gamma); \quad \forall i \in 1..n.\, \Gamma[x := A_i] \Vdash B[x := A_i]\,\rho[x := A_i]}{x \overline{\in}\{A_1, \ldots, A_n\}, \Gamma \Vdash B\,\rho}$$

Fig. 4. Restriction Satisfaction/Utilisation Judgements ($\Gamma \Vdash B\rho$)

Let $\Delta \vdash^{\boldsymbol{R}} A : B : C$ stand for $\Delta \vdash^{\boldsymbol{R}} A : B$ and $\Delta \vdash^{\boldsymbol{R}} B : C$. If $\boldsymbol{R}$ is omitted from $\vdash^{\boldsymbol{R}}$, then the reader should infer it.

As we see in Fig. 5, the λ- and f-cubes only differ in rules (start), (app) and (conv). For the f-cube, (start) is an obvious generalisation of that of the λ-cube (checking that the B_js have the correct type), whereas (app) and (conv) use Fig. 4 to check that only well behaved restrictions are used. Here, $\mathsf{rdec}(\Delta) \Vdash A\,\rho$ *and* $\mathsf{rdec}(\Delta) \Vdash B\overline{\in}\{C\}$ *ensure that the restrictions via FSDs are activated according to Fig. 4 so that if $\rho = \overline{\in}\{C_1, \cdots, C_n\}$, then for all i, $A =_\beta C_i$ modulo substitutions based on FSDs in* $\mathsf{rdec}(\Delta)$*. Thus, if there are no FSDs, i.e.* $\mathsf{rdec}(\Delta) = \varepsilon$*, then the* $\mathsf{rdec}(\Delta) \Vdash B\overline{\in}\{C\}$ *of (conv) becomes the $B =_\beta C$ in the λ-cube.*[1]

$$\text{(axiom)}\ \varepsilon \vdash^{\boldsymbol{R}} * : \square \qquad\qquad \text{(weak)}\ \frac{\Delta, \delta \vdash^{\boldsymbol{R}} A : B; \qquad \Delta \vdash^{\boldsymbol{R}} C : D}{\Delta, \delta \vdash^{\boldsymbol{R}} C : D}$$

$$\text{(start)}\ \frac{\left(\begin{array}{l} x^{\varsigma} \notin \mathsf{vars}(\Delta); \qquad \Delta \vdash^{\boldsymbol{R}} A : \varsigma; \\ \text{if } \rho = \overline{\in}\{B_1, \cdots, B_n\} \text{ then } \forall j \in 1..n.\, \Delta \vdash^{\boldsymbol{R}} B_j : A \end{array}\right)}{\Delta, x^{\varsigma}\,\rho{:}A \vdash^{\boldsymbol{R}} x^{\varsigma} : A}$$

$$(\Pi)\ \frac{\Delta, x\,\rho{:}A \vdash^{\boldsymbol{R}} B : \varsigma; \qquad \Delta \vdash^{\boldsymbol{R}} A : \varsigma'; \qquad (\varsigma', \varsigma) \in \boldsymbol{R}}{\Delta \vdash^{\boldsymbol{R}} \Pi x\,\rho{:}A.\, B : \varsigma}$$

$$(\lambda)\ \frac{\Delta, \delta \vdash^{\boldsymbol{R}} B' : B; \qquad \Delta \vdash^{\boldsymbol{R}} \Pi\delta.\, B : \varsigma}{\Delta \vdash^{\boldsymbol{R}} \lambda\delta.\, B' : \Pi\delta.\, B}$$

$$\text{(app)}\ \frac{\Delta \vdash^{\boldsymbol{R}} F : (\Pi x\,\rho{:}C.\, B); \qquad \Delta \vdash^{\boldsymbol{R}} A : C; \qquad (\text{ if } \rho \neq \diamond \text{ then } \mathsf{rdec}(\Delta) \Vdash A\,\rho)}{\Delta \vdash^{\boldsymbol{R}} F\,A : B[x := A]}$$

$$\text{(conv)}\ \frac{\Delta \vdash^{\boldsymbol{R}} A : B; \qquad \Delta \vdash^{\boldsymbol{R}} C : \varsigma; \qquad \mathsf{rdec}(\Delta) \Vdash B\overline{\in}\{C\}}{\Delta \vdash^{\boldsymbol{R}} A : C}$$

- In the λ-cube, the if-then statements of (start) and (app) do not apply, and the $\mathsf{rdec}(\Delta) \Vdash B\overline{\in}\{C\}$ of (conv) becomes $b =_\beta C$ by Figure 4.
- We write $\Delta \vdash^{\boldsymbol{R}}_{\lambda} A : B$ resp. $\Delta \vdash^{\boldsymbol{R}}_{\mathsf{f}} A : B$ for type derivation in the λ- resp. f-cube.

Fig. 5. Typing rules of the λ- and f-cubes.

[1] The (weak) rule differs slighly from that of the λ-cube, but a simple check shows that this formalisation of the λ-cube is equivalent to that of [1].

The next definition gives the function TE which erases types and all information at degree 1 or more from elements of Term to return pure untyped λ-terms. TE is like the function E of [9], but is simpler because we only need $\mathsf{TE}(A)$ to be meaningful when $\Delta \vdash_{\mathsf{f}} A : B : *$. If A is not legal or the sort (type of the type) of A is not $*$, then we do not care whether $\mathsf{TE}(A)$ is defined or if so what it is.

Definition 5 (Type Erasure). *Let* $\mathsf{TE} \in \mathsf{Term} \to \mathsf{LTerm}$ *be the smallest function where:* $\mathsf{TE}(x) = x$ *and*

$$\begin{array}{llll} \mathsf{TE}(A\,B) = \mathsf{TE}(A)\,\mathsf{TE}(B) & \textit{if } \natural(B) = 0 & \mathsf{TE}(\lambda x^{*}\,\rho : A.\,B) = \lambda x^{*}.\,\mathsf{TE}(B) \\ \mathsf{TE}(A\,B) = \mathsf{TE}(A) & \textit{if } \natural(B) = 1 & \mathsf{TE}(\lambda x^{\Box}\,\rho : A.\,B) = \mathsf{TE}(B) \end{array}$$

Definition 4 stated how we can type explicily typed terms (those of Term). The next definition states how to type pure type-free terms (those of LTerm).

Definition 6 (Typability of Pure λ-Terms). *A pure* λ*-term* $\dot{M}$ *is* typable *iff there exist* Δ, A, *and* B *such that* $\Delta \vdash_f A : B : *$ *and* $\mathsf{TE}(A) = \dot{M}$.

4 Implementing Intersection Types

This section defines intersection types using FSDs and shows that Urzyczyn's famous term is typable in the f-cube. Throughout, assume we are using one of the 2 systems that allow forming functions "from types to types" ("type constructors") and "from types to terms" ("type polymorphism"). Thus, prefix every statement with "If $\{(\Box,\Box),(\Box,*)\} \subseteq \boldsymbol{R}$, then $\cdots$" and read every "$\vdash$" as "$\vdash_{\mathsf{f}}^{\boldsymbol{R}}$".

The next definitions give pieces of syntax and abbreviations that are needed to define intersection types in the f-cubes.

Definition 7 (General Syntax Abbreviations).

- $A \to B = \Pi w^{\varsigma} : A.\,B$ *where* $w^{\varsigma} \notin \mathsf{FV}(B)$ *and* $\varsigma = \mathsf{tsort}(A)$.
  $\to$ *associates to the right, that is,* $A \to B \to C$ *stands for* $A \to (B \to C)$.
- $*_0 = *$ *and* $*_{i+1} = * \to *_i$.
- *Given names for declarations* $\delta^{v_1}, \ldots, \delta^{v_n}$, *define:* $\Delta^{v_1,\ldots,v_n} = \delta^{v_1},\ldots,\delta^{v_n}$.

Definition 8 (Pieces of Syntax Used in Intersection Types). *The translations use the* y_j*'s to represent type variables, use the* x_i*'s to build type-choice combinators, and use the* z_q^j*'s as variables restricted to range over type-choice combinators. We implement these specialized purposes by using the declarations, restrictions, and terms defined for* $i, j \in \mathbb{N}$ *and* $q \in \mathbb{N}_1$ *by:*

$$\begin{array}{lll} \delta^{y_j} & = & y_j^{\Box} \diamond : * \\ \delta^{x_i} & = & x_i^{\Box} \diamond : * \\ P_{i,q} & = & \lambda\delta^{x_1}.\cdots.\lambda\delta^{x_q}.\,x_i \qquad \textit{where } i \in 1..q \quad (P \textit{ for ``projection''}) \\ \rho^{P_{\cdot\cdot q}} & = & \overline{\in}\{P_{1,q},\ldots,P_{q,q}\} \\ \delta^{z_q^j} & = & z_q^{j\Box}\,\rho^{P_{\cdot\cdot q}} : *_q \\ \gamma^{z_q^j} & = & \mathsf{rdec}(\delta^{z_q^j}) \quad = \quad z_q^j\,\rho^{P_{\cdot\cdot q}} \end{array}$$

We are ready to define intersection types in the f-cube. We only take the intersection of terms whose degree is 1 and hence whose required sort is $\Box$ (these terms correspond to types). From Definition 8, $z_q^j\,\rho^{P_{\cdot\cdot q}}$ is $z_q^j\,\overline{\in}\{P_{1,q},\ldots,P_{q,q}\}$ and hence whichever $P_{i,q}$ is chosen from $\overline{\in}\{P_{1,q},\ldots,P_{q,q}\}$ for z_q^j, we get $(z_q^j\,A_1\cdots A_q) =_\beta A_i$ and we see that $\Pi\,\delta^{z_q^j}.(z_q^j\,A_1\cdots A_q)$ is the intersection of $A_1,\cdots,A_q$.

Definition 9 (Intersection Types in the f-cube). *Given Δ-terms $A_1,\ldots,$ A_q where $q \in \mathbb{N}_1$ and $\sharp(A_1) = \cdots = \sharp(A_q) = 1$, the intersection of $A_1,\ldots,A_q$ is defined as:*

$$\sqcap\{A_1,\ldots,A_q\} \;=\; \Pi\,\delta^{z_q^j}.(z_q^j\,A_1\cdots A_q) \quad \text{where } z_q^j \notin \mathsf{FV}(A_i) \text{ for } i \in 1..q.$$

Definition 10 (Syntax Abbreviations for Intersection Types).
- *For translations that use only y_0 from the y's, let: $y = y_0$ and $\delta^y = \delta^{y_0}$.*
- *For examples that use only one of the z's at a particular arity $q \in \mathbb{N}_1$, let:* $z_q = z_q^0 \qquad \delta^{z_q} = \delta^{z_q^0} \qquad \gamma^{z_q} = \gamma^{z_q^0}.$
- *Let* $\overline{A} = A \to A$ $\ \widetilde{A} = \overline{A} \to A$ $\ \underline{A} = (A \to \widetilde{A}) = A \to ((A \to A) \to A)$ $\overline{A}^0 = A$ *and* $\overline{A}^{i+1} = \overline{\overline{A}^i}$ $\ \underline{A}_0 = A$ *and* $\underline{A}_{i+1} = \underline{\underline{A}_i}$.

The following lemma sets a type-building toolkit to be used in our examples. Its proof is straightforward using the machinery of PTSs.

Lemma 1 (Type-Building Toolkit for Examples). *The following hold:*
1. *For $i,j \in \mathbb{N}$ and $q \in \mathbb{N}_1$, $\varepsilon \vdash *_i : \Box$; $\varepsilon \vdash P_{i,q} : *_q$ for $i \in 1..q$; $\delta^{z_q^j} \vdash z_q^j : *_q$.*
2. *If Δ is legal and $u^\varsigma\,\rho : A \in \Delta$, then $\Delta \vdash u^\varsigma : A : \varsigma$.*
3. *Let $j \in \mathbb{N}$, let $i \in \mathbb{N}_1$, let $n \in 1..i$, and let $u_1,\ldots,u_n \in \{y_k \mid k \in \mathbb{N}\}$. Suppose for $l \in 1..n$ that $A_l \in \{u_l, \overline{u_l}\}$. Let Δ be legal such that $\delta^{z_i^j} \in \Delta$ and for all $l \in 1..n$, $\delta^{u_l} \in \Delta$. Then $\Delta \vdash z_i^j A_1 \ldots A_n : *_{i-n} : \Box$.*
4. *If $q \in \mathbb{N}_1$, and $\Delta \vdash A : *_q$, and $\Delta \vdash B_i : *$ for $i \in [0..q)$, then for $j \in [0..q)$ it holds that $\Delta \vdash A\,B_0 \cdots B_j : *_{q-(j+1)}$.*
5. *If $\Delta \vdash A : *$ and $\Delta \vdash B : *$ then $\Delta \vdash A \to B : *$.*
6. *If $\Delta \vdash A : *$ and $i \in \mathbb{N}$ then $\Delta \vdash \overline{A}^i : *$ and $\Delta \vdash \underline{A}_i : *$ and $\Delta \vdash \widetilde{A} : *$.*

4.1 Simple Examples

Definition 11 (Needed Terms and Declarations). *Define the following:*

$U = z_2\,y\,\overline{y} \qquad \delta^u = u{:}U$ *where* $u \not\equiv z_2$ *and* $u \not\equiv y \qquad V = z_2\,\overline{y}\,\overline{y}^2$

$W' = (\lambda\delta^{z_2}.\lambda\delta^u.u) \qquad W = (\Pi\,\delta^{z_2}.\Pi\,\delta^u.U) = (\Pi\,\delta^{z_2}.(U \to U)) \qquad \delta^w = w{:}W$

Example 1 (Derivation Simulating Polymorphic Identity with Intersection Types). All the derivations in this example follow from Lemma 1 and the typing rules.

1. $\Delta^{y,z_2} \vdash U : *$ by Lemma 1.
2. $\Delta^{y,z_2,u} \vdash u : U$ by Lemma 1.
3. $\Delta^{y,z_2} \vdash (\lambda\delta^u.u) : (\Pi\,\delta^u.U) : *$ by (λ) and (app).
4. $\delta^y \vdash W' : W : *$ by (λ) and (app).

We have a polymorphic identity function W', but the type $W = \Pi\,\delta^{z_2}.\,(\Pi\,\delta^u.\,U) = \Pi\,\delta^{z_2}.\,(U \to U)$ doesn't look like an intersection type. Let's see if we can reach something that looks more like an intersection type instead.

5. Δ^{y,z_2} is legal
6. $\Delta^{y,z_2} \vdash y : *$ and $\Delta^{y,z_2} \vdash \overline{y} : *$ and $\Delta^{y,z_2} \vdash \overline{y}^2 : *$ by Lemma 1.
7. $\Delta^{y,z_2} \vdash z_2 : *_2$ and $\Delta^{y,z_2} \vdash V : *$ by Lemma 1.
8. $\forall i \in 1..2.\ (\Pi\,\delta^u.\,U)[z_2 := P_{i,2}] = (P_{i,2}\,y\,\overline{y}) \to (P_{i,2}\,y\,\overline{y}) =_\beta \overline{y}^2 =_\beta (P_{i,2}\,\overline{y}\,\overline{y}^2) = V[z_2 := P_{i,2}]$
9. $\forall i \in 1..2.\ \varepsilon \Vdash (\Pi\,\delta^u.\,U)[z_2 := P_{i,2}]\,\overline{\in}\{V[z_2 := P_{i,2}]\}$ by (ref) of Fig. 4.
10. $\gamma^{z_2} \Vdash \Pi\,\delta^u.\,U\,\overline{\in}\{V\}$ by (ctR) of Fig. 4.
11. $\Delta^{y,z_2} \vdash (\lambda\delta^u.\,u) : V : *$ by 3., 10., and (conv).
12. $\delta^y \vdash W' : (\Pi\,\delta^{z_2}.\,V) : *$ by 11., and (λ).

The result type here looks better: $\Pi\,\delta^{z_2}.\,V = \Pi\,\delta^{z_2}.\,(z_2\,\overline{y}\,\overline{y}^2) = \bar{\cap}\{\overline{y}, \overline{y}^2\}$. It is more obvious that one can simply choose either $\overline{y}$ or $\overline{y}^2$, just like with the intersection type $\overline{y} \cap \overline{y}^2$. So what would that choice look like? Instantiating $\Pi\,\delta^{z_2}.\,V$ to either $\overline{y}$ or $\overline{y}^2$ goes like this:

13. δ^y is legal (as a context)
14. $\forall i \in 1..2.\ \delta^y \vdash P_{i,2} : *_2 : \square$ by Lemma 1 and (weak).
15. $\forall i \in 1..2.\ \varepsilon \Vdash P_{i,2}\,\overline{\in}\{P_{1,2}, P_{2,2}\}$ by (ref) of Fig. 4.
16. $\forall i \in 1..2.\ \mathsf{rdec}(\delta^y) \Vdash P_{i,2}\,\overline{\in}\{P_{1,2}, P_{2,2}\}$ by (ctR) of Fig. 4.
17. $\forall i \in 1..2.\ \delta^y \vdash (\lambda\delta^u.\,u)[z_2 := P_{i,2}] : V[z_2 := P_{i,2}] : *$ by 11., 15., substitution.
18. $\forall i \in 1..2.\ (\lambda\delta^u.\,u)[z_2 := P_{i,2}] = (\lambda u{:}(P_{i,2}\,y\,\overline{y}).\,u) \to_\beta (\lambda u{:}\overline{y}^{i-1}.\,u)$
19. $\forall i \in 1..2.\ V[z_2 := P_{i,2}] = (P_{i,2}\,\overline{y}\,\overline{y}^2) \to_\beta \overline{y}^i$
20. $\forall i \in 1..2.\ \delta^y \vdash (\lambda u{:}\overline{y}^{i-1}.\,u) : \overline{y}^i : *$ by 17., 18., 19., and subject reduction.

So both 4., and 12., above are roughly like $(\lambda u.\,u) : \overline{y} \cap \overline{y}^2$ with intersection types and the instantiations are like $(\lambda u.\,u) : \overline{y}$ and $(\lambda u.\,u) : \overline{y}^2$.

Example 2 (Derivation for $(\lambda w.\,w\,w)\,(\lambda u.\,u)$ in Intersection Types Style). We make use of 1., 4., 14., and 15. of Example 1 in the following.

21. $\delta^y \vdash W : * : \square$ by 1., of Example 1.
22. $\Delta^{y,w} \vdash w : W : *$ by 21., & (start).
23. $\Delta^{y,w}$ is legal by 22., & Definition 4.
24. $\forall i \in 1..2.\ \Delta^{y,w} \vdash P_{i,2} : *_2 : \square$ by 23., & 14., of Example 1
25. $\forall i \in 1..2.\ \mathsf{rdec}(\Delta^{y,w}) \Vdash P_{i,2}\,\overline{\in}\{P_{1,2}, P_{2,2}\}$ by 16., of Example 1.
26. $\forall i \in 1..2.\ \Delta^{y,w} \vdash w\,P_{i,2} : (\Pi\delta^u.U)[z_2 := P_{i,2}] : *$ by 22., 24., 25., & (app).
27. $\forall i \in 1..2.\ \Delta^{y,w} \vdash w\,P_{i,2} : (\Pi\,u{:}(P_{i,2}\,y\,\overline{y}).\,(P_{i,2}\,y\,\overline{y})) : *$ by 26.
28. $\Delta^{y,w} \vdash w\,P_{1,2} : \overline{y} : *$ by 27.
29. $\Delta^{y,w} \vdash w\,P_{2,2} : \overline{y} \to \overline{y} : *$ by 27.
30. $\Delta^{y,w} \vdash (w\,P_{2,2}\,(w\,P_{1,2})) : \overline{y} : *$ by 28., 29., & (app)
31. $\delta^y \vdash (\lambda\delta^w.\,w\,P_{2,2}\,(w\,P_{1,2})) : W \to \overline{y} : *$ by 30., & (λ)
32. $\delta^y \vdash (\lambda\delta^w.\,w\,P_{2,2}\,(w\,P_{1,2}))\,W' : \overline{y} : *$ by 4., of Example 1, 31.

This is the equivalent of typing $(\lambda w.\,w\,w)\,(\lambda u.\,u)$ with intersection types.

4.2 Typing Urzyczyn's Untypable Term

Urzyczyn [17] proved $\dot{U} = (\lambda r.\, h(r(\lambda f \lambda s.\, f\, s))(r(\lambda q.\lambda g.\, g\, q)))(\lambda o.\, o\, o\, o)$ is untypable in F_ω. [9] proved every pure λ-term is typable in F_ω iff it is typable in the λ-cube. Hence $\dot{U}$ is untypable in the λ-cube. This section types $\dot{U}$ in the f-cube by using finite-set declarations.

Definition 12 (Terms of Type $*$ and Sort $\Box$ for Urzyczyn's Term).

$$
\begin{array}{ll}
F = z_3\, \overline{y}^3\, \overline{y}^2\, \overline{y} & Q = z_3\, \underline{y}\, y\, \underline{y} \\
S = z_3\, \overline{y}^2\, \overline{y}^1\, y & G = z_3\, \underset{\sim}{\underline{y}_2}\, \overline{y}\, \overline{(\underline{y})} \\
 & M = z_3\, (\underline{y})\, y\, \underline{y} \\
B = F \to S \to S & A = Q \to G \to M \\
E_1 = \overline{y}^4 & D_1 = \underline{y} \to \underline{y}_2 \to \widetilde{(\underline{y})} \\
E_2 = \overline{y}^3 & D_2 = \underline{y} \\
E_3 = \overline{y}^2 & D_3 = \underline{y}_2 \\
E = \Pi\, \delta^{z_3}.\, B & D = \Pi \delta^{z_3}.A \\
C_1 = \overline{y}^2 & R' = O \to C \\
C_2 = \widetilde{(\underline{y})} & R_1 = E \to C_1 \\
C = z_2\, C_1\, C_2 & R_2 = D \to C_2 \\
O = z_2\, E\, D & R = \Pi \delta^{z_2}.R'
\end{array}
$$

The proof of the following lemma is straightforward from the typing rules.

Lemma 2. *Let $H \in \{F, S, B, Q, G, M, A\}$ and $J \in \{E, D, R\}$. The following hold: $\delta^y, \delta^{z_3} \vdash H : *$ and $\delta^y \vdash J : *$ and $\delta^y, \delta^{z_2} \vdash C : *$ and $\delta^y, \delta^{z_2} \vdash R' : *$.*

Example 3 (Viewing E, D, and R as Intersection Types).

E	$= \Pi\delta^{z_3}.\ F$	$\to S$	$\to S$			
$\mathsf{nf}(B[z_3 :=P_{1,3}])$	$=\ \overline{y}^3$	$\to \overline{y}^2$	$\to \overline{y}^2$	$=\overline{y}^4$	$=E_1$
$\mathsf{nf}(B[z_3 :=P_{2,3}])$	$=\ \overline{y}^2$	$\to \overline{y}^1$	$\to \overline{y}^1$	$=\overline{y}^3$	$=E_2$
$\mathsf{nf}(B[z_3 :=P_{3,3}])$	$=\ \overline{y}$	$\to y$	$\to y$	$=\overline{y}^2$	$=E_3$
D	$= \Pi\delta^{z_3}.\ Q$	$\to G$	$\to M$		
$\mathsf{nf}(A[z_3 :=P_{1,3}])$	$=\ \underline{y}$	$\to \underline{y}_2$	$\to \widetilde{(\underline{y})}$		$\dot{=}D_1$
$\mathsf{nf}(A[z_3 :=P_{2,3}])$	$=\ y$	$\to \overline{y}$	$\to y$	$=\underline{y}$	$=D_2$
$\mathsf{nf}(A[z_3 :=P_{3,3}])$	$=\ \underline{y}$	$\to \overline{(\underline{y})}$	$\to \underline{y}$	$=\underline{y}_2$	$=D_3$
R	$= \Pi\delta^{z_2}.\ O$	$\to C$			
$\mathsf{nf}(R'[z_2 :=P_{1,2}])$	$=\ E$	$\to C_1$			$=R_1$
$\mathsf{nf}(R'[z_2 :=P_{2,2}])$	$=\ D$	$\to C_2$			$=R_2$

Consider the type E and its component types F and S which we list in separate columns in the table above. Both F and S act like tuples of 3 types. The restriction in the declaration of z_3 forces whatever replaces z_3 to simply pick one of the three types. By looking at the above table, we see that the column with F at the top lists the components of F in the three rows below, and the columns with S at the top work similarly. The first row lists E and the three rows below list the results of the three possible instantiations of E. In effect, E works like the intersection type $\overline{y}^4 \cap \overline{y}^3 \cap \overline{y}^2 = E_1 \cap E_2 \cap E_3$.

The same argument shows that the type D works like the intersection type $D_1 \cap D_2 \cap D_3$ and that the type R works like the intersection type $R_1 \cap R_2$.

Definition 13 (Declarations for Urzyczyn's Term). *Let* $\delta^h = h{:}(C_1 \to C_2 \to y)$; $\delta^r = r{:}R$; $\delta^o = o{:}O$; $\delta^f = f{:}F$; $\delta^s = s{:}S$; $\delta^q = q{:}Q$; *and* $\delta^g = g{:}G$.

Definition 14 (Terms of Sort $*$ for Urzyczyn's Term). *Let*
$T = \lambda\delta^{z_3}.\lambda\delta^f.\lambda\delta^s.f\,s$ $\quad J = \lambda\delta^{z_3}.\lambda\delta^q.\lambda\delta^g.g\,q$ $\quad L = h\,(r\ P_{1,2}\,T)\,(r\ P_{2,2}\,J)$
$V = \lambda\delta^{z_2}.\lambda\delta^o.o\ P_{1,3}\,(o\ P_{2,3})\,(o\ P_{3,3})$ $\quad U = (\lambda\delta^r.L)\,V$

Again the following lemma is straightforward according to the typing rules.

Lemma 3. *The following hold:*

1. (a) $\gamma^{z_3} \Vdash F \,\overline{\in}\, \{S \to S\}$
   (b) $\gamma^{z_3} \Vdash G \,\overline{\in}\, \{Q \to M\}$,
   (c) $\gamma^{z_2} \Vdash O \,\overline{\in}\, \{\Pi\delta^{z_3}.(z_2\ B\ A)\}$
2. $\delta^y \vdash T : E : *$.
3. $\delta^y \vdash J : D : *$.
4. (a) $\Delta^{y,z_2,o} \vdash (o\ P_{i,3}) : (z_2\ E_i\ D_i) : *$ *for* $i \in \{1,2,3\}$.
   (b) $\Delta^{y,z_2,o} \vdash (o\,P_{1,3})(o\,P_{2,3})(o\,P_{3,3}) : C : *$.
   (c) $\delta^y \vdash V : R : *$.
5. (a) $\Delta^{y,h,r} \vdash (r\ P_{i,2}) : R_i : *$ *for* $i \in \{1,2\}$.
   (b) $\Delta^{y,h,r} \vdash (r\ P_{1,2}\ T) : C_1 : *$.
   (c) $\Delta^{y,h,r} \vdash (r\ P_{2,2}\ J) : C_2 : *$.
6. $\Delta^{y,h,r} \vdash L : y : *$ *and* $\Delta^{y,h} \vdash \lambda\delta^r.L : \Pi\delta^r.y : *$.
7. $\Delta^{y,h} \vdash U : y : *$.

Now we show that Urzyczyn's famous term is typable in the f-cube.

Example 4 (Urzyczyn's Term Is Typable). Clearly, Urzyczyn's term $\dot{U} = \mathsf{TE}(U)$. Since Lemma 3.7 shows that $\Delta^{y,h} \vdash U : y : *$, then by Definition 6, $\dot{U}$ is typable.

5 Conclusion

In this paper we introduced an extension of the PTS λ-cube using finite set declarations that allow us to translate intersection types as λ-terms. We gave the translation of Urzyczyn's famous term U (which is untypable in the λ-cube) in the f-cube and showed that this term is indeed typable in the f-cube. The set up and machinery presented in this paper can be followed to prove that the f-cube characterizes all strongly normalising terms.

References

1. Barendregt, H.P.: Lambda calculi with types. In: Abramsky, S., Gabbay, D.M., Maibaum, T.S.E. (eds.) Handbook of Logic in Computer Science, vol. 2. Oxford University Press, Oxford (1992)
2. Berardi, S.: Type dependency and constructive mathematics. Ph.D. thesis, Carnegie Mellon University and Università di Torino (1990)
3. Bloo, R., Kamareddine, F., Nederpelt, R.: The Barendregt cube with definitions and generalised reduction. Inform. Comput. **126**(2), 123–143 (1996)
4. Bono, V., Venneri, B., Bettini, L.: A typed lambda calculus with intersection types. Theoret. Comput. Sci. **398**, 95–113 (2008)
5. Capitani, B., Loreti, M., Venneri, B.: Hyperformulae, parallel deductions and intersection types. Electron. Notes Theor. Comput. Sci. **50**, 178–195 (2001). Proceedings of ICALP 2001 workshop: Bohm's Theorem: Applications to Computer Science Theory (BOTH 2001), Crete, Greece, 2001-07-13
6. Compagnoni, A.B., Pierce, B.C.: Higher-order intersection types and multiple inheritance. Math. Structures Comput. Sci. **6**(5), 469–501 (1996)
7. Coppo, M., Dezani-Ciancaglini, M.: An extension of the basic functionality theory for the λ-calculus. Notre Dame J. Formal Logic **21**(4), 685–693 (1980)
8. Dunfield, J.: Elaborating intersection and union types. J. Funct. Program. **24**(2–3) (2014)
9. Giannini, P., Honsell, F., Ronchi Della Rocca, S.: Type inference: some results, some problems. Fund. Inform. **19**(1/2), 87–125 (1993)
10. Liquori, L., Ronchi Della Rocca, S.: Intersection-types à la Church. Inf. Comput. **205**(9), 1371–1386 (2007)
11. Oliveira, B.D., Shi, Z., Alpuim, J.: Disjoint intersection types. In: Proceedings of ICFP (2016)
12. Pottinger, G.: A type assignment for the strongly normalizable λ-terms. In: Hindley, J.R., Seldin, J.P. (eds.) To H. B. Curry: Essays on Combinatory Logic, Lambda Calculus, and Formalism. Academic Press (1980)
13. Della Rocca, S.R., Roversi, L.: Intersection logic. In: Fribourg, L. (ed.) CSL 2001. LNCS, vol. 2142, pp. 414–429. Springer, Heidelberg (2001). https://doi.org/10.1007/3-540-44802-0_29
14. Ronchi Della Rocca, S.: Intersection typed lambda-calculus. Intersection Types and Related Systems, ITRS 2002. Electronic Notes in Theoretical Computer Science, vol. 70, pp. 163–181 (2002)
15. Severi, P., Poll, E.: Pure type systems with definitions. In: Nerode, A., Matiyasevich, Y.V. (eds.) LFCS 1994. LNCS, vol. 813, pp. 316–328. Springer, Heidelberg (1994). https://doi.org/10.1007/3-540-58140-5_30
16. Terlouw, J.: Een nadere bewijstheoretische analyse van GSTT's. Manuscript (1989)
17. Urzyczyn, P.: Type reconstruction in F_ω. Math. Struct. Comput. Sci. **7**(4) (1997)
18. van Oostrom, V.: Confluence for Abstract and Higher-Order Rewriting. Ph.D. thesis, Vrije Universiteit Amsterdam (1994)
19. Venneri, B.: Intersection types as logical formulae. J. Logic Comput. **4**(2), 109–124 (1994)
20. Wells, J.B., Dimock, A., Muller, R., Turbak, F.: A calculus with polymorphic and polyvariant flow types. J. Funct. Program. **12**(3), 183–227 (2002)
21. Wells, J.B., Haack, C.: Branching types. In: Le Métayer, D. (ed.) ESOP 2002. LNCS, vol. 2305, pp. 115–132. Springer, Heidelberg (2002). https://doi.org/10.1007/3-540-45927-8_9

Syntactic Concept Lattice Models for Infinitary Action Logic

Stepan L. Kuznetsov[1,2](✉)

[1] Steklov Mathematical Institute of RAS, 8 Gubkina Street, Moscow, Russia
sk@mi-ras.ru

[2] HSE University, 11 Pokrovsky Blvd., Moscow, Russia

Abstract. We introduce models for infinitary action logic, i.e., the infinitary extension of multiplicative-additive Lambek calculus with the Kleene star, on syntactic concept lattices. This semantics is a variant of language semantics, which is in a sense more natural from the linguistic point of view. Extending the argument of Wurm (2017), we prove completeness for the whole infinitary action logic, while standard language models enjoy completeness only for small fragments of this system. As a corollary, we obtain completeness of infinitary action logic w.r.t. action lattices which are complete in the lattice-theoretic sense.

Keywords: Infinitary action logic · Syntactic concept lattices · Lambek calculus · Completeness

1 Introduction

The *Lambek calculus* was introduced by Lambek [21] in 1958 to provide a mathematical description of natural language syntactic structures. From the point of view of algebraic logic, the Lambek calculus is the logic of partially ordered semigroups with residual operations (divisions). Thus, the principal operations of the Lambek calculus are $\cdot$ (product), $\backslash$ (left division), and $/$ (right division). If the partial order forms a lattice structure, then its meet ($\wedge$) and join ($\vee$) operations may be added to the language, along with constants $\mathbf{1}$ (unit for product) and $\mathbf{0}$ (the least element, also zero for product). This results in the *multiplicative-additive Lambek calculus* (**MALC**), also called the *bounded full Lambek calculus* (see [1,9,12,22]), which is the algebraic logic of *bounded residuated lattices.*

Yet another extension of **MALC** is obtained by adding the iteration operation, or *Kleene star.* Bounded residuated lattices extended with Kleene star are called *action lattices* (or *residuated Kleene lattices*). This notion goes back to the works of Pratt [26] and Kozen [16], who also introduced *action logic* (**ACT**)—the logic of action lattices, where Kleene star is axiomatised as a least fixpoint:

$$a^* = \min\{b \mid \mathbf{1} \vee a \cdot b \leq b\}.$$

Later, Buszkowski [5] and Palka [23] introduced a stronger system called *infinitary action logic* ($\mathbf{ACT}_\omega$). In $\mathbf{ACT}_\omega$ Kleene star is axiomatised by an ω-rule.

G. Metcalfe et al. (Eds.): WoLLIC 2024, LNCS 14672, pp. 93–107, 2024.
https://doi.org/10.1007/978-3-031-62687-6_7

Algebraically, this corresponds to considering a narrower class of action lattices, so-called $*$-*continuous* ones, where Kleene star is defined as follows:

$$a^* = \sup\{a^n \mid n \geq 0\}.$$

The condition of $*$-continuity reflects the original language-theoretic notion of Kleene star, so throughout this paper we shall focus on $\mathbf{ACT}_\omega$ rather than $\mathbf{ACT}$.

The sequent-style formulation of $\mathbf{ACT}_\omega$, given by Palka [23], is as follows. Formulae are built from variables and constants $\mathbf{0}$ and $\mathbf{1}$ using the aforementioned operations: $\cdot$, $\backslash$, $/$, $\wedge$, $\vee$, and * (here the last operation is unary, written in the postfix form, all other operations are binary).[1] Sequents are expressions of the form $A_1, \ldots, A_n \to B$, where $n \geq 0$ and $A_1, \ldots, A_n, B$ are formulae. Formulae are denoted by capital Latin letters. Capital Greek letters are used for sequences of formulae; A^n is the sequence of n copies of A. Axioms and inference rules of $\mathbf{ACT}_\omega$ are those of $\mathbf{MALC}$, plus two rules for Kleene star:[2]

$$\frac{}{A \to A}\ \mathrm{Id} \qquad \frac{}{\Gamma, \mathbf{0}, \Delta \to C}\ \mathbf{0}\mathrm{L} \qquad \frac{\Gamma, \Delta \to C}{\Gamma, \mathbf{1}, \Delta \to C}\ \mathbf{1}\mathrm{L} \qquad \frac{}{\to \mathbf{1}}\ \mathbf{1}\mathrm{R}$$

$$\frac{\Pi \to A \quad \Gamma, B, \Delta \to C}{\Gamma, \Pi, A \backslash B, \Delta \to C}\ \backslash\mathrm{L} \qquad \frac{A, \Pi \to B}{\Pi \to A \backslash B}\ \backslash\mathrm{R} \qquad \frac{\Gamma, A, B, \Delta \to C}{\Gamma, A \cdot B, \Delta \to C}\ \cdot\mathrm{L}$$

$$\frac{\Pi \to A \quad \Gamma, B, \Delta \to C}{\Gamma, B / A, \Pi, \Delta \to C}\ /\mathrm{L} \qquad \frac{\Pi, A \to B}{\Pi \to B / A}\ /\mathrm{R} \qquad \frac{\Gamma \to A \quad \Delta \to B}{\Gamma, \Delta \to A \cdot B}\ \cdot\mathrm{R}$$

$$\frac{\Gamma, A, \Delta \to C}{\Gamma, A \wedge B, \Delta \to C} \quad \frac{\Gamma, B, \Delta \to C}{\Gamma, A \wedge B, \Delta \to C}\ \wedge\mathrm{L} \qquad \frac{\Pi \to A \quad \Pi \to B}{\Pi \to A \wedge B}\ \wedge\mathrm{R}$$

$$\frac{\Gamma, A, \Delta \to C \quad \Gamma, B, \Delta \to C}{\Gamma, A \vee B, \Delta \to C}\ \vee\mathrm{L} \qquad \frac{\Pi \to A}{\Pi \to A \vee B} \quad \frac{\Pi \to B}{\Pi \to A \vee B}\ \vee\mathrm{R}$$

$$\frac{\left(\Gamma, A^n, \Delta \to C\right)_{n=0}^{\infty}}{\Gamma, A^*, \Delta \to C}\ {*}\mathrm{L}_\omega \qquad \frac{\Pi_1 \to A \quad \ldots \quad \Pi_n \to A}{\Pi_1, \ldots, \Pi_n \to A^*}\ {*}\mathrm{R}_n,\ n \geq 0$$

[1] In some presentations of the bounded full Lambek calculus, like Wurm's one [30], there is also the "top" constant $\top$ for the maximal element of the residuated lattice. However, it is easily expressible using zero: $\top = \mathbf{0} / \mathbf{0}$, so we omit it.

[2] Throughout this paper, we consider the version of the Lambek calculus which has the unit constant and allows empty left-hand sides of sequents. Some linguistic applications motivate considering the calculus with so-called "Lambek's non-emptiness restriction" (all left-hand sides must be non-empty), which was used in Lambek's original work [21]. This version can be extended with a modification of Kleene star, namely, Kleene plus (positive iteration), and results of the present paper will generally keep valid. We refrain from considering this version, due to space constraints.

$$\frac{\Pi \to A \quad \Gamma, A, \Delta \to C}{\Gamma, \Pi, \Delta \to C} \text{ Cut}$$

The $*\mathrm{L}_\omega$ rule has infinitary many premises—it is an ω-rule. Thus, derivations in $\mathbf{ACT}_\omega$ may be infinite, but are required to be well-founded (each path from the goal sequent should reach an axiom in finitely many steps). For "pure" derivability (theoremhood), the cut elimination theorem holds [23]. However, we shall also consider derivations from sets of hypotheses (non-logical axioms), where the presence of Cut is essential. Sets of hypotheses also may be infinite, and compactness does not hold (e.g., $p^* \to q$ is derivable from the set $\{ \to q; p \to q; p^2 \to q; \ldots\}$, but not from any of its finite subsets).

The original linguistic motivation of the Lambek calculus suggest the following semantics, called language models, or *L-models*. Given an alphabet Σ (usually finite, but this is not required), each variable is interpreted as a formal language over Σ by a valuation function $\alpha\colon \mathrm{Var} \to \mathcal{P}(\Sigma^*)$. This forms an L-model as a pair $\mathcal{M} = (\mathcal{P}(\Sigma^*), \alpha)$. The valuation function is then propagated to arbitrary formulae, yielding the interpretation function $\bar{\alpha}$:

$$\begin{aligned}
&\bar{\alpha}(p) = \alpha(p), \text{ where } p \text{ is a variable;}\\
&\bar{\alpha}(\mathbf{1}) = \{\varepsilon\} \ (\varepsilon \text{ is the empty word}); \qquad \bar{\alpha}(\mathbf{0}) = \varnothing;\\
&\bar{\alpha}(A \cdot B) = \bar{\alpha}(A) \cdot \bar{\alpha}(B) = \{uv \mid u \in \bar{\alpha}(A), v \in \bar{\alpha}(B)\};\\
&\bar{\alpha}(A \setminus B) = \bar{\alpha}(A) \setminus \bar{\alpha}(B) = \{v \in \Sigma^* \mid (\forall u \in \bar{\alpha}(A))\, uv \in \bar{\alpha}(B)\};\\
&\bar{\alpha}(B \,/\, A) = \bar{\alpha}(B) \,/\, \bar{\alpha}(A) = \{u \in \Sigma^* \mid (\forall v \in \bar{\alpha}(A))\, uv \in \bar{\alpha}(B)\};\\
&\bar{\alpha}(A \wedge B) = \bar{\alpha}(A) \cap \bar{\alpha}(B); \qquad \bar{\alpha}(A \vee B) = \bar{\alpha}(A) \cup \bar{\alpha}(B);\\
&\bar{\alpha}(A^*) = \bar{\alpha}(A)^* = \{u_1 \ldots u_n \mid n \geq 0; u_1, \ldots, u_n \in \bar{\alpha}(A)\}.
\end{aligned}$$

A sequent of the form $A_1, \ldots, A_n \to B$ is true in this L-model, $\mathcal{M} \models A_1, \ldots, A_n \to B$, if $\bar{\alpha}(A_1) \cdot \ldots \cdot \bar{\alpha}(A_n) \subseteq \bar{\alpha}(B)$. For $n = 0$ the truth definition is different: $\mathcal{M} \models \ \to B$, if $\varepsilon \in \bar{\alpha}(B)$.

The calculus **MALC** and its extension $\mathbf{ACT}_\omega$ is *strongly sound* w.r.t. L-models. Namely, if a sequent $\Pi \to B$ is derivable from a set of hypotheses $\mathcal{H}$ (denoted by $\mathcal{H} \vdash \Pi \to B$), then for any L-model $\mathcal{M}$ the following holds:

$$((\forall (\Gamma \to A) \in \mathcal{H})\ \mathcal{M} \models \Gamma \to A) \Rightarrow \mathcal{M} \models \Pi \to B;$$

in other words, $\Pi \to B$ is semantically entailed by $\mathcal{H}$ on the class of L-models. The latter is briefly denoted by $\mathcal{H} \models \Pi \to B$.

The opposite implication, if $\mathcal{H} \models \Pi \to B$, then $\mathcal{H} \vdash \Pi \to B$, is called *strong completeness*. *Weak completeness* is completeness without hypotheses: if $\Pi \to B$ is true in any $\mathcal{M}$, then it is derivable. Unlike soundness, completeness holds only for specific fragments, but not for $\mathbf{ACT}_\omega$ or even **MALC** in whole. On one hand, there are the following known completeness results.

1. The fragment of **MALC** with only $\setminus$, $/$, and $\wedge$ is strongly complete w.r.t. L-models, as follows from the construction by Buszkowski [3]. Below (Sect. 3) we

shall extend this result to the fragment of $\backslash$, $/$, $\wedge$, and *, with a restriction that Kleene star is allowed only in denominators of divisions (i.e., in subformulae of the form $A^* \backslash B$ and B / A^*).[3]
2. As proved by Pentus [24,25], the fragment of **MALC** with $\backslash$, $/$, and $\cdot$ (i.e., the Lambek calculus) is weakly complete w.r.t. L-models. Strong completeness in the presence of product does not hold [6]. Weak completeness with four connectives, $\backslash$, $/$, $\cdot$, and $\wedge$, is an open question.

At the same time, there are the following obstacles to completeness w.r.t. L-models, even in the weak sense.

1. In the presence of both $\wedge$ and $\vee$, L-models satisfy the distributivity law $(A \vee B) \wedge C \to (A \wedge C) \vee (B \wedge C)$, which is not derivable in **MALC**. Issues connected to distributivity also block weak completeness w.r.t. classes of distributive models in the fragments with the following sets of connectives: $\{\backslash, /, \vee\}$ [14] and $\{/, \cdot, \wedge, {}^*\}$ [18].
2. In the presence of at least one of the constants, $\mathbf{0}$ or $\mathbf{1}$, weak completeness also fails, as combinations like $\mathbf{1} / A$ and $\mathbf{0} / A$ obey certain structural rules from finite-valued logics, which are invalid in **MALC** (see [17]).

A modification of L-models, which fixes the aforementioned issues and enjoys completeness of the whole **MALC**, except for constant $\mathbf{0}$ (see Appendix), was proposed by Wurm [29,30]. Wurm introduced the notion of *syntactic concept lattices* (SCL) and interpretations of **MALC** on SCLs. The difference from L-models (which Wurm calls "canonical" L-models) is in the usage of a closure operator. Given a fixed language L_0, each language M in an SCL is extended to its closure, denoted by $M^{\rhd\lhd}$. This closure includes all words from M and also all words which appear in the same contexts w.r.t. L_0:

$$v \in M^{\rhd\lhd} \iff \forall (x, y) \in \Sigma^* \times \Sigma^* \left((\forall w \in M \; xwy \in L_0) \Rightarrow xvy \in L_0 \right).$$

(Accurate definitions of Wurm's SCL models are given in the next section.)

From the point of view of linguistic meaning of the Lambek calculus, models based on SCLs in fact seem more appropriate than L-models. In Lambek categorial grammars, formulae denote *syntactic types*, i.e., grammatic categories assigned to words and phrases. For example, *John*, *Mary*, or *the professor* receive syntactic type np, "noun phrase," and *loves* or *reads* are of type $(np \backslash s) / np$ which is the category of transitive verbs (s is for "sentence"). The interpretation of a syntactic category (Lambek formula) should be the set of all words and phrases of the given category: $\bar{\alpha}(np)$ is the set of all noun phrases, $\bar{\alpha}(s)$—of all sentences, $\bar{\alpha}((np \backslash s) / np)$—of all transitive verb groups, etc. Linguistic intuitions suggest, however, that if a word or phrase can appear exactly in the same contexts as words or phrases of type A, then it should also belong to type A. For example, *John* is a noun phrase and may appear in contexts like __ *loves Mary* or *Mary met* __ *yesterday*, etc. *Pete* may appear in the very same contexts, so

[3] The corresponding result for the variant of $\mathbf{ACT}_\omega$ with Lambek's non-emptiness restriction and Kleene plus instead of Kleene star was presented in [19].

it also should belong to the *np* type. The closure used in SCLs, with $L_0 = \alpha(s)$ being the set of all correct sentences, exactly augments the language for each type with such possible new words and phrases.

The aim of the present paper is to extend Wurm's SCL approach with Kleene star, i.e., from **MALC** to $\mathbf{ACT}_\omega$, as well as to present some new results on Wurm's models for **MALC**. The rest of the paper is organised as follows.

In Sect. 2 we give the definition of syntactic concept lattices and models upon them, in the language of $\mathbf{ACT}_\omega$. The corresponding correctness-of-definition statement for Kleene star (Proposition 1) is proved. In Sect. 3, we prove completeness of $\mathbf{ACT}_\omega$ without $\mathbf{0}$ w.r.t. SCL-models. Unlike Wurm, we prove strong completeness, for derivability/entailment from sets of hypotheses, possibly infinite ones. We also provide some interesting corollaries. Namely, we get strong completeness of $\mathbf{ACT}_\omega$ w.r.t. abstract algebraic models on residuated Kleene lattices which are complete as lattices. We get completeness w.r.t. L-models (in the original sense) for the fragment of $\mathbf{ACT}_\omega$ with $\backslash$, $/$, $\wedge$, and *, where Kleene star is allowed only in denominators. We also prove strong conservativity of $\mathbf{ACT}_\omega$ over **MALC** (recall that with hypotheses we do not have cut elimination).

Section 4 contains the reduction of SCL-models to a two-letter alphabet. This fixes the following gap: in the completeness proofs of Wurm and in the present paper's Sect. 3, the alphabets used in SCLs are infinite (countable), while in practical examples they are finite; the reduction yields completeness over two-letter alphabets. Finally, Sect. 5 contains a remark on SCL-models where the language L_0 is regular. We show that weak completeness still holds also for $\mathbf{ACT}_\omega$ (Wurm proves it for **MALC**), while strong completeness fails already for **MALC**, due to complexity reasons.

In the arguments, we face some issues with constants $\mathbf{0}$ and $\mathbf{1}$, so the results are formulated without one or both of them. In the Appendix, we discuss the issues with constants in more detail.

This paper focuses on the SCL variant of language models. Extending concept lattice versions of relational models, also considered by Wurm [30], to $\mathbf{ACT}_\omega$, is left for further study. Another species of semantics, based on powerset monoids (Σ^* is the free monoid) and closure operations, is phase semantics [10,11,13]. The study of phase semantics for $\mathbf{ACT}_\omega$, possibly connected to SCL semantics, is an interesting direction of further research.

2 Syntactic Concept Lattices

The notion of syntactic concept lattice (SCL) which we are going to recall in this section goes back to the works of Clark [7] and Wurm [29,30]. SCLs form a specific kind of concept lattices, the notion which is the core of *Formal Concept Analysis* (see [8,20,28]). Formal Concept Analysis is widely used in data science, including machine learning, data mining, knowledge representation, etc. The ideas of SCL are closely related to *distributional semantics,* an approach in structural linguistics which studies words and phrases by considering the contexts they could appear in.

Let us recall the definitions, extending them with Kleene star. SCL-models, as well as L-models, are a specific case of models on *$*$-continuous residuated Kleene lattices (RKL)*. Models on $*$-continuous RKLs are the most general algebraic models for $\mathbf{ACT}_\omega$.

Definition 1. *A $*$-continuous residuated Kleene lattice is a partially ordered algebraic structure* $(\mathbf{K}; \leq, \cdot, \backslash, /, \wedge, \vee, {}^*, 0, 1)$, *where*

1. $(\mathbf{K}; \leq, \wedge, \vee)$ *is a lattice with* 0 *being its least element;*
2. $(\mathbf{K}; \cdot, 1)$ *is a monoid;*
3. $\backslash$ *and* $/$ *are residuals of* $\cdot$ *w.r.t. the* $\leq$ *partial order:* $b \leq a \backslash c \Leftrightarrow a \cdot b \leq c \Leftrightarrow a \leq c \,/\, b$;
4. $a^* = \sup\{a^n \mid n \geq 0\}$.

It follows from the residuation condition that $(\mathbf{K}; \cdot, \vee)$ is a semiring. It is also well-known that $\wedge$, $\vee$, $\cdot$, * in such structures are monotone on both argument, and $\backslash$, $/$ are monotone on the numerator and antitone on the denominator. Finally, it is worth noticing that the standard (Kozen's [15]) definition of $*$-continuous Kleene algebra uses a stronger version of the $*$-continuity condition: $b \cdot a^* \cdot c = \sup\{b \cdot a^n \cdot c \mid n \geq 0\}$. In the presence of residuals, however, it follows from condition 4 of our Definition 1.

Definition 2. *A model $\mathcal{M}$ on a $*$-continuous RKL is defined using the interpretation function $\bar{\alpha}$ from formulae to elements of* $\mathbf{K}$, *which is defined arbitrarily on variables and commutes with the operations;* $\bar{\alpha}(\mathbf{0}) = 0, \bar{\alpha}(\mathbf{1}) = 1$. *A sequent* $A_1, \ldots, A_n \to B$ *is true in* $\mathcal{M}$ *if* $\bar{\alpha}(A_1) \cdot \ldots \cdot \bar{\alpha}(A_n) \leq \bar{\alpha}(B)$; *for* $n = 0$, $1 \leq \bar{\alpha}(B)$.

L-models are nothing but models on RKLs of formal languages, where $\mathbf{K} = \mathcal{P}(\Sigma^*)$ and the RKL operations are defined in the natural way.

Now let us define SCLs and SCL-models. We start with a fixed alphabet Σ and a language $L_0 \subseteq \Sigma^*$ and define two maps, ${}^{\triangleright} \colon \mathcal{P}(\Sigma^*) \to \mathcal{P}(\Sigma^* \times \Sigma^*)$ and ${}^{\triangleleft} \colon \mathcal{P}(\Sigma^* \times \Sigma^*) \to \mathcal{P}(\Sigma^*)$, as follows:

$$M^{\triangleright} = \{(x, y) \in \Sigma^* \times \Sigma^* \mid (\forall w \in M)\, xwy \in L_0\}, \text{ for } M \subseteq \Sigma^*;$$
$$C^{\triangleleft} = \{v \in \Sigma^* \mid (\forall (x, y) \in C)\, xvy \in L_0\}, \text{ for } C \subseteq \Sigma^* \times \Sigma^*.$$

It is easy to show that the composition of this two maps, $M \mapsto M^{\triangleright\triangleleft}$, is a closure operator, as well as the dual one: $C \mapsto C^{\triangleleft\triangleright}$. Closed languages (such that $M = M^{\triangleright\triangleleft}$) form elements of the syntactic concept lattice, denoted by $\mathcal{B}_{L_0}$. They are in the Galois correspondence (given by the pair of maps ${}^{\triangleright}$ and ${}^{\triangleleft}$) with closed *contexts* $C \subseteq \Sigma^* \times \Sigma^*$ (such that $C = C^{\triangleleft\triangleright}$).

The partial order on $\mathcal{B}_{L_0}$ is the same subset order ($M_1 \subseteq M_2$) as in the lattice of all formal languages over Σ. Since for $M_1, M_2 \in \mathcal{B}_{L_0}$ their intersection $M_1 \cap M_2$ is also a closed language, meet in $\mathcal{B}_{L_0}$ is intersection: $M_1 \sqcap M_2 = M_1 \cap M_2$. Join, however, is not union, as $M_1 \cup M_2$ may not be closed. In order to compute join, one needs to apply closure: $M_1 \sqcup M_2 = (M_1 \cup M_2)^{\triangleright\triangleleft}$.

The new lattice, $(\mathcal{B}_{L_0}, \sqcap, \sqcup)$, is not distributive anymore. This removes obstacles for completeness, which are connected with distributivity (see above).

Next, the remaining operations of RKL are defined. For divisions, it is easy to check that they keep the languages closed (namely, if M_2 is closed, then $M_1 \setminus M_2$ and $M_2 \,/\, M_1$ are also closed). Thus, $\setminus$ and $/$ are defined on $\mathcal{B}_{L_0}$ exactly as on $\mathcal{P}(\Sigma^*)$. Product and iteration may yield non-closed languages, so closure must be added, as we did for union: $M_1 \circ M_2 = (M_1 \cdot M_2)^{\rhd\lhd}$; $M^{\circledast} = (M^*)^{\rhd\lhd}$. Finally, zero and unit are also replaced by their closures: $\mathbb{0} = \varnothing^{\rhd\lhd}$ and $\mathbb{1} = \{\varepsilon\}^{\rhd\lhd}$. Again, these new zero and unit do not obey extra principles not derivable in **MALC**.

Proposition 1. *The algebraic structure* $(\mathcal{B}_{L_0}; \subseteq, \circ, \setminus, /, \sqcap, \sqcup, {}^{\circledast}, \mathbb{0}, \mathbb{1})$ *is a* $*$*-continuous RKL.*

Proof. The only new case, in comparison with Wurm [30], is Kleene star:

$$M^{\circledast} = \sup(\{\mathbb{1}\} \cup \{\underbrace{M \circ \ldots \circ M}_{n} \mid n \geq 1\}).$$

We shall also recall, however, the proof of associativity for $\circ$, by establishing a stronger statement:

$$(M_1 \circ M_2) \circ M_3 = (M_1 \cdot M_2 \cdot M_3)^{\rhd\lhd} = M_1 \circ (M_2 \circ M_3).$$

It is sufficient to prove the first equality: $((M_1 \cdot M_2)^{\rhd\lhd} \cdot M_3)^{\rhd\lhd} = (M_1 \cdot M_2 \cdot M_3)^{\rhd\lhd}$. On one hand, we have $M_1 \cdot M_2 \subseteq (M_1 \cdot M_2)^{\rhd\lhd}$, and by monotonicity of product and the closure operator $(M_1 \cdot M_2 \cdot M_3)^{\rhd\lhd} \subseteq ((M_1 \cdot M_2)^{\rhd\lhd} \cdot M_3)^{\rhd\lhd}$. Now let $v \in ((M_1 \cdot M_2)^{\rhd\lhd} \cdot M_3)^{\rhd\lhd}$, and let us show that $v \in (M_1 \cdot M_2 \cdot M_3)^{\rhd\lhd}$. Take such a pair (x, y) that for any $w = w_1 w_2 w_3 \in M_1 \cdot M_2 \cdot M_3$ ($w_i \in M_i$) we have $x w_1 w_2 w_3 y \in L_0$. For the pair $(x, w_3 y)$, the we also have $x w' w_3 y \in L_0$ for any $w' \in (M_1 \cdot M_2)^{\rhd\lhd}$. Therefore, $x w'' y$ belongs to L_0 for any word $w'' \in (M_1 \cdot M_2)^{\rhd\lhd} \cdot M_3$ (w'' is of the form $w' w_3$). Since $v \in ((M_1 \cdot M_2)^{\rhd\lhd} \cdot M_3)^{\rhd\lhd}$, we get $x v y \in L_0$. This concludes the proof of $v \in (M_1 \cdot M_2 \cdot M_3)^{\rhd\lhd}$.

By induction on n, we show that $(M_1 \circ M_2) \circ \ldots \circ M_n = (M_1 \cdot M_2 \cdot \ldots \cdot M_n)^{\rhd\lhd}$ for any n.

Now we have $M^{\circledast} = (M^*)^{\rhd\lhd}$, $\mathbb{1} = \{\varepsilon\}^{\rhd\lhd}$, and $\underbrace{M \circ \ldots \circ M}_{n} = (\underbrace{M \cdot \ldots \cdot M}_{n})^{\rhd\lhd}$ for each $n \geq 1$. By monotonicity of the closure operator we have:

$$\{\varepsilon\} \subseteq M^* \Rightarrow \mathbb{1} \subseteq M^{\circledast}; \qquad M^n \subseteq M^* \Rightarrow \underbrace{M \circ \ldots \circ M}_{n} \subseteq M^{\circledast}, \text{ for } n \geq 1.$$

Thus, $M^{\circledast}$ is an upper bound for $\{\mathbb{1}\} \cup \{\underbrace{M \circ \ldots \circ M}_{n} \mid n \geq 1\}$. Let us show that it is the supremum. Let $N \in \mathcal{B}_{L_0}$ be another upper bound, i.e., $\mathbb{1} \subseteq N$ and $\underbrace{M \circ \ldots \circ M}_{n} \subseteq N$ for each $n \geq 1$. We have the following:

$$\{\varepsilon\} \subseteq \mathbb{1} \subseteq N, \qquad M^n \subseteq \underbrace{M \circ \ldots \circ M}_{n} \subseteq N,$$

and therefore $M^* \subseteq N$. By monotonicity of the closure operator, and due to the fact that N is closed ($N \in \mathcal{B}_{L_0}$), we have $M^{\circledast} = (M^*)^{\rhd\lhd} \subseteq N^{\rhd\lhd} = N$, which is what we need. □

In the next section we prove strong completeness of $\mathbf{ACT}_\omega$ w.r.t. SCL-models.

3 Completeness Proof and Corollaries

The proof of completeness is based on the following representation theorem, which extends the corresponding construction of Wurm [30, Sect. 3].

Theorem 1. *For any $*$-continuous RKL over a set $\mathbf{K}$ there exist an alphabet Σ, a language $L_0 \subseteq \Sigma^*$, and an injective mapping $h \colon \mathbf{K} \to \mathcal{B}_{L_0}$, which preserves all operations and constants, except $\mathbf{0}$. In other words, any $*$-continuous RKL can be embedded into an appropriate SCL almost homomorphically (up to $\mathbf{0}$).*

Proof. The construction exactly resembles Wurm's one. Define two alphabets, $\overline{\Sigma} = \{\bar{b} \mid b \in \mathbf{K}\}$ and $\underline{\Sigma} = \{\underline{b} \mid b \in \mathbf{K}\}$, and let $\Sigma = \overline{\Sigma} \cup \underline{\Sigma}$.[4] For any word $w = \bar{b}_1 \dots \bar{b}_n \in \overline{\Sigma}^*$, let $w^\bullet = b_1 \cdot \ldots \cdot b_n$ (in $\mathbf{K}$). Next, we define the designated language L_0:

$$L_0 = \{w\underline{b}u \mid w, u \in \overline{\Sigma}^* \text{ and } w^\bullet \le b, u^\bullet \le 1 \text{ in } \mathbf{K}\}.$$

Finally, the needed mapping h is defined as follows, given $b \in \mathbf{K}$:

$$h(b) = \{(\varepsilon, \underline{b})\}^{\lhd} = \{w \in \Sigma^* \mid w\underline{b} \in L_0\}$$

(by definition of L_0 we have $h(b) \subseteq \overline{\Sigma}^*$ for all b).

Wurm proves that h is injective, commutes with all operations, except Kleene star, and correctly maps the constants [30, Prop. 7, Lem. 8, 9]. Moreover, Wurm shows that $w \in h(b) \Leftrightarrow w^\bullet \le b$ in $\mathbf{K}$, for any $w \in \overline{\Sigma}^*$ and $b \in \mathbf{K}$ [30, Lem. 6].

It remains to show that, for any $a \in \mathbf{K}$,

$$h(a^*) = \big(h(a)\big)^{\circledast}.$$

The $\supseteq$ inclusion is easier. Since $h(a^*)$ is closed and $\big(h(a)\big)^{\circledast}$ is the closure of $(h(a))^*$, it is sufficient to show that $(h(a))^* \subseteq h(a^*)$. Let $w = w_1 \dots w_n$, where $n \ge 0$, $w_i \in h(a)$. The latter yields $w_i^\bullet \le a$ in $\mathbf{K}$, whence $w^\bullet = w_1^\bullet \cdot \ldots \cdot w_n^\bullet \le a \cdot \ldots \cdot a \le a^*$ (in $\mathbf{K}$). Therefore, $w \in h(a^*)$.

For the $\subseteq$ inclusion, we take an arbitrary $w \in h(a^*)$ and prove that $w \in \big(h(a)\big)^{\circledast} = \big((h(a))^*\big)^{\rhd\lhd}$. By [30, Lem. 6] we have $w^\bullet \le a^*$. Take a pair $(x, y) \in \Sigma^* \times \Sigma^*$, such that for any $w' \in (h(a))^*$ we have $xw'y \in L_0$. We need to prove $xwy \in L_0$.

[4] Wurm uses the same set $\mathbf{K}$ instead of $\overline{\Sigma}$; we perform a renaming for clarity.

In particular, as $\overline{a}$ obviously belongs to $h(a)$, let us take $w' = \overline{a}^n$, for an arbitrary $n \geq 0$. Each word $x\overline{a}^n y$ should belong to L_0, thus, xy includes exactly one letter of the form $\underline{b}$; other letters belong to $\overline{\Sigma}$.

Consider two cases.

Case 1: $\underline{b}$ is in y, i.e., $y = y_1\underline{b}y_2$. By definition of L_0 we have $x^\bullet \cdot a^n \cdot y_1^\bullet = (x\overline{a}^n y_1)^\bullet \leq b$ in $\mathbf{K}$. Hence, $a^n \leq x^\bullet \setminus b \,/\, y_1^\bullet$ for any n, and therefore $w^\bullet \leq a^* \leq x^\bullet \setminus b \,/\, y_1^\bullet$, or $x^\bullet \cdot w^\bullet \cdot y_1^\bullet \leq b$. Moreover, $y_2^\bullet \leq 1$, whence $xwy = xwy_1\underline{b}y_2 \in L_0$.

Case 2: $\underline{b}$ is in x, i.e., $x = x_1\underline{b}x_2$. Using the same argument, as in Case 1, we prove $x_1^\bullet \leq b$ and $x_2^\bullet \cdot w^\bullet \cdot y^\bullet \leq 1$, whence $xwy = x_1\underline{b}x_2wy \in L_0$. □

Now we are ready to prove completeness. This completeness result strengthens Wurm's one [30, Thm. 4] in two ways. First, it includes Kleene star, i.e., features completeness for a broader, infinitary system $\mathbf{ACT}_\omega$. Second, this completeness result is a strong one, including entailment from (potentially infinite) sets of hypotheses.

Theorem 2. *The fragment of* $\mathbf{ACT}_\omega$ *without* $\mathbf{0}$ *is strongly complete w.r.t. SCL-models. In other words, for a given sequent* $\Pi \to B$ *and a set of sequents* $\mathcal{H}$, *if* $\Pi \to B$ *is not derivable from* $\mathcal{H}$ *in* $\mathbf{ACT}_\omega$, *then there exists an SCL-model* $\mathcal{M}$ *which makes* $\Pi \to B$ *false and all sequents from* $\mathcal{H}$ *true.*

Proof. The standard Lindenbaum–Tarski argument (for a general presentation see, e.g., [2]) establishes strong completeness of $\mathbf{ACT}_\omega$ w.r.t. to its general class of algebraic models, namely, models on $*$-continuous RKLs. Thus, for the given $\mathcal{H}$ and $\Pi \to B$ there exists an RKL on some set $\mathbf{K}$ and an interpretation function $\bar{\alpha}$ which validates $\mathcal{H}$ and falsifies $\Pi \to B$. Let us apply Theorem 1 and construct an SCL $\mathcal{B}_{L_0}$ and a injective mapping $h \colon \mathbf{K} \to \mathcal{B}_{L_0}$. Now consider the new interpretation function $\bar{\alpha}' = h \circ \bar{\alpha}$, which gives an interpretation of formulae on the SCL $\mathcal{B}_{L_0}$. Since h preserves operations and $\mathbf{1}$ and $\bar{\alpha}$ is a correct interpretation function, the function $\bar{\alpha}'$ commutes with operations and respects constant $\mathbf{1}$. Thus, we have correctly defined an SCL-model. Moreover, the new model validates exactly the same sequents which were true in the original model on $\mathbf{K}$. Thus, it falsifies $\Pi \to B$ and validates $\mathcal{H}$, which is what we need. □

Now let us extract some corollaries of Theorem 2. The first one considers abstract algebraic models of $\mathbf{ACT}_\omega$ on RKLs which are complete in the lattice-theoretic sense (i.e., which include all infinite suprema and infima). This is a narrower class than the class of $*$-continuous RKLs, since $*$-continuity requires existence only of suprema of a very specific form.[5] Weak completeness w.r.t. such models is actually due to Buszkowski [5], who proved the finite model property (FMP) for $\mathbf{ACT}_\omega$: any finite lattice is complete. For strong completeness, the FMP does not work. SCLs, however, are complete as lattices, which does the job. Actually, the closure construction used is quite close to Dedekind – McNeille completions used in lattice theory.

[5] In the presence of all suprema, the RKL is always $*$-continuous, even if originally Kleene star was defined in a fixpoint fashion. This is a well-known fact which Restall attributes to Pratt, calling it "Pratt's normality theorem" [27, Thm. 9.44].

Corollary 1. *The fragment of* $\mathbf{ACT}_\omega$ *without* $\mathbf{0}$ *is strongly complete w.r.t. models on RKLs which are complete as lattices.*

Another corollary is completeness of a fragment of $\mathbf{ACT}_\omega$ w.r.t. L-models (in the original sense).

Corollary 2. *The fragment of* $\mathbf{ACT}_\omega$ *in the language of* $\backslash$, $/$, $\wedge$, *and* *, *where* * *is allowed to be used only in subformulae of the form* $A^* \backslash B$ *and* B / A^*, *is strongly complete w.r.t. L-models.*

Proof. The idea here is that the listed operations, including the composite operations $A^* \backslash B$ and B / A^*, behave in the same way in L-models and SCL-models. For $\backslash$, $/$, and $\wedge$, this was already mentioned above.

For iteration in denominators, we have to prove the following: $M_1^* \backslash M_2 = M_1^{\circledast} \backslash M_2$, for any $M_1, M_2 \in \mathcal{B}_{L_0}$; the case of $/$ is symmetric. The $\supseteq$ inclusion follows from $M_1^* \subseteq M_1^{\circledast}$ and the fact that $\backslash$ is antitone on the denominator. Let us prove the $\subseteq$ inclusion. Suppose $u \in M_1^* \backslash M_2$ and let $v \in M_1^{\circledast}$. We have to show that $vu \in M_2$. Since M_2 is closed, it is sufficient to show $vu \in M_2^{\rhd\lhd}$. Let $(x, y) \subseteq \Sigma^* \times \Sigma^*$ be such a pair that for any $w \in M_2$ we have $xwy \in L_0$.

Let us consider the pair (x, uy). For any $v' = v_1 \dots v_n \in M_1^*$, since $u \in M_1^* \backslash M_2$, we have $w = v'u \in M_2$. Hence, $xwy \in L_0$. Next, we have $v \in M_1^{\circledast} = (M_1^*)^{\rhd\lhd}$, whence $xvuy \in L_0$, which is what we need. □

Finally, we semantically establish *strong conservativity* of $\mathbf{ACT}_\omega$ over **MALC**.

Corollary 3. *If* $\mathcal{H}$ *and* $\Pi \to B$ *do not include Kleene star and* $\mathbf{0}$, *then* $\Pi \to B$ *is derivable from* $\mathcal{H}$ *in* $\mathbf{ACT}_\omega$ *if and only if this holds for* **MALC**.

Proof. Strong completeness (Theorem 2) can be proved for **MALC** without $\mathbf{0}$ as well as $\mathbf{ACT}_\omega$: one just removes the cases for Kleene star. Thus, if $\Pi \to B$ is not derivable from $\mathcal{H}$ in **MALC**, then there exists an SCL-model satisfying $\mathcal{H}$ and falsifying $\Pi \to B$. Therefore $\Pi \to B$ is not derivable from $\mathcal{H}$ in $\mathbf{ACT}_\omega$ (strong soundness). The opposite is obvious: $\mathbf{ACT}_\omega$ extends **MALC**. □

4 SCL-Models over a Two-Letter Alphabet

The alphabets used in L-models and SCL-models, as defined above, are allowed to be infinite. Moreover, the completeness argument used in the previous section (as well as Wurm's original argument) essentially uses this feature: two letters for each element of an abstract algebraic model are used. In linguistic practice, however, the alphabets are usually finite. Thus, it would be nice to have a completeness result for SCL-models over finite alphabets.

For weak completeness, this can be obtained using the FMP, as shown in the next section. For strong completeness the FMP does not hold, and we shall show how to reduce an arbitrary SCL with a countable (or finite) Σ to an SCL over the two-letter alphabet $\Sigma_2 = \{e, f\}$. The reducing function is due to Pentus [24], who used it for L-models. We show that it is also suitable for SCL-models.

Let $\Sigma = \{a_1, a_2, \ldots\}$ be an infinite alphabet and let $g \colon \Sigma^* \to \Sigma_2^*$ be a homomorphism defined (on letters) as follows: $g(a_i) = ef^i e$. The homomorphism g can also be applied to languages: $g(M) = \{g(w) \mid w \in M\}$.

Lemma 1. *If $M \ni w \neq \varepsilon$ and $M^{\triangleright} \neq \varnothing$, then $g(M^{\triangleright\triangleleft}) = \big(g(M)\big)^{\triangleright\triangleleft}$. The closure operator in $\mathcal{B}_{L_0}$ and in $\mathcal{B}_{g(L_0)}$, resp., is taken w.r.t. L_0 and $g(L_0)$.*

Proof. Let $v \in g(M^{\triangleright\triangleleft})$, i.e., $v = g(v')$, where $v' \in M^{\triangleright\triangleleft}$. Take a pair $(x, y) \in \Sigma_2^* \times \Sigma_2^*$, such that for any $w \in g(M)$ we have $xwy \in g(L_0)$. There is a non-empty $w \in g(M)$, therefore, x and y are also of the form $g(x')$ and $g(y')$ respectively. Moreover, for any $w' \in M$ we have $x'w'y' \in L_0$. Therefore, since $v' \in M^{\triangleright\triangleleft}$, we have $x'v'y' \in L_0$, whence $xvy \in g(L_0)$. This yields $v \in \big(g(M)\big)^{\triangleright\triangleleft}$. The inclusion $g(M^{\triangleright\triangleleft}) \subseteq \big(g(M)\big)^{\triangleright\triangleleft}$ is established.

Now let $v \in \big(g(M)\big)^{\triangleright\triangleleft}$. Since $M^{\triangleright}$ is non-empty, there exists a pair $(x', y') \in \Sigma^* \times \Sigma^*$, such that $x'w'y' \in L_0$ for any $w' \in M$. Apply the mapping g: $x = g(x')$, $y = g(y')$. For the pair (x, y), we have $xvy \in g(L_0)$. Hence, v is of the form $g(v')$ for some $v' \in \Sigma^*$. Let us show that $v' \in M^{\triangleright\triangleleft}$. Take an arbitrary pair $(x', y') \in M^{\triangleright}$ and apply g as above. For any $w' \in M$, we have $x'w'y' \in L_0$, whence $xwy \in g(L_0)$. Since $v \in \big(g(M)\big)^{\triangleright\triangleleft}$ and w is an arbitrary element of $g(M)$, we get $xvy \in g(L_0)$, whence $x'v'y' \in L_0$. This yields $v' \in M^{\triangleright\triangleleft}$, and therefore $v \in g(M^{\triangleright\triangleleft})$. This establishes the inclusion $g(M^{\triangleright\triangleleft}) \supseteq \big(g(M)\big)^{\triangleright\triangleleft}$. □

Both non-emptiness conditions here are crucial. In what follows, we shall check them when applying this lemma. (Similar issues were dealt with by Pentus.)

Theorem 3. *The fragment of* $\mathbf{ACT}_\omega$ *without constants* **0** *and* **1** *is strongly complete w.r.t. SCL-models over the two-letter alphabet Σ_2.*

Proof. The set of variables is countable, whence so are the RKLs given by the Lindenbaum–Tarski construction. Thus, the alphabet Σ used in SCL-models obtained by Theorem 1 is also countable. We shall to reduce Σ to Σ_2 using g.

Let us inspect the proof of Theorem 2. In the construction of the SCL-model, each formula A is interpreted by the language $\bar{\alpha}(A) = h(a)$, where a is the element of $\mathbf{K}$ corresponding to formula A (Lindenbaum–Tarski construction). We always have $\overline{a} \in h(a)$ and $h(a)^{\triangleright} = \{(\varepsilon, \underline{a})\}^{\triangleleft\triangleright} \ni (\varepsilon, \underline{a})$. Therefore, any language of the form $M = \bar{\alpha}(A)$ satisfies the conditions of Lemma 1.

Now let us construct a new SCL-model $\mathcal{M}'$ over the two-letter alphabet Σ_2, taking $\alpha' = g \circ \alpha$. Let us show that $\bar{\alpha}'(A) = g(\bar{\alpha}(A))$ for each formula A.

Obviously, g commutes with meet (set-theoretic intersection): $\bar{\alpha}'(A \wedge B) = g(\bar{\alpha}(A) \cap \bar{\alpha}(B)) = g(\bar{\alpha}(A)) \cap g(\bar{\alpha}(B))$. It also commutes with division, provided its denominator (which is of the form $\bar{\alpha}(A)$) is non-empty. Finally, as an injective homomorphism, g of course commutes with standard language-theoretic union, product, and Kleene iteration. However, here the closure operator also comes into play:

$$g(\bar{\alpha}(A \vee B)) = g((\bar{\alpha}(A) \cup \bar{\alpha}(B))^{\triangleright\triangleleft}) = (g(\bar{\alpha}(A) \cup \bar{\alpha}(B)))^{\triangleright\triangleleft} = (g(\bar{\alpha}(A)) \cup g(\bar{\alpha}(B)))^{\triangleright\triangleleft} = (\bar{\alpha}'(A) \cup \bar{\alpha}'(B))^{\triangleright\triangleleft} = \bar{\alpha}'(A \vee B);$$

$$g(\bar{\alpha}(A \cdot B)) = g((\bar{\alpha}(A) \cdot \bar{\alpha}(B))^{\triangleright\triangleleft}) = (g(\bar{\alpha}(A) \cdot \bar{\alpha}(B)))^{\triangleright\triangleleft} = \\ (g(\bar{\alpha}(A)) \cdot g(\bar{\alpha}(B)))^{\triangleright\triangleleft} = (\bar{\alpha}'(A) \cdot \bar{\alpha}'(B))^{\triangleright\triangleleft} = \bar{\alpha}'(A \cdot B);$$

$$g(\bar{\alpha}(A^*)) = g((\bar{\alpha}(A)^*)^{\triangleright\triangleleft}) = (g(\bar{\alpha}(A)^*))^{\triangleright\triangleleft} = \\ (g(\bar{\alpha}(A))^*)^{\triangleright\triangleleft} = (\bar{\alpha}'(A)^*)^{\triangleright\triangleleft} = \bar{\alpha}'(A^*).$$

The second equality, which is the only interesting one, in each line here is due to Lemma 1. Applying Lemma 1, however, requires checking the non-emptiness conditions for languages M of the form $\bar{\alpha}(A) \cup \bar{\alpha}(B)$, $\bar{\alpha}(A) \cdot \bar{\alpha}(B)$, and $\bar{\alpha}(A)^*$. Since $\bar{\alpha}(A)$ and $\bar{\alpha}(B)$ include non-empty words, so does M. For the non-emptiness of $M^{\triangleright}$, the arguments are based on the facts that $M^{\triangleright} = M^{\triangleright\triangleleft\triangleright}$ and $\bar{\alpha}(C)^{\triangleright} \neq \varnothing$ for any formula C:

$$(\bar{\alpha}(A) \cup \bar{\alpha}(B))^{\triangleright} = (\bar{\alpha}(A) \cup \bar{\alpha}(B))^{\triangleright\triangleleft\triangleright} = \bar{\alpha}(A \vee B)^{\triangleright} \neq \varnothing;$$
$$(\bar{\alpha}(A) \cdot \bar{\alpha}(B))^{\triangleright} = (\bar{\alpha}(A) \cdot \bar{\alpha}(B))^{\triangleright\triangleleft\triangleright} = \bar{\alpha}(A \cdot B)^{\triangleright} \neq \varnothing;$$
$$(\bar{\alpha}(A)^*)^{\triangleright} = (\bar{\alpha}(A)^*)^{\triangleright\triangleleft\triangleright} = \bar{\alpha}(A^*)^{\triangleright} \neq \varnothing.$$

Finally, the new SCL-model $(\mathcal{B}_{g(L_0)}, \alpha')$ validates exactly the same sequents as $(\mathcal{B}_{L_0}, \alpha)$ from Theorem 2. This yields strong completeness over Σ_2. □

5 Regular SCL-Models

In this final section, we shall briefly discuss *regular SCL-models.*

Definition 3. *An SCL $\mathcal{B}_{L_0}$ is regular, if the language L_0 is a regular language.*

Regular SCL-models are actually finite models, due to the following fact: $\mathcal{B}_{L_0}$ is finite iff it is regular [30, Lem. 11]. This yields the following:

Theorem 4. *Neither* **ACT**$_\omega$, *nor even* **MALC** *is strongly complete w.r.t. regular SCL-models.*

Proof. Suppose the contrary. Since regular SCL-models are special kinds of finite ones, this makes **MALC** strongly complete w.r.t. finite (algebraic) models. Hence, the algorithmic problem of deriving sequents from finite sets of sequents, in **MALC**, is both enumerable (proof search) and co-enumerable (finite countermodel search). By Post's theorem, it is decidable. On the other hand, it is known that this is not the case [4]. Contradiction. □

We leave it as an open question to construct a concrete example of $\mathcal{H}$ and $\Pi \to B$ such that $\Pi \to B$ is not derivable from **MALC**, but is semantically entailed on the class of regular SCL-models. The weak completeness result, however, extends from **MALC** to **ACT**$_\omega$ in a straightforward way.

Theorem 5. **ACT**$_\omega$ *is weakly complete w.r.t. regular SCL-models.*

Proof. By the FMP for $\mathbf{ACT}_\omega$ [5], any sequent, which is not derivable in $\mathbf{ACT}_\omega$, is falsified by an interpretation on a finite RKL. By [30, Lem. 12], the language L_0 constructed from this RKL (in Theorem 1) is regular. This yields the desired regular SCL-model falsifying the sequent. □

Acknowledgments. This paper was prepared within the framework of the HSE University Basic Research Program. The work was supported by the Theoretical Physics and Mathematics Advancement Foundation "BASIS." The author thanks C. Wurm and S. O. Kuznetsov for fruitful discussions and the reviewers for their valuable comments.

Disclosure of Interests. The author declares that he has no competing interests.

Appendix

In this Appendix, we discuss issues with constants $\mathbf{0}$ and $\mathbf{1}$. Namely, in our formulation Theorem 2 works only for the fragment of $\mathbf{ACT}_\omega$ without $\mathbf{0}$, and the stronger Theorem 3 is even more restrictive, working only without both constants.

The first issue, connected with constant $\mathbf{0}$, actually goes back to Wurm [30]. Wurm claims completeness of the bounded full Lambek calculus (which he denotes by $\mathbf{FL}_\perp$, in our notation **MALC**; Wurm uses $\perp$ for $\mathbf{0}$). However, the interpretation used for $\mathbf{0}$ is non-standard. Namely, if 0 is the zero element of $\mathbf{K}$, then the interpretation for $\mathbf{0}$ is $\{\overline{0}\}^{\triangleright\triangleleft}$, which is not the same as $\emptyset = \varnothing^{\triangleright\triangleleft}$ [30, p. 194]. Our Theorem 2 would also work if we adopt this non-standard interpretation of $\mathbf{0}$. However, our definition of SCL-models uses the standard interpretation, which leaves $\mathbf{0}$ beyond the completeness result.

The question of whether $\mathbf{ACT}_\omega$ or even **MALC** is complete w.r.t. SCL-models with the standard interpretation of $\mathbf{0}$ is left open. We conjecture a negative answer.

For the other constant, $\mathbf{1}$, the situation is as follows. Wurm's argument and its strong infinitary extension presented in Theorem 2 correctly handle this constant, using its standard interpretation: $\mathbb{1} = \{\varepsilon\}^{\triangleright\triangleleft}$. In contrast, the argument used in our Theorem 3, which reduces an arbitrary countable alphabet Σ to the two-letter alphabet Σ_2, fails for $\mathbf{1}$.

Namely, if one takes the closure $\{\varepsilon\}^{\triangleright\triangleleft}$ in the new SCL $\mathcal{B}_{g(L_0)}$, one just gets $\{\varepsilon\}$. Indeed, let 1 be the unit of $\mathbf{K}$, then we have $\underline{1} \in L_0$ and $g(\underline{1}) \in g(L_0)$. Let $g(\underline{1}) = ef^je$, where j is the number of the letter $\underline{1}$ in Σ. By definition, in $\mathcal{B}_{g(L_0)}$,

$$\{\varepsilon\}^{\triangleright} = \{(x,y) \in \Sigma_2^* \times \Sigma_2^* \mid xy \in g(L_0)\}.$$

In particular, this set includes any pair (x, y) such that $xy = ef^je$. Now let $\{\varepsilon\}^{\triangleright\triangleleft}$ include a non-empty word v. Take $x = ef^j$ and $y = e$. The word v should end with an f, because otherwise xvy ends with ee, which is impossible for a word from the image of g. But now if we take $x = ef^je$ and $y = \varepsilon$, we get $ef^jev \in g(L_0)$. The latter is impossible, as no word from the image of g ends with an f. Therefore, no non-empty word belongs to $\{\varepsilon\}^{\triangleright\triangleleft}$.

The fact that, in $\mathcal{B}_{g(L_0)}$, constant $\mathbf{1}$ is interpreted by $\{\varepsilon\}$, makes this SCL unsuitable for proving completeness in the presence of $\mathbf{1}$. Namely, interpretations of formulae of the form $\mathbf{1} / A$ are restricted to three possibilities: $\varnothing$, $\{\varepsilon\}$, and Σ_2^*, and for such interpretations extra principles become valid, like $\mathbf{1} / A \to (\mathbf{1} / A) \cdot (\mathbf{1} / A)$ (see [17]).

Thus, completeness of the fragment of $\mathbf{ACT}_\omega$ (or even **MALC**) without $\mathbf{0}$, but with $\mathbf{1}$, w.r.t. SCL-models over a two-letter alphabet, also remains an open question.

References

1. van Benthem, J.: Language in Action: Categories, Lambdas, and Dynamic Logic. North Holland, Amsterdam (1991)
2. Blok, W.J., Pigozzi, D.: Algebraizable Logic. Memoirs of the American Mathematical Society, vol. 77, no. 396. AMS (1989)
3. Buszkowski, W.: Compatibility of a categorial grammar with an associated category system. Z. Math. Logik Grundl. Math. **28**, 229–238 (1982). https://doi.org/10.1002/malq.19820281407
4. Buszkowski, W.: Some decision problems in the theory of syntactic categories. Z. Math. Logik Grundl. Math. **28**, 539–548 (1982). https://doi.org/10.1002/malq.19820283308
5. Buszkowski, W.: On action logic: equational theories of action algebras. J. Logic Comput. **17**(1), 199–217 (2007). https://doi.org/10.1093/logcom/exl036
6. Buszkowski, W.: Lambek calculus and substructural logics. Linguist. Anal. **36**(1–4), 15–48 (2010)
7. Clark, A.: A learnable representation for syntax using residuated lattices. In: de Groote, P., Egg, M., Kallmeyer, L. (eds.) FG 2009. LNCS (LNAI), vol. 5591, pp. 183–198. Springer, Heidelberg (2011). https://doi.org/10.1007/978-3-642-20169-1_12
8. Davey, B.A., Priestley, H.A.: Introduction to Lattices and Order, 2nd edn. Cambridge University Press, Cambridge (2002). https://doi.org/10.1017/CBO9780511809088
9. Galatos, N., Jipsen, P., Kowalski, T., Ono, H.: Residuated Lattices: An Algebraic Glimpse at Substructural Logics. Studies in Logic and Foundations of Mathematics, vol. 151. Elsevier (2007)
10. Girard, J.-Y.: Linear logic: its syntax and semantics. In: Girard, J.-Y., Lafont, Y., Regnier, L. (eds.) Advances in Linear Logic. London Mathematical Society Lecture Note Series, vol. 222, pp. 1–42. Cambridge University Press, Cambridge (1995). https://doi.org/10.1017/CBO9780511629150
11. de Groote, P.: On the expressive power of the Lambek calculus extended with a structural modality. In: Casadio, C., Scott, P. J., Seely, R. A. G. (eds.) Language and Grammar. CSLI Lecture Notes, vol. 168, pp. 95–111. Stanford University (2005)
12. Kanazawa, M.: The Lambek calculus enriched with additional connectives. J. Logic Lang. Inform. **1**(2), 141–171 (1992). https://doi.org/10.1007/BF00171695
13. Kanovich, M.I., Okada, M., Terui, K.: Intuitionistic phase semantics is almost classical. Math. Struct. Comput. Sci. **16**(1), 67–86 (2006). https://doi.org/10.1017/S0960129505005062

14. Kanovich, M., Kuznetsov, S., Scedrov, A.: Language models for some extensions of the Lambek calculus. Inform. and Comput. **287**, 104760, 16 pp. (2022). https://doi.org/10.1016/j.ic.2021.104760
15. Kozen, D.: On induction vs. *-continuity. In: Kozen, D. (ed.) Logic of Programs 1981. LNCS, vol. 131, pp. 167–176. Springer, Heidelberg (1981). https://doi.org/10.1007/BFb0025782
16. Kozen, D.: On action algebras. In: van Eijck, J., Visser, A. (eds.) Logic and Information Flow, pp. 78–88. MIT Press (1994)
17. Kuznetsov, S.L.: Trivalent logics arising from L-models for the Lambek calculus with constants. J. Appl. Non-Class. Log. **14**(1–2), 132–137 (2014). https://doi.org/10.1080/11663081.2014.911522
18. Kuznetsov, S.: *-continuity vs. induction: divide and conquer. In: Bezhanishvili, G., D'Agostino, G., Metcalfe, G., Studer, T. (eds.) Proceedings of 12th Conference "Advances in Modal Logic". Advances in Modal Logic, vol. 12, pp. 493–510. College Publications, London (2018)
19. Kuznetsov, S.L., Ryzhkova, N.S.: A restricted fragment of the Lambek calculus with iteration and intersection operations. Algebra Logic **59**(2), 129–146 (2020). https://doi.org/10.1007/s10469-020-09586-9
20. Kuznetsov, S.O.: Mathematical aspects of concept analysis. J. Math. Sci. **80**(2), 1654–1698 (1996). https://doi.org/10.1007/BF02362847
21. Lambek, J.: The mathematics of sentence structure. Am. Math. Mon. **65**, 154–170 (1958). https://doi.org/10.1080/00029890.1958.11989160
22. Lambek, J.: On the calculus of syntactic types. In: Jakobson, R. (ed.) Structure of Language and Its Mathematical Aspects, pp. 166–178. AMS (1961)
23. Palka, E.: An infinitary sequent system for the equational theory of *-continuous action lattices. Fundam. Inform. **78**(2), 295–309 (2007)
24. Pentus, M.: Models for the Lambek calculus. Ann. Pure Appl. Logic **75**(1–2), 179–213 (1995). https://doi.org/10.1016/0168-0072%2894%2900063-9
25. Pentus, M.: Free monoid completeness of the Lambek calculus allowing empty premises. In: Larrazabal, M., Lascar, D., Mints, G. (eds.) Proceedings of Logic Colloquium 1996. Lecture Notes in Logic, vol. 12, pp. 171–209. Cambridge University Press, Cambridge (1998). https://doi.org/10.1017/9781316716816.008
26. Pratt, V.: Action logic and pure induction. In: van Eijck, J. (ed.) JELIA 1990. LNCS, vol. 478, pp. 97–120. Springer, Heidelberg (1991). https://doi.org/10.1007/BFb0018436
27. Restall, G.: An Introduction to Substructural Logics. Routledge, London (2000)
28. Wille, R.: Concept lattices and conceptual knowledge systems. Comput. Math. Applic. **23**(6–9), 493–515 (1992). https://doi.org/10.1016/0898-1221%2892%2990120-7
29. Wurm, C.: Completeness of full Lambek calculus for syntactic concept lattices. In: Morrill, G., Nederhof, M.-J. (eds.) FG 2012-2013. LNCS, vol. 8036, pp. 126–141. Springer, Heidelberg (2013). https://doi.org/10.1007/978-3-642-39998-5_8
30. Wurm, C.: Language-theoretic and finite relation models for the (full) Lambek calculus. J. Logic Lang. Inform. **26**(2), 179–214 (2017). https://doi.org/10.1007/s10849-017-9249-z

Rules of Partial Orthomodularity

Mena Leemhuis[1(✉)], Diedrich Wolter[1], and Özgür L. Özçep[2]

[1] University of Lübeck, Lübeck, Germany
{m.leemhuis,diedrich.wolter}@uni-luebeck.de
[2] University of Hamburg, Hamburg, Germany
oezguer.oezcep@uni-hamburg.de

Abstract. The rule of orthomodularity is important, for example due to its foundational role in quantum logic. However, orthomodularity is a restriction that is not always suitable. For example, orthomodularity is not fulfilled by certain geometric structures such as the lattice of closed convex cones, which is different from the lattice considered in quantum logic, namely that of closed subspaces of a Hilbert space. Thus, the question arises whether the rule of orthomodularity can be relaxed such that the relaxed rule is still stronger than the ortholattice rule and such that each orthomodular lattice fulfills also the relaxed rule. Therefore, we present two rules of partial orthomodularity of different strength, (pOM) and (pOM$_{ex}$), which keep some of the advantages of the rule of orthomodularity but are relaxations of it. We show the validity and usefulness of these rules by proving a subalgebra theorem for (pOM), by showing that an algebraic representation theorem for orthomodularity can be relaxed as to be based on the rules of partial orthomodularity and by proving a connection to Johansson's minimal rule.

Keywords: Orthomodularity · Ortholattices · Quantum Logic

1 Introduction

Soon after the start of modern classical logic by Boole and Frege, the need to weaken certain of its rules was recognized. Within the resulting plethora of non-classical logics some of the earliest approaches weaken the rule of distributivity of the "or" connector $\vee$ over the "and" connector $\wedge$. Formally, distributivity reads as $a \vee (b \wedge c) = (a \vee b) \wedge (a \vee c)$. As of now one can observe a growing interest in so-called non-distributive logics [5].

A prominent weakening of distributivity is the rule of orthomodularity which was introduced by Birkhoff and von Neumann [1] in the context of quantum logic and which is intensively discussed in the context of lattice theory (see, e.g., the monograph of Kalmbach [12]). Formally, orthomodularity reads as follows: if $a \leq b$ and $a^{\perp} \leq c$, then $a \vee (b \wedge c) = (a \vee b) \wedge (a \vee c)$. Here $a^{\perp}$ denotes the orthocomplement of a. In other words, orthomodularity amounts to distributivity under the conditions that a is smaller than b and that the orthocomplement of a is smaller than c. Though orthomodularity is an interesting restriction, it

G. Metcalfe et al. (Eds.): WoLLIC 2024, LNCS 14672, pp. 108–121, 2024.
https://doi.org/10.1007/978-3-031-62687-6_8

may already be too strong in some cases. One example can be found in lattices of geometric objects: the rule of orthomodularity holds for lattices of closed subspaces of a Hilbert space (where lattice-meet is set-intersection, lattice-join is the convex hull and negation is defined as orthogonality). However, lattices of closed convex cones, for example, do not satisfy orthomodularity (again based on set-intersection and convex hull).

This leads to the question of whether there is a rule which is as similar to the orthomodularity as possible, while still allowing a wider diversity of lattices. There are solutions of this problem [2,3,7] who consider orthomodularity rules which are similar to the orthomodularity in an ortholattice, however, different when ortholattices are not considered. We aim to stick to ortholattices since they have interesting properties. For example, the ortholattice of closed convex cones has proved useful for geometrically constrained embeddings [13–15]. Our aim is thus to investigate relaxations of the orthomodularity rule in the context of ortholattices.

In this paper, we propose and discuss the two rules of partial orthomodularity (pOM) and (pOM_{ex}) which are based on the idea of considering two forms of the Sasaki hook and thus combining two different definitions orthomodularity to define a weaker form of orthomodularity. Based on a combination of these two forms, it seems impossible to find any other versions of the partial orthomodularity, as all other relaxations based on these rules lead to contradictory or trivial results, as will be discussed in Sect. 3. This further motivates investigating (pOM) and (pOM_{ex}). Both rules are considered in the context of ortholattices. Moreover, not all lattices satisfy (pOM) and (pOM_{ex}) (e.g., in the context of permutohedrons, the lattice $R(B_2)$ [17], see Fig. 3), showing that they may characterize a potentially interesting restriction.

(pOM) and (pOM_{ex}) are in fact weakenings of orthomodularity, as each orthomodular lattice (each Boolean algebra too) fulfills both rules. The rules of partial orthomodularity share also other attributes of (OMr): (pOM) can be, similar to (OMr), characterized with the help of a subalgebra theorem, i.e., there is a lattice which is not allowed to be a subalgebra of a lattice fulfilling (pOM).

As Goldblatt [8] proved, there is an algebraic representation of orthomodular logic. This representation theorem can be adapted to a representation theorem based on (pOM), resp. (pOM_{ex}). These underlines the appropriateness of the rules of partial orthomodularity further and strengthens the connection to the rule of orthomodularity.

The remainder of the paper is structured as follows: After a short introduction of lattices and orthologics in Sect. 2, the rules of partial orthomodularity are introduced in Sect. 3. After that, the forbidden subalgebra theorem of (pOM) is given in Sect. 4 and the algebraic representation is discussed in Sect. 5.

2 Preliminaries

We summarize essential notions and results from lattice theory and orthologics.

A thorough introduction to lattice theory can be found, e.g., in [9] and to ortholattices, e.g., in [12]. A *lattice* $(L, \leq)$ is a structure with a partial order $\leq$

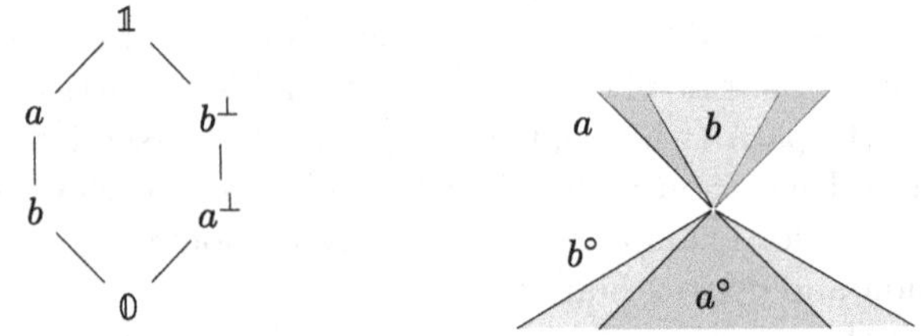

Fig. 1. Left: Ortholattice O_6; right: Cone embedding of O_6

such that for any pair of elements $a, b \in L$ there is a smallest upper bound $a \vee b$ and a largest lower bound $a \wedge b$. It is *bounded* if it contains a smallest element $\mathbb{0}$ and a largest element $\mathbb{1}$. Element b covers element a, for short $a <: b$ if and only if for all c with $a \leq c \leq b$ either $c = a$ or $c = b$. An element a is called an *atom* if it covers $\mathbb{0}$. A lattice is called *atomistic* if every element is a join of atoms. A lattice is called *distributive* if and only if for all $a, b, c \in L$: $a \wedge (b \vee c) = (a \wedge b) \vee (a \wedge c)$ (and dually: $a \vee (b \wedge c) = (a \vee b) \wedge (a \vee c)$).

An element a^* is called a *complement of* a if and only if $a \wedge a^* = \mathbb{0}$ and $a \vee a^* = \mathbb{1}$. A lattice is said to be *complemented (uniquely complemented)* if and only if each a has a complement (has exactly one complement). A bounded lattice L is called an *ortholattice* if and only if it has an orthocomplement $\cdot^{\perp}$, i.e., a unary operation such that for all $a, b \in L$ the following conditions hold:

- $a \leq b$ entails $b^{\perp} \leq a^{\perp}$ (antitonicity)
- $a^{\perp\perp} = a$ (double negation elimination)
- $\mathbb{0} = a \wedge a^{\perp}$ (intuitionistic absurdity)

Any ortholattice satisfies de Morgan's laws, i.e., for any $a, b \in L$ it holds that $(a \wedge b)^{\perp} = a^{\perp} \vee b^{\perp}$ (and dually: $(a \vee b)^{\perp} = a^{\perp} \wedge b^{\perp}$). Thus, ortholattices are a weakening of Boolean algebras.

An ortholattice is called *orthomodular* if and only if one of the following equivalent conditions [16, pp. 35–36] of orthomodularity holds:

(OMr) If $a \leq b$ and $a^{\perp} \leq c$, then $a \vee (b \wedge c) = (a \vee b) \wedge (a \vee c)$.
(orthomodularity)

(sOMr) If $a \leq b$, then $b = a \vee (a^{\perp} \wedge b)$.
(short form orthomodularity)

(dsOMr) If $b \leq a$, then $b = a \wedge (a^{\perp} \vee b)$.
(dual short form of orthomodularity)

Just for the sake of completeness, we state here that there is next to the order-based notion of a lattice L also an algebraic notion of a lattice $(L; \wedge; \vee)$. These notions are equivalent in the sense that each lattice L induces an algebra $(L; \wedge; \vee)$ and vice versa. Construction of substructures differs, though. A lattice $(K; \wedge; \vee)$ is a *subalgebra* of the lattice $(L; \wedge; \vee)$ if K is a non-empty subset of L and if K is closed under $\wedge$ and $\vee$ in $(L; \wedge; \vee)$. *sub*(H) denotes the *subalgebra of*

Axioms

$A \vdash A \quad A \,\&\, B \vdash A \quad A \,\&\, B \vdash B \quad A \dashv\vdash \sim\sim A$

$A \,\&\, \sim A \vdash B \quad A \bigvee B \dashv\vdash \sim(\sim A \,\&\, \sim B)$

Rules

$$\frac{A \vdash B,\, B \vdash C}{A \vdash C} \qquad \frac{A \vdash B,\, A \vdash C}{A \vdash B \,\&\, C} \qquad \frac{A \vdash B}{\sim B \vdash \sim A}$$

Fig. 2. Minimal Orthologic *Omin*

L generated by H, thus the smallest subset of L containing H and being closed under $\wedge$ and $\vee$.

In lattice theory there are characterizations of lattices fulfilling some given property (rule, axiom) by so-called *forbidden subalgebra theorems.* Consider the hexagon lattice on the left hand side of Fig. 1, also called O_6 in the literature [12, p. 22]. It is easy to check that the hexagon is indeed a lattice and that it is orthocomplemented. However, this lattice is not orthomodular according to (dsOMr): we have $b \leq a$, but also $b \neq a \wedge (a^\perp \vee b) = a \wedge \mathbb{1} = a$. Now the forbidden subalgebra theorem for ortholattices L [12, p. 22] states that L is orthomodular if and only if it excludes O_6 as a subalgebra. In Sect. 4 we state a similar theorem for one of the rules of partial orthomodularity.

Ortholattices as defined above can be logically characterized by orthologics [8]. Let $P = \{P_i \mid i \in \mathbb{N}\}$ be a set of proposition symbols and assume that we have logical symbols for binary conjunction &, unary negation $\sim$, and binary disjunction $\bigvee$. The set of propositional formulae $\mathcal{F}(P)$ over P is defined as usual. A, B, C stand for propositional formulae in $\mathcal{F}(P)$.

We consider a deduction calculus with a derivability relation $\vdash$. We use the short notation $A \dashv\vdash B$ for $A \vdash B$ and $B \vdash A$. Moreover, for a finite set of formulae $\Gamma = \{B_1, \ldots, B_n\}$ the notation $\Gamma \vdash A$ is a shorthand for $B_1 \,\&\, \ldots \,\&\, B_n \vdash A$. The calculus of *minimal orthologic Omin* according to Goldblatt [8] is given in Fig. 2.

Any logic $\mathcal{L}$ containing the rules of Fig. 2 is called an *orthologic.* For any orthologic the well-known Lindenbaum-Tarski construction leads to an ortholattice: The binary relation $\dashv\vdash$ can be shown to be an equivalence relation inducing for each formula C an equivalence class $[C]$. Define operations $\wedge$, $\vee$, $^\perp$ on the equivalence classes by setting $[C] \wedge [D] = [C \,\&\, D]$, $[C] \vee [D] = [C \bigvee D]$ and $[C]^\perp = [\sim C]$. These yield an ortholattice.

Goldblatt [8] defines the semantics of orthologics based on a structure $(X, \perp)$ called an *orthoframe.* It consists of a domain (carrier) X and a binary *orthogonality relation* $\perp \subseteq X \times X$, i.e., a relation that is irreflexive and symmetric. An orthoframe induces an operation $(\cdot)^*$ over subsets $Y \subseteq X$ defined by $Y^* = \{x \in X \mid x \perp Y\} = \{x \in X \mid x \perp y \text{ for all } y \in Y\}$. A set $Y \subseteq X$ is called $\perp$*-closed* if and only if $Y = Y^{**}$. This means that if $x \notin Y$ then there is a z such that not $x \perp z$, and for all $y \in Y$: $z \perp y$.

An *orthomodel* for a logic $\mathcal{L}$ over $\mathcal{F}(P)$ is defined as structure $\mathcal{I} = (X, \perp, (\cdot)^{\mathcal{I}})$ such that $(X, \perp)$ is an orthoframe and $(\cdot)^{\mathcal{I}}$ assigns to each $P_i \in P$ a $\perp$-closed set over X. In a natural way one can extend the assignment function to arbitrary formulae $(A \ \&\ B)^{\mathcal{I}} = (A)^{\mathcal{I}} \cap (B)^{\mathcal{I}}$, $(\sim A)^{\mathcal{I}} = ((A)^{\mathcal{I}})^*$ where $\bigvee$ is treated by de Morgan's law. The *semantical entailment relation* $\models$ then can be defined as $\mathcal{I} : A \models B$ if and only if $(A)^{\mathcal{I}} \subseteq (B)^{\mathcal{I}}$. If U is a class of orthoframes, then $A \models_U B$ means that $\mathcal{I} : A \models B$ for any orthomodel definable in any orthoframe in U. In establishing correctness and completeness results w.r.t. the orthomodel semantics, Goldblatt [8] constructs for each orthologic $\mathcal{L}$ a canonical model. In order to define this canonical model, he considers maximally consistent sets called $\mathcal{L}$-full sets: a set Y of formulae is said to be $\mathcal{L}$-*full* if and only if it is closed w.r.t. derivability and w.r.t. conjunction & and is consistent (i.e., Y is different from the set of all formulae $\mathcal{F}(P)$). Based on the following fact [8]

$$\Gamma \vdash_{\mathcal{L}} A \text{ if and only if } \mathcal{I}_{\mathcal{L}} : \Gamma \models A \text{ for any orthologic } \mathcal{L} \tag{1}$$

and using a canonical-model construction, Goldblatt establishes in the following (soundness and) completeness result for the class θ of all orthoframes that A is derivable in Omin if and only if it is within the class of all orthoframes.

Proposition 1 ([8]). *$\Gamma \vdash_{Omin} A$ if and only if $\Gamma \models_\theta A$.*

3 Rules of Partial Orthomodularity

Let us motivate the need for rules for partial orthomodularity by an example.

Example 1. Orthomodularity can be motivated based on the lattice of closed subspaces of a Hilbert space [1]. However, when considering other geometric structures, the resulting lattice is not necessarily orthomodular. Consider the lattice of closed convex cones in $\mathbb{R}^n$: a *closed convex cone* a is a set such that from $x, y \in a$ it follows that $\lambda x + \mu y \in a$ for any $\lambda, \mu \in \mathbb{R}_{\geq 0}$ and that is topologically closed in the canonical topology of $\mathbb{R}^n$. One of the nice properties of closed convex cones is that they allow for a polarity operation that takes the role of an orthocomplement. The *polar cone* a° for a is defined for Euclidean spaces with a dot product $\langle \cdot, \cdot \rangle$ as $a^\circ = \{x \in \mathbb{R}^n \mid \forall y \in a : \langle x, y \rangle \leq 0\}$. Now consider the subset-relation $\sqsubseteq = \subseteq$ on closed convex cones in $\mathbb{R}^n$ as a partial order. Closed convex cones are closed under set intersection, so $\cap$ is a meet operator $\wedge$ w.r.t. $\leq$. Closed convex cones are not closed under set union. Instead they have to be closed up by the conic hull operator. The *conic hull* of a set b, for short $ch(b)$, is the smallest convex cone containing b. So, we can define the join operation $\vee$ by $a \vee b = ch(a \cup b)$. Considering $\mathbb{R}^n$ as the largest lattice element $\mathbb{1}$ and $\{0\}$, for $0 \in \mathbb{R}^n$, as the smallest lattice element $\mathbb{0}$ makes the resulting structure a bounded lattice. The polarity operator for closed convex cones fulfills the properties of an orthocomplement. Hence the set of all closed convex cones (over $\mathbb{R}^n$) forms an ortholattice. However, the lattice of closed convex cones does not fulfill the rule of orthomodularity as the forbidden subalgebra for orthomodularity can be represented by cones (see Fig. 1). Thus, the question arises whether there is a weaker form of the rule of orthomodularity to describe such cone lattices further. We answer this positively for the case of closed convex cones in $\mathbb{R}^2$ in the remainder of this section by introducing the rules of partial orthomodularity and will come back to this example in Example 2.

One idea of weakening the rule of orthomodularity is to stick to the conclusion of the orthomodularity rule but to change the premise in order to circumvent O_6 as counterexample, while being as close to (OMr) as possible. Therefore, an additional premise is added. This is done as follows: First, consider two of the variants of orthomodularity, (dsOMr) and (sOMr) (where for (sOMr) the naming of the variables is changed):

$$\text{If } b \leq a, \text{ then } a = b \vee (a \wedge b^{\perp})$$

$$\text{If } b \leq a, \text{ then } b = a \wedge (a^{\perp} \vee b)$$

Obviously, both rules are not fulfilled if (OMr) is not fulfilled. $a \wedge (a^{\perp} \vee b)$ is usually denoted as *Sasaki product* (or *Sasaki hook*) and an important notion, e.g., because of its implication-like behavior in orthomodular lattices and as basis for residuated lattices [6] and thus a suitable candidate for considering a relaxation of the orthomodularity rule. The basic idea is now to consider these rules for all elements $a, b \in L$ and enforce some form of homogeneity for these elements so that either both rules, (sOMr) and (dsOMr), are fulfilled for one a, b or neither of the two rules. This leads to the following definition of the rule of partial orthomodularity:

(pOM) If $b \leq a$ and $a = b \vee (a \wedge b^{\perp})$, then $b = a \wedge (a^{\perp} \vee b)$.

This is actually a weakening of the orthomodularity rule, as on the one hand, each lattice fulfilling (OMr) fulfills (pOM) and on the other hand, not all lattices that fulfill (pOM) also fulfill (OMr).

Proposition 2. *If an ortholattice L fulfills (OMr), then it fulfills (pOM) but not vice versa.*

Proof. The first follows trivially out of the definition of (pOM). The second follows with O_6, depicted in Fig. 1, as it depicts the forbidden subalgebra for (OMr) but fulfills (pOM).

On the other hand, (pOM) actually is a restriction of the ortholattice, thus, there are ortholattices not fulfilling (pOM).

Proposition 3. *Not every ortholattice fulfills (pOM).*

Proof. As counterexample, e.g., the lattice MC_{10} in Fig. 3 can be considered. The premise is fulfilled, however, $a \wedge (a^{\perp} \vee b) = d \neq b$.

Another more involved counterexample is $R(B_2)$, a lattice appearing in the context of considerations on permutohedrons [17], see the middle of Fig. 3. It is possible to define several equivalent variants of (pOM), particularly the following two: First, it is possible to dismiss the restriction of $b \leq a$:

(pOM$_1$) If $a = b \vee (a \wedge b^{\perp})$, then $b = a \wedge (a^{\perp} \vee b)$.

Second, it is also possible to mimic the equivalence of (sOMr) and (dsOMr) for orthomodularity by exchanging the implication of (pOM) with an equivalence:

(pOM$_2$) $a = b \vee (a \wedge b^{\perp})$ if and only if $b = a \wedge (a^{\perp} \vee b)$.

Proposition 4. *For an ortholattice L, following assertions are equivalent:*

- *L fulfills (pOM),*
- *L fulfills (pOM$_1$) and*
- *L fulfills (pOM$_2$).*

Proof. – (pOM) → (pOM$_1$): let (pOM) be valid and let the premise of (pOM$_1$) be fulfilled, thus $a = b \vee (a \wedge b^{\perp})$ and therefore $b \leq a$ and thus with (pOM) follows $b = a \wedge (a^{\perp} \vee b)$.
- (pOM$_1$) → (pOM$_2$): let (pOM$_1$) be valid and let $b = a \wedge (a^{\perp} \vee b)$ be fulfilled (the other direction is trivial). Then, $b^{\perp} = a^{\perp} \vee (a \wedge b^{\perp})$ and with (pOM$_1$) $a^{\perp} = b^{\perp} \wedge (a^{\perp} \vee b)$ and thus $a = b \vee (a \wedge b^{\perp})$.
- (pOM$_2$) → (pOM) follows trivially.

Another idea of adapting (pOM) is to dismiss both the restriction of $b \leq a$ and exchanging equality with less or equal:

(pOM$_{ex}$) If $a \leq b \vee (a \wedge b^{\perp})$, then $a \wedge (a^{\perp} \vee b) \leq b$.

Note that when having (pOM$_1$) as a basis, this relaxation of the equality is a natural one, having (OMr) and (pOM) as special cases. Other variants of relaxing the equality are contradictory or trivial and thus are not considered.

This rule is not equivalent to (pOM) but presents a stronger restriction.

Proposition 5. *If an ortholattice fulfills (pOM$_{ex}$), then it fulfills (pOM) but not vice versa.*

Proof. Let an ortholattice L be given and let it fulfill (pOM$_{ex}$) and assume $a = b \vee (a \wedge b^{\perp})$. With (pOM$_{ex}$) it follows that $a \wedge (a^{\perp} \vee b) \leq b$ and with $b \leq a$ it follows that $a \wedge (a^{\perp} \vee b) = b$.

For a counterexample for a lattice fulfilling (pOM) but not (pOM$_{ex}$), see Fig. 3 on the right. That lattice fulfills (pOM) (as can be determined by testing all conditions or by using the forbidden subalgebra theorem of Theorem 1 by observing that MC_{10} is not a subalgebra). It does not fulfill (pOM$_{ex}$), as $a < b \vee (a \wedge b^{\perp}) = \mathbb{1}$ but $a \wedge (a^{\perp} \vee b) = d \not\leq b$.

However, analogous to the case of (pOM), each orthomodular lattice also fulfills (pOM$_{ex}$) but not vice versa.

Proposition 6. *If an ortholattice L fulfills (OMr), then it fulfills (pOM$_{ex}$) but not vice versa.*

Proof. Let L be a lattice and (OMr) be fulfilled. Assume the premise of (pOM$_{ex}$) is fulfilled, thus $a \leq b \vee (a \wedge b^{\perp})$. If $a = b \vee (a \wedge b^{\perp})$, then the conclusion follows, as $b \leq a$. Thus, assume $a < b \vee (a \wedge b^{\perp})$ and let $c = a^{\perp} \vee b$. Then, $b \leq c$ and thus with (OMr) $b = c \wedge (c^{\perp} \vee b) = (a^{\perp} \vee b) \wedge ((a \wedge b^{\perp}) \vee b)$ and with $b \vee (a \wedge b^{\perp}) > a$ it follows that $b \geq (a^{\perp} \vee b) \wedge a$, thus the conclusion of (pOM$_{ex}$).

For a counterexample for a lattice fulfilling (pOM$_{ex}$) but not (OMr), the counterexample for (pOM), i.e. MC_{10}, can be used, because, as shown in Proposition 5, (pOM$_{ex}$) can only be fulfilled if (pOM) is fulfilled.

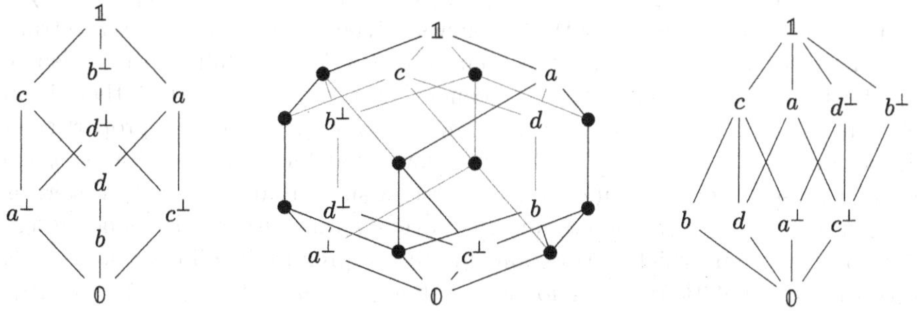

Fig. 3. Left: lattice MC_{10}, not fulfilling (pOM); middle: $R(B_2)$ [17], another counterexample for (pOM); right: example for a lattice fulfilling (pOM) but not (pOM$_{ex}$).

The rule (pOM$_{ex}$) can be considered as a weakening of another rule, namely Johansson's minimal rule (LLJ) [10], established in the context of Dunn's Kite of negation.

In its original form, it reads as follows.

(LLJ) If $a \wedge b \leq c$, then $a \wedge c^{\perp} \leq b^{\perp}$

Here, for clarity, an adapted version is used, assuming the context of an ortholattice:

(LLJ') If $a \leq b \vee c$, then $a \wedge c^{\perp} \leq b$.

When $c = a \wedge b^{\perp}$ is chosen, then this results in (pOM$_{ex}$). Thus (pOM$_{ex}$) can be considered as a specialization of (LLJ).

As further contrast between (pOM)/(pOM$_{ex}$) and (OMr), atomicity can be considered. Whereas a lattice fulfilling (OMr) is atomistic, this is not in general the case for a lattice fulfilling (pOM)/(pOM$_{ex}$), as especially lattice O_6 is not atomistic but fulfills (pOM) and (pOM$_{ex}$).

Proposition 7. *An ortholattice fulfilling (pOM) or (pOM$_{ex}$) is not necessarily atomistic.*

Now, we come back to the example at the beginning of this section and show that though the lattice of closed convex cones in $\mathbb{R}^2$ is not orthomodular, it fulfills (pOM$_{ex}$) (and thus also (pOM)).

Example 2 (Example 1 *continued).* In the following, we show that the lattice of two-dimensional closed convex cones actually fulfills (pOM$_{ex}$) and therefore also (pOM).

Proposition 8. *The lattice of closed convex cones in* $\mathbb{R}^2$ *as defined in Example 1 fulfills (pOM$_{ex}$).*

Proof. Consider cones in $\mathbb{R}^2$. Let $a \notin \{\mathbb{R}^2, \{0\}\}$ and $a \cap b^\circ \notin \{\mathbb{R}^2, \{0\}\}$ and $a^\circ \nsubseteq b$ and $b \nsubseteq a^\circ$, as otherwise (pOM$_{ex}$) follows trivially. Now let a, b be arbitrary closed convex cones such that the premise of (pOM$_{ex}$) is fulfilled and assume for the sake of contradiction that the conclusion is not fulfilled, thus, there is an element $x_a \in a \cap ch(a^\circ \cup b)$ with $x_a \in a$, but $x_a \notin b$. Due to the properties of convexity and as $a \cap b^\circ \notin \{\mathbb{R}^2, \{0\}\}$, it follows that for all $x_{a^\circ} \in a^\circ$ and $x_b \in b$ it is the case that $x_a \in ch(x_{a^\circ} \cup x_b)$. First, assume that $x_b \notin a$. However, as $x_a \in a$ and $x_{a^\circ} \notin a$, it follows due to convexity that either a is a line trough the point of origin which means that due to the premise it follows that $x_a \in b$, a contradiction. Otherwise, it follows that $a \subseteq ch(a^\circ \cup b)$. As $a \cap b^\circ \neq \{0\}$, this means that $(a \cap b^\circ) \cap ch(a^\circ \cup b) \neq \{0\}$, a contradiction. Therefore, $x_b \in a$ has to be the case for all $x_b \in b$ and therefore $b \subseteq a$. Then, it is the case that $a = ch(b \cup (a \cap b^\circ))$ and thus for all $x_{b'} \in b, x_{a \cap b^\circ} \in a \cap b^\circ$ it follows that $x_a \in ch(x_{b'} \cup x_{a \cap b^\circ})$. Therefore, due to convexity it is the case that either $x_{a \cap b^\circ} \in ch(a^\circ \cup b)$ or $x_{a^\circ} \in ch(x_a \cup x_{a \cap b^\circ})$, both a contradiction. (The proof contains a slight simplification, as for half spaces, there is an additional third point necessary such that $Y = ch(x \cup y)$ and $x \nsubseteq y$, $y \nsubseteq x$ if and only if there are points $a \in x$, $b \in y$ and $c \in x \cup y$ with $Y = ch(a \cup b \cup c)$. Such a point, however, can be added in the above proof such that the result follows analogously.)

For cone lattices in $\mathbb{R}^n$ with $n > 2$, (pOM) and (pOM$_{ex}$) are still too strong and not fulfilled. For a counterexample, see the appendix. On the other hand, cone lattices in $\mathbb{R}^2$ are not characterized by (pOM$_{ex}$), as, e.g., due to Helly's theorem, the small dimension restricts the expressivity.

4 A Forbidden Subalgebra Theorem for Partial Orthomodularity

In the following, we state a characterization theorem for (pOM), thus we show that an ortholattice fulfills (pOM) if and only if it does not contain the lattice MC_{10} as a subalgebra.

Theorem 1. *An ortholattice L fulfills (pOM) if and only if it excludes* MC_{10}.

Proof. The proof is conducted analogously to the subalgebra theorem for orthomodular lattices of Kalmbach [12, p. 22]. The equivalence of the following three statements is proven:

(i) L fulfills (pOM)
(ii) MC_{10} is not a subalgebra of L
(iii) if $a = b \vee (a \wedge b^{\perp})$, then $sub\{a, b, a^{\perp}, b^{\perp}\}$ is a Boolean subalgebra of L.

- *(i)* → *(ii)*: Let MC_{10} be a subalgebra of L, then the premises are fulfilled, but $a \wedge (a^{\perp} \vee b) = d > b$ and therefore (pOM) is not fulfilled.
- *(ii)* → *(iii)*: Assume for the sake of contradiction that (iii) is not fulfilled, thus $a = b \vee (a \wedge b^{\perp})$ and $sub\{a, b, a^{\perp}, b^{\perp}\}$ not distributive. Since MC_{10} is not a subalgebra, $a \wedge (a^{\perp} \vee b) = b$ and $b^{\perp} \wedge (b \vee a^{\perp}) = a^{\perp}$ must be valid and would imply that $sub\{a, b, a^{\perp}, b^{\perp}\} = \{\perp, \top, a, a^{\perp}, b, b^{\perp}, a \wedge b^{\perp}, b \vee a^{\perp}\}$ is distributive. It can be assumed that $a \wedge (a^{\perp} \vee b) = d > b$ (then $sub\{a, b, a^{\perp}, b^{\perp}\}$ is not distributive), then MC_{10} is a subalgebra of L and *(iii)* does not hold.
- *(iii)* → *(i)*: If (pOM) is not fulfilled, then $a \wedge (a^{\perp} \vee b) > b$ (as $a \wedge (a^{\perp} \vee b) < b$ is not possible, as $b \leq a$), therefore, the subalgebra $sub\{a, b, a^{\perp}, b^{\perp}\}$ is not Boolean.

5 A Representation Theorem for Partial Orthomodularity

Orthoframes prove to be adequate semantic interpretations for orthologics because the class of orthoframes is complete for orthologics. Goldblatt [8] strengthens this result for orthomodular logics. Therefore, he uses the notion of relative closure: X is called *⊥-closed in Z* if and only if: when $x \notin X$ then there is some $y \in Z$ such that $y \perp X$ but not $x \perp y$. Based on that definition, Goldblatt shows for any orthomodel $\mathfrak{M}$:

$$B \text{ is } \perp\text{-closed in } A \text{ if and only if } \mathfrak{M} : A \;\&\; (\sim A \bigvee B) \models B \tag{2}$$

It represents the fact that orthomodularity in orthomodels can be represented by relative closure. This enables him to define so called quantum frames as a specific class of orthoframes and to show a representation theorem for orthomodular logic and quantum frames analog to the representation theorem for orthologic and orthoframes. To further underline the connection between orthomodularity and partial orthomodularity, we show in the following that it is possible to adapt this result such that for a specific class of orthoframes (called c-frames in the following) a representation theorem for (pOM) and (pOM_{ex}) can be found. Both rules are, for completeness, given as logical rules in Fig. 4. (pOM) is given here in a slightly changed form but with the results of Proposition 4 this is clearly equivalent to (pOM). In the following, the representation theorem for (pOM) is shown which is, as will turn out at the end of this section, easily adaptable to a representation theorem for (pOM_{ex}).

Now c-frames can be defined, adapting the notion of quantum frames by Goldblatt [8] and being a specialization of orthoframes introduced in Sect. 2. Whereas point 1. of the definition mimics the definition of an orthoframe, point 2. ensures the validity of (pOM) in c-frames. Whereas for quantum frames, it is sufficient to guarantee the relative closure of Eq. (2) for all ⊥-closed subsets, for (pOM) it is necessary to relax this condition by stating (following the motivation

$$\frac{\begin{array}{l} B \vdash A \\ A \vdash B \bigvee (A \,\&\, {\sim} B) \end{array}}{A \,\&\, ({\sim} A \bigvee B) \vdash B} \qquad \frac{A \vdash B \bigvee (A \,\&\, {\sim} B)}{A \,\&\, ({\sim} A \bigvee B) \vdash B}$$

Fig. 4. Left: (pOM); Right: (pOM_{ex})

of (pOM)) that if one variant of the relative closure is valid, then the other one needs to be valid, too.

Definition 1. *A* c-frame $(X, \perp, \xi)$ *is a structure where* $(X, \perp)$ *is an orthoframe and where* ξ *is a collection of* $\perp$*-closed subsets* X *such that:*

1. ξ *is closed under set intersection and the* $\perp$*-induced polarity operator* $Y^* = \{x \mid \text{for all } y \in Y : x \perp y\}$
2. *if* $A, B \in \xi$ *and* $B \subseteq A$ *and* ${\sim} A$ *is* $\perp$*-closed in* ${\sim} B$ *then* B *is* $\perp$*-closed in* A

A c-model $(X, \perp, \xi, (\cdot)^{\mathcal{I}})$ *is an orthomodel with c-frame* $(X, \perp, \xi)$ *and assigns to each* P_i *a set from* ξ, $(P_i)^{\mathcal{I}} \in \xi$.

This is indeed a suitable definition, as all c-models verify (pOM).

Proposition 9. *All c-models verify (pOM).*

Proof. Let the premise of (pOM) be valid for an arbitrary $\mathfrak{M}$, thus $B \subseteq A$ and $A \vdash B \bigvee (A \,\&\, {\sim} B)$. This can be reformulated to $\mathfrak{M} : {\sim} B \,\&\, (B \bigvee {\sim} A) \models {\sim} A$ and with Eq. (2) it follows that ${\sim} A$ is $\perp$-closed in ${\sim} B$. With Definition 1 it follows that B is $\perp$-closed in A and with Eq. (2) it follows that $\mathfrak{M} : A \,\&\, ({\sim} A \bigvee B) \models B$. Hence, if the premise of (pOM) is valid the conclusion is valid too and thus a c-model verifies (pOM).

With a reasoning equivalent of Goldblatt [8] for orthomodularity it can be shown that any orthologic $\mathcal{L}$ that contains (pOM) is captured semantically by orthomodels over c-frames. For proving soundness and completeness the canonical c-model is created for proving equivalence to (pOM), analogue to the canonical orthomodel for proving it for ortholattices. For any formula A and logic $\mathcal{L}$ let $f_{\mathcal{L}}(A)$ be the set of all $\mathcal{L}$-full sets containing A.

Definition 2. *Let* $\mathcal{L}$ *be a logic fulfilling (pOM). The canonical c-model for* $\mathcal{L}$ *is the structure* $\mathfrak{C}_{\mathcal{L}} = \langle X_{\mathcal{L}}, \perp_{\mathcal{L}}, \xi_{\mathcal{L}}, (\cdot)^{\mathcal{I}_{(pOM)}} \rangle$ *where* $X_{\mathcal{L}} = \{x \subseteq \mathcal{F}(P) : x \text{ is } \mathcal{L}\text{-full}\}$, $x \perp_{\mathcal{L}} y$ *if and only if there is an* A *such that* ${\sim} A \in x, A \in y$ *and* $\xi_{\mathcal{L}} = \{f_{\mathcal{L}_{(pOM)}}(A) \mid A \in \mathcal{F}(P)\}$ *and the assignment function* $(P_i)^{\mathcal{I}_{(pOM)}} = f_{\mathcal{L}}(P_i)$.

It is now easy to see that $\mathfrak{C}_L$ is a c-model: the property of Definition 1 follows directly from [8], only the property of Definition 2 remains to be shown. Analogue to the proof of Proposition 9, this follows with (pOM) and Eq. (2).

This proposition allows us to show soundness and completeness of the representation of (pOM) in an algebraic way via canonical c-models.

Theorem 2. $\Gamma \vdash_{\mathcal{L}_{(pOM)}} A$ *if and only if* $\Gamma \vDash_{c-frame} A$

Proof. "$\rightarrow$"(soundness): This works by induction on the length of the derivation considering each rule case by case. This is done for the rules of O_{min} by Goldblatt (see his soundness proof [8, p. 26]). It has to be shown now for (pOM). Assume that $\mathcal{I}$ is a c-model making the premises of (pOM) true. Then with Definition 1 $\sim A$ is $\perp$-closed in $\sim B$ and B is $\perp$-closed in A. With Eq. (2) the conclusion of (pOM) directly follows.

"$\leftarrow$"(completeness): Let $\Gamma \nvdash_{\mathcal{L}_{(pOM)}} A$. Since $\mathfrak{C}_L$ is a c-model, structure $\mathcal{I}_{\mathcal{L}_{(pOM)}}$ is a c-model. Moreover, $\mathcal{I}_{\mathcal{L}_{(pOM)}}$ is a canonical model of $\mathcal{L}_{(pOM)}$ and so we can use Eq. (1) to infer that $\mathcal{I}_{(pOM)} : \Gamma \nvDash A$ which entails that the desired relation $\Gamma \nvDash_{c-frame} A$ holds.

An analogous result can be proven for (pOM$_{ex}$) by dismissing the restriction of $B \subseteq A$ in Definition 1 and adapting the other proofs accordingly.

6 Related Work

Non-distributivity is a widely studied topic, e.g., Conradie et al. [4] argue for it and present a representation theorem for a non-distributive class of logics.

Orthomodularity is an important rule in the area of quantum logic. It was introduced by Birkhoff and von Neumann [1] (and, indepently, by Husimi [11]) and extensively studied since then, on the one hand in the context of a characterization of the logic of closed subspaces of a Hilbert space and on the other hand in its own interest, e.g., based on the properties of orthomodular lattices (see, e.g., the monograph of Kalmbach [12]). Chadja and Länger [3], Bonzio and Chajda [2] and Giuntini, Ledda and Paoli [7] proposed a weakening of the orthomodularity rule, however, by dismissing the ortholattice rules. Fussner and St. John [6] consider a relaxation of the orthomodularity rule by considering residuated ortholattices, also based on a construction based on the Sasaki hook, however, in a more general setting and not related to the partial orthomodularity rules considered here. In contrast to other well-known lattice rules such as Mac Lane's condition [18, p. 111] or semimodularity [18, p. 2], which are either stronger or independent of (OMr), the rules of partial orthomodularity (pOM) and (pOM$_{ex}$) are actual relaxations of (OMr).

7 Conclusion

In this paper we have motivated the need to investigate new weakenings of orthomodularity. Using the structure of convex cones as one example for a structure not characterized by existing rules, we propose (pOM) and (pOM$_{ex}$) as two new intuitive weakenings that are also related to the geometric structure of cones. While we are already able to give a forbidden subalgebra theorem for (pOM), a similar characterization for (pOM$_{ex}$) is more involved and seems to require a different approach. Another interesting question is whether lattices fulfilling (pOM) or (pOM$_{ex}$) form a variety in the sense that they are an equationally definable class of algebras. Further investigating (pOM$_{ex}$), the varieties and obtaining a general characterization of cone structures is left for future work.

Appendix

Counterexample for the Validity of (pOM) in Cones in $\mathbb{R}^3$

Proposition 10. *A lattice based on cones in $\mathbb{R}^n$ with $n \geq 3$ does not necessarily fulfills (pOM) (and thus also not necessarily (pOM_{ex})).*

Proof. In the following, a counterexample for (pOM) in $\mathbb{R}^3$ is given: Let the cones be as follows:

$$\begin{aligned} a &= ch(\left[0\ 0\ 1\right]^T, \left[0\ 1\ 0\right]^T, \left[1\ 1\ -1\right]^T) \\ b &= ch(\left[0\ 1\ 0\right]^T, \left[1\ 1\ -1\right]^T) \\ d &= ch(\left[0\ 1\ 0\right]^T, \left[1\ 1\ -1\right]^T, \left[1\ 1\ 0\right]^T) \end{aligned}$$

It is the case that $b \subsetneq d$, as $\left[1\ 1\ 0\right]^T \in d$ but not in b, $b \subseteq a$, $ch(b \cup (a \cap b^\circ)) = a$ and $a \cap b^\circ = a \cap d^\circ$. However, as

$$ch(a^\circ \cup b^\circ) = ch(\left[1\ 0\ 0\right]^T, \left[0\ 1\ 0\right]^T, \left[-1\ 0\ 0\right]^T, \left[0\ -1\ 0\right]^T, \left[0\ 0\ -1\right]^T),$$

it follows that $a \cap ch(a^\circ \cap b) = d \neq b$.

References

1. Birkhoff, G., von Neumann, J.: The logic of quantum mechanics. Ann. Math. **37**, 823–843 (1936)
2. Bonzio, S., Chajda, I.: A note on orthomodular lattices. Int. J. Theor. Phys. **56**(12), 3740–3743 (2016). https://doi.org/10.1007/s10773-016-3258-6
3. Chajda, I., Länger, H.: Weakly orthomodular and dually weakly orthomodular lattices. Order **35**(3), 541–555 (2018). https://doi.org/10.1007/s11083-017-9448-x
4. Conradie, W., Palmigiano, A., Robinson, C., Wijnberg, N.: Non-distributive logics: from semantics to meaning. arXiv e-prints arXiv:2002.04257 (2020)
5. Dalla Chiara, M.L.: A general approach to non-distributive logics. Stud. Logica. **35**(2), 139–162 (1976). https://doi.org/10.1007/bf02120877
6. Fussner, W., St. John, G.: Negative translations of orthomodular lattices and their logic. Electron. Proc. Theor. Comput. Sci. **343**, 37–49 (2021). https://doi.org/10.4204/EPTCS.343.3
7. Giuntini, R., Ledda, A., Paoli, F.: A new view of effects in a hilbert space. Stud. Logica. **104**(6), 1145–1177 (2016). https://doi.org/10.1007/s11225-016-9670-3
8. Goldblatt, R.I.: Semantic analysis of orthologic. J. Philos. Log. **3**(1), 19–35 (1974). https://doi.org/10.1007/BF00652069
9. Grätzer, G.: Lattice Theory: Foundation. Springer, Basel (2011). https://doi.org/10.1007/978-3-0348-0018-1
10. Hartonas, C.: Reasoning with incomplete information in generalized galois logics without distribution: the case of negation and modal operators. In: Bimbó, K. (ed.) J. Michael Dunn on Information Based Logics. OCL, vol. 8, pp. 279–312. Springer, Cham (2016). https://doi.org/10.1007/978-3-319-29300-4_14

11. Husimi, K.: Studies on the foundation of quantum mechanics. i. Proceedings of the Physico-Mathematical Society of Japan. 3rd Series, vol. 19, pp. 766–789 (1937). https://doi.org/10.11429/ppmsj1919.19.0_766
12. Kalmbach, G.: Orthomodular Lattices. Academic Press, Cambridge (1983)
13. Leemhuis, M., Özçep, Ö.L.: Conceptual orthospaces - convexity meets negation. Int. J. Approx. Reason. **162**, 109013 (2023). https://doi.org/10.1016/J.IJAR.2023.109013
14. Leemhuis, M., Özçep, Ö.L., Wolter, D.: Learning with cone-based geometric models and orthologics. Ann. Math. Artif. Intell. **90**(11–12), 1159–1195 (2022). https://doi.org/10.1007/S10472-022-09806-1
15. Özçep, Ö.L., Leemhuis, M., Wolter, D.: Embedding ontologies in the description logic ALC by axis-aligned cones. J. Artif. Intell. Res. **78**, 217–267 (2023). https://doi.org/10.1613/JAIR.1.13939
16. Rédei, M.: Quantum Logic in Algebraic Approach. Fundamental Theories of Physics. Springer, Dordrecht (1998). https://doi.org/10.1007/978-94-015-9026-6
17. Santocanale, L., Wehrung, F.: The extended permutohedron on a transitive binary relation. Eur. J. Comb. **42**, 179–206 (2014). https://doi.org/10.1016/j.ejc.2014.06.004
18. Stern, M.: Semimodular Lattices. Vieweg+Teubner Verlag (1991). https://doi.org/10.1007/978-3-663-12478-8

Labelled Sequent Calculi for Inquisitive Modal Logics

Valentin Müller(✉)

78315 Radolfzell am Bodensee, Germany
valentin.johannes.mueller@gmail.com

Abstract. We present cut-free labelled sequent calculi for various systems of inquisitive modal logic, including *inquisitive epistemic logic* and *inquisitive doxastic logic*. Inquisitive modal logic extends the framework of standard modal logic with a question-forming operator and an inquisitive modal operator. Under an epistemic interpretation, this modal operator may be used to express not only the information available to an agent, but also the issues entertained by the agent. Each of our proof systems is shown to satisfy cut-admissibility, height-preserving admissibility of weakening and contraction, and height-preserving invertibility of all rules. The completeness of our calculi is established proof-theoretically.

Keywords: Inquisitive semantics · Team semantics · Modal logic · Epistemic logic · Doxastic logic · Proof theory · Labelled sequent calculi

1 Introduction

Inquisitive modal logic is a semantic framework introduced in [2,3,5] which allows to reason about declarative and interrogative aspects of meaning in a uniform way. This is achieved by enriching the framework of Kripke-style modal logic with an inquisitive disjunction $\mathbin{\rotatebox[origin=c]{-90}{$\geqslant$}}$ and an inquisitive modality $\boxplus$. The connective $\mathbin{\rotatebox[origin=c]{-90}{$\geqslant$}}$ is used to form alternative questions within the object language, so $\varphi \mathbin{\rotatebox[origin=c]{-90}{$\geqslant$}} \psi$ stands for the question *whether* φ *or* ψ. The modality $\boxplus$ can be interpreted in various different ways, depending on the intended application. For example, in an *epistemic* setting, $\boxplus$ may be used to express not only the *knowledge* of an agent, but also the *issues* entertained by the agent at a possible world [2,5]. As shown by Ciardelli [3], inquisitive modal logic is strictly more expressive than standard modal logic, even when restricted to purely declarative formulas.

In this paper, we provide modular labelled sequent calculi for a family of inquisitive modal logics previously considered in [3]. Labelled sequent calculi play an important role in the proof theory of non-classical logics [6,12] and can be seen as an extension of the standard sequent-style formalism introduced by Gentzen [7,8]. The basic idea is to enrich the language of a sequent calculus with labels in order to incorporate the semantics of a logic directly into the syntax of the proof system. A labelled sequent calculus for basic inquisitive logic (without any modalities) was described by Chen and Ma [1]. A more comprehensive study of labelled

G. Metcalfe et al. (Eds.): WoLLIC 2024, LNCS 14672, pp. 122–139, 2024.
https://doi.org/10.1007/978-3-031-62687-6_9

sequent calculi for inquisitive logics was provided by Müller [10], who also considers inquisitive logics with Kripke modalities (but without the operator $\boxplus$). The proof systems presented here extend the class of calculi proposed in [10, Ch. 5] with additional rules accounting for the semantics of the modality $\boxplus$.

The paper is structured as follows. In Sect. 2, we will introduce various systems of inquisitive modal logic, including *inquisitive epistemic logic* (IEL) and *inquisitive doxastic logic* (IDL). In Sect. 3, we will then define cut-free labelled sequent calculi for the full class of these logics. The structural properties of our calculi are investigated in Sect. 4. Each of our proof systems is shown to satisfy cut-admissibility, height-preserving admissibility of weakening and contraction, and height-preserving invertibility of all rules. The completeness of our proof systems is established in Sect. 5, using the admissibility of the cut rule.

2 Inquisitive Modal Logic

We start by providing a short introduction to inquisitive modal logic. Further details can be found in [2–5]. Inquisitive semantics is a generalization of truth-conditional approaches to meaning which allows to analyse the semantic content of statements and questions in a uniform way. Rather than specifying what it means for a formula to be *true* in relation to a state of affairs (a possible world), inquisitive logic specifies what it means for a formula to be *supported* by a state of information. Such a state of information can be modelled as a set of possible worlds, namely, those worlds that are compatible with the information available in the state. Thus, an *information state* over a set of worlds W simply amounts to a subset $s \subseteq W$ [4, p. 16]. Declarative and interrogative aspects of meaning can now be represented using the concept of an *inquisitive proposition* [3, p. 252].

Definition 1 (Inquisitive Proposition). *An* inquisitive proposition *over a set of worlds W is a non-empty set of information states $\Pi \subseteq \mathcal{P}(W)$ which is downward closed, i.e., for all states $s, t \subseteq W$, if $s \in \Pi$ and $t \subseteq s$, then $t \in \Pi$.*

An inquisitive proposition Π can be seen as a uniform representation of both information and issues. The *informative content* of Π is given by the information state $\bigcup \Pi$, i.e., by the union of all states contained in Π. And the *issue* described by Π is the one which is settled by a state s if and only if s is a member of Π.

The basic system of inquisitive modal logic will be denoted by InqM. Recall that, in ordinary modal logic, a Kripke frame can be seen as a pair $\langle W, \sigma \rangle$, where W is a set of worlds and $\sigma : W \to \mathcal{P}(W)$ is a function which assigns, to each world w, an information state $\sigma(w)$, namely, the set of all worlds *accessible* from w. In InqM, a frame is equipped with a function $\Sigma : W \to \mathcal{PP}(W)$, assigning to each $w \in W$ an *inquisitive proposition* $\Sigma(w)$. Under an epistemic interpretation, $\Sigma(w)$ might be conceived as a combined representation of the *information* available to an agent and the *issues* entertained by the agent at w [3, pp. 253–254].

Definition 2 (Inquisitive Modal Model). *An* inquisitive frame *is a pair $F = \langle W, \Sigma \rangle$, where $W \neq \emptyset$ is a set of worlds and $\Sigma : W \to \mathcal{PP}(W)$ is a function* *which assigns, to each $w \in W$, an inquisitive proposition $\Sigma(w)$. An* inquisitive modal model *for a set of atomic formulas* P *is a triple* $M = \langle W, \Sigma, V \rangle$*, where* $\langle W, \Sigma \rangle$ *is an inquisitive frame and* $V : W \times \mathsf{P} \to \{0, 1\}$ *is a valuation function.*

Given a frame $F = \langle W, \Sigma \rangle$ and a world $w \in W$, we also write $\sigma(w)$ for the *informative content* of $\Sigma(w)$, so $\sigma(w) := \bigcup \Sigma(w)$. In what follows, we will assume a fixed set P of atomic propositions, denoted by the meta-variables p and q. The language of InqM, notation $\mathcal{L}^{\boxplus}$, is generated by the following grammar:

$$\varphi ::= p \mid \bot \mid \varphi \wedge \varphi \mid \varphi \rightarrow \varphi \mid \varphi \vee\!\!\!\vee \varphi \mid \Box\varphi \mid \boxplus\varphi \qquad (p \in \mathsf{P}).$$

We also put $\neg\varphi := \varphi \rightarrow \bot$, $\varphi \leftrightarrow \psi := (\varphi \rightarrow \psi) \wedge (\psi \rightarrow \varphi)$ and $\varphi \vee \psi := \neg(\neg\varphi \wedge \neg\psi)$. The operator $\vee\!\!\!\vee$, known as *inquisitive disjunction*, allows to form alternative questions within the language of InqM, so $\varphi \vee\!\!\!\vee \psi$ stands for the question *whether* φ *or* ψ. The operator $\boxplus$ is an *inquisitive modality* and allows to express properties of the proposition $\Sigma(w)$ assigned to a world w in a model. For example, in an epistemic setting, $\boxplus\varphi$ may be read as 'The agent entertains the issue raised by φ' [4, p. 155]. The semantics of InqM is given by spelling out the support conditions for all formulas in $\mathcal{L}^{\boxplus}$. Intuitively, a state s supports a formula φ, if s implies the informative content of φ, and it also resolves the issue raised by φ.

Definition 3 (Support). *For any model M and state $s \subseteq W$, we define:*

- $M, s \models p \;:\Leftrightarrow\; V(w, p) = 1$ *for all* $w \in s$,
- $M, s \models \bot \;:\Leftrightarrow\; s = \emptyset$,
- $M, s \models \varphi \wedge \psi \;:\Leftrightarrow\; M, s \models \varphi$ *and* $M, s \models \psi$,
- $M, s \models \varphi \rightarrow \psi \;:\Leftrightarrow$ *for all* $t \subseteq s$*: if* $M, t \models \varphi$*, then* $M, t \models \psi$,
- $M, s \models \varphi \vee\!\!\!\vee \psi \;:\Leftrightarrow\; M, s \models \varphi$ *or* $M, s \models \psi$,
- $M, s \models \Box\varphi \;:\Leftrightarrow$ *for all* $w \in s$*:* $M, \sigma(w) \models \varphi$,
- $M, s \models \boxplus\varphi \;:\Leftrightarrow$ *for all* $w \in s$ *and for all* $t \in \Sigma(w)$*:* $M, t \models \varphi$.

If $M, s \models \varphi$ holds, then φ is said to be *supported* by s. It is easy to check that support in InqM is *persistent*: if $M, s \models \varphi$ and $t \subseteq s$, then also $M, t \models \varphi$. Moreover, the empty state supports every formula, so we always have $M, \emptyset \models \varphi$.

We will write $\Gamma \models \varphi$ and say that φ is *entailed* by Γ, if for every state s over any model M, it is the case that $M, s \models \psi$ for all $\psi \in \Gamma$ implies $M, s \models \varphi$. And a formula φ is said to be *true* at a world w of a model M, notation $M, w \models \varphi$, if it holds $M, \{w\} \models \varphi$. The semantic difference between statements and questions is formalized using the concept of truth-conditionality. Formally, φ is called *truth-conditional*, if for all models M and all states s, we have: $M, s \models \varphi$ if and only if $M, w \models \varphi$ for all $w \in s$. A formula φ is now said to be a *statement*, if it is truth-conditional, and it is said to be a *question* otherwise. The set of *declarative formulas*, notation $\mathcal{L}^{\boxplus}_{d}$, is generated by the following grammar [3, p. 260]:

$$\alpha ::= p \mid \bot \mid \Box\varphi \mid \boxplus\varphi \mid \alpha \wedge \alpha \mid \alpha \rightarrow \alpha \qquad (p \in \mathsf{P} \text{ and } \varphi \in \mathcal{L}^{\boxplus}).$$

Declarative formulas will be denoted by the meta-variables α and β.

Proposition 1. *Every declarative formula* $\alpha \in \mathcal{L}_d^{\boxplus}$ *is truth-conditional.*[1]

The proof proceeds by induction on the structure of α (cf. [3, Prop. 7.1.20]). As in standard modal logic, one can define various extensions of the basic system by requiring models to satisfy certain additional constraints. Following [3], we only consider the four constraints presented in Table 1. Given any collection C of these constraints, we define a corresponding extension L of InqM by restricting the entailment relation $\models$ to models satisfying each of the constraints in C. The resulting entailment relation will be denoted by $\models_L$. *Inquisitive epistemic logic* (IEL) is the logic of models satisfying factivity as well as positive and negative introspection, and *inquisitive doxastic logic* (IDL) is the logic of models satisfying consistency as well as positive and negative introspection [3, p. 293].

Table 1. Possible constraints for models and corresponding axiom schemes.

Model Constraint	Axiom Scheme
Factivity: $w \in \sigma(w)$ for all $w \in W$	(T) $\boxplus\alpha \to \alpha \quad (\alpha \in \mathcal{L}_d^{\boxplus})$
Consistency: $\sigma(w) \neq \emptyset$ for all $w \in W$	(D) $\neg\boxplus\bot$
Positive introspection: if $u \in \sigma(w)$, then $\Sigma(u) \subseteq \Sigma(w)$	(4) $\boxplus\varphi \to \boxplus\boxplus\varphi$
Negative introspection: if $u \in \sigma(w)$, then $\Sigma(w) \subseteq \Sigma(u)$	(5) $\neg\boxplus\varphi \to \boxplus\neg\boxplus\varphi$

A natural deduction system for InqM was provided by Ciardelli [3, Sect. 7.3.4]. An equivalent Hilbert-style system, denoted HinqM, is presented in Fig. 1. Given any inquisitive modal logic L determined by imposing zero or more of the constraints from Table 1, one can obtain a Hilbert-style system HinqM_L for L by adding the corresponding set of axiom schemes $S \subseteq \{\mathtt{T}, \mathtt{D}, \mathtt{4}, \mathtt{5}\}$ to the system HinqM (see the right column of Table 1). The provability relation of HinqM_L will be denoted by $\vdash^{\mathrm{H}}_L$, so we write $\Gamma \vdash^{\mathrm{H}}_L \varphi$ and say that φ is *provable* from Γ in HinqM_L, if one of the following holds: (1) φ is an element of Γ, or (2) φ is an axiom of HinqM_L, or (3) there is some $\psi \in \mathcal{L}^{\boxplus}$ such that $\Gamma \vdash^{\mathrm{H}}_L \psi$ and $\Gamma \vdash^{\mathrm{H}}_L \psi \to \varphi$, or (4) there is some $\psi \in \mathcal{L}^{\boxplus}$ and some $\boxtimes \in \{\Box, \boxplus\}$ such that $\varphi = \boxtimes\psi$ and $\vdash^{\mathrm{H}}_L \psi$.

Theorem 1 (Completeness). *Let* L *be an extension of* InqM *determined by some combination of the constraints from Table 1. The proof system* HinqM_L *is sound and complete with respect to* L*, so we have:* $\Gamma \vdash^{\mathrm{H}}_L \varphi$ *iff* $\Gamma \models_L \varphi$.

Proof. See Appendix A. □

3 Labelled Sequent Calculi for Inquisitive Modal Logics

We will now define cut-free labelled sequent calculi for the family of extensions of InqM introduced in the previous section. Each of our calculi will be equipped

[1] The converse does not hold. For example, $p \vee p$ is truth-conditional, but $(p \vee p) \notin \mathcal{L}_d^{\boxplus}$.

(A1) $\varphi \to (\psi \to \varphi)$	(A2) $(\varphi \to (\psi \to \chi)) \to ((\varphi \to \psi) \to (\varphi \to \chi))$
(A3) $(\varphi \wedge \psi) \to \varphi,\ (\varphi \wedge \psi) \to \psi$	(A4) $\varphi \to (\psi \to (\varphi \wedge \psi))$
(A5) $\varphi \to (\varphi \vee \psi),\ \psi \to (\varphi \vee \psi)$	(A6) $(\varphi \to \chi) \to ((\psi \to \chi) \to ((\varphi \vee \psi) \to \chi))$
(A7) $\bot \to \varphi$	(Ds) $\Box(\varphi \vee \psi) \to (\Box\varphi \vee \Box\psi)$
(K$_\Box$) $\Box(\varphi \to \psi) \to (\Box\varphi \to \Box\psi)$	(K$_\boxplus$) $\boxplus(\varphi \to \psi) \to (\boxplus\varphi \to \boxplus\psi)$
(C) $\Box\alpha \leftrightarrow \boxplus\alpha \quad (\alpha \in \mathcal{L}_d^{\boxplus})$	(Dn) $\neg\neg\alpha \to \alpha \quad (\alpha \in \mathcal{L}_d^{\boxplus})$
(S) $(\alpha \to (\varphi \vee \psi)) \to ((\alpha \to \varphi) \vee (\alpha \to \psi)) \quad (\alpha \in \mathcal{L}_d^{\boxplus})$	

- *Modus ponens*: from $\Gamma \vdash \varphi$ and $\Gamma \vdash \varphi \to \psi$, infer $\Gamma \vdash \psi$.
- *Necessitation*: from $\vdash \varphi$, infer $\Gamma \vdash \boxtimes\varphi$, for any $\boxtimes \in \{\Box, \boxplus\}$ and any $\Gamma \subseteq \mathcal{L}^{\boxplus}$.

Fig. 1. The Hilbert-style system HinqM.

with two sorts of labels, referred to as *state labels* and *proposition labels.* State labels will be used to denote information states, and proposition labels will be used to denote the propositions $\Sigma(w)$ assigned to the worlds in a model. As in [10], we assume two infinite sets of *state variables*, denoted by $\mathfrak{S}$ and $\mathfrak{A}$. The variables in $\mathfrak{S}$ stand for *singleton states*, and the variables in $\mathfrak{A}$ stand for *states of arbitrary size.* In order to avoid confusion, we will always use the meta-variables u, v, w for elements of $\mathfrak{S}$ and the meta-variables x, y, z for elements of $\mathfrak{A}$.

Definition 4 (Labels). *The set of* state labels, *notation* SL, *consists of all expressions generated by the following grammar, where* $w \in \mathfrak{S}$ *and* $x \in \mathfrak{A}$:

$$\pi ::= w \mid x \mid \emptyset \mid \pi \cup \pi \mid \sigma(w).$$

The set of proposition labels, *notation* PL, *is given by* $\mathsf{PL} := \{\Sigma(w) \mid w \in \mathfrak{S}\}$. *And the set of all labels, notation* Lab, *is defined by* $\mathsf{Lab} := \mathsf{SL} \cup \mathsf{PL}$.

We will henceforth use the meta-variables π, τ, μ for arbitrarily complex state labels from SL. Labels are interpreted in the obvious way. So, in particular, $\emptyset$ represents the empty state, and $\pi \cup \tau$ represents the union of the states denoted by π and τ. A proposition label $\Sigma(w)$ stands for the proposition assigned to the unique world contained in the singleton w, and a state label of the form $\sigma(w)$ represents the informative content of this proposition (see Sect. 2).

By a *labelled formula*, we will mean an expression of the form $\pi : \varphi$, where $\pi \in \mathsf{SL}$ is a state label and $\varphi \in \mathcal{L}^{\boxplus}$ is a formula. Labelled formulas will be used to incorporate the support semantics of InqM directly into the syntax of our calculi. So, intuitively, $\pi : \varphi$ stands for the statement 'φ is supported by the state π'.

A *relational atom* is defined to be an expression of the form $\pi \subseteq \tau$ or an expression of the form $\pi \in \Sigma(w)$, where $\pi, \tau \in \mathsf{SL}$ are state labels and $\Sigma(w) \in \mathsf{PL}$ is a proposition label. Intuitively, $\pi \subseteq \tau$ may be read as 'State π is a subset of state τ', and $\pi \in \Sigma(w)$ may be read as 'π is an element of the proposition $\Sigma(w)$'.

A *sequent* is now defined to be an expression of the form $\Gamma \Rightarrow \Delta$, where Γ is a finite multiset containing labelled formulas and relational atoms, and Δ is a finite multiset containing only labelled formulas (but no relational atoms).

Initial Sequents (Axioms)

$$\mathsf{ax}\,\frac{}{w : p, \Gamma \Rightarrow \Delta, w : p} \qquad \mathsf{ax}_{\bot}\,\frac{}{w : \bot, \Gamma \Rightarrow \Delta} \qquad \mathsf{ax}_{\emptyset}\,\frac{}{w \subseteq \emptyset, \Gamma \Rightarrow \Delta}$$

Logical Rules

$$\mathsf{p}_L\,\frac{w : p, w \subseteq \pi, \pi : p, \Gamma \Rightarrow \Delta}{w \subseteq \pi, \pi : p, \Gamma \Rightarrow \Delta} \qquad \mathsf{p}_R\,\frac{w \subseteq \pi, \Gamma \Rightarrow \Delta, w : p}{\Gamma \Rightarrow \Delta, \pi : p}\,(\ddagger, *)$$

$$\bot_L\,\frac{w : \bot, w \subseteq \pi, \pi : \bot, \Gamma \Rightarrow \Delta}{w \subseteq \pi, \pi : \bot, \Gamma \Rightarrow \Delta} \qquad \bot_R\,\frac{w \subseteq \pi, \Gamma \Rightarrow \Delta, w : \bot}{\Gamma \Rightarrow \Delta, \pi : \bot}\,(\ddagger, *)$$

$$\wedge_L\,\frac{\pi : \varphi, \pi : \psi, \Gamma \Rightarrow \Delta}{\pi : \varphi \wedge \psi, \Gamma \Rightarrow \Delta} \qquad \wedge_R\,\frac{\Gamma \Rightarrow \Delta, \pi : \varphi \qquad \Gamma \Rightarrow \Delta, \pi : \psi}{\Gamma \Rightarrow \Delta, \pi : \varphi \wedge \psi}$$

$$\mathbin{\vee\!\!\!\vee}_L\,\frac{\pi : \varphi, \Gamma \Rightarrow \Delta \qquad \pi : \psi, \Gamma \Rightarrow \Delta}{\pi : \varphi \mathbin{\vee\!\!\!\vee} \psi, \Gamma \Rightarrow \Delta} \qquad \mathbin{\vee\!\!\!\vee}_R\,\frac{\Gamma \Rightarrow \Delta, \pi : \varphi, \pi : \psi}{\Gamma \Rightarrow \Delta, \pi : \varphi \mathbin{\vee\!\!\!\vee} \psi}$$

$$\rightarrow_L\,\frac{\pi \subseteq \tau, \tau : \varphi \rightarrow \psi, \Gamma \Rightarrow \Delta, \pi : \varphi \qquad \pi \subseteq \tau, \tau : \varphi \rightarrow \psi, \pi : \psi, \Gamma \Rightarrow \Delta}{\pi \subseteq \tau, \tau : \varphi \rightarrow \psi, \Gamma \Rightarrow \Delta}$$

$$\rightarrow_R\,\frac{x \subseteq \pi, x : \varphi, \Gamma \Rightarrow \Delta, x : \psi}{\Gamma \Rightarrow \Delta, \pi : \varphi \rightarrow \psi}\,(\S)$$

$$\Box_L\,\frac{\sigma(w) : \varphi, w \subseteq \pi, \pi : \Box\varphi, \Gamma \Rightarrow \Delta}{w \subseteq \pi, \pi : \Box\varphi, \Gamma \Rightarrow \Delta} \qquad \Box_R\,\frac{w \subseteq \pi, \Gamma \Rightarrow \Delta, \sigma(w) : \varphi}{\Gamma \Rightarrow \Delta, \pi : \Box\varphi}\,(\ddagger)$$

$$\boxplus_L\,\frac{\tau : \varphi, w \subseteq \pi, \tau \in \Sigma(w), \pi : \boxplus\varphi, \Gamma \Rightarrow \Delta}{w \subseteq \pi, \tau \in \Sigma(w), \pi : \boxplus\varphi, \Gamma \Rightarrow \Delta} \qquad \boxplus_R\,\frac{w \subseteq \pi, x \in \Sigma(w), \Gamma \Rightarrow \Delta, x : \varphi}{\Gamma \Rightarrow \Delta, \pi : \boxplus\varphi}\,(\ddagger, \S)$$

Order Rules

$$\mathsf{tr}\,\frac{\pi \subseteq \mu, \pi \subseteq \tau, \tau \subseteq \mu, \Gamma \Rightarrow \Delta}{\pi \subseteq \tau, \tau \subseteq \mu, \Gamma \Rightarrow \Delta} \qquad \mathsf{sg}\,\frac{\pi \subseteq \emptyset, \pi \subseteq w, \Gamma \Rightarrow \Delta \qquad w \subseteq \pi, \pi \subseteq w, \Gamma \Rightarrow \Delta}{\pi \subseteq w, \Gamma \Rightarrow \Delta}$$

$$\mathsf{rf}\,\frac{\pi \subseteq \pi, \Gamma \Rightarrow \Delta}{\Gamma \Rightarrow \Delta} \qquad \mathsf{ul}\,\frac{\pi \cup \tau \subseteq \mu, \pi \subseteq \mu, \tau \subseteq \mu, \Gamma \Rightarrow \Delta}{\pi \subseteq \mu, \tau \subseteq \mu, \Gamma \Rightarrow \Delta} \qquad \mathsf{ur}\,\frac{\pi_i \subseteq \pi_1 \cup \pi_2, \Gamma \Rightarrow \Delta}{\Gamma \Rightarrow \Delta}\,(i = 1, 2)$$

$$\mathsf{id}\,\frac{\sigma(w) \subseteq \sigma(u), w \subseteq u, \Gamma \Rightarrow \Delta}{w \subseteq u, \Gamma \Rightarrow \Delta} \qquad \mathsf{cd}\,\frac{w \subseteq \pi, w \subseteq \pi \cup \tau, \Gamma \Rightarrow \Delta \quad w \subseteq \tau, w \subseteq \pi \cup \tau, \Gamma \Rightarrow \Delta}{w \subseteq \pi \cup \tau, \Gamma \Rightarrow \Delta}$$

$$\mathsf{sig}{\downarrow}\,\frac{\pi \subseteq \sigma(w), \pi \in \Sigma(w), \Gamma \Rightarrow \Delta}{\pi \in \Sigma(w), \Gamma \Rightarrow \Delta} \qquad \mathsf{sig}{\uparrow}\,\frac{w \in \Sigma(u), w \subseteq \sigma(u), \Gamma \Rightarrow \Delta}{w \subseteq \sigma(u), \Gamma \Rightarrow \Delta}$$

***Side conditions*: ($\ddagger$) means that $w \in \mathfrak{S}$ must be fresh, and ($\S$) means that $x \in \mathfrak{A}$ must be fresh. In rules marked with ($*$), we require π to be a non-singleton state label, so $\pi \in \mathsf{SL}$ and $\pi \notin \mathfrak{S}$.**

Fig. 2. The labelled sequent calculus GinqM.

Definition 5. *A* variable interpretation *over a model $M = \langle W, \Sigma, V\rangle$ is a function $I : \mathfrak{S} \cup \mathfrak{A} \rightarrow \mathcal{P}(W)$ which assigns to each $w \in \mathfrak{S}$ a singleton state $I(w) \subseteq W$ and to each $x \in \mathfrak{A}$ an arbitrary state $I(x) \subseteq W$. Such a function I is extended to all labels by putting $I(\emptyset) := \emptyset$, $I(\pi \cup \tau) := I(\pi) \cup I(\tau)$ as well as $I(\sigma(w)) := \sigma(u)$ and $I(\Sigma(w)) := \Sigma(u)$, where u is the unique world such that $I(w) = \{u\}$.*

A labelled formula $\pi : \varphi$ is *satisfied* by an interpretation I over a model M, if we have $M, I(\pi) \models \varphi$. And relational atoms $\pi \subseteq \tau$ and $\pi \in \Sigma(w)$ are satisfied by I, if it holds $I(\pi) \subseteq I(\tau)$ and $I(\pi) \in I(\Sigma(w))$, respectively. We also say that a sequent $\Gamma \Rightarrow \Delta$ is *valid*, if for every interpretation I over any model M, it holds: if I satisfies all elements of Γ, then I satisfies at least one element of Δ.

$$\mathsf{t}\frac{w \subseteq \sigma(w), \Gamma \Rightarrow \Delta}{\Gamma \Rightarrow \Delta} \qquad \mathsf{d}\frac{u \subseteq \sigma(w), \Gamma \Rightarrow \Delta}{\Gamma \Rightarrow \Delta}(u \text{ fresh})$$

$$4\frac{\pi \in \Sigma(w), u \subseteq \sigma(w), \pi \in \Sigma(u), \Gamma \Rightarrow \Delta}{u \subseteq \sigma(w), \pi \in \Sigma(u), \Gamma \Rightarrow \Delta} \qquad 5\frac{\pi \in \Sigma(u), u \subseteq \sigma(w), \pi \in \Sigma(w), \Gamma \Rightarrow \Delta}{u \subseteq \sigma(w), \pi \in \Sigma(w), \Gamma \Rightarrow \Delta}$$

Fig. 3. Special order rules corresponding to the constraints from Table 1.

A labelled sequent calculus GinqM for the basic system InqM is depicted in Fig. 2. Note that, in the figure, w and u range over variables from $\mathfrak{S}$, x ranges over variables from $\mathfrak{A}$, and π, τ, μ range over arbitrary state labels from SL. Moreover, some rules are subject to additional side conditions. For instance, w must be fresh in all rules marked with (‡), and x must be fresh in all rules marked with (§). Here, 'fresh' means that the corresponding variable does not occur in the sequent acting as the conclusion of the rule. The fresh variables involved in the rules p_R, $\bot_R$, $\to_R$, $\Box_R$, $\boxplus_R$ are said to be the *eigenvariables* of these rules. As can be seen, the *logical rules* of our system simply mirror the support conditions for the formulas of InqM, and the *order rules* reflect the set-theoretic properties of information states and inquisitive propositions (see also [10, Sect. 3.1]).

The calculus GinqM can be extended modularly to cover not only the basic system InqM, but also any of the extensions of InqM introduced in Sect. 2. This is achieved by translating the model constraints from Table 1 into equivalent order rules. The resulting rules are displayed in Fig. 3. Given any inquisitive modal logic L determined by some combination of the constraints from Table 1, one can obtain a labelled sequent calculus GinqM_L for L by adding the corresponding set of order rules $R \subseteq \{\mathsf{t}, \mathsf{d}, 4, 5\}$ to the system GinqM. Provability in any of the systems GinqM_L is defined as follows: we write $\Gamma \vdash^{\mathsf{G}}_{L} \varphi$ and say that φ *is provable from* $\Gamma \subseteq \mathcal{L}^{\boxplus}$ in GinqM_L, if there exists a finite subset $\Delta \subseteq \Gamma$ and a state variable $x \in \mathfrak{A}$ such that the sequent $x : \Delta \Rightarrow x : \varphi$ is derivable in GinqM_L, where $(x : \Delta) := \{x : \psi \mid \psi \in \Delta\}$. Later on, we will see that the concrete choice of the variable x does not matter: if $x : \Delta \Rightarrow x : \varphi$ is derivable for *some* $x \in \mathfrak{A}$, then it is also derivable for *every* $x \in \mathfrak{A}$ (see Proposition 2). If it holds $\emptyset \vdash^{\mathsf{G}}_{L} \varphi$, then we will also write $\vdash^{\mathsf{G}}_{L} \varphi$ and say that φ *is provable* in GinqM_L.

In each of the rules and axioms from Figs. 2 and 3, Γ is called the *left context* and Δ is called the *right context*. An expression occurring in an axiom or in the conclusion of a rule is called *principal*, if it does not belong to the context. In order to make sure that contraction is admissible, we also adopt the well-known *closure condition* from [11–13]: if an instance of an order rule of GinqM_L produces a duplication of a principal relational atom A in the conclusion of the rule, then also the contracted instance of the rule (in which the two occurrences of A are replaced by a single one) is assumed to be part of the system GinqM_L.

Lemma 1. *All sequents of the following form are derivable in* GinqM*:*

1. $\pi \subseteq \tau, \tau : \varphi, \Gamma \Rightarrow \Delta, \pi : \varphi$,
2. $\pi : \varphi, \Gamma \Rightarrow \Delta, \pi : \varphi$,
3. $\pi \subseteq \emptyset, \Gamma \Rightarrow \Delta, \pi : \varphi$,
4. $\pi : \bot, \Gamma \Rightarrow \Delta, \pi : \varphi$.

Proof. By induction on φ. See also [10, Sect. 3.2.1 and Lemmas 5.4.1–5.4.2]. □

4 Structural Properties

We will now investigate the structural properties of our sequent calculi. We will see that each of the systems GinqM_L satisfies cut-admissibility, height-preserving admissibility of weakening and contraction, and height-preserving invertibility of all rules. Throughout the rest of this paper, let L be an arbitrary extension of InqM obtained by imposing zero or more of the constraints from Table 1, and let GinqM_L be the corresponding sequent calculus introduced in Sect. 3.

By the *height* of a derivation $\mathcal{D}$, we mean the length of a longest branch in $\mathcal{D}$. As usual, a rule is said to be *height-preserving admissible* (or *hp-admissible*), if whenever all premises of the rule are derivable by a proof tree of height at most n, then also the conclusion of the rule is derivable by a proof tree of height at most n. If the admissibility of a rule is not height-preserving, then the rule is simply called *admissible.* And a rule is said to be *height-preserving invertible* (or *hp-invertible*), if whenever the conclusion of the rule is derivable by a proof tree of height at most n, then so is each premise of the rule [14, pp. 19–20].

Given any variable $s \in \mathfrak{S} \cup \mathfrak{A}$, a state label $\pi \in \mathsf{SL}$ and an arbitrary label $\lambda \in \mathsf{Lab}$, we define $\lambda(\pi/s)$ to be the result of replacing every occurrence of s in λ by π. As in [10, p. 46], we also write $\Gamma(\pi/s)$ for the result of substituting π for s in each label occurring in a multiset Γ. The *substitution rules* are given by

$$(u/w)\frac{\Gamma \Rightarrow \Delta}{\Gamma(u/w) \Rightarrow \Delta(u/w)} \qquad \text{and} \qquad (\pi/x)\frac{\Gamma \Rightarrow \Delta}{\Gamma(\pi/x) \Rightarrow \Delta(\pi/x)}$$

where u and w are variables from $\mathfrak{S}$, x is a variable from $\mathfrak{A}$, and π is an arbitrary state label from SL. Note that, in particular, we allow variables from $\mathfrak{S}$ to be replaced only by other variables from $\mathfrak{S}$, but not by any other state label.

Proposition 2. *The substitution rules are hp-admissible in* GinqM_L.

The proof works in the same way as in [10, p. 47]. We can now prove the desired results: the rules of *weakening* and *contraction*, displayed in Fig. 4, are hp-admissible in GinqM_L. Furthermore, all rules of GinqM_L are hp-invertible.

$$\mathtt{W}_L\frac{\Gamma \Rightarrow \Delta}{E, \Gamma \Rightarrow \Delta}(\dagger) \qquad \mathtt{W}_R\frac{\Gamma \Rightarrow \Delta}{\Gamma \Rightarrow \Delta, \pi : \varphi} \qquad \mathtt{C}_L\frac{E, E, \Gamma \Rightarrow \Delta}{E, \Gamma \Rightarrow \Delta}(\dagger) \qquad \mathtt{C}_R\frac{\Gamma \Rightarrow \Delta, \pi : \varphi, \pi : \varphi}{\Gamma \Rightarrow \Delta, \pi : \varphi}$$

$$\mathtt{cut}\frac{\Gamma \Rightarrow \Delta, \pi : \varphi \qquad \pi : \varphi, \Pi \Rightarrow \Phi}{\Gamma, \Pi \Rightarrow \Delta, \Phi}$$

(†) In the rules $\mathtt{W}_L$ and $\mathtt{C}_L$, E may be either a relational atom or a labelled formula.

Fig. 4. The structural rules of weakening, contraction and cut.

Proposition 3. *The weakening rules are hp-admissible in* GinqM_L.

Proof. For both of the rules $\mathtt{W}_L$ and $\mathtt{W}_R$, hp-admissibility is proved by induction on the height of a derivation $\mathcal{D}$ for the premise of the rule. In the inductive step, we consider the last rule applied in $\mathcal{D}$. If this rule has no eigenvariables, we simply apply the induction hypothesis to the premises and then the same rule again. Otherwise, we first use Proposition 2 in order to introduce fresh eigenvariables not clashing with the variables in the weakening formula. See [10, pp. 47–48]. □

Proposition 4. *All rules of* GinqM_L *are hp-invertible.*

Proof. The logical rules for atoms and for the symbols $\bot$, $\wedge$, $\mathbb{V}$, $\rightarrow$, $\Box$ are treated in the same way as in [10, p. 48 and p. 105]. Moreover, the hp-invertibility of $\boxplus_L$ and the order rules follows from the hp-admissibility of weakening. In order to prove the hp-invertibility of $\boxplus_R$, let $\mathcal{D}$ be a derivation for $\Gamma \Rightarrow \Delta, \pi : \boxplus\varphi$, let n be the height of $\mathcal{D}$ and let $w \in \mathfrak{S}$ and $x \in \mathfrak{A}$ be fresh. Using induction on n, we show that there is a derivation $\mathcal{D}'$ of height $\leq n$ for $w \subseteq \pi, x \in \Sigma(w), \Gamma \Rightarrow \Delta, x : \varphi$.

For the base case, let $n = 0$. This means that $\Gamma \Rightarrow \Delta, \pi : \boxplus\varphi$ is an initial sequent, so $\pi : \boxplus\varphi$ cannot be principal. Hence, the sequent $w \subseteq \pi, x \in \Sigma(w), \Gamma \Rightarrow \Delta, x : \varphi$ is also an axiom and thus derivable by a proof tree of height $n = 0$.

For the inductive step, let $n \geq 1$. If $\mathcal{D}$ ends with a rule for which $\pi : \boxplus\varphi$ is not principal, we apply the induction hypothesis to the premises of the rule (possibly together with a renaming of eigenvariables), and we then use the same rule again. If $\mathcal{D}$ ends with an application of $\boxplus_R$ for which $\pi : \boxplus\varphi$ is principal, then $\mathcal{D}$ contains a subderivation of height $n - 1$ for $u \subseteq \pi, y \in \Sigma(u), \Gamma \Rightarrow \Delta, y : \varphi$, where $u \in \mathfrak{S}$ and $y \in \mathfrak{A}$ are both fresh. Using height-preserving substitutions, this yields the desired derivation of height $\leq n$ for $w \subseteq \pi, x \in \Sigma(w), \Gamma \Rightarrow \Delta, x : \varphi$. □

Proposition 5. *The contraction rules are hp-admissible in* GinqM_L.

Proof. The hp-admissibility of $\mathtt{C}_L$ and $\mathtt{C}_R$ is proved *simultaneously*, by induction on the height of a derivation for the premise. Let $\mathcal{D}$ be a derivation for $\Gamma \Rightarrow \Delta$, let n be the height of $\mathcal{D}$ and suppose that either Γ or Δ contains a duplication of a relational atom or labelled formula E. Using induction on n, we show that also the contracted version of $\Gamma \Rightarrow \Delta$ is derivable by a proof tree of height $\leq n$.

The base case is easy. For the inductive step, let $n \geq 1$. If $\mathcal{D}$ ends with a rule for which E is not principal, we apply the induction hypothesis to the premises of the rule, and then the rule again. Otherwise, we consider the following cases.

Case 1: E is a relational atom. If only one of the two occurrences of E is principal in the last rule applied in $\mathcal{D}$, we proceed as above. And if both occurrences of E are principal, we use the *closure condition* (see Sect. 3).

Case 2: E is a labelled formula. In this case, we make use of the hp-invertibility of the logical rules of GinqM_L. For instance, if $\mathcal{D}$ ends with an application of $\bot_R$ for which E is principal, $\Gamma \Rightarrow \Delta$ must be of the form $\Gamma \Rightarrow \Phi, \pi : \bot, \pi : \bot$ and $\mathcal{D}$ contains a subderivation of height $n - 1$ for $w \subseteq \pi, \Gamma \Rightarrow \Phi, w : \bot, \pi : \bot$, where $w \in \mathfrak{S}$ is fresh. Using the hp-invertibility of $\bot_R$ and a subsequent height-preserving substitution, this yields a derivation of height $\leq n-1$ for $w \subseteq \pi, w \subseteq \pi, \Gamma \Rightarrow \Phi, w : \bot, w : \bot$. But then, by the induction hypothesis and an application of $\bot_R$, we obtain a derivation of height $\leq n$ for $\Gamma \Rightarrow \Phi, \pi : \bot$, as desired. □

Next, we will show that the *cut rule* is admissible in GinqM_L (see Fig. 4). The proof follows the general pattern outlined in [14, Sect. 2.4], so we proceed by a main induction on the complexity of the cut formula, with a subinduction on the height of the cut. However, when measuring the complexity of a cut formula $\pi : \varphi$, we must take into account not only the complexity of φ, but also the complexity of the associated label π. The *degree of a state label* π, notation $dg(\pi)$, is defined as follows: we put $dg(\pi) := 0$, if $\pi \in \mathfrak{S}$ is a singleton variable, and we put $dg(\pi) := 1$ otherwise. The *degree of a formula* φ, notation $dg(\varphi)$, is defined to be the number of occurrences of the symbols $\bot, \wedge, \rightarrow, \mathbin{\rotatebox[origin=c]{-90}{$\geqslant$}}, \Box, \boxplus$ in φ. And the *rank of a labelled formula* $\pi : \varphi$ is the pair of integers given by $rk(\pi : \varphi) := (dg(\varphi), dg(\pi))$. Ranks of labelled formulas will be compared using a *lexicographic ordering*. Thus, we write $rk(\pi : \varphi) < rk(\tau : \psi)$ and say that the rank of $\pi : \varphi$ is *smaller* than the rank of $\tau : \psi$, if we either have $dg(\varphi) < dg(\psi)$, or we have both $dg(\varphi) = dg(\psi)$ and $dg(\pi) < dg(\tau)$. Note that, as a consequence, we always have $rk(w : \varphi) < rk(\pi : \varphi)$ for $w \in \mathfrak{S}$ and $\pi \notin \mathfrak{S}$. By the *rank of a cut rule application*, we mean the rank of the associated cut formula $\pi : \varphi$. And the *height of a cut* is the sum of the heights of the two subderivations ending with the premises of the cut.

Theorem 2 (Cut-Admissibility). *The cut rule is admissible in* GinqM_L.

Proof. We perform a main induction on the rank of a cut rule application and a subinduction on the height of the cut. Most cases are treated in the same way as in [10, Sect. 3.2.3]. If one of the premises of the cut is an axiom or if the cut formula is not principal on one side, then the conclusion is always itself an axiom, or the cut can be permuted upwards in order to obtain a cut of lower height. If neither of the two premises is an axiom and the cut formula is principal on both sides, then we distinguish cases, depending on the form of the cut formula. For instance, if the cut formula is atomic, then the cut must be of the form

$$\dfrac{\mathsf{p}_R\dfrac{\begin{matrix}\mathcal{D}_1\\ w \subseteq \pi, \Gamma \Rightarrow \Delta, w : p\end{matrix}}{\Gamma \Rightarrow \Delta, \pi : p} \qquad \mathsf{p}_L\dfrac{\begin{matrix}\mathcal{D}_2\\ u : p, u \subseteq \pi, \pi : p, \Pi \Rightarrow \Phi\end{matrix}}{u \subseteq \pi, \pi : p, \Pi \Rightarrow \Phi}}{u \subseteq \pi, \Gamma, \Pi \Rightarrow \Delta, \Phi}\,\mathsf{cut}$$

where $\pi \notin \mathfrak{S}$ is a non-singleton state label and $w \in \mathfrak{S}$ is a fresh variable. Using the admissibility of substitution and contraction, this cut is transformed into

$$\mathtt{mp}\,\dfrac{\Gamma \Rightarrow x : \varphi \quad \Delta \Rightarrow x : \varphi \rightarrow \psi}{\Gamma, \Delta \Rightarrow x : \psi} \qquad \mathtt{nec}_{\Box}\,\dfrac{\Rightarrow x : \varphi}{\Rightarrow x : \Box\varphi} \qquad \mathtt{nec}_{\boxplus}\,\dfrac{\Rightarrow x : \varphi}{\Rightarrow x : \boxplus\varphi} \qquad \mathtt{tc}\,\dfrac{w \subseteq \pi, \Gamma \Rightarrow \Delta, w : \alpha}{\Gamma \Rightarrow \Delta, \pi : \alpha}\,(\dagger)$$

(†) In the rule tc, we require $\alpha \in \mathcal{L}_d^{\boxplus}$ to be declarative and $w \in \mathfrak{S}$ to be fresh.

Fig. 5. Further admissible rules.

$$
\mathtt{C}_L,\mathtt{C}_R\,\dfrac{\mathtt{cut}\,\dfrac{(u/w)\,\dfrac{\overset{\mathcal{D}_1}{w \subseteq \pi, \Gamma \Rightarrow \Delta, w : p}}{u \subseteq \pi, \Gamma \Rightarrow \Delta, u : p} \qquad \mathtt{cut}\,\dfrac{\mathtt{P}_R\,\dfrac{\overset{\mathcal{D}_1}{w \subseteq \pi, \Gamma \Rightarrow \Delta, w : p}}{\Gamma \Rightarrow \Delta, \pi : p} \qquad \overset{\mathcal{D}_2}{u : p, u \subseteq \pi, \pi : p, \Pi \Rightarrow \Phi}}{u : p, u \subseteq \pi, \Gamma, \Pi \Rightarrow \Delta, \Phi}}{u \subseteq \pi, u \subseteq \pi, \Gamma, \Gamma, \Pi \Rightarrow \Delta, \Delta, \Phi}}{u \subseteq \pi, \Gamma, \Pi \Rightarrow \Delta, \Phi}
$$

The first cut is of lower height than the original one. And since $u \in \mathfrak{S}$ and $\pi \notin \mathfrak{S}$, we have $rk(u : p) < rk(\pi : p)$, so the second cut is of lower rank. If, on the other hand, the cut formula is of the form $\pi : \boxplus\varphi$, then the derivation looks like this:

$$
\mathtt{cut}\,\dfrac{\boxplus_R\,\dfrac{\overset{\mathcal{D}_1}{w \subseteq \pi, x \in \Sigma(w), \Gamma \Rightarrow \Delta, x : \varphi}}{\Gamma \Rightarrow \Delta, \pi : \boxplus\varphi} \qquad \boxplus_L\,\dfrac{\overset{\mathcal{D}_2}{\tau : \varphi, u \subseteq \pi, \tau \in \Sigma(u), \pi : \boxplus\varphi, \Pi \Rightarrow \Phi}}{u \subseteq \pi, \tau \in \Sigma(u), \pi : \boxplus\varphi, \Pi \Rightarrow \Phi}}{u \subseteq \pi, \tau \in \Sigma(u), \Gamma, \Pi \Rightarrow \Delta, \Phi}
$$

where $w \in \mathfrak{S}$ and $x \in \mathfrak{A}$ are both fresh. This cut is transformed into

$$
\mathtt{C}_L,\mathtt{C}_R\,\dfrac{\mathtt{cut}\,\dfrac{(u/w),(\tau/x)\,\dfrac{\overset{\mathcal{D}_1}{w \subseteq \pi, x \in \Sigma(w), \Gamma \Rightarrow \Delta, x : \varphi}}{u \subseteq \pi, \tau \in \Sigma(u), \Gamma \Rightarrow \Delta, \tau : \varphi} \qquad \overset{\mathcal{D}}{\tau : \varphi, u \subseteq \pi, \tau \in \Sigma(u), \Gamma, \Pi \Rightarrow \Delta, \Phi}}{u \subseteq \pi, u \subseteq \pi, \tau \in \Sigma(u), \tau \in \Sigma(u), \Gamma, \Gamma, \Pi \Rightarrow \Delta, \Delta, \Phi}}{u \subseteq \pi, \tau \in \Sigma(u), \Gamma, \Pi \Rightarrow \Delta, \Phi}
$$

where the subderivation $\mathcal{D}$ is of the form

$$
\mathtt{cut}\,\dfrac{\boxplus_R\,\dfrac{\overset{\mathcal{D}_1}{w \subseteq \pi, x \in \Sigma(w), \Gamma \Rightarrow \Delta, x : \varphi}}{\Gamma \Rightarrow \Delta, \pi : \boxplus\varphi} \qquad \overset{\mathcal{D}_2}{\tau : \varphi, u \subseteq \pi, \tau \in \Sigma(u), \pi : \boxplus\varphi, \Pi \Rightarrow \Phi}}{\tau : \varphi, u \subseteq \pi, \tau \in \Sigma(u), \Gamma, \Pi \Rightarrow \Delta, \Phi}
$$

The cut on $\pi : \boxplus\varphi$ is of lower height, and the cut on $\tau : \varphi$ is of lower rank. □

Figure 5 comprises a number of additional rules that can be shown to be admissible in GinqM_L. The rules $\mathtt{mp}$, $\mathtt{nec}_\Box$, $\mathtt{nec}_\boxplus$ correspond to *modus ponens* and *necessitation*, respectively, and the rule $\mathtt{tc}$ reflects the *truth-conditionality* of declarative formulas in InqM (see Proposition 1). The admissibility of $\mathtt{mp}$ follows from the invertibility of $\rightarrow_R$ and the admissibility of $\mathtt{cut}$. In the case of $\mathtt{nec}_\Box$ and $\mathtt{nec}_\boxplus$, one can use the admissibility of substitution and weakening (see also [10, Lemmas 3.3.6 and 5.5.7]). The admissibility of $\mathtt{tc}$ is proved by induction on the structure of α, using the invertibility of the logical rules for $\Box$, $\boxplus$, $\wedge$, $\rightarrow$. The details are essentially the same as in [10, Prop. 3.2.14 and 5.4.10].

5 Soundness and Completeness

We will now prove that GinqM_L is sound and complete with respect to the corresponding extension L of InqM. The soundness of our calculi follows directly from the following statement: if a sequent $\Gamma \Rightarrow \Delta$ is derivable in GinqM_L, then it is also *L-valid*, i.e., for every interpretation I over an L-model M, it is the case that, if I satisfies all elements of Γ, then it also satisfies at least one element of Δ. The proof proceeds by induction on the structure of a derivation in GinqM_L.

Lemma 2 (Soundness). *The calculus* GinqM_L *is sound with respect to* L. *That is, for any set of formulas* $\Gamma \cup \{\varphi\} \subseteq \mathcal{L}^{\boxplus}$, *we have: if* $\Gamma \overset{\mathrm{G}}{\underset{L}{\vdash}} \varphi$, *then* $\Gamma \models_L \varphi$.

In order to prove the completeness of GinqM_L, we first show that GinqM_L is complete with respect to the Hilbert-style system HinqM_L defined in Sect. 2.

Lemma 3. *Let* $\Gamma \cup \{\varphi\} \subseteq \mathcal{L}^{\boxplus}$ *be an arbitrary set of formulas. If* $\Gamma \overset{\mathrm{H}}{\underset{L}{\vdash}} \varphi$ *holds in the Hilbert-style system* HinqM_L, *then* $\Gamma \overset{\mathrm{G}}{\underset{L}{\vdash}} \varphi$ *holds in the calculus* GinqM_L.

Proof. By induction on the structure of a Hilbert-style proof for $\Gamma \overset{\mathrm{H}}{\underset{L}{\vdash}} \varphi$. We already know that the rules of modus ponens and necessitation are admissible in GinqM_L (see Sect. 4). Thus, it suffices to show that all axioms of HinqM_L are provable in GinqM_L. For the schemes (A1)–(A7), this is straightforward. The provability of (Ds) and ($\mathtt{K}_\Box$) can be established in the same way as in [10, Lemma 5.5.6]. Derivations for the schemes ($\mathtt{K}_\boxplus$), (Dn) and (S) are provided in Appendix B. And the two directions of (C) can be proved in the following way:

$$
\begin{array}{rc}
 & \text{By Lemma 1 (1)} \\
\hdashline
\mathtt{sig}\!\downarrow & z \subseteq \sigma(w), \sigma(w) : \alpha, w \subseteq y, z \in \Sigma(w), y \subseteq x, y : \Box\alpha \Rightarrow z : \alpha \\
\hline
\Box_L & \sigma(w) : \alpha, w \subseteq y, z \in \Sigma(w), y \subseteq x, y : \Box\alpha \Rightarrow z : \alpha \\
\hline
\boxplus_R & w \subseteq y, z \in \Sigma(w), y \subseteq x, y : \Box\alpha \Rightarrow z : \alpha \\
\hline
\to_R & y \subseteq x, y : \Box\alpha \Rightarrow y : \boxplus\alpha \\
\hline
 & \Rightarrow x : \Box\alpha \to \boxplus\alpha
\end{array}
$$

$$
\begin{array}{rc}
 & \text{By Lemma 1 (2)} \\
\hdashline
\boxplus_L & u : \alpha, u \in \Sigma(w), u \subseteq \sigma(w), w \subseteq y, y \subseteq x, y : \boxplus\alpha \Rightarrow u : \alpha \\
\hline
\mathtt{sig}\!\uparrow & u \in \Sigma(w), u \subseteq \sigma(w), w \subseteq y, y \subseteq x, y : \boxplus\alpha \Rightarrow u : \alpha \\
\hline
\mathtt{tc} & u \subseteq \sigma(w), w \subseteq y, y \subseteq x, y : \boxplus\alpha \Rightarrow u : \alpha \\
\hline
\Box_R & w \subseteq y, y \subseteq x, y : \boxplus\alpha \Rightarrow \sigma(w) : \alpha \\
\hline
\to_R & y \subseteq x, y : \boxplus\alpha \Rightarrow y : \Box\alpha \\
\hline
 & \Rightarrow x : \boxplus\alpha \to \Box\alpha
\end{array}
$$

Note that, in the second derivation, we also used the admissible rule tc from Fig. 5. It remains to show that each of the special axioms from Table 1 is provable by means of the associated sequent rule depicted in Fig. 3. The corresponding derivations for the schemes (T), (D) and (4) are provided in Appendix C. The provability of (5) can be established in a similar way. □

Theorem 3 (Soundness and Completeness). *The sequent calculus* GinqM_L *is sound and complete with respect to the corresponding extension* L *of* InqM. *That is, for any subset* $\Gamma \cup \{\varphi\} \subseteq \mathcal{L}^{\boxplus}$, *we have:* $\Gamma \overset{\mathrm{G}}{\underset{L}{\vdash}} \varphi$ *iff* $\Gamma \models_L \varphi$.

Proof. The claim follows directly from Theorem 1, Lemma 2 and Lemma 3. □

6 Conclusion

We conclude our investigation by pointing out some directions for future work. First of all, it might be interesting to transfer the ideas presented here to other logics based on support semantics or team semantics. For example, one could try to find labelled sequent calculi for a larger family of inquisitive modal logics or for various systems of *dependence logic* (see, e.g., [15–17]). In addition, it would be desirable to find terminating proof search procedures for GinqM and for the class of calculi presented in [10]. Here, a *proof search procedure* for a labelled sequent calculus S is understood to be an algorithm that, given any formula φ as input, either outputs an S-derivation for a sequent of the form $\Rightarrow x : \varphi$ or a finite countermodel for φ. Various difficulties associated with root-first proof search for basic (i.e., non-modal) inquisitive logic are discussed in [10, Sect. 3.4]. Only recently, the decidability of InqM was established by Marić and Perkov [9], using the method of filtrations. A proof search procedure for GinqM would allow us to establish this result in an alternative and more 'syntactic' way.

Acknowledgments. I would like to thank Marianna Girlando for her support during the writing of my master's thesis, which already contains much of the material presented here. I am also grateful to Stipe Marić and Tin Perkov for sending me their manuscript [9] and to the anonymous reviewers for their insightful comments and suggestions.

Disclosure of Interests. The author has no competing interests to declare that are relevant to the content of this article.

A Proof of Theorem 1

We first recall an axiomatization of inquisitive modal logic provided by Ciardelli [3, Sects. 7.3–7.4]. A slightly modified version of Ciardelli's [3, Sect. 7.3.4] natural deduction system for InqM is depicted in Fig. 6. This modified system will henceforth be denoted by NinqM.[2] In order to obtain natural deduction systems for stronger inquisitive modal logics, we first convert the axiom schemes from Table 1 into equivalent natural deduction rules. The resulting rules are displayed in Fig. 7. Given any inquisitive modal logic L determined by some combination of the constraints from Table 1, one can obtain a natural deduction system NinqM_L for L by adding the corresponding set of special rules $R \subseteq \{\mathtt{t}, \mathtt{d}, 4, 5\}$ to the system NinqM (cf. [3, Sect. 7.4]). Provability in any of the systems NinqM_L is defined as follows: we write $\Gamma \vdash^{\mathrm{N}}_{L} \varphi$ and say that φ is *provable* from Γ in NinqM_L, if there exists a deduction $\mathcal{D}$ in NinqM_L such that φ is the conclusion of $\mathcal{D}$ and all open hypotheses of $\mathcal{D}$ are contained in Γ. The following theorem is a direct consequence of the completeness result presented in [3, Theorem 7.4.18].

Theorem 4. *Let L be an extension of* InqM *determined by imposing zero or more of the constraints from Table 1. The natural deduction system* NinqM_L *is sound and complete with respect to L, so we have: $\Gamma \vdash^{\mathrm{N}}_{L} \varphi$ iff $\Gamma \models_L \varphi$.*

[2] The system NinqM differs from Ciardelli's axiomatization only with respect to the *necessitation rules* $\mathtt{N}_\Box$ and $\mathtt{N}_\boxplus$. In the system from [3, Sect. 7.3.4], these rules are replaced by so-called *monotonicity rules*. However, using the rules $\mathtt{K}_\Box$ and $\mathtt{K}_\boxplus$, it is easy to show that the two versions of the system are equivalent. See also [3, p. 281].

$$\wedge_I\frac{\varphi \quad \psi}{\varphi\wedge\psi} \qquad \wedge_E\frac{\varphi_1\wedge\varphi_2}{\varphi_i}\ (i=1,2) \qquad \mathbb{V}_I\frac{\varphi_i}{\varphi_1\mathbin{\mathbb{V}}\varphi_2}\ (i=1,2) \qquad \bot_E\frac{\bot}{\varphi}$$

$$\to_I\frac{\begin{matrix}[\varphi]\\ \vdots\\ \psi\end{matrix}}{\varphi\to\psi} \qquad \to_E\frac{\varphi\to\psi \quad \varphi}{\psi} \qquad \mathbb{V}_E\frac{\varphi\mathbin{\mathbb{V}}\psi \quad \begin{matrix}[\varphi]\\ \vdots\\ \chi\end{matrix} \quad \begin{matrix}[\psi]\\ \vdots\\ \chi\end{matrix}}{\chi} \qquad \neg\neg_E\frac{\neg\neg\alpha}{\alpha}\ (\alpha\in\mathcal{L}_d^{\boxplus})$$

$$\mathsf{S}\frac{\alpha\to(\varphi\mathbin{\mathbb{V}}\psi)}{(\alpha\to\varphi)\mathbin{\mathbb{V}}(\alpha\to\psi)}\ (\alpha\in\mathcal{L}_d^{\boxplus}) \qquad \mathsf{Ds}\frac{\Box(\varphi\mathbin{\mathbb{V}}\psi)}{\Box\varphi\vee\Box\psi} \qquad \mathsf{K}_{\Box}\frac{\Box(\varphi\to\psi)}{\Box\varphi\to\Box\psi} \qquad \mathsf{K}_{\boxplus}\frac{\boxplus(\varphi\to\psi)}{\boxplus\varphi\to\boxplus\psi}$$

$$\mathsf{C}{\downarrow}\frac{\boxplus\alpha}{\Box\alpha}\ (\alpha\in\mathcal{L}_d^{\boxplus}) \qquad \mathsf{C}{\uparrow}\frac{\Box\alpha}{\boxplus\alpha}\ (\alpha\in\mathcal{L}_d^{\boxplus}) \qquad \mathsf{N}_{\Box}\frac{\varphi}{\Box\varphi}(\dagger) \qquad \mathsf{N}_{\boxplus}\frac{\varphi}{\boxplus\varphi}(\dagger)$$

(†) In the rules $\mathsf{N}_{\Box}$ and $\mathsf{N}_{\boxplus}$, the subtree ending with φ must not contain any open hypotheses.

Fig. 6. The natural deduction system NinqM.

$$\mathsf{t}\frac{\boxplus\alpha}{\alpha}\ (\alpha\in\mathcal{L}_d^{\boxplus}) \qquad \mathsf{d}\frac{}{\neg\boxplus\bot} \qquad \mathsf{4}\frac{\boxplus\varphi}{\boxplus\boxplus\varphi} \qquad \mathsf{5}\frac{\neg\boxplus\varphi}{\boxplus\neg\boxplus\varphi}$$

Fig. 7. Special natural deduction rules corresponding to the axioms from Table 1.

So, in order to establish Theorem 1, it suffices to show that each of our Hilbert-style calculi HinqM_L is sound and complete with respect to the corresponding natural deduction system NinqM_L. For this purpose, let now L be an arbitrary extension of InqM determined by some combination of the constraints from Table 1. First of all, using induction on the definition of $\Gamma\vdash^{\mathrm{H}}_{L}\varphi$, one can easily verify that the provability relation of the Hilbert-style system HinqM_L is *monotonic*, i.e., if we have $\Gamma\vdash^{\mathrm{H}}_{L}\varphi$ and $\Gamma\subseteq\Delta$, then also $\Delta\vdash^{\mathrm{H}}_{L}\varphi$. Furthermore, it is possible to show that HinqM_L satisfies the *deduction theorem.*

Theorem 5. *In the system* HinqM_L*, we have:* $\Gamma,\varphi\vdash^{\mathrm{H}}_{L}\psi$ *iff* $\Gamma\vdash^{\mathrm{H}}_{L}\varphi\to\psi$.

Proof. For the right-to-left direction, suppose that $\Gamma\vdash^{\mathrm{H}}_{L}\varphi\to\psi$. By monotonicity, this yields $\Gamma,\varphi\vdash^{\mathrm{H}}_{L}\varphi\to\psi$. Since we also have $\Gamma,\varphi\vdash^{\mathrm{H}}_{L}\varphi$ by definition of the relation $\vdash^{\mathrm{H}}_{L}$, it now follows $\Gamma,\varphi\vdash^{\mathrm{H}}_{L}\psi$ by an application of modus ponens.

For the left-to-right direction, assume that $\Gamma,\varphi\vdash^{\mathrm{H}}_{L}\psi$. We prove $\Gamma\vdash^{\mathrm{H}}_{L}\varphi\to\psi$ by induction on the definition of $\Gamma,\varphi\vdash^{\mathrm{H}}_{L}\psi$. There are the following possibilities.

Case 1: ψ is an element of $\Gamma\cup\{\varphi\}$, so it holds $\psi\in\Gamma$ or $\psi=\varphi$. If we have $\psi\in\Gamma$, then we also have $\Gamma\vdash^{\mathrm{H}}_{L}\psi$ by definition of $\vdash^{\mathrm{H}}_{L}$. Using axiom (A1) and an application of modus ponens, this implies $\Gamma\vdash^{\mathrm{H}}_{L}\varphi\to\psi$. And if we have $\psi=\varphi$, then we can easily derive $\Gamma\vdash^{\mathrm{H}}_{L}\varphi\to\psi$ using the schemes (A1), (A2) and (A7).

Case 2: ψ is an axiom of HinqM_L. In this case, we must also have $\Gamma \vdash^{\mathrm{H}}_{L} \psi$. Thus, using axiom (A1) and modus ponens, it follows again $\Gamma \vdash^{\mathrm{H}}_{L} \varphi \to \psi$.

Case 3: There exists some $\chi \in \mathcal{L}^{\boxplus}$ such that $\Gamma, \varphi \vdash^{\mathrm{H}}_{L} \chi$ and $\Gamma, \varphi \vdash^{\mathrm{H}}_{L} \chi \to \psi$. By induction hypothesis, we first obtain $\Gamma \vdash^{\mathrm{H}}_{L} \varphi \to \chi$ and $\Gamma \vdash^{\mathrm{H}}_{L} \varphi \to (\chi \to \psi)$. Since $(\varphi \to (\chi \to \psi)) \to ((\varphi \to \chi) \to (\varphi \to \psi))$ is an instance of axiom scheme (A2), we may now conclude $\Gamma \vdash^{\mathrm{H}}_{L} \varphi \to \psi$ using two applications of modus ponens.

Case 4: There exists some $\chi \in \mathcal{L}^{\boxplus}$ and some $\boxtimes \in \{\Box, \boxplus\}$ such that $\psi = \boxtimes\chi$ and $\vdash^{\mathrm{H}}_{L} \chi$. From $\vdash^{\mathrm{H}}_{L} \chi$, it follows $\Gamma \vdash^{\mathrm{H}}_{L} \boxtimes\chi$ and therefore $\Gamma \vdash^{\mathrm{H}}_{L} \psi$ by necessitation. But then, using axiom (A1) and modus ponens, we also obtain $\Gamma \vdash^{\mathrm{H}}_{L} \varphi \to \psi$. □

We are now ready to prove the desired statement: the Hilbert system HinqM_L is sound and complete with respect to the natural deduction system NinqM_L.

Proposition 6. *For any $\Gamma \cup \{\varphi\} \subseteq \mathcal{L}^{\boxplus}$, we have: $\Gamma \vdash^{\mathrm{H}}_{L} \varphi$ holds in the Hilbert-style system HinqM_L iff $\Gamma \vdash^{\mathrm{N}}_{L} \varphi$ holds in the natural deduction system NinqM_L.*

Proof. For the left-to-right direction, one proceeds by induction on the definition of $\Gamma \vdash^{\mathrm{H}}_{L} \varphi$. This is straightforward, since each axiom of HinqM_L is obviously provable in NinqM_L, and modus ponens and necessitation are also available in NinqM_L. For the right-to-left direction, one can use induction on the structure of a natural deduction proof $\mathcal{D}$ for $\Gamma \vdash^{\mathrm{N}}_{L} \varphi$. This is also not difficult, since most of the rules of NinqM_L correspond directly to some axiom or rule of HinqM_L, and the discharging of hypotheses can be 'simulated' using the deduction theorem for HinqM_L. For example, suppose that $\mathcal{D}$ ends with an application of $\to_I$, so φ is of the form $\varphi = \psi \to \chi$ and $\mathcal{D}$ contains an immediate subdeduction for $\Gamma, \psi \vdash^{\mathrm{N}}_{L} \chi$. Using the induction hypothesis, we first obtain $\Gamma, \psi \vdash^{\mathrm{H}}_{L} \chi$ in the system HinqM_L. By the deduction theorem, this yields $\Gamma \vdash^{\mathrm{H}}_{L} \psi \to \chi$ and therefore $\Gamma \vdash^{\mathrm{H}}_{L} \varphi$. □

Theorem 1 now follows as a corollary of Theorem 4 and Proposition 6.

B Derivations for Some of the Axioms from Figure 1

As shown by the following three derivations, each of the schemes ($\mathtt{K}_{\boxplus}$), (Dn) and (S) is provable in GinqM (and therefore also in any of its extensions). In the derivations for (Dn) and (S), we use the admissible rule tc from Fig. 5.

$$
\to_R\dfrac{\to_R\dfrac{\boxplus_R\dfrac{\boxplus_L\dfrac{\mathtt{tr}\dfrac{\boxplus_L\dfrac{\mathtt{rf}\dfrac{\to_L\dfrac{\dfrac{\text{By Lemma 1 (2)}}{\ldots, x_0 : \varphi \Rightarrow x_0 : \psi, x_0 : \varphi} \qquad \dfrac{\text{By Lemma 1 (2)}}{\ldots, x_0 : \psi \Rightarrow x_0 : \psi}}{\ldots, x_0 \subseteq x_0, x_0 : \varphi \to \psi, w \subseteq y, x_0 : \varphi, w \subseteq z, x_0 \in \Sigma(w), z \subseteq y, y \subseteq x \Rightarrow x_0 : \psi}}{\ldots, x_0 : \varphi \to \psi, w \subseteq y, x_0 : \varphi, w \subseteq z, x_0 \in \Sigma(w), z \subseteq y, y \subseteq x \Rightarrow x_0 : \psi}}{w \subseteq y, x_0 : \varphi, w \subseteq z, x_0 \in \Sigma(w), z \subseteq y, y \subseteq x, y : \boxplus(\varphi \to \psi), z : \boxplus\varphi \Rightarrow x_0 : \psi}}{x_0 : \varphi, w \subseteq z, x_0 \in \Sigma(w), z \subseteq y, y \subseteq x, y : \boxplus(\varphi \to \psi), z : \boxplus\varphi \Rightarrow x_0 : \psi}}{w \subseteq z, x_0 \in \Sigma(w), z \subseteq y, y \subseteq x, y : \boxplus(\varphi \to \psi), z : \boxplus\varphi \Rightarrow x_0 : \psi}}{z \subseteq y, y \subseteq x, y : \boxplus(\varphi \to \psi), z : \boxplus\varphi \Rightarrow z : \boxplus\psi}}{y \subseteq x, y : \boxplus(\varphi \to \psi) \Rightarrow y : \boxplus\varphi \to \boxplus\psi}}{\Rightarrow x : \boxplus(\varphi \to \psi) \to (\boxplus\varphi \to \boxplus\psi)}
$$

$$
{\to_R}\,\dfrac{\texttt{tc}\,\dfrac{{\to_L}\,\dfrac{{\to_R}\,\dfrac{\texttt{sg}\,\dfrac{\dfrac{\text{By Lemma 1 (3)}}{z \subseteq \emptyset, \ldots \Rightarrow w : \alpha, z : \bot} \quad \dfrac{\text{By Lemma 1 (1)}}{w \subseteq z, \ldots, z : \alpha \Rightarrow w : \alpha, z : \bot}}{z \subseteq w, w \subseteq y, y \subseteq x, y : \neg\neg\alpha, z : \alpha \Rightarrow w : \alpha, z : \bot}}{w \subseteq y, y \subseteq x, y : \neg\neg\alpha \Rightarrow w : \alpha, w : \neg\alpha} \quad \texttt{ax}_\bot\,\dfrac{}{w : \bot, \ldots \Rightarrow w : \alpha}}{w \subseteq y, y \subseteq x, y : \neg\neg\alpha \Rightarrow w : \alpha}}{y \subseteq x, y : \neg\neg\alpha \Rightarrow y : \alpha}}{\Rightarrow x : \neg\neg\alpha \to \alpha}
$$

$$
{\to_R}\,\dfrac{{\mathbin{\vee\!\!\!\vee}_R}\,\dfrac{{\to_R}\,\dfrac{{\to_R}\,\dfrac{\texttt{ul}\,\dfrac{{\to_L}\,\dfrac{\begin{matrix}\mathcal{D}_1\\ \ldots, y : \alpha, z : \alpha \Rightarrow \ldots, y \cup z : \alpha\end{matrix} \qquad \begin{matrix}\mathcal{D}_2\\ \ldots, y \cup z : \varphi \mathbin{\vee\!\!\!\vee} \psi \Rightarrow y : \varphi, z : \psi\end{matrix}}{y \cup z \subseteq x_0, z \subseteq x_0, y \subseteq x_0, x_0 \subseteq x, x_0 : \alpha \to (\varphi \mathbin{\vee\!\!\!\vee} \psi), y : \alpha, z : \alpha \Rightarrow y : \varphi, z : \psi}}{z \subseteq x_0, y \subseteq x_0, x_0 \subseteq x, x_0 : \alpha \to (\varphi \mathbin{\vee\!\!\!\vee} \psi), y : \alpha, z : \alpha \Rightarrow y : \varphi, z : \psi}}{y \subseteq x_0, x_0 \subseteq x, x_0 : \alpha \to (\varphi \mathbin{\vee\!\!\!\vee} \psi), y : \alpha \Rightarrow y : \varphi, x_0 : \alpha \to \psi}}{x_0 \subseteq x, x_0 : \alpha \to (\varphi \mathbin{\vee\!\!\!\vee} \psi) \Rightarrow x_0 : \alpha \to \varphi, x_0 : \alpha \to \psi}}{x_0 \subseteq x, x_0 : \alpha \to (\varphi \mathbin{\vee\!\!\!\vee} \psi) \Rightarrow x_0 : (\alpha \to \varphi) \mathbin{\vee\!\!\!\vee} (\alpha \to \psi)}}{\Rightarrow x : (\alpha \to (\varphi \mathbin{\vee\!\!\!\vee} \psi)) \to ((\alpha \to \varphi) \mathbin{\vee\!\!\!\vee} (\alpha \to \psi))}
$$

where $\mathcal{D}_1$ and $\mathcal{D}_2$ are the following two subderivations:

$$
\texttt{tc}\,\dfrac{\texttt{cd}\,\dfrac{\dfrac{\text{By Lemma 1 (1)}}{w \subseteq y, \ldots, y : \alpha, z : \alpha \Rightarrow \ldots, w : \alpha} \quad \dfrac{\text{By Lemma 1 (1)}}{w \subseteq z, \ldots, y : \alpha, z : \alpha \Rightarrow \ldots, w : \alpha}}{w \subseteq y \cup z, \ldots, y : \alpha, z : \alpha \Rightarrow \ldots, w : \alpha}}{\ldots, y : \alpha, z : \alpha \Rightarrow \ldots, y \cup z : \alpha}
$$

$$
{\mathbin{\vee\!\!\!\vee}_L}\,\dfrac{\texttt{ur}\,\dfrac{\dfrac{\text{By Lemma 1 (1)}}{y \subseteq y \cup z, \ldots, y \cup z : \varphi \Rightarrow y : \varphi, z : \psi}}{\ldots, y \cup z : \varphi \Rightarrow y : \varphi, z : \psi} \quad \texttt{ur}\,\dfrac{\dfrac{\text{By Lemma 1 (1)}}{z \subseteq y \cup z, \ldots, y \cup z : \psi \Rightarrow y : \varphi, z : \psi}}{\ldots, y \cup z : \psi \Rightarrow y : \varphi, z : \psi}}{\ldots, y \cup z : \varphi \mathbin{\vee\!\!\!\vee} \psi \Rightarrow y : \varphi, z : \psi}
$$

C Derivations for the Special Axioms from Table 1

We need to show that each of the special axioms from Table 1 is provable by means of the corresponding sequent rule depicted in Fig. 3. For the schemes `(T)`, `(D)` and `(4)`, this is achieved by constructing the following derivations. Note that, in the first derivation, we use again the admissible rule `tc` from Fig. 5.

$$
{\to_R}\,\dfrac{\texttt{tc}\,\dfrac{\texttt{t}\,\dfrac{\texttt{sig}{\uparrow}\,\dfrac{\boxplus_L\,\dfrac{\dfrac{\text{By Lemma 1 (2)}}{w : \alpha, w \in \Sigma(w), w \subseteq \sigma(w), w \subseteq y, y \subseteq x, y : \boxplus\alpha \Rightarrow w : \alpha}}{w \in \Sigma(w), w \subseteq \sigma(w), w \subseteq y, y \subseteq x, y : \boxplus\alpha \Rightarrow w : \alpha}}{w \subseteq \sigma(w), w \subseteq y, y \subseteq x, y : \boxplus\alpha \Rightarrow w : \alpha}}{w \subseteq y, y \subseteq x, y : \boxplus\alpha \Rightarrow w : \alpha}}{y \subseteq x, y : \boxplus\alpha \Rightarrow y : \alpha}}{\Rightarrow x : \boxplus\alpha \to \alpha}
$$

$$
{\to_R}\dfrac{{\bot_R}\dfrac{\mathtt{d}\dfrac{\mathtt{sig}\!\uparrow\dfrac{\boxplus_L\dfrac{\mathtt{ax}_\bot\dfrac{}{u:\bot, u \in \Sigma(w), u \subseteq \sigma(w), w \subseteq y, y \subseteq x, y : \boxplus\bot \Rightarrow w:\bot}}{u \in \Sigma(w), u \subseteq \sigma(w), w \subseteq y, y \subseteq x, y : \boxplus\bot \Rightarrow w:\bot}}{u \subseteq \sigma(w), w \subseteq y, y \subseteq x, y : \boxplus\bot \Rightarrow w:\bot}}{w \subseteq y, y \subseteq x, y : \boxplus\bot \Rightarrow w:\bot}}{y \subseteq x, y : \boxplus\bot \Rightarrow y:\bot}}{\Rightarrow x : \neg\boxplus\bot}
$$

By Lemma 1 (2)

$$
{\to_R}\dfrac{\boxplus_R\dfrac{\boxplus_R\dfrac{\mathtt{sig}\!\downarrow\dfrac{\mathtt{tr}\dfrac{\mathtt{4}\dfrac{\boxplus_L\dfrac{\dots, z:\varphi, z \in \Sigma(w), u \subseteq \sigma(w), y \subseteq \sigma(w), u \subseteq y, z \in \Sigma(u), w \subseteq x_0, x_0 : \boxplus\varphi \Rightarrow z:\varphi}{\dots, z \in \Sigma(w), u \subseteq \sigma(w), y \subseteq \sigma(w), u \subseteq y, z \in \Sigma(u), w \subseteq x_0, x_0 : \boxplus\varphi \Rightarrow z:\varphi}}{u \subseteq \sigma(w), y \subseteq \sigma(w), u \subseteq y, z \in \Sigma(u), w \subseteq x_0, y \in \Sigma(w), x_0 \subseteq x, x_0 : \boxplus\varphi \Rightarrow z:\varphi}}{y \subseteq \sigma(w), u \subseteq y, z \in \Sigma(u), w \subseteq x_0, y \in \Sigma(w), x_0 \subseteq x, x_0 : \boxplus\varphi \Rightarrow z:\varphi}}{u \subseteq y, z \in \Sigma(u), w \subseteq x_0, y \in \Sigma(w), x_0 \subseteq x, x_0 : \boxplus\varphi \Rightarrow z:\varphi}}{w \subseteq x_0, y \in \Sigma(w), x_0 \subseteq x, x_0 : \boxplus\varphi \Rightarrow y:\boxplus\varphi}}{x_0 \subseteq x, x_0 : \boxplus\varphi \Rightarrow x_0 : \boxplus\boxplus\varphi}}{\Rightarrow x : \boxplus\varphi \to \boxplus\boxplus\varphi}
$$

The derivation for axiom scheme (5) is similar to the derivation for (4).

References

1. Chen, J., Ma, M.: Labelled sequent calculus for inquisitive logic. In: Baltag, A., Seligman, J., Yamada, T. (eds.) Logic, Rationality, and Interaction (LORI). LNCS, vol. 10455, pp. 526–540. Springer, Berlin and Heidelberg (2017). https://doi.org/10.1007/978-3-662-55665-8_36
2. Ciardelli, I.: Modalities in the realm of questions: axiomatizing inquisitive epistemic logic. In: Goré, R., Kooi, B., Kurucz, A. (eds.) Advances in Modal Logic (AiML), vol. 10, pp. 94–113. College Publications, London (2014)
3. Ciardelli, I.: Questions in Logic, Ph.D. thesis. Institute for Logic, Language and Computation, University of Amsterdam (2016). https://projects.illc.uva.nl/inquisitivesemantics/assets/files/theses/Ciardelli2016_QuestionsInLogic.pdf
4. Ciardelli, I., Groenendijk, J., Roelofsen, F.: Inquisitive Semantics. Oxford University Press, Oxford (2018). https://doi.org/10.1093/oso/9780198814788.001.0001
5. Ciardelli, I., Roelofsen, F.: Inquisitive dynamic epistemic logic. Synthese **192**(6), 1643–1687 (2015). https://doi.org/10.1007/s11229-014-0404-7
6. Dyckhoff, R., Negri, S.: Proof analysis in intermediate logics. Archiv. Math. Logic **51**, 71–92 (2012). https://doi.org/10.1007/s00153-011-0254-7
7. Gentzen, G.: Untersuchungen über das logische Schließen. I. Mathematische Zeitschrift **39**(2), 176–210 (1935). https://doi.org/10.1007/BF01201353
8. Gentzen, G.: Untersuchungen über das logische Schließen. II. Mathematische Zeitschrift **39**(3), 405–431 (1935). https://doi.org/10.1007/BF01201363
9. Marić, S., Perkov, T.: Decidability of Inquisitive Modal Logic via Filtrations (2024). Unpublished manuscript
10. Müller, V.: On the Proof Theory of Inquisitive Logic, M.Sc. thesis. Institute for Logic, Language and Computation, University of Amsterdam (2023). https://eprints.illc.uva.nl/id/eprint/2278/1/MoL-2023-26.text.pdf

11. Negri, S.: Contraction-free sequent calculi for geometric theories with an application to Barr's theorem. Archiv. Math. Logic **42**, 389–401 (2003). https://doi.org/10.1007/s001530100124
12. Negri, S.: Proof analysis in modal logic. J. Philos. Logic **34**, 507–544 (2005). https://doi.org/10.1007/s10992-005-2267-3
13. Negri, S., Von Plato, J.: Cut elimination in the presence of axioms. Bullet. Symbol. Logic **4**(4), 418–435 (1998). https://doi.org/10.2307/420956
14. Negri, S., Von Plato, J.: Structural Proof Theory. Cambridge University Press, Cambridge (2001). https://doi.org/10.1017/CBO9780511527340
15. Väänänen, J.: Dependence Logic: A New Approach to Independence Friendly Logic. Cambridge University Press, Cambridge (2007). https://doi.org/10.1017/CBO9780511611193
16. Yang, F.: On Extensions and Variants of Dependence Logic: A Study of Intuitionistic Connectives in the Team Semantics Setting, Ph.D. thesis. University of Helsinki (2014). http://urn.fi/URN:ISBN:978-952-10-9787-4
17. Yang, F., Väänänen, J.: Propositional logics of dependence. Annal. Pure Appl. Logic **167**, 557–589 (2016). https://doi.org/10.1016/j.apal.2016.03.003

Correspondence Theory on Vector Spaces

Alessandra Palmigiano[1,2], Mattia Panettiere[1](✉), and Ni Wayan Switrayni[1]

[1] Vrije Universiteit Amsterdam, Amsterdam, The Netherlands
{a.palmigiano,m.panettiere,n.w.switrayni}@vu.nl
[2] Department of Mathematics and Applied Mathematics, University of Johannesburg, Johannesburg, South Africa

Abstract. This paper extends correspondence theory to the framework of $\mathbb{K}$-algebras, i.e. vector spaces endowed with a bilinear operation, seen as 'Kripke frames'. For every $\mathbb{K}$-algebra, the lattice of its subspaces can be endowed with the structure of a complete (non necessarily monoidal) residuated lattice. Hence, a sequent of the logic of residuated lattices can be interpreted as a property of its lattice of subspaces. Thus, correspondence theory can be developed between the propositional language of this logic and the first order language of $\mathbb{K}$-algebras, analogously to the well known correspondence theory between classical normal modal logic and the first-order language of Kripke frames. In this paper, we develop such a theory for the class of analytic inductive inequalities.

Keywords: Correspondence theory · Non classical logics · Residuated lattices · Vector spaces

1 Introduction

This papers builds on [8], where, motivated by a research program aimed at integrating the compositional and the distributional approaches in computational linguistics [3,4], a complete semantics has been introduced for the basic Lambek calculus enriched with tense modal operators. This semantics is based on *vector spaces*, which, rather than being regarded as algebraic structures, provide a Kripke-style interpretation of the propositional (i.e. additive) fragment of the Lambek calculus via the lattice of their subspaces (which plays a role analogous to the Boolean algebra reduct of the complex algebra of a Kripke frame), while the semantics of the multiplicative fragment of the Lambek calculus is supported by an additional bilinear operation which makes the given vector space a $\mathbb{K}$-algebra. Regarding its graph as a ternary relation, this bilinear operation

The first author acknowledges the NWO grant KIVI.2019.001.
The third author is supported by the Indonesian Education Scholarship, Ref. Number: 1027/J5.2.3/BPI.LG/VIII/2022.
The authors have received support from the EU's Horizon 2020 research and innovation programme under the Marie Skłodowska-Curie grant agreement No. 101007627.

G. Metcalfe et al. (Eds.): WoLLIC 2024, LNCS 14672, pp. 140–156, 2024.
https://doi.org/10.1007/978-3-031-62687-6_10

on vector spaces generates the binary operations on their associated lattice of subspaces interpreting the multiplicative fragment of the Lambek calculus in a way that is completely analogous to the interpretation of the same connectives in the Routley-Meyer semantics [14].

In [8], complete semantics for a finite number of well-known axiomatic extensions of the Lambek calculus was introduced via dual characterizations (cf. [8, Proposition 5.7]), using arguments similar to those well known from modal correspondence theory [15]. Building on notions, results, and insights pertaining to unified correspondence [5,6], we extend the results of [8, Proposition 5.7] to the class of *analytic inductive inequalities* (cf. Definition 2). This class has been introduced in [10], where it has been identified as the class of axioms which can be captured by analytic structural rules of proper display calculi. That is, analytic inductive axioms are exactly those which can be equivalently transformed into proof rules with an optimal proof-theoretic and computational behaviour (see [10] for an expanded discussion). Thus, the results of the present paper lend themselves to being applied within a research line in type-logical theory referred to as *structural control* [12], which is aimed at accounting for various forms of grammatical exceptions in formal linguistics.

Structure of the paper. In Sect. 2 we recall some basic notions. In Sect. 3, we show how any analytic inductive inequality in the language of non-necessarily monoidal residuated lattices can be equivalently rewritten a system of inequalities containing only joins and products. In Sect. 4, we extend correspondence theory to algebras over a field seen as frames. Finally, we conclude in Sect. 5.

2 Preliminaries

In the present section, we recall some basic algebraic definitions and facts, and the definition of (analytic) inductive inequality in [6] recasted to the residuated lattice setting. Throughout the rest of the paper, we stick to the convention of implicitly universally closing equations and quasi-equations.

2.1 Algebras over a Field and Their Complex Algebras

Let $\mathbb{K} = (K, +, \cdot, 0, 1)$ be a field. A *vector space* over $\mathbb{K}$ is a tuple $\mathbb{V} = (V, +, \cdot, 0)$ s.t. $(V, +, 0)$ is an abelian group, $\cdot : \mathbb{K} \times V \to V$, and for all $\alpha, \beta \in \mathbb{K}, u, v \in V$

$$\alpha \cdot (\beta \cdot v) = (\alpha\beta) \cdot v \quad 1 \cdot v = v \quad \alpha \cdot (u + v) = \alpha \cdot u + \alpha \cdot v \quad (\alpha + \beta)v = \alpha \cdot v + \beta \cdot v.$$

A *subspace* $\mathbb{U}$ of a vector space $\mathbb{V}$ is a non-empty subset $U \subseteq V$ closed under $+$ and $\cdot$. For any subset $X \subseteq V$, we denote by $\mathsf{span}(X)$ the smallest subspace of $\mathbb{V}$ containing X. Also, a subspace $\mathbb{U} \subseteq \mathbb{V}$ is called the internal direct sum of a family $\mathcal{A} = \{\mathbb{U}_i \mid i \in I\}$ of subspaces of $\mathbb{V}$, denoted by $\bigoplus \mathcal{A}$ or $\bigoplus_{i \in I} \mathbb{U}_i$, if $\mathbb{U} = \sum_{i \in I} \mathbb{U}_i := \mathsf{span}(\bigcup_i \mathbb{U}_i)$ and for each $i \in I$, $\mathbb{U}_i \cap \sum_{j \neq i} \mathbb{U}_j = \{0\}$.

An *algebra over* a field $\mathbb{K}$ (or $\mathbb{K}$-*algebra*) is a pair $(\mathbb{V}, \star)$ where $\mathbb{V}$ is a vector space over $\mathbb{K}$ and $\star : V \times V \to V$ is *bilinear*, i.e., for all $\alpha, \beta \in \mathbb{K}$ and $u, v, w \in V$,

$$u \star (v + w) = (u \star v) + (u \star w), \quad (u + v) \star w = (u \star w) + (v \star w),$$
$$(\alpha \cdot u) \star (\beta \cdot v) = (\alpha\beta) \cdot (u \star v).$$

An algebraic structure $\mathbb{A} = (A, \wedge, \vee, \cdot, \backslash, /)$ is a *pre-residuated lattice* if $(A, \wedge, \vee)$ is a lattice and the *residuation rule* holds, i.e., $x \cdot y \leq z$ iff $x \leq z/y$ iff $y \leq x\backslash z$ for all $x, y, z \in A$. If $\mathbb{A}$ also contains a constant 1 and $(A, \cdot, 1)$ is a monoid, then $\mathbb{A}$ is a *residuated lattice.* A complete *pre-residuated lattice* is a *quantale* [13].

Example 1. For any monoid X, $\mathbb{A} = (\mathcal{P}(X), \cap, \cup, \cdot, \backslash, /, \{1\})$ is a residuated lattice where $\cdot$ is defined by $A \cdot B = \{a \cdot b \mid a \in A, b \in B\}$, and $\backslash, /$ are respectively defined by $A\backslash B = \{u \mid \forall b \forall a((b = a \cdot u \text{ and } a \in A) \Rightarrow b \in B)\}$, $A/B = \{u \mid \forall a \forall b((a = u \cdot b \text{ and } b \in B) \Rightarrow a \in A)\}$.

For any $\mathbb{K}$-algebra $\mathbb{V} = (V, \star)$, the poset $(\mathcal{S}(\mathbb{V}), \subseteq)$ of the subspaces of $\mathbb{V}$ is a complete lattice, where for any $\mathcal{A} = \{\mathbb{W}_i \mid i \in I\} \subseteq \mathcal{S}(\mathbb{V})$,

$$\bigwedge \mathcal{A} = \bigcap \mathcal{A} \qquad \text{and} \qquad \bigvee \mathcal{A} = \mathsf{span}(\bigcup\nolimits_{W_i \in \mathcal{A}} W_i) = \sum\nolimits_{i \in I} W_i.$$

Moreover, the operation $\otimes : \mathcal{S}(\mathbb{V}) \times \mathcal{S}(\mathbb{V}) \to \mathcal{S}(\mathbb{V})$ defined by $\mathbb{U} \otimes \mathbb{W} = \mathsf{span}(\{u \star w \mid u \in U, w \in W\})$ is completely join preserving in both coordinates; hence its residuals $\backslash$ and $/$ exist, i.e. binary operations s.t. for every $\mathbb{U}, \mathbb{W}, \mathbb{Z} \in \mathcal{S}(\mathbb{V})$,

$$\mathbb{U} \otimes \mathbb{W} \subseteq \mathbb{Z} \quad \text{iff} \quad \mathbb{W} \subseteq \mathbb{U}\backslash\mathbb{Z} \quad \text{iff} \quad \mathbb{U} \subseteq \mathbb{Z}/\mathbb{W}.$$

where $\mathbb{U}\backslash\mathbb{Z} = \mathsf{span}(\{w \mid \forall u \forall z((z = u \star w \text{ and } u \in U) \Rightarrow z \in Z)\})$ and $\mathbb{Z}/\mathbb{W} = \mathsf{span}(\{u \mid \forall w \forall z((z = u \star w \text{ and } w \in W) \Rightarrow z \in Z)\})$. For any $\mathbb{K}$-algebra $\mathbb{V} = (V, \star)$, the *complex algebra* $\mathbb{V}^+$ of $\mathbb{V}$ is the complete pre-residuated lattice $(\mathcal{S}(\mathbb{V}), \subseteq, \wedge, \vee, \otimes, \backslash, /)$.

Lemma 1. *Let V be a vector space and $\mathcal{S}(V)$ its lattice of subspaces. For any subspace $S \in \mathcal{S}(V)$, S is completely join irreducible*[1] *iff* $\mathsf{dim}\, S = 1$.

Proof. Let S be a completely join irreducible element in $\mathcal{S}(\mathbb{V})$ and $S = \mathsf{span}(\{a_i \mid i \in I\})$. Then, $S = \sum_{i \in I} \mathsf{span}(\{a_i\}) = \bigvee\{\mathsf{span}(\{a_i\}) \mid i \in I\}$; thus, $S = \mathsf{span}(\{a_i\})$ for some $i \in I$ and, hence, S is a 1-dimensional subspace of $\mathbb{V}$. Conversely, let $S = \mathsf{span}(\{a\})$ for some $a \neq 0$, and $S = \bigvee\{A_i \mid i \in I\} = \sum_{i \in I} A_i$. Since $S \neq \{0\}$, then there exists $i_0 \in I$ such that $\mathsf{dim} A_{i_0} = 1$; hence $S = A_{i_0}$.

Lemma 2. *For any vector space V, the set of completely join irreducible subspaces of $\mathcal{S}(V)$ is join-dense in $\mathcal{S}(V)$, i.e., any subspace of V is the join of a set of completely join irreducible subspaces of V.*

Proof. Let S be any subspace of $\mathbb{V}$ and $B = \{b_i \mid i \in I\}$ be a basis of S. Then, $S = \bigoplus_{i \in I} \mathsf{span}(\{b_i\})$, and hence $S = \bigvee\{\mathsf{span}(\{b_i\}) \mid i \in I\}$. Thus, by Lemma 1, S is the join of completely join irreducible subspaces of $\mathbb{V}$.

[1] An element $x \neq \bot$ of a lattice L is completely join irreducible whenever for any set $A \subseteq L$, $x = \bigvee A$ implies $x \in A$.

2.2 Analytic Inductive Inequalities in Residuated Lattices

Let $\mathcal{V}$ be a denumerably infinite set of propositional variables, whose elements are denoted by p, q, r, etc., possibly indexed. The language $\mathcal{L}_{\mathrm{PRL}}$ is generated by

$$\varphi ::= p \mid \varphi \wedge \varphi \mid \varphi \vee \varphi \mid \varphi \cdot \varphi \mid \varphi \backslash \varphi \mid \varphi / \varphi,$$

where p ranges over $\mathcal{V}$. The language $\mathcal{L}_{\mathrm{RL}}$ (resp. $\mathcal{L}_{\mathrm{BRL}}$) expands $\mathcal{L}_{\mathrm{PRL}}$ with the constant 1 (resp. $\top$ and $\bot$). The concepts throughout this section apply to all these languages; hence, we will just refer a generic one of such languages $\mathcal{L}$.

An *order type* over $n \in \mathbb{N}$ is a sequence in $\{1, \partial\}^n$. For every order-type ε, we denote its *opposite* order-type by ε^∂, that is, $\varepsilon_i^\partial = \varepsilon^\partial(i) = 1$ iff $\varepsilon_i = \varepsilon(i) = \partial$ for every $1 \leq i \leq n$, and $\varepsilon_i^\partial = \varepsilon^\partial(i) = \partial$ iff $\varepsilon_i = \varepsilon(i) = 1$ for every $1 \leq i \leq n$.

Definition 1 (Signed Generation Tree). *The* positive *(resp.* negative*)* generation tree *of any $\mathcal{L}$-term s is defined by labelling the root node of the syntax tree of s with the sign $+$ (resp. $-$), and propagating as follows:*

1. *For any node labelled with $\wedge$ or $\vee$ or $\cdot$, assign the same sign to its children.*
2. *For any node labelled with $\backslash$ (resp. $/$), assign the same (resp. the opposite) sign to its right (resp. left) child and the opposite (resp. same) sign to its left (resp. right) child.*

Nodes in signed generation trees are *positive* (resp. *negative*) if they are signed $+$ (resp. $-$). The concept of generation trees will be used in the context of term-inequalities $s \leq t$ in $\mathcal{L}$ in which we refer to the positive generation tree $+s$ for the left-hand side and the negative one $-t$ for the right hand side.[2] A term-inequality $s \leq t$ is *uniform* in a given variable p if all occurrences of p in both $+s$ and $-t$ have the same sign. We will also write $\varphi[t/x]$ to indicate the formula obtained from φ by substituting t for x, and $\varphi[(t_1, \cdots, t_n)/(x_1, \cdots, x_n)]$ for the formula obtained from φ by simultaneously substituting every x_i by t_i.[3]

For any term $s(p_1, \ldots p_n)$, any order-type ε over n, and any $1 \leq i \leq n$, an *ε-critical node* in a signed generation tree of s is a leaf node $+p_i$ if $\varepsilon(i) = 1$, and a leaf node $-p_i$ if $\varepsilon(i) = \partial$. An *$\varepsilon$-critical branch* in the tree is a branch the leaf of which is an ε-critical node. Finally, we will write $\varepsilon(\gamma) \prec *s$ (resp. $\varepsilon^\partial(\gamma) \prec *s$) to indicate that the signed subtree γ, with the sign inherited from $*s$, contains only ε-critical (resp. ε^∂-critical) leaves.[4]

A branch in a signed generation tree $*s$, with $* \in \{+, -\}$, is called a *good branch* if it is the concatenation of two paths P_1 and P_2, such that P_1 is a path

[2] A $+$ (resp. $-$) sign in a node u of $+s$ (resp. $-t$) indicates that s (resp. t) is monotone w.r.t. the subterm rooted in u, while a $-$ (resp. $+$) sign indicates that is antitone.

[3] Although we use the symbol $\backslash$ to denote both a connective in the language and the substitution symbol, in the remainder of the paper no ambiguity ever arises, since the terms in substitutions will not contain any explicit occurrence of $\backslash$.

[4] An order type over the variables of a term specifies which polarity serves to compute the minimal valuation for each variable [6]. Hence, ε-critical nodes are the occurrences of the variables in such polarities.

from the leaf consisting, apart from variable nodes, only of *PIA* nodes, i.e. nodes in $\{-\vee, +\wedge, +/, +\backslash, -\cdot\}$, and P_2 consists only of *Skeleton* nodes, i.e. nodes in $\{+\vee, -\wedge, -/, -\backslash, +\cdot\}$. A node in $\{+/, +\backslash, -\cdot\}$ is an *SRR* node.[5]

Definition 2 (Inductive Inequalities). *Given an order type ε and an irreflexive and transitive relation Ω on the variables $p_1, \cdots, p_n$, the generation tree $*s$, $* \in \{+, -\}$, of a term $s(p_1, \cdots, p_n)$ is (Ω, ε)-inductive if*

1. *every ε-critical branch with leaf p_i is good,*
2. *every SRR node $\gamma_0 \circledast \gamma_1$ in a critical branch passing by any γ_j (with $j \in \{0, 1\}$) is s.t. $\varepsilon^\partial(\gamma_{1-j}) \prec *s$ and any variable $q \neq p_i$ occurring in γ_j is s.t. $q <_\Omega p_i$.*

We will refer to $<_\Omega$ as the dependency order. *An inequality $s \leq t$ is (Ω, ε)-*inductive *if the signed generation trees $+s$ and $-t$ are (Ω, ε)-inductive. An inequality $s \leq t$ is* inductive *if it is (Ω, ε)-inductive for some Ω and ε.*

Furthermore, an inductive inequality is *analytic* if every branch is good. If an inequality does not contain any occurrence of / and \, it is *quasi-left primitive.*

Definition 3. *We will refer to formulas φ as positive (resp. negative)* PIA *formulas (resp.* Skeleton *formulas) if only PIA (resp. skeleton) nodes occur in $+\varphi$ (resp. $-\varphi$). Moreover, a positive or negative* PIA *(resp.* skeleton*) φ is definite if it does not contain occurrences of $-\vee$ and $+\wedge$ (resp. $+\vee$ and $-\wedge$). More explicitly, a negative PIA is built out of only constants, variables, and the connectives $\cdot$ and $\vee$. Positive PIAs are either variables, constants, or formulas $\alpha_1 \wedge \alpha_2$, α/β, or $\beta\backslash\alpha$, where α, α_1 and α_2 positive PIAs, and β is a negative PIA.*

From the interactions between $\cdot$, / and \ with $\vee$ and $\wedge$, the following lemma follows straightforwardly by induction, with the idea of distributing $\vee$ and $\wedge$ as up as possible in the syntax tree. Notice that (definite) positive (resp. negative) skeletons are negative (resp. positive) PIAs.

Lemma 3. *For any (bounded) (pre)residuated lattice $\mathbb{A}$, any positive (resp. negative) PIA is equivalent in $\mathbb{A}$ to a meet (resp. join) of definite positive (resp. negative) PIAs.*

Following [2], we will often represent analytic (Ω, ε)-inductive inequalities as follows: $(\varphi \leq \psi)[\overline{\alpha}/\overline{x}, \overline{\beta}/\overline{y}]$, where $\varphi \leq \psi$ contains only skeleton nodes, is positive (resp. negative) in $\overline{x}$ (resp. $\overline{y}$), each α in $\overline{\alpha}$ (resp. β in $\overline{\beta}$) is a positive (resp. negative) PIA, and it is *scattered*, i.e. each variable in $\overline{x}$ and $\overline{y}$ occurs only once. Intuitively speaking, since every branch in the signed generation tree of the inequality is good, there must be an upper portion of the tree (represented by $\varphi(\overline{x}, \overline{y})$ and $\psi(\overline{x}, \overline{y})$) which contains only Skeleton nodes, and all the other nodes must be PIA nodes.

---

5 The acronym PIA means *positive implies atomic.* It was first introduced in [1] and used as in this context in [6]. The acronym SRR stands for *syntactical right residual.*

3 Rewriting Analytic Inductive Inequalities

We show that any analytic inductive $\mathcal{L}_{\mathrm{PRL}}$-inequality is equivalent for pre-residuated lattices to a system of inequalities whose terms only contain the connectives $\cdot$, $\vee$, and then we show that a similar result can be obtained for (bounded) residuated lattices. We proceed in two steps. Firstly, we show that any analytic inductive inequality is equivalent to a system of inequalities which are (Ω, ε)-inductive for the order type ε such that every non-uniformly negative variable is critical in its positive occurrences. Consequently, the algorithm ALBA can eliminate all the variables in the positive coordinates of any given input analytic inductive inequality, and we use this fact to rewrite the inequalities in the system in such a way that no occurrence of $/$ and $\backslash$ is needed.

For a given inequality, we will equivalently consider order types over the number of variables occurring in the inequality to be maps from the variables occurring in the inequality to $\{1, \partial\}$, so as to avoid to explicitly define an ordering of the variables of an inequality and its terms.

3.1 Analytic Inductive Shape in Residuated Lattices

In the present section we show that analytic inductive inequalities in $\mathcal{L}_{\mathrm{PRL}}$ are equivalent to (systems of) inequalities with a rather simple shape. The reader is referred to Example 2 and Example 3 in Appendix A.

Remark 1. Throughout the rest of the paper, we write $\alpha(x, \overline{q})$ to denote a definite positive PIA whose (unique) positive coordinate contains x (either a variable or a constant), and whose negative variable occurrences are the variables in the vector $\overline{q}$. We also write $\varphi(\overline{p})$ or $\beta(\overline{p})$ to denote a refined positive skeleton (or, equivalently, a definite negative PIA) whose variable occurrences are in $\overline{p}$.

Lemma 4. *For any definite positive PIA $\alpha(y, \overline{z})$ there is a formula $\alpha^\flat(x, \overline{z})$ which contains only the operator $\cdot$, such that for any (bounded) (pre)residuated lattice $\mathbb{L}$, ${\alpha^\flat}^{\mathbb{L}}(x, \overline{z})$ is left residual of $\alpha^{\mathbb{L}}(y, \overline{z})$. That is, for every $x, y, z_1, \ldots, z_n \in \mathbb{L}$, ${\alpha^\flat}^{\mathbb{L}}(x, z_1, \ldots, z_n) \leq y$ iff $x \leq \alpha^{\mathbb{L}}(y, z_1, \ldots, z_n)$, where $\alpha^{\mathbb{L}}$ and ${\alpha^\flat}^{\mathbb{L}}$ denote the term functions of α and $\alpha^\flat$ in $\mathbb{L}$, respectively.*

Proof. We prove it by induction on the length of the path from the root of α to x. If $\alpha(y, \overline{z}) = y$, then $\alpha^\flat(x, \overline{z}) = x$. Otherwise, $\alpha(y, \overline{z})$ is either $\alpha'(y, \overline{z_1})/\beta(\overline{z_2})$ or $\beta(\overline{z_2})\backslash\alpha'(y, \overline{z_1})$, where $\alpha'(y, \overline{z_1})$ (resp. $\beta(\overline{z_2})$) is a definite positive (resp. negative) PIA and the variables in $\overline{z}$ are the union of the variables in $\overline{z_1}$ and $\overline{z_2}$. By induction hypothesis, there is a formula ${\alpha'}^\flat(x, \overline{z_1})$ which is left residual of $\alpha'(y, \overline{z_1})$ in (bounded) (pre)residuated lattices; hence ${\alpha^\flat}^{\mathbb{L}}(x, \overline{z})$ can be ${\alpha'}^\flat(\beta(\overline{z_2}) \cdot x, \overline{z_1})$ if the root of α is $\backslash$, and ${\alpha'}^\flat(x \cdot \beta(\overline{z_2}), \overline{z_1})$ if the root of α is $/$.

The reader is referred to Example 2 and 3 while reading the following lemma.

Lemma 5. *For any (bounded) (pre)residuated lattice $\mathbb{L}$, any analytic inductive $\mathcal{L}_{(\mathrm{B})(\mathrm{P})\mathrm{RL}}$-inequality can be rewritten as a system of inequalities*

$$\varphi(\overline{x})[\overline{\xi}/\overline{x}] \leq \bigvee_i \beta_i(\overline{r_i}),$$

where each ξ in $\overline{\xi}$ is a meet of definite positive PIAs, i.e. it has shape $\bigwedge_j \alpha_j(x_j, \overline{y_j})$, where each x_j is a constant or a variable, and each β_i is a definite negative PIA.

Proof. Let $(\varphi \leq \psi)[\overline{\alpha}/\overline{x}, \overline{\beta}/\overline{y}]$ be an analytic inductive inequality as above, so each α_i in $\overline{\alpha}$ (resp. β_i in $\overline{\beta}$) is a positive (resp. negative) PIA, and variables in $\overline{x}$ (resp. $\overline{y}$) occur only once and in positive (resp. negative) coordinates of $\varphi \leq \psi$. Since positive (resp. negative) skeletons are negative (resp. positive) PIAs, φ (resp. ψ) is equivalent to a join $\bigvee_k \varphi_k$ (resp. meet $\bigwedge_h \psi_h$) of definite positive (resp. negative) skeletons. Hence, the inequality is equivalent to $(\bigvee_k \varphi_k \leq \bigwedge_h \psi_h)[\overline{\alpha}/\overline{x}, \overline{\beta}/\overline{y}]$, which is equivalent to the system of inequalities $(\varphi_k \leq \psi_h)[\overline{\alpha}/\overline{x}, \overline{\beta}/\overline{y}]$, for every index h and k. By writing ψ_h as $\psi_h(y, \overline{z})$ using notation in Remark 1, so y is positive in ψ_h and the variables in $\overline{z}$ are negative. By Lemma 4, ψ_h has a left adjoint $\psi_h^\flat(w, \overline{z})$, which is positive in all coordinates and such that the variables in $\overline{z}$ are amongst those of $\overline{x}$; therefore the inequality is equivalent to $(\psi_h^\flat(\varphi_k, \overline{z}) \leq y)[\overline{\alpha}/\overline{x}, \overline{\beta}/\overline{y}]$, where the variables of φ_k and $\overline{z}$ constitute precisely the variables in $\overline{x}$, and y is the only variable in $\overline{y}$. Of course, $\psi_h^\flat(\varphi_k, \overline{z})$ is a definite positive Skeleton, let us denote it by $\varphi_k'(\overline{x})$.

By Lemma 3, the inequality $(\varphi_k \leq \psi_h)[\overline{\alpha}/\overline{x}, \overline{\beta}/\overline{y}]$ is equivalent to

$$\varphi_k'(\overline{x}) \left[\left(\bigwedge_j \alpha_{1,j}, \ldots, \bigwedge_j \alpha_{n,j} \right) / \overline{x} \right] \leq \bigvee \beta_i',$$

where each $\alpha_{i,j}$ (resp. β_i') is a definite positive (resp. negative) PIA.

By applying the same rewritings for each $\varphi_k \leq \psi_h$, the system of inequalities in the target shape is obtained.

3.2 Solving in the Positive Coordinates

Let us fix an arbitrary analytic (Ω, ε)-inductive inequality which can be rewritten by Lemma 5 as a system of inequalities. Let us consider a generic inequality $\varphi \leq \psi$ in the system, and let us also assume w.l.o.g. that Ω is the smallest dependency order such that $\varphi \leq \psi$ is (Ω, ε)-inductive, i.e., it is the intersection of all such orders. Via an iterative process, we show that the inequality is also analytic (Ω', ε')-inductive with ε' such that $\varepsilon'(p) = 1$ for every p. We can assume that $\varepsilon(p) = 1$ for every uniformly negative variable, since only critical variable occurrences generate constraints in Definition 2.

Let us denote by $\varepsilon^{(i)}$ and $\Omega^{(i)}$ the order type and dependency order which we obtain after the i-th iteration, and let us denote $\varepsilon^{(0)} = \varepsilon$ and $\Omega^{(0)} = \Omega$. After the i-th iteration, the iterative process shows that the variable v_i can be made critical in its positive occurrences; hence, $\varepsilon^{(i)}(v_i) := 1$ and $\varepsilon^{(i)}(p) := \varepsilon^{(i-1)}(p)$ for every other variable p. If n is the number of variables v for which $\varepsilon(v) = \partial$, we pick the variables $v_1, \ldots, v_n$ for each iteration in such a way that $v_i \neq v_j$ for every $i \neq j$, and each at the i-th iteration, the picked variable v_i is maximal amongst the remaining variables with respect to $\Omega^{(i-1)}$, i.e., $v_i \not<_{\Omega^{(i-1)}} v_j$ for every $j > i$. We need to show that the input inequality is $(\Omega^{(i)}, \varepsilon^{(i)})$-inductive after each iteration, so that after the n-th iteration the desired positive order type is found, since all the non-uniformly negative variables v for which $\varepsilon(v) = \partial$ are such that $\varepsilon^{(n)}(v) = 1$.

Since each v_i is not uniformly negative in the inequality, then it occurs in the positive coordinate of some positive definite PIAs $\alpha_{i_1}(v_i, \overline{q_{i_1}}), \ldots, \alpha_{i_m}(v_i, \overline{q_{i_m}})$. Let us denote by Q_i the set of all the variables occurring negatively in such positive definite PIAs, i.e. the variables in some $\overline{q_{i_j}}$. Let us put

$$\Omega^{(i)} := (\Omega^{(i-1)^-} \cup \{(q, v_i) : q \in Q_i\})^+,$$

where $(\cdot)^+$ denotes the transitive closure of the relation, and $\Omega^{(i-1)^-}$ denotes $\Omega^{(i-1)}$ where all the pairs forced by negative critical occurrences of v_i are removed, i.e. $\Omega^{(i-1)^-} := \Omega^{(i-1)} \setminus (V \times \{v_i\})$, where V is the set of variables occurring in the inequality. Example 5 showcases the procedure.

Lemma 6. *For any i in $\{1, \ldots, n\}$ such that $\varphi \leq \psi$ is $(\Omega^{(j)}, \varepsilon^{(j)})$-inductive for every $j < i$, the inequality is also $(\Omega^{(i)}, \varepsilon^{(i)})$-inductive.*

Proof. Notice that every variable $q \in Q_i$ is such that $\varepsilon^{(i-1)}(q) = 1$; indeed, if $\varepsilon^{(i-1)}(q)$ were ∂, then $v_i <_{\Omega^{(i-1)}} q$, and therefore q would coincide with some v_j with $j < i$, against $\varepsilon^{(j)}(v_j) = 1 = \varepsilon^{(i-1)}(q)$. Hence, setting v_i to critical does not require us to consider more constraints than those enforced by the PIAs in which v_i is critical.

We need to show that $\Omega^{(i)}$ is irreflexive. Since the starting inequality is inductive, $v_i \notin Q_i$, for otherwise $v_i <_\Omega v_i$ for every suitable Ω, by item 2 of Definition 2. Since $\Omega^{(i-1)}$ is irreflexive and transitive, any loop introduced in $\Omega^{(i)}$ must involve one of the newly added edges $q <_{\Omega^{(i)}} v_i$; so, the loop has shape $q <_{\Omega^{(i)}} v_i <_{\Omega^{(i)}} u_1 <_{\Omega^{(i)}} \cdots <_{\Omega^{(i)}} u_m <_{\Omega^{(i)}} q$, where $v_i <_{\Omega^{(i-1)}} u_1 <_{\Omega^{(i-1)}} \cdots <_{\Omega^{(i-1)}} u_m <_{\Omega^{(i-1)}} q$. Therefore, it follows that $v_i <_{\Omega^{(i-1)}} q$. There are two cases to analyze. If $\varepsilon^{(0)}(q) = 1$, then v_i occurs negatively in one of the positive PIAs where q occurs critically; hence, since the inequality is (Ω, ε)-inductive, also $\varepsilon^{(0)}(v_i) = 1$, against the assumption that $\varepsilon^{(0)}(v_i) = \partial$.

Otherwise, $\varepsilon^{(i)}(q) = 1$ because has $q = v_j$ for some $j < i$; hence $\varepsilon^{(j)}(v_i) = 1$, as $v_i \neq v_k$ for every $k < j$. This contradicts the assumption that $\varepsilon^{(i)}(v_i) = \partial$. By definition of $\Omega^{(i)}$ and the fact that the inequality is $(\Omega^{(i-1)}, \varepsilon^{(i-1)})$-inductive by assumption, it follows straightforwardly that it is $(\Omega^{(i)}, \varepsilon^{(i)})$-inductive.

Corollary 1. *Any inductive $\mathcal{L}_{\mathrm{PRL}}$-inequality is (Ω, ε) inductive for the order type ε such that $\varepsilon(p) = 1$ for every non-uniformly negative variable p.*

3.3 From Analytic Inductive to Quasi Left Primitive

In the previous subsection we have shown that, without loss of generality, any analytic inductive inequality is equivalent to a system of inequalities, each of which is (Ω, ε)-inductive, where $\varepsilon(p) = 1$ for every non-uniform variable p occurring in the inequality. This order type can be easily used in the algorithm ALBA (see [6]) to show that any analytic inductive $\mathcal{L}_{\mathrm{PRL}}$-inequality is equivalent to a quasi-left primitive inequality.

In the present section, we show a rather self-contained presentation of ALBA tailored for the residuated lattices case, which we use to show that each of the inequalities in the system is equivalent to a quasi left primitive inequality.

Since every inductive inequality is *canonical* [6, Theorem 7.1], i.e. it holds in a preresiduated lattice if and only if it holds in its canonical extension, we can restrict ourselves to the canonical extensions of preresiduated lattices.[6] Let us fix an arbitrary pre-residuated lattice $\mathbb{L}$. We will write symbols $\mathbf{i}, \mathbf{j}$ (resp. $\mathbf{m}, \mathbf{n}$), possibly with subscripts, to denote variables which are implicitly (universally) quantified over $J^\infty(\mathbb{L}^\delta)$ (resp. $M^\infty(\mathbb{L}^\delta)$).

Let us consider any analytic inductive $\mathcal{L}_{\mathrm{PRL}}$-inequality which, by Lemma 5, can be rewritten as a system of inequalities $\varphi(\overline{x})[\overline{\xi}/\overline{x}] \leq \bigvee_i \beta_i(\overline{r_i})$, and let us consider each one of these inequalities separately.

Remark 2. From now on we will assume that the inequality does not contain uniformly negative variables. Indeed, any uniformly negative variable can be equivalently substituted by $\bot$ (which is interpreted as the minimum of $\mathbb{L}^\delta$). Indeed, the left (resp. right) side of the inequality is antitone (resp. monotone) w.r.t. every uniformly negative variable u; hence

$$\varphi(\overline{x})[\overline{\xi}/\overline{x}] \leq \varphi(\overline{x})[\overline{\xi}/\overline{x}][\bot/u] \leq (\bigvee_i \beta_i(\overline{r_i}))[\bot/u] \leq \bigvee_i \beta_i(\overline{r_i}).$$

Any occurrence of $\bot$ will be removed before returning to the language $\mathcal{L}_{\mathrm{PRL}}$.

Since $\mathbb{L}^\delta$ is join-generated (resp. meet generated) by $J^\infty(\mathbb{L}^\delta)$ (resp. $M^\infty(\mathbb{L}^\delta)$), each $\xi_i = \bigvee\{\mathbf{j}_i : \mathbf{j}_i \leq \xi_i\}$ (resp. $\bigvee_i \beta_i(\overline{r_i}) = \bigwedge\{\mathbf{m} : \bigvee_i \beta_i(\overline{r_i}) \leq \mathbf{m}\}$); therefore $\varphi(\overline{x})[\overline{\xi}/\overline{x}] \leq \bigvee_i \beta_i(\overline{r_i})$ is equivalent to

$$\varphi(\overline{x}) \left[\left(\bigvee\{\mathbf{j}_1 : \mathbf{j}_1 \leq \xi_1\}, \ldots, \bigvee\{\mathbf{j}_n : \mathbf{j}_n \leq \xi_n\}\right) /\overline{x}\right] \leq \bigwedge\{\mathbf{m} : \bigvee_i \beta_i(\overline{r_i}) \leq \mathbf{m}\}.$$

[6] The canonical extension $\mathbb{L}^\delta$ of a preresiduated lattice $\mathbb{L}$ is a completion of $\mathbb{L}$, with a lattice embedding $e : \mathbb{L} \to \mathbb{L}^\delta$. The canonical extension of a lattice $\mathbb{L}$ is a quantale which is join-generated (resp. meet generated) by the set $K(\mathbb{L}^\delta)$ (resp. $O(\mathbb{L}^\delta)$) of elements which are in the meet closure (resp. join closure) in $\mathbb{L}^\delta$ of $e[\mathbb{L}]$, which are called *closed* (resp. *open*) elements. Furthermore, the operations $\cdot$, $/$, and $\backslash$ are extended to $\mathbb{L}^\delta$ in such a way that they still satisfy residuation rules; hence,

$$\begin{array}{lll} \bigvee_{s\in S} s \cdot a = \bigvee_{s\in S}(s \cdot a) & a \cdot \bigvee_{s\in S} s = \bigvee_{s\in S}(a \cdot s) & \text{for every } a \in \mathbb{L}^\delta, S \subseteq \mathbb{L}^\delta, \\ \bigwedge_{s\in S} s/a = \bigwedge_{s\in S}(s/a) & a/\bigvee_{s\in S} s = \bigwedge_{s\in S}(a/s) & \text{for every } a \in \mathbb{L}^\delta, S \subseteq \mathbb{L}^\delta, \\ \bigvee_{s\in S} s\backslash a = \bigwedge_{s\in S}(s\backslash a) & a\backslash \bigwedge_{s\in S} s = \bigwedge_{s\in S}(a\backslash s) & \text{for every } a \in \mathbb{L}^\delta, S \subseteq \mathbb{L}^\delta. \end{array}$$

It can be shown that $\mathbb{L}^\delta$ is join generated (resp. meet generated) by a subset of $K(\mathbb{L}^\delta)$ (resp. $O(\mathbb{L}^\delta)$), i.e., the set $J^\infty(\mathbb{L}^\delta)$ (resp. $M^\infty(\mathbb{L}^\delta)$) of completely join irreducible (resp. completely meet irreducible) elements of $\mathbb{L}^\delta$ (see [7, Corollary 2.10]).

Since φ contains only the connective $\cdot$, which is completely join preserving in $\mathbb{L}^\delta$, the inequality above is equivalent to

$$\bigvee\{\varphi(\overline{x})[\overline{\mathbf{j}}/\overline{x}] : \mathbf{j}_1 \leq \xi_1, \ldots, \mathbf{j}_n \leq \xi_n\} \leq \bigwedge\{\mathbf{m} : \bigvee_i \beta_i(\overline{r_i}) \leq \mathbf{m}\},$$

which by basic order theoretic facts is equivalent to[7]

$$\mathbf{j}_1 \leq \xi_1, \ldots, \mathbf{j}_n \leq \xi_n, \bigvee_i \beta_i(\overline{r_i}) \leq \mathbf{m} \Rightarrow \varphi(\overline{x})[\overline{\mathbf{j}}/\overline{x}] \leq \mathbf{m},$$

that, given the shape of each ξ_i (such as in Lemma 5) can be rewritten as

$$\mathbf{j}_1 \leq \bigwedge\nolimits_j^{m_1} \alpha_j^1(p_j^1, \overline{q_j^1}), \ldots, \mathbf{j}_n \leq \bigwedge\nolimits_j^{m_n} \alpha_j^n(p_j^n, \overline{q_j^n}), \bigvee_i \beta_i(\overline{r_i}) \leq \mathbf{m} \Rightarrow \varphi(\overline{x})[\overline{\mathbf{j}}/\overline{x}] \leq \mathbf{m}.$$

The antecedent can be rewritten using residuation (Lemma 4) as follows

$$\begin{array}{l}
\alpha_1^{1^\flat}(\mathbf{j}_1, \overline{q_1^1}) \leq p_1^1, \ \ldots, \ \alpha_{m_1}^{1}{}^\flat(\mathbf{j}_1, \overline{q_{m_1}^1}) \leq p_{m_1}^1, \\
\alpha_1^{2^\flat}(\mathbf{j}_2, \overline{q_1^2}) \leq p_1^2, \ \ldots, \ \alpha_{m_2}^{2}{}^\flat(\mathbf{j}_2, \overline{q_{m_2}^2}) \leq p_{m_2}^2, \\
\vdots \qquad\qquad\qquad \vdots \qquad\qquad\qquad \vdots \\
\alpha_1^{n^\flat}(\mathbf{j}_n, \overline{q_1^n}) \leq p_1^n, \ \ldots, \ \alpha_{m_n}^{n}{}^\flat(\mathbf{j}_n, \overline{q_{m_n}^n}) \leq p_{m_n}^n, \\
\qquad\qquad \bigvee_i \beta_i(\overline{r_i}) \leq \mathbf{m} \Rightarrow \varphi(\overline{x})[\overline{\mathbf{j}}/\overline{x}] \leq \mathbf{m}.
\end{array}$$

For every variable p consider the set $M_p := \{\alpha_j^{i^\flat}(\mathbf{j}_i, \overline{q_j^i}) : p = p_j^i\}$. If $\{p_1, \ldots, p_k\}$ is the set of variables occurring in the inequality, the quasi-inequality holds iff

$$\bigvee M_1 \leq p_1, \ldots, \bigvee M_k \leq p_k, \bigvee_i \beta_i(\overline{r_i}) \leq \mathbf{m} \Rightarrow \varphi(\overline{x})[\overline{\mathbf{j}}/\overline{x}] \leq \mathbf{m}.$$

The starting inequality being inductive guarantees that the Ackermann Lemma can be applied (see [6]);[8] hence the quasi inequality above is equivalent to

$$\begin{aligned}
&\bigvee_i \beta_i(\overline{r_i})[\bigvee M_1/p_1] \cdots [\bigvee M_k/p_k] \leq \mathbf{m} \Rightarrow \varphi(\overline{x})[\overline{\mathbf{j}}/\overline{x}] \leq \mathbf{m}, \\
&\text{iff } \varphi(\overline{x})[\overline{\mathbf{j}}/\overline{x}] \leq \bigvee_i \beta_i(\overline{r_i})[\bigvee M_1/p_1] \cdots [\bigvee M_k/p_k].
\end{aligned}$$

---

[7] For all $A, B \subseteq \mathbb{L}^\delta$, $\bigvee A \leq \bigwedge B$ iff $(\forall a \in A)(\forall b \in B) a \leq b$.

[8] The Ackermann Lemma in this setting implies that for any residuated lattice $\mathbb{L}$, any variable p, and any formulas $\alpha, \beta_1, \ldots, \beta_n, \gamma_1, \ldots, \gamma_n, \xi$, and ζ such that p does not occur in α, is positive in each β_i and ζ, and negative in each γ_i and ξ, the following quasi-inequalities are equivalent in $\mathbb{L}$

$$\alpha \leq p, \beta_1 \leq \gamma_1, \ldots, \beta_n \leq \gamma_n \Rightarrow \xi \leq \zeta \quad \text{iff} \quad (\beta_1 \leq \gamma_1, \ldots, \beta_n \leq \gamma_n \Rightarrow \xi \leq \zeta)[\alpha/p].$$

The conditions on the polarity of each variable in the other inequalities are trivially satisfied here. The condition that states that the eliminated variable does not occur in α (in this case it is equivalent to saying that p_i does not occur in $\bigvee M_i[\bigvee M_1/p_1] \cdots [\bigvee M_{i-1}/p_{i-1}]$) is implied by item 2 of Definition 2 (see [6]).

Since all the formulas in each M_i contain only the connective $\cdot$, the inequality above only contains $\vee$, and $\cdot$. Moreover, by associating a variable $p_{\mathbf{j}}$ to each $\mathbf{j}$, such an inequality is equivalent to

$$\varphi(\overline{x})[\overline{p}_{\mathbf{j}}/\overline{x}] \leq \bigvee_i \beta_i(\overline{r_i})[\bigvee M_1/p_1]\cdots[\bigvee M_k/p_k][\overline{p}_{\mathbf{j}}/\overline{\mathbf{j}}]. \tag{1}$$

Indeed, since every $p_{\mathbf{j}} = \bigvee\{\mathbf{j} : \mathbf{j} \leq p_{\mathbf{j}}\}$, such an inequality is equivalent to

$$\mathbf{j}_1 \leq p_{\mathbf{j}_1}, \ldots, \mathbf{j}_n \leq p_{\mathbf{j}_n} \Rightarrow \varphi(\overline{x})[\overline{\mathbf{j}}/\overline{x}] \leq \bigvee_i \beta_i(\overline{r_i})[\bigvee M_1/p_1]\cdots[\bigvee M_k/p_k][\overline{p}_{\mathbf{j}}/\overline{\mathbf{j}}],$$

which is trivially equivalent (by the Ackermann Lemma) to

$$\varphi(\overline{x})[\overline{\mathbf{j}}/\overline{x}] \leq \bigvee_i \beta_i(\overline{r_i})[\bigvee M_1/p_1]\cdots[\bigvee M_k/p_k].$$

Remark 3. Notice that, since by Remark 2 the variables in each $\overline{r_i}$ are amongst $\{p_1, \ldots, p_k\}$, the variables contained in the right hand side of the equivalent quasi left-primitive inequality are amongst those in $\overline{p}_{\mathbf{j}}$, i.e. amongst those found in the left hand side of the inequality.

The obtained inequality (1) is equivalent in $\mathbb{L}^\delta$ to the starting inequality $\varphi(\overline{x})[\overline{\xi}/\overline{x}] \leq \bigvee_i \beta_i(\overline{r_i})$, which holds if and only if $\varphi(\overline{x})[\overline{\xi}/\overline{x}] \leq \bigvee_i \beta_i(\overline{r_i})$ holds in $\mathbb{L}$. Let us call $\zeta_1 \leq \zeta_2$ the inequality resulting from the substitution of every (negative) occurrence of $\bot$ with a fresh variable $v_\bot$ in (1). Notice that every occurrence of $\bot$ has negative polarity, as all these equivalent rewritings do not change any polarity. By an argument analogous to that of Remark 2, $\zeta_1 \leq \zeta_2$ is equivalent to (1) in $\mathbb{L}^\delta$, and, since $\zeta_1 \leq \zeta_2$ is an analytic inductive $\mathcal{L}_{\mathrm{PRL}}$-inequality, $\zeta_1 \leq \zeta_2$ holds in $\mathbb{L}^\delta$ iff it holds in $\mathbb{L}$; thus $\mathbb{L} \models \varphi(\overline{x})[\overline{\xi}/\overline{x}] \leq \bigvee_i \beta_i(\overline{r_i})$ iff $\mathbb{L} \models \zeta_1 \leq \zeta_2$. From the above discussion the following theorem follows.

Theorem 1. *For any pre-residuated lattice* $\mathbb{L}$ *and any analytic inductive* $\mathcal{L}_{\mathrm{PRL}}$*-inequality* $\varphi \leq \psi$ *there is a system of quasi-left primitive* $\mathcal{L}_{\mathrm{PRL}}$*-inequalities* $\varphi'_1 \leq \psi'_1, \ldots, \varphi'_n \leq \psi'_n$ *such that*

$$\mathbb{L} \models \varphi \leq \psi \quad \textit{iff} \quad \mathbb{L} \models \varphi'_1 \leq \psi'_1, \ldots, \mathbb{L} \models \varphi'_n \leq \psi'_n.$$

As mentioned at the start of the section, a similar result can be applied to (bounded) residuated lattices. It remains to check what happens when the only positive coordinate of some definite positive PIA $\alpha^i_j(c, \overline{q})$ contains a constant c, as it would not be possible to apply the Ackermann Lemma after residuating, so as to make it possible to reassemble the inequality after rewriting the residuals $/$ and $\backslash$ as $\cdot$. If the constant c is $\top$, the whole definite PIA is equivalent to $\top$, as the positive coordinates of the residuals are completely meet preserving; hence they preserve the empty meet, i.e. $\top$. When c is 1 or $\bot$, there is no obvious transformation. The result above can be generalized as follows.

Theorem 2. *Let $\mathbb{L}$ be a (bounded) (pre)residuated lattice. For any analytic inductive $\mathcal{L}_{(B)(P)RL}$-inequality $\varphi \leq \psi$ there is a system of $\mathcal{L}_{(B)(P)RL}$-inequalities $\varphi'_1 \leq \psi'_1, \ldots, \varphi'_n \leq \psi'_n$ such that*

$$\mathbb{L} \models \varphi \leq \psi \quad \textit{iff} \quad \mathbb{L} \models {\varphi'}_1 \leq {\psi'}_1, \ldots, \mathbb{L} \models {\varphi'}_n \leq {\psi'}_n,$$

and every ${\varphi'}_i \leq {\psi'}_i$ is either quasi-left primitive or it contains an occurrence of $\bot$ or 1 in the positive coordinate of some / or \. Furthermore, if $\varphi \leq \psi$ does not contain any occurrence of $\bot$ or 1 in the positive coordinate of some / or \, every $\varphi'_i \leq \psi'_i$ is quasi-left primitive.

4 Correspondence

In the present section, we make use of the results in Sect. 3 to characterize the first order conditions in the first order language of $\mathbb{K}$-algebras which correspond to analytic inductive inequalities in lattices of subspaces of $\mathbb{K}$-algebras.

Let us denote by $\mathcal{L}_{\mathrm{KA}}$ the language of the lattice of subspaces of $\mathbb{K}$-algebras, containing the connectives $\cap$, $+$, $\otimes$, $/$, $\backslash$, $\top$, and $\bot$, and let us denote by $\mathcal{L}_{\mathrm{FO}}$ the first order language with identity of $\mathbb{K}$-algebras, containing function symbols for $\star$, $+$, $\cdot$, 1, 0, and two sorts of variables: $u, v, \ldots$ for vectors, and $\alpha, \beta, \ldots$ for scalars. Let us also denote by $\mathcal{L}^+_{\mathrm{KA}}$ an extension of $\mathcal{L}_{\mathrm{KA}}$ containing also a new sort of variables called *nominals* denoted by $\mathbf{i}$ and $\mathbf{j}$, possibly with subscripts. For any $\mathbb{K}$-algebra $\mathbb{A}$, any formulas $\varphi \in \mathcal{L}_{\mathrm{FO}}$, $\psi \in \mathcal{L}^+_{\mathrm{KA}}$, we write $\mathbb{A} \models \varphi$ to say that φ holds in $\mathbb{A}$ (seen as a first order structure), and $\mathbb{A} \models \psi$ to denote that ψ holds interpreting variables as subspaces of $\mathbb{A}$ and nominals as one dimensional subspaces of $\mathbb{A}$. Let us define the following translation from formulas in a subset of $\mathcal{L}^+_{\mathrm{KA}}$ to terms of $\mathcal{L}_{\mathrm{FO}}$.

Definition 4. *Let $\varphi \in \mathcal{L}^+_{\mathrm{KA}}$ such that φ does not contain any variable, and which only contains the connectives $\otimes$, $\top$, and $\bot$. The translation $\tau : \mathcal{L}^+_{\mathrm{KA}} \to$ $\mathsf{Terms}(\mathcal{L}_{\mathrm{FO}})$ is defined recursively as follows:*

$$\tau(\mathbf{j}) = v_{\mathbf{j}} \qquad \tau(\top) = v_{\top} \qquad \tau(\bot) = 0 \qquad \tau(\varphi \otimes \psi) = \tau(\varphi) \star \tau(\psi),$$

where $v_{\mathbf{j}}$ is a fresh variable for each nominal $\mathbf{j}$, and $v_{\top}$ is another fresh variable.

Theorem 3. *For every analytic inductive $\mathcal{L}_{\mathrm{KA}}$-inequality $\varphi \leq \psi$ such that φ does not contain $\bot$ in the positive coordinate of some / or \, there is a first order formula $\chi \in \mathcal{L}_{\mathrm{FO}}$ which is a conjunction of conjuncts with shape*

$$\forall v_1 \cdots \forall v_n \exists \alpha_1 \cdots \exists \alpha_k \;\; t(\overline{v}) = \alpha_1 \cdot s_1(\overline{v}) + \ldots + \alpha_k \cdot s_k(\overline{v}),$$

where $t(\overline{v})$ and each $s_i(\overline{v})$ are terms built only from variables (not necessarily all) in $v_1, \ldots, v_n$ and the connectives 0 and $\star$, such that for every $\mathbb{K}$-algebra $\mathbb{A}$,

$$\mathbb{A} \models \varphi \leq \psi \qquad \textit{iff} \qquad \mathbb{A} \models \chi.$$

Proof. The lattice of subspaces of $\mathbb{A}$ is a bounded pre-residuated lattice, and, by Theorem 2, there is a system of quasi left primitive inequalities $\varphi'_1 \leq \psi'_1, \ldots, \varphi'_n \leq \psi'_n$ which holds in $\mathbb{A}$ iff $\varphi \leq \psi$ holds. We show that each inequality in the system corresponds to one of the conjuncts of the formula χ we want to construct. By following the proof in Sect. 3.3, every $\varphi'_h \leq \psi'_h$ has shape

$$\varphi(\overline{x})[\overline{p}_{\mathbf{j}}/\overline{x}] \leq \bigvee_i \beta_i(\overline{r_i})[\bigvee M_1/p_1] \cdots [\bigvee M_k/p_k][\overline{p}_{\mathbf{j}}/\overline{\mathbf{j}}].$$

Since each β_i only contains the connective $\otimes$, which is join preserving in both coordinates, and since also the formulas in each M_i contain only the connective $\otimes$, the inequality above is equivalent to (by also renaming variables) $\varphi(\overline{x}) \leq \bigvee_i \gamma_i(\overline{y}_i)$, where φ and each γ_i are formulas containing only the connective $\otimes$, φ contains all the variables in $\overline{x}$, and, by Remark 3, each $\overline{y}_i$ contains a subset of variables of $\overline{x}$. Since $\otimes$ is completely join preserving, and, by Lemma 2, $\mathbb{A}$ is join generated by the one dimensional spaces,

$$\begin{array}{ll} \varphi(\overline{x}) \leq \bigvee_i \gamma_i(\overline{x}) & \\ \text{iff } \varphi(\overline{x})[(\bigvee\{\mathbf{j}_1 : \mathbf{j}_1 \leq x_1\}, \ldots, \bigvee\{\mathbf{j}_n : \mathbf{j}_n \leq x_n\})/\overline{x}] \leq \bigvee_i \gamma_i(\overline{y}_i) & \\ \text{iff } \bigvee\{\varphi(\overline{x})[\overline{\mathbf{j}}/\overline{x}] : \mathbf{j}_1 \leq x_1, \ldots, \mathbf{j}_n \leq x_n\} \leq \bigvee_i \gamma_i(\overline{y}_i) & \\ \text{iff } \mathbf{j}_1 \leq x_1, \ldots, \mathbf{j}_n \leq x_n \Rightarrow \varphi(\overline{x})[\overline{\mathbf{j}}/\overline{x}] \leq \bigvee_i \gamma_i(\overline{y}_i) & \\ \text{iff } \varphi(\overline{x})[\overline{\mathbf{j}}/\overline{x}] \leq \bigvee_i \gamma_i(\overline{y}_i)[\overline{\mathbf{j}}/\overline{x}] & \text{by Ackermann Lemma} \end{array}$$

Since all the variables in each $\overline{y}_i$ are amongst those in $\overline{x}$, the resulting inequality does not contain variables and contains only the connectives $\otimes$ and $\vee$. It is now straightforward to check that $\mathbb{A} \models \varphi(\overline{x})[\overline{\mathbf{j}}/\overline{x}] \leq \bigvee_i \gamma_i(\overline{y}_i)[\overline{\mathbf{j}}/\overline{x}]$ if and only if $\mathsf{span}(\{\tau(\varphi(\overline{x})[\overline{\mathbf{j}}/\overline{x}])\}) \subseteq \sum_i^k \mathsf{span}(\{\tau(\gamma_i(\overline{y}_i)[\overline{\mathbf{j}}/\overline{x}])\})$, which is equivalent to

$$\chi_h := \forall v_\top \forall v_{\mathbf{j}_1} \cdots \forall v_{\mathbf{j}_n} \exists \alpha_1 \cdots \exists \alpha_k \\ \tau(\varphi(\overline{x})[\overline{\mathbf{j}}/\overline{x}]) = \alpha_1 \cdot \tau(\gamma_1(\overline{y}_1)[\overline{\mathbf{j}}/\overline{x}]) + \cdots + \tau(\gamma_k(\overline{y}_k)[\overline{\mathbf{j}}/\overline{x}]).$$

By repeating the argument for each $\varphi'_h \leq \psi'_h$, $\chi := \bigwedge_h \chi_h$.

5 Conclusions

This paper develops correspondence theory on vector spaces seen as frames, and shows semantically equivalent reformulations of analytic inductive inequalities in residuated lattices.

In [10], it has been shown that there is a procedure that uses correspondence theory to transform analytic inductive inequalities into rules which generate well behaved display calculi for the basic (distributive) lattice expansion logic extended with such inequalities as axioms. This approach has also been used to construct multi-type display calculi in several settings (e.g. [9,11]), and such multi-type environments have been proposed as a calculus for structural control [11, Sect. 7] to capture certain grammatical exceptions. In [3,4], geometrical and type-logical approaches to meaning have been mixed by considering *meaning spaces* which are objects of the compact closed category **FVect** $\times$ P, where **FVect** is the category of finite dimensional vector spaces, and P is the pregroup generated by the basic types of a natural language. We plan on investigating the connection between the multitype environments for structural control and such meaning spaces. Finally, since the results of the paper up to Theorem 2 hold also when considering modules instead of vector spaces, we plan on exploring what first order shape is obtained in a context in which Lemma 1 and 2 do not hold.

A Examples

The present section collects some examples that showcase the results in the paper.

Example 2. The inequality $(p \vee q) \otimes (r/(p \otimes q)) \leq (q \otimes (p \vee r))/((p\backslash q) \vee r)$ is analytic (Ω, ε)-inductive for $\varepsilon(p, q, r) = (1, 1, 1)$ and $p < q < r$. By distributing $\otimes$ over $\vee$ and following the fact that $/$ is join reversing on its right coordinate, we get the inequality:

$$(p \otimes (r/(p \otimes q))) \vee (q \otimes (r/(p \otimes q))) \leq (((q \otimes p) \vee (q \otimes r))/(p\backslash q)) \wedge (((q \otimes p) \vee (q \otimes r))/r),$$

which is equivalent to the system

$$\begin{aligned}
p \otimes (r/(p \otimes q)) &\leq ((q \otimes p) \vee (q \otimes r))/(p\backslash q)\\
q \otimes (r/(p \otimes q)) &\leq ((q \otimes p) \vee (q \otimes r))/(p\backslash q)\\
p \otimes (r/(p \otimes q)) &\leq ((q \otimes p) \vee (q \otimes r))/r\\
q \otimes (r/(p \otimes q)) &\leq ((q \otimes p) \vee (q \otimes r))/r.
\end{aligned}$$

By residuation, the system can be rewritten as follows (thus reaching the shape in Lemma 5)

$$\begin{aligned}
(p \otimes (r/(p \otimes q))) \otimes (p\backslash q) &\leq (q \otimes p) \vee (q \otimes r)\\
(q \otimes (r/(p \otimes q))) \otimes (p\backslash q) &\leq (q \otimes p) \vee (q \otimes r)\\
(p \otimes (r/(p \otimes q))) \otimes r &\leq (q \otimes p) \vee (q \otimes r)\\
(q \otimes (r/(p \otimes q))) \otimes r &\leq (q \otimes p) \vee (q \otimes r).
\end{aligned}$$

Using notation in Lemma 5, the first inequality has shape $\varphi(\overline{x})[\overline{\xi}/\overline{x}] \leq \bigvee_i \beta_i(\overline{r_i})$, where $\varphi(x_1, x_2, x_3) := (x_1 \otimes x_2) \otimes x_3$, $\xi_1 := \alpha_1(p) := p$, $\xi_2 := \alpha_2(r, p, q) = r/(p \otimes q)$, $\xi_3 := \alpha_3(p, q) := p\backslash q$, $\beta_1(q, p) := q \otimes p$, and $\beta_2(q, r) := q \otimes r$.

Example 3. The inequality $(((q \otimes r)\backslash p) \vee s) \otimes ((s\backslash q) \otimes (p/s)) \leq ((p/(s \otimes r))\backslash(p \otimes s)) \wedge ((s \otimes (p \otimes q))/((p/s) \wedge r))$ is analytic (Ω, ε)-inductive with $\varepsilon(p, q, r, s) = (\partial, 1, \partial, 1)$ and $s < q < p < r$. By distributing $\otimes$ over $\vee$ we get

$$\begin{aligned}
&(((q \otimes r)\backslash p) \otimes ((s\backslash q) \otimes (p/s))) \vee (s \otimes ((s\backslash q) \otimes (p/s)))\\
&\leq ((p/(s \otimes r))\backslash(p \otimes s)) \wedge ((s \otimes (p \otimes q))/((p/s) \wedge r)),
\end{aligned}$$

which is equivalent (by also applying residuation) to the system:

$$\begin{aligned}
&(p/(s\otimes r))\otimes(((q\otimes r)\backslash p)\otimes((s\backslash q)\otimes(p/s))) &&\leq p\otimes s\\
&(p/(s\otimes r))\otimes(s\otimes((s\backslash q)\otimes(p/s))) &&\leq p\otimes s\\
&(((q\otimes r)\backslash p)\otimes((s\backslash q)\otimes(p/s)))\otimes((p/s)\wedge r) &&\leq s\otimes(p\otimes q)\\
&(s\otimes((s\backslash q)\otimes(p/s)))\otimes((p/s)\wedge r) &&\leq s\otimes(p\otimes q).
\end{aligned}$$

Example 4. Let us find the correspondent of the first inequality in the system in Example 2. First we show that it is equivalent to a quasi-left primitive.

$$\begin{aligned}
&\quad(p\otimes(r/(p\otimes q)))\otimes(p\backslash q)\leq(q\otimes p)\vee(q\otimes r)\\
&\text{iff } (\bigvee\{\mathbf{j}_1:\mathbf{j}_1\leq p\}\otimes\bigvee\{\mathbf{j}_2:\mathbf{j}_2\leq r/(p\otimes q)\})\otimes\bigvee\{\mathbf{j}_3:\mathbf{j}_3\leq p\backslash q\}\leq\bigwedge\{\mathbf{m}:(q\otimes p)\vee(q\otimes r)\leq\mathbf{m}\}\\
&\text{iff } \bigvee\{(\mathbf{j}_1\otimes\mathbf{j}_2)\otimes\mathbf{j}_3:\mathbf{j}_1\leq p,\mathbf{j}_2\leq r/(p\otimes q),\mathbf{j}_3\leq p\backslash q\}\leq\bigwedge\{\mathbf{m}:(q\otimes p)\vee(q\otimes r)\leq\mathbf{m}\}\\
&\text{iff } \mathbf{j}_1\leq p,\mathbf{j}_2\leq r/(p\otimes q),\mathbf{j}_3\leq p\backslash q,(q\otimes p)\vee(q\otimes r)\leq\mathbf{m}\Rightarrow(\mathbf{j}_1\otimes\mathbf{j}_2)\otimes\mathbf{j}_3\leq\mathbf{m}\\
&\text{iff } \mathbf{j}_1\leq p,\mathbf{j}_2\otimes(p\otimes q)\leq r,p\otimes\mathbf{j}_3\leq q,(q\otimes p)\vee(q\otimes r)\leq\mathbf{m}\Rightarrow(\mathbf{j}_1\otimes\mathbf{j}_2)\otimes\mathbf{j}_3\leq\mathbf{m}\\
&\text{iff } \mathbf{j}_2\otimes(\mathbf{j}_1\otimes q)\leq r,\mathbf{j}_1\otimes\mathbf{j}_3\leq q,(q\otimes\mathbf{j}_1)\vee(q\otimes r)\leq\mathbf{m}\Rightarrow(\mathbf{j}_1\otimes\mathbf{j}_2)\otimes\mathbf{j}_3\leq\mathbf{m}\\
&\text{iff } \mathbf{j}_2\otimes(\mathbf{j}_1\otimes(\mathbf{j}_1\otimes\mathbf{j}_3)\leq r,((\mathbf{j}_1\otimes\mathbf{j}_3)\otimes\mathbf{j}_1)\vee((\mathbf{j}_1\otimes\mathbf{j}_3)\otimes r)\leq\mathbf{m}\Rightarrow(\mathbf{j}_1\otimes\mathbf{j}_2)\otimes\mathbf{j}_3\leq\mathbf{m}\\
&\text{iff } ((\mathbf{j}_1\otimes\mathbf{j}_3)\otimes\mathbf{j}_1)\vee((\mathbf{j}_1\otimes\mathbf{j}_3)\otimes(\mathbf{j}_2\otimes(\mathbf{j}_1\otimes(\mathbf{j}_1\otimes\mathbf{j}_3))))\leq\mathbf{m}\Rightarrow(\mathbf{j}_1\otimes\mathbf{j}_2)\otimes\mathbf{j}_3\leq\mathbf{m}\\
&\text{iff } (\mathbf{j}_1\otimes\mathbf{j}_2)\otimes\mathbf{j}_3\leq((\mathbf{j}_1\otimes\mathbf{j}_3)\otimes\mathbf{j}_1)\vee((\mathbf{j}_1\otimes\mathbf{j}_3)\otimes(\mathbf{j}_2\otimes(\mathbf{j}_1\otimes(\mathbf{j}_1\otimes\mathbf{j}_3))))\\
&\text{iff } (p_{\mathbf{j}_1}\otimes p_{\mathbf{j}_2})\otimes p_{\mathbf{j}_3}\leq((p_{\mathbf{j}_1}\otimes p_{\mathbf{j}_3})\otimes p_{\mathbf{j}_1})\vee((p_{\mathbf{j}_1}\otimes p_{\mathbf{j}_3})\otimes(p_{\mathbf{j}_2}\otimes(p_{\mathbf{j}_1}\otimes(p_{\mathbf{j}_1}\otimes p_{\mathbf{j}_3})))).
\end{aligned}$$

Hence, by Theorem 3, the inequality correspond to the $\mathcal{L}_{\mathrm{FO}}$-formula

$$\begin{aligned}
&\forall v_{\mathbf{j}_1}\forall v_{\mathbf{j}_2}\forall v_{\mathbf{j}_3}\exists\alpha_1\exists\alpha_2\\
&(v_{\mathbf{j}_1}\star v_{\mathbf{j}_2})\star v_{\mathbf{j}_3}=\alpha_1\cdot((v_{\mathbf{j}_1}\star v_{\mathbf{j}_3})\star v_{\mathbf{j}_1})+\alpha_2\cdot((v_{\mathbf{j}_1}\star v_{\mathbf{j}_3})\star(v_{\mathbf{j}_2}\star(v_{\mathbf{j}_1}\star(v_{\mathbf{j}_1}\star v_{\mathbf{j}_3})))).
\end{aligned}$$

Example 5. The inequality $(p\otimes(q/r))\otimes((s\backslash q)\wedge(s/t))\leq(t\wedge(r/s))\backslash(t\otimes(p\vee q))$ is analytic (Ω,ε)-inductive for $\varepsilon(p,q,r,s,t)=(\partial,\partial,\partial,\partial,1)$ and $t<q<r<s$, $t<p$. By distributing $\otimes$ over $\vee$ and applying the residuation rule, we get

$$(t\wedge(r/s))\otimes((p\otimes(q/r))\otimes((s\backslash q)\wedge(s/t)))\leq(t\otimes p)\vee(t\otimes q).$$

We show by the procedure in Sect. 3.2 that the inequality is inductive also for $\varepsilon'(p,q,r,s,t)=(1,1,1,1,1)$. The definite positive PIAs in the formula are

$$\begin{array}{lll}
\alpha_1(t)\quad:=t & \alpha_2(r,s):=r/s & \alpha_3(p)\quad:=p\\
\alpha_4(q,r):=q/r & \alpha_5(q,s):=s\backslash q & \alpha_6(s,t):=s/t;
\end{array}$$

hence, the sets Q_v are

$$\begin{array}{lll}
Q_p=\{\} & Q_q=\{r,s\} & Q_r=\{s\}\\
Q_s=\{t\} & Q_t=\{\}. &
\end{array}$$

Of course, $\varepsilon^{(0)}(p,q,r,s,t)=(\partial,\partial,\partial,\partial,1)$ and $\Omega^{(0)}$ is the smallest relation for which it is inductive, i.e. $\{(t,p),(t,q),(r,s),(q,r),(q,s),(t,r),(t,s)\}$.

The following table represents the steps of the procedure. At the i-th step, a variable v_i such that $\varepsilon^{(i-1)}(v_i)=\partial$ maximal w.r.t. $\Omega^{(i-1)}$ is picked, all the edges where it is an endpoint are removed from $\Omega^{(i-1)}$ (this is denoted by $\Omega^{(i-1)-}$), and the edges in $Q_{v_i}\times\{v_i\}$ are added in $\Omega^{(i)}$.

Step	v_i	$\varepsilon^{(i)}(p, q, r, s, t)$	$\Omega^{(i-1)-}$	$\Omega^{(i)}$
0	-	$(\partial, \partial, \partial, \partial, 1)$	-	$t < q < r < s,\ t < p$
1	s	$(\partial, \partial, \partial, 1, 1)$	$t < q < r,\ t < p$	$t < q < r,\ t < p,\ t < s$
2	p	$(1, \partial, \partial, 1, 1)$	$t < q < r,\ t < s$	$t < q < r,\ t < s$
3	r	$(1, \partial, 1, 1, 1)$	$t < q,\ t < s$	$t < q,\ t < s < r$
4	q	$(1, 1, 1, 1, 1)$	$t < s < r$	$t < s < r < q$

By Lemma 6, the inequality is $(\varepsilon^{(i)}, \Omega^{(i)})$-inductive for every $i \in \{0, 1, 2, 3, 4\}$.

References

1. van Benthem, J.: Minimal predicates, fixed-points, and definability. J. Symbol. Logic **70**(3), 696–712 (2005). https://doi.org/10.2178/jsl/1122038910
2. Chen, J., Greco, G., Palmigiano, A., Tzimoulis, A.: Syntactic completeness of proper display calculi. ACM Trans. Comput. Logic **23**(4), 1–46 (2022). https://doi.org/10.1145/3529255
3. Coecke, B., Grefenstette, E., Sadrzadeh, M.: Lambek vs. Lambek: functorial vector space semantics and string diagrams for Lambek calculus. Annals Pure Appl. Logic **164**(11), 1079–1100 (2013). https://doi.org/10.1016/j.apal.2013.05.009, special issue on Seventh Workshop on Games for Logic and Programming Languages (GaLoP VII)
4. Coecke, B., Sadrzadeh, M., Clark, S.: Mathematical foundations for a compositional distributional model of meaning. arXiv preprint arXiv:1003.4394 (2010)
5. Conradie, W., Ghilardi, S., Palmigiano, A.: Unified correspondence. In: Baltag, A., Smets, S. (eds.) Johan van Benthem on Logic and Information Dynamics, Outstanding Contributions to Logic, vol. 5, pp. 933–975. Springer, Cham (2014). https://doi.org/10.1007/978-3-319-06025-5_36
6. Conradie, W., Palmigiano, A.: Algorithmic correspondence and canonicity for non-distributive logics. Ann. Pure Appl. Logic **170**(9), 923–974 (2019)
7. Dunn, J.M., Gehrke, M., Palmigiano, A.: Canonical extensions and relational completeness of some substructural logics. J. Symbolic Logic **70**(3), 713–740 (2005). http://www.jstor.org/stable/27588391
8. Greco, G., Liang, F., Moortgat, M., Palmigiano, A., Tzimoulis, A.: Vector spaces as Kripke frames. IfCoLoG J. Logic. Appl. **7**(5), 853–873 (2020)
9. Greco, G., Liang, F., Moshier, M.A., Palmigiano, A.: Multi-type display calculus for semi De Morgan logic. In: Kennedy, J., de Queiroz, R.J. (eds.) Logic, Language, Information, and Computation, pp. 199–215. Springer, Heidelberg (2017). https://doi.org/10.1007/978-3-662-55386-2_14
10. Greco, G., Ma, M., Palmigiano, A., Tzimoulis, A., Zhao, Z.: Unified correspondence as a proof-theoretic tool. J. Log. Comput. **28**(7), 1367–1442 (2018)
11. Greco, G., Palmigiano, A.: Linear logic properly displayed. ACM Trans. Comput. Logic **24**(2), 1–56 (2023). https://doi.org/10.1145/3570919
12. Kurtonina, N., Moortgat, M.: Structural control. In: Specifying Syntactic Structures, pp. 75–113 (1997)

13. Rosenthal, K.: Quantales and Their Applications. Pitman Research Notes in Mathematics Series. Longman Scientific & Technical (1990)
14. Routley, R., Meyer, R.K.: The semantics of entailment: III. J. Philos. Logic **1**(2), 192–208 (1972). http://www.jstor.org/stable/30226036
15. Sahlqvist, H.: Completeness and correspondence in the first and second order semantics for modal logic. In: Studies in Logic and the Foundations of Mathematics, vol. 82, pp. 110–143. Elsevier (1975)

An EXPTIME-Complete Entailment Problem in Separation Logic

Nicolas Peltier(✉)

Université Grenoble Alpes, CNRS, LIG, 38000 Grenoble, France
Nicolas.Peltier@imag.fr

Abstract. Separation logic (SL) is extensively employed in verification to analyze programs that manipulate dynamically allocated memory. The entailment problem, when dealing with inductively defined predicates or data constraints, is undecidable for SL formulas. Our focus is on addressing a specific fragment of this issue, wherein the consequent is restricted to clauses of some particular form, devoid of inductively defined predicates. We present an algorithm designed to determine the validity of such entailments and demonstrate that the problem is decidable and ExpTime complete under some conditions on the data theory. This algorithm serves the purpose of verifying that the data structures outlined by a given SL formula (the antecedent) adhere to certain shape constraints expressed by the consequent.

1 Introduction

Separation logic (SL) [19] is a variant of bunched logic [18] introduced in program verification for reasoning about programs that manipulate dynamically allocated memory. This logic employs a specific connective, called the separating conjunction and denoted by $*$, to assert that two formulas hold on disjoint sections of memory, facilitating more concise specifications. The main advantage of SL is that it supports *local reasoning*, meaning that program properties can be asserted and proven by referencing only the portion of memory affected by the program, without considering the global state of the system. The expressive power of the logic can be strongly augmented by utilizing *inductively defined predicates*, enabling the definition of recursive data structures of unbounded sizes, such as lists or trees. For example, the following rules define a predicate $\mathtt{lseg}(x, y)$ denoting a list segment from x to y (with no data): $\{\mathtt{lseg}(x, y) \Leftarrow \mathtt{emp} \wedge x \simeq y,\ \mathtt{lseg}(x, y) \Leftarrow \exists z.(x \mapsto (z) * \mathtt{lseg}(z, y))\}$. Informally, x, y, z represent locations (i.e., memory addresses), $\mathtt{emp}$ asserts that the heap is empty, $x \mapsto (z)$ asserts that location x is allocated and points to a tuple only containing location z, and the separating conjunction $x \mapsto (z) * \mathtt{lseg}(z, y)$ indicates that the heap contains a list segment $\mathtt{lseg}(z, y)$ along with an additional memory cell x pointing to z (implicitly ensuring that x is distinct from all memory locations allocated in the list segment from z to y). The first rule corresponds to the case where the list segment is empty (in which

This work has been partially funded by the French National Research Agency project ANR-21-CE48-0011.

G. Metcalfe et al. (Eds.): WoLLIC 2024, LNCS 14672, pp. 157–174, 2024.
https://doi.org/10.1007/978-3-031-62687-6_11

case we must have $x = y$). These predicates can be either hard-coded or defined by the user to handle custom data structures. In the fragment of separation logic known as *symbolic heaps* (formally defined later), satisfiability is decidable for formulas with inductively defined predicates [2], but entailment is undecidable (entailment cannot be reduced to satisfiability since the fragment does not include negations).

In this present paper, our focus lies on a specific fragment of the entailment problem in SL, and we show that this fragment is decidable and ExpTime-complete (under some particular conditions on the data theory). These entailments exhibit dissymmetry: the antecedent and consequent belong to distinct classes of formulas. Formal definitions will be provided subsequently, but in essence, the antecedent is a symbolic heap describing data structures of unbounded size (with constraints on the data contained within those structures) whereas the consequent is a clause that articulates shape constraints over these structures, and assert conditions on the allocated and referenced locations and on the data stored in the structures. Such clauses may be used to assert that a structure contains—or does not contain—some specific patterns. For example, the following (valid) entailment problem asserts that, in all structures satisfying $\mathtt{lseg}(x, y)$, all referenced locations are allocated, except for the one associated with y ($\top$ denotes the atom true and $\mathtt{alloc}(z')$ states that z' is allocated): $\mathtt{lseg}(x, y) \models \forall z \forall z' (\neg(z \mapsto (z') * \top) \vee z' \simeq y \vee \mathtt{alloc}(z'))$. Another instance expresses that each location is referenced only once: $\mathtt{lseg}(x, y) \models \forall z \forall z' \forall z'' \neg(z \mapsto (z'') * z' \mapsto (z'') * \top)$. The latter is deemed invalid as $\mathtt{lseg}(x, y)$ possesses models representing cyclic lists (where y is allocated, and referenced twice). Now, consider a predicate $\mathtt{dll}(x, y, z)$ denoting a doubly linked list segment (with data) from x to y (z denotes the element preceding x): $\{\mathtt{dll}(x, y, z) \Leftarrow \mathtt{emp} \wedge (x \simeq y), \mathtt{dll}(x, y, z) \Leftarrow \exists x' \exists w (x \mapsto (z, w, x') * \mathtt{dll}(x', y, x))\}$. Here, each location refers to a tuple (x', w, x'') where x' and x'' are pointers to the previous and next elements, respectively, and w is the data stored in the current cell. The (valid) problem $\mathtt{dll}(x, y, z) \models \phi$, with ϕ is the formula: $\forall x_1 \forall x_2 \forall x_3 \forall x_1' \forall x_2' \forall w_1 \forall w_2 (\neg(x_1 \mapsto (x_1', w_1, x_2) * x_2 \mapsto (x_2', w_2, x_3)) \vee x_2' \simeq x_1)$ ensures that the "previous" pointer of the successor of any location x_1 is indeed x_1. The (non valid) problem $\mathtt{dll}(x, y, z) \models \psi$ where ψ is $\forall x_1 \forall x_2 \forall x_3 \forall x_1' \forall x_2' \forall w_1 \forall w_2 (\neg(x_1 \mapsto (x_1', w_1, x_2) * x_2 \mapsto (x_2', w_2, x_3)) \vee w_1 < w_2)$ asserts that the list is sorted in strict ascending order.

Related Work. A significant portion of research within automated reasoning in SL is directed toward decidable fragments of entailment problems. As the entailment problem is undecidable when dealing with formulas with inductively defined predicates, substantial effort has been expended to pinpoint decidable fragments and design corresponding proof procedures (see, e.g., [1,3,6,7,12,13]). Most works focus on formulas of some particular form, called *symbolic heaps* (defined as existentially quantified conjunctions and separated conjunctions of atoms). A very general class of decidable entailment problems (specifically for formulas involving no theory beyond equality) is devised in [14], obtained by restricting the considered inductive definitions to so-called PCE (for Progressing, Connected and Established) rules. The decidability result rests upon the decidability of the satisfiability problem for monadic second-order logic over graphs with bounded treewidth. A more recent advancement is the proposal of a 2-ExpTime algorithm for such entailments [17]. In [8] the optimality of this bound is established, and in [9,10], novel algorithms are introduced, capable of handling more expressive classes of inductive definitions. More recently, a proof procedure has been devised [11] for the PCE fragment. In the pursuit of computational efficiency, less expressive fragments have been explored, leading to the development of more efficient algorithms. For instance, in [15], a strict subclass of PCE entailments is identified, with an ExpTime complexity derived through a reduction to the language inclusion problem for tree automata [5]. Another example is found in [12], where an algorithm is devised to handle various types of (potentially nested) singly linked lists, relying on a reduction to the membership problem for tree automata. A polynomial proof procedure was also proposed for the specific case of singly linked lists [6]. The tractability result is extended to more expressive fragments [4], incorporating formulas defined on a unique nonlinear compositional inductive predicate with distinguished source, destination, and static parameters. Recently [16], a polynomial-time cyclic proof procedure has been introduced to efficiently solve the entailment problem, subject to certain conditions on the inductive rules.

Our contribution diverges from previous work in two key aspects: on one hand, we impose no syntactic restrictions on the considered inductive definitions[1], which may in particular contain data constraints (with some conditions on the data theory). On the other hand, we concentrate on entailment problems where the consequents are simpler than their corresponding antecedents, in the sense that they contain no inductive predicates. It is important to note that, even if the considered inductive definitions satisfy the PCE conditions of [14], the entailment problems we consider still do not fall in the scope of the previously cited results, because the consequents are not symbolic heaps. They cannot be expressed either as guarded formulas (in the sense of [17]).

2 Separation Logic with Inductive Definitions

We define the syntax and semantics of SL with inductively defined predicates and data constraints. Most definitions in this section are standard.

Basic Notations. For every finite set S, $card(S)$ denotes the number of elements in S. For every partial function f, $dom(f)$ denotes the domain of f. Partial functions will be taken as relations, e.g., if $x_1, \ldots, x_n$ are pairwise distinct, then $\{(x_i, y_i) \mid i \in \{1, \ldots, n\}\}$ denotes the function f of domain $\{x_1, \ldots, x_n\}$ such that $f(x_i) = y_i$ for all $i \in \{1, \ldots, n\}$ ($\emptyset$ is the function with an empty domain). An *extension* of a partial function f to a set S, is a function g such that $dom(g) = dom(f) \cup S$ coinciding with f on $dom(f)$ (then f is called a *restriction* of g to $dom(f)$). We sometimes identify tuples with sets when the order and number of repetitions is unimportant, i.e., we may write $\boldsymbol{x} \subseteq S$ to state that every component of the tuple $\boldsymbol{x}$ occurs in the set S, or $y \in \boldsymbol{x}$ to state that y occurs in $\boldsymbol{x}$.

Syntax. Let $\mathcal{S} = \{\mathtt{loc}, \mathtt{data}\}$ be the set of *sort symbols*, where $\mathtt{loc}$ denotes locations (i.e., memory addresses) and $\mathtt{data}$ denotes data. Let $\mathcal{V}$ be a countably infinite set of *variables* and let C be a finite set of *constant symbols*. Let $\mathcal{T} = \mathcal{V} \cup C$ be the set of *terms*. Every term x is associated with a unique sort $\mathtt{sort}(x) \in \mathcal{S}$, and $\mathcal{T}(\mathtt{s})$ denotes the set of terms of sort $\mathtt{s}$. Let $\mathcal{P}_s$ and $\mathcal{P}_d$ be two finite sets of predicate symbols, denoting *spatial*

[1] except from the fact that the right-hand side of the inductive rules must be a symbolic heap.

predicates and *data predicates*, respectively. Each symbol in $p \in \mathcal{P}_s$ (resp. $p \in \mathcal{P}_d$) is associated with a unique *profile* $\mathtt{pr}(p) \in \mathcal{S}^*$ (resp. $\mathtt{pr}(p) \in \{\mathtt{data}\}^*$).

Definition 2.1 (Syntax of SL). *A separation logic formula ϕ (or simply formula) is built inductively as follows:*

$$\mathtt{emp} \mid \mid p(x_1, \dots, x_n) \mid u \mapsto (v_1, \dots, v_k) \mid \mathtt{alloc}(u) \mid \mathtt{ref}(u) \mid \top \mid u \simeq v \mid$$

$$(\phi_1 * \phi_2) \mid (\phi_1 \vee \phi_2) \mid (\phi_1 \wedge \phi_2) \mid \neg\psi \mid \exists x\, \psi$$

where $k, n \in \mathbb{N}$, p is a predicate in $\mathcal{P}_s \cup \mathcal{P}_d$, of some profile $(\mathtt{s}_1, \dots, \mathtt{s}_n)$, $x_i \in \mathcal{T}(\mathtt{s}_i)$, $u, v \in \mathcal{T}(\mathtt{loc})$, $v_i \in \mathcal{T}$, $x \in \mathcal{V}$ and ϕ_1, ϕ_2, ψ are formulas.

The separating implication is not considered in our framework. Formal definitions will be provided later, but the atoms $\mathtt{alloc}(x)$ and $\mathtt{ref}(x)$ are intended to state that x is allocated and referenced in the heap, respectively. A *data atom* (resp. a spatial predicate atom) is of the form $p(x_1, \dots, x_n)$ where $p \in \mathcal{P}_d$ (resp. $p \in \mathcal{P}_s$). A *data literal* is either a data atom or its negation. A formula of the form $u \mapsto (v_1, \dots, v_k)$ is a *points-to atom*. A *spatial atom* is either a points-to atom or a spatial predicate atom. A *pure atom* is either a data atom or an equational atom $x \simeq y$ or $\top$. A *pure literal* is either a pure atom or the negation of a pure atom. We denote by $fv(\phi)$ the set of variables freely occurring in ϕ. We assume (by α-renaming) that distinct quantifiers bind distinct variables and that the set of free and bound variables are disjoint. A *substitution* is a partial function mapping every variable x to a term of sort $\mathtt{sort}(x)$. For every substitution σ and expression (term, tuple of terms or formula) ϕ we denote by $\phi\sigma$ the expression obtained from ϕ by replacing every free occurrence of a variable $x \in dom(\sigma)$ by $\sigma(x)$.

Inductive Rules. The semantics of the spatial predicates is defined using inductive rules of some particular form:

Definition 2.2 (Symbolic Heaps and Inductive Rules). *We recall that a* symbolic heap *is a formula of the form $\exists \mathbf{x}[(\alpha_1 * \dots * \alpha_n) \wedge \bigwedge_{j=1}^{m} \beta_j]$, where α_i (for all $i \in \{1, \dots, n\}$) is a spatial atom and β_j (for all $j \in \{1, \dots, m\}$) is a pure literal. A* disjunctive symbolic heap *(DSH) is a formula of the form $\bigvee_{i=1}^{n} \phi_i$ where ϕ_i (for all $i \in \{1, \dots, n\}$) is a symbolic heap. An* inductive rule *is an expression of the form $p(x_1, \dots, x_n) \Leftarrow \xi$ where p is a spatial predicate of profile $(\mathtt{s}_1, \dots, \mathtt{s}_n)$, $x_1, \dots, x_n$ are pairwise distinct variables of sort $\mathtt{s}_1, \dots, \mathtt{s}_n$ (respectively) and ξ is a DSH with $fv(\xi) \subseteq \{x_1, \dots, x_n\}$.*

Let $\mathcal{R}$ be a finite set of inductive rules. We write $\phi \leadsto_{\mathcal{R}} \psi$ if ψ is obtained from the formula ϕ by replacing one occurrence of a spatial atom $p(x_1, \dots, x_n)$ by a formula $\xi\sigma$ where $p(y_1, \dots, y_n) \Leftarrow \xi$ is a rule in $\mathcal{R}$ and $\sigma = \{(y_i, x_i) \mid i \in \{1, \dots, n\}\}$. Then $\leadsto_{\mathcal{R}}^*$ denotes the reflexive and transitive closure of $\leadsto_{\mathcal{R}}$. We assume that the existential variables in ξ are renamed to avoid any collision with variables already occurring in ϕ.

Semantics. Let $\mathcal{L}$ be a countably infinite set of *locations* and let $\mathcal{D}$ be an arbitrary set of *data*. The domain of a sort $\mathtt{s}$ is $\mathcal{D}$ if $\mathtt{s} = \mathtt{data}$ and $\mathcal{L}$ if $\mathtt{s} = \mathtt{loc}$. We assume that every predicate $p \in \mathcal{P}_d$ of profile $\mathtt{data}^n$ is mapped to a subset $\langle p \rangle$ of $\mathcal{D}^n$, and that every constant c of sort $\mathtt{data}$ is associated with an element $\langle c \rangle \in \mathcal{D}$. Note that the interpretation of data constants and data predicates is fixed in our setting.

Definition 2.3 (SL Structures). *A* store $\mathfrak{s}$ *is a partial function mapping every term x to an element of $\mathcal{L}$ if x is of sort* `loc` *or to an element of $\mathcal{D}$ if x is of sort* `data`*, where $C \subseteq dom(\mathfrak{s})$ and $\mathfrak{s}(c) = \langle c \rangle$ if $c \in C$ and $\mathtt{sort}(c) = \mathtt{data}$. A* heap $\mathfrak{h}$ *is a partial function mapping locations in $\mathcal{L}$ to tuples $(\ell_1, \dots, \ell_n)$ with $n \geq 0$ and $\ell_i \in \mathcal{L} \cup \mathcal{D}$ (for all $i \in \{1, \dots, n\}$) such that $dom(\mathfrak{h})$ is finite. A* structure *is a pair $(\mathfrak{s}, \mathfrak{h})$ where $\mathfrak{s}$ is a store and $\mathfrak{h}$ is a heap.*

A location ℓ is *allocated* in $\mathfrak{h}$ if $\ell \in dom(\mathfrak{h})$ and an element $e \in \mathcal{L} \cup \mathcal{D}$ is *referenced* in $\mathfrak{h}$ if there exists $\ell \in dom(\mathfrak{h})$ such that $e \in \mathfrak{h}(\ell)$. A variable x is *allocated* (resp. *referenced*) in a structure $(\mathfrak{s}, \mathfrak{h})$ if $\mathfrak{s}(x)$ is allocated (resp. referenced) in $\mathfrak{h}$. Two heaps $\mathfrak{h}_1, \mathfrak{h}_2$ are *disjoint* if $dom(\mathfrak{h}_1) \cap dom(\mathfrak{h}_2) = \emptyset$, in which case $\mathfrak{h}_1 \cup \mathfrak{h}_2$ denotes the heap of domain $dom(\mathfrak{h}_1) \cup dom(\mathfrak{h}_2)$, coinciding with $\mathfrak{h}_i$ on $dom(\mathfrak{h}_i)$ (for all $i \in \{1, 2\}$).

Definition 2.4 (Semantics of SL). *Let $\mathcal{R}$ be a finite set of inductive rules. Let $(\mathfrak{s}, \mathfrak{h})$ be a structure. For every formula ϕ with $fv(\phi) \subseteq dom(\mathfrak{s})$, we write $(\mathfrak{s}, \mathfrak{h}) \models_{\mathcal{R}} \phi$ (and say that $(\mathfrak{s}, \mathfrak{h})$ is an $\mathcal{R}$-model of ϕ) if one of the following conditions holds:*

- *ϕ is $\top$; or ϕ is* `emp` *and $\mathfrak{h} = \emptyset$; or ϕ is $x \simeq y$ and $\mathfrak{s}(x) = \mathfrak{s}(y)$;*
- *$\phi = x \mapsto (y_1, \dots, y_n)$ and $\mathfrak{h} = \{(\mathfrak{s}(x), \mathfrak{s}(y_1), \dots, \mathfrak{s}(y)\}$;*
- *$\phi = p(x_1, \dots, x_n)$, $p \in \mathcal{P}_d$ and $(\mathfrak{s}(x_1), \dots, \mathfrak{s}(x_n)) \in \langle p \rangle$;*
- *or $\phi = \neg\psi$ and $(\mathfrak{s}, \mathfrak{h}) \not\models_{\mathcal{R}} \psi$;*
- *$\phi = \phi_1 \vee \phi_2$ (resp. $\phi_1 \wedge \phi_2$) and $(\mathfrak{s}, \mathfrak{h}) \models_{\mathcal{R}} \phi_i$, for some $i \in \{1, 2\}$ (resp. for all $i \in \{1, 2\}$);*
- *$\phi = \phi_1 * \phi_2$ and there exist disjoint heaps $\mathfrak{h}_1, \mathfrak{h}_2$ with $\mathfrak{h} = \mathfrak{h}_1 \cup \mathfrak{h}_2$, and for all $i \in \{1, 2\}$, $(\mathfrak{s}, \mathfrak{h}_i) \models_{\mathcal{R}} \phi_i$;*
- *$\phi = \exists x \psi$ and there exists an extension $\mathfrak{s}'$ of $\mathfrak{s}$ with $dom(\mathfrak{s}') = dom(\mathfrak{s}) \cup \{x\}$ and $(\mathfrak{s}', \mathfrak{h}) \models_{\mathcal{R}} \psi$;*
- *$\phi = \mathtt{alloc}(x)$ and $\mathfrak{s}(x) \in dom(\mathfrak{h})$; or $\phi = \mathtt{ref}(x)$ and $\exists \ell \in dom(\mathfrak{h})$ s.t. $\mathfrak{s}(x) \in \mathfrak{h}(\ell)$;*
- *$\phi = p(x_1, \dots, x_n)$, $p \in \mathcal{P}_s$ and there is a formula ψ containing no spatial predicate symbol such that $\phi \leadsto^*_{\mathcal{R}} \psi$ and $(\mathfrak{s}, \mathfrak{h}) \models_{\mathcal{R}} \psi$.*

If S is a set of formulas, then $(\mathfrak{s}, \mathfrak{h}) \models_{\mathcal{R}} S$ holds iff $\forall \phi \in S$ $(\mathfrak{s}, \mathfrak{h}) \models_{\mathcal{R}} \phi$. If ϕ, ψ are formulas, we write $\phi \models_{\mathcal{R}} \psi$ if the implication $(\mathfrak{s}, \mathfrak{h}) \models_{\mathcal{R}} \phi \implies (\mathfrak{s}, \mathfrak{h}) \models_{\mathcal{R}} \psi$ holds for every structure $(\mathfrak{s}, \mathfrak{h})$ with $dom(\mathfrak{s}) \supseteq fv(\phi) \cup fv(\psi)$.

Formulas are taken modulo associativity and commutativity of $*$ and $\wedge, \vee$, modulo neutrality of `emp` for $*$, modulo commutativity of $\exists$ (i.e. $\exists x \exists y \phi$ is equivalent to $\exists y \exists x \phi$) modulo contraction for $\wedge$ and $\vee$ and modulo contraction of pure atoms for $*$ (i.e., $\phi * \phi \equiv \phi$ if ϕ is pure, note that the contraction does not hold for spatial atoms). If $\boldsymbol{x} = (x_1, \dots, x_n)$ (with $n \geq 0$), we may write $\exists \boldsymbol{x}\, \phi$ for $\exists x_1 \dots \exists x_n\, \phi$ (if $\boldsymbol{x}$ is empty then $\exists \boldsymbol{x}\, \phi$ is ϕ). For any formula ϕ, $|\phi|$ denotes the size of ϕ.

Example 2.5 (Sorted Lists). The rules below define an atom $\mathtt{sls}(x, y)$ describing sorted lists starting at x, ending at a constant `nil`, and containing only elements bigger or equal to y:

$$\mathtt{sls}(x, y) \Leftarrow x \mapsto (\mathtt{nil}) \qquad \mathtt{sls}(x, y) \Leftarrow \exists x' \exists y' [x \mapsto (x', y') * \mathtt{sls}(x', y') \wedge y' \geq y]$$

Each location (other than the last one) in the list points to a pair (ℓ, v) where ℓ denotes the next element and v is the stored value. The profile of `sls` is (`loc`, `data`). The variables x, x' are of sort `loc` and the variables y, y' are of sort `data`. The formula $\exists y, y' (\mathtt{sls}(x, y) * \mathtt{sls}(x', y') \wedge y \geq y') \vee \mathtt{emp}$ is a DSH.

We make the following assumptions on the data theory, which are all essential to the soundness of the results.

1. The set of data predicates $\mathcal{P}_d$ contains in particular the equality predicate $\approx$ interpreted as usual.
2. The satisfiability problem is decidable for conjunctions of data literals.
3. Every formula of the form $\exists x\, \phi$ where ϕ is a conjunction of data literals is equivalent to a formula $\bigvee_{i=1}^{n} \phi_i$, where ϕ_i (for all $i \in \{1, \ldots, n\}$) is a conjunction of data literals, with $fv(\phi_i) \subseteq fv(\exists x\, \phi)$.

Assumptions (1) and (2) are natural, but Assumption (3) is rather strong, as the set of constants and the set of data predicates are both finite (of course, this cannot be overcome since we want to get a decidable entailment problem with fixpoint computations). The conditions are satisfied for instance by the theory of reals (or rational numbers) with predicates $\approx, <, \leq$.

3 The Entailment Problem Ent(DSH,HC)

We now define the entailment problem we are considering in the present paper. As explained in the introduction, this entailment problem is dissymmetric: the antecedent and consequent belong to different fragments of SL. The antecedent is a disjunctive symbolic heap, and the consequent is a universally quantified disjunction of literals (with no inductive predicates) of some specific form:

Definition 3.1 (𝔥**-Clauses).** *A* 𝔥-atom *is either a data atom, or a formula of the form* $\mathtt{alloc}(x)$, $\mathtt{ref}(x)$, $x \bowtie y$ *(with* $\bowtie \in \{\simeq, \not\simeq\}$*), or a separating conjunction* $\alpha_1 * \cdots * \alpha_n$ *where* α_i *is either a points-to atoms or* $\top$ *(spatial predicate atoms are not allowed). Formulas of the latter form are called* spatial 𝔥*-atoms. A* 𝔥-literal *is either a* 𝔥*-atom (positive* 𝔥*-literal) or the negation of a* 𝔥*-atom (negative* 𝔥*-literal). The* 𝔥*-literal* complementary to some 𝔥*-literal* ϕ *is either* $\neg\phi$ *if* ϕ *is positive or* ψ *if* $\phi = \neg\psi$*. A* 𝔥*-clause (HC) is of the form* $\forall x_1 \ldots \forall x_n\, \phi$*, where* ϕ *is a disjunction of* 𝔥*-literals (*ϕ *may contain variables not occurring in* $\{x_1, \ldots, x_n\}$*).*

Example 3.2. Consider the following 𝔥-clauses:

$$
\begin{array}{ll}
\xi_1 : & \forall x \forall x' \forall y' \, (\neg(x \mapsto (x', y') * \top) \vee y' \geq y) \\
\xi_2 : & \forall x_1 \forall x_2 \forall y_1 \forall y_2 \forall x' \, \neg(x_1 \mapsto (x', y_1) * x_2 \mapsto (x', y_2) * \top) \\
\xi_3 : & \forall x_1 \forall x_2 \forall x'_1 \forall x'_2 \forall y \, \neg(x_1 \mapsto (x'_1, y) * x_2 \mapsto (x'_2, y) * \top)
\end{array}
$$

With the conventions of Example 2.5, ξ_1 asserts that the list contains no element strictly lower than y, ξ_2 states that every location is referenced at most once and ξ_3 states that all elements are pairwise distinct.

Definition 3.3 (Ent**(DSH,HC)).** *The entailment problem* Ent*(DSH,HC) consists in determining, given a finite set of inductive rules* $\mathcal{R}$*, a disjunctive symbolic heap* ξ *and a* 𝔥*-clause* γ*, whether the entailment* $\xi \models_{\mathcal{R}} \gamma$ *holds.*

Example 3.4. With the definitions of Examples 2.5 and 3.2, $p(x, y) \models_{\mathcal{R}} \xi_i$ is an instance of ENT(DSH,HC) for all $i \in \{1, 2, 3\}$. It is valid if $i \in \{1, 2\}$ and not valid if $i = 3$. Additional instances of ENT(DSH,HC) can be found in the introduction. One specific instance of ENT(DSH,HC) consists to test whether a given a symbolic heap ξ is *established* (in the sense of [14]), i.e., that all the locations occurring in the heap of the models of ξ are either allocated or equal to some free variable: $\xi \models_{\mathcal{R}} \forall x[\mathtt{alloc}(x) \vee \neg\mathtt{ref}(x) \vee x \simeq y_1 \vee \cdots \vee x \simeq y_n)]$, with $\{y_1, \ldots, y_n\} = \{y \in fv(\phi) \mid \mathtt{sort}(y) = \mathtt{loc}\}$.

4 Abstracting Structures

The decision procedure operates by computing abstractions of the models of the antecedent. Intuitively, these abstractions will encompass information pertaining to the key characteristics of these models which is adequate for determining whether these models satisfy the consequent. We firstly define a notion of an *E-relation*, denoting an equality relation between terms:

Definition 4.1 (*E*-Relation). *An E-relation $\sim$ (for a set of variables $V \subseteq \mathcal{V}$) is an equivalence relation on $V \cup C$ satisfying the following conditions: (i) if $x \sim y$ then* $\mathtt{sort}(x) = \mathtt{sort}(y)$*; and (ii) if x, y are constants of sort* $\mathtt{data}$ *then $x \sim y \iff \langle x \rangle = \langle y \rangle$. For every term x, we denote by $x\downarrow_\sim$ a unique representative of the equivalence class of x, e.g., the minimal term y (w.r.t. to some arbitrary but fixed order on terms) such that $x \sim y$. This notation is extended to any formula ϕ, where $\phi\downarrow_\sim$ denotes the formula obtained form ϕ by replacing every term x by $x\downarrow_\sim$. A formula ϕ is* $\sim$-normalized *if $\phi = \phi\downarrow_\sim$. We denote by $\mathcal{E}(V)$ the set of E-relations for V.*

If V is clear from the context, then we shall denote an E-relation $\sim$ by a set of equations S, with the convention that $\sim$ is the smallest E-relation for V such that $x \sim y$ holds for all $(x \simeq y) \in S$. We then define the notion of a *consistent set*, which denotes the set of data atoms that are true in some specific structure.

Definition 4.2 (Consistency). *For every set of variables V and E-relation $\sim$, we denote by $\mathcal{A}^D_\sim(V)$ the set of $\sim$-normalized data atoms ϕ such that $fv(\phi) \subseteq V$. A subset S of $\mathcal{A}^D_\sim(V)$ is* consistent *(w.r.t. $\sim$ and V) if there exists an injective store $\mathfrak{s}$ such that for all $\sim$-normalized data atoms α in $\mathcal{A}^D_\sim(V)$: $(\mathfrak{s}, \emptyset) \models_{\mathcal{R}} \alpha \iff \alpha \in S$.*

Definition 4.3 (Abstraction). *An* abstraction *is a tuple $(V, \sim, A, R, \Phi, \Delta)$ where V is a set of variables, $\sim\in \mathcal{E}(V)$, A and R are sets of $\sim$-normalized terms, Φ is a $\sim$-normalized spatial $\mathfrak{h}$-atom and Δ is a consistent subset of $\mathcal{A}^D_\sim(V)$.*

Intuitively, $(V, \sim, A, , R, \Phi, \Delta)$ encapsulates crucial information about a structure. The set V denotes the variables in the domain of the store. The relation $\sim$ is the equality relation between terms. The sets A and R respectively contain the sets of allocated and referenced terms. The formula Φ is a spatial $\mathfrak{h}$-atom describing the part of the heap that corresponds to locations and data associated with variables in V and abstracting away the remainder of the heap. Finally, Δ is the set of data atoms that are true in the considered model. The formalization of the relationship between structures and abstractions is provided by Definitions 4.4 and 4.6.

Definition 4.4. *For every structure* $(\mathfrak{s}, \mathfrak{h})$*, for every set of variables* $V \subseteq dom(\mathfrak{s})$ *and for every E-relation* $\sim$*, we denote by* $\Phi_\sim(\mathfrak{s}, \mathfrak{h})$ *the* $\mathfrak{h}$*-atom* $\Phi^1_\sim(\mathfrak{s}, \mathfrak{h}) * \Phi^2_\sim(\mathfrak{s}, \mathfrak{h})$*, where:*

- $\Phi^1_\sim(\mathfrak{s}, \mathfrak{h}) = \alpha_1 * \cdots * \alpha_n$*, where* $\{\alpha_i \mid i \in \{1, \ldots, n\}\}$ *is the set of atoms of the form* $x_0 \mapsto (x_1, \ldots, x_k)$ *such that* $x_0, \ldots, x_k$ *are* $\sim$*-normalized terms in* $dom(\mathfrak{s})$*,* $\mathfrak{s}(x_0) \in dom(\mathfrak{h})$ *and* $\mathfrak{h}(\mathfrak{s}(x_0)) = (\mathfrak{s}(x_1), \ldots, \mathfrak{s}(x_k))$ *(if this set is empty then* $n = 0$ *and* $\Phi^1_\sim(\mathfrak{s}, \mathfrak{h}) = \mathtt{emp}$*).*
- $\Phi^2_\sim(\mathfrak{s}, \mathfrak{h})$ *is* $\mathtt{emp}$ *if* $card(dom(\mathfrak{h})) = n$ *and* $\top$ *otherwise.*

In particular, if $\mathfrak{h} = \emptyset$*, then* $\Phi_\sim(\mathfrak{s}, \mathfrak{h}) = \mathtt{emp} * \mathtt{emp} = \mathtt{emp}$*, and if* $dom(\mathfrak{s}) = \emptyset$ *and* $\mathfrak{h} \neq \emptyset$ *then* $\Phi_\sim(\mathfrak{s}, \mathfrak{h}) = \mathtt{emp} * \top = \top$*.*

Example 4.5. Let $\mathcal{L} = \mathbb{N}$, $\mathcal{D} = \mathbb{Q}$ and let $\mathfrak{h}$ be the heap $\{(2, 1, 0.5), (1, 0, -0.5)\}$. Let $\mathfrak{s} = \{(x, 2), (y, 1), (z_1, 0.5), (z_2, -0.5), (\mathtt{nil}, 0)\}$ and $\mathfrak{s}' = \{(u, 1), (v, 1), (w, -0.5), (\mathtt{nil}, 0)\}$.

Then $\Phi_\sim(\mathfrak{s}, \mathfrak{h})$ is $x \mapsto (y, z_1) * y \mapsto (\mathtt{nil}, z_2)$ and $\Phi_\sim(\mathfrak{s}', \mathfrak{h})$ is $u \mapsto (\mathtt{nil}, w) * \top$ (assuming that the representative of the class of $\{u, v\}$ is u).

Definition 4.6 (Abstraction of a Structure). *Let* $k \in \mathbb{N}$*,* $W \subseteq \mathcal{V}$*, Let* $(\mathfrak{s}, \mathfrak{h})$ *be a structure, and let* $\mathcal{A} = (V, \sim, A, R, \Phi, \Delta)$ *be an abstraction. The abstraction* $\mathcal{A}$ *is called an* abstraction of $(\mathfrak{s}, \mathfrak{h})$ *(written* $\mathcal{A} \triangleright (\mathfrak{s}, \mathfrak{h})$*) if all the following conditions hold. (1)* $dom(\mathfrak{s}) = V \cup C$*; (2) For all terms* $x, y \in V \cup C$*,* $x \sim y \iff \mathfrak{s}(x) = \mathfrak{s}(y)$*; (3)* A *is the set of* $\sim$*-normalized terms in* $V \cup C$ *such that* $\mathfrak{s}(x) \in dom(\mathfrak{h})$*; (4)* R *is the set of* $\sim$*-normalized terms of sort* $\mathtt{loc}$ *in* $V \cup C$ *such that there exists* $\ell \in dom(\mathfrak{h})$ *with* $\mathfrak{s}(x) \in \mathfrak{h}(\ell)$*; (5)* $\Phi = \Phi_\sim(\mathfrak{s}, \mathfrak{h})$*; (6)* Δ *is the set of data atoms in* $\mathcal{A}^D_\sim(V)$*, such that* $(\mathfrak{s}, \emptyset) \models_{\mathcal{R}} \phi$*.*

Note that, when the representative of each term equivalence class is fixed, each structure has a unique abstraction, where the components $V, \sim, A, R, \Phi$ and Δ are defined in accordance with conditions (1)-(6).

Example 4.7. With the definitions of Example 4.5, and with $\mathcal{P}_d = \{\approx, \geq\}$, the abstractions of $(\mathfrak{s}, \mathfrak{h})$ and $(\mathfrak{s}', \mathfrak{h})$ are $\mathcal{A}$ and $\mathcal{A}'$, respectively, with:

$$\begin{aligned}
\mathcal{A} &= (\{x, y, z_1, z_2\}, \emptyset, \{x, y\}, \{y, \mathtt{nil}\}, x \mapsto (y, z_1) * y \mapsto (\mathtt{nil}, z_2), \Delta) \\
\Delta &= \{z_1 \geq z_2, z_1 \approx z_1, z_1 \geq z_1, z_2 \approx z_2, z_2 \geq z_2\} \\
\mathcal{A}' &= (\{u, v, w\}, \{u \simeq v\}, \{u\}, \{\mathtt{nil}\}, u \mapsto (\mathtt{nil}, w) * \top, \{w \geq w, w \approx w\})
\end{aligned}$$

We show (see Lemma 4.10) that the truth value of a $\mathfrak{h}$-literal in a structure depends solely on the structure's abstraction. This allows for testing the validity of entailments in ENT(DSH,HC) by solely considering abstractions (Proposition 4.11). For this purpose, Definition 4.8 offers a simple criterion for determining whether an abstracted structure satisfies a particular $\mathfrak{h}$-literal or set of $\mathfrak{h}$-literals.

Definition 4.8. *For all spatial* $\mathfrak{h}$*-atoms* ϕ, ψ*, we write* $\phi \prec \psi$ *if* ϕ *and* ψ *are respectively of the form (up to AC)* $\phi_1 * \top$ *and* $\phi_1 * \phi_2$ *(with possibly* $\phi_2 = \mathtt{emp}$*). For all abstractions* $\mathcal{A} = (V, \sim, A, R, \Phi, \Delta)$ *and* $\mathfrak{h}$*-literal* ϕ*,* $\mathcal{A} \models \phi$ *iff* $fv(\phi) \subseteq V$ *and one of the following conditions holds: (1)* $\phi = (x \simeq y)$ *and* $x \sim y$*; (2)* $\phi = \mathtt{alloc}(x)$ *and* $x\downarrow_\sim \in A$*; (3)* $\phi = \mathtt{ref}(x)$ *and* $x\downarrow_\sim \in R$*; (4)* $\phi\downarrow_\sim \preceq \Phi$*; (5)* $\phi\downarrow_\sim \in \Delta$*; or (6)* $\phi = \neg\psi$ *and* $\mathcal{A} \not\models \psi$*. For any set of* $\mathfrak{h}$*-literals* S*,* $\mathcal{A} \models S$ *iff* $\forall \phi \in S\ \mathcal{A} \models \phi$*.*

Example 4.9. With the definitions of Example 4.7, we have (for instance):

$$\mathcal{A} \models \{\texttt{alloc}(y),\ \texttt{ref}(y),\ x \not\simeq y,\ x \mapsto (y, z_1) * \top, z_2 \not\simeq z_1,\ \neg(x \mapsto (y, z_1))\}$$
$$\mathcal{A}' \models \{\texttt{alloc}(v),\ \neg\texttt{ref}(u),\ u \simeq v,\ u \mapsto (\texttt{nil}, w) * \top,\ \neg\texttt{emp}\}$$

Lemma 4.10. *Let ϕ be a $\mathfrak{h}$-literal. If $\mathcal{A} \triangleright (\mathfrak{s}, \mathfrak{h})$ and $dom(\mathfrak{s}) \supseteq fv(\phi)$ then $(\mathfrak{s}, \mathfrak{h}) \models_{\mathcal{R}} \phi$ iff $\mathcal{A} \models \phi$.*

Proof. Let $\mathcal{A} = (V, \sim, A, R, \Phi, \Delta)$. Note that, due to $\mathcal{A} \triangleright (\mathfrak{s}, \mathfrak{h})$, $x \sim y$ holds iff $\mathfrak{s}(x) = \mathfrak{s}(y)$ (for all $x, y \in V \cup C$). For conciseness, we focus on the case where ϕ is a spatial $\mathfrak{h}$-atom (the other cases are covered in Appendix A). By the previous remark, $(\mathfrak{s}, \mathfrak{h}) \models_{\mathcal{R}} \phi \iff (\mathfrak{s}, \mathfrak{h}) \models_{\mathcal{R}} \phi\downarrow_{\sim}$. By definition of $\mathfrak{h}$-atoms, $\phi\downarrow_{\sim}$ can be written on the form $\alpha_1 * \cdots * \alpha_n * \beta$ where α_i (for all $i \in \{1, \dots, n\}$) is a points-to atom $x_i \mapsto (\mathbf{y}_i)$, and β is either $\top$ or emp. Moreover, by Definition 4.6 (5), we have $\Delta = \Phi_{\sim}(\mathfrak{s}, \mathfrak{h})$, thus, by Definition 4.4, Δ is of the form $\alpha'_1 * \cdots * \alpha'_m * \beta'$, where: $\{\alpha'_i \mid i \in \{1, \dots, m\}\}$ is the set of atoms of the form $x'_i \mapsto (\mathbf{y}'_i)$ such that $x'_i, \mathbf{y}'_i$ only contain $\sim$-normalized terms in $V \cup C$, $\mathfrak{s}(x'_i) \in dom(\mathfrak{h})$, $\mathfrak{h}(\mathfrak{s}(x'_i)) = (\mathfrak{s}(\mathbf{y}'_i))$, and β' is emp if $card(dom(\mathfrak{h})) = m$ and $\top$ otherwise. Note that by definition the atoms α'_i for $i \in \{1, \dots, m\}$ are pairwise distinct. We establish the double implication.

- ⇒ Assume that $(\mathfrak{s}, \mathfrak{h}) \models_{\mathcal{R}} \phi$ (hence $(\mathfrak{s}, \mathfrak{h}) \models_{\mathcal{R}} \phi\downarrow_{\sim}$). Then $\mathfrak{h} = \bigcup_{i=0}^{n} \mathfrak{h}_i$, where $\mathfrak{h}_0, \dots, \mathfrak{h}_n$ are pairwise disjoint heaps such that $(\mathfrak{s}, \mathfrak{h}_i) \models_{\mathcal{R}} \alpha_i$ (for all $i \in \{1, \dots, n\}$) and $(\mathfrak{s}, \mathfrak{h}_0) \models_{\mathcal{R}} \beta$. This entails that $\mathfrak{h}_i = \{(\mathfrak{s}(x_i), \mathfrak{s}(\mathbf{y}_i))\}$ (for all $i \in \{1, \dots, n\}$), so that $\mathfrak{s}(x_i) \in dom(\mathfrak{h})$ and $\mathfrak{h}(\mathfrak{s}(x_i)) = (\mathfrak{s}(\mathbf{y}_i))$. As α_i is normalized, this entails that each atom α_i necessarily occurs in $\{\alpha'_1, \dots, \alpha'_m\}$. Assume by symmetry that $\alpha_i = \alpha'_i$ for all $i \in \{1, \dots, n\}$ (with $n \leq m$). If $\beta = \top$ then we get $\phi\downarrow_{\sim} = (\alpha_1 * \cdots * \alpha_n) * \top$ and $\Delta = (\alpha_1 * \cdots * \alpha_n) * (\alpha'_{n+1} * \dots \alpha'_m * \beta')$, so that $\phi\downarrow_{\sim} < \Delta$, whence $\mathcal{A} \models \phi$ by Definition 4.8 (4). Otherwise (i.e., if $\beta = \texttt{emp}$), we must have $card(dom(\mathfrak{h})) = n$, which entails that $m = n = card(dom(\mathfrak{h}))$ (as $card(dom(\mathfrak{h})) \geq m$ by definition of $\{\alpha'_1, \dots, \alpha'_m\}$). Therefore, $\beta' = \texttt{emp}$ and $\phi\downarrow_{\sim} = \Delta$, so that $\mathcal{A} \models \phi$ by Definition 4.8 (4).
- ⇐ Assume that $\mathcal{A} \models \phi$, i.e., by Definition 4.8, $\phi\downarrow_{\sim} \leq \Delta$. We may assume by symmetry that $\alpha_i = \alpha'_i$ for all $i \in \{1, \dots, n\}$ (with $n \leq m$), and β is either β' (with $n = m$) or $\top$. By definition of the set $\{\alpha'_1, \dots, \alpha'_m\}$, we have $\mathfrak{h}(\mathfrak{s}(x'_i)) = \mathfrak{s}(\mathbf{y}'_i)$. As the atoms α'_i are pairwise distinct and $\sim$-normalized, this entails that the locations $\mathfrak{s}(x'_i)$ are pairwise distinct: indeed, if $\mathfrak{s}(x'_i) = \mathfrak{s}(x'_j)$ with $i \neq j$, then $x'_i = x'_j$ as x'_i, x'_j are $\sim$ -normalized, thus $\mathfrak{s}(\mathbf{y}'_i) = \mathfrak{s}(\mathbf{y}'_j)$ hence $\mathbf{y}'_i = \mathbf{y}'_j$ (as $\mathbf{y}'_i, \mathbf{y}'_j$ are $\sim$-normalized), hence $\alpha'_i = \alpha'_j$, which contradicts the fact that the atoms α'_i are pairwise distinct. Consequently there exist disjoint subheaps $\mathfrak{h}_i = \{(\mathfrak{s}(x'_i), \mathfrak{s}(\mathbf{y}'_i))\}$ of $\mathfrak{h}$ (for all $i \in \{1, \dots, m\}$) such that $(\mathfrak{s}, \mathfrak{h}_i) \models_{\mathcal{R}} \alpha'_i$. If $\beta = \top$ then we get $(\mathfrak{s}, \mathfrak{h}_1 \cup \cdots \cup \mathfrak{h}_n) \models_{\mathcal{R}} \alpha'_1 * \cdots * \alpha'_n = \alpha_1 * \cdots * \alpha_n$ hence $(\mathfrak{s}, \mathfrak{h}) \models_{\mathcal{R}} \alpha_1 * \cdots * \alpha_n * \top$ (as $\mathfrak{h}_1 \cup \cdots \cup \mathfrak{h}_n \subseteq \mathfrak{h}$) and the proof is completed. Otherwise we must have $\beta = \beta'$ and $n = m$ so that $(\mathfrak{s}, \mathfrak{h}_1 \cup \cdots \cup \mathfrak{h}_m) \models_{\mathcal{R}} \alpha'_1 * \dots \alpha'_m = \alpha_1 * \dots \alpha_n = \phi\downarrow_{\sim}$.

For every formula ϕ and for every set of variables W, we denote by $\mathcal{A}_{\mathcal{R}}(\phi, W)$ the set of abstractions of the models $(\mathfrak{s}, \mathfrak{h})$ that interpret exactly the variables in W, i.e., $\mathcal{A}_{\mathcal{R}}(\phi, W) = \{\mathcal{A} \mid (\mathfrak{s}, \mathfrak{h}) \models_{\mathcal{R}} \phi,\ dom(\mathfrak{s}) = W \cup C,\ \mathcal{A} \triangleright (\mathfrak{s}, \mathfrak{h})\}$. The following lemma stems from Lemma 4.10 and from the definitions of $\Phi_{\sim}(\mathfrak{s}, \mathfrak{h})$ and $\mathcal{A}_{\mathcal{R}}(\xi, W)$ (see Appendix B):

Lemma 4.11. *For every $\mathfrak{h}$-clause γ, we denote by $\overline{\gamma}$ the set of $\mathfrak{h}$-literals complementary to those occurring in γ. Let $\xi \models_{\mathcal{R}} \gamma$ be an instance of* Ent*(DSH,HC), with $fv(\xi) \cup fv(\gamma) \subseteq V$. The entailment $\xi \models_{\mathcal{R}} \gamma$ is valid iff for all $\mathcal{A} \in \mathcal{A}_{\mathcal{R}}(\xi, V)$, $\mathcal{A} \not\models \overline{\gamma}$.*

5 Computing Abstractions

We now show how to compute abstractions. To achieve this, we introduce two basic operations on abstractions. The first one consists in removing a variable from V. If $\mathcal{A} = (V, \sim, A, R, \Phi, \Delta)$ and $x \in V$ then we denote by $\mathcal{A} \setminus \{x\}$ the abstraction of the form $(V \setminus \{x\}, \sim', A', R', \Phi', \Delta')$ where $\sim' = \{(u, v) \mid u \sim v, u \neq x, v \neq x\}$, and:

- If there exists a term $y \neq x$ such that $x \sim y$ then A', R', Φ' and Δ' are obtained from A, R, Φ and Δ respectively by replacing all occurrences of x by $y\downarrow_{\sim'}$.
- Otherwise, $A' = A \setminus \{x\}$, $R' = R \setminus \{x\}$, Φ' is obtained from Φ by replacing every atom containing x by $\top$ and Δ' is the set of formulas in Δ that do not contain x.

Example 5.1. With the definitions of Example 4.7 we have:

$$\begin{aligned}
\mathcal{A} \setminus \{x\} &= (\{y, z_1, z_2\}, \emptyset, \{y\}, \{y, \texttt{nil}\}, \top * y \mapsto (\texttt{nil}, z_2), \Delta) \\
\mathcal{A}' \setminus \{u\} &= (\{v, w\}, \emptyset, \{v\}, \{w, \texttt{nil}\}, v \mapsto (\texttt{nil}, w) * \top, \{w \geq w, w \approx w\}) \\
\mathcal{A}' \setminus \{w\} &= (\{u, v\}, \{u \simeq v\}, \{u\}, \{\texttt{nil}\}, \top, \emptyset)
\end{aligned}$$

The second operation consists in computing the disjoint union of two abstractions. Let $\mathcal{A}_i = (V_i, \sim_i, A_i, R_i, \Phi_i, \Delta_i)$ be two abstractions (with $i \in \{1, 2\}$). The abstraction $\mathcal{A}_1 * \mathcal{A}_2$ is defined if $V_1 = V_2$, $\sim_1 = \sim_2$, $A_1 \cap A_2 = \emptyset$ and $\Delta_1 = \Delta_2$, and in this case $\mathcal{A}_1 * \mathcal{A}_2$ is $(V_1, \sim_1, A_1 \cup A_2, R_1 \cup R_2, \Phi_1 * \Phi_2, \Delta_1)$.

Example 5.2. Consider the abstraction $\mathcal{A}$ of Example 4.7 together with:

$$\mathcal{A}_1 = (\{x, x', y, z_1, z_2\}, \emptyset, \emptyset, \emptyset, \top, \Delta) \qquad \mathcal{A}_2 = (\{x, y, z_1, z_2\}, \emptyset, \{x\}, \emptyset, \top, \Delta)$$
$$\mathcal{A}_3 = (\{x, y, z_1, z_2\}, \emptyset, \{\texttt{nil}\}, \{x\}, \texttt{nil} \mapsto (x), \Delta)$$

Then $\mathcal{A} * \mathcal{A}_i$ is undefined if $i = 1$ (as $\mathcal{A}_1$ has a variable x' that is not in $\mathcal{A}$) or if $i = 2$ (as $\mathcal{A}$ and $\mathcal{A}_2$ both allocate x), and $\mathcal{A} * \mathcal{A}_3$ is:

$$(\{x, y, z_1, z_2\}, \emptyset, \{x, y, \texttt{nil}\}, \{x, y, \texttt{nil}\}, x \mapsto (y, z_1) * y \mapsto (\texttt{nil}, z_2) * \texttt{nil} \mapsto (x), \Delta)$$

Lemma 5.3 relates these operators to the corresponding operations on the abstracted structures (the proof is given in Appendix C).

Lemma 5.3. *The two following assertions hold:*

1. *If $\mathcal{A}_i \triangleright (\mathfrak{s}, \mathfrak{h}_i)$, for all $i \in \{1, 2\}$, $dom(\mathfrak{h}_1) \cap dom(\mathfrak{h}_2) = \emptyset$ and $\mathcal{A}_1 * \mathcal{A}_2$ is defined, then $\mathcal{A}_1 * \mathcal{A}_2 \triangleright (\mathfrak{s}, \mathfrak{h}_1 \cup \mathfrak{h}_2)$.*
2. *If $\mathcal{A} \triangleright (\mathfrak{s}, \mathfrak{h})$, and $\mathfrak{s}'$ is the restriction of $\mathfrak{s}$ to the variables distinct from x, then $\mathcal{A} \setminus \{x\} \triangleright (\mathfrak{s}', \mathfrak{h})$.*

Using the above operations on abstraction, we define a set of rules (Fig. 1) that inductively compute the set of abstractions $\mathcal{A}^*_{\mathcal{R}}(\phi, W)$, for all DSH ϕ. The first two rules correspond to base cases, where ϕ is atomic. The first rule tackles the case where $\phi = \mathtt{emp}$. In this case, both A and R are empty (as the heap is empty) and Φ is $\mathtt{emp}$. The second rule handles the case where ϕ is a points-to atom $x_0 \mapsto (x_1, \ldots, x_n)$. Then A contains the representative of x_0 (as it is the only allocated location), R contains the representatives of the location terms in $x_1, \ldots, x_n$, and Φ is simply the $\sim$-normalized form of ϕ. The next four rules cover conjunctions of the form $\phi \wedge \alpha$ where ϕ is a symbolic heap and α is either an equational literal or a data literal. In each case, one only has to compute abstractions of ϕ and check whether α is satisfied. Note that it is impossible to compute abstractions of α as the latter formula is not a symbolic heap. Abstractions of existential quantifications $\exists x\, \phi$ are computed by removing the variable x from the abstractions of ϕ using the operation $\mathcal{A} \setminus \{x\}$ defined above, and abstractions of separating conjunctions $\phi_1 * \phi_2$ are computed by combining abstractions of ϕ_1 and ϕ_2 using the operator $*$. The last rules handle the case of disjunctions and inductive definitions, respectively (the computation is straightforward in both cases).

Remark 5.4. Note that abstractions may contain variables not occurring in the considered formula, and are defined to associate a truth value with every equation and data atom (this is why we may assume, when combining abstractions $(V_i, \sim_i, A_i, R_i, \Phi_i, \Delta_i)$ using the operator $*$, that $V_1 = V_2$, $\sim_1 = \sim_2$ and $\Delta_1 = \Delta_2$). This design choice was made for the sake of readability and conciseness, but it leads to some computational overhead, as not all of these variables and atoms are necessarily relevant for evaluating the formulas at hand. In practice, variables and constraints should be added on demand, when they become necessarily to check that the premises of the rules in Fig. 1 are satisfied.

Lemma 5.5 asserts that the rules for computing abstractions are correct and complete, i.e., that the computed set of abstractions $\mathcal{A}^*_{\mathcal{R}}(\phi, W)$ is indeed the set of all abstractions of the models of ϕ. The result crucially relies on Assumption 3 (see Appendix D).

Lemma 5.5. *For all DSH ϕ and all $W \supseteq fv(\phi)$, $\mathcal{A}^*_{\mathcal{R}}(\phi, W) = \mathcal{A}_{\mathcal{R}}(\phi, W)$.*

Lemmata 4.11 and 5.5 yield an algorithm for testing the validity of entailment $\xi \models_{\mathcal{R}} \gamma$ in ENT(DSH,HC), described in the proof of Theorem 5.6.

Theorem 5.6. *The problem* ENT*(DSH,HC) is decidable, and it is* EXPTIME*-complete if the satisfiability test is in* EXPTIME *for data constraints.*

Proof. The lower bound stems from the EXPTIME-hardness of the satisfiability problem for symbolic heaps [2] (with $\mathcal{P}_d = \{\approx\}$). The decision procedure runs as follows. Consider an instance $\xi \models_{\mathcal{R}} \gamma$ of ENT(DSH,HC). We first compute the set $\mathcal{A}^*_{\mathcal{R}}(\xi, V)$ using the rules in Fig. 1, where $V = fv(\xi) \cup fv(\gamma)$. To this purpose, we only have to compute the sets $\mathcal{A}^*_{\mathcal{R}}(\phi, W)$ for formulas ϕ occurring either in ξ or in some instance of a rule in $\mathcal{R}$, where W contains all variables occurring in ξ, γ or $\mathcal{R}$. By Lemma 5.5, we have $\mathcal{A}^*_{\mathcal{R}}(\phi, V) = \mathcal{A}_{\mathcal{R}}(\phi, V)$. Then, by Lemma 4.11, to test whether $\xi \models_{\mathcal{R}} \gamma$, it suffices to test whether $\mathcal{A} \not\models \overline{\gamma}$ holds for all $\mathcal{A} \in \mathcal{A}^*_{\mathcal{R}}(\xi, V)$.

We now briefly analyze the complexity of the procedure. We first observe that the number of formulas ϕ to consider is simply exponential w.r.t. $|\xi| + |\mathcal{R}|$ (up to a renaming

$$\frac{\Delta \subseteq \mathcal{A}^D_{\sim}(V) \quad \sim \in \mathcal{E}(V)}{(V, \sim, \emptyset, \emptyset, \mathtt{emp}, \Delta) \in \mathcal{A}^*_{\mathcal{R}}(\mathtt{emp}, V)}$$

$$\frac{\sim \in \mathcal{E}(V) \quad \Delta \subseteq \mathcal{A}^D_{\sim}(V) \quad \Phi = \{x_0 \downarrow_{\sim} \mapsto (x_1 \downarrow_{\sim}, \ldots, x_n \downarrow_{\sim}\}}{(V, \sim, \{x_0 \downarrow_{\sim}\}, \{x_i \downarrow_{\sim} \mid i \in \{1, \ldots, n\}, \mathtt{sort}(x_i) = \mathtt{loc}\}, \Phi, \Delta) \in \mathcal{A}^*_{\mathcal{R}}(x_0 \mapsto (x_1, \ldots, x_n), V)}$$

$$\frac{x \sim y \quad (V, \sim, A, R, \Phi, \Delta) \in \mathcal{A}^*_{\mathcal{R}}(\phi, V)}{(V, \sim, A, R, \Phi, \Delta) \in \mathcal{A}^*_{\mathcal{R}}(\phi \wedge (x \simeq y), V)} \quad \frac{x \not\sim y \quad (V, \sim, A, R, \Phi, \Delta) \in \mathcal{A}^*_{\mathcal{R}}(\phi, V)}{(V, \sim, A, R, \Phi, \Delta) \in \mathcal{A}^*_{\mathcal{R}}(\phi \wedge (x \not\simeq y), V)}$$

$$\frac{\alpha \in \Delta \quad (V, \sim, A, R, \Phi, \Delta) \in \mathcal{A}^*_{\mathcal{R}}(\phi, V)}{(V, \sim, A, R, \Phi, \Delta) \in \mathcal{A}^*_{\mathcal{R}}(\phi \wedge \alpha, V)} \quad \frac{\alpha \notin \Delta \quad (V, \sim, A, R, \Phi, \Delta) \in \mathcal{A}^*_{\mathcal{R}}(\phi, V)}{(V, \sim, A, R, \Phi, \Delta) \in \mathcal{A}^*_{\mathcal{R}}(\phi \wedge \neg\alpha, V)}$$

$$\frac{\mathcal{A} \in \mathcal{A}^*_{\mathcal{R}}(\phi, V)}{\mathcal{A} \setminus \{x\} \in \mathcal{A}^*_{\mathcal{R}}(\exists x\, \phi, V \setminus \{x\})} \quad \frac{\forall i \in \{1,2\}\, \mathcal{A}_i \in \mathcal{A}^*_{\mathcal{R}}(\phi_i, V) \quad \mathcal{A}_1 * \mathcal{A}_2 \text{ is defined}}{\mathcal{A}_1 * \mathcal{A}_2 \in \mathcal{A}^*_{\mathcal{R}}(\phi_1 * \phi_2, V)}$$

$$\frac{\mathcal{A} \in \mathcal{A}_{\mathcal{R}}(\phi_i, V) \quad i \in \{1,2\} \quad fv(\phi_1 \vee \phi_2) \subseteq V}{\mathcal{A} \in \mathcal{A}_{\mathcal{R}}(\phi_1 \vee \phi_2, V)}$$

$$\frac{\mathcal{A} \in \mathcal{A}^*_{\mathcal{R}}(\phi, V) \quad p(\mathbf{x}) \leadsto_{\mathcal{R}} \phi \quad p \in \mathcal{P}_s}{\mathcal{A} \in \mathcal{A}^*_{\mathcal{R}}(p(\mathbf{x}), V)}$$

Fig. 1. Inductive rules for computing abstractions of a formula

of variables). The test $\mathcal{A} \models \overline{\gamma}$ is decidable in polynomial time (see Definition 4.8). Furthermore, the size of the abstractions is polynomial in $|\xi| + |\gamma| + |\mathcal{R}|$. Indeed, it is possible to prove that it is sufficient to compute abstractions with variables occurring in W, so that the number of terms is bounded by $card(W \cup C) \leq |\xi| + |\gamma| + |\mathcal{R}|$ thus the E-relation $\sim$ is of quadratic size, the sets A and R are of linear size and the set of data atoms Δ is of size $O(card(\mathcal{P}_d) \times (|\xi| + |\mathcal{R}|)^n)$, where n denotes the maximal arity of the predicates in $\mathcal{P}_d$ (which is fixed in the context). Finally, the size of points-to atoms is bounded by $|\xi| + |\gamma| + |\mathcal{R}|$, and the maximal number of points-to atom occurring in a spatial $\mathfrak{h}$-atom is bounded by $card(W \cup C)$ (as the same term cannot be allocated twice, otherwise the $\mathfrak{h}$-atom is trivially unsatisfiable). This entails that there is exponentially many such abstractions (assuming, w.l.o.g., that every constant and inductive predicate occurs in ξ, γ or $\mathcal{R}$). Finally, it is straightforward to check that each rule in Fig. 1 can be applied in exponential time w.r.t. the size of the abstractions (assuming the satisfiability problem is in ExpTime for data constraints). Thus the algorithm runs in exponential time.

6 Conclusion

A new decidable fragment of the entailment problem in SL has been identified. It is ExpTime-complete (if the satisfiability problem for data constraints is in ExpTime) and incomparable with previously known decidable fragments. A natural follow-up involves implementing the decision procedure and enhancing its efficiency, as outlined in Remark 5.4. Although the theoretical complexity of the procedure remains unaffected, this approach has the potential to significantly improve the practical efficiency of the procedure by reducing the number of abstractions to be considered. One could also try to relax the assumptions on the data theory, by imposing additional syntactic restrictions on data literals.

A Proof of Lemma 4.10

We handle the cases that have not been already covered in the body of the paper:

- If $\phi = (x \simeq y)$, then $(\mathfrak{s}, \mathfrak{h}) \models_{\mathcal{R}} \phi \iff \mathfrak{s}(x) = \mathfrak{s}(y)$ (Definition 2.4). By Definition 4.6 (2), $\mathfrak{s}(x) = \mathfrak{s}(y) \iff x \sim y$, and by Definition 4.8 (1) $x \sim y \iff \mathcal{A} \models \phi$.
- $\phi = \mathtt{alloc}(x)$, then $(\mathfrak{s}, \mathfrak{h}) \models_{\mathcal{R}} \phi \iff \mathfrak{s}(x) \in dom(\mathfrak{h})$ (Definition 2.4). As $\mathfrak{s}(x) = \mathfrak{s}(x\downarrow_{\sim})$, we get $(\mathfrak{s}, \mathfrak{h}) \models_{\mathcal{R}} \phi \iff \mathfrak{s}(x\downarrow_{\sim}) \in dom(\mathfrak{h})$. By Definition 4.6 (3), $\mathfrak{s}(x\downarrow_{\sim}) \in dom(\mathfrak{h}) \iff x\downarrow_{\sim} \in A$ (as $x\downarrow_{\sim}$ is $\sim$-normalized by definition). By Definition 4.8 (2) we have $x\downarrow_{\sim} \in A \iff \mathcal{A} \models \mathtt{alloc}(x)$. Thus $(\mathfrak{s}, \mathfrak{h}) \models_{\mathcal{R}} \phi \iff \mathcal{A} \models \phi$.
- $\phi = \mathtt{ref}(x)$, then $(\mathfrak{s}, \mathfrak{h}) \models_{\mathcal{R}} \phi \iff \exists \ell \in dom(\mathfrak{h})$ s.t. $\mathfrak{s}(x) \in \mathfrak{h}(\ell)$ (Definition 2.4). As $\mathfrak{s}(x) = \mathfrak{s}(x\downarrow_{\sim})$, we get $(\mathfrak{s}, \mathfrak{h}) \models_{\mathcal{R}} \phi \iff \exists \ell \in dom(\mathfrak{h})$ s.t. $\mathfrak{s}(x\downarrow_{\sim}) \in \mathfrak{h}(\ell)$. By Definition 4.6 (4), we deduce $(\mathfrak{s}, \mathfrak{h}) \models_{\mathcal{R}} \phi \iff x\downarrow_{\sim} \in R$ (as $x\downarrow_{\sim}$ is $\sim$-normalized). By Definition 4.8 (3) we get $(\mathfrak{s}, \mathfrak{h}) \models_{\mathcal{R}} \phi \iff \mathcal{A} \models \phi$.
- If ϕ is a data atom, then $(\mathfrak{s}, \mathfrak{h}) \models_{\mathcal{R}} \phi \iff (\mathfrak{s}, \emptyset) \models_{\mathcal{R}} \phi\downarrow_{\sim}$ (as the truth value of ϕ does not depend on the heap). By Definition 4.6 (6), we get $(\mathfrak{s}, \mathfrak{h}) \models_{\mathcal{R}} \phi \iff \phi\downarrow_{\sim} \in \Delta$ (since $\phi\downarrow_{\sim} \in \mathcal{A}^{D}_{\sim}(V)$, by definition, as $\phi\downarrow_{\sim}$ is $\sim$-normalized and $fv(\phi\downarrow_{\sim}) \subseteq V$), thus by Definition 4.8 (5) $(\mathfrak{s}, \mathfrak{h}) \models_{\mathcal{R}} \phi \iff \mathcal{A} \models \phi$.
- If $\phi = \neg\psi$, then by the previous items we get $(\mathfrak{s}, \mathfrak{h}) \models_{\mathcal{R}} \psi \iff \mathcal{A} \models \psi$. Moreover $(\mathfrak{s}, \mathfrak{h}) \models_{\mathcal{R}} \phi \iff (\mathfrak{s}, \mathfrak{h}) \not\models_{\mathcal{R}} \psi$ (Definition 2.4) and $\mathcal{A} \models \phi \iff \mathcal{A} \not\models \psi$ by Definition 4.8 (6) so that $(\mathfrak{s}, \mathfrak{h}) \models_{\mathcal{R}} \phi \iff \mathcal{A} \models \phi$.

B Proof of Lemma 4.11

By definition, $\xi \models_{\mathcal{R}} \gamma$ iff $(\mathfrak{s}, \mathfrak{h}) \models_{\mathcal{R}} \xi \implies (\mathfrak{s}, \mathfrak{h}) \models_{\mathcal{R}} \gamma$ holds for all structures $(\mathfrak{s}, \mathfrak{h})$ where $dom(\mathfrak{s}) \supseteq fv(\xi) \cup fv(\gamma)$. By definition of $\overline{\gamma}$, $(\mathfrak{s}, \mathfrak{h}) \models_{\mathcal{R}} \gamma$ holds iff $(\hat{\mathfrak{s}}, \mathfrak{h}) \not\models_{\mathcal{R}} \overline{\gamma}$, for all extensions $\hat{\mathfrak{s}}$ of $\mathfrak{s}$ to $fv(\gamma) \setminus dom(\mathfrak{s})$ (moreover, as we assume that the variables that are bound in γ do not occur in $fv(\xi)$, we have $(\hat{\mathfrak{s}}, \mathfrak{h}) \models_{\mathcal{R}} \xi \iff (\mathfrak{s}, \mathfrak{h}) \models_{\mathcal{R}} \xi$). Thus $\xi \models_{\mathcal{R}} \gamma$ holds iff $(\hat{\mathfrak{s}}, \mathfrak{h}) \models_{\mathcal{R}} \xi \implies (\hat{\mathfrak{s}}, \mathfrak{h}) \not\models_{\mathcal{R}} \overline{\gamma}$ holds for all structures $(\hat{\mathfrak{s}}, \mathfrak{h})$ where $dom(\hat{\mathfrak{s}}) = V$. By definition of $\mathcal{A}_{\mathcal{R}}(\xi, fv(\gamma))$, $(\hat{\mathfrak{s}}, \mathfrak{h}) \models_{\mathcal{R}} \xi$ with $dom(\hat{\mathfrak{s}}) = V$ iff there exists an abstraction $\mathcal{A} \in \mathcal{A}_{\mathcal{R}}(\xi, V)$ such that $\mathcal{A} \triangleright (\hat{\mathfrak{s}}, \mathfrak{h})$. By Lemma 4.10, for all such structures $(\hat{\mathfrak{s}}, \mathfrak{h})$ and abstractions $\mathcal{A}$, $(\hat{\mathfrak{s}}, \mathfrak{h}) \not\models_{\mathcal{R}} \overline{\gamma}$ iff $\mathcal{A} \not\models \overline{\gamma}$. Consequently, $\xi \models_{\mathcal{R}} \gamma$ holds iff $\mathcal{A} \not\models \overline{\gamma}$ for all abstractions $\mathcal{A} \in \mathcal{A}_{\mathcal{R}}(\xi, V)$.

C Proof of Lemma 5.3

Assertion 1. Let $\mathcal{A}_i = (V_i, \sim_i, A_i, R_i, \Phi_i, \Delta_i)$, $\mathfrak{h} = \mathfrak{h}_1 \cup \mathfrak{h}_2$, and $\mathcal{A} = (V, \sim, A, R, \Phi, \Delta)$, with (since $\mathcal{A}_1 * \mathcal{A}_2 = \mathcal{A}$) $V_1 = V_2 = V$, $\sim_1 = \sim_2 = \sim$, $A = A_1 \cup A_2$, $A_1 \cap A_2 = \emptyset$, $R = R_1 \cup R_2$, $\Phi = \Phi_1 * \Phi_2$, $\Delta_1 = \Delta_2 = \Delta$. We have $\{x\downarrow_{\sim} \mid \mathfrak{s}(x) \in dom(\mathfrak{h})\} = \bigcup_{i=1}^{2} \{x\downarrow_{\sim} \mid \mathfrak{s}(x) \in dom(\mathfrak{h}_i)\} = A_1 \cup A_2$ (by Cond. 3 in Definition 4.6). Thus $\{x\downarrow_{\sim} \mid \mathfrak{s}(x) \in dom(\mathfrak{h})\} = A$. Similarly, $\{x\downarrow_{\sim} \mid$

$\exists \ell \in dom(\mathfrak{h})$ s.t. $\mathfrak{s}(x) \in \mathfrak{h}(\ell)\} = \bigcup_{i=1}^{2}\{x\downarrow_{\sim} \mid \exists \ell \in dom(\mathfrak{h}_i)$ s.t. $\mathfrak{s}(x) \in \mathfrak{h}_i(\ell)\} = R_1 \cup R_2 = R$. Finally, $\Phi_{\sim}(\mathfrak{s}, \mathfrak{h}) = \alpha_1 * \cdots * \alpha_n * \Phi^2_{\sim}(\mathfrak{s}, \mathfrak{h})$, where $\{\alpha_1, \ldots, \alpha_n\}$ is the set of $\sim$-normalized atoms $v_0 \mapsto (v_1, \ldots, v_k)$ such that $\mathfrak{h}(\mathfrak{s}(v_0)) = (\mathfrak{s}(v_1), \ldots, \mathfrak{s}(v_n))$ and $\Phi^2_{\sim}(\mathfrak{s}, \mathfrak{h}) = \texttt{emp}$ if $card(dom(\mathfrak{h})) = n$ and $\top$ otherwise. Similarly, $\Phi_{\sim}(\mathfrak{s}, \mathfrak{h}_i) = \alpha^i_1 * \cdots * \alpha^i_{n_i} * \Phi^2_{\sim}(\mathfrak{s}, \mathfrak{h}_i)$, where $\{\alpha^i_1, \ldots, \alpha^i_{n_i}\}$ is the set of $\sim$-normalized atoms $v_0 \mapsto (v_1, \ldots, v_k)$ such that $\mathfrak{h}_i(\mathfrak{s}(v_0)) = (\mathfrak{s}(v_1), \ldots, \mathfrak{s}(v_n))$ and $\Phi^2_{\sim}(\mathfrak{s}, \mathfrak{h}_i) = \texttt{emp}$ if $card(dom(\mathfrak{h}_i)) = n_i$ and $\top$ otherwise. As $\mathfrak{h}$ is the disjoint union of $\mathfrak{h}_1$ and $\mathfrak{h}_2$, $\{\alpha_1, \ldots, \alpha_n\} = \bigcup_{i=1}^{2}\{\alpha^i_1, \ldots, \alpha^i_{n_i}\}$ with $n = n_1 + n_2$, thus $\alpha_1 * \cdots * \alpha_n = \alpha^1_1 * \cdots * \alpha^1_{n_1} * \alpha^2_1 * \cdots * \alpha^2_{n_2}$. Moreover, $\Phi^2_{\sim}(\mathfrak{s}, \mathfrak{h}) = \top$ iff $card(dom(\mathfrak{h})) > n$, i.e., iff $card(dom(\mathfrak{h}_i)) > n_i$ for some $i \in \{1, 2\}$, thus $\Phi^2_{\sim}(\mathfrak{s}, \mathfrak{h}_i) = \Phi^2_{\sim}(\mathfrak{s}, \mathfrak{h}_1) * \Phi^2_{\sim}(\mathfrak{s}, \mathfrak{h}_2)$ (up of neutrality of $\texttt{emp}$ and contraction of $\top$). Consequently, $\Phi_{\sim}(\mathfrak{s}, \mathfrak{h}) = \Phi_{\sim}(\mathfrak{s}, \mathfrak{h}_1) * \Phi_{\sim}(\mathfrak{s}, \mathfrak{h}_2) = \Phi_1 * \Phi_2 = \Phi$ and $\mathcal{A} \triangleright (\mathfrak{s}, \mathfrak{h})$.

Assertion 2. Let $\mathcal{A} = (V, \sim, A, R, \Phi, \Delta)$ and $\mathcal{A} \setminus \{x\} = (V \setminus \{x\}, \sim', A', R', \Phi', \Delta')$.

- If $\mathfrak{s}(x) = \mathfrak{s}(y)$ for some $y \in (V \setminus \{x\} \cup C$ then A', R', Φ' and Δ' are identical to A, R, Φ and Δ, up to the replacement of the variable x by $y\downarrow_{\sim}$, and it is straightforward to check that all the conditions of Definition 4.6 hold. Thus $\mathcal{A} \setminus \{x\} \triangleright (\mathfrak{s}', \mathfrak{h})$.
- Now assume that $\mathfrak{s}(x) \notin \mathfrak{s}((V \setminus \{x\}) \cup C)$. This entails that $u\downarrow_{\sim} = u\downarrow_{\sim'}$ for all terms $u \in (V \setminus \{x\}) \cup C$. We show that all the conditions of Definition 4.6 hold.
  1 As $\mathcal{A} \triangleright (\mathfrak{s}, \mathfrak{h})$, we have $dom(\mathfrak{s}) = V \cup C$. By definition $dom(\mathfrak{s}') = dom(\mathfrak{s}) \setminus \{x\} = (V \cup C) \setminus \{x\} = (V \setminus \{x\}) \cup C$.
  2 For all $u, v \in (V \setminus \{x\}) \cup C$, we have $u \sim v \iff \mathfrak{s}(u) = \mathfrak{s}(v)$, (as $\mathcal{A} \triangleright (\mathfrak{s}, \mathfrak{h})$). Moreover $u \sim v \iff u \sim' v$ (as $\sim'$ is the restriction of $\sim$ to pairs not containing x), and, since $\mathfrak{s}'$ is the restriction of $\mathfrak{s}$ to variables other than x, $\mathfrak{s}(u) = \mathfrak{s}'(u)$ and $\mathfrak{s}(v) = \mathfrak{s}'(v)$. Thus $u \sim' v \iff \mathfrak{s}'(u) = \mathfrak{s}'(v)$.
  3 Let u be a $\sim'$-normalized term in $(V \setminus \{x\}) \cup C$. Then $u \in V \cup C$ and u is $\sim$-normalized (since $\mathfrak{s}(x) \notin (V \setminus \{x\}) \cup C)$, hence $u \in A \iff \mathfrak{s}(u) \in dom(\mathfrak{h})$. As $u \neq x$, $u \in A' \iff u \in A$ and $\mathfrak{s}'(u) = \mathfrak{s}(u)$. Consequently $u \in A' \iff \mathfrak{s}'(u) \in dom(\mathfrak{h})$.
  4 We prove in the same way that for all $\sim'$-normalized terms of sort `loc` $u \in (V \setminus \{x\}) \cup C$, $u \in R' \iff \exists \ell \in dom(\mathfrak{h})$ s.t. $\mathfrak{s}'(u) \in \mathfrak{h}(\ell)$.
  5 It is clear that all atoms in $\Phi^1_{\sim}(\mathfrak{s}', \mathfrak{h})$ also occur in $\Phi^1_{\sim}(\mathfrak{s}, \mathfrak{h})$, since $\mathfrak{s}'$ is a restriction of $\mathfrak{s}$ and $u\downarrow_{\sim} = u\downarrow_{\sim'}$ for all terms in $(V \setminus \{x\}) \cup C$. If $\Phi^1_{\sim}(\mathfrak{s}', \mathfrak{h}) = \Phi^1_{\sim}(\mathfrak{s}, \mathfrak{h})$, then by Definition 4.4 we also have $\Phi^2_{\sim}(\mathfrak{s}', \mathfrak{h}) = \Phi^2_{\sim}(\mathfrak{s}, \mathfrak{h})$, so that $\Phi_{\sim}(\mathfrak{s}', \mathfrak{h}) = \Phi_{\sim}(\mathfrak{s}, \mathfrak{h})$. Otherwise, we must have $\Phi^2_{\sim}(\mathfrak{s}', \mathfrak{h}) = \top$, so that $\Phi_{\sim}(\mathfrak{s}', \mathfrak{h})$ may be obtained from $\Phi_{\sim}(\mathfrak{s}, \mathfrak{h})$ (up to contraction $\top * \top = \top$) by replacing all atoms containing x by $\top$.
  6 Let $\phi \in \mathcal{A}^D_{\sim'}(V \setminus \{x\})$. Then we have $\phi \in \mathcal{A}^D_{\sim}(V)$, thus $\phi \in \Delta \iff (\mathfrak{s}, \emptyset) \models_{\mathcal{R}} \phi$. As $x \notin fv(\phi)$, we get $(\mathfrak{s}, \emptyset) \models_{\mathcal{R}} \phi \iff (\mathfrak{s}', \emptyset) \models_{\mathcal{R}} \phi$ and $\phi \in \Delta \iff \phi \in \Delta'$, so that $\phi \in \Delta' \iff (\mathfrak{s}', \emptyset) \models_{\mathcal{R}} \phi$.

D Proof of Lemma 5.5

$\mathcal{A}^*_{\mathcal{R}}(\phi, W) \subseteq \mathcal{A}_{\mathcal{R}}(\phi, W)$

We need to establish a stronger inductive lemma, formalized as follows.

Lemma D.1. *A store* $\mathfrak{s}$ *is* compatible *with a set of variables* V*, an E-relation* $\sim$ *and a set of* $\sim$*-normalized data atoms* Δ *if the three following conditions hold: (i)* $dom(\mathfrak{s}) = V \cup C$*; (ii) for all* $x, y \in V \cup C$, $x \sim y \iff \mathfrak{s}(x) = \mathfrak{s}(y)$*; and (iii) for all* $\psi \in \mathcal{A}^D_\sim(V)$, $(\mathfrak{s}, \emptyset) \models_\mathcal{R} \psi \iff \psi \in \Delta$*.*

For every abstraction $\mathcal{A} = (V, \sim, A, R, \Phi, \Delta) \in \mathcal{A}^*_\mathcal{R}(\phi, V)$ *and every store* $\mathfrak{s}$ *compatible with* $V, \sim$ *and* Δ*, there exists a heap* $\mathfrak{h}$ *such that* $(\mathfrak{s}, \mathfrak{h}) \models_\mathcal{R} \phi$ *and* $\mathcal{A} \triangleright (\mathfrak{s}, \mathfrak{h})$*.*

Lemma D.1 entails that $\mathcal{A}^*_\mathcal{R}(\phi, W) \subseteq \mathcal{A}_\mathcal{R}(\phi, W)$. Indeed, if an abstraction $\mathcal{A} = (V, \sim, A, , R, \Phi, \Delta)$ is in $\mathcal{A}^*_\mathcal{R}(\phi, W)$ then necessarily $V = W$ and Δ is consistent w.r.t. $\sim$ and V, thus there exists a store $\mathfrak{s}$ such that for all $\alpha \in \mathcal{A}^D_\sim(V)$: $(\mathfrak{s}, \emptyset) \models_\mathcal{R} \alpha \iff \alpha \in \Delta$. As Δ is $\sim$-normalized, this store may be transformed into a store $\hat{\mathfrak{s}}$ compatible with $W, \sim$ and Δ by letting: $\hat{\mathfrak{s}}(x) = \mathfrak{s}(x\downarrow_\sim)$, for all terms $x \in W \cup C$. By Lemma D.1, we deduce that there exists a heap $\mathfrak{h}$ such that $(\hat{\mathfrak{s}}, \mathfrak{h}) \models_\mathcal{R} \phi$ and $\mathcal{A} \triangleright (\hat{\mathfrak{s}}, \mathfrak{h})$, so that $\mathcal{A} \in \mathcal{A}_\mathcal{R}(\phi, W)$ by definition.

Proof (of Lemma D.1*).* The proof is by induction on $\mathcal{A}^*_\mathcal{R}(\phi, W)$. We distinguish several cases, according to the rule in Fig. 1 used to derive the conclusion $\mathcal{A} \in \mathcal{A}^*_\mathcal{R}(\phi, W)$.

- Assume that $\phi = \mathtt{emp}$, $A = R = \emptyset$, $\Phi = \mathtt{emp}$, with $\Delta \subseteq \mathcal{A}^D_\sim(V)$ and $\sim \in \mathcal{E}(V)$. Taking $\mathfrak{h} = \emptyset$, we get $(\mathfrak{s}, \mathfrak{h}) \models_\mathcal{R} \phi$. Moreover, by Definition 4.4 $\Phi_\sim(\mathfrak{s}, \mathfrak{h}) = \mathtt{emp}$, so that $\mathcal{A} \triangleright (\mathfrak{s}, \mathfrak{h})$ by Definition 4.6 (as $dom(\mathfrak{h}) = \emptyset$).
- Assume that $\phi = \psi \wedge (x \simeq y)$ and $\mathcal{A} \in \mathcal{A}^*_\mathcal{R}(\psi, W)$, with $\Delta \subseteq \mathcal{A}^D_\sim(V)$, $\sim \in \mathcal{E}(V)$ and $x \sim y$. By the induction hypothesis, there exists a heap $\mathfrak{h}$ such that $(\mathfrak{s}, \mathfrak{h}) \models_\mathcal{R} \psi$ and $\mathcal{A} \triangleright (\mathfrak{s}, \mathfrak{h})$. As $\sim \in \mathcal{E}(V)$ and $\mathfrak{s}$ is compatible with $\sim$, we also have $(\mathfrak{s}, \mathfrak{h}) \models_\mathcal{R} x \simeq y$, so that $(\mathfrak{s}, \mathfrak{h}) \models_\mathcal{R} \phi$.
- The proof is similar if ϕ is of the form $\psi \wedge x \not\simeq y$ or $\psi \wedge \alpha$ where α is a data literal.
- Assume that $\phi = x_0 \mapsto (x_1, \ldots, x_n)$, $A = \{x_0 \downarrow_\sim\}$, $R = \{x_i \downarrow_\sim \mid i \in \{1, \ldots, n\}, \mathtt{sort}(x_i) = \mathtt{loc}\}$ and $\Phi = x_0 \downarrow_\sim \mapsto (x_1 \downarrow_\sim, \ldots, x_n \downarrow_\sim)$. Let $\mathfrak{h} = \{(\mathfrak{s}(x_0), \ldots, \mathfrak{s}(x_n))\}$. By definition, $(\mathfrak{s}, \mathfrak{h}) \models_\mathcal{R} \phi$. Moreover, by Definition 4.4 we have $\Phi_\sim(\mathfrak{s}, \mathfrak{h}) = \mathfrak{s}(x_0 \downarrow_\sim) \mapsto (\mathfrak{s}(x_1 \downarrow_\sim, \ldots, \mathfrak{s}(x_n \downarrow_\sim)) = \phi\downarrow_\sim$, $dom(\mathfrak{h}) = \{\mathfrak{s}(x_0)\} = \mathfrak{s}(A)$, and $\{x \in V\downarrow_\sim \mid \exists \ell \in dom(\mathfrak{h}) \text{ s.t. } \mathfrak{s}(x) \in \mathfrak{h}(\ell)\} = \mathfrak{s}(R)$. Thus $\mathcal{A} \triangleright (\mathfrak{s}, \mathfrak{h})$.
- Assume that $\phi = \exists x \phi'$, $\mathcal{A} = \mathcal{A}' \setminus \{x\}$, with $\mathcal{A}' = (V', \sim', A', R', \Phi', \Delta') \in \mathcal{A}^*_\mathcal{R}(\psi, W \cup \{x\})$. We first construct an extension $\hat{\mathfrak{s}}$ of $\mathfrak{s}$ to $\{x\}$ that is compatible with $\sim'$ and Δ'. This is straightforward if x is of sort $\mathtt{loc}$, as $\mathcal{L}$ is infinite: if $x \sim y$ for some $y \neq x$ then we let $\hat{\mathfrak{s}}(x) = \mathfrak{s}(y)$, otherwise, $\hat{\mathfrak{s}}(x)$ is some arbitrary chosen location not occurring in the image of $\mathfrak{s}$. If x is of sort $\mathtt{data}$, we assume that $\hat{\mathfrak{s}}$ does not exist and we derive a contradiction. The assumption entails that $(\mathfrak{s}, \emptyset)$ falsifies the formula $\psi = \exists x \bigwedge_{\rho \in \Delta'} \rho \wedge \bigwedge_{\rho \in \mathcal{A}^D_\sim(V') \setminus \Delta'} \neg \rho$. As $\mathcal{A}'$ is an abstraction, Δ is necessarily consistent w.r.t. $V', \sim'$, hence ψ admits a model $(\mathfrak{s}', \emptyset)$. By Assumption 3, there exists a formula ψ' that is equivalent to ψ and contains no quantifier, with $fv(\psi') \subseteq fv(\psi)$. By definition, ψ' only contains atoms in $\mathcal{A}^D_\sim(V)$. Since $\mathfrak{s}$ is compatible with $V, \sim, \Delta$, $(\mathfrak{s}, \emptyset)$ and $(\mathfrak{s}', \emptyset)$ coincide on all atoms in $\mathcal{A}^D_\sim(V)$, which entails that $(\mathfrak{s}, \emptyset) \models_\mathcal{R} \psi'$, i.e., $(\mathfrak{s}, \emptyset) \models_\mathcal{R} \psi$, which contradicts our assumption. Thus $\hat{\mathfrak{s}}$ necessarily exists. By the induction hypothesis, this entails that there exists a heap $\mathfrak{h}$ such that $(\hat{\mathfrak{s}}, \mathfrak{h}) \models_\mathcal{R} \phi'$ and $\mathcal{A}' \triangleright (\hat{\mathfrak{s}}, \mathfrak{h})$. Then $(\mathfrak{s}, \mathfrak{h}) \models_\mathcal{R} \phi$, and by Lemma 5.3 (2), $\mathcal{A} \triangleright (\mathfrak{s}, \mathfrak{h})$.
- Assume that $\phi = \phi_1 * \phi_2$, with $\mathcal{A}_i = (V_i, \sim_i, A_i, R_i, \Phi_i, \Delta_i) \in \mathcal{A}^*_\mathcal{R}(\phi_i, W)$ (for all $i \in \{1, 2\}$) and $\mathcal{A} = \mathcal{A}_1 * \mathcal{A}_2$. Note that since $\mathcal{A}_1 * \mathcal{A}_2$ is defined we must have $V_i = V$, $\sim_i = \sim$, $\Delta_i = \Delta$ and $A_1 \cap A_2 = \emptyset$. By the induction hypothesis, there exist

heaps $\mathfrak{h}_i$ (for all $i \in \{1,2\}$) such that $(\mathfrak{s}, \mathfrak{h}_i) \models_{\mathcal{R}} \phi_i$, and $\mathcal{A}_i \triangleright (\mathfrak{s}, \mathfrak{h}_i)$. By renaming locations if needed, we may assume that $\mathfrak{h}_1$ and $\mathfrak{h}_2$ share no location, other than those in the image of $\mathfrak{s}$. As $A_1 \cap A_2 = \emptyset$, and $A_i = \{x\downarrow_\sim \mid \mathfrak{s}(x) \in dom(\mathfrak{h}_i)\}$ (by Cond. 3 in Definition 4.6)), this entails that $\mathfrak{h}_1$ and $\mathfrak{h}_2$ are disjoint. By Lemma 5.3 (1) we get $\mathcal{A} \triangleright (\mathfrak{s}, \mathfrak{h}_1 \cup \mathfrak{h}_2)$.

- Assume that $\phi = \phi_1 \vee \phi_2$, with $\mathcal{A} \in \mathcal{A}^*_{\mathcal{R}}(\phi_i, W)$ (for some $i \in \{1,2\}$). By the induction hypothesis there exists a heap $\mathfrak{h}$ such that $(\mathfrak{s}, \mathfrak{h}) \models_{\mathcal{R}} \phi_i$ and $\mathcal{A} \triangleright (\mathfrak{s}, \mathfrak{h})$. This entails that $(\mathfrak{s}, \mathfrak{h}) \models_{\mathcal{R}} \phi$ hence the proof is completed.
- Assume that ϕ is a spatial predicate atom, $\phi \leadsto_{\mathcal{R}} \psi$, and $\mathcal{A} \in \mathcal{A}^*_{\mathcal{R}}(\psi, W)$. Then there exists a heap $\mathfrak{h}$ such that $(\mathfrak{s}, \mathfrak{h}) \models_{\mathcal{R}} \psi$ and $\mathcal{A} \triangleright (\mathfrak{s}, \mathfrak{h})$. This entails that $(\mathfrak{s}, \mathfrak{h}) \models_{\mathcal{R}} \phi$ thus the proof is completed.

$\mathcal{A}_{\mathcal{R}}(\phi, W) \subseteq \mathcal{A}^*_{\mathcal{R}}(\phi, W)$

Let $\mathcal{A} = (V, \sim, A, , R, \Phi, \Delta) \in \mathcal{A}_{\mathcal{R}}(\phi, V)$. By definition, there is a structure $(\mathfrak{s}, \mathfrak{h})$ such that $(\mathfrak{s}, \mathfrak{h}) \models_{\mathcal{R}} \phi$, $\mathcal{A} \triangleright (\mathfrak{s}, \mathfrak{h})$ and $dom(\mathfrak{s}) = V \cup C$. By definition of the semantics of inductive predicates, there is a (minimal) natural number $\kappa(\phi)$ such that $\phi \leadsto^{\kappa(\phi)}_{\mathcal{R}} \phi'$, ϕ' contains no spatial predicates and $(\mathfrak{s}, \mathfrak{h}) \models_{\mathcal{R}} \phi'$. We show that $\mathcal{A} \in \mathcal{A}^*_{\mathcal{R}}(\phi, V)$ by induction on the pair $(\kappa(\phi), |\phi|)$. We distinguish several cases according to the form of ϕ.

- If $\phi = \texttt{emp}$, then by definition $\mathfrak{h} = \emptyset$. As $\mathcal{A} \triangleright (\mathfrak{s}, \mathfrak{h})$, we get, by Definition 4.6, $A = R = \emptyset$, and $\Phi = \Phi_\sim(\mathfrak{s}, \emptyset) = \texttt{emp}$. Then $\mathcal{A} \in \mathcal{A}^*_{\mathcal{R}}(\phi, V)$ using the first rule in Fig. 1.
- If ϕ is a points-to atom $x_0 \mapsto (x_1, \ldots, x_n)$, then by definition $\mathfrak{h} = (\mathfrak{s}(x_0), \ldots, \mathfrak{s}(x_n))$. As $\mathcal{A} \triangleright (\mathfrak{s}, \mathfrak{h})$, $\mathfrak{s}$ is compatible with $\sim$, hence $\mathfrak{s}(x_i \downarrow_\sim) = \mathfrak{s}(x_i)$ (for all $i \in \{0, \ldots, n\}$). Thus $\mathfrak{h} = (\mathfrak{s}(x_0 \downarrow_\sim), \ldots, \mathfrak{s}(x_n \downarrow_\sim))$. Moreover, $A = \{x_0 \downarrow_\sim\}$ and $R = \{x_i \downarrow_\sim \mid i \in \{1, \ldots, n\}, \texttt{sort}(x_i) = \texttt{loc}\}$. By Definition 4.4, we have $\Phi_\sim(\mathfrak{s}, \mathfrak{h}) = x_0 \downarrow_\sim \mapsto (x_1 \downarrow_\sim, \ldots, x_n \downarrow_\sim)$, so that $\mathcal{A} \in \mathcal{A}^*_{\mathcal{R}}(\phi, W)$ using the second rule in Fig. 1.
- if ϕ is of the form $\psi \wedge x \simeq y$, then $(\mathfrak{s}, \mathfrak{h}) \models_{\mathcal{R}} \psi$ (with $\kappa(\psi) = \kappa(\phi)$ as no inductive rule applies on $x \simeq y$), $\{x, y\} \subseteq dom(\mathfrak{s})$ and $\mathfrak{s}(x) = \mathfrak{s}(y)$. Since $\mathcal{A} \triangleright (\mathfrak{s}, \mathfrak{h})$, this entails that (by Definition 4.6) that $x \sim y$. By the induction hypothesis, we deduce that $\mathcal{A} \in \mathcal{A}^*_{\mathcal{R}}(\phi, W)$ so that $\mathcal{A} \in \mathcal{A}^*_{\mathcal{R}}(\phi, W)$ using the third rule in Fig. 1.
- The proof is similar if $\phi = \psi \wedge \alpha$ and α is a disequation (using the fourth rule in Fig. 1) or a data literal (using the fifth or sixth rule depending on the sign of α).
- Assume that $\phi = \exists x \psi$. There exists a formula ϕ' with no inductive predicate such that $\phi \leadsto^{\kappa(\phi)}_{\mathcal{R}} \phi'$ and $(\mathfrak{s}, \mathfrak{h}) \models_{\mathcal{R}} \phi$. This entails that $\psi \leadsto^{\kappa(\phi)}_{\mathcal{R}} \psi'$ with $\phi' = \exists x \psi'$, and there exists an extension $\hat{\mathfrak{s}}$ of $\mathfrak{s}$ to $\{x\}$ such that $(\hat{\mathfrak{s}}, \mathfrak{h}) \models_{\mathcal{R}} \psi'$, hence $(\hat{\mathfrak{s}}, \mathfrak{h}) \models_{\mathcal{R}} \psi$. Let $\mathcal{A}'$ be the (necessarily unique, if the representative of each variable is fixed) abstraction such that $\mathcal{A}' \triangleright (\hat{\mathfrak{s}}, \mathfrak{h})$. By the induction hypothesis, we have $\mathcal{A}' \in \mathcal{A}^*_{\mathcal{R}}(\psi, W \cup \{x\})$, so that $\mathcal{A}' \setminus \{x\} \in \mathcal{A}^*_{\mathcal{R}}(\phi, W)$ using the seventh rule in Fig. 1. By Lemma 5.3 (2) we get $\mathcal{A}' \setminus \{x\} \triangleright (\mathfrak{s}, \mathfrak{h})$, and using the unicity of the abstraction of a structure, we deduce that $\mathcal{A} = \mathcal{A}' \setminus \{x\}$, hence $\mathcal{A} \in \mathcal{A}^*_{\mathcal{R}}(\phi, W)$.
- Assume that $\phi = \phi_1 * \phi_2$. Then there exist heaps $\mathfrak{h}_1, \mathfrak{h}_2$ such that $(\mathfrak{s}, \mathfrak{h}_i) \models_{\mathcal{R}} \phi_i$ (for all $i \in \{1,2\}$) and $\mathfrak{h} = \mathfrak{h}_1 * \mathfrak{h}_2$. It is clear that $\kappa(\phi) = \kappa(\phi_1) + \kappa(\phi_2)$, so that $\kappa(\phi_i) \leq \kappa(\phi)$ for all $i \in \{1,2\}$. Let $\mathcal{A}_i$ be be the abstraction of $(\mathfrak{s}, \mathfrak{h}_i)$. By the induction hypothesis, we have $\mathcal{A}_i \in \mathcal{A}^*_{\mathcal{R}}(\phi_i, W)$, so that $\mathcal{A}_1 * \mathcal{A}_2 \in \mathcal{A}^*_{\mathcal{R}}(\phi, W)$ using the eighth rule in

Fig. 1. Using Lemma 5.3 (1) and the unicity of the abstraction of $(\mathfrak{s}, \mathfrak{h})$, we deduce that $\mathcal{A} \in \mathcal{A}^*_{\mathcal{R}}(\phi, W)$.

- Assume that $\phi = \phi_1 \vee \phi_2$. Then $(\mathfrak{s}, \mathfrak{h}_i) \models_{\mathcal{R}} \phi_i$, for some $i \in \{1, 2\}$. We get $\mathcal{A} \in \mathcal{A}^*_{\mathcal{R}}(\phi_i, W)$, so that $\mathcal{A} \in \mathcal{A}^*_{\mathcal{R}}(\phi, W)$ by the penultimate rule in Fig. 1.
- Assume that ϕ is a spatial predicate atom. Then there exists a formula ψ such that $\phi \leadsto_{\mathcal{R}} \psi$, with $(\mathfrak{s}, \mathfrak{h}) \models_{\mathcal{R}} \psi$ and $\kappa(\psi) = \kappa(\phi) - 1$. This entails, by the induction hypothesis, that $\mathcal{A} \in \mathcal{A}^*_{\mathcal{R}}(\psi, W)$, so that $\mathcal{A} \in \mathcal{A}^*_{\mathcal{R}}(\phi, W)$, using the last rule in Fig. 1.

References

1. Berdine, J., Calcagno, C., O'Hearn, P.W.: A decidable fragment of separation logic. In: Lodaya, K., Mahajan, M. (eds.) FSTTCS 2004: Foundations of Software Technology and Theoretical Computer Science, pp. 97–109. Springer, Heidelberg (2004). https://doi.org/10.1007/978-3-540-30538-5_9
2. Brotherston, J., Fuhs, C., Pérez, J.A.N., Gorogiannis, N.: A decision procedure for satisfiability in separation logic with inductive predicates. In: CSL 2014, pp. 25:1–25:10. ACM (2014)
3. Calcagno, C., Yang, H., O'Hearn, P.W.: Computability and complexity results for a spatial assertion language for data structures. In: Hariharan, R., Vinay, V., Mukund, M. (eds.) FST TCS 2001: Foundations of Software Technology and Theoretical Computer Science, pp. 108–119. Springer, Heidelberg (2001). https://doi.org/10.1007/3-540-45294-X_10
4. Chen, T., Song, F., Wu, Z.: Tractability of separation logic with inductive definitions: beyond lists. In: Meyer, R., Nestmann, U. (eds.) CONCUR 2017, LIPIcs, vol. 85, pp. 37:1–37:17. Schloss Dagstuhl - Leibniz-Zentrum für Informatik (2017)
5. Comon, H., et al.: Tree automata techniques and applications (2007). http://www.grappa.univ-lille3.fr/tata. Release 12th October 2007
6. Cook, B., Haase, C., Ouaknine, J., Parkinson, M., Worrell, J.: Tractable reasoning in a fragment of separation logic. In: Katoen, J.-P., König, B. (eds.) CONCUR 2011—Concurrency Theory, pp. 235–249. Springer, Heidelberg (2011). https://doi.org/10.1007/978-3-642-23217-6_16
7. Demri, S., Galmiche, D., Larchey-Wendling, D., Méry, D.: Separation logic with one quantified variable. In: Hirsch, E.A., Kuznetsov, S.O., Pin, J.-É., Vereshchagin, N.K. (eds.) Computer Science - Theory and Applications. LNCS, vol. 476, pp. 125–138. Springer, Cham (2014). https://doi.org/10.1007/978-3-319-06686-8_10
8. Echenim, M., Iosif, R., Peltier, N.: Entailment checking in separation logic with inductive definitions is 2-exptime hard. In: LPAR 2020. EPiC Series in Computing, vol. 73, pp. 191–211. EasyChair (2020)
9. Echenim, M., Iosif, R., Peltier, N.: Decidable entailments in separation logic with inductive definitions: beyond establishment. In: CSL 2021, EPiC Series in Computing. EasyChair (2021)
10. Echenim, M., Iosif, R., Peltier, N.: Unifying decidable entailments in separation logic with inductive definitions. In: Platzer, A., Sutcliffe, G. (eds.) Automated Deduction. CADE 28. LNCS, vol. 12699, pp. 183–199. Springer, Cham (2021). https://doi.org/10.1007/978-3-030-79876-5_11
11. Echenim, M., Peltier, N.: A proof procedure for separation logic with inductive definitions and data. J. Autom. Reason. **67**(3), 30 (2023)
12. Enea, C., Lengál, O., Sighireanu, M., Vojnar, T.: Compositional entailment checking for a fragment of separation logic. Formal Methods Syst. Des. **51**(3), 575–607 (2017)

13. Enea, C., Sighireanu, M., Wu, Z.: On automated lemma generation for separation logic with inductive definitions. In: ATVA, vol. 2015, pp. 80–96 (2015)
14. Iosif, R., Rogalewicz, A., Simacek, J.: The tree width of separation logic with recursive definitions. In: Automated Deduction. CADE-24. LNCS, vol. 7898, pp. 21–38. Springer, Heidelberg (2013). https://doi.org/10.1007/978-3-642-38574-2_2
15. Iosif, R., Rogalewicz, A., Vojnar, T.: Deciding entailments in inductive separation logic with tree automata. In: Cassez, F., Raskin, J.-F. (eds.) Automated Technology for Verification and Analysis. LNCS, vol. 8837, pp. 201–218. Springer, Cham (2014). https://doi.org/10.1007/978-3-319-11936-6_15
16. Le, Q.L., Le, X.-B.D.: An efficient cyclic entailment procedure in a fragment of separation logic. In: Kupferman, O., Sobocinski, P. (eds.) Foundations of Software Science and Computation Structures: 26th International Conference, FoSSaCS 2023, ETAPS 2023. LNCS, vol. 13992, pp. 477–497. Springer, Cham (2023). https://doi.org/10.1007/978-3-031-30829-1_23
17. Matheja, C., Pagel, J., Zuleger, F.: A decision procedure for guarded separation logic complete entailment checking for separation logic with inductive definitions. ACM Trans. Comput. Log. **24**(1), 1:1–1:76 (2023)
18. O'Hearn, P.W., Pym, D.J.: The logic of bunched implications. Bull. Symb. Log. **5**(2), 215–244 (1999)
19. Reynolds, J.: Separation logic: a logic for shared mutable data structures. In: LICS 2002 (2002)

(In)consistency Operators on Quasi-Nelson Algebras

Umberto Rivieccio[1(✉)] and Aldo Figallo-Orellano[2]

[1] Universidad Nacional de Educación a Distancia, Madrid 28040, Spain
umberto@fsof.uned.es

[2] IME, University of São Paulo, São Paulo, Brazil

Abstract. We propose a preliminary study of (in)consistency operators on quasi-Nelson algebras, a variety that generalizes both Nelson and Heyting algebras; our aim is to pave the way for introducing logics of formal inconsistency (LFIs) in a non-necessarily involutive setting. We show how several results that were obtained for LFIs based on distributive involutive residuated lattices can be extended to quasi-Nelson algebras and their logic. We prove that the classes of algebras thus obtained are equationally axiomatizable, and provide a twist representation for them. Having obtained some insight on filters and congruences, we characterize the directly indecomposable members of these varieties, showing in particular that two of them are semisimple. Further logical developments and extensions of the present approach are also discussed.

Keywords: Quasi-Nelson · Logics of formal inconsistency · Twist-structures · Residuated lattices

1 Introduction

Logics of formal inconsistency (LFIs) are among the most well-known and time-honoured among the inconsistency-tolerant, or paraconsistent, logical systems. Formally, an LFI is usually presented as a standard (propositional) consequence relation ($\vdash$) over a language which includes a conjunction ($\wedge$), a disjunction ($\vee$), an implication ($\Rightarrow$), truth constants ($\bot, \top$) and a negation ($\sim$) that crucially fails to satisfy the *principle of explosion*: $\varphi \wedge {\sim}\varphi \vdash \bot$. To this language one usually adds a unary *consistency* connective $\circ$ that allows one to recover explosion in a more controlled way. The intended meaning of $\circ\varphi$ is "φ is consistent", and the following weaker principle is postulated:

$$\varphi \wedge {\sim}\varphi \wedge \circ\varphi \vdash \bot \tag{1}$$

(the *finite gentle principle of explosion* of [4, p. 50]), which can be informally read as follows: "if φ is consistent and contradictory, then φ explodes".

In addition (or alternatively) to $\circ$, a dual *inconsistency* connective $\bullet$ may be employed, and $\bullet\varphi$ is interpreted as "φ is inconsistent". One may require $\bullet$ to be

G. Metcalfe et al. (Eds.): WoLLIC 2024, LNCS 14672, pp. 175–192, 2024.
https://doi.org/10.1007/978-3-031-62687-6_12

the negation-dual of $\circ$ (perhaps even taking $\bullet\varphi := {\sim}\circ\varphi$ as a definition) or may impose independent postulates on both. For instance, dualizing (1), one obtains:

$$\vdash \varphi \vee {\sim}\varphi \vee \bullet\varphi \tag{2}$$

which is indeed a valid principle of some LFIs. Under certain assumptions on the negation, it is also easily verified that (1) and (2) are equivalent via the definition $\bullet\varphi := {\sim}\circ\varphi$ (or its dual $\circ\varphi := {\sim}\bullet\varphi$; more on this below).

The starting point of the present work is the paper [5], which investigates a family of LFIs that result from adding a consistency connective to certain extensions of the *Full Lambek Calculus with Exchange and Weakening* (FL_{ew}), the substructural logic determined by the class of *commutative integral bounded residuated lattices*. The approach of [5] is fairly general and modular, but it only applies to involutive logics (i.e. those that satisfy the double negation law, ${\sim}{\sim}\varphi \Rightarrow \varphi$): the present work is a first attempt at extending this research project beyond the involutive setting.

To any given class K of residuated lattices one can associate two logical consequences in a standard way, the *truth-preserving* logic $\vdash^{\top}_{\mathsf{K}}$ and the *order-preserving* $\vdash^{\leq}_{\mathsf{K}}$. Both share the same set of valid formulas, but in general they do not coincide: $\vdash^{\top}_{\mathsf{K}}$ is the stronger one and satisfies the principle of explosion, while $\vdash^{\leq}_{\mathsf{K}}$ typically does not. The latter thus provides a natural candidate for an LFI based on residuated lattices. Assuming an axiomatization for $\vdash^{\leq}_{\mathsf{K}}$ is given (see [1]), the paper [5] describes a method for axiomatizing the order-preserving logic $\vdash^{\leq}_{\mathsf{K}^{\circ}}$ obtained by endowing each algebra in K with a consistency operator $\circ$ satisfying (the algebraic counterpart of) the gentle principle of explosion (1).

The procedure sketched above may be applied to several well-known order-preserving companions of substructural logics, including Łukasiewicz logic, Nelson's constructive logic with strong negation [11] and nilpotent minimum logic [7]; in specific cases, further insight on the resulting logics is also gained thanks to the peculiar structure of prelinear algebras (for Łukasiewicz and nilpotent minimum) and the twist representation of Nelson algebras. The method of [5] does not apply, however, to many well-known logics based on residuated lattices—e.g. Hájek's basic logic, product logic and FL_{ew} itself—because the algebras in K are required to be distributive and involutive (see below for the relevant definitions). These limitations are due to technical reasons, and the main aim of the present paper is indeed to explore the possibility of relaxing them.

We are going to show how the results of [5] can be extended if we take K to be the variety of *quasi-Nelson algebras*, a recently-introduced generalization of Nelson (and Heyting) algebras. Such a setting seems to be particularly promising for potential future research: for, on the one hand, quasi-Nelson algebras are distributive but not necessarily involutive residuated lattices; on the other, they can be represented through a Nelson-type twist construction that affords powerful insight into their structure. We therefore propose the present study as a preliminary investigation on the possibilities of extending the approach described above to more general classes of algebras and logics. We shall focus on laying the algebraic foundations, and in particular on the question of how to define and represent (in)consistency operators on quasi-Nelson algebras; we stress, however, that all the results we will establish have a straightforward logical interpretation in the setting of logics extending FL_{ew} (see Sect. 4).

The paper is organized as follows. In Sect. 2 we recall preliminary definitions and results on quasi-Nelson logic and its algebraic counterpart, the variety QN of quasi-Nelson algebras. In Sect. 3 we study inconsistency operators on quasi-Nelson algebras. The choice of focusing on inconsistency (rather than consistency) operators is motivated by the technical observation that, in the absence of involutivity, it is easier to work with the quasi-equational defining properties of inconsistency operators (Definitions 2 and 3) than with those of consistency operators (see Sect. 4.1). The difference, as we shall see, cannot be appreciated in an involutive setting such as that of [5], where consistency and inconsistency operators are perfect duals of one another. Following [5], we consider three possible definitions for an inconsistency operator (Definitions 2 and 3), which give rise to three classes of expanded quasi-Nelson algebras. We prove that all three are equationally definable (Theorems 1 and 3), thus also settling an issue left open in [5]. We extend the twist representation to quasi-Nelson algebras endowed with inconsistency operators (Theorem 4) and use it to obtain information on the congruences and filters of these new classes of algebras; we also see how the insight thus gained can improve our understanding of subvarieties. In the concluding Sect. 4 we sketch a plan for future work, focusing in particular on three directions: how to introduce consistency operators on quasi-Nelson algebras (Sect. 4.1); the logical translation of the algebraic results established so far (Sect. 4.2); and the future study of (in)consistency operators in wider settings (Sect. 4.3). To improve readability and respect space limitations, all proofs are included in the Appendix.

2 Quasi-Nelson Logic and Algebras

The class of quasi-Nelson algebras (QN) was introduced in [12] and further investigated in a number of subsequent publications [8,10,13–15]. Formally, QN can be viewed either as a subvariety of residuated lattices or as a generalization of both Nelson algebras (the algebraic counterpart of Nelson's logic) and Heyting algebras. Taking the former approach, we may define a quasi-Nelson algebra as a *commutative, integral and bounded residuated lattice*[1] $\mathbf{A} = \langle A; \wedge, \vee, *, \Rightarrow, 0, 1\rangle$ that further satisfies the *Nelson equation*:

$$(x \Rightarrow (x \Rightarrow y)) \wedge ({\sim} y \Rightarrow ({\sim} y \Rightarrow {\sim} x)) \leq x \Rightarrow y \qquad \text{(Nelson)}$$

where ${\sim} x := x \Rightarrow 0$. While (Nelson) entails that quasi-Nelson algebras satisfy distributivity ($x \wedge (y \vee z) = (x \wedge y) \vee (x \wedge z)$) and 3-potency ($x^3 = x^2$), they are not involutive, i.e. they need not satisfy the double negation equation ${\sim}{\sim} x = x$. In fact, the involutive members of QN are precisely the Nelson algebras, and the idempotent ones (those satisfying $x^2 = x$) are precisely the Heyting algebras.

[1] See [9] for all the unexplained terminology of universal algebra, substructural logics and (residuated) lattice theory.

Quasi-Nelson logic, the logical counterpart of QN, may be obtained by adding the *Nelson axiom* to FL_{ew} (see [9]):

$$((\varphi \Rightarrow (\varphi \Rightarrow \psi)) \wedge (\sim\psi \Rightarrow (\sim\psi \Rightarrow \sim\varphi))) \Rightarrow (\varphi \Rightarrow \psi).$$

The interest in quasi-Nelson algebras/logic is manyfold, and can be motivated from a number of perspectives (e.g. constructive logics, order theory, and universal algebra; see the above-mentioned papers for further details). In the present context we are mainly interested in QN as a first step in the extension of the approach of [5] to LFIs beyond the involutive setting.

A prominent feature of quasi-Nelson algebras is the twist representation, which allows one to construct each algebra $\mathbf{A} \in$ QN as a special binary product of a *nuclear Heyting algebra*, i.e. a Heyting algebra $\langle H; \wedge, \vee, \rightarrow, \neg, 0, 1\rangle$ endowed with a unary *nucleus* operator $\Box$ satisfying $\Box 0 = 0$ and $x \rightarrow \Box y = \Box x \rightarrow \Box y$ (see e.g. [16] for further background on nuclei). The details of the construction are given in Definition 1 below. Recall that the set $D(\mathbf{H})$ of *dense elements* on a (nuclear) Heyting algebra $\mathbf{H}$ is given by $D(\mathbf{H}) := \{a \in H : \neg a = 0\}$.

Definition 1. *Let* $\mathbf{H} = \langle H; \wedge, \vee, \rightarrow, \neg, \Box, 0, 1\rangle$ *be a nuclear Heyting algebra, and let* $\nabla \subseteq H$ *be a lattice filter of* $\mathbf{H}$ *such that* $D(\mathbf{H}) \subseteq \nabla$*. Define the* quasi-Nelson twist-algebra $Tw(\mathbf{H}, \nabla) = \langle A; \wedge, \vee, *, \Rightarrow, 0, 1\rangle$ *with universe:*

$$A := \{\langle a_1, a_2\rangle \in H \times H : a_2 = \Box a_2,\ a_1 \vee a_2 \in \nabla,\ a_1 \wedge a_2 = 0\}$$

and operations given, for all $\langle a_1, a_2\rangle, \langle b_1, b_2\rangle \in H \times H$, *by:*

$$\begin{aligned}
1 &:= \langle 1, 0\rangle \\
0 &:= \langle 0, 1\rangle \\
\langle a_1, a_2\rangle * \langle b_1, b_2\rangle &:= \langle a_1 \wedge b_1, (a_1 \rightarrow b_2) \wedge (b_1 \rightarrow a_2)\rangle \\
\langle a_1, a_2\rangle \wedge \langle b_1, b_2\rangle &:= \langle a_1 \wedge b_1, \Box(a_2 \vee b_2)\rangle \\
\langle a_1, a_2\rangle \vee \langle b_1, b_2\rangle &:= \langle a_1 \vee b_1, a_2 \wedge b_2\rangle \\
\langle a_1, a_2\rangle \Rightarrow \langle b_1, b_2\rangle &:= \langle (a_1 \rightarrow b_1) \wedge (b_2 \rightarrow a_2), \Box a_1 \wedge b_2\rangle.
\end{aligned}$$

The negation (defined as $\sim x := x \Rightarrow 0$) is given by $\sim\langle a_1, a_2\rangle = \langle a_2, \Box a_1\rangle$. Thus, if the nucleus $\Box$ is not the identity map (as an example, take $\Box x := \neg\neg x$) then $Tw(\mathbf{H}, \nabla)$ is not involutive. Each twist-algebra $Tw(\mathbf{H}, \nabla)$ belongs to QN and, conversely, the twist representation result states that *every quasi-Nelson algebra can be constructed according to Definition* 1 (see e.g. [13,16] for further details).

Before we proceed, we need to introduce a notion that plays a prominent role in the study of LFIs based on residuated lattices. The *Boolean elements* $B(\mathbf{A})$ of a bounded integral residuated lattice $\mathbf{A}$ may be defined in the following three alternative ways: (i) $B(\mathbf{A}) := \{a \in A : \exists b \in A \text{ s.t. } a \vee b = 1, a \wedge b = 0\}$; (ii) $B(\mathbf{A}) := \{a \in A : a \vee \sim a = 1\}$; (iii) $B(\mathbf{A}) := \{a \in A : a \wedge \sim a = 0\}$. Our official definition will be (ii), which is equivalent to (i), but in practice easier to work with. On the other hand, in a non-involutive setting (iii) gives a weaker notion: this is essentially because, on every residuated lattice, $a \vee \sim a = 1$ entails

$a \wedge {\sim} a = 0$, but not the other way round. $B(\mathbf{A})$ is the universe of a sublattice of $\mathbf{A}$; note that, on a quasi-Nelson twist-algebra $Tw(\mathbf{H}, \nabla)$, the Boolean elements are precisely those of the form $\langle a, \neg a \rangle$ for some $a \in B(\mathbf{H})$.

3 Inconsistency Operators

Drawing inspiration from [5], we consider three possible definitions for an inconsistency operator. As mentioned earlier, the informal reading of $\bullet a$ is "the value a is inconsistent", and we may further allow this proposition to assume only crisp (i.e. Boolean) values or not. In the involutive case, our approach is equivalent to that of [5], for the consistency operator can then be recovered as $\circ x := {\sim} \bullet x$.

3.1 The min and Bmin Operators

Definition 2. *A* min-inconsistency operator *on a quasi-Nelson algebra* $\mathbf{A}$ *is a unary operator* $\bullet$ *that satisfies the following quasi-equations:*

$$x \vee {\sim} x \vee y = 1 \qquad \textit{if and only if} \qquad \bullet x \leq y.$$

A Bmin-inconsistency operator *is a* min-*inconsistency operator that further satisfies the equation* $\bullet x \vee {\sim} \bullet x = 1$ *(ensuring that* $\bullet a$ *is a Boolean element).*

We denote by $\mathsf{QN}^{\bullet}$ (respectively, $\mathsf{QN}^{\bullet}_{\mathsf{Bm}}$) the class of all algebras $\langle \mathbf{A}, \bullet \rangle$ such that $\mathbf{A} \in \mathsf{QN}$ and $\bullet$ is a min- (resp., a Bmin-)inconsistency operator on $\mathbf{A}$. From an order-theoretic point of view, Definition 2 is precisely saying that, for each $a \in A$, the element $\bullet a$ is the dual pseudo-complement (see Definition 4) of $a \vee {\sim} a$. Such an element is unique if it exists, for one has:

$$\bullet\, a = \min\{b \in A : a \vee {\sim} a \vee b = 1\}. \tag{3}$$

Existence can be guaranteed on a finite $\mathbf{A} \in \mathsf{QN}$ (or, more generally, any algebra having a complete and completely distributive lattice reduct), for one can let:

$$\bullet\, a = \bigwedge \{b \in A : a \vee {\sim} a \vee b = 1\}. \tag{4}$$

However, the element $\bullet a$ given by (4) may fail to satisfy $\bullet a \vee {\sim} \bullet a = 1$, so a Bmin-inconsistency operator may not be definable, even when $\mathbf{A}$ is finite (see Example 2).

Example 1. Let $\mathbf{A} \in \mathsf{QN}$ be a subdirectly irreducible quasi-Nelson algebra. Defining $\bullet 0 = \bullet 1 = 0$ and $\bullet a = 1$ for $a \notin \{0, 1\}$, one obtains a min-inconsistency (in fact, a Bmin-inconsistency) operator. To see this, recall from [9, p. 202] that $\mathbf{A}$ has a unique co-atom, say $c \in A$. Then, for every element $0 < a \leq c$, we have ${\sim} a \leq c$ as well. For, otherwise, from ${\sim} a = 1$ we would have $a \leq {\sim}{\sim} a = {\sim} 1 = 0$, against the assumption that $0 < a$. Thus $a \vee {\sim} a \leq c$, which gives us $\bullet a = 1$ by (3). By the same token, for every $\langle \mathbf{A}, \bullet \rangle \in \mathsf{QN}^{\bullet}$ s.t. $\mathbf{A}$ is a subdirectly irreducible quasi-Nelson algebra, the $\bullet$ operator must be defined as indicated above. This example will also be used to show that both classes $\mathsf{QN}^{\bullet}$ and $\mathsf{QN}^{\bullet}_{\mathsf{Bm}}$ extend QN conservatively (see Theorem 2).

Proposition 1. *Let* $\langle \mathbf{A}, \bullet \rangle \in \mathsf{QN}^\bullet$ *and* $a, b \in A$.

(i) $a \in B(\mathbf{A})$ *if and only if* $\bullet a = 0$ *(in particular,* $\bullet 1 = \bullet 0 = 0$*).*
(ii) $\bullet a = \bullet(a \vee {\sim} a)$.
(iii) $\bullet {\sim} a = \bullet {\sim}{\sim} a$.
(iv) $a \vee {\sim} a \vee \bullet a = 1$.
(v) $\bullet a = \bullet a * \bullet a$.
(vi) $\bullet a \leq b \vee \bullet(a \vee {\sim} a \vee b)$.

Item (i) above suggests that the behaviour of $\bullet$ on each algebra $\mathbf{A} \in \mathsf{QN}$ may be read as a measure of "how Boolean" $\mathbf{A}$ is: indeed, $\mathbf{A}$ is a Boolean algebra if and only if $\bullet a = 0$ for all $a \in A$. Note that, in contrast to the involutive case of [5], it may in general happen that $\bullet {\sim} a \neq \bullet a \neq \bullet(a \wedge {\sim} a)$. This will be clarified by the twist representation for the algebras in $\mathsf{QN}^\bullet$ (see Proposition 5).

Theorem 1. *The conditions in Definition 2 are equivalent to the following equations:*

(i) $\bullet x \leq y \vee \bullet(x \vee {\sim} x \vee y)$.
(ii) $x \vee {\sim} x \vee \bullet x = 1$.
(iii) $\bullet 1 = 0$.

Hence, $\mathsf{QN}^\bullet$ and $\mathsf{QN}^\bullet_{\mathsf{Bm}}$ are varieties. Note that Theorem 1 applies to residuated lattices in general, thereby settling an issue that was left open in [5]. The following result establishes that both $\mathsf{QN}^\bullet$ and $\mathsf{QN}^\bullet_{\mathsf{Bm}}$ extend QN conservatively.

Theorem 2. *The variety* QN *of quasi-Nelson algebras is precisely the class of* $\{\bullet\}$*-free subreducts of* $\mathsf{QN}^\bullet_{\mathsf{Bm}}$ *(and,* a fortiori*, also of* $\mathsf{QN}^\bullet$*).*

3.2 The minB Operator

Definition 3. *A unary operator* $\bullet_{\mathsf{B}}$ *on a quasi-Nelson algebra* $\mathbf{A}$ *is a* minB-inconsistency operator *if the following (quasi-)equations are satisfied:*

(i) $x \vee {\sim} x \vee \bullet_{\mathsf{B}} x = 1$.
(ii) $\bullet_{\mathsf{B}} x \vee {\sim} \bullet_{\mathsf{B}} x = 1$.
(iii) $x \vee {\sim} x \vee y = 1$ *and* $y \vee {\sim} y = 1$ *imply* $\bullet_{\mathsf{B}} x \leq y$.

Denote by $\mathsf{QN}^\bullet_{\mathsf{mB}}$ the class of algebras $\langle \mathbf{A}, \bullet_{\mathsf{B}} \rangle$ such that $\mathbf{A} \in \mathsf{QN}$ and $\bullet_{\mathsf{B}}$ is a minB-inconsistency operator on $\mathbf{A}$. Every Bmin-inconsistency operator (Definition 2) is a minB-inconsistency operator, so $\mathsf{QN}^\bullet_{\mathsf{Bm}} = \mathsf{QN}^\bullet \cap \mathsf{QN}^\bullet_{\mathsf{mB}}$, implying that Theorem 2 applies to $\mathsf{QN}^\bullet_{\mathsf{mB}}$ as well. But neither $\mathsf{QN}^\bullet$ nor $\mathsf{QN}^\bullet_{\mathsf{mB}}$ is contained in the other (see Example 2). A minB-inconsistency operator is unique, if it exists, for we have:

$$\bullet_{\mathsf{B}}\, a = \min\{b \in B(\mathbf{A}) : a \vee {\sim} a \vee b = 1\}. \tag{5}$$

Similarly to the case of min-operators, if the sublattice of Boolean elements $B(\mathbf{A})$ is complete, then the operator $\bullet_{\mathsf{B}}$ is definable on $\mathbf{A}$ by:

$$\bullet_{\mathsf{B}}\, a := \bigwedge \{b \in B(\mathbf{A}) : a \vee {\sim} a \vee b = 1\}.$$

The following example should help further clarify the relationships among the classes of algebras under consideration.

Example 2. [5, Fig. 2, p. 1236] depicts an eight-element *nilpotent minimum algebra* (let us call it $\mathbf{A}_8$) on which two different consistency operators $\circ$ and $\circ_{\mathsf{B}}$ are definable (note that there is a mistake in the table of the monoid operation: it should have $f * f = f$ instead of $f * f = a$). Nilpotent minimum algebras are a subvariety of Nelson algebras (see e.g. [8]), so $\mathbf{A}_8 \in \mathsf{QN}$. Dualizing the definitions (i.e. letting $\bullet x := {\sim}\circ x$ and $\bullet_{\mathsf{B}} x := {\sim}\circ_{\mathsf{B}} x$), we can endow $\mathbf{A}_8$ with a (necessarily unique) min-inconsistency operator $\bullet$ and an (also unique) minB-inconsistency operator $\bullet_{\mathsf{B}}$ which do not coincide. Thus $\langle \mathbf{A}_8, \bullet \rangle \in \mathsf{QN}^{\bullet} - \mathsf{QN}^{\bullet}_{\mathsf{mB}}$ and $\langle \mathbf{A}_8, \bullet_{\mathsf{B}} \rangle \in \mathsf{QN}^{\bullet}_{\mathsf{mB}} - \mathsf{QN}^{\bullet}$. Since $\langle \mathbf{A}_8, \bullet \rangle \notin \mathsf{QN}^{\bullet}_{\mathsf{Bm}}$, we also see that it is not possible to define a Bmin-inconsistency operator on $\mathbf{A}_8$.

The counterpart of Proposition 1 for minB-inconsistency operators is the following:

Proposition 2. *Let $\langle \mathbf{A}, \bullet \rangle \in \mathsf{QN}^{\bullet}_{\mathsf{mB}}$ and $a, b \in A$.*

(i) $a \in B(\mathbf{A})$ *if and only if* $\bullet_{\mathsf{B}} a = 0$ *(thus* $\bullet_{\mathsf{B}} 1 = \bullet_{\mathsf{B}} 0 = 0$ *and* $\bullet_{\mathsf{B}} \bullet_{\mathsf{B}} a = 0$*).*
(ii) $\bullet_{\mathsf{B}} a = \bullet_{\mathsf{B}}(a \vee {\sim} a) = {\sim}{\sim} \bullet_{\mathsf{B}} a$.
(iii) $\bullet_{\mathsf{B}} {\sim} a = \bullet_{\mathsf{B}} {\sim}{\sim} a$.
(iv) $\bullet_{\mathsf{B}} a \vee b \vee \bullet_{\mathsf{B}} b \in B(\mathbf{A})$.
(v) $\bullet_{\mathsf{B}} a \leq b \vee \bullet_{\mathsf{B}}(b \vee {\sim} b) \vee \bullet_{\mathsf{B}}(a \vee {\sim} a \vee b)$.

Also in this case the class of algebras introduced in Definition 3 is equational, thus settling the corresponding open issue from [5].

Theorem 3. *The conditions in Definition 3 are equivalent to the following equations:*

(i) $x \vee {\sim} x \vee \bullet_{\mathsf{B}} x = 1$.
(ii) $\bullet_{\mathsf{B}} x \vee {\sim} \bullet_{\mathsf{B}} x = 1$.
(iii) $\bullet_{\mathsf{B}} 1 = 0$.
(iv) $\bullet_{\mathsf{B}} x \leq y \vee \bullet_{\mathsf{B}}(y \vee {\sim} y) \vee \bullet_{\mathsf{B}}(x \vee {\sim} x \vee y)$.

Hence, $\mathsf{QN}^{\bullet}_{\mathsf{mB}}$ *is a variety.*

3.3 Twist Representation

We now proceed to extend the twist representation of quasi-Nelson algebras given in Sect. 2 to algebras in $\mathsf{QN}^{\bullet}$. This will provide us with further insight into their structure and a useful tool for establishing arithmetical properties.

Definition 4. *Given a (nuclear) Heyting algebra* $\mathbf{H}$*, we shall denote by* $\neg$ *the unary operation that realizes the* dual pseudo-complement (dpc) *given (whenever it exists) by* $\neg a = \min\{b \in H : a \vee b = 1\}$ *for all* $a \in H$.

Proposition 3. *Let* $\mathbf{A} = Tw(\mathbf{H}, \nabla)$ *be a twist-algebra over a nuclear Heyting algebra* $\mathbf{H}$*. Assume the element* $\neg\, b$ *exists for all* $b \in \nabla$*. Then, defining* $\bullet\langle a_1, a_2 \rangle := \langle \neg(a_1 \vee a_2), \neg\neg(a_1 \vee a_2) \rangle$ *for all* $\langle a_1, a_2 \rangle \in A$*, we have* $\langle \mathbf{A}, \bullet \rangle \in \mathsf{QN}^{\bullet}$.

Proposition 4. *Let* $\mathbf{A} = Tw(\mathbf{H}, \nabla) \in \mathsf{QN}$ *be endowed with an operation* $\bullet$ *such that* $\langle \mathbf{A}, \bullet \rangle \in \mathsf{QN}^{\bullet}$. *Then the element* $\ulcorner b$ *exists for all* $b \in \nabla$, *and* $\bullet\langle a_1, a_2\rangle := \langle \ulcorner(a_1 \vee a_2), \neg\ulcorner(a_1 \vee a_2)\rangle$ *for all* $\langle a_1, a_2\rangle \in A$.

Propositions 3 and 4 give us the announced representation result.

Theorem 4. *Every quasi-Nelson algebra endowed with a* min-*inconsistency operator* $\bullet$ *can be constructed as* $Tw(\mathbf{H}, \nabla)$ *in accordance with Proposition 3.*

Theorem 4 can be used to establish an equivalence between an algebraic category based on $\mathsf{QN}^{\bullet}$ and a suitably defined category having as objects tuples of type $\langle \mathbf{H}, \nabla \rangle$, as done in [6] for Nelson algebras. In turn, on such an equivalence one might build a "two-sorted" topological duality for $\mathsf{QN}^{\bullet}$ (see [17]).

The twist representation also provides us with an easy way to establish arithmetical properties of $\mathsf{QN}^{\bullet}$ and its subvarieties. For instance, it is easy to verify that the following (in)equalities are satisfied on twist-algebras – the two inequalities being, in general, strict (cf. Proposition 1): $\bullet{\sim}(x \wedge {\sim}x) = \bullet(x \wedge {\sim}x) \leq \bullet{\sim}x \leq \bullet x = \bullet x * \bullet x$. As another application, in the next proposition we consider, from the perspective of twist-algebras, a few (in)equalities (corresponding to subvarieties of $\mathsf{QN}^{\bullet}$) that play a prominent role in the study of logics of formal inconsistency.

Proposition 5. *Let* $\langle \mathbf{A} = Tw(\mathbf{H}, \nabla), \bullet \rangle \in \mathsf{QN}^{\bullet}$, *let* $a \in \nabla$ *and* $\langle b_1, b_2\rangle \in A$.

(i) $\bullet x \leq \bullet(x \wedge {\sim}x)$ *holds iff* $\ulcorner a = \ulcorner \Box a$.
(ii) $\bullet{\sim}x \leq \bullet(x \wedge {\sim}x)$ *holds iff* $\Box b_1 \vee b_2 \vee \ulcorner\Box(b_1 \vee b_2) = 1$.
(iii) $\bullet x \leq \bullet{\sim}x$ *holds iff* $b_1 \vee b_2 \vee \ulcorner(\Box b_1 \vee b_2) = 1$.
(iv) $x \wedge \bullet x = 0$ *holds iff* $\nabla = \{1\}$ *(and* $\mathbf{H}$ *is a Boolean algebra).*
(v) ${\sim}x \wedge \bullet x = 0$ *holds iff* $\Box a = \Box b_1 \vee \neg b_1 = 1$.
(vi) $\bullet x \vee {\sim}\bullet x = 1$ *holds iff* $\ulcorner a \vee \neg\ulcorner a = 1$.

3.4 Filters and Congruences

In this section we take a look at filters and congruences on quasi-Nelson algebras endowed with inconsistency operators; here, too, we shall profit from the insight gained with the twist representation.

An *implicative filter* of a residuated lattice $\mathbf{A}$ is a lattice filter $F \subseteq A$ that is further closed under the monoid operation, i.e., $a * b \in F$ whenever $a, b \in F$. Implicative filters are in one-to-one correspondence with congruences on commutative residuated lattices [9, Thm 3.47] via the maps defined as follows. To an implicative filter $F \subseteq A$ one associates the congruence $\theta_F := \{\langle a, b\rangle \in A \times A : a \Rightarrow b, b \Rightarrow a \in F\}$, and to a congruence $\theta \in \mathrm{Con}(\mathbf{A})$ one associates the implicative filter $1/\theta$.

The above correspondence applies to quasi-Nelson algebras as well. Given $\langle \mathbf{A}, \bullet \rangle \in \mathsf{QN}^{\bullet}$ and a congruence $\theta \in \mathrm{Con}(\mathbf{A}, \bullet)$, —that is, θ is compatible with the operations of $\mathbf{A}$ and also with the $\bullet$ operator—the associated implicative filter $1/\theta$ will satisfy the following: if $a \Rightarrow b, b \Rightarrow a \in 1/\theta$, then $\bullet a \Rightarrow \bullet b \in 1/\theta$.

We say that an implicative filter F closed under this rule is a $\bullet$-*filter* (cf. the definition of $\circ$-filter in [5, Fig. 2, p. 1236], and note that we do not need to impose condition (F2), because we know to be dealing with varieties). It is easy to verify that each $\bullet$-filter F is also closed under the following rule: if $a \in F$, then $\sim \bullet a \in F$ (in fact, Corollary 1 entails that this rule is not only necessary but also sufficient for defining $\bullet$-filters). Indeed, from $a \in F$ we have $1 \Rightarrow a = a \in F$ and $a \Rightarrow 1 = 1 \in F$, so we immediately obtain $\bullet a \Rightarrow \bullet 1 = \bullet a \Rightarrow 0 = \sim \bullet a \in F$.

The isomorphism between implicative filters and congruences of each $\mathbf{A} \in \mathsf{QN}$ is preserved when we consider an algebra $\langle \mathbf{A}, \bullet \rangle \in \mathsf{QN}^\bullet$ and its $\bullet$-filters: indeed, it is easy to verify that θ_F is compatible with $\bullet$ if (and only if) F is a $\bullet$-filter. This entails, in particular, that any algebra $\langle \mathbf{A}, \bullet \rangle$ constructed as in Example 1 is simple (i.e. has exactly two congruences). Indeed, if $\langle \mathbf{A}, \bullet \rangle$ had a non-trivial congruence $Id_A \neq \theta \neq A \times A$, then $1/\theta$ would be a non-trivial $\bullet$-filter. But there are no $\bullet$-filters on $\mathbf{A}$ except $\{1\}$ and A itself, for $a \in 1/\theta$ implies $\sim \bullet a = \sim 1 = 0 \in 1/\theta$ whenever $0 \neq a \neq 1$. A similar reasoning shows that the algebra defined in Example 2 (endowed either with $\bullet$ or with $\bullet_{\mathsf{B}}$) is also simple. Indeed, any algebra $\langle \mathbf{A}, \bullet \rangle$ will be simple as long as $\mathbf{A}$ is subdirectly irreducible, and the algebra in Example 2 witnesses that the converse is not true: $\langle \mathbf{A}_8, \bullet \rangle$ is simple even though $\mathbf{A}_8$ is not a subdirectly irreducible residuated lattice.

$\bullet$-filters can be characterized via the twist construction, building on a description of implicative filters on quasi-Nelson twist-algebras [16, Prop. 4.1].

Proposition 6. *A subset* $G \subseteq A$ *of* $\mathbf{A} = Tw(\mathbf{H}, \nabla) \in \mathsf{QN}$ *is an implicative filter if and only if* $G = (F \times H) \cap A$*, where* F *is a lattice filter of* $\mathbf{H}$.

Consider an algebra $\langle \mathbf{A} = Tw(\mathbf{H}, \nabla), \bullet \rangle \in \mathsf{QN}^\bullet$. By the preceding result, every $\bullet$-filter $G \subseteq A$ has the shape $G = (F \times H) \cap A$, with F a lattice filter of $\mathbf{H}$. In such a case, moreover, one will have $\neg \ulcorner a \in F$ whenever $a \in \nabla \cap F$. This property appears to be a relativized version of the *normality* considered in [18]: the latter, indeed, corresponds precisely to the special case where $F \subseteq \nabla$. This consideration suggests the following definition.

Definition 5. *Let* $\mathbf{H}$ *be a (nuclear) Heyting algebra and le* $\nabla \subseteq H$ *be a filter such that* $\ulcorner a$ *exists for all* $a \in \nabla$*. Given a lattice filter* $F \subseteq H$*, we say that* F *is* ∇-normal *if* $\neg \ulcorner a \in F$ *whenever* $a \in \nabla \cap F$.

The family of all ∇-normal filters (for a fixed ∇) is closed under arbitrary intersections, and so forms a complete lattice. Two alternative characterizations of ∇-normality are given in the following lemma.

Lemma 1. *Let* $\mathbf{H}$ *be a Heyting algebra and let* $\nabla, F \subseteq H$ *be lattice filters. Assuming* $\ulcorner a$ *exists for all* $a \in \nabla$*, the following are equivalent:*

(i) F *is* ∇*-normal.*
(ii) For all $a, b \in \nabla$*, if* $a \to b \in F$*, then* $\ulcorner b \to \ulcorner a \in F$.
(iii) For all $a, b \in \nabla$*, if* $a \to b, b \to a \in F$*, then* $\ulcorner a \to \ulcorner b \in F$.

Having singled out the notion of ∇-normality allows us to smoothly extend Proposition 6 as follows.

Proposition 7. *A subset $G \subseteq A$ of an algebra $\langle \mathbf{A} = Tw(\mathbf{H}, \nabla), \bullet \rangle \in \mathsf{QN}^\bullet$ is a $\bullet$-filter if and only if $G = (F \times H) \cap A$, where F is a ∇-normal filter of $\mathbf{H}$.*

The preceding result implicitly contains a characterization of the congruences on each algebra $\langle \mathbf{A} = Tw(\mathbf{H}, \nabla), \bullet \rangle \in \mathsf{QN}^\bullet$ in terms of Con($\mathbf{H}$), and suggests that further insight on $\mathsf{QN}^\bullet$ might be obtained by importing results on normal filters (e.g. Thm. 4.3, Cor. 4.5) from [18]. Before explaining this, let us note that Proposition 7 entails (Lemmas 4.7, 4.8 and) Theorem 4.9 from [5]. Indeed, phrased in our notation, the latter states that, given $\langle \mathbf{A} = Tw(\mathbf{H}, \nabla), \bullet \rangle \in \mathsf{QN}^\bullet$, we have that:

(i) $G := (\nabla \times H) \cap A$ is a proper $\bullet$-filter $\mathbf{A}$ iff ∇ is proper and normal;
(ii) if ∇ is the minimal filter of $\mathbf{H}$, then G is the minimal filter of $\mathbf{A}$.

The only mismatch is that the normality mentioned in (i) is the standard notion from [18]; but normality and ∇-normality here coincide, because $F = \nabla$. The following characterization of $\bullet$-filters also follows from Proposition 7.

Corollary 1. *Let $\langle \mathbf{A} = Tw(\mathbf{H}, \nabla), \bullet \rangle \in \mathsf{QN}^\bullet$ and let $G \subseteq A$ be an implicative filter of $\mathbf{A}$. The following are equivalent:*

(i) G is a $\bullet$-filter.
(ii) $\sim \bullet a \in G$ whenever $a \in G$.

Unlike some of the previous propositions, the proof of Corollary 1 appears to rely in an essential way on the twist representation; we therefore do not know whether the result applies to more general classes of residuated lattices, or even to the involutive ones considered in [5]. While the twist representation does not seem essential to the following result, it enables us to provide a straightforward proof (cf. [5, Thm. 3.8]).

Theorem 5. *An algebra $\langle \mathbf{A}, \bullet \rangle \in \mathsf{QN}^\bullet$ is directly indecomposable if and only if $B(\mathbf{A}) = \{0, 1\}$. In consequence, we also have that $B(\mathbf{A}) = \{0, 1\}$ whenever $\langle \mathbf{A}, \bullet \rangle$ is subdirectly irreducible.*

In the case of a quasi-Nelson algebra $\mathbf{A} = Tw(\mathbf{H}, \nabla)$, we know that the lattice of congruences Con($\mathbf{A}$) is isomorphic to the lattice $\mathrm{Con}\langle H; \wedge, \vee, \rightarrow, \neg, 0, 1 \rangle$ of congruences of $\mathbf{H}$ viewed simply as a Heyting algebra (the nucleus $\Box$ does not alter the congruences of the underlying Heyting algebra reduct). This result, proved in [13, Prop. 8], may also be obtained as a corollary of Proposition 6, and we may employ Proposition 7 to obtain a similar result about $\mathrm{Con}\langle \mathbf{A}, \bullet \rangle$.

As observed earlier, for each algebra $\langle \mathbf{A} = Tw(\mathbf{H}, \nabla), \bullet \rangle \in \mathsf{QN}^\bullet$, we have that $\mathrm{Con}\langle \mathbf{A} = Tw(\mathbf{H}, \nabla), \bullet \rangle$ is isomorphic to the lattice of $\bullet$-filters on $\langle \mathbf{A}, \bullet \rangle$, which is isomorphic (by Proposition 7) to the lattice of ∇-normal filters of $\mathbf{H}$. These, in turn, are easily seen to be in one-to-one correspondence with the Heyting algebra congruences of $\mathbf{H}$ that satisfy the following property: for all $a, b \in \nabla$ such that $\langle a, b \rangle \in \theta$, we have $\langle \ulcorner a, \ulcorner b \rangle \in \theta$. This result may not appear very informative, but one needs to keep in mind that the role of $\mathbf{H}$ in the representation given in Theorem 4 is not exactly that of a standard algebra, for the dual pseudo-complement operation is only required to be defined on the elements of ∇. Obviously, when $\nabla = H$, we recover the well-known correspondence between the congruences of a Heyting algebra endowed with a dual pseudo-complement and its normal filters [18, Thm. 3.3].

We state below a stronger version of Theorem 5 for quasi-Nelson algebras endowed with a minB-inconsistency operator (cf. [5, Thm. 3.16]).

Theorem 6. *For each $\langle \mathbf{A}, \bullet_{\mathsf{B}} \rangle \in \mathsf{QN}^{\bullet}_{\mathsf{mB}}$, the following are equivalent:*

(i) $\langle \mathbf{A}, \bullet_{\mathsf{B}} \rangle$ *is simple.*
(ii) $\langle \mathbf{A}, \bullet_{\mathsf{B}} \rangle$ *is subdirectly irreducible.*
(iii) $\langle \mathbf{A}, \bullet_{\mathsf{B}} \rangle$ *directly indecomposable.*
(iv) $B(\mathbf{A}) = \{0, 1\}$.

Hence, $\mathsf{QN}^{\bullet}_{\mathsf{mB}}$ *(and* $\mathsf{QN}^{\bullet}_{\mathsf{Bm}}$*) are semisimple varieties.*

4 Future Work

4.1 Consistency Operators

On every quasi-Nelson algebra $\mathbf{A}$, a max-consistency operator $\circ$ may be introduced, as in [5, Def. 3.3], by the prescription:

$$x \wedge {\sim} x \wedge y = 0 \qquad \text{if and only if} \qquad y \leq \circ x$$

giving us $\circ a = \max\{b \in A : a \wedge {\sim} a \wedge b = 0\}$ for all $a \in A$. Many of the results established in the previous sections, including the twist representation (see below), can be obtained for the consistency operator $\circ$ as well. There are, however, certain additional technical difficulties. For instance, it is not clear at this point whether an analogue of Theorem 3 (entailing that the resulting class of algebras is equational) can be established: this is essentially due to the fact that the term $y \vee {\sim} y$ appearing in item (iv) of Theorem 3 is the same that defines the Boolean elements, but its negation-dual $y \wedge {\sim} y$, as we have observed, does have the same effect in a non-involutive setting. Strategies for overcoming such difficulties will have to be explored in future research.

On the other hand, a twist representation can be established, and the analogue of Theorem 4 would state that the consistency operator is given, on every twist-algebra, by $\circ\langle a_1, a_2 \rangle := \langle \neg - (a_1 \vee a_2), -(a_1 \vee a_2) \rangle$, where the unary operation $-$ is defined as follows:

$$-\, a = \min\{b \in \Box[H] : \Box(a \vee b) = 1\}. \tag{6}$$

(6) is precisely saying that $-a$ is the dual pseudo-complement of $a \in \Box[H]$ computed in the Heyting algebra $\Box[H] := \{a \in H : \Box a = a\}$ of fixpoints of the nucleus operator. Using this representation it is not hard to verify, for instance, that when both a min-inconsistency operator $\bullet$ and a max-consistency operator $\circ$ are defined on a quasi-Nelson algebra $\mathbf{A} = Tw(\mathbf{H}, \nabla)$, the inequality

$\sim \bullet x \leq \circ x$ is always satisfied. On the other hand, the converse inequality ($\circ x \leq \sim \bullet x$) holds if and only if $-a = \Box \neg a$ for all $a \in \nabla$, in which case the term $\sim \bullet x$ may be taken as a definition of $\circ x$. A perfect duality between the two operators, however, is only reached if we impose the stronger requirement $\neg a = -a$ for all $a \in \nabla$ (in which case we may also define $\bullet x := \sim \circ x$, as in the involutive setting). These considerations suggest that the exploration of non-involutive algebras simultaneously endowed with consistency and inconsistency operators may also prove to be an interesting direction for future research.

4.2 LFIs Based on Quasi-Nelson Algebras

As mentioned earlier, the logical interpretation of the results presented in the previous sections is straightforward. Following [5], we can proceed by first defining truth-preserving logics $\vdash_{\mathsf{K}}^{\top}$ for $\mathsf{K} \in \{\mathsf{QN}^{\bullet}, \mathsf{QN}^{\bullet}_{\mathsf{Bm}}, \mathsf{QN}^{\bullet}_{\mathsf{mB}}\}$. For $\mathsf{K} = \mathsf{QN}^{\bullet}$, the counterparts of the rules (A1), (Max) and (CNG) of [5, Definition 5.1] would be the following:

$$\text{(A1')} \quad \frac{}{\varphi \vee \sim\varphi \vee \bullet\varphi} \qquad \text{(Min)} \quad \frac{\varphi \vee \sim\varphi \vee \psi}{\bullet\varphi \Rightarrow \psi} \qquad \text{(CNG)} \quad \frac{\varphi \Rightarrow \psi, \psi \Rightarrow \varphi}{\bullet\varphi \Rightarrow \bullet\psi}$$

(Note that these formulations of (A1') and (Min) appear closer to their algebraic counterparts than (A1) and (Max) in [5].) In a similar way one may define rules for the truth-preserving logic $\vdash_{\mathsf{K}}^{\top}$ with $\mathsf{K} \in \{\mathsf{QN}^{\bullet}_{\mathsf{Bm}}, \mathsf{QN}^{\bullet}_{\mathsf{mB}}\}$. By restricting the application of these rules as indicated in [5, Def. 5.5], we can then obtain order-preserving logics $\vdash_{\mathsf{K}}^{\leq}$ for $\mathsf{K} \in \{\mathsf{QN}^{\bullet}, \mathsf{QN}^{\bullet}_{\mathsf{Bm}}, \mathsf{QN}^{\bullet}_{\mathsf{mB}}\}$, thus recovering the subsequent logical results of [5, Section 5] in the setting of quasi-Nelson algebras endowed with inconsistency operators. We intend to pursue this in future publications, alongside the study of logics based on algebras endowed with consistency operators (defined as in the preceding subsection) and logics that include both consistency and inconsistency connectives.

4.3 (In)consistency Operators Beyond the Quasi-Nelson Setting

As mentioned in the Introduction, the present paper aims at establishing an algebraic background for extending the approach of [5] to LFIs beyond the setting of distributive involutive residuated lattices. Quasi-Nelson algebras, while non-necessarily involutive, are still a quite special subclass of residuated lattices (members of QN are, in particular, distributive and 3-potent), but some of the results presented here can be proved in a more general setting. As a next step in this direction, we speculate that the classes of residuated lattices introduced in the recent papers [2,3] might be a promising starting point. These are much more general residuated lattices that, while not necessarily satisfying any of the above-mentioned requirements (involutivity, distributivity, n-potency, integrality or commutativity), are still representable as twist-algebras. One may thus hope to obtain suitable generalizations of the results presented in the present paper, including those that appear to rely more heavily on the twist construction (e.g. Proposition 7 and Corollary 1). We leave this as a last suggestion for future investigations.

Acknowledgements. A. Figallo-Orellano acknowledges the support from São Paulo Research Foundation (FAPESP) through the *Jovem Pesquisador* grant 2021/04883-0. U. Rivieccio acknowledges support from the 2023-PUNED-0052 grant Investigadores tempranos UNED-SANTANDER, and from the I+D+i research project PID2022-142378NB-I00 "PHIDELO" funded by the Ministry of Science and Innovation of Spain.

Appendix: Proofs

Proof (Proposition 1). Items (i) to (iv) are straightforward consequences of Definition 2. We shall prove (v) later on, as it follows directly from the twist representation. Let us prove (vi). Using Definition 2, it suffices to show that $a \vee {\sim} a \vee b \vee \bullet(a \vee {\sim} a \vee b) = 1$ for all $a, b \in A$. Since $a \leq a \vee {\sim} a \vee b$, we have $a \vee {\sim} a \vee b \geq {\sim} a \geq {\sim}(a \vee {\sim} a \vee b)$. Hence, we can use item (iv) to obtain the result: $a \vee {\sim} a \vee b \vee \bullet(a \vee {\sim} a \vee b) = (a \vee {\sim} a \vee b) \vee {\sim}(a \vee {\sim} a \vee b) \vee \bullet(a \vee {\sim} a \vee b) = 1$.

Proof (Theorem 1). We have seen in Proposition 1 that the three conditions in the statement are consequences of Definition 2. Conversely, assume conditions (i)–(iii) hold on a quasi-Nelson algebra $\mathbf{A}$, and let a, b be such that $a \vee {\sim} a \vee b = 1$. By (i) and (iii), we have $\bullet a \leq b \vee \bullet(a \vee {\sim} a \vee b) = b \vee \bullet 1 = b \vee 0 = b$, as required. Conversely, assume $\bullet a \leq b$. Then, by (ii), we have $1 = a \vee {\sim} a \vee \bullet a \leq a \vee {\sim} a \vee b$, as required.

Proof (Theorem 2). Recall that all the classes under consideration are varieties. Thus, assuming an equation $\varphi = \psi$ in the $\{\bullet\}$-free language does not hold in QN, let $\mathbf{A} \in \mathsf{QN}$ be a subdirectly irreducible algebra witnessing this. We can then apply Example 1 to obtain an algebra $\langle \mathbf{A}, \bullet \rangle \in \mathsf{QN}^{\bullet}_{\mathsf{Bm}}$ that does not satisfy $\varphi = \psi$.

Proof (Proposition 2). Items (i)–(iii) are immediate consequences of Definition 3. Regarding (iv), using items (ii) and (i) of Definition 3, we have:

$$
\begin{aligned}
&(\bullet_{\mathsf{B}} a \vee b \vee \bullet_{\mathsf{B}} b) \vee {\sim}(\bullet_{\mathsf{B}} a \vee b \vee \bullet_{\mathsf{B}} b) \\
&= (\bullet_{\mathsf{B}} a \vee b \vee \bullet_{\mathsf{B}} b) \vee ({\sim} \bullet_{\mathsf{B}} a \wedge {\sim} b \wedge {\sim} \bullet_{\mathsf{B}} b) \\
&= (\bullet_{\mathsf{B}} a \vee b \vee \bullet_{\mathsf{B}} b \vee {\sim} \bullet_{\mathsf{B}} a) \wedge (\bullet_{\mathsf{B}} a \vee b \vee \bullet_{\mathsf{B}} b \vee {\sim} b) \wedge (\bullet_{\mathsf{B}} a \vee b \vee \bullet_{\mathsf{B}} b \vee {\sim} b {\sim} \bullet_{\mathsf{B}} b) \\
&\geq (\bullet_{\mathsf{B}} a \vee {\sim} \bullet_{\mathsf{B}} a) \wedge (b \vee \bullet_{\mathsf{B}} b \vee {\sim} b) \wedge (\bullet_{\mathsf{B}} b \vee {\sim} \bullet_{\mathsf{B}} b) = 1 \wedge 1 \wedge 1 = 1.
\end{aligned}
$$

Let us now prove (v). Note that, by the previous items (ii) and (iv), we have $b \vee \bullet_{\mathsf{B}}(b \vee {\sim} b) \vee \bullet_{\mathsf{B}}(a \vee {\sim} a \vee b) = \bullet_{\mathsf{B}}(a \vee {\sim} a \vee b) \vee b \vee \bullet_{\mathsf{B}} b \in B(\mathbf{A})$. Then, by Definition 3 (iii), it will be sufficient to show that $a \vee {\sim} a \vee b \vee \bullet_{\mathsf{B}}(b \vee {\sim} b) \vee \bullet_{\mathsf{B}}(a \vee {\sim} a \vee b) = 1$. Indeed, following the proof of Proposition 1 (vi), we can show that $a \vee {\sim} a \vee b \vee \bullet_{\mathsf{B}}(a \vee {\sim} a \vee b) = 1$. From $a \leq a \vee {\sim} a \vee b$, we have $a \vee {\sim} a \vee b \geq {\sim} a \geq {\sim}(a \vee {\sim} a \vee b)$. Hence, Definition 3 (i) gives us the required result: $a \vee {\sim} a \vee b \vee \bullet(a \vee {\sim} a \vee b) = (a \vee {\sim} a \vee b) \vee {\sim}(a \vee {\sim} a \vee b) \vee \bullet(a \vee {\sim} a \vee b) = 1$.

Proof (Theorem 3). We have seen in Proposition 2 that an operator $\bullet_{\mathsf{B}}$ given as per Definition 3 satisfies all the equations in the statement. Conversely, supposing these equations hold, let us prove that Definition 3 (iii) is satisfied. Let then $a, b \in A$ be elements of $\mathbf{A} \in \mathsf{QN}$ such that $a \vee\sim a \vee b = b \vee\sim b = 1$. Then, using (iv) and (iii), we have $\bullet_{\mathsf{B}} a \leq b \vee \bullet_{\mathsf{B}}(b \vee\sim b) \vee \bullet_{\mathsf{B}}(a \vee\sim a \vee b) = b \vee \bullet_{\mathsf{B}} 1 \vee \bullet_{\mathsf{B}} 1 = b \vee 0 \vee 0 = b$, as required.

Proof (Proposition 3). Let us preliminarily note that $Tw(\mathbf{H}, \nabla)$ is closed under the new operation. Indeed, on the one hand, if $\langle a_1, a_2 \rangle \in A$, then $a_1 \vee a_2 \in \nabla$, so $\ulcorner(a_1 \vee a_2)$ exists in $\mathbf{H}$. Furthermore, we have $\ulcorner(a_1 \vee a_2) \wedge \neg \ulcorner(a_1 \vee a_2) = 0$ and, since $\Box \neg x = \neg x$, also $\Box \neg \ulcorner(a_1 \vee a_2) = \neg \ulcorner(a_1 \vee a_2)$.

To prove the main statement, for the "if" part, let us check that $\langle a_1, a_2 \rangle \vee \sim\langle a_1, a_2 \rangle \vee \bullet\langle a_1, a_2 \rangle = \langle 1, 0 \rangle$. Recalling that $\Box a_1 \wedge a_2 \leq \Box a_1 \wedge \Box a_2 = \Box(a_1 \wedge a_2) = \Box 0 = 0$, we easily obtain: $\langle a_1, a_2 \rangle \vee \sim\langle a_1, a_2 \rangle \vee \bullet\langle a_1, a_2 \rangle = \langle a_1 \vee a_2 \vee \ulcorner(a_1 \vee a_2), a_2 \wedge \Box a_1 \wedge \neg \ulcorner(a_1 \vee a_2) \rangle = \langle 1, 0 \wedge \neg \ulcorner(a_1 \vee a_2) \rangle = \langle 1, 0 \rangle$.

For the "only if" part, assume $\langle a_1, a_2 \rangle \vee \sim\langle a_1, a_2 \rangle \vee \langle b_1, b_2 \rangle = \langle 1, 0 \rangle$. In the light of the preceding computations, we note that only the first component gives us some information; namely that $a_1 \vee a_2 \vee b_1 = 1$. Then, by the property of the dpc, we have $-(a_1 \vee a_2) \leq b_1$. As to the second component, we need to show that $b_2 \leq \neg \ulcorner(a_1 \vee a_2)$. By the property of the pseudo-complement, this is equivalent to $\ulcorner(a_1 \vee a_2) \wedge b_2 = 0$. The latter, in turn, follows from $\ulcorner(a_1 \vee a_2) \leq b_1$ and the assumption that $b_1 \wedge b_2 = 0$, for we have $\ulcorner(a_1 \vee a_2) \wedge b_2 \leq b_1 \wedge b_2 = 0$.

Proof (Proposition 4). Let $b \in \nabla$. Then $\langle b, 0 \rangle \in A$. Let $\bullet\langle b, 0 \rangle = \langle a_1, a_2 \rangle$. We claim that $a_1 = \ulcorner b$. We therefore need to show that, for all $c \in H$, we have $b \vee c = 1$ iff $a_1 \leq c$. Assume $a_1 \leq c$. From Definition 2 we have: $\langle 1, 0 \rangle = \langle b, 0 \rangle \vee \sim\langle b, 0 \rangle \vee \bullet\langle b, 0 \rangle = \langle b \vee 0 \vee a_1, 0 \wedge \Box b \wedge a_2 \rangle = \langle b \vee a_1, 0 \rangle$, which, in particular, gives us $1 = b \vee a_1 \leq b \vee c$, as required.

Conversely, assume $b \vee c = 1$. Then, considering for instance the element $\langle c, \neg c \rangle \in A$, we have: $\langle b, 0 \rangle \vee \sim\langle b, 0 \rangle \vee \langle c, \neg c \rangle = \langle b \vee 0 \vee c, 0 \wedge \Box b \wedge \neg c \rangle = \langle b \vee c, 0 \rangle = \langle 1, 0 \rangle$. Thus, we may apply Definition 2 to obtain $\bullet\langle b, 0 \rangle \leq \langle c, \neg c \rangle$, giving us in particular $a_1 \leq c$, as required.

For the second claim in the statement, given $\langle a_1, a_2 \rangle \in A$, let $\bullet\langle a_1, a_2 \rangle = \langle b_1, b_2 \rangle$. By Proposition 1 (i), it suffices to compute $\bullet(\langle a_1, a_2 \rangle \vee \sim\langle a_1, a_2 \rangle) = \bullet\langle a_1 \vee a_2, 0 \rangle$. Since $a_1 \vee a_2 \in \nabla$, we can apply the above reasoning to obtain $b_1 = \ulcorner(a_1 \vee a_2)$. Hence $\bullet\langle a_1, a_2 \rangle = \langle \ulcorner(a_1 \vee a_2), b_2 \rangle$, and we know that $\ulcorner(a_1 \vee a_2) \wedge b_2 = 0$, i.e. (by the property of the pseudo-complement) $b_2 \leq \neg \ulcorner(a_1 \vee a_2)$. It remains to show that $\neg \ulcorner(a_1 \vee a_2) \leq b_2$. Since $\langle a_1, a_2 \rangle \vee \sim\langle a_1, a_2 \rangle \vee \langle \ulcorner(a_1 \vee a_2), \neg \ulcorner(a_1 \vee a_2) \rangle = \langle 1, 0 \rangle$, by Definition 4 we have $\langle b_1, b_2 \rangle \leq \langle \ulcorner(a_1 \vee a_2), \neg \ulcorner(a_1 \vee a_2) \rangle$, giving us, in particular, $\neg \ulcorner(a_1 \vee a_2) \leq b_2$.

Proof (Proposition 5). Let us preliminarily verify that the following (in)equalities hold on every twist-algebra: $\bullet\sim(x \wedge \sim x) = \bullet(x \wedge \sim x) \leq \bullet\sim x \leq \bullet x = \bullet x * \bullet x$. Given $\langle b_1, b_2 \rangle \in A$, to establish $\bullet\sim(x \wedge \sim x) = \bullet(x \wedge \sim x)$, let us compute: $\bullet(\langle b_1, b_2 \rangle \wedge \sim\langle b_1, b_2 \rangle) = \bullet\langle 0, \Box(b_2 \vee \Box b_1) \rangle = \bullet\langle 0, \Box(b_1 \vee b_2) \rangle = \langle \ulcorner \Box(b_1 \vee b_2), \neg \ulcorner \Box(b_1 \vee b_2) \rangle = \bullet\langle \Box(b_1 \vee b_2), 0 \rangle = \bullet\sim\langle 0, \Box(b_1 \vee b_2) \rangle = \bullet\sim(\langle b_1, b_2 \rangle \wedge \sim\langle b_1, b_2 \rangle)$. Now observe that from $\Box b_1 \vee b_2 \leq \Box(b_1 \vee b_2) = \Box(\Box b_1 \vee b_2)$ we have $\ulcorner \Box(b_1 \vee b_2) \leq \ulcorner$

$(\Box b_1 \vee b_2)$, which justifies the inequality $\bullet(x \wedge {\sim} x) \leq \bullet {\sim} x$. To justify the inequality $\bullet {\sim} x \leq \bullet x$, suffice it to observe that $\neg(\Box b_1 \vee b_2) \leq \neg(b_1 \vee b_2)$ because $b_1 \vee b_2 \leq \Box b_1 \vee b_2$. Finally, regarding $\bullet = \bullet x * \bullet x$, recall that the idempotent elements on a twist-algebra are precisely those of the form $\langle b_1, \neg b_1 \rangle$ for some $b_1 \in H$.

(i). By the preceding observations, we have $\bullet\langle b_1, b_2 \rangle \leq \bullet(\langle b_1, b_2 \rangle \wedge {\sim}\langle b_1, b_2 \rangle)$ if and only if $\neg(b_1 \vee b_2) \leq \neg\Box(b_1 \vee b_2)$. Note that the inequality $\neg\Box(b_1 \vee b_2) \leq \neg (b_1 \vee b_2)$ holds in general. Since $b_1 \vee b_2 \in \nabla$, the result easily follows.

(ii). Recalling the preliminary observations, we easily see that $\bullet {\sim}\langle b_1, b_2 \rangle \leq \bullet(\langle b_1, b_2 \rangle \wedge {\sim}\langle b_1, b_2 \rangle)$ if and only if $\neg (\Box b_1 \vee b_2) \leq \neg \Box(b_1 \vee b_2)$ if and only if $\neg (\Box b_1 \vee b_2) = \neg \Box(b_1 \vee b_2)$. By the property of the dpc, the latter is in turn equivalent to $\Box b_1 \vee b_2 \vee \neg\Box(b_1 \vee b_2) = 1$.

(iii). As with the preceding item, we have $\bullet\langle b_1, b_2 \rangle \leq \bullet {\sim}\langle b_1, b_2 \rangle$ iff $\neg (b_1 \vee b_2) \leq \neg (\Box b_1 \vee b_2)$ iff $\neg (b_1 \vee b_2) = \neg (\Box b_1 \vee b_2)$. By the property of the dpc, the latter is equivalent to $b_1 \vee b_2 \vee \neg (\Box b_1 \vee b_2) = 1$.

(iv). Assume $\mathbf{A} \models x \wedge \bullet x = 0$, and let $a \in \nabla$. Then, considering $\langle a, 0 \rangle \in A$, compute $\langle a, 0 \rangle \wedge \bullet\langle a, 0 \rangle = \langle a \wedge \neg a, \Box(0 \vee \neg \neg a) \rangle$. The assumption then gives us, in particular, $\Box(0 \vee \neg \neg a) = \Box(\neg \neg a) = 1$. From the latter, recalling that $\neg\Box x = \neg x$, we obtain $\neg\Box\neg \neg a = \neg\neg \neg a = 0 = \neg 1$. Since $\neg a \leq \neg\neg \neg a$, we conclude that $\neg a = 0$. The latter gives us $a = a \vee 0 = a \vee \neg a = 1$. So $\nabla = \{1\}$. Notice that, by construction, $D(\mathbf{H}) \subseteq \nabla$. Since $D(\mathbf{H}) = \{b \vee \neg b : b \in H\}$, we see that $\nabla = \{1\}$ entails that $\mathbf{H}$ is a Boolean algebra (and, in consequence, the nucleus is the identity map).

Conversely, assume $\nabla = \{1\}$. Then $\bullet\langle b_1, b_2 \rangle = \langle \neg 1, \neg \neg 1 \rangle = \langle 0, 1 \rangle$ for all $\langle b_1, b_2 \rangle \in A$.

(v). Assume $\mathbf{A} \models {\sim} x \wedge \bullet x = 0$, and let $\langle b_1, b_2 \rangle \in A$. Let us compute ${\sim}\langle b_1, b_2 \rangle \wedge \bullet\langle b_1, b_2 \rangle = \langle b_2 \wedge \neg (b_1 \vee b_2), \Box(\Box b_1 \vee \neg \neg (b_1 \vee b_2)) \rangle = \langle b_2 \wedge \neg (b_1 \vee b_2), \Box(b_1 \vee \neg \neg (b_1 \vee b_2)) \rangle$. We thus see that the assumption implies, in particular, $b_2 \wedge \neg (b_1 \vee b_2) = 0$, which (by the property of the pseudo-complement $\neg$) is equivalent to $\neg (b_1 \vee b_2) \leq \neg b_2$. By the property of the dpc, the latter is in turn equivalent to $b_1 \vee b_2 \vee \neg b_2 = 1$. But $b_1 \leq \neg b_2$ (because $b_1 \wedge b_2 = 0$), so $b_1 \vee b_2 \vee \neg b_2 = b_2 \vee \neg b_2$. This means that, for every $b_2 \in \Box[H]$, we have $b_2 \vee \neg b_2 = 1$. Thus, in particular, the Heyting algebra $\mathbf{H}_\Box$ is Boolean; notice also that $b_2 \vee \neg b_2 = 1$ is equivalent to the statement $\Box c \vee \neg c = 1$ for all $c \in H$, because $\Box b_2 = b_2$ and $\neg\Box c = \neg c$.

Now let $a \in \nabla$, so $\langle a, 0 \rangle, \langle 0, \Box a \rangle \in A$. Taking then $b_1 = 0$ and $b_2 = \Box a$, ${\sim}\langle 0, \Box a \rangle \wedge \bullet\langle 0, \Box a \rangle = \langle \Box a \wedge \neg \Box a, \Box(0 \vee \neg \neg \Box a) \rangle = \langle 0, 1 \rangle$. From the second component, we have $\Box\neg \neg\Box a = \neg \neg\Box a = 1$, which negating both sides gives us $\neg\neg \neg\Box a = 0 = \neg 1$. Since $x \leq \neg\neg x$, we thus have $\neg \Box a = 0$. Then $1 = \Box a \vee \neg \Box a = \Box a \vee 0 = \Box a$, as claimed.

Conversely, let $\langle b_1, b_2 \rangle \in A$. We need to show that $b_2 \wedge \neg (b_1 \vee b_2) = 0$ and $\Box(b_1 \vee \neg \neg (b_1 \vee b_2)) = 1$. Since $b_2 \in \Box[H]$, the assumptions give us $b_2 \vee \neg b_2 = 1$. The latter gives us $b_1 \vee b_2 \vee \neg b_2 = 1$, which is equivalent (by the property of the dpc) to $\neg (b_1 \vee b_2) \leq \neg b_2$. By the property of the pseudo-complement, the latter is in turn equivalent to $b_2 \wedge \neg (b_1 \vee b_2) = 0$, which is the first required equality. To obtain the second, from $b_2 \wedge \neg (b_1 \vee b_2) = 0$ we have, again by the property of the pseudo-complement, $b_2 \leq \neg \ulcorner (b_1 \vee b_2)$. From $b_2 \leq \neg \ulcorner (b_1 \vee b_2)$ we obtain $b_1 \vee b_2 \leq b_1 \vee \neg \ulcorner (b_1 \vee b_2)$. Since $b_1 \vee b_2 \in \nabla$, we have that $b_1 \vee \neg \ulcorner (b_1 \vee b_2) \in \nabla$ as well. So we may use the assumptions to conclude that $\Box(b_1 \vee \neg \ulcorner (b_1 \vee b_2)) = 1$.

(vi). Observe that $\bullet\langle a_1, a_2\rangle \vee \sim \bullet\langle a_1, a_2\rangle = \langle \ulcorner (a_1 \vee a_2) \vee \neg \ulcorner (a_1 \vee a_2), \neg \ulcorner (a_1 \vee a_2) \wedge \Box \ulcorner (a_1 \vee a_2)\rangle = \langle \ulcorner (a_1 \vee a_2) \vee \neg \ulcorner (a_1 \vee a_2), 0\rangle$. The latter equality follows from the nucleus properties: we have $\neg \ulcorner (a_1 \vee a_2) \wedge \Box \ulcorner (a_1 \vee a_2) \leq \Box \neg \ulcorner (a_1 \vee a_2) \wedge \Box \ulcorner (a_1 \vee a_2) = \Box(\neg \ulcorner (a_1 \vee a_2) \wedge \ulcorner (a_1 \vee a_2)) = \Box 0 = 0$. The only non-trivial condition imposed by the identity $\bullet x \vee \sim \bullet x = 1$ is thus $\ulcorner (a_1 \vee a_2) \vee \neg \ulcorner (a_1 \vee a_2) = 1$.

Proof (Lemma 1). It will be useful to preliminary state the following lemma (we write $\ulcorner a, \ulcorner b$ etc. meaning that the relevant properties hold whenever the dual pseudo-complements of the elements a, b etc. exist in the Heyting algebra **H**).

Lemma 2. *For every Heyting algebra* **H** *and for every* $a, b \in H$, *we have* $\neg \ulcorner (a \to b) \leq \ulcorner b \to \ulcorner a$.

Proof. Since $\ulcorner$ is order-reversing and $\ulcorner (x \wedge y) = \ulcorner x \vee \ulcorner y$, from $a \wedge (a \to b) \leq b$ we have $\ulcorner b \leq \ulcorner (a \wedge (a \to b)) = \ulcorner a \vee \ulcorner (a \to b)$. From the latter inequality, using distributivity, we obtain $\ulcorner b \wedge \neg \ulcorner (a \to b) \leq (\ulcorner a \vee \ulcorner (a \to b)) \wedge \neg \ulcorner (a \to b) = (\ulcorner a \wedge \neg \ulcorner (a \to b)) \vee (\ulcorner (a \to b) \wedge \neg \ulcorner (a \to b)) = (\ulcorner a \wedge \neg \ulcorner (a \to b)) \vee 0 = \ulcorner a \wedge \neg \ulcorner (a \to b)$. Thus, in particular, we have $\ulcorner b \wedge \neg \ulcorner (a \to b) \leq \ulcorner a$, which by residuation gives us $\neg \ulcorner (a \to b) \leq \ulcorner b \to \ulcorner a$, as required.

We can now easily prove the equivalence among the three items in the statement of Lemma 1. To show that (i) entails (ii), assume F is ∇-normal and $a \to b \in F$ for some $a, b \in \nabla$. Then $\neg \ulcorner (a \to b) \in F$, so we can apply Lemma 2 (iii) to obtain $\ulcorner b \to \ulcorner a$, as required. It is clear that (ii) entails (iii). To conclude the proof, assuming F satisfies (iii), let us prove (i). Let $a \in \nabla \cap F$. Then $a \to 1 = 1 \in F$ and $1 \to a = a \in F$. Hence we can apply the hypothesis to obtain $\ulcorner a \to \ulcorner 1 \in F$. But $\ulcorner a \to \ulcorner 1 = \ulcorner a \to 0 = \neg \ulcorner a$, so we are done.

Proof (Proposition 7). We know that every implicative filter $G \subseteq \mathbf{A}$ has the shape $G = (F \times H) \cap A$, where F is a lattice filter of **H** (Proposition 6). It remains to show that G is a $\bullet$-filter if and only if F is ∇-normal. Let us first assume that G is a $\bullet$-filter, and let $a \in \nabla \cap F$. Then $\langle a, 0\rangle \in G$ and, as observed earlier, $\bullet\langle a, 0\rangle \Rightarrow \langle 0, 1\rangle = \sim \bullet\langle a, 0\rangle = \langle \neg \ulcorner a, \Box \ulcorner a\rangle \in G$. This means that $\neg \ulcorner a \in F$, as required.

Conversely, assume F is ∇-normal and $\langle a_1, a_2\rangle \Rightarrow \langle b_1, b_2\rangle, \langle b_1, b_2\rangle \Rightarrow \langle a_1, a_2\rangle \in G$. This means, in particular, that $a_1 \to b_1, b_1 \to a_1, a_2 \to b_2, b_2 \to a_2 \in F$. Since $x \to y \leq x \to (y \vee z)$, from $a_1 \to b_1, a_2 \to b_2 \in F$ we obtain $a_1 \to (b_1 \vee b_2), a_2 \to (b_1 \vee b_2) \in F$, hence $(a_1 \to (b_1 \vee b_2)) \wedge (a_2 \to (b_1 \vee b_2)) = (a_1 \vee a_2) \to (b_1 \vee b_2) \in F$ as well. Symmetrically, from $b_1 \to a_1, b_2 \to a_2 \in F$ we obtain $(b_1 \vee b_2) \to (a_1 \vee a_2) \in F$. Since $a_1 \vee a_2, b_1 \vee b_2 \in \nabla$, we can use Lemma 1 to obtain $\ulcorner (a_1 \vee a_2) \to \ulcorner (b_1 \vee b_2) \in F$. Since $\ulcorner (a_1 \vee a_2) \to \ulcorner (b_1 \vee b_2)$ is the first component of $\bullet\langle a_1, a_2\rangle \Rightarrow \bullet\langle b_1, b_2\rangle$, this allows us to conclude that $\bullet\langle a_1, a_2\rangle \Rightarrow \bullet\langle b_1, b_2\rangle \in G$, as required.

Proof (Corollary 1). We have already observed that every $\bullet$-filter satisfies (ii). For the converse, let $\mathbf{A} = Tw(\mathbf{H}, \nabla)$, so we can use Proposition 7. Hence, $G = (F \times H) \cap A$, where F is a ∇-normal lattice filter of $\mathbf{H}$. Let $a = \langle a_1, a_2\rangle$ and $b = \langle b_1, b_2\rangle$ be such that $\langle a_1, a_2\rangle \Rightarrow \langle b_1, b_2\rangle, \langle b_1, b_2\rangle \Rightarrow \langle a_1, a_2\rangle \in G$. This means, in particular, that $a_1 \to b_1, b_1 \to a_1, a_2 \to b_2, b_2 \to a_2 \in F$. Since $x \to y \leq x \to (y \vee z)$ holds on Heyting algebras, from $a_1 \to b_1, a_2 \to b_2 \in F$ we obtain $a_1 \to (b_1 \vee b_2), a_2 \to (b_1 \vee b_2) \in F$, hence $(a_1 \to (b_1 \vee b_2)) \wedge (a_2 \to (b_1 \vee b_2)) = (a_1 \vee a_2) \to (b_1 \vee b_2) \in F$ as well. Symmetrically, from $b_1 \to a_1, b_2 \to a_2 \in F$ we obtain $(b_1 \vee b_2) \to (a_1 \vee a_2) \in F$. Since $a_1 \vee a_2, b_1 \vee b_2 \in \nabla$, we can use Lemma 1 to obtain $\ulcorner(a_1 \vee a_2) \to \ulcorner(b_1 \vee b_2) \in F$. Since $\ulcorner(a_1 \vee a_2) \to \ulcorner(b_1 \vee b_2)$ is the first component of $\bullet\langle a_1, a_2\rangle \Rightarrow \bullet\langle b_1, b_2\rangle$, this allows us to conclude that $\bullet\langle a_1, a_2\rangle \Rightarrow \bullet\langle b_1, b_2\rangle = \bullet a \Rightarrow \bullet b \in G$, as required.

Proof (Theorem 5). Supposing $\mathbf{A}$ is not directly indecomposable, let $\mathbf{A} = \mathbf{B} \times \mathbf{C}$. Then the element $\langle 1^{\mathbf{B}}, 0^{\mathbf{C}}\rangle$ is Boolean and $B(\mathbf{A}) \neq \{0, 1\}$. Conversely, let $\mathbf{A} = Tw(\mathbf{H}, \nabla)$. As observed earlier, every Boolean element is involutive and an idempotent, that is, every element in $B(\mathbf{A})$ is of type $a = \langle a_1, \neg a_1\rangle$ for some $a_1 \in H$ with $a_1 = \Box a_1$ and $a_1 \vee \neg a_1 = 1$ (hence, a_1 is a Boolean element of $\mathbf{H}$). Now, assuming $a \in B(\mathbf{A}) - \{0, 1\}$, let us consider the up-set $G := [a)$. We claim that G is a $\bullet$-filter. It is easy to see that G is closed under $*$ (hence, it is an implicative filter). It follows that $G = (F \times H) \cap A$, where $F = [a_1)$. Since a_1 is Boolean, we have $a_1 = \neg \ulcorner a_1$ (Lemma 2). It follows that F is ∇-normal. Indeed, letting $b_1 \in \nabla \cap F$ (i.e. $a_1 \leq b_1$), we have $\ulcorner b_1 \leq \ulcorner a_1$ and $a_1 = \neg\ulcorner a_1 \leq \neg\ulcorner b_1$. Hence, F is ∇-normal and, by Proposition 7, G is a $\bullet$-filter. A similar reasoning shows that $J := [\sim a)$ is a $\bullet$-filter. Note that in the lattice of $\bullet$-filters of $\mathbf{A}$, we have $G \wedge J = \{1\}$ and $G \vee J = A$. The former claim follows from the observation that $c \geq a, \sim a$ entails $c \geq a \vee \sim a = 1$. As to the latter, we have that $a, \sim a \in G \vee J$ entails $a \wedge \sim a = 0 \in G \vee J$. Thus, considering the associated congruences θ_G and θ_J, we have $\theta_G \wedge \theta_J = Id_A$ and $\theta_G \vee \theta_J = A \times A$. Hence, θ_G and θ_J are (non-trivial) factor congruences of $\mathbf{A}$ (it is obvious that they permute, for quasi-Nelson algebras (as a subclass of residuated lattices) are congruence-permutable). We would then conclude that $\mathbf{A} = \mathbf{A}/\theta_G \times \mathbf{A}/\theta_J$, contradicting our hypothesis that $\mathbf{A}$ was directly indecomposable.

Proof (Theorem 6). Clearly (i) implies (ii), which implies (iii). The only non-trivial implications are from (iii) to (iv) and from (iv) to (i). For the former, we can reason as in the proof of Theorem 5. As to the latter, assuming $B(\mathbf{A}) = \{0, 1\}$, we have $\bullet_{\mathrm{B}} a = 1$ for all $a \in A - B(\mathbf{A})$ (item (iii) of Proposition 2). It follows that the only $\bullet_{\mathrm{B}}$-filters of $\mathbf{A}$ are $\{1\}$ and A itself. Hence, $\mathbf{A}$ has only two congruences, and is simple.

References

1. Bou, F., et al.: Logics preserving degrees of truth from varieties of residuated lattices. J. Log. Comput. **19**(6), 1031–1069 (2009)
2. Busaniche, M., Galatos, N., Marcos, M.A.: Twist structures and Nelson Conuclei. Stud. Logica **110**(4), 949–987 (2022)

3. Busaniche, M., Rivieccio, U.: Nelson Conuclei and nuclei: the twist construction beyond involutivity. Studia Logica (To appear)
4. Carnielli, W.A., Marcos, J.: A taxonomy of C-systems. In: Paraconsistency, pp. 1–94. CRC Press (2002)
5. Esteva, F., Figallo-Orellano, A., Flaminio, T., Godo, L.: Logics of formal inconsistency based on distributive involutive residuated lattices. J. Log. Comput. **31**(5), 1226–1265 (2021)
6. Esteva, F., Figallo-Orellano, A., Flaminio, T., Godo, L.: Some categorical equivalences for Nelson algebras with consistency operators. In: 19th World Congress of the International Fuzzy Systems Association (IFSA), 12th Conference of the European Society for Fuzzy Logic and Technology (EUSFLAT)
7. Esteva, F., Godo, L.: Monoidal t-norm based logic: towards a logic for left-continuous t-norms. Fuzzy Sets Syst. **124**(3), 271–288 (2001)
8. Flaminio, T., Rivieccio, U.: Prelinearity in (quasi-)Nelson logic. Fuzzy Sets Syst. **445**, 66–89 (2022)
9. Galatos, N., Jipsen, P., Kowalski, T., Ono, H.: Residuated Lattices: an algebraic glimpse at substructural logics. In: Studies in Logic and the Foundations of Mathematics, vol. 151. Elsevier, Amsterdam (2007)
10. Nascimento, T., Rivieccio, U.: Negation and implication in quasi-Nelson logic. Logic. Investig. **27**(1), 107–123 (2021)
11. Nelson, D.: Constructible falsity. J. Symb. Log. **14**, 16–26 (1949)
12. Rivieccio, U., Spinks, M.: quasi-Nelson algebras. Electron. Notes Theor. Comput. Sci. **344**, 169–188 (2019)
13. Rivieccio, U., Spinks, M.: Quasi-Nelson; or, non-involutive Nelson algebras. In: Fazio, D., Ledda, A., Paoli, F. (eds.) Algebraic Perspectives on Substructural Logics. LNCS, vol. 57, pp. 133–168. Springer, Cham (2021). https://doi.org/10.1007/978-3-030-52163-9_8
14. Rivieccio, U.: Fragments of quasi-Nelson: two negations. J. Appl. Log. **7**, 499–559 (2020)
15. Rivieccio, U.: Fragments of Quasi-Nelson: the algebraizable core. Logic J. IGPL **30**(5), 807–839 (2021). https://doi.org/10.1093/jigpal/jzab023
16. Rivieccio, U.: Quasi-N4-lattices. Soft. Comput. **26**(6), 2671–2688 (2022)
17. Rivieccio, U., Jung, A.: A duality for two-sorted lattices. Soft. Comput. **25**(2), 851–868 (2021)
18. Sankappanavar, H.: Heyting algebras with dual pseudocomplementation. Pacific J. Math. **117**(2), 405–415 (1985)

Lambek Calculus with Banged Atoms for Parasitic Gaps

Mehrnoosh Sadrzadeh[1(✉)] and Lutz Straßburger[2]

[1] University College London, London, UK
m.sadrzadeh@ucl.ac.uk
[2] INRIA Saclay, Ile-de-France, Palaiseau, France

Abstract. Lambek Calculus is a non-commutative substructural logic for formalising linguistic constructions. However, its domain of applicability is limited to constructions with local dependencies. We propose here a simple extension that allows us to formalise a range of relativised constructions with long distance dependencies, notably medial extractions and the challenging case of parasitic gaps. In proof theoretic terms, our logic combines commutative and non-commutative behaviour, as well as linear and non-linear resource management. This is achieved with a single restricted modality. But unlike other extensions of Lambek Calculus with modalities, our logic remains decidable, and the complexity of proof search (i.e., sentence parsing) is the same as for the basic Lambek calculus. Furthermore, we provide not only a sequent calculus, and a cut elimination theorem, but also proof nets.

Keywords: Substructural Logics · Permutation and Contraction · Exponentials · Proof Nets · Polarised Systems · Natural Language · Relativisation · Long Distance Dependencies

1 Introduction

The *Lambek Calculus* [21] is a well-estabished tool in formal linguistics. It is a cut-free proof calculus for a logic with a non-commutative multiplication and two directional divisions. Proof search in the Lambek calculus is **NP**-complete [37]. It has been implemented in automatic parsers—the most recent using deep neural network technology—and applied to verify the grammaticality of sentences and phrases of languages such as English, Dutch and French [18,19,28,29]. However, the non-commutative nature of Lambek Calculus means that it can only model the elementary fragments of these languages.

Natural Languages, on the other hand, witnesses long distance dependencies in a range of constructions such as relativisation, topicalisation, and wh-questions. In these cases, a syntactic element such as an object of a verb e.g. the direct object "articles" of the verb "read" in (a) below, is withdrawn from its original place, i.e. after the verb, and placed at a different part of the sentence, for instance to the head of the relative clause. In such cases, a relative pronoun such as "that" *relates* the head to the rest of the clause. Traditionally, withdrawal places are called *gaps* and marked with $-$, as in the examples below:

G. Metcalfe et al. (Eds.): WoLLIC 2024, LNCS 14672, pp. 193–209, 2024.
https://doi.org/10.1007/978-3-031-62687-6_13

(a) articles that reviewers read – yesterday
(b) articles that reviewers accepted $-_1$ without reading $-_2$
(c) articles that reviewers accepted $-_1$ after skimming $-_2$ without reading $-_3$
(d) the article that a review about $-_1$ in a blog post made $-_2$ famous
(e) articles that chairs persuaded every reviewer of $-_1$ to accept $-_2$

A relative clause can have multiple gaps, where often some of the gaps, for instance $-_2$ in (b) and $-_2$ and $-_3$ in (c), become *parasitic.* As the name suggests, for a gap to be parasitic means that its presence relies on the existence of another gap [3,5,26]. In other words, the second and third gaps did not exist if the first gap was not there in the first place. In order to see this, note that phrases such as "articles that reviewers read them" are not grammatical. In (b), the main gap $-_1$ is after the verb "accepted" and the *parasitic* gap $-_2$ occurs after the gerund "reading". In (c), we have a similar situation, but one main gap $-_1$ and two parasitic ones $-_2$ and $-_3$. The parasitic gap can be the first gap, as is the case for $-_1$ in (d). In this case, both gaps are arguments of the verb "made". Gaps can also be nested, as in (e), where the parasitic gap $-_2$ is the object of "accept", itself nested within a complement of"persuaded".

Naturally, the Lambek calculus has been extended in various ways with different modalities and additional binary connectives to model long distance dependencies, for example [2,11,12,24,25,31–34,36]. There has been some recent interest in this by adding the linear logic exponentials [6] and subexponentials [35] to the Lambek calculus [13,14]. However, the presence of exponentials or subexponentials with contraction in a system with non-commutative connectives leads immediately to an undecidable proof system [15,16,39]. The existing solution [13,14] is imposing an external bound on the number of copies. Apart from needing *a priori* knowledge about the bound, this solution contradicts the compositional nature of language constructions. Furthermore, even with such a bound, the complexity of parsing is much higher [22].

We propose here an alternative solution that simply restricts the structure of the formulas under the modalities. For the linguistic applications mentioned above, it is enough to allow the exponentials only for atomic formulas. With this insight, we are able to present a cut-free proof system with the same proof search complexity as the original Lambek calculus.

Besides the aforementioned linguistic motivation for our proof system, there is also an independent proof theoretical interest. Since the advent of linear logic, there has been a dichtonomy between linear resources (that can be used exactly once) and classical resources (that can be used unlimited). From the beginning, there have been attempts to merge the two in a single proof system, starting with linear logic itself with the exponentials added, leading to sophisticated systems like Girard's LU [7], merging all the connectives of classical and linear logic. We take here the opposite direction, allowing the duplication only for a selected set of atoms, which leads to a very simple proof system.

Another dichotomy in substructural proof theory is the one between commutativity and non-commutativity—again with various existing proposals to merge the two in a single proof system [1,8,9,38]. All of these follow the idea of having both, commutative and non-commutative connectives in the logic. Our approach here is fundamentally different. We only have non-commutative connectives, but we allow to permute a selected set of atoms.

The result is a very simple proof system, that allows us to obtain a notion of proofs nets that is very similar to the one for plain MLL.

In summary, this paper presents a sequent calculus for a logic that is based on the Lambek calculus, but allows the duplication and permutation of atomic formulas that are marked by the !-modality. We prove cut elimination and provide a notion of proof nets with a simple correctness criterion, and we show decidability and **NP**-completeness of the provability problem. This is achieved by translating our system into a one-sided proof system that is based on cyclic MLL [40] and uses the methods presented in [20]. Finally, we show how our calculus can be applied for linguistic purposes.

$$\frac{\Gamma_1, a, \Gamma_2 \vdash C}{\Gamma_1, !a, \Gamma_2 \vdash C}\,!_{\mathsf{L}} \qquad \frac{}{!a \vdash !a}\,\mathsf{id}_! \qquad \frac{}{a \vdash a}\,\mathsf{id}$$

$$\frac{\Gamma_1, A, B, \Gamma_2 \vdash C}{\Gamma_1, A \cdot B, \Gamma_2 \vdash C}\,\cdot_{\mathsf{L}} \qquad \frac{\Gamma \vdash A \quad \Delta \vdash B}{\Gamma, \Delta \vdash A \cdot B}\,\cdot_{\mathsf{R}} \qquad \frac{\Gamma_1, !a, !a, \Gamma_2 \vdash C}{\Gamma_1, !a, \Gamma_2 \vdash C}\,\mathsf{con}$$

$$\frac{\Delta \vdash A \quad \Gamma_1, B, \Gamma_2 \vdash C}{\Gamma_1, \Delta, A \backslash B, \Gamma_2 \vdash C}\,\backslash_{\mathsf{L}} \qquad \frac{A, \Gamma \vdash B}{\Gamma \vdash A \backslash B}\,\backslash_{\mathsf{R}} \qquad \frac{\Gamma_1, !a, \Delta, \Gamma_2 \vdash C}{\Gamma_1, \Delta, !a, \Gamma_2 \vdash C}\,\mathsf{perm}_1$$

$$\frac{\Gamma_1, B, \Gamma_2 \vdash C \quad \Delta \vdash A}{\Gamma_1, B/A, \Delta, \Gamma_2 \vdash C}\,/_{\mathsf{L}} \qquad \frac{\Gamma, A \vdash B}{\Gamma \vdash B/A}\,/_{\mathsf{R}} \qquad \frac{\Gamma_1, \Delta, !a, \Gamma_2 \vdash C}{\Gamma_1, !a, \Delta, \Gamma_2 \vdash C}\,\mathsf{perm}_2$$

Fig. 1. System $\mathsf{L}_!$

2 The System

We start by defining the set $\mathcal{L}$ of ***formulas*** of our calculus. Formulas are denoted by capital Latin letters $A, B, \ldots$, and are generated from a countable set $\mathcal{A} = \{a, b, \ldots, s, n, gp, \ldots\}$ of ***atoms*** via the following grammar

$$\mathcal{L} ::= \mathcal{A} \mid !\mathcal{A} \mid \mathcal{L} \cdot \mathcal{L} \mid \mathcal{L} \backslash \mathcal{L} \mid \mathcal{L} / \mathcal{L}$$

Observe that the modality ! operates only on atoms, whereas the binary connectives $\cdot$, $\backslash$, and $/$ operate on arbitrary formulas, the modality ! can only be applied to atoms, and we call those atom ***banged atoms***. We use capital Greek letters $\Gamma, \Delta, \ldots$, to denote finite lists of formulas, separated by comma: $\Gamma = A_1, \ldots, A_n$. A ***sequent*** is a pair $\Gamma \vdash A$. The inference rules of our system, denoted by $\mathsf{L}_!$ and shown in Fig. 1, consist of the standard Lambek calculus [21], extended by inference rules dealing with the !-modality. As discussed in the introduction, banged atoms can be duplicated and freely permuted with other formulas. This is achieved by the rules con (*contraction*) and perm_1 and perm_2 (*permutation*)[1] In order to be able to *use* banged atoms in a proof, we need to release the modality eventually. This is done by the $!_{\mathsf{L}}$-rule.

[1] Note that we do not have *weakening*. This has linguistic reasons as well as proof theoretical reasons [10].

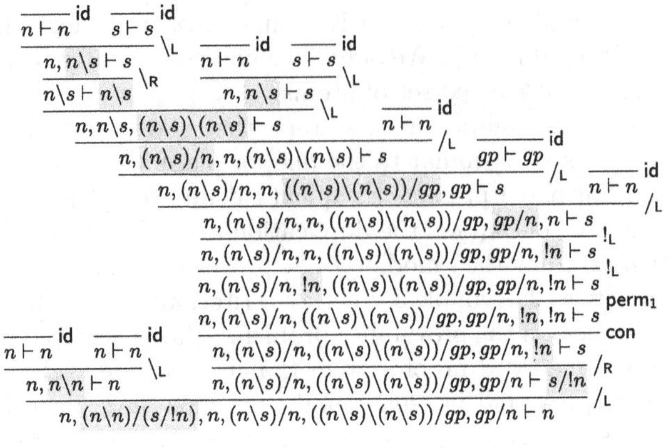

Fig. 2. Derivation in $\mathsf{L}_!$ for example (*b*)

In order to have cut elimination, to be discussed in the next section, we also need a $!_R$-rule. The reader familiar with rules for modalities in the sequent calculus, might immediately think of the following three options:

$$\frac{a \vdash b}{!a \vdash !b}\,!^1_{\mathsf{R}} \qquad \frac{a_1, \ldots, a_n \vdash b}{!a_1, \ldots, !a_n \vdash !b}\,!^2_{\mathsf{R}} \qquad \frac{!a_1, \ldots, !a_n \vdash b}{!a_1, \ldots, !a_n \vdash !b}\,!^3_{\mathsf{R}} \tag{1}$$

All three rules would ensure the cut elimination result. Now observe that $!^1_{\mathsf{R}}$ is a special case of $!^2_{\mathsf{R}}$, and $!^2_{\mathsf{R}}$ is derivable from $!^3_{\mathsf{R}}$ with the $!_{\mathsf{L}}$-rule. Thus, in the general case, the three rules have increasing strength. However, since there is no weakening and the ! is restricted to atoms, all three rules are equivalent. This is easy to see by observing that $!a_1, \ldots, !a_n \vdash b$ is only provable if $n = 1$ and $a_1 = b$. For this reason, it is sufficient to have $!_{\mathsf{R}} = !^1_{\mathsf{R}}$.

However, as the sequent $a \vdash b$ is only provable if $a = b$, and in that case the proof consists of a single application of the id-rule, we can replace $!_{\mathsf{R}}$ by the $\mathsf{id}_!$-rule.[2]

Finally, we have the so-called *Lambek restriction* which demands that we never have an empty left-hand side in a sequent. Looking at our rules, this is equivalent to asking that in the rules $\backslash_{\mathsf{R}}$ and $/_{\mathsf{R}}$, the Γ must not be empty.[3]

The cut-rule has the usual form: $\dfrac{\Delta \vdash A \quad \Gamma_1, A, \Gamma_2 \vdash C}{\Gamma_1, \Delta, \Gamma_2 \vdash C}\,\mathsf{cut}$

Theorem 2.1. *If a sequent is provable in* $\mathsf{L}_! + \mathsf{cut}$, *then it is also provable in* $\mathsf{L}_!$.

---

[2] We thank an anonymous referee for this simplification. However, if the reader insists on a system with only atomic id-rules, then $\dfrac{}{!a \vdash !a}\,\mathsf{id}_!$ can be replaced by $\dfrac{a \vdash b}{!a \vdash !b}\,!_{\mathsf{R}}$, yielding an equivalent system, not affecting any of the results in this paper.

[3] Observe that since we only allow atoms under the !, we do not have the issue discussed in [17].

We show the proof in the next section, and we end this section with the observation that even though the id-rule is restricted to atoms, its general form is derivable.

Proposition 2.2. *The rule* $\dfrac{}{A \vdash A}\,\mathsf{id}$ *is derivable in* $\mathsf{L}_!$.

Proof. Straightforward induction on A. □

Example 2.3. Figure 2 shows the derivation for our example (b), which will serve as the running example for this paper. For better readability we highlighted for each inference rule instance the principal formula in the conclusion.

3 Cut Elimination

We prove Theorem 2.1 with the help of the following reduction lemma:

Lemma 3.1. *If we have a proof*

$$\dfrac{\overset{\pi_1}{\Delta \vdash A} \qquad \overset{\pi_2}{\Gamma_1, A, \Gamma_2 \vdash C}}{\Gamma_1, \Delta, \Gamma_2 \vdash C}\,\mathsf{cut}$$

where π_1 *and* π_2 *are proofs in* $\mathsf{L}_!$ *that do not contain any cuts, then* $\Gamma_1, \Delta, \Gamma_2 \vdash C$ *is also provable in* $\mathsf{L}_!$ *without the* cut*-rule.*

For proving this lemma, we need the following notions. For a formula A, we define $|A|$ to be the ***size*** of A, i.e., the number of symbols needed to write A. For a proof π, we define $|\pi|$ to be the ***size*** of π, i.e., the number of inference rule instances used in π.

Proof (of Lemma 3.1*).* The proof is standard and proceeds by induction on the lexicographic pair $\langle |A|, |\pi_1|+|\pi_2| \rangle$ and a case analysis on the bottom-most rule instances in π_1 and π_2.

1. If the bottommost rule instance in π_1 or in π_2 does not operate on the cut-formula A, then we can do a simple rule permutation and proceed by induction hypothesis (since $|\pi_1|+|\pi_2|$ has decreased).
2. We now consider the cases where the bottommost rules instances in π_1 and in π_2 do operate on the cut-formula A. If $A = a$ for some atom a, then the cut disappears trivially.
3. If $A = A'/A''$, then we can replace

$$\dfrac{\dfrac{\overset{\pi_1'}{\Delta, A'' \vdash A'}}{\Delta \vdash A'/A''}\,/_{\mathsf{R}} \qquad \dfrac{\overset{\pi_2'}{\Gamma_1, A', \Gamma_2 \vdash C} \quad \overset{\pi_2''}{\Lambda \vdash A''}}{\Gamma_1, A'/A'', \Lambda, \Gamma_2 \vdash C}\,/_{\mathsf{L}}}{\Gamma_1, \Delta, \Lambda, \Gamma_2 \vdash C}\,\mathsf{cut} \quad \rightsquigarrow \quad \dfrac{\dfrac{\overset{\pi_2''}{\Lambda \vdash A''} \quad \overset{\pi_1'}{\Delta, A'' \vdash A'}}{\Delta, \Lambda \vdash A'}\,\mathsf{cut} \qquad \overset{\pi_2'}{\Gamma_1, A', \Gamma_2 \vdash C}}{\Gamma_1, \Delta, \Lambda, \Gamma_2 \vdash C}\,\mathsf{cut}$$

and proceed by induction hypothesis.

4. If $A = A' \backslash A''$ or $A = A' \cdot A''$, we proceed similarly.
5. Let us now look at the cases when $A = !a$ for some atom a. There are four possibilities for the bottommost rule in π_2. In the case for $!_{\mathsf{L}}$ we have

$$\dfrac{\dfrac{}{!a \vdash !a}\,\mathsf{id}_! \qquad \dfrac{\overset{\pi_2'}{\Gamma_1, a, \Gamma_2 \vdash C}}{\Gamma_1, !a, \Gamma_2 \vdash C}\,!_{\mathsf{L}}}{\Gamma_1, !a, \Gamma_2 \vdash C}\,\mathsf{cut} \quad \rightsquigarrow \quad \dfrac{\overset{\pi_2'}{\Gamma_1, a, \Gamma_2 \vdash C}}{\Gamma_1, !a, \Gamma_2 \vdash C}\,!_{\mathsf{L}}$$

and in the case of the con-rule we have

$$\dfrac{\dfrac{}{!a \vdash !a}\,\mathsf{id}_! \qquad \dfrac{\overset{\pi_2'}{\Gamma_1, !a, !a, \Gamma_2 \vdash C}}{\Gamma_1, !a, \Gamma_2 \vdash C}\,\mathsf{con}}{\Gamma_1, !a, \Gamma_2 \vdash C}\,\mathsf{cut} \quad \rightsquigarrow \quad \dfrac{\overset{\pi_2'}{\Gamma_1, !a, !a, \Gamma_2 \vdash C}}{\Gamma_1, !a, \Gamma_2 \vdash C}\,\mathsf{con}$$

Finally, the cases of the perm_1- and perm_2-rules is similar to case 1 above. □

Proof (of Theorem 2.1). By induction on the number of cuts in the derivation, using Lemma 3.1. □

4 A One-Sided System

In this section we present a system equivalent to $\mathsf{L}_!$, but with the (non-commutative versions of the) two connectives $\otimes$ and $\mathbin{⅋}$ from multiplicative linear logic (MLL). For this, we closely follow the presentation of [20]. The main ingredient is the distinction of the formulas that would occur on the left-hand side of the sequent turnstile from the ones on the right-hand side, using the polarities $\bullet$ (called ***input***) and $\circ$ (called ***output***).

The *raison d'être* of this exercise is to give the proof nets in the next section, which will essentially be the proof nets for cyclic MLL restricted to the Lambek calculus as presented in [20], with some additional conditions for accommodating our !-atoms.

First, let us recall MLL in its cyclic version [40]. While doing so, we add the necessary modalities that will correspond to the one of $\mathsf{L}_!$. We denote this logic by $\mathsf{CyMLL}_{!?}$,[4]. For defining its set $\mathcal{M}$ of formulas, we introduce a set $\mathcal{A}^\perp = \{a^\perp, b^\perp, \ldots, s^\perp, n^\perp, gp^\perp, \ldots\}$ of dual atoms, isomorphic to $\mathcal{A}$. We let $\mathcal{X} = \mathcal{A} \cup \mathcal{A}^\perp$ and define $\mathcal{M}$ via the following grammar:

$$\mathcal{M} ::= \mathcal{X} \mid !\mathcal{X} \mid ?\mathcal{X} \mid \mathcal{M} \otimes \mathcal{M} \mid \mathcal{M} \mathbin{⅋} \mathcal{M}$$

The operation $(\cdot)^\perp$ can be extended to all formulas via $a^{\perp\perp} = a$, and $(!a)^\perp = ?a^\perp$, and $(?a)^\perp = !a^\perp$, and $(A \otimes B)^\perp = B^\perp \mathbin{⅋} A^\perp$, and $(A \mathbin{⅋} B)^\perp = B^\perp \otimes A^\perp$.[5] Sequents of $\mathsf{CyMLL}_{!?}$ are simply finite lists of formulas $\vdash \Gamma = \vdash A_1, \ldots, A_n$, i.e., everything is one-sided, and we can write $⅋\Gamma$ for $A_1 \mathbin{⅋} \cdots \mathbin{⅋} A_n$. The inference

[4] Note that even though the language is similar to cyclic MELL, the logic is very different.

[5] Note the inversion of the order of the arguments, which is crucial.

$$\frac{}{\vdash a, a^{\perp}}\,\mathsf{id} \qquad \frac{\vdash \Gamma, A, B, \Delta}{\vdash \Gamma, A \parr B, \Delta}\,\parr \qquad \frac{\vdash \Gamma, A \quad \vdash B, \Delta}{\vdash \Gamma, A \otimes B, \Delta}\,\otimes \qquad \frac{\vdash \Delta, \Gamma}{\vdash \Gamma, \Delta}\,\mathsf{cyc}$$

$$\frac{}{\vdash ?a, !a^{\perp}}\,\mathsf{id}_! \qquad \frac{\vdash \Gamma_1, a, \Gamma_2}{\vdash \Gamma_1, ?a, \Gamma_2}\,? \qquad \frac{\vdash \Gamma_1, ?a, ?a, \Gamma_2}{\vdash \Gamma_1, ?a, \Gamma_2}\,\mathsf{con} \qquad \frac{\vdash \Gamma_1, \Delta, ?a, \Gamma_2}{\vdash \Gamma_1, ?a, \Delta, \Gamma_2}\,\mathsf{perm}$$

Fig. 3. Inference rules for $\mathsf{CyMLL}_{!?}$

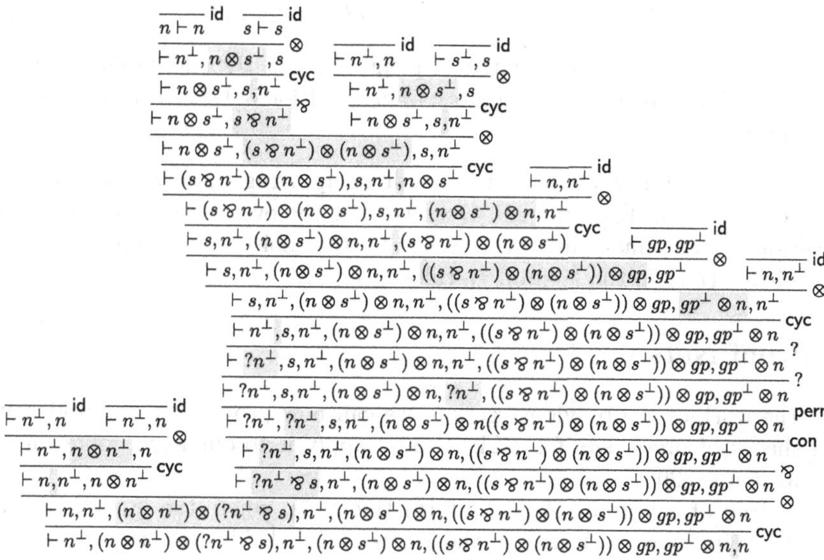

Fig. 4. Example of a derivation in $\mathsf{CyMLL}_{!?}$

rules are shown in Fig. 3, and as expected, the cut-rule (in its one-sided version) is admissible.[6]

There is the obvious mapping $(\cdot)^{\flat} \colon \mathcal{L} \to \mathcal{M}$, defined via:[7]

$$a^{\flat} = a \qquad (!a)^{\flat} = !a \qquad (A \cdot B)^{\flat} = B^{\flat} \otimes A^{\flat}$$
$$(A \backslash B)^{\flat} = B^{\flat} \parr (A^{\flat})^{\perp} \qquad (B/A)^{\flat} = (A^{\flat})^{\perp} \parr B^{\flat}$$

Let us now characterize the image of that translation. For this, we define ***polarized formulas***:

$$\mathcal{M}^{\bullet} ::= \mathcal{A}^{\perp} \mid ?\mathcal{A}^{\perp} \mid \mathcal{M}^{\bullet} \parr \mathcal{M}^{\bullet} \mid \mathcal{M}^{\bullet} \otimes \mathcal{M}^{\circ} \mid \mathcal{M}^{\circ} \otimes \mathcal{M}^{\bullet}$$
$$\mathcal{M}^{\circ} ::= \mathcal{A} \mid !\mathcal{A} \mid \mathcal{M}^{\circ} \otimes \mathcal{M}^{\circ} \mid \mathcal{M}^{\circ} \parr \mathcal{M}^{\bullet} \mid \mathcal{M}^{\bullet} \parr \mathcal{M}^{\circ}$$

[6] There is only one perm-rule in $\mathsf{CyMLL}_{!?}$ because the other one is derivable with the help of the cyc-rule.

[7] Here we also invert the order, even though this is not strictly needed (and also not done in [20]). We do it here to ease the use of the system for the linguistic applications.

It immediately follows that $\mathcal{M}^\bullet \cap \mathcal{M}^\circ = \emptyset$ and $\mathcal{M}^\bullet \cup \mathcal{M}^\circ \subsetneq \mathcal{M}$, and that $(\cdot)^\perp$ inverts the polarity.

The purpose of this is to have access to the following two propositions that we can now formulate. For the first one, we define $\mathcal{L}^\flat$ to be the image of $\mathcal{L}$ under $(\cdot)^\flat$.

Proposition 4.1 ([20]). *We have* $\mathcal{L}^\flat = \mathcal{M}^\circ$.

Proposition 4.2 ([20]). *A sequent* $A_1, \ldots, A_n \vdash B$ *is provable in* $\mathsf{L}_!$ *if and only if the sequent* $\vdash (A_1^\flat)^\perp, \ldots, (A_1^\flat)^\perp, B^\flat$ *is provable in* $\mathsf{CyMLL}_{!?}$.

Observe that such a translated sequent has exactly one formula with $\circ$-polarity and (because of the non-empty LHS condition of $\mathsf{L}_!$) at least one formula of $\bullet$-polarity.

Example 4.3. In Fig. 4 we show the result of applying these two propositions to the derivation in Example 2.3. Observe that the overal structure of the two derivations is the same. This is the reason for the choice of which premise is left and which is right in the $\backslash_\mathsf{L}$- and $/_\mathsf{L}$-rules in Fig. 1.[8]

5 Proof Nets

With the work of the previous section, we can now profit from the well developed theory of proof nets for MLL [4], and apply it to our logic, following the presentation in [20].

The ***tree*** of a formula A is the term tree of A, where the inner nodes are labeled by binary connectives and the leaves are labeled by atoms or atoms with a modality.[9] A ***prenet*** π is a pair $\langle \Gamma, \ell \rangle$ where Γ is a finite list of formulas from $\mathcal{M}$ and ℓ is an ***(axiom) linking***, which is a symmetric binary relation on the leaves of the sequent forest Γ, such that

(i) every non-modal atom is related to exactly one other non-modal atom or ?-atom that is dual to it, and
(ii) every !-atom is connected to exactly one ?-atom that is dual to it, and
(iii) every ?-atom is connected only to non-modal atoms or !-atoms that are all dual to it, and it has to be connected to at least one such atom.

Such a related pair of leaves is called an ***axiom link***. We can draw a prenet by simply writing Γ and adding the axiom links on top of it by simply connecting the corresponding atoms by an edge, as in the example below:

$$\vdash n^\perp, (n \otimes n^\perp) \otimes (?n^\perp \parr s), n^\perp, (n \otimes s^\perp) \otimes n, ((s \parr n^\perp) \otimes (n \otimes s^\perp)) \otimes gp, gp^\perp \otimes n, n \tag{2}$$

[8] Furthermore, the order of the formulas in the conclusion is the same in the two derivations in Examples 2.3 and 4.3. This is the reason for inverting the order in the definition of $(\cdot)^\flat$.

[9] To simplify the presentation, we consider the modalities not as unary inner nodes, but as part of the leaves.

The ***graph*** $\mathcal{G}(\pi)$ of the prenet $\pi = \langle \Gamma, \ell \rangle$ is obtained from the sequent forest of Γ by adding an edge between any leaves that are in ℓ-relation. For example, below is the graph of the prenet above:

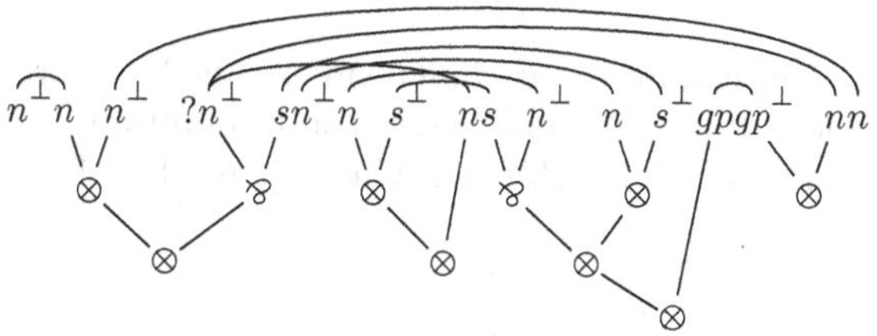

(3)

A ***subnet*** of a prenet π is a prenet π' whose graph $\mathcal{G}(\pi')$ is a subgraph of $\mathcal{G}(\pi)$.

It is straightforward to translate a $\mathsf{CyMLL}_{!?}$ sequent proof into a prenet $\langle \Gamma, \ell \rangle$: Γ is always the endsequent of the proof, and ℓ is constructed inductively as follows: The id-axiom creates a single axiom link between the two atoms in its conclusion. The rules $⅋$, ?, !, cyc, and perm have the same leaves in the premise as in the conclusion and therefore preserve the linking ℓ. The $\otimes$-rule simply takes the union of the linkings of the premises, and the con-rule links the $?a$ in the conclusion to all atoms which are linked to one of the two $?a$ in the premise, and preserves all other links for Γ, Δ (see Fig. 3). A $\mathsf{L}_!$***-proof net*** is a prenet that is obtained in this manner from a $\mathsf{CyMLL}_{!?}$ sequent proof that is the translation of a $\mathsf{L}_!$ sequent proof according to the previous section.

Example 5.1. The prenet in (2) is an $\mathsf{L}_!$-proof net, as it is obtained from the $\mathsf{CyMLL}_{!?}$-proof in Example 4.3, which is the translation of the $\mathsf{L}_!$-proof in Example 2.3.

Now we give a correctness criterion that allows us to distinguish the proof nets without having to resort to the sequent calculus. For this, we are going to adapt the results of [20] to the presence of our modalities. We start with the standard MLL-criterion. A ***DR-switching*** of a prenet π is obtained from $\mathcal{G}(\pi)$ by removing for each $⅋$ node one of the edges connecting it to its childen, and for each ?-leaf all but one axiom edges. Now, a prenet $\pi = \langle \Gamma, \ell \rangle$ is $\mathsf{L}_!$***-correct*** iff the following conditions hold:

1. every DR-switiching of π is a connected and acyclic graph;
2. $⅋\Gamma \in \mathcal{M}^{\circ}$;
3. the graph obtained from $\mathcal{G}(\pi)$ by removing all axiom edges connected to a ?-leaf is planar; and
4. every subnet of π has at least two conclusions.

Theorem 5.2. *A prenet is a* $\mathsf{L}_!$*-proof net iff it is* $\mathsf{L}_!$*-correct.*

Proof (Sketch). The first condition is the standard MLL-correctness criterion, where our contaction rule con behaves like a $⅋$-rule on atoms. The second condition is the restriction to the intuitionistic setting (exactly one formula on the right-hand side of the $\vdash$). The third condition is about the non-commutativity of the logic (with the exception of the ?-atoms), and the last condition encodes the Lambek restriction that forces a non-empty left-hand side. The details are similar to existing proofs in the literature (e.g., [20]), as the adjustments to the presence of our ?-atoms are straightforward. □

Remark 5.3. The four conditions are independent, and their presence or absence leads to different logics. For example, having only conditions 1 and 3 would lead to a correctness criterion for $\mathsf{CyMLL}_{!?}$, which might be of independent proof theoretical interest.

6 Decidability and Complexity

Theorem 6.1. *(i) The logic* $\mathsf{L}_!$ *is decidable. (ii) Moreover, the complexity of proof search is* **NP***-complete.*

Proof. Every axiom link connects a positive and a negative atom. The number of positive atoms is fixed by the endsequent. Only negative atoms can be duplicated by the con-rule. This means that the size of the sequents in a proof is limited, and decidability follows immediately. Furthermore, the size of a sequent is also linear in the size of the endsequent, which means the size of the whole proof is bound by a polynomial and can therefore be guessed by an **NP**-algorithm.[10] Finally, **NP**-hardness follows from **NP**-hardness of the standard Lambek calculus. □

Remark 6.2. The same holds for the logic $\mathsf{CyMLL}_{!?}$, but the proof is a bit more involved, because in $\mathsf{CyMLL}_{!?}$ the con-rule can also duplicate positive atoms. However, the number of possible duplications is still bounded by a polynomial because the DR-switching condition forbids an axiom link between two ?-atoms.

7 Application to Relativisation in Natural Language

In this section, we put $\mathsf{L}_!$ to use and show how it is employed in linguistic reasoning. The simplest cases of relativisation are when the extraction site is either at the front or rear of the original sentence. For instance, at the subject position of a verb in (f) below, or its object position in (g) below.

(f) articles that – disappeared
(g) articles that reviewers read –

These are still derivable in Lambek Calculus without permutation or contraction. One starts to face challenges when the extraction sites are medial, as is the case for all of the examples presented in the introduction. In order to demonstrate the differences, we first present a derivation for (g), and then show how our calculus deals with (a)–(c) from the introduction. Derivations for (d) and (e)

[10] Note that we can restrict the number of consecutive applications of the cyc- and perm-rules.

are provided in the appendix. The proof of (f) is straightforward. In order to model these clauses, we first design a *lexicon*, which is an assignment of $\mathcal{L}$ to the vocabulary used in the examples, where s is a declarative sentence, n a noun phrase, and gp a gerund phrase (or gerundive verb):

$$\begin{array}{rcl}
\text{articles, reviewers} & :: & n \\
\text{that} & :: & (n\backslash n)/(!n\backslash s) \text{ or } (n\backslash n)/(s/!n) \\
\text{disappeared} & :: & (n\backslash s) \\
\text{read, accepted} & :: & (n\backslash s)/n \\
\text{reading, skimming} & :: & gp/n \\
\text{yesterday} & :: & (n\backslash s)\backslash(n\backslash s) \\
\text{without, after} & :: & ((n\backslash s)\backslash(n\backslash s))/gp \text{ or } ((n\backslash s)\backslash(n\backslash s))/n
\end{array} \tag{4}$$

The syntactic categories of "that" take care of its roles, as a subject or an object relative pronoun. In its subject role in (f), it needs a sentence with a missing noun somewhere at its front (before its verb), expressed by the $\backslash$ connective in its subtype $(!n\backslash s)$. In the object role in (g), it is expecting a sentence with a missing noun somewhere at is rear (after its verb), expressed by the use of $/$ in its subtype $(s/!n)$. In either case, $!n$ indicates that the missing noun can be any where (before or after the verb, respectively) and any number of times. This reasoning about the subtype $(s/!n)$ is expressible using the cut-rule, as shown in the derivation of (g) below:

$$\dfrac{\dfrac{\dfrac{\dfrac{\dfrac{}{n\vdash n}\,\mathsf{id} \quad \dfrac{\dfrac{}{n\vdash n}\,\mathsf{id}\quad \dfrac{}{s\vdash s}\,\mathsf{id}}{n, n\backslash s\vdash s}\,\backslash_{\mathsf{L}}}{n, (n\backslash s)/n, n\vdash s}\,/_{\mathsf{L}}}{n, (n\backslash s)/n, !n\vdash s}\,!_{\mathsf{L}}}{n, (n\backslash s)/n\vdash s/!n}\,/_{\mathsf{R}} \qquad \dfrac{\dfrac{}{s/!n\vdash s/!n}\,\mathsf{id} \quad \dfrac{\dfrac{}{n\vdash n}\,\mathsf{id}\quad\dfrac{}{n\vdash n}\,\mathsf{id}}{n, n\backslash n\vdash n}\,\backslash_{\mathsf{L}}}{n, (n\backslash n)/(s/!n), (s/!n)\vdash n}\,/_{\mathsf{L}}}{n, (n\backslash n)/(s/!n), n, (n\backslash s)/n\vdash n}\,\mathsf{cut}$$

After eliminating the cut-rule, the first rule that is applied is the $/_{\mathsf{L}}$-rule, which leads to a linguistically unintuitive proof. The reason ! is used in the type of the relative pronoun rather than the type of the noun is since nouns takes other – non contractive – roles in the absence of "that". The proof net corresponding to either derivation, however, is the same and is shown below:

$$n^{\perp}, (n\otimes n^{\perp})\otimes(?n^{\perp}\parr s), n^{\perp}, (n\otimes s^{\perp})\otimes n, n$$

In (a), we have an extraction from the middle of the incomplete sentence and need to permute the missing noun, as shown below.

$$\dfrac{\dfrac{\dfrac{\dfrac{\dfrac{\text{as before}}{n, (n\backslash s)/n, n, (n\backslash s)\backslash(n\backslash s)\vdash s}\,/_{\mathsf{L}}}{n, (n\backslash s)/n, !n, (n\backslash s)\backslash(n\backslash s)\vdash s}\,!_{\mathsf{L}}}{n, (n\backslash s)/n, (n\backslash s)\backslash(n\backslash s), !n\vdash s}\,\mathsf{perm}_2}{n, (n\backslash s)/n, (n\backslash s)\backslash(n\backslash s)\vdash s/!n}\,/_{\mathsf{R}} \qquad \dfrac{\dfrac{\dfrac{\dfrac{}{n\vdash n}\,id}{!n\vdash !n}\,!_{\mathsf{R}} \quad \dfrac{}{s\vdash s}\,id}{s/!n, !n\vdash s}\,/_{\mathsf{R}} \quad \dfrac{\dfrac{}{n\vdash n}\,id \quad \dfrac{}{n\vdash n}\,id}{n, n\backslash n\vdash n}\,\backslash_{\mathsf{L}}}{n, (n\backslash n)/(s/!n), s/!n\vdash n}\,/_{\mathsf{L}}}{n, (n\backslash n)/(s/!n), n, (n\backslash s)/n, (n\backslash s)\backslash(n\backslash s)\vdash n}\,\mathsf{cut}$$

$$n^{\perp}, (n \otimes n^{\perp}) \otimes (?n^{\perp} \parr s), n^{\perp}, (n \otimes s^{\perp}) \otimes n, (s \parr n^{\perp}) \otimes (n \otimes s), n$$

For (b) we need contraction as well as permutation, see the derivation below. The cut-free variant of this derivation is our running Example 2.3 and its proof net is provided in (2).

$$\dfrac{\dfrac{\dfrac{\dfrac{\dfrac{\dfrac{\dfrac{\dfrac{\dfrac{}{n \vdash n}\,id \quad \dfrac{\dfrac{\text{as before}}{n, n\backslash s, ((n\backslash s)\backslash(n\backslash s))/gp, gp \vdash s}\,/_{\mathsf{L}}}{n, n\backslash s, ((n\backslash s)\backslash(n\backslash s))/gp, gp/n, n \vdash s}\,/_{\mathsf{L}}}{n, (n\backslash s)/n, n, ((n\backslash s)\backslash(n\backslash s))/gp, gp/n, n \vdash s}\,/_{\mathsf{L}}}{n, (n\backslash s)/n, n, ((n\backslash s)\backslash(n\backslash s))/gp, gp/n, !n \vdash s}\,!_{\mathsf{L}}}{n, (n\backslash s)/n, !n, ((n\backslash s)\backslash(n\backslash s))/gp, gp/n, !n \vdash s}\,!_{\mathsf{L}}}{n, (n\backslash s)/n, ((n\backslash s)\backslash(n\backslash s))/gp, gp/n, !n, !n \vdash s}\,\mathsf{perm}_2}{n, (n\backslash s)/n, ((n\backslash s)\backslash(n\backslash s))/gp, gp/n, !n \vdash s}\,\mathsf{con}}{n, (n\backslash s)/n, ((n\backslash s)\backslash(n\backslash s))/gp, gp/n \vdash s/!n}\,/_{\mathsf{R}} \quad \dfrac{\text{as before}}{n, (n\backslash n)/(s/!n), s/!n \vdash n}\,/_{\mathsf{L}}}{n, (n\backslash n)/(s/!n), n, (n\backslash s)/n, ((n\backslash s)\backslash(n\backslash s))/gp, gp/n \vdash n}\,\mathsf{cut}$$

When there is more than one parasitic extraction, as in (c), we need more applications of the con and $!_{\mathsf{L}}$ rules. See below for an abridged derivation and the appendix for the full tree and the proof net:

$$\dfrac{\dfrac{\dfrac{\dfrac{\dfrac{\dfrac{\text{as above}}{\Upsilon, n, \Phi, n, \Psi, n \vdash s}\,/_{\mathsf{L}}}{\Upsilon, !n, \Phi, !n, \Psi, !n \vdash s}\,!_{\mathsf{L}} \times 3}{\Upsilon, \Phi, \Psi, !n, !n, !n \vdash s}\,\mathsf{perm}_2 \times 2}{\Upsilon, \Phi, \Psi, !n \vdash s}\,\mathsf{con} \times 2}{\Upsilon, \Phi, \Psi \vdash s/!n}\,/_{\mathsf{R}} \quad \dfrac{\text{as above}}{n, (n\backslash n)/(s/!n), s/!n \vdash n}\,/_{\mathsf{L}}}{n, (n\backslash n)/(s/!n), \underbrace{n, (n\backslash s)/n,}_{\Upsilon} \underbrace{((n\backslash s)\backslash(n\backslash s))/gp, gp/n,}_{\Phi} \underbrace{((n\backslash s)\backslash(n\backslash s))/gp, gp/n}_{\Psi} \vdash n}\,\mathsf{cut}$$

Relative clauses with parasitic gaps and more adverbs, as in "articles that reviewers accepted $-_1$ immediately without reading $-_2$ properly" are derivable with more, in this case 2, applications of perm_2 rule. Cases when the gap is in the co-argument, as in (d) and (f), are also derivable. Other types of extraction are also derivable, e.g. infinitival, as in "men that John assured Mary to be reliable most of the time". We present some examples in the appendix.

8 Discussion and Conclusion

We developed an extension of Lambek Calculus with the Linear Logic exponential, where it is only applicable to atoms. The system has a cut-elimination theorem and proof nets, and is decidable.

Our system can successfully model a range of parasitic gap phenomena. However, whenever a logic is applied to natural language, there is a risk of over generation and our system is not exempt from it. Traditionally, over generation is overcome by adding key-and-lock *bracket* modalities to modal Lambek calculi [2,24]. Modal Lambek Calculi without bracket modalities [13–15,23] will all naturally over generate. The dilemma is that existing systems with both contraction and bracket modalities are undecidable [16]. We conjecture that our system extended with bracket modalities is still decidable. We are also currently investigating the possibility of developing proof nets for this extended system, along the work of [30].

A Appendix

Let us first show the full proof tree of (c) "articles that reviewers accepted after skimming without reading", and the resulting proof net:

$$\dfrac{\dfrac{}{n \vdash n}\,id \quad \dfrac{}{n \vdash n}\,id}{n, (n\backslash s) \vdash s}\,\backslash_L$$

$$\dfrac{n, (n\backslash s) \vdash s \quad \dfrac{}{n\backslash s \vdash n\backslash s}\,id}{n, (n\backslash s), ((n\backslash s)\backslash(n\backslash s)) \vdash s}\,\backslash_L$$

$$\dfrac{n, (n\backslash s), ((n\backslash s)\backslash(n\backslash s)) \vdash s \quad \dfrac{}{n\backslash s \vdash n\backslash s}\,id}{n, (n\backslash s), ((n\backslash s)\backslash(n\backslash s)), ((n\backslash s)\backslash(n\backslash s)) \vdash s}\,\backslash_L$$

$$\dfrac{n, (n\backslash s), ((n\backslash s)\backslash(n\backslash s)), ((n\backslash s)\backslash(n\backslash s)) \vdash s \quad \dfrac{}{n \vdash n}\,id}{n, (n\backslash s)/n, n, ((n\backslash s)\backslash(n\backslash s)), ((n\backslash s)\backslash(n\backslash s)) \vdash s}\,/_L$$

$$\dfrac{n, (n\backslash s)/n, n, ((n\backslash s)\backslash(n\backslash s)), ((n\backslash s)\backslash(n\backslash s)) \vdash s \quad \dfrac{}{n \vdash n}\,id}{n, (n\backslash s)/n, n, ((n\backslash s)\backslash(n\backslash s))/gp, gp, ((n\backslash s)\backslash(n\backslash s)) \vdash s}$$

$$\dfrac{n, (n\backslash s)/n, n, ((n\backslash s)\backslash(n\backslash s))/gp, gp, ((n\backslash s)\backslash(n\backslash s)) \vdash s \quad \dfrac{}{n \vdash n}\,id}{n, (n\backslash s)/n, n, ((n\backslash s)\backslash(n\backslash s))/gp, gp/n, n, ((n\backslash s)\backslash(n\backslash s)) \vdash s}\,/_L$$

$$\dfrac{n, (n\backslash s)/n, n, ((n\backslash s)\backslash(n\backslash s))/gp, gp/n, n, ((n\backslash s)\backslash(n\backslash s)) \vdash s \quad \dfrac{}{gp \vdash gp}\,id}{n, (n\backslash s)/n, n, ((n\backslash s)\backslash(n\backslash s))/gp, gp/n, n, ((n\backslash s)\backslash(n\backslash s))/gp, gp \vdash s}\,/_L$$

$$\dfrac{n, (n\backslash s)/n, n, ((n\backslash s)\backslash(n\backslash s))/gp, gp/n, n, ((n\backslash s)\backslash(n\backslash s))/gp, gp \vdash s \quad \dfrac{}{n \vdash n}\,id}{n, (n\backslash s)/n, n, ((n\backslash s)\backslash(n\backslash s))/gp, gp/n, n, ((n\backslash s)\backslash(n\backslash s))/gp, gp/n, n \vdash s}\,/_L$$

$$\dfrac{n, (n\backslash s)/n, n, ((n\backslash s)\backslash(n\backslash s))/gp, gp/n, n, ((n\backslash s)\backslash(n\backslash s))/gp, gp/n, n \vdash s}{n, (n\backslash s)/n, !n, ((n\backslash s)\backslash(n\backslash s))/gp, gp/n, n, ((n\backslash s)\backslash(n\backslash s))/gp, gp/n, n \vdash s}\,!_L$$

$$\dfrac{n, (n\backslash s)/n, !n, ((n\backslash s)\backslash(n\backslash s))/gp, gp/n, n, ((n\backslash s)\backslash(n\backslash s))/gp, gp/n, n \vdash s}{n, (n\backslash s)/n, !n, ((n\backslash s)\backslash(n\backslash s))/gp, gp/n, !n, ((n\backslash s)\backslash(n\backslash s))/gp, gp/n, n \vdash s}\,!_L$$

$$\dfrac{n, (n\backslash s)/n, !n, ((n\backslash s)\backslash(n\backslash s))/gp, gp/n, !n, ((n\backslash s)\backslash(n\backslash s))/gp, gp/n, n \vdash s}{n, (n\backslash s)/n, !n, ((n\backslash s)\backslash(n\backslash s))/gp, gp/n, !n, ((n\backslash s)\backslash(n\backslash s))/gp, gp/n, !n \vdash s}\,!_L$$

$$\dfrac{n, (n\backslash s)/n, !n, ((n\backslash s)\backslash(n\backslash s))/gp, gp/n, !n, ((n\backslash s)\backslash(n\backslash s))/gp, gp/n, !n \vdash s}{n, (n\backslash s)/n, !n, ((n\backslash s)\backslash(n\backslash s))/gp, gp/n, ((n\backslash s)\backslash(n\backslash s))/gp, gp/n, !n, !n \vdash s}\,\mathsf{perm}_2$$

$$\dfrac{n, (n\backslash s)/n, !n, ((n\backslash s)\backslash(n\backslash s))/gp, gp/n, ((n\backslash s)\backslash(n\backslash s))/gp, gp/n, !n, !n \vdash s}{n, (n\backslash s)/n, ((n\backslash s)\backslash(n\backslash s))/gp, gp/n, ((n\backslash s)\backslash(n\backslash s))/gp, gp/n, !n, !n, !n \vdash s}\,\mathsf{perm}_2$$

$$\dfrac{n, (n\backslash s)/n, ((n\backslash s)\backslash(n\backslash s))/gp, gp/n, ((n\backslash s)\backslash(n\backslash s))/gp, gp/n, !n, !n, !n \vdash s}{n, (n\backslash s)/n, ((n\backslash s)\backslash(n\backslash s))/gp, gp/n, ((n\backslash s)\backslash(n\backslash s))/gp, gp/n, !n, !n \vdash s}\,\mathsf{con}$$

$$\dfrac{n, (n\backslash s)/n, ((n\backslash s)\backslash(n\backslash s))/gp, gp/n, ((n\backslash s)\backslash(n\backslash s))/gp, gp/n, !n, !n \vdash s}{n, (n\backslash s)/n, ((n\backslash s)\backslash(n\backslash s))/gp, gp/n, ((n\backslash s)\backslash(n\backslash s))/gp, gp/n, !n \vdash s}\,\mathsf{con}$$

$$\dfrac{n, (n\backslash s)/n, ((n\backslash s)\backslash(n\backslash s))/gp, gp/n, ((n\backslash s)\backslash(n\backslash s))/gp, gp/n, !n \vdash s}{n, (n\backslash s)/n, ((n\backslash s)\backslash(n\backslash s))/gp, gp/n, ((n\backslash s)\backslash(n\backslash s))/gp, gp/n \vdash s/!n}\,/_R$$

$$\dfrac{\text{as before}}{n, (n\backslash n)/(s/!n), s/!n \vdash n}\,/_L$$

$$\dfrac{n, (n\backslash s)/n, ((n\backslash s)\backslash(n\backslash s))/gp, gp/n, ((n\backslash s)\backslash(n\backslash s))/gp, gp/n \vdash s/!n \quad n, (n\backslash n)/(s/!n), s/!n \vdash n}{n, (n\backslash n)/(s/!n), n, (n\backslash s)/n, ((n\backslash s)\backslash(n\backslash s))/gp, gp/n, ((n\backslash s)\backslash(n\backslash s))/gp, gp/n \vdash n}\,\mathsf{cut}$$

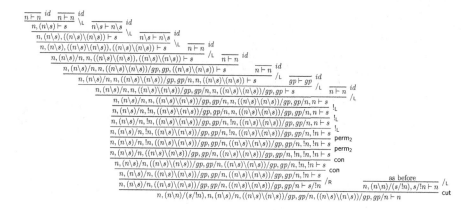

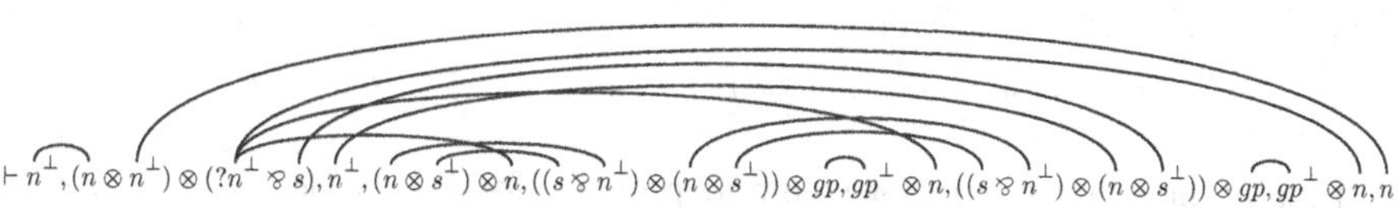

$$\vdash n^{\perp}, (n \otimes n^{\perp}) \otimes (?n^{\perp} \parr s), n^{\perp}, (n \otimes s^{\perp}) \otimes n, ((s \parr n^{\perp}) \otimes (n \otimes s^{\perp})) \otimes gp, gp^{\perp} \otimes n, ((s \parr n^{\perp}) \otimes (n \otimes s^{\perp})) \otimes gp, gp^{\perp} \otimes n, n$$

In order to model (e) and (f) we need new atoms. We use the atoms used in [27] for adjective phrases and infinitives of verbs. A few shortcuts are also implemented to keep the size of the proof trees manageable. For instance instead of typing "a" separately and "review" and "blog post" separately, we assign the type n to "a review", similarly to "a blog post" in one step. The new assignments are presented below:

$$\begin{array}{rcl}
\text{chairs, a blog post, a review} & :: & n \\
\text{famous} & :: & ap \\
\text{accept} & :: & if/n \\
\text{persuaded} & :: & ((n\backslash s)/to)/n \\
\text{made} & :: & ((n\backslash s)/ap)/n \\
\text{every} & :: & (n/n) \\
\text{to} & :: & to/if \\
\text{in, about} & :: & (n\backslash n)/n
\end{array} \qquad (5)$$

Here are the proof tree and proof net for (d) "articles that chairs persuaded every reviewer of to accept":

$$\dfrac{n \vdash n\ id \qquad s \vdash s\ id}{n, ((n\backslash s) \vdash s}\ \backslash_L$$

$$\dfrac{n, ((n\backslash s) \vdash s \qquad to \vdash to\ id}{n, ((n\backslash s)/to), to \vdash s}\ /_L$$

$$\dfrac{n, ((n\backslash s)/to), to \vdash s \qquad n \vdash n\ id}{n, ((n\backslash s)/to)/n), n, to \vdash s}\ /_L$$

$$\dfrac{n, ((n\backslash s)/to)/n), n, to \vdash s \qquad n \vdash n\ id}{n, ((n\backslash s)/to)/n), n/n, n, to \vdash s}\ /_L$$

$$\dfrac{n, ((n\backslash s)/to)/n), n/n, n, to \vdash s \qquad n \vdash n\ id}{n, ((n\backslash s)/to)/n), n/n, n/n, n, to \vdash s}\ /_L$$

$$\dfrac{n, ((n\backslash s)/to)/n), n/n, n/n, n, to \vdash s \qquad if \vdash if\ id}{n, ((n\backslash s)/to)/n), n/n, n/n, n, to/if, if \vdash s}\ /_L$$

$$\dfrac{n, ((n\backslash s)/to)/n), n/n, n/n, n, to/if, if \vdash s \qquad n \vdash n\ id}{n, ((n\backslash s)/to)/n), n/n, n/n, n, to/if, if/n, n \vdash s}\ /_L$$

$$\dfrac{n, ((n\backslash s)/to)/n), n/n, n/n, n, to/if, if/n, n \vdash s}{n, ((n\backslash s)/to)/n), n/n, n/n, !n, to/if, if/n, !n \vdash s}\ !_L \times 2$$

$$\dfrac{n, ((n\backslash s)/to)/n), n/n, n/n, !n, to/if, if/n, !n \vdash s}{n, ((n\backslash s)/to)/n), n/n, n/n, to/if, if/n, !n, !n \vdash s}\ \mathsf{perm}_2$$

$$\dfrac{n, ((n\backslash s)/to)/n), n/n, n/n, to/if, if/n, !n, !n \vdash s}{n, ((n\backslash s)/to)/n), n/n, n/n, to/if, if/n, !n \vdash s}\ \mathsf{con}$$

$$\dfrac{n, ((n\backslash s)/to)/n), n/n, n/n, to/if, if/n, !n \vdash s}{n, ((n\backslash s)/to)/n), n/n, n/n, to/if, if/n \vdash s/!n}\ /_R \qquad \dfrac{\text{as before}}{n, (n\backslash n)/(s/!n), s/!n \vdash n}\ /_L$$

$$\dfrac{n, ((n\backslash s)/to)/n), n/n, n/n, to/if, if/n \vdash s/!n \qquad n, (n\backslash n)/(s/!n), s/!n \vdash n}{n, (n\backslash n)/(s/!n), n, ((n\backslash s)/to)/n), n/n, n/n, to/if, if/n \vdash n}\ \mathsf{cut}$$

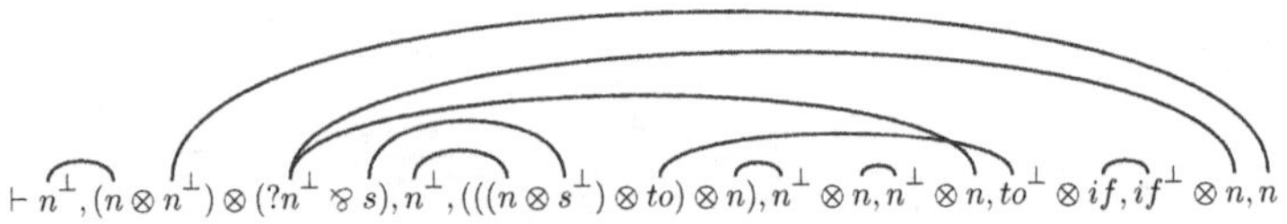

Finally, here are the proof tree and prof net for (e) "articles that a review about in a blog post made famous":

$$\dfrac{n \vdash n\ id \qquad s \vdash s\ id}{n, (n\backslash s) \vdash s}\ \backslash_L$$

$$\dfrac{n \vdash n\ id \qquad n, (n\backslash s) \vdash s}{n, (n\backslash n), (n\backslash s) \vdash s}\ \backslash_L$$

$$\dfrac{n, (n\backslash n), (n\backslash s) \vdash s \qquad n \vdash n\ id}{n, (n\backslash n)/n, n, (n\backslash s) \vdash s}\ /_L$$

$$\dfrac{n, (n\backslash n)/n, n, (n\backslash s) \vdash s \qquad n \vdash n\ id}{n, (n\backslash n)/n, n, n\backslash n, (n\backslash s) \vdash s}\ \backslash_L$$

$$\dfrac{n, (n\backslash n)/n, n, n\backslash n, (n\backslash s) \vdash s \qquad n \vdash n\ id}{n, (n\backslash n)/n, n, (n\backslash n)/n, n, (n\backslash s) \vdash s}\ /_L$$

$$\dfrac{n, (n\backslash n)/n, n, (n\backslash n)/n, n, (n\backslash s) \vdash s \qquad ap \vdash ap\ id}{n, (n\backslash n)/n, n, (n\backslash n)/n, n, ((n\backslash s)/ap), ap \vdash s}\ /_L$$

$$\dfrac{n, (n\backslash n)/n, n, (n\backslash n)/n, n, ((n\backslash s)/ap), ap \vdash s \qquad n \vdash n\ id}{n, (n\backslash n)/n, n, (n\backslash n)/n, n, ((n\backslash s)/ap)/n, n, ap \vdash s}\ /_L$$

$$\dfrac{n, (n\backslash n)/n, n, (n\backslash n)/n, n, ((n\backslash s)/ap)/n, n, ap \vdash s}{n, (n\backslash n)/n, !n, (n\backslash n)/n, n, ((n\backslash s)/ap)/n, !n, ap \vdash s}\ !_L \times 2$$

$$\dfrac{n, (n\backslash n)/n, !n, (n\backslash n)/n, n, ((n\backslash s)/ap)/n, !n, ap \vdash s}{n, (n\backslash n)/n, (n\backslash n)/n, n, ((n\backslash s)/ap)/n, ap, !n, !n \vdash s}\ \mathsf{perm}_2$$

$$\dfrac{n, (n\backslash n)/n, (n\backslash n)/n, n, ((n\backslash s)/ap)/n, ap, !n, !n \vdash s}{n, (n\backslash n)/n, (n\backslash n)/n, n, ((n\backslash s)/ap)/n, ap, !n \vdash s}\ \mathsf{con}$$

$$\dfrac{n, (n\backslash n)/n, (n\backslash n)/n, n, ((n\backslash s)/ap)/n, ap, !n \vdash s}{n, (n\backslash n)/n, (n\backslash n)/n, n, ((n\backslash s)/ap)/n, ap \vdash s/!n}\ /_R \qquad \dfrac{\text{as before}}{n, (n\backslash n)/(s/!n), s/!n \vdash n}\ /_L$$

$$\dfrac{n, (n\backslash n)/n, (n\backslash n)/n, n, ((n\backslash s)/ap)/n, ap \vdash s/!n \qquad n, (n\backslash n)/(s/!n), s/!n \vdash n}{n, (n\backslash n)/(s/!n), n, (n\backslash n)/n, (n\backslash n)/n, n, ((n\backslash s)/ap)/n, ap \vdash n}\ \mathsf{cut}$$

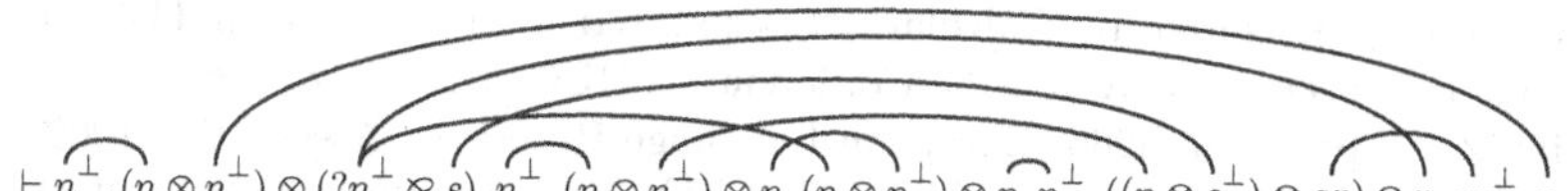

$$\vdash n^\perp, (n \otimes n^\perp) \otimes (?n^\perp \parr s), n^\perp, (n \otimes n^\perp) \otimes n, (n \otimes n^\perp) \otimes n, n^\perp, ((n \otimes s^\perp) \otimes ap) \otimes n, ap^\perp, n$$

References

1. Abrusci, V.M., Ruet, P.: Non-commutative logic I: the multiplicative fragment. Ann. Pure Appl. Logic **101**, 29–64 (2000)
2. Barry, G., Hepple, M., Leslie, N., Morrill, G.: Proof figures and structural operators for categorial grammar. In: Kunze, J., Reimann, D. (eds.) EACL 1991, 5th Conference of the European Chapter of the Association for Computational Linguistics, 9–11 April 1991, Congress Hall, Alexanderplatz, Berlin, Germany, pp. 198–203. The Association for Computer Linguistics (1991)
3. Culicover, P., Postal, P. (eds.): Parasitic Gaps. MIT Press, Cambridge (2001)
4. Danos, V., Regnier, L.: The structure of multiplicatives. Arch. Math. Log. **28**(3), 181–203 (1989)
5. Engdahl, E.: Parasitic gaps. Linguist. Philos. **6**(1), 5–34 (1983)
6. Girard, J.-Y.: Linear logic. Theoret. Comput. Sci. **50**, 1–102 (1987)
7. Girard, J.-Y.: On the unity of logic. Ann. Pure Appl. Logic **59**, 201–217 (1993)
8. Guglielmi, A.: A system of interaction and structure. ACM Trans. Comput. Logic **8**(1), 1–64 (2007)
9. Guglielmi, A., Straßburger, L.: Non-commutativity and MELL in the calculus of structures. In: Fribourg, L. (ed.) CSL 2001. LNCS, vol. 2142, pp. 54–68. Springer, Heidelberg (2001). https://doi.org/10.1007/3-540-44802-0_5
10. Heijltjes, W., Houston, R.: Proof equivalence in MLL is PSPACE-complete. Log. Methods Comput. Sci. **12**(1) (2016)
11. Jäger, G.: Anaphora and Type Logical Grammar, vol. 24. Springer, Dordrecht (2006). https://doi.org/10.1007/1-4020-3905-0
12. Kanazawa, M.: The lambek calculus enriched with additional connectives. J. Logic Lang. Inform. **1**(2), 141–171 (1992)
13. Kanovich, M.I., Kuznetsov, S.L., Nigam, V., Scedrov, A.: Subexponentials in non-commutative linear logic. Math. Struct. Comput. Sci. **29**(8), 1217–1249 (2019)
14. Kanovich, M., Kuznetsov, S., Nigam, V., Scedrov, A.: Soft subexponentials and multiplexing. In: Peltier, N., Sofronie-Stokkermans, V. (eds.) IJCAR 2020. LNCS (LNAI), vol. 12166, pp. 500–517. Springer, Cham (2020). https://doi.org/10.1007/978-3-030-51074-9_29
15. Kanovich, M., Kuznetsov, S., Scedrov, A.: Undecidability of the lambek calculus with a relevant modality. In: Foret, A., Morrill, G., Muskens, R., Osswald, R., Pogodalla, S. (eds.) FG 2015-2016. LNCS, vol. 9804, pp. 240–256. Springer, Heidelberg (2016). https://doi.org/10.1007/978-3-662-53042-9_14
16. Kanovich, M., Kuznetsov, S., Scedrov, A.: Undecidability of the lambek calculus with subexponential and bracket modalities. In: Klasing, R., Zeitoun, M. (eds.) FCT 2017. LNCS, vol. 10472, pp. 326–340. Springer, Heidelberg (2017). https://doi.org/10.1007/978-3-662-55751-8_26

17. Kanovich, M.I., Kuznetsov, S.L., Scedrov, A.: Reconciling lambek's restriction, cut-elimination and substitution in the presence of exponential modalities. J. Log. Comput. **30**(1), 239–256 (2020)
18. Kogkalidis, K., Moortgat, M., Moot, R.: Æthel: automatically extracted typelogical derivations for Dutch. In: Calzolari, N., et al. (eds.) Proceedings of The 12th Language Resources and Evaluation Conference, LREC 2020, Marseille, France, 11–16 May 2020, pp. 5257–5266. European Language Resources Association (2020)
19. Kogkalidis, K., Moortgat, M., Moot, R.: SPINDLE: spinning raw text into lambda terms with graph attention. In: Croce, D., Soldaini, L. (eds.) Proceedings of the 17th Conference of the European Chapter of the Association for Computational Linguistics. EACL 2023 - System Demonstrations, Dubrovnik, Croatia, 2–4 May 2023, pp. 128–135. Association for Computational Linguistics (2023)
20. Lamarche, F., Retoré, C.: Proof nets for the Lambek-calculus — an overview. In: Michele Abrusci, V., Casadio, C. (eds.) Proceedings of the Third Roma Workshop "Proofs and Linguistic Categories", pp. 241–262. CLUEB, Bologna (1996)
21. Lambek, J.: The mathematics of sentence structure. Am. Math. Monthly **65**, 154–170 (1958)
22. Lazić, R., Schmitz, S.: Nonelementary complexities for branching VASS, MELL, and extensions. ACM Trans. Comput. Logic **16**(3), 1–30 (2015)
23. Mcpheat, L., Wijnholds, G., Sadrzadeh, M., Correia, A., Toumi, A.: Anaphora and ellipsis in lambek calculus with a relevant modality: Syntax and semantics. J. Cogn. Sci. **22**, 1–34 (2021)
24. Moortgat, M.: Multimodal linguistic inference. J. Logic Lang. Inform. **5**(3–4), 349–385 (1996)
25. Moortgat, M., Oehrle, R.: Structural abstractions. In: Proofs and Linguistic Categories: Application of Logic to the Analysis and Implementation of Natural Language, Proceedings of the 1996 Roma Workshop (1996)
26. Moortgat, M., Sadrzadeh, M., Wijnholds, G.: A frobenius algebraic analysis for parasitic gaps. FLAP **7**(5), 823–852 (2020)
27. Moortgat, M., Sadrzadeh, M., Wijnholds, G.: A frobenius algebraic analysis for parasitic gaps. J. Appl. Log. **7**, 823–852 (2020)
28. Moot, R.: Semi-automated extraction of a wide-coverage type-logical grammar for French. In: Langlais, P., Gagnon, M. (eds.) Actes de la 17e conférence sur le Traitement Automatique des Langues Naturelles. Articles courts, TALN 2010, Montréal, Canada, July 2010, pp. 189–194. ATALA (2010)
29. Moot, R.: The grail theorem prover: type theory for syntax and semantics. CoRR, abs/1602.00812 (2016)
30. Moot, R., Puite, Q.: Proof nets for the multimodal lambek calculus. Stud. Logica. **71**, 415–442 (2002)
31. Morrill, G., Leslie, N., Hepple, M., Barry, G.: Categorial deductions and structural operations. Studies in Categorial Grammar. Edinburgh Working Papers in Cognitive Science (1990)
32. Morrill, G., Valentín, O.: Computational coverage of TLG: Nonlinearity. In: Proceedings of Third Workshop on Natural Language and Computer Science, vol. 32, pp. 51–63. EasyChair Publications (2015)
33. Morrill, G., Valentín, O.: On the logic of expansion in natural language. In: Amblard, M., de Groote, P., Pogodalla, S., Retoré, C. (eds.) LACL 2016. LNCS, vol. 10054, pp. 228–246. Springer, Heidelberg (2016). https://doi.org/10.1007/978-3-662-53826-5_14
34. Morrill, G., Valentín, O., Fadda, M.: The displacement calculus. J. Logic Lang. Inform. **20**(1), 1–48 (2011)

35. Nigam, V., Miller, D.: Algorithmic specifications in linear logic with subexponentials. In: ACM SIGPLAN Conference on Principles and Practice of Declarative Programming (PPDP), pp. 129–140 (2009)
36. Oehrle, R.T.: Resource-sensitivity–a brief guide. In: Kruijff, G.-J.M., Oehrle, R.T. (eds.) Resource-Sensitivity, Binding and Anaphora, pp. 231–255. Springer, Dordrecht (2003). https://doi.org/10.1007/978-94-010-0037-6_9
37. Pentus, M.: Lambek calculus is np-complete. Theor. Comput. Sci. **357**(1–3), 186–201 (2006)
38. Retoré, C.: Pomset logic: a non-commutative extension of classical linear logic. In: de Groote, P., Roger Hindley, J. (eds.) TLCA 1997. LNCS, vol. 1210, pp. 300–318. Springer, Heidelberg (1997). https://doi.org/10.1007/3-540-62688-3_43
39. Straßburger, L.: System NEL is undecidable. In: De Queiroz, R., Pimentel, E., Figueiredo, L. (eds.) 10th Workshop on Logic, Language, Information and Computation (WoLLIC). Electronic Notes in Theoretical Computer Science, vol. 84, pp. 166–177 (2003)
40. Yetter, D.N.: Quantales and (noncommutative) linear logic. J. Symb. Log. **55**(1), 41–64 (1990)

Completeness of Finitely Weighted Kleene Algebra with Tests

Igor Sedlár(✉)

The Czech Academy of Sciences, Institute of Computer Science, Prague, Czech Republic
sedlar@cs.cas.cz

Abstract. Building on Ésik and Kuich's completeness result for finitely weighted Kleene algebra, we establish relational and language completeness results for finitely weighted Kleene algebra with tests. Similarly as Ésik and Kuich, we assume that the finite semiring of weights is commutative, partially ordered and zero-bounded, but we also assume that it is integral. We argue that finitely weighted Kleene algebra with tests is a natural framework for equational reasoning about weighted programs in cases where an upper bound on admissible weights is assumed.

1 Introduction

Ésik and Kuich [4] generalize the completeness result of Kozen [8], which connects Kleene algebras with the algebra of regular languages, to the case of weighted regular languages, or formal power series. In particular, their result applies to a weighted generalization of Kleene algebra where the semiring of weights is finite, commutative, zero-bounded (or positive) and partially ordered. Building on their work, we establish two completeness results for a weighted generalization of Kleene algebras with tests [9]. First, we establish completeness with respect to the algebra of weighted guarded languages using a reduction to weighted regular languages similar to the one used by Kozen and Smith [10] to prove completeness for non-weighted Kleene algebras with tests. Second, we establish completeness with respect to weighted transition systems by using a Cayley-like construction going back to the work of Pratt [13] on (non-weighted) dynamic algebras. In addition to the assumptions of Ésik and Kuich, we need to assume that the semiring of weights is also integral.

Weighted Kleene algebras with tests provide a framework for equational reasoning about properties of weighted programs [1], a generalization of standard programs articulating the idea that computation may carry some sort of weight. We have pointed out this connection in earlier work [16]; this paper contributes with a slightly simpler but more general definition of a weighted Kleene algebra with tests, and the completeness results. We also argue that although *finitely* weighted structures are a simplification with respect to the cases usually studied when weighted computation is concerned [3,12,15] they are still practically relevant since they represent the assumption of an upper bound on admissible weights.

G. Metcalfe et al. (Eds.): WoLLIC 2024, LNCS 14672, pp. 210–224, 2024.
https://doi.org/10.1007/978-3-031-62687-6_14

The paper is organized as follows. Section 2 recalls semirings, their interpretation in terms of weights, and discusses formal power series and weighted relations. Section 3 introduces weighted Kleene algebras with tests and outlines their applications in reasoning about weighted programs. Completeness of finitely weighted Kleene algebras with tests with respect to the algebra of weighted guarded languages is established in Sect. 4 and Sect. 5 establishes completeness with respect to weighted transition systems. The concluding Sect. 6 summarizes the paper and outlines some interesting problems we leave for future work. Details of some of the proofs are given in the technical appendix.

2 Semirings and Weighted Structures

In this section we recall the basic background information on semirings, and we discuss their interpretation as algebras of weights. Then we recall two kinds of weighted structures that will be important in this paper: formal power series (weighted languages) and weighted relations (square matrices over a semiring). Our discussion is based on [12], and details are provided for the benefit of the non-specialist reader. At the end of the section, we discuss the usefulness of working with finite semirings of weights.

Recall that a *semiring* is a structure $\langle X, +, \cdot, 0, 1\rangle$ where $\langle X, \cdot, 1\rangle$ is a monoid, $\langle X, +, 0\rangle$ is a commutative monoid, multiplication $\cdot$ distributes over addition $+$ from both sides, and 0 is the multiplicative annihilator ($0 \cdot x = 0 = x \cdot 0$ for all $x \in X$). A semiring X is *commutative* if $x \cdot y = y \cdot x$ for all $x, y \in X$; it is (additively) *idempotent* iff $x + x = x$ for all $x \in X$; and X is *partially ordered* if there is a partial order $\leq$ on X such that both $\cdot$ and $+$ are monotone with respect to $\leq$. A partially ordered semiring X is *zero-bounded* if $0 \leq x$ for all $x \in X$, and it is *integral* if $x \leq 1$ for all $x \in X$. Note that each idempotent semiring is partially ordered ($x \leq y$ iff $x+y = y$) and zero-bounded. A commutative partially ordered zero-bounded semiring is called a *copo-semiring*; a copo-semiring which is also integral is called a *copi-semiring.*

Semirings are natural models of *weights* (for instance, the amount of some resource needed to perform an action). Multiplication represents merge of weights ($x \cdot y$ as weight x together with weight y), the multiplicative unit 1 represents inert weight (resp. no weight) and the annihilator 0 represents absolute weight. Partially ordered semirings represent the idea that weights are ordered, but the order may not be linear. In zero-bounded ordered semirings 0 is the "worst" weight and in integral semirings 1 is the "best" one. Idempotent semirings come with a natural interpretation of addition, which can be seen as selecting the "best" weight out of a pair of weights.

Example 1. A familiar example of a finite semiring is the *Boolean semiring* $\langle \{0, 1\}, \vee, \wedge, 0, 1\rangle$, representing an "all or nothing" perspective on weights. Real numbers $\mathbb{R}$ with their usual addition and multiplication also form a semiring, as do their subalgebras such as integers $\mathbb{Z}$ and natural numbers $\mathbb{N}$. A semiring often used in connection with shortest paths is the *tropical semiring* over extended natural numbers $\mathbb{N} \cup \{\infty\}$ where semiring multiplication is addition on $\mathbb{N} \cup \{\infty\}$

(where $\infty + x = \infty = x + \infty$) and semiring addition is the minimum function, which is idempotent. This means that the multiplicative identity 0 (the natural number zero) is the greatest element with respect to the partial order induced by min and ∞, where the latter is the annihilator and the least element. A semiring often used in modelling imprecise or vague notions is the *Łukasiewicz semiring* on the real unit interval $[0, 1]$ where max is semiring addition (idempotent) and the semiring multiplication is the Łukasiewicz t-norm: $x \otimes y = \max\{0, x+y-1\}$. Of course, 1 is the multiplicative identity and 0 is the annihilator.

Recall that if Σ is a set, then Σ^* is the set of all finite sequences of elements of Σ, including the empty sequence ϵ. If Σ is seen as an alphabet, Σ^* can be seen as the set of all finite words over Σ. Algebraically speaking, Σ^* is the free monoid generated by Σ with ϵ as the multiplicative identity and word concatenation as multiplication. A *language* over Σ is a subset of Σ^*. A *formal power series* over Σ with coefficients in a semiring S is a function from Σ^* to S. Formal power series can be seen as *weighted languages* and languages over Σ correspond to formal power series over Σ with coefficients in the Boolean semiring. The set of all formal power series over Σ with coefficients in S is usually denoted as $S\langle\langle\Sigma^*\rangle\rangle$. A *polynomial* is a formal power series r such that the set of $w \in \Sigma^*$ with $r(w) \neq 0$ is finite. The set of polynomials in $S\langle\langle\Sigma^*\rangle\rangle$ is usually denoted as $S\langle\Sigma^*\rangle$. Examples of polynomials in $S\langle\Sigma^*\rangle$ include formal power series usually denoted as sw, for $s \in S$ and $w \in \Sigma^*$, such that $sw(u) = s$ if $w = u$ and $sw(u) = 0$ otherwise. It is customary to denote $s\epsilon$ as s and $1w$ as w for $w \neq \epsilon$. The set $S\langle\langle\Sigma^*\rangle\rangle$ has a structure of a semiring where $0, 1 \in S\langle\langle\Sigma^*\rangle\rangle$ are polynomials of the type just mentioned, and

$$(r_1 + r_2)(w) = r_1(w) + r_2(w) \qquad (r_1 \cdot r_2)(w) = \sum_{w = w_1 w_2} r_1(w_1) \cdot r_2(w_2) \, .$$

(Note that the sum exists in arbitrary S since there are only finitely many w_1, w_2 such that $w = w_1 w_2$.) If S is finite, then we may define $s^* = \sum_{n \in \omega} s^n$, where $s^0 = 1$ and $s^{n+1} = s^n \cdot s$.[1] The * may be lifted to formal power series:

$$r^*(w) = \sum_{w_1 \ldots w_n \in [w]} r(w_1) \cdot \ldots \cdot r(w_n) \, ,$$

where $[w]$ is the set of all factors of w. (Equivalently, $r^*(w) = \sum_{n \in \omega} r^n(w)$.) Addition, multiplication and star are known as *rational operations* on formal power series. The smallest set of formal power series in $S\langle\langle\Sigma^*\rangle\rangle$ that contains all polynomials and is closed under the rational operations is known as the set of *rational power series* and denoted as $S^{\mathrm{rat}}\langle\langle\Sigma^*\rangle\rangle$. Rational power series over Σ with coefficients in the Boolean semiring are the *regular languages* over Σ.

Let S be a semiring. An *S-weighted relation* on a set Q is a function from $Q \times Q$ to S. An S-weighted relation on Q may be seen as a (potentially infinite)

[1] Not only if S is finite, of course, but we need not consider this more general setting in this paper. See [3,12,15].

$Q \times Q$ matrix with entries in S. Matrix addition can then be used to define weighted union of relations on Q and, if S is finite, matrix multiplication can be used to define weighted relational composition of relations on Q:

$$(M+N)_{q,q'} = M_{q,q'} + N_{q,q'} \qquad (M \cdot N)_{q,q'} = \sum_{p \in Q} M_{q,p} \cdot N_{p,q'} \,.$$

The set of all S-weighted relations on Q ($Q \times Q$ matrices with entries in S) forms a semiring, where 0 is the zero matrix (all entries are 0) and 1 is the identity matrix (the diagonal matrix where all entries on the diagonal are 1). If S is finite, then the star of a $Q \times Q$ matrix with entries in S [2,12] represents weighted reflexive transitive closure of the corresponding S-weighted relation on Q: $M^* = \sum_{n \in \omega} M^n$, where $M^0 = 1$ and $M^{n+1} = M^n \cdot M$. Alternatively, $M^*_{q,q'} = \sum_{x \in [q,q']} M(x)$ where $[q,q']$ is the set of all finite paths from q to q' and $M(q_1 \ldots q_n) = M_{q_1,q_2} \cdot \ldots \cdot M_{q_{n-1},q_n}$.

Weighted relations represent the idea that the transition from q to q' carries a weight, $M_{q,q'}$. For instance, if $\mathbb{N} \cup \{\infty\}$ is used and M gives each edge in a directed graph over Q a weight of $1 \in \mathbb{N}$, then $M_{q,q'}$ is the length of the shortest path from q to q' – literally the smallest number of steps in the graph you need to take in order to get from q to q' (∞ if there is no path from q to q'). Assuming an infinite semiring of weights, such as $\mathbb{N} \cup \{\infty\}$, means that "no path is too long *a priori*". On the other hand, in most practical situations it is sensible (or even necessary), to set a cut-off point beyond which all paths *are* "too long". Reasoning about weights with a cut-off point in place corresponds to working with a *finite* semiring of weights.

Example 2. A *finite tropical semiring* is any $N \cup \{\infty\}$ where N is a non-empty initial segment of $\mathbb{N}$, semiring multiplication is truncated addition ($n + m = \infty$ if the "ordinary sum" of n and m is not in N), semiring addition is min, the multiplicative identity is 0 and the annihilator is ∞. For $n > 1$, the *n-element Łukasiewicz semiring* is defined on the domain $\{\frac{m}{n-1} \mid m \in [0, n-1]\}$ and the operations are defined as in the infinite case. Note that both of these examples yield *nilpotent* semirings: for each $s \neq 1$ there is $n \in \omega$ such that $s^n = 0$.

3 Weighted Kleene Algebra with Tests

In this section, we recall Kleene algebras [8], we formulate a notion of weighted Kleene algebra based on Ésik and Kuich's definition [4], and we state their completeness result (Sect. 3.1). Then we recall Kleene algebras with tests and we formulate a notion of weighted Kleene algebras with tests (3.2). Finally, applications to reasoning about weighted programs are outlined (3.3).

3.1 Kleene Algebras

Recall that a *Kleene algebra* [8] is an idempotent semiring X with a unary operation * satisfying, for all $x, y, z \in X$ the following *unrolling* (left column) and *fixpoint* laws (right column):

$$1 + (x \cdot x^*) = x^* \qquad y + (x \cdot z) \le z \implies x^* \cdot y \le z \tag{1}$$

$$1 + (x^* \cdot x) = x^* \qquad y + (z \cdot x) \le z \implies y \cdot x^* \le z\,. \tag{2}$$

Ésik and Kuich [4] do not assume the unrolling law $1 + (x^* \cdot x) = x^*$ but it can be shown that it can be derived from the rest. We usually write xy instead of $x \cdot y$. Some useful equalities that follow from these axioms are the *sliding* and *denesting* laws: $(xy)^*x = x(yx)^*$ and $(x + y)^* = x^*(yx^*)^*$.

Definition 1. *Let S be a finite semiring. A* Kleene S-algebra *is a Kleene algebra X together with a binary operation*

$$\odot : X \times S \to X$$

such that (the additive monoid reduct of) X forms a right S-semimodule and

$$(x \cdot y) \odot s = x \cdot (y \odot s) = (x \odot s) \cdot y \tag{3}$$

$$1 \odot s^* \le (1 \odot s)^* \tag{4}$$

(Recall that $s^* = \sum_{n \in \omega} s^n$.) It follows that $(1 \odot s^*) = (1 \odot s)^*$; see [4].[2]

The class of all Kleene S-algebras for a fixed S is denoted as $\mathsf{KA}(S)$; moreover, we define $\mathsf{KA(X)} = \bigcup_{S \in \mathsf{X}} \mathsf{KA}(S)$. Ésik and Kuich use the *left* S-action on K instead of the right one (that is, $\odot : S \times X \to X$).

The following syntactic definition is not used explicitly by Ésik and Kuich, but we will need it in this paper. (Ésik and Kuich state their result using the notion of free algebra.)

Definition 2. *Let Σ be a finite alphabet and S a finite semiring. The set of (Σ, S)-expressions* $\mathrm{Exp}(\Sigma, S)$ *is defined using the following grammar:*

$$e, f := \mathsf{a} \mid e \odot s \mid e + f \mid e \cdot f \mid e^* \mid \mathsf{0} \mid \mathsf{1}$$

where $\mathsf{a} \in \Sigma$ and $s \in S$.

A Kleene S-algebra *model* is a Kleene S-algebra X together with a homomorphism $h : \mathrm{Exp}(\Sigma, S) \to X$, where it is understood that $h(e \odot s) = h(e) \odot s$. The notions of validity of an equation in a class of Kleene S-algebras, and equational theory of a class of Kleene S-algebras are defined in the usual way. Note that $S^{\mathrm{rat}}\langle\langle\Sigma^*\rangle\rangle \in \mathsf{KA}(S)$.

Theorem 1 (Ésik and Kuich [4]). *If S is a finite copo-semiring, then, for all $e, f \in \mathrm{Exp}(\Sigma, S)$,*

$$\mathsf{KA}(S) \models e \approx f \iff S^{\mathrm{rat}}\langle\langle\Sigma^*\rangle\rangle \models e \approx f\,.$$

[2] A similar definition could be formulated for the case of infinite S where it is assumed that s^* is defined for all s. For instance, one could assume that S is a Kleene algebra.

The *standard language interpretation* of $\mathrm{Exp}(\Sigma, S)$ is the unique homomorphism $\mathscr{L} : \mathrm{Exp}(\Sigma, S) \to S\langle\langle\Sigma^*\rangle\rangle$ such that $\mathscr{L}(\mathsf{a}) = 1\mathsf{a}$.

Corollary 1. *If S is a finite copo-semiring, then, for all $e, f \in \mathrm{Exp}(\Sigma, S)$,*

$$\mathsf{KA}(S) \models e \approx f \iff \mathscr{L}(e) = \mathscr{L}(f)\,.$$

Proof. The non-trivial implication follows from the fact that for every $r \in S^{\mathrm{rat}}\langle\langle\Sigma^*\rangle\rangle$ there is e_r such that $r = \mathscr{L}(e_r)$. □

3.2 Kleene Algebras with Tests

Recall that a Kleene algebra with tests [9] is a Kleene algebra X with a distinguished $B \subseteq X$ such that $\langle B, +, \cdot, 0, 1\rangle$ is a subalgebra of X and a bounded distributive lattice, and $\bar{}$ is an unary operation on B such that $x \cdot \bar{x} = 0$ and $x + \bar{x} = 1$ for all $x \in B$. Hence, B forms a Boolean algebra. Intuitively, elements of B represent *Boolean tests.*

Definition 3. *Let S be a semiring. A* Kleene S-algebra with tests *is a Kleene S-algebra X that is also a Kleene algebra with tests.*

Recall that every Kleene algebra is also a Kleene algebra with tests (take $B = \{0, 1\}$ with $\bar{}$ defined in the obvious way). Hence, every Kleene S-algebra is a Kleene S-algebra with tests. Conversely, every Kleene S-algebra with tests becomes a Kleene S-algebra if one "disregards" the tests. The class of all Kleene S-algebras with tests for a fixed S is denoted as $\mathsf{KAT}(S)$, and $\mathsf{KAT}(\mathsf{X})$ is defined in the obvious way. Concrete examples of Kleene S-algebras with tests will be discussed in the following two sections.

Definition 4. *Let S be a finite semiring and Σ, Φ be two finite mutually disjoint alphabets. The set of Φ-tests* $\mathrm{Te}(\Phi)$ *is defined using the following grammar:*

$$b, c := \mathsf{p} \mid \bar{b} \mid b + c \mid b \cdot c \mid \mathsf{0} \mid \mathsf{1}\,,$$

where $\mathsf{p} \in \Phi$. The set of (Σ, Φ, S)-expressions $\mathrm{Exp}(\Sigma, \Phi, S)$ *is defined using the following grammar:*

$$e, f := \mathsf{a} \mid b \mid e \odot s \mid e + f \mid e \cdot f \mid e^*\,,$$

where $\mathsf{a} \in \Sigma$, $s \in S$, and $b \in \mathrm{Te}(\Phi)$.

A $\mathsf{KAT}(S)$-*model* is a Kleene S-algebra with tests X together with a homomorphism $h : \mathrm{Exp}(\Sigma, \Phi, S) \to X$ where $h(e \odot s) = h(e) \odot s$ and $h(\mathsf{p}) \in B$. The notion of validity in a class of Kleene S-algebras with tests and the equational theory of a class of Kleene S-algebras with tests are defined in the usual way.

3.3 Weighted Programs

Batz et al. [1] consider an extension of the language of *while programs* (containing variable assignment commands, the skip command, sequential composition, conditionals and while loops) with *non-deterministic branching* and *weighting.* For an element $s \in S$ of some fixed semiring of weights, the command "add s" merges the weight of the current computation path with s. Batz et al. [1] argue that these *weighted programs* constitute a useful formalism that captures certain mathematical models (such as optimization problems) in an intuitive algorithmic way. They also argue that weighted programs generalize *probabilistic programs.* For further details, the reader is referred to [1].

It is well known that Kleene algebras with tests are able to express the control flow commands of while programs: sequential composition $e; f$ is expressed as $e \cdot f$; **skip** is 1; **if** b **then** e **else** f is $be + \bar{b}f$; and **while** b **do** e is $(be)^*\bar{b}$. Non-deterministic branching corresponds directly to $e+f$. Importantly, the expression $e \odot s$ represents the sequential composition of e with the weighting by s: "do e and then add weight s".

Example 3. As an example, we formalize the *Ski Rental Problem* of [1] as an expression of Kleene S-algebra with tests. The *SRP* is based on the following scenario: "A person does not own a pair of skis but is going on a skiing trip for n days. At the beginning of each day, the person can chose between two options: Either rent a pair of skis, costing 1 EUR for that day; or buy a pair of skis, costing n EUR (and then go skiing for all subsequent days free of charge)." [1, p. 3]. The semiring of weights in $\mathbb{N} \cup \{\infty\}$. The weighted program representing the situation is:

$$\textbf{while } \mathtt{n} > \mathtt{0} \textbf{ do } (\mathtt{n} := \mathtt{n} - \mathtt{1}; (\odot \mathbf{1} + (\odot s; \mathtt{n} := \mathtt{0})))$$

(Note that $\mathbf{1}$ represents the natural number one and s represents the cost of the skis.) This program can be represented by the expression

$$(\mathtt{p}\,(\mathtt{a} \odot \mathbf{1} + (\mathtt{a} \odot s)\mathtt{b}))^*\, \bar{\mathtt{p}}$$

Example 4. As discussed in [1] *probabilistic choice* "do e with probability $s \in [0, 1]$ and f with probability $1 - s$" can be expressed in the language of weighted programs. Using weighted Kleene algebra (Boolean tests are not necessary), we can express probabilistic choice as

$$(e \odot s) + (f \odot (1 - s))\,.$$

A more thorough examination of the relation of weighted Kleene algebra to *probabilistic regular expressions* [14] is left for another occasion.

4 Language Completeness

In this section we define a weighted version of guarded strings (Sect. 4.1) and we prove our first completeness result connecting Kleene S-algebras with tests and guarded formal power series over S (Sect. 4.2).

4.1 Guarded Strings

Take a finite alphabet Φ and assume that it is ordered in some arbitrary but fixed way as $\mathsf{p}_1, \ldots, \mathsf{p}_n$. Recall from [9] that a *Φ-atom* is a string $a_1 \ldots a_n$ over literals $\Lambda = \Phi \cup \bar{\Phi} = \Phi \cup \{\bar{\mathsf{p}} \mid \mathsf{p} \in \Phi\}$ where $a_i \in \{\mathsf{p}_i, \bar{\mathsf{p}}_i\}$. Let $\mathrm{At}(\Phi)$ be the set of all Φ-atoms. For $G \in \mathrm{At}(\Phi)$ and $\mathsf{p} \in \Phi$, we write $G \models \mathsf{p}$ if there is $i \leq n$ such that $G(i) = \mathsf{p}$. $\mathrm{At}(\Phi)$ represents all possible assignments of truth values to propositional letters in Φ. A *guarded string over Σ and Φ* is a string in $(\mathrm{At}(\Phi) \cdot \Sigma)^* \cdot \mathrm{At}(\Phi)$; in other words, it is a string of the form

$$G_1 \mathsf{a}_1 G_2 \ldots \mathsf{a}_{n-1} G_n \,,$$

where $G_i \in \mathrm{At}(\Phi)$ and $\mathsf{a}_j \in \Sigma$. The set of guarded strings over Σ and Φ will be denoted as $\mathrm{Gs}(\Sigma, \Phi)$. We do not distinguish between non-empty words $a_1 \ldots a_n$ over $(\Sigma \cup \Lambda)$ and the corresponding expressions $a_1 \cdot \ldots \cdot a_n$ (assuming some fixed bracketing). Hence, every guarded string can also be seen as an expression in $\mathrm{Exp}(\Sigma, \Phi, S)$ or even as an expression in $\mathrm{Exp}(\Sigma \cup \Lambda, S)$.

For a guarded string $\sigma = G_1 \mathsf{a}_1 G_2 \ldots \mathsf{a}_{n-1} G_n$, we define $\mathsf{head}(\sigma) = G_1$, $\mathsf{tail}(\sigma) = G_n$ and $\mathsf{body}(\sigma) = \mathsf{a}_1 G_2 \ldots \mathsf{a}_{n-1} G_n$ (not a guarded string). The *fusion product* is a partial binary operation $\diamond$ on $\mathrm{Gs}(\Sigma, \Phi)$ such that

$$\sigma \diamond \sigma' = \begin{cases} \mathsf{head}(\sigma)\mathsf{body}(\sigma') & \mathsf{tail}(\sigma) = \mathsf{head}(\sigma'); \\ \text{undefined} & \mathsf{tail}(\sigma) \neq \mathsf{head}(\sigma'). \end{cases}$$

(For instance, $G\mathsf{a}H \diamond H\mathsf{b}G = G\mathsf{a}H\mathsf{b}G$, but $G\mathsf{a}H \diamond G\mathsf{a}H$ is undefined if $G \neq H$.) Fusion product is lifted to a total binary operation on subsets of $\mathrm{Gs}(\Sigma, \Phi)$ in the obvious way.

The free multimonoid of guarded strings Σ^*_Φ is the partial monoid with universe $\mathrm{Gs}(\Sigma, \Phi)$, partial multiplication $\diamond$, and $\mathrm{At}(\Phi)$ as the set of unit elements.[3]

Definition 5. *Let S be a finite semiring. The set of* guarded formal power series *over (Σ, Φ and S) is the set $S\langle\langle \Sigma^*_\Phi \rangle\rangle$ of mappings from $\mathrm{Gs}(\Sigma, \Phi)$ to S. The* rational operations *on $S\langle\langle \Sigma^*_\Phi \rangle\rangle$ are defined point-wise as follows:*

- *unit:* $1(w) = 1$ *if* $w \in \mathrm{At}(\Phi)$ *and* $1(w) = 0$ *otherwise;*
- *annihilator:* $0(w) = 0$ *for all* w*;*
- *addition:* $(r_1 + r_2)(w) = r_1(w) + r_2(w)$*;*
- *multiplication:* $(r_1 \cdot r_2)(w) = \sum\{r_1(v_1) \cdot r_2(v_2) \mid w = v_1 \diamond v_2\}$*;*
- *scalar multiplication for* $s \in S$*:* $(r \odot s)(w) = r(w) \cdot s$*;*
- *Kleene star:* $r^*(w) = \sum_{n \in \omega} r^n(w)$*, where* $r^0 = 1$ *and* $r^{n+1} = r^n \cdot r$*.*

A polynomial *in $S\langle\langle \Sigma^*_\Phi \rangle\rangle$ is any $r \in S\langle\langle \Sigma^*_\Phi \rangle\rangle$ such that the set of $w \in \mathrm{Gs}(\Sigma, \Phi)$ where $r(w) \neq 0$ is finite. The set $S^{\mathrm{rat}}\langle\langle \Sigma^*_\Phi \rangle\rangle$ of* rational guarded formal power series *is the least subset of $S\langle\langle \Sigma^*_\Phi \rangle\rangle$ that contains all polynomials and is closed under the rational operations.*

---

[3] For much more on multimonoids, see [11] and [5].

Note that $\sum_{n\in\omega} r^n(w)$ exists since S is assumed to be finite.

It is easily seen that $S^{\text{rat}}\langle\langle\Sigma^*_\Phi\rangle\rangle$ is an idempotent semiring. If $K \subseteq \text{Gs}(\Sigma,\Phi)$ is finite and $s \in S$, then s_K denotes the formal power series (in fact, a polynomial) such that $s_K(w) = s$ if $w \in K$ and $s_K(w) = 0$ otherwise. Given the definition of fusion product, the subalgebra of $S^{\text{rat}}\langle\langle\Sigma^*_\Phi\rangle\rangle$ with the universe $\{1_K \mid K \subseteq \text{At}(\Phi)\}$ is a distributive lattice, naturally extended to a Boolean algebra by defining $\overline{(1_K)} = 1_{\text{At}(\Phi)\setminus K}$. In this way, we obtain a Kleene S-algebra with tests:

Lemma 1. *$S^{\text{rat}}\langle\langle\Sigma^*_\Phi\rangle\rangle$ is a Kleene S-algebra with tests.*

Definition 6. *The* standard language interpretation *of* $\text{Exp}(\Sigma,\Phi,S)$ *is the unique homomorphism* $\mathscr{G} : \text{Exp}(\Sigma,\Phi,S) \to S\langle\langle\Sigma^*_\Phi\rangle\rangle$ *such that*

$$\mathscr{G}(\mathsf{a}) = 1_{\{G\mathsf{a}H \mid G,H\in\text{At}(\Phi)\}} \quad \textit{and} \quad \mathscr{G}(\mathsf{p}) = 1_{\{G \mid G\vDash \mathsf{p}\}}\,.$$

It is easily seen that, in fact, $\mathscr{G} : \text{Exp}(\Sigma,\Phi,S) \to S^{\text{rat}}\langle\langle\Sigma^*_\Phi\rangle\rangle$.

4.2 The Language Completeness Result

This section establishes our first result: if S is a finite copi-semiring, then the equational theory of $\mathsf{KAT}(S)$ coincides with the equational theory of a "canonical model" consisting of S-weighted guarded formal power series.

From now on we assume that every expression $e \in \text{Exp}(\Sigma,\Phi,S)$ is in *Boolean normal form*, that is, $\bar{b}$ occurs in e only if $b \in \Phi$. Recall that every expression $e \in \text{Exp}(\Sigma,\Phi,S)$ in Boolean normal form can be seen as an expression in $\text{Exp}(\Sigma \cup \Phi \cup \bar{\Phi}, S)$, and so it makes sense to consider the standard language interpretation $\mathscr{L}(e) \in S\langle\langle(\Sigma\cup\Lambda)^*\rangle\rangle$ of e.

Our proof of the language completeness result for $\mathsf{KAT}(S)$ is very similar to Kozen and Smith's proof of the language completeness result for KAT [10]; what gives some novelty to our proof is that we need to take weights into account. The proof strategy is the following one: we identify a set of expressions $F \subseteq \text{Exp}(\Sigma,\Phi,S)$ such that $\mathscr{L}(f) = \mathscr{G}(f)$ for all $f \in F$, and we show that every $e \in \text{Exp}(\Sigma,\Phi,S)$ is $\mathsf{KAT}(S)$-equivalent to some $f \in F$.

Definition 7. *A* guarded expression *(over Σ, Φ and S) is any expression of the form $0 \odot 1$, $G \odot s$ or $GeH \odot s$ where $G, H \in \text{At}(\Phi)$, $e \in \text{Exp}(\Sigma,\Phi,S)$, and $s \in S$. A* guarded sum *is any expression of the form $\sum_{i<n} e_i$ where each e_i is a guarded expression. (The empty sum is defined to be the guarded expression $0 \odot 1$.)*

We define $\mathsf{head}(G\odot s) = G = \mathsf{head}(GeH\odot s)$, $\mathsf{tail}(H\odot s) = H = \mathsf{tail}(GeH\odot s)$, $\mathsf{body}(H \odot s) = \epsilon$, $\mathsf{body}(GeH \odot s) = eH$, *and* $\mathsf{weight}(e \odot s) = s$. *For guarded expressions e, f, we define*

$$e \bullet f = \begin{cases} (e \cdot \mathsf{body}(f)) \odot (\mathsf{weight}(e)\cdot\mathsf{weight}(f)) & \mathsf{tail}(e) = \mathsf{head}(f); \\ 0 \odot 1 & \mathsf{tail}(e) \neq \mathsf{head}(f). \end{cases}$$

Definition 8. *We define the following operations on guarded sums:*

- $[1] = \sum_{G\in\text{At}(\Phi)}(G \odot 1)$ *and* $[0] = 0 \odot 1$;

- $e\ [+]\ f = e + f$;
- $(e_1 + \ldots + e_n)\ [\cdot]\ (f_1 + \ldots + f_m) = \sum_{i \le n, j \le m}(e_i \bullet f_j)$;
- $(e_1 \odot s_1 + \ldots + e_n \odot s_n)\ [\odot t] = (e_1 \odot (s_1 \cdot t) + \ldots + e_n \odot (s_n \cdot t))$;
- $(g_1 + \ldots + g_n)^{[*]}$ *is defined by induction on* n *as follows:*
  1. $(0 \odot 1)^{[*]} = [1] = (G \odot s)^{[*]}$;
  2. $(GeH \odot s)^{[*]} = \begin{cases} [1] + (GeH \odot s) & G \neq H; \\ [1] + (Ge(Ge \odot s)^* H \odot s) & G = H; \end{cases}$
  3. *If* $e = (g_1 + \ldots + g_{n-1})$ *for guarded expressions* $g_1, \ldots, g_{n-1}$ *and* g *is a guarded expression, then*
  $$(e+g)^{[*]} = e^{[*]} + \left(e^{[*]}\ [\cdot]\ f^{[*]}\ [\cdot]\ g\ [\cdot]\ e^{[*]}\right),$$
  where $f = \big(\mathsf{head}(g)\mathsf{body}(g)(e^{[*]})\mathsf{head}(g)\big) \odot \mathsf{weight}(g)$.

Note that, in the definition of $(e+g)^{[*]}$, f is a guarded expression and so $f^{[*]}$ is provided by the induction steps 1 or 2. Note also that the set of guarded sums $\mathrm{Gsu}(\Sigma, \Phi, S)$ endowed with the operations defined in Definition 8 can be seen as a term algebra of the Kleene S-algebra type.

Definition 9. *For all* $e \in \mathrm{Exp}$, *we define* $\widehat{e} \in \mathrm{Gsu}$ *by induction on* e *as follows:*

$$\widehat{\mathsf{a}} = \sum_{G,H \in \mathrm{At}(\Phi)} G\mathsf{a}H \odot 1 \qquad \widehat{\mathsf{p}} = \sum_{G \models \mathsf{p}} G \odot 1 \qquad \widehat{\bar{\mathsf{p}}} = \sum_{G \not\models \mathsf{p}} G \odot 1$$

$$\widehat{1} = [1] \qquad \widehat{0} = [0] \qquad \widehat{e+f} = \widehat{e}\ [+]\ \widehat{f} \qquad \widehat{e \cdot f} = \widehat{e}\ [\cdot]\ \widehat{f}$$

$$\widehat{e \odot s} = \widehat{e}\ [\odot s] \qquad \widehat{e^*} = (\widehat{e})^{[*]}$$

Lemma 2. *For every* $e \in \mathrm{Exp}$*:*

1. $\mathsf{KAT}(S) \models e \approx \widehat{e}$;
2. $\mathscr{G}(\widehat{e}) = \mathscr{L}(\widehat{e})$.

Proof. See Appendix A.1. We note that our assumption that S be integral seems to be required in the proof. □

Theorem 2. *For all* $e, f \in \mathrm{Exp}(\Sigma, \Phi, S)$,

$$\mathsf{KAT}(S) \models e \approx f \iff S^{\mathrm{rat}}\langle\langle \Sigma^*_\Phi \rangle\rangle \models e \approx f\,.$$

Proof. The implication from left to right follows from Lemma 1. The converse implication is established as follows:

$S^{\mathrm{rat}}\langle\langle \Sigma^*_\Phi \rangle\rangle \models e \approx f$	
$S^{\mathrm{rat}}\langle\langle \Sigma^*_\Phi \rangle\rangle \models \widehat{e} \approx \widehat{f}$	by Lemma 2(1) and Lemma 1
$\mathscr{G}(\widehat{e}) = \mathscr{G}(\widehat{f})$	by definition
$\mathscr{L}(\widehat{e}) = \mathscr{L}(\widehat{f})$	by Lemma 2(2)
$\mathsf{KA}(S) \models \widehat{e} \approx \widehat{f}$	by Theorem 1, Corollary 1
$\mathsf{KAT}(S) \models \widehat{e} \approx \widehat{f}$	
$\mathsf{KAT}(S) \models e \approx f$	by Lemma 2(1)

□

Corollary 2. *For all* $e, f \in \text{Exp}(\Sigma, \Phi, S)$,

$$\mathsf{KAT}(S) \models e \approx f \iff \mathscr{G}(e) = \mathscr{G}(f).$$

5 Relational Completeness

In this section we define S-transition systems (Sect. 5.1) and we prove our second completeness result connecting Kleene S-algebras with tests and S-transition systems (Sect. 5.2). Our proof uses a Cayley-like construction going back to the work of Pratt [13] on dynamic algebras; see also the relational completeness result for Kleene algebras with tests [10].

5.1 Transition Systems

Definition 10. *Let S be a finite semiring. An S-*transition system *for Σ and Φ is a triple $M = \langle Q, \mathsf{rel}_M, \mathsf{sat}_M \rangle$ where Q is a countable non-empty set and*

$$\mathsf{rel}_M : \Sigma \to S^{Q \times Q} \qquad \mathsf{sat}_M : \Phi \to S^Q$$

As discussed in Sect. 2, M can be seen as a function assigning to each $\mathsf{a} \in \Sigma$ a (possibly infinite) $Q \times Q$ matrix $M(\mathsf{a})$ with entries in S, and to $\mathsf{p} \in \Phi$ a (possibly infinite) $Q \times Q$ diagonal matrix $M(\mathsf{p})$ with entries in $\{0, 1\}$. M can be extended to a function from $\text{Exp}(\Sigma, \Phi, S)$ to (possibly infinite) $Q \times Q$-matrices over S using the notions introduced in Sect. 2:

$$M(e + f) = M(e) + M(f) \quad M(e \cdot f) = M(e) \cdot M(f) \quad M(e^*) = M(e)^*$$
$$M(e \odot s) = M(e) \cdot M(s) \quad M(1) = 1 \quad M(0) = 0 \quad M(\bar{b}) = \overline{M(b)}$$

where $M(s)$ is the diagonal $Q \times Q$ matrix where the entries in the main diagonal are all s; 1 is the $Q \times Q$ identity matrix and 0 is the $Q \times Q$ zero matrix; and where $\overline{N}$ for a matrix N with entries in $\{0, 1\}$ is the matrix that results from N by switching all 1s to 0s and vice versa. We denote as $\text{Mat}(Q, S)$ the set of all $Q \times Q$ matrices with entries in S.

Lemma 3. *For all Q and finite S,* $\text{Mat}(Q, S) \in \mathsf{KAT}(S)$.

5.2 The Relational Completeness Result

Theorem 3. *For all* $e, f \in \text{Exp}(\Sigma, \Phi, S)$,

$$\mathsf{KAT}(S) \models e \approx f \iff (\forall M)(M(e) = M(f)).$$

Proof. The implication from left to right follows from Lemma 3. The converse implication is established as follows. Define $\mathsf{cay} : S^{\text{rat}}\langle\langle \Sigma_\Phi^* \rangle\rangle \to \text{Mat}(\text{Gs}(\Sigma, \Phi), S)$ as follows:

$$\mathsf{cay}(r)_{w,v} = \begin{cases} r(u) & v = w \diamond u \\ 0 & \text{otherwise.} \end{cases}$$

The function cay is injective. Indeed, if there is w such that $r_0(w) \neq r_1(w)$, then take the head of w, that is, the unique $H \in \mathrm{At}(\Phi)$ such that $w = H \diamond w$. Note that $\mathsf{cay}(r_0)_{H,w} = r_0(w) \neq r_1(w) = \mathsf{cay}(r_1)_{H,w}$. Define $M = \langle \mathrm{Gs}, \mathsf{rel}_M, \mathsf{sat}_M \rangle$ by $\mathsf{rel}_M(\mathsf{a}) = \mathsf{cay}(\mathscr{G}(\mathsf{a}))$ for all $\mathsf{a} \in \Sigma$ and $\mathsf{sat}_M(\mathsf{p}) = \mathsf{cay}(\mathscr{G}(\mathsf{p}))$ for all $\mathsf{p} \in \Phi$. Now we claim the following:

Claim. For all e, $\mathsf{cay}(\mathscr{G}(e)) = M(e)$.

The theorem is then immediate: If $\mathsf{KAT}(S) \not\models e \approx f$, then $\mathscr{G}(e) \neq \mathscr{G}(f)$ by Corollary 2, hence $\mathsf{cay}(\mathscr{G}(e)) \neq \mathsf{cay}(\mathscr{G}(f))$, and so $M(e) \neq M(f)$. It remains to prove the claim, which we do in Appendix A.2. □

6 Conclusion

We extended Ésik and Kuich's [4] completeness result for finitely weighted Kleene algebras to finitely valued Kleene algebras with tests. This result contributes, we hope, to a better understanding of the properties of frameworks that may be used to formalize reasoning about weighted programs [1].

A number of interesting problems need to be left for the future. First, we would like to prove that the equational theory of $\mathsf{KAT}(S)$ is decidable and establish its complexity. Second, we will work on adapting Kozen and Smith's [10] argument showing that the quasi-equational theory of $\mathsf{KAT}(S)$ where all assumptions are of the form $e \approx 0$ reduces to the equational theory. Third, it would be interesting to extend Ésik and Kuich's completeness result to Kleene algebras weighted in a more general class of semirings (including, for instance, the Łukasiewicz semiring) and then to use this result to provide a similar generalization for weighted Kleene algebras with tests. Indeed, it would be interesting to figure out a weighted generalization of other completeness proofs for Kleene algebra, such as [7]. An intriguing problem is also to extend our result to variants of Kleene algebra with tests where tests do not form a Boolean algebra [6].

Acknowledgement. This work was supported by the grant 22-16111S of the Czech Science Foundation. The author is grateful to three anonymous reviewers for their comments.

A Technical appendix

A.1 Proof of Lemma 2

It is clear that if $\mathsf{KAT} \models e \approx f$ for e, f without occurrences of $\odot$, then $\mathsf{KAT}(S) \models e \approx f$ for all S. We write $e \equiv f$ instead of $\mathsf{KAT}(S) \models e \approx f$. A Kleene S-algebra model for $\mathrm{Exp}(\Sigma \cup \Lambda, S)$ is defined as expected (elements of Λ are mapped into arbitrary elements of the model). If $\mathsf{KA}(S) \models e \approx f$ for $e, f \in \mathrm{Exp}(\Sigma \cup \Lambda, S)$, then we write $e \equiv_{\mathsf{KA}} f$. Recall that we write Exp instead of $\mathrm{Exp}(\Sigma, \Phi, S)$ and Exp_Λ instead of $\mathrm{Exp}(\Sigma \cup \Lambda, S)$.

Lemma 4. *The following hold:*

1. $1 \equiv \texttt{[1]}$ *and* $0 \equiv \texttt{[0]}$*;*
2. $e\ \texttt{[+]}\ e' \equiv e + f$ *for all guarded sums* e *and* e'*;*
3. $e\texttt{[}\odot s\texttt{]} \equiv e \odot s$*;*
4. $e\ \texttt{[}\cdot\texttt{]}\ e' \equiv e \cdot e'$ *for all guarded sums* e *and* e'*;*
5. $e^* \equiv e^{\texttt{[*]}}$ *for all guarded sums* e*.*

Proof. The first three claims are straightforward. The fourth claim follows from the fact that $g_1 \bullet g_2 \equiv g_1 \cdot g_2$ for all guarded expressions g_1, g_2.

The fifth claim is established by induction on the number n of guarded expressions in the sum $e = g_1 + \ldots + g_n$. If $n = 1$, then we have three possibilities to consider:

- $e = 0 \odot 1$. Then $e^* \equiv 0^* \equiv 1 \equiv \texttt{[1]} = (0 \odot 1)^{\texttt{[*]}} = e^{\texttt{[*]}}$.
- $e = G \odot s$. Then $e^* \equiv (G \odot s)^* \equiv 1 \equiv \texttt{[1]} = e^{\texttt{[*]}}$. We note that $(G \odot s)^* \equiv 1$ holds since $G \leqq 1$ (meaning that $G + 1 \equiv 1$) and $s \leq 1$ imply $(G \odot s)^* \leqq (1 \odot 1)^* \equiv 1^* \equiv 1$. The argument does not seem to go through if $s \not\leq 1$.
- $e = Ge_1H \odot s$. Let us define $f = Ge_1H$ to simplify notation. Then $e^* \equiv 1 + (f \odot s)^*(f \odot s)$. We have two possibilities, depending on whether $G = H$:
  (a) If $G \neq H$, then $e^{\texttt{[*]}} = \texttt{[1]} + (f \odot s)$, and it is sufficient to show that $(f \odot s)^*(f \odot s) \equiv (f \odot s)$. The $\geqq$ claim follows from $(f \odot s)^* \geqq 1$ and the $\leqq$ claim is established by applying the right-fixpoint law of Kleene algebra to the assumption $(f \odot s) + (f \odot s)(f \odot s) \leqq (f \odot s)$. This assumption holds since $(f \odot s)(f \odot s) \leqq (f \odot s)$ follows from the fact that $(f \odot s)(f \odot s) \equiv (ff \odot s) \odot s \equiv 0$ ($ff \equiv 0$ since $G \neq H$).
  (b) If $G = H$, then we reason as follows:

$$
\begin{gathered}
e^* \equiv 1 + (f \odot s)(f \odot s)^* \equiv 1 + (Ge_1(H \odot s))\,(Ge_1(H \odot s))^* \equiv \\
1 + Ge_1\left((H \odot s)Ge_1\right)^*(H \odot s) \equiv 1 + Ge_1(HGe_1 \odot s)^*(H \odot s) \equiv \\
\texttt{[1]} + (Ge_1(Ge_1 \odot s)^* H \odot s) \equiv e^{\texttt{[*]}}\,.
\end{gathered}
$$

Now assume that the claim holds of all guarded sums $f = g_1 + \ldots + g_m$ for some $g_1, \ldots, g_m$, and take $e = g_1 + \ldots + g_m + g$ for some g. We reason as follows, writing f for $g_1 + \ldots + g_m$:

$$
\begin{aligned}
e^* = (f+g)^* &\equiv f^*(gf^*)^* \equiv f^* + f^*gf^*(gf^*)^* \\
&\equiv f^* + f^*gf^*\,(\mathsf{head}(g)gf^*)^* \equiv f^* + f^*\,(gf^*\mathsf{head}(g))\,gf^* \\
&\equiv f^* + f^*\,(\mathsf{head}(g)\mathsf{body}(g)f^*\mathsf{head}(g) \odot \mathsf{weight}(g))^*\,gf^* \\
\equiv f^{\texttt{[*]}} + f^{\texttt{[*]}} &\left(\mathsf{head}(g)\mathsf{body}(g)f^{\texttt{[*]}}\mathsf{head}(g) \odot \mathsf{weight}(g)\right)^* gf^{\texttt{[*]}} \equiv (f+g)^{\texttt{[*]}} \equiv e^{\texttt{[*]}}
\end{aligned}
$$

□

Definition 11. *A guarded expression* e *is called* proper *iff* $\mathscr{L}(e) = \mathscr{G}(e)$*. A guarded sum is called proper iff it is a sum of proper guarded expressions.*

Lemma 5. *The set of proper guarded sums is closed under* $\texttt{[1]}$, $\texttt{[0]}$, $\texttt{[+]}$, $\texttt{[}\cdot\texttt{]}$, $\texttt{[}\oplus s\texttt{]}$ *and* $^{\texttt{[*]}}$.

Lemma 2. *For all* $e \in \text{Exp}$:

1. $e \equiv \widehat{e}$;
2. $\mathscr{L}(\widehat{e}) = \mathscr{G}(\widehat{e})$

Proof. Both claims are established by induction on the complexity of e.

1. The base case for $e \in \Sigma \cup \Lambda$ is easily established using the semimodule axioms for $\odot$, which establish that $(e+f) \odot s \equiv (e \odot s) + (f \odot s)$ and $e \odot 1 \equiv e$, and KAT reasoning. The induction step is established using Lemma 4.
2. The base case follows from Definition 9 and the induction step is easily established using Lemma 5.

□

A.2 Proof of Theorem 3

Let $M = \langle \text{Gs}, \mathsf{rel}_M, \mathsf{sat}_M \rangle$ where $\mathsf{rel}_M(\mathsf{a}) = \mathsf{cay}(\mathscr{G}(\mathsf{a}))$ for $\mathsf{a} \in \Sigma$ and $\mathsf{sat}_M(\mathsf{p}) = \mathsf{cay}(\mathscr{G}(\mathsf{p}))$ for $\mathsf{p} \in \Phi$. We prove by induction on the structure of $e \in \text{Exp}(\Sigma, \Phi, S)$ that $\mathsf{cay}(\mathscr{G}(e)) = M(e)$. We write $[e]$ instead of $\mathsf{cay}(\mathscr{G}(e))$.

The base cases for $\mathsf{a} \in \Sigma$ and $\mathsf{p} \in \Phi$ hold by definition of M. The case for $\mathsf{0}$ is trivial. The case for $\mathsf{1}$ follows from the definition of $\mathscr{G}$. In particular, $\mathscr{G}(\mathsf{1}) = 1_{\text{At}}$ is the function that assigns 1 to atoms and 0 to all other guarded strings. Hence, $\mathsf{cay}(1_{\text{At}})$ is the identity matrix.

Induction step for $e \odot s$ is established by showing that $[e \odot s]_{w,v} = [e]_{w,v} \cdot s$. It is sufficient to check this in the case that $w = v \diamond u$. Then $[e \odot s]_{w,v} = (\mathscr{G}(e) \odot s)(u) = \mathscr{G}(e)(u) \cdot s = [e]_{w,v} \cdot s$ by the induction hypothesis.

The case for $e + f$ is routine. The case for $e \cdot f$ is established by showing that $[e \cdot f]_{w,v} = \sum_{u \in \text{Gs}} [e]_{w,u} \cdot [f]_{u,v}$. It is sufficient to check this for w, v such that $v = w \diamond w'$. Then

$$
\begin{aligned}
[e \cdot f]_{w,v} = \mathscr{G}(e \cdot f)(w') &= \sum \{\mathscr{G}(e)(u') \cdot \mathscr{G}(f)(v') \mid w' = u' \diamond v'\} \\
&= \sum \{\mathscr{G}(e)(u') \cdot \mathscr{G}(f)(v') \mid v = w \diamond (u' \diamond v')\} \\
&= \sum \{\mathscr{G}(e)(u') \cdot \mathscr{G}(f)(v') \mid v = u \diamond v' \ \ \& \ \ u = w \diamond u'\} \\
&= \sum \{[e]_{w,u} \cdot [f]_{u,v} \mid v = u \diamond v' \ \ \& \ \ u = w \diamond u'\} \\
&= \sum_{u \in \text{Gs}} [e]_{w,u} \cdot [f]_{u,v} \,.
\end{aligned}
$$

The case for e^* is established by showing that $[e^*]_{w,v} = \sum_{n \in \omega} [e]^n_{w,v}$. This is implied by the following claim which is established easily by induction on n:

Claim. For all $n \in \omega$: for all $e \in \text{Exp}$ and all $w, u, v \in \text{Gs}$, if $v = w \diamond u$, then $\mathscr{G}(e)^n(u) = \sum_{x \in [w,v], |x| = n} M(e)(x)$.

The case for $\bar{b}$ is established by showing that $\mathscr{C}(\bar{b})_{w,v} = \overline{[b]}_{w,v}$. Since $[b]$ is a diagonal matrix, it is sufficient to check the case $w = v$. Then $[\bar{b}]_{w,w} = \mathscr{G}(\bar{b})(G)$ for the tail G of w, that is, the unique $G \in \text{At}$ such that $w = w \diamond G$. It follows that $\mathscr{G}(\bar{b})(G) = \overline{\mathscr{G}(b)(G)} = \overline{[b]}_{w,w}$. □

References

1. Batz, K., Gallus, A., Kaminski, B.L., Katoen, J.P., Winkler, T.: Weighted programming: a programming paradigm for specifying mathematical models. Proc. ACM Program. Lang. **6**(OOPSLA1) (2022). https://doi.org/10.1145/3527310
2. Conway, J.H.: Regular Algebra and Finite Machines. Chapman and Hall Ltd., London (1971)
3. Droste, M., Kuich, W., Vogler, H. (eds.): Handbook of Weighted Automata. Springer, Heidelberg (2009). https://doi.org/10.1007/978-3-642-01492-5
4. Ésik, Z., Kuich, W.: A generation of Kozen's axiomatization of the equational theory of the regular sets. In: Ito, M., Paun, G., Yu, S. (eds.) Words, Semigroups, and Transductions - Festschrift in Honor of Gabriel Thierrin, pp. 99–114. World Scientific (2001). https://doi.org/10.1142/9789812810908_0008
5. Fahrenberg, U., Johansen, C., Struth, G., Ziemiański, K.: Catoids and modal convolution algebras. Algebra Universalis **84**(2) (2023). https://doi.org/10.1007/s00012-023-00805-9
6. Gomes, L., Madeira, A., Barbosa, L.S.: Generalising KAT to verify weighted computations. Sci. Ann. Comput. Sci. **29**(2), 141–184 (2019)
7. Kappé, T.: Completeness and the finite model property for Kleene algebra, reconsidered. In: Glück, R., Santocanale, L., Winter, M. (eds.) RAMiCS 2023. LNCS, vol. 13896, pp. 158–175. Springer, Cham (2023). https://doi.org/10.1007/978-3-031-28083-2_10
8. Kozen, D.: A completeness theorem for Kleene algebras and the algebra of regular events. Inf. Comput. **110**(2), 366–390 (1994). https://doi.org/10.1006/inco.1994.1037
9. Kozen, D.: Kleene algebra with tests. ACM Trans. Program. Lang. Syst. **19**(3), 427–443 (1997). https://doi.org/10.1145/256167.256195
10. Kozen, D., Smith, F.: Kleene algebra with tests: completeness and decidability. In: van Dalen, D., Bezem, M. (eds.) CSL 1996. LNCS, vol. 1258, pp. 244–259. Springer, Heidelberg (1997). https://doi.org/10.1007/3-540-63172-0_43
11. Kudryavtseva, G., Mazorchuk, V.: On multisemigroups. Portugaliae Math. **72**(1), 47–80 (2015). https://doi.org/10.4171/pm/1956
12. Kuich, W., Salomaa, A.: Semirings, Automata, Languages. EATCS Monographs on Theoretical Computer Science, vol. 5. Springer, Heidelberg (1986). https://doi.org/10.1007/978-3-642-69959-7
13. Pratt, V.: Dynamic algebras and the nature of induction. In: Proceedings of Twelfth Annual ACM Symposium on Theory of Computing (STOC 1980), pp. 22–28. ACM (1980). https://doi.org/10.1145/800141.804649
14. Różowski, W., Silva, A.: A completeness theorem for probabilistic regular expressions. Technical report (2023). https://doi.org/10.48550/ARXIV.2310.08779. https://arxiv.org/abs/2310.08779. Accepted to LICS 2024
15. Salomaa, A., Soittola, M.: Automata-Theoretic Aspects of Formal Power Series. Monographs in Computer Science, 1st edn. Springer, New York (1978). https://doi.org/10.1007/978-1-4612-6264-0
16. Sedlár, I.: Kleene algebra with tests for weighted programs. In: Proceedings of IEEE 53rd International Symposium on Multiple-Valued Logic (ISMVL 2023), pp. 111–116 (2023). https://doi.org/10.1109/ISMVL57333.2023.00031. http://arxiv.org/abs/2303.00322

Modal Hyperdoctrine: Higher-Order and Non-normal Extensions

Florrie Verity(✉) and Yoshihiro Maruyama

School of Computing, Australian National University, Canberra, ACT 2602, Australia
{florrie.verity,yoshihiro.maruyama}@anu.edu.au

Abstract. Lawvere hyperdoctrines give categorical semantics for intuitionistic predicate logic but are flexible enough to be applied to other logics and extended to higher-order systems. We return to Ghilardi's hyperdoctrine semantics for first-order modal logic [3] and extend it in two directions—to weaker, non-normal modal logics and to higher-order modal logics. We also relate **S4** modal hyperdoctrines to intuitionistic hyperdoctrines via a hyperdoctrinal version of the Gödel-McKinsey-Tarski translation. This work is intended to complement the other categorical semantics that have been developed for quantified modal logic, and may also be regarded as first steps to extend coalgebraic modal logic to first-order and higher-order settings via hyperdoctrines.

Keywords: Categorical logic · Modal logic · Higher-order logic · Hyperdoctrines

1 Introduction

Moving from propositional modal logic to quantified modal logic is less straightforward than one might hope. For example, traditional Kripke semantics do not automatically extend to the first-order case, with several instances of well-motivated but incomplete extensions of Kripke-complete propositional logics [5]. Turning to alternative semantics, category-theoretic methods have been used extensively by Ghilardi and Meloni [7–11] for mathematical and philosophical investigations of quantified modal logic beyond the reach of Kripke semantics.

Amongst the category-theoretic tools deployed are Lawvere's *hyperdoctrines* [15]. Hyperdoctrines provide semantics for first-order logics that reduce to familiar algebraic semantics on the propositional level. Originally conceived for intuitionistic predicate logic, they are flexible enough to be applied to other logics and extended to higher-order systems. Hyperdoctrine semantics for first-order normal modal logics are presented in [3], where they are used by Ghilardi as a unifying tool for studying other non-Kripkean modal semantics, while Awodey, Kishida and Kotzsch [2,13] provide topos-theoretic hyperdoctrine semantics for higher-order modal logic based on intuitionistic **S4**.

We make three contributions to modal hyperdoctrine. The first is a very general presentation. Ghilardi's presentation in [3] concerns a single-sorted typed

G. Metcalfe et al. (Eds.): WoLLIC 2024, LNCS 14672, pp. 225–242, 2024.
https://doi.org/10.1007/978-3-031-62687-6_15

language and a base propositional modal logic of **S4**, while advising that it is straightforward to generalise. We follow this guidance to present modal hyperdoctrine semantics for a many-sorted typed language and a base propositional modal logic of the weaker *non-normal* class. To this end, we introduce hyperdoctrines in Sect. 2, present the syntax of the modal logic in Sect. 3, and give the semantics in Sect. 4. The second contribution is to connect modal hyperdoctrines—in the case of **S4** modal logics—to intuitionstic hyperdoctrines via a translation theorem (Sect. 4.3). The third is to define higher-order modal hyperdoctrines for non-normal modal logics and prove their soundness and completeness (Sect. 5). This complements the aforementioned work of Awodey et al., in which the topos-theoretic nature of their semantics prohibits generalising to bases weaker than **S4**. In Sect. 6 we conclude with future directions.

2 Hyperdoctrine Semantics

In this section, we define a hyperdoctrine and consider when a logic has semantics in a hyperdoctrine. Many decisions are made in choosing a quantified modal logic, from the base propositional logic to the interaction between the modal operators and quantifiers. We take the perspective: if we want sound and complete hyperdoctrine semantics for modal logic, what does it require of our logic?

Lawvere hyperdoctrines are fibred algebras indexed by categories, where the algebras represent the propositional logic and the indexing category provides a type structure. Let $\mathbf{C}$ be a category with finite products and $\mathbf{HA}$ be the category of Heyting algebras and finite meet preserving functions between them. A hyperdoctrine is a functor

$$P : \mathbf{C}^{\mathrm{op}} \to \mathbf{HA}$$

capturing quantification by the following requirements. For any projection $\pi : X \times Y \to Y$ in $\mathbf{C}$, the image $P(\pi) : P(Y) \to P(X \times Y)$ has right and left adjoints

$$\forall_\pi : P(X \times Y) \to P(Y) \text{ and } \exists_\pi : P(X \times Y) \to P(Y).$$

These adjoints satisfy corresponding Beck-Chevalley conditions: for $\forall_\pi$, this says that the following diagram commutes for any $f : Z \to Y$ in $\mathbf{C}$, where $\pi' : X \times Z \to Z$ is a projection[1]:

$$\begin{array}{ccc} P(X \times Y) & \xrightarrow{\forall_\pi} & P(Y) \\ {\scriptstyle P(\mathsf{id}_X \times f)}\downarrow & & \downarrow{\scriptstyle P(f)} \\ P(X \times Z) & \xrightarrow[\forall_{\pi'}]{} & P(Z) \end{array} \tag{1}$$

The indexing category $\mathbf{C}$ represents a type structure that acts as a domain of reasoning for the logic. In this way, hyperdoctrines adopt the view that "a logic

[1] The left adjoint must also satisfy the *Frobenius reciprocity condition*, omitted here as we are only concerned with classical logic, in which the quantifiers are interdefined.

is always a logic over a type theory" [12]. This is more natural from a category-theoretic perspective and subsumes untyped logics via reduction to a single type.

The restrictions placed on the syntax of our logic if we wish to equip it with hyperdoctrine semantics are as follows. The syntax is a typed version, built on top of a type signature and term calculus, detailed in Sect. 3. The functoriality of P means that substitution commutes with all of the logical connectives. This is clear when we consider the syntactic hyperdoctrine in Sect. 4, where we see that in order for the image of a map in the base category to be an algebra homomorphism, it is necessary that substitution commutes with the propositional connectives. Considering the syntactic hyperdoctrine also demonstrates that the Beck-Chevalley condition corresponds logically to the quantifiers commuting with substitution, and so we also require this of our syntax.

3 Typed First-Order Non-normal Modal Logic

Non-normal modal logics are a particularly weak class of modal logics, as distinct from *normal* modal logics such as **K** and **S4**. In this section, we present a typed version of first-order non-normal modal logics, following [1] for the logic and [19] for the typing. The resulting system is essentially a multi-sorted, non-normal version of the single-sorted, normal logic in [3].

3.1 Term Calculus

The logic is built on a typed (many-sorted) *signature* Σ, consisting of *type symbols* σ, *function symbols* $F : \sigma_1, \dots, \sigma_n \to \tau$ and *relation (predicate) symbols* $R \subseteq \sigma_1, \dots, \sigma_n$. For each type σ there are *variables* $x, y, z, \dots$, and the formal expression $x : \sigma$ is a *type judgement* expressing that x is a variable of type σ. A *context* is a finite list of type judgements $x_1 : \sigma_1, \dots, x_n : \sigma_n$, denoted by Γ.

On top of the signature is a *term calculus*. The basic term calculus consists of *terms-in-context*, which are judgements $M : \sigma\ [\Gamma]$, expressing that M is a well-formed term of type σ in context Γ. The well-formed terms-in-context in the basic term calculus are inductively generated by the following rules:

- $x : \sigma\ [\Gamma, x : \sigma, \Gamma']$ is a term;
- if $F : \sigma_1, \dots, \sigma_n \to \tau$ is a function symbol and $M_1 : \sigma_1\ [\Gamma], \dots, M_n : \sigma_n\ [\Gamma]$ (abbreviated $\vec{M} : \vec{\sigma}$) are terms, then $F(M_1, \dots, M_n) : \tau\ [\Gamma]$ is a term.

The meta-theoretic operation of *substitution over a term* of a term for a variable is defined by induction on the structure of an untyped term N:

- if $N = x_i$ then $N[\vec{M}/\vec{x}] = M_i$;
- if $N = F(N_1, \dots, N_n)$ then $N[\vec{M}/\vec{x}] = F(N_1[\vec{M}/\vec{x}], \dots, N_n[\vec{M}/\vec{x}])$.

A *formula-in-context* is a judgement $\phi\ [\Gamma]$ expressing that ϕ is a well-formed formula in context Γ. For each relation symbol $R \subseteq \sigma_1, \dots, \sigma_n$, if $M_1 : \sigma_1\ [\Gamma], \dots,$ $M_n : \sigma_n[\Gamma]$ are terms, then $R(M_1, \dots, M_n)\ [\Gamma]$ is an *atomic formula. Compound formulae* are built from the atomic formulae and the constant $\bot$ with the rules:

- $\bot\ [\Gamma]$ is a formula;
- if $\phi\ [\Gamma]$ and $\psi\ [\Gamma]$ are formulae then $\phi \supset \psi\ [\Gamma]$ is a formula;
- if $\phi\ [x : \sigma, \Gamma]$ is a formula then $\forall x \phi\ [\Gamma]$ is a formula;
- if $\phi\ [\Gamma]$ is a formula then $\Box\phi\ [\Gamma]$ is a formula.

The remaining connectives are treated as abbreviations in the usual manner; this includes equivalence of formulae $\phi \supset\subset \psi$, abbreviating $\phi \supset \psi \wedge \psi \subset \phi$.

If $\phi\ [\Gamma]$ is a formula with $\Gamma = x_1 : \sigma_1, \ldots, x_n : \sigma_n$ and $M_1 : \sigma_1\ [\Gamma'], \ldots, M_n : \sigma_n\ [\Gamma']$ are terms, we want to define a formula $\phi[\vec{M}/\vec{x}]\ [\Gamma']$, where every instance of the variable x_i is replaced by the term M_i, for every i. Since every formula is built in a unique way from atomic subformulae and the rules for forming compound formulae, substitution into a formula is defined on these subformulae as follows. Substitution over atomic formulae:

$$R(N_1, \ldots, N_n)[\vec{M}/\vec{x}]\ [\Gamma'] := R(N_1[\vec{M}/\vec{x}], \ldots, N_n[\vec{M}/\vec{x}])\ [\Gamma']$$

Substitution on subformulae (where x_{m+1} is a fresh variable):

- $\bot[\vec{M}/\vec{x}]\ [\Gamma'] := \bot\ [\Gamma']$
- $(\phi_1 \supset \phi_2)[\vec{M}/\vec{x}]\ [\Gamma'] := (\phi_1[\vec{M}/\vec{x}]) \supset (\phi_2[\vec{M}/\vec{x}])\ [\Gamma']$
- $(\forall x_{n+1}\psi)[\vec{M}/\vec{x}]\ [\Gamma'] := \forall x_{m+1}(\psi[\vec{M}/\vec{x}, x_{m+1}/x_{n+1}])\ [\Gamma']$
- $(\Box\psi)[\vec{M}/\vec{x}]\ [\Gamma'] := \Box(\psi[\vec{M}/\vec{x}])\ [\Gamma']$

3.2 Logical Calculus

A Hilbert-style system for (typed) non-normal propositional modal logics is given by any axiomatisation of propositional logic, plus the rules and axiom schema

$$\frac{\phi \supset\subset \psi\ [\Gamma]}{\Box\phi \supset\subset \Box\psi\ [\Gamma]}(\mathrm{RE}) \qquad \frac{\phi\ [\Gamma] \quad \phi \supset \psi\ [\Gamma]}{\psi\ [\Gamma]}(\mathrm{MP}) \qquad \Diamond\phi \supset\subset \neg\Box\neg\phi\ [\Gamma]\ (\mathrm{E})$$

and zero or more of the following axiom schemata:

$$\Box(\phi \wedge \psi) \supset (\Box\phi \wedge \Box\psi) \quad [\Gamma] \tag{M}$$

$$(\Box\phi \wedge \Box\psi) \supset \Box(\phi \wedge \psi) \quad [\Gamma] \tag{C}$$

$$\Box\top \quad [\Gamma] \tag{N}$$

The smallest non-normal propositional modal logic is called **E**; the non-normal extensions are denoted by $\mathbf{E}_X$, where X is a subset of $\{\mathbf{M}, \mathbf{N}, \mathbf{C}\}$ and $\mathbf{E}_X$ is the smallest system containing every instance of the axiom schemata in X. The system **EMCN** is equivalent to the smallest normal modal logic **K**. The system **S4** is **K** plus the schemata $\Box\phi \supset \phi\ [\Gamma]$ (T) and $\Box\phi \supset \Box\Box\phi\ [\Gamma]$ (4).

To extend any propositional non-normal modal logic **S** to a (typed) first-order logic **TFOL** + **S**, we add the following axiom schema and rules:[2]

$$(\forall x\phi)[x_1,\ldots,x_n] \supset \phi \quad [x:\sigma,\Gamma] \qquad (\forall\text{-}Elim)$$

$$\frac{\phi[x_1,\ldots,x_n] \supset \psi \quad [x:\sigma,\Gamma]}{\phi \supset \forall x\psi \quad [\Gamma]}\ (\forall\text{-}Intro) \qquad \frac{\phi \quad [\Gamma]}{\phi[\vec{M}/\vec{x}] \quad [\Gamma']}\ (Inst)$$

where $\Gamma = x_1:\sigma_1,\ldots,x_n:\sigma_n$ and $\vec{M}$ abbreviates the terms $M_1:\sigma_1\ [\Gamma']$, ..., $M_n:\sigma_n\ [\Gamma']$. The formula $\phi[x_1,\ldots,x_n]$ evidentiates the free variables of ϕ, since the rule requires that x is not free in ϕ. It differs from the formula $\phi\ [\Gamma]$ by the renaming of bound variables.

A *derivation* of a formula $\phi\ [\Gamma]$ is a finite sequence of formulae $\phi_1\ [\Gamma_1]$, $\phi_2\ [\Gamma_2]$, ..., $\phi_n\ [\Gamma_n]$ such that each formula is either an instance of an axiom schema or follows from earlier formulae by one of the rules of inference. A formula $\phi\ [\Gamma]$ is said to be *derivable* in the axiom system **TFOL** + **S** if there exists a derivation of $\phi\ [\Gamma]$ in this axiom system, denoted $\vdash_{\mathbf{TFOL}\,+\,\mathbf{S}} \phi\ [\Gamma]$.

4 Hyperdoctrine Semantics for TFOL + $\mathbf{E_X}$

Before defining a modal hyperdoctrine, we present the standard algebraic semantics for modal logic, to which the hyperdoctrine semantics reduce on the propositional level. Algebraic semantics for modal logic **S4** were developed by McKinsey and Tarski, extended to normal modal logics in [16], and even weaker modal logics in [6]. We adopt this last, most general, definition of modal algebra.

Definition 1. *A* modal algebra A *is a Boolean algebra* $(A, \wedge_A, \vee_A, \neg_A, \top_A, \bot_A)$ *together with a unary operator* $\Box_A$ *satisfying zero or more conditions, such as:*

$$\Box_A(x \wedge_A y) \leq \Box_A(x) \wedge_A \Box_A(y) \qquad (\mathrm{M}_A)$$

$$\Box_A(x) \wedge_A \Box_A(y) \leq \Box_A(x \wedge_A y) \qquad (\mathrm{C}_A)$$

$$\Box_A(\top_A) = \top_A \qquad (\mathrm{N}_A)$$

$$\Box_A(x) \leq x \qquad (\mathrm{T}_A)$$

$$\Box_A(x) \leq \Box_A\Box_A(x) \qquad (4_A)$$

There are secondary operations $x \supset_A y := \neg_A x \vee_A y$ *and* $\Diamond_A(x) := \neg_A\Box_A(\neg_A x)$.

We use the same notation for the operations on the algebra as for the logical connectives, to highlight their correspondence. The algebraic operations are subscripted with the underlying set when it is helpful to have a reminder that we are in the algebraic setting. A poset structure is inherited from the Boolean algebra, given by the order $x \leq y$ if and only if $x \wedge_A y = x$. Modal algebras and finite meet preserving functions between them form the category **MA**.

[2] This axiomatisation deviates from [1], instead following [3] in taking two separate principles of *replacement*—corresponding to the *Instantiation* rule—and *agreement*—corresponding to the ∀ *-Introduction* rule—to more readily accommodate the proofs.

Possible conditions on $\Box_A$ correspond to axiom schemata of the logical calculus to be captured. In the proofs that follow, we only specify the strength of modal algebra to which the category **MA** refers when necessary. Since we are concerned with the level of predicates, most proofs operate independently of the specific axioms satisfied by the modal operator.

4.1 Modal Hyperdoctrine Semantics

In this section we adapt the definition of Lawvere hyperdoctrine from intuitionistic logic to modal logic, define *interpretation* in a modal hyperdoctrine, and prove that this gives sound and complete semantics for $\mathbf{TFOL} + \mathbf{E}_X$.

Definition 2. *Let* $\mathbf{C}$ *be a category with finite products. A* modal hyperdoctrine *is a contravariant functor* $P : \mathbf{C}^{\mathrm{op}} \to \mathbf{MA}$ *such that for any projection* $\pi : X \times Y \to Y$ *in* $\mathbf{C}$, $P(\pi) : P(Y) \to P(X \times Y)$ *has a right adjoint satisfying the Beck-Chevalley condition (1).*

Since our modal logic is classical, our definition of modal hyperdoctrine does not treat the existential quantifier independently.

Definition 3. *Fix a modal hyperdoctrine* $P : \mathbf{C}^{\mathrm{op}} \to \mathbf{MA}$*. An* interpretation $[\![\text{-}]\!]$ *of* $\mathbf{TFOL} + \mathbf{E}_X$ *in* P *consists of the following:*

- *assignment of an object* $[\![\sigma]\!]$ *in* $\mathbf{C}$ *to each basic type* σ *in* $\mathbf{TFOL} + \mathbf{E}_X$*;*
- *assignment of an arrow* $[\![F]\!] : [\![\sigma_1]\!] \times \cdots \times [\![\sigma_n]\!] \to [\![\tau]\!]$ *in* $\mathbf{C}$ *to each function symbol* $F : \sigma_1, \ldots, \sigma_n \to \tau$ *in* $\mathbf{TFOL} + \mathbf{E}_X$*;*
- *assignment of an element* $[\![R\ [\Gamma]]\!]$ *in the modal algebra* $P([\![\Gamma]\!])$ *to each typed predicate symbol* $R\ [\Gamma]$ *in* $\mathbf{TFOL} + \mathbf{E}_X$*; if the context* Γ *is* $x_1 : \sigma_1, ..., x_n : \sigma_n$*, then* $[\![\Gamma]\!]$ *denotes* $[\![\sigma_1]\!] \times ... \times [\![\sigma_n]\!]$.

The interpretation of a term is defined by induction on its derivation, as follows:

- $[\![x : \sigma\ [\Gamma, x : \sigma, \Gamma']]\!]$ *is defined as the following projection in* $\mathbf{C}$*:*

$$\pi : [\![\Gamma]\!] \times [\![\sigma]\!] \times [\![\Gamma']\!] \to [\![\sigma]\!];$$

- $[\![F(M_1, \ldots, M_n) : \tau\ [\Gamma]]\!] := [\![F]\!] \circ \langle [\![M_1 : \sigma_1\ [\Gamma]]\!], \ldots, [\![M_n : \sigma_n\ [\Gamma]]\!] \rangle$.

Formulae are interpreted inductively in the following manner:

- $[\![R(M_1, \ldots, M_n)\ [\Gamma]]\!] := P(\langle [\![M_1 : \sigma_1\ [\Gamma]]\!], \ldots, [\![M_n : \sigma_n\ [\Gamma]]\!] \rangle)([\![R]\!])$.
- *For the propositional connectives:*

$$[\![\phi \wedge \psi\ [\Gamma]]\!] := [\![\phi\ [\Gamma]]\!] \wedge_{P([\![\Gamma]\!])} [\![\psi\ [\Gamma]]\!]$$
$$[\![\phi \vee \psi\ [\Gamma]]\!] := [\![\phi\ [\Gamma]]\!] \vee_{P([\![\Gamma]\!])} [\![\psi\ [\Gamma]]\!]$$
$$[\![\phi \supset \psi\ [\Gamma]]\!] := [\![\phi\ [\Gamma]]\!] \supset_{P([\![\Gamma]\!])} [\![\psi\ [\Gamma]]\!]$$
$$[\![\neg\phi\ [\Gamma]]\!] := \neg_{P([\![\Gamma]\!])}[\![\phi\ [\Gamma]]\!] \qquad [\![\bot\ [\Gamma]]\!] := \bot_{P([\![\Gamma]\!])}$$
$$[\![\Box\phi\ [\Gamma]]\!] := \Box_{P([\![\Gamma]\!])}([\![\phi\ [\Gamma]]\!]) \qquad [\![\top[\Gamma]]\!] := \top_{P([\![\Gamma]\!])}$$

- *For the quantifiers:*

$$[\![\forall x\phi\ [\Gamma]]\!] := \forall_\pi([\![\phi\ [x:\sigma,\Gamma]]\!]) \quad and \quad [\![\exists x\phi\ [\Gamma]]\!] := \exists_\pi([\![\phi\ [x:\sigma,\Gamma]]\!])$$

where $\pi : [\![\sigma]\!] \times [\![\Gamma]\!] \to [\![\Gamma]\!]$ *is a projection in* $\mathbf{C}$.

For a formula $\phi\ [\Gamma]$, where $\Gamma = x_1 : \sigma_1, \ldots, x_n : \sigma_n$, and terms $M_1 : \sigma_1\ [\Gamma'], \ldots, M_n : \sigma_n\ [\Gamma']$, the interpretation of substitution by $\vec{M}$ is:

$$[\![\phi[\vec{M}/\vec{x}]\ [\Gamma']]\!] = P(\langle [\![M_1 : \sigma_1\ [\Gamma']]\!], \ldots, [\![M_n : \sigma_n\ [\Gamma']]\!]\rangle)([\![\phi\ [\Gamma]]\!]).$$

This can be proved by induction on the structure of ϕ. Weakening of the context of a formula $\phi\ [\Gamma]$ to the context $x : \sigma, \Gamma$ is the following special case:

$$[\![\phi\ [x:\sigma,\Gamma]]\!] = P(\pi)([\![\phi\ [\Gamma]]\!])$$

where $\pi : [\![\sigma]\!] \times [\![\Gamma]\!] \to [\![\Gamma]\!]$ is a projection map.

Definition 4. *A formula* $\phi\ [\Gamma]$ *is* satisfied *in an interpretation* $[\![\text{-}]\!]$ *in a modal hyperdoctrine* P *if and only if* $[\![\phi]\!] = \top_{P([\![\Gamma]\!])}$.

Since $a \leq_A \top_A$ holds for every element a in a Boolean algebra A, showing the satisfiability of $\phi\ [\Gamma]$ amounts to showing $\top_{P([\![\Gamma]\!])} \leq [\![\phi]\!]$. Note that the definition of satisfaction here differs from that in [19], which is concerned with the satisfiability of sequents rather than formulae.

4.2 Soundness and Completeness

We proceed by proving the soundness and completeness of $\mathbf{TFOL} + \mathbf{E}_X$ with respect to the modal hyperdoctrine semantics. We make use of an equivalent condition for the satisfaction of an implication $\phi \supset \psi\ [\Gamma]$ in an interpretation:

$$\top \leq [\![\phi \supset \psi\ [\Gamma]]\!] \text{ if and only if } [\![\phi\ [\Gamma]]\!] \leq [\![\psi\ [\Gamma]]\!]. \tag{2}$$

This follows from the fact that in a Boolean algebra, the pair of functions $\text{-} \wedge x : A \to A$ and $x \supset \text{-} : A \to A$ determine an adjunction, that is, for all $y, z \in A$, $z \leq x \supset y$ if and only if $z \wedge x \leq y$. Letting $z = \top$ and using the fact that $\top \wedge x = x$, we have $\top \leq x \supset y$ if and only if $x \leq y$.

We will also use the following bijection, coming from the adjointness condition on the universal quantifier:

$$\frac{P(\pi)(A) \leq_{P(X\times Y)} B}{A \leq_{P(Y)} \forall_\pi(B)} \tag{3}$$

The following soundness proof is with respect to the systems $\mathbf{TFOL} + \mathbf{E}_X$, but we note that the proof applies to other systems $\mathbf{TFOL} + \mathbf{S}$, provided we strengthen the conditions on the modal operator in correspondence with the axiom schemata of $\mathbf{S}$. This generality is possible given how the predicate and propositional components interact in the semantics, that is, the structure on the predicate part governs the interaction between the modal algebras, while preserving their internal structure.

Proposition 1. *If ϕ $[\Gamma]$ has a derivation in* $\mathbf{TFOL} + \mathbf{E}_X$*, then it is satisfied in any interpretation in any modal hyperdoctrine.*

Proof. See Appendix A.

Towards proving completeness, we now define the syntactic hyperdoctrine of $\mathbf{TFOL} + \mathbf{S}$. For the base category $\mathbf{C}$, let the objects be contexts Γ up to α-equivalence (renaming of variables). This is equivalent to taking as objects lists of types $\sigma_1, \ldots, \sigma_n$, rather than a list of variable-type pairs. A context morphism from $\sigma_1, \ldots, \sigma_n$ to $\Gamma' = \tau_1, \ldots, \tau_m$ is given by a list of terms $t_1 : \tau_1[\Gamma], \ldots, t_m : \tau_m[\Gamma]$, abbreviated $[t_1, \ldots, t_m] : \Gamma \to \Gamma'$. We take as arrows equivalence classes of context morphisms under the relation $[t_1, \ldots, t_n] = [s_1, \ldots, s_n]$ if and only if t_i is equivalent—as terms—to s_i, for all i. Contexts up to α-equivalence and context morphisms up to term-equivalence form a category.

Definition 5. *For a context Γ, let* $\mathrm{Form}_\Gamma := \{\phi \mid \phi \text{ is a formula in context } \Gamma\}$. *The* syntactic hyperdoctrine $P : \mathbf{C}^{\mathrm{op}} \to \mathbf{MA}$ *sends objects Γ to*

$$P(\Gamma) := \mathrm{Form}_\Gamma / \sim$$

where $\sim$ is the equivalence relation $\phi \sim \psi$ if and only if $\vdash_{\mathbf{TFOL+S}} \phi \supset\subset \psi\ [\Gamma]$. The object $P(\Gamma)$ has a modal algebra structure induced by the logical connectives.

The syntactic hyperdoctrine sends arrows $[t_1, \ldots, t_m] : \Gamma \to \Gamma'$ to

$$P([t_1, \ldots, t_m]) : P(\Gamma') \to P(\Gamma),$$

defined by $P([t_1, \ldots, t_m])(\phi) := \phi[t_1/y_1, \ldots, t_m/y_m]$.

Proposition 2. *The syntactic hyperdoctrine $P : \mathbf{C}^{\mathrm{op}} \to \mathbf{MA}$ is a modal hyperdoctrine.*

Proof. See Appendix B.

There is the obvious canonical interpretation (generic model) of $\mathbf{TFOL} + \mathbf{S}$ in the syntactic hyperdoctrine, about which we can say the following:

Proposition 3. *If ϕ $[\Gamma]$ is satisfied in the canonical interpretation in the syntactic hyperdoctrine then it is deducible in* $\mathbf{TFOL} + \mathbf{S}$.

From this it follows that if ϕ $[\Gamma]$ is satisfied in any interpretation in any modal hyperdoctrine, then it is deducible in $\mathbf{TFOL} + \mathbf{S}$.

4.3 Hyperdoctrinal Translation Theorem for TFOL + S4

Having categorical semantics for a logic allows us to investigate that logic using the structure of category theory; in the following, we compose an **S4** modal hyperdoctrine with a translation functor from modal to intuitionistic logic to get a hyperdoctrinal translation theorem. One direction of the Gödel-McKinsey-Tarski translation between modal and intuitionistic logic (see, e.g., [18]) can be expressed as the functor

$$\mathsf{Fix}_{\Box} : \mathbf{MA} \to \mathbf{HA}$$

sending a modal algebra A to a Heyting algebra on the set $\{a \in A \mid \Box a = a\}$, and an **MA**-homomorphism $h : A \to B$ to an **HA**-homomorphism

$$\mathsf{Fix}_{\Box}(h) : \mathsf{Fix}_{\Box}(A) \to \mathsf{Fix}_{\Box}(B).$$

For the functor to send modal algebras to Heyting algebras, the modal algebra must satisfy all the axioms in Definition 1, and thus the translation theorem only works for modal logics **S4** and stronger.

Proposition 4. *Let* $P : \mathbf{C}^{\mathrm{op}} \to \mathbf{MA}$ *be a modal hyperdoctrine. The functor*

$$P_{\mathsf{Fix}} := \mathsf{Fix}_{\Box} \circ P : \mathbf{C}^{\mathrm{op}} \to \mathbf{HA}$$

is an intuitionistic hyperdoctrine.

Proof. Firstly, we show that there are right and left adjoints, $\forall_{\pi}^{\Box}$ and $\exists_{\pi}^{\Box}$, to

$$P_{\mathsf{Fix}}(\pi) : P_{\mathsf{Fix}}(Y) \to P_{\mathsf{Fix}}(X \times Y),$$

where $\pi : X \times Y \to Y$ is a projection function in **C**. Since P is a modal hyperdoctrine, there exist maps $\forall_{\pi}, \exists_{\pi} : P(X \times Y) \to P(Y)$ right and left adjoint to $P(\pi)$. We restrict these maps to the domain $P_{\mathsf{Fix}}(X \times Y)$ to define the right and left adjoints to $P_{\mathsf{Fix}}(\pi)$ as follows. For $\psi \in P_{\mathsf{Fix}}(X \times Y)$,

$$\forall_{\pi}^{\mathsf{Fix}}(\psi) := \mathsf{Fix}_{\Box}(\forall_{\pi}(\psi)) \quad \text{and} \quad \exists_{\pi}^{\mathsf{Fix}}(\psi) := \mathsf{Fix}_{\Box}(\exists_{\pi}(\psi)).$$

To show that $\forall_{\pi}^{\mathsf{Fix}}$ is right adjoint to $P_{\mathsf{Fix}}(\pi)$, let $\phi \in P_{\mathsf{Fix}}(Y)$ and suppose $P_{\mathsf{Fix}}(\pi)(\phi) \leq \psi$. Since $P_{\mathsf{Fix}}(\pi)$ is just the restriction $P(\pi)|_{P_{\mathsf{Fix}}(Y)}$, we have $P(\pi)(\phi) \leq \psi$, and since $P(\pi)$ is left adjoint to $\forall_{\pi}$, this means $\phi \leq \forall_{\pi}(\psi)$. But $\psi \in P_{\mathsf{Fix}}(X \times Y)$, so $\forall_{\pi}^{\mathsf{Fix}}(\psi) = \forall_{\pi}(\psi)$ and $\phi \leq \forall_{\pi}^{\mathsf{Fix}}(\psi)$. Since this argument is entirely reversible, the other direction of the bijection holds. A similar argument can be made to show $\exists_{\pi}^{\mathsf{Fix}}$ is left adjoint to $P_{\mathsf{Fix}}(\pi)$.

5 Higher-Order Modal Hyperdoctrine

From the hyperdoctrine perspective of "logic over type theory", moving from first-order logic to higher-order logic corresponds to adding more structure to the indexing category **C**. After specifying the higher-order syntax, we define a higher-order modal hyperdoctrine and prove soundness and completeness.

5.1 Higher-Order Modal Logic

We present a higher-order version of a typed modal system **S**, called **HoS**. This is achieved by two augmentations to the type structure of **TFOL** + **S**: to enable quantification over predicates, we add a special type of propositions to the signature; we also add rules for arrow and finite product types to the term calculus to give a simply typed λ-calculus. These changes follow [12] and [19].

Simply Typed $\lambda 1_{\times}$-calculus. In addition to the basic types of our signature Σ we add *compound types* by including the usual type formation rules for arrow (exponent) types $\rightarrow$ and finite product types $1, \times$. We also add the usual introduction, elimination and computation rules for terms of these types: for arrow types, these are λ-abstraction, application, and β- and η-conversion; for finite product types, these are pairing, projection, and their conversion rules. Substitution is extended to these terms in the usual way (see [12, Section 2]).

Distinguished Type Prop. To be able to quantify over propositions as well as inhabitants of types σ, we add the distinguished type Prop to those listed in the signature. Like the other types, Prop has a list of variables $x, y, z, \ldots$.

On top of the signature, terms-in-context $M : \sigma\ [\Gamma]$ and formulae-in-context $\phi\ [\Gamma]$ are given the same inductive definition as in Sect. 3. Terms of type Prop (in context) are constructed as follows. For each relation symbol $R \subseteq \sigma_1, \ldots, \sigma_n$ in the signature, introduce a corresponding function symbol with codomain Prop:

$$R : \sigma_1, \ldots, \sigma_n \rightarrow \mathsf{Prop}.$$

Then for $M_1 : \sigma_1\ [\Gamma], \ldots, M_n : \sigma_n\ [\Gamma]$, there is a term $R(M_1, \ldots, M_n)$ of type Prop. Further terms of type Prop are constructed by the logical connectives:

$$\frac{\phi : \mathsf{Prop}\ [\Gamma] \quad \psi : \mathsf{Prop}\ [\Gamma]}{\phi * \psi : \mathsf{Prop}\ [\Gamma]} \text{ for } * \in \{\wedge, \vee, \supset\}$$

$$\frac{\phi : \mathsf{Prop}\ [\Gamma]}{*\phi : \mathsf{Prop}\ [\Gamma]} \text{ for } * \in \{\neg, \Box\} \qquad \frac{\phi : \mathsf{Prop}\ [x : \sigma, \Gamma]}{*_{x:\sigma}\phi : \mathsf{Prop}\ [\Gamma]} \text{ for } * \in \{\forall, \exists\}$$

Substitution over these terms is defined in the usual way (see [12] for full details).

On top of this term calculus, we still have the judgement $\vdash_{\mathbf{HoS}} \phi\ [\Gamma]$, saying that there is a derivation of $\phi\ [\Gamma]$ as governed by the first-order logic rules in Sect. 3. It remains to relate the notion of logical equivalence between formulae[3] to the notion of equality of terms of type Prop via the following rule:

$$\frac{\vdash_{\mathbf{HoS}} \phi \supset \psi\ [\Gamma] \quad \vdash_{\mathbf{HoS}} \psi \supset \phi\ [\Gamma]}{\phi = \psi : \mathsf{Prop}\ [\Gamma]}\ (Prop),$$

where $\phi = \psi$: Prop is judgemental (computational) equality of terms, that is, one term may be converted to the other following the rules of the λ-calculus. Propositions are now terms internal to the type theory.

[3] For convenience in the proofs to come, we express it as two separate conditionals rather than the biconditional $\supset\subset$.

5.2 Modal Tripos

Definition 6. *A* modal tripos, *or* higher-order modal hyperdoctrine, *is a modal hyperdoctrine* $P : \mathbf{C}^{\mathrm{op}} \to \mathbf{MA}$ *where the base category is cartesian closed and there is a* truth-value object Ω *in* $\mathbf{C}$ *with a natural isomorphism*

$$P(C) \simeq Hom_{\mathbf{C}}(C, \Omega)$$

Modal tripos semantics are given by the following definition.

Definition 7. *Fix a modal tripos* $P : \mathbf{C}^{\mathrm{op}} \to \mathbf{MA}$. *An interpretation* $[\![\text{-}]\!]$ *of* **HoS** *in* P *is given by the interpretation in Definition 3, augmented as follows.*

- *arrow and finite product types,* $\sigma \to \tau$ *and* $1, \sigma \times \tau$, *are interpreted by exponentiation* $[\![\tau]\!]^{[\![\sigma]\!]}$ *and categorical product* $[\![\sigma]\!] \times [\![\tau]\!]$ *in* $\mathbf{C}$;
- *the following cases are added to the inductively-defined interpretation of a term:* λ*-abstraction,* λ*-application, pairing and projections are interpreted by categorical transpose, evaluation, pairing and projection respectively in* $\mathbf{C}$;
- *the type* Prop *is assigned to the truth-value object* Ω *in* $\mathbf{C}$, *i.e.* $[\![\mathsf{Prop}]\!] = \Omega$;
- *a term* $\phi : \mathsf{Prop}\ [\Gamma]$ *is assigned to the arrow* $[\![\phi]\!] : [\![\Gamma]\!] \to [\![\mathsf{Prop}]\!]$ *in* $\mathbf{C}$ *that corresponds to* $[\![\phi\ [\Gamma]]\!] \in P([\![\Gamma]\!])$ *via the defining isomorphism of* P.

5.3 Soundness and Completeness

Proposition 5. *If* $\phi\ [\Gamma]$ *has a derivation in* $\mathbf{HoE}_X$, *then it is satisfied in any interpretation in any modal tripos.*

Proof. Fix a modal tripos P and an interpretation $[\![\text{-}]\!]$ in P. With the soundness of modal hyperdoctrine semantics established in Proposition 1, it remains to show that satisfaction of the *Prop* rule is preserved. Suppose $[\![\phi \supset \psi]\!]$ and $[\![\psi \supset \phi]\!]$ are true in $P([\![\Gamma]\!])$, and so we have

$$\top \leq [\![\phi]\!] \supset [\![\psi]\!] \text{ and } \top \leq [\![\psi]\!] \supset [\![\phi]\!].$$

By 2, this is equivalent to $[\![\phi]\!] \leq [\![\psi]\!]$ and $[\![\psi]\!] \leq [\![\phi]\!]$, from which it follows that $[\![\phi]\!] = [\![\psi]\!]$ in $P([\![\Gamma]\!])$. By the isomorphism in the definition of a modal tripos, $[\![\phi]\!], [\![\psi]\!] \in P([\![\Gamma]\!])$ correspond to arrows $[\![\phi]\!], [\![\psi]\!] : [\![\Gamma]\!] \to [\![\mathsf{Prop}]\!]$ in $\mathbf{C}$ that must be equal. These arrows are the interpretations of the terms $\phi : \mathsf{Prop}[\Gamma]$ and $\psi : \mathsf{Prop}[\Gamma]$ respectively, and so we have:

$$[\![\phi : \mathsf{Prop}[\Gamma]]\!] = [\![\psi : \mathsf{Prop}[\Gamma]]\!]$$

which is the same as $[\![\phi = \psi : \mathsf{Prop}\ [\Gamma]]\!]$.

Towards proving completeness, we are interested in the syntactic tripos of **HoS**, which is defined in the same way as the syntactic hyperdoctrine. Here we prove that it is in fact a modal tripos.

Proposition 6. *The syntactic hyperdoctrine defined in 5 is a modal tripos.*

Proof. The existence of finite products and exponentials in **C** is guaranteed by the existence of finite product types and function types in the type theory. To show the existence of a truth value object, we need a context up to α-equivalence satisfying the required isomorphism. Take $\Omega = x : \mathsf{Prop}$, noting that this is essentially the same as taking Prop itself when considering $x : \mathsf{Prop}$ as a (single variable) context up to α-equivalence. The required isomorphism then becomes

$$P(\Gamma) \simeq \mathrm{Hom}_{\mathbf{C}}(\Gamma, x : \mathsf{Prop}).$$

By the definition of the syntax, for every formula $\phi\ [\Gamma]$—built from atomic formulae $R(M_1, \ldots, M_n)\ [\Gamma]$ and the logical connectives—there is a corresponding term $\phi : \mathsf{Prop}\ [\Gamma]$—built in the same way from the logical connectives and atomic propositions $R(M_1, \ldots, M_n) : \mathsf{Prop}\ [\Gamma]$. We may consider the term $\phi : \mathsf{Prop}\ [\Gamma]$ as a context morphism in the base category of the modal tripos, that is, as a list of terms of length one, $[\phi] : \Gamma \to \mathsf{Prop}$. This gives the following isomorphism:

$$P(\Gamma) \simeq P(\Gamma, \mathsf{Prop}).$$

To show that this isomorphism is natural, for contexts $\Gamma = \sigma_1, \ldots, \sigma_n$ and $\Gamma' = \tau_1, \ldots, \tau_m$, for any morphism $[t_1, \ldots, t_m] : \Gamma \to \Gamma'$ in the base category, where $t_i : \tau_i\ [\Gamma]$, we require that the following square commutes:

$$\begin{array}{ccc} P(\Gamma') & \xrightarrow{\mathrm{PaF}'_{\Gamma}} & \mathrm{Hom}_{\mathbf{C}}(\Gamma', \mathsf{Prop}) \\ {\scriptstyle P([t_1,\ldots,t_m])}\downarrow & & \downarrow{\scriptstyle \mathrm{Hom}_{\mathbf{C}}([t_1,\ldots,t_m], x:\mathsf{Prop})} \\ P(\Gamma) & \xrightarrow[\mathrm{PaF}_{\Gamma}]{} & \mathrm{Hom}_{\mathbf{C}}(\Gamma, \mathsf{Prop}) \end{array}$$

where PaF ("Propositions as functions") denotes the isomorphism. This is given by the calculation:

$$\begin{aligned} &\mathrm{Hom}_{\mathbf{C}}([t_1, \ldots, t_m], x : \mathsf{Prop}) \circ \mathrm{PaF}_{\Gamma}(\phi\ [\Gamma']) \\ &= \mathrm{Hom}_{\mathbf{C}}([t_1, \ldots, t_m], x : \mathsf{Prop})(\phi : \mathsf{Prop}\ [\Gamma']) \\ &= \phi[t_1/x_1, \ldots, t_m/x_m] : \mathsf{Prop}\ [\Gamma] \\ &= \mathrm{PaF}_{\Gamma}(\phi[t_1/x_1, \ldots, t_m/x_m][\Gamma]) \\ &= \mathrm{PaF}_{\Gamma} \circ P([t_1, \ldots, t_m])(\phi[\Gamma']). \end{aligned}$$

It is straightforward to see that if $\phi\ [\Gamma]$ is valid in the canonical interpretation in the syntactic tripos, then it is provable in **HoS**. The standard counter-model argument then immediately gives completeness. Combined with soundness, we obtain the following theorem.

Theorem 1. *$\phi\ [\Gamma]$ is provable in* **HoS** *iff it is valid in any interpretation in any modal tripos.*

6 Conclusion

We have established both first-order and higher-order completeness for non-normal modal logics via hyperdoctrine semantics; we have also shown a hyperdoctrinal translation theorem for normal modal hyperdoctrines. The straightforward nature of these results is demonstrative of the power of hyperdoctrine.

Coalgebraic logic has been highly successful for a unified treatment of various propositional modal logics [4,17], and in future work, we plan to apply coalgebraic logic, especially duality-theoretical results such as in [14], to construct models of modal hyperdoctrines; the predicate functors of Stone-type dual adjunctions often form hyperdoctrines. More ambitiously, we plan to extend coalgebraic modal logic to first-order and higher-order settings via hyperdoctrine semantics.

Acknowledgments. We thank the anonymous reviewers for their helpful feedback. This work was supported by JST (JPMJMS2033-02; JPMJFR206P).

A Soundness of Modal Hyperdoctrine Semantics

Proof. Fix a modal hyperdoctrine P and an interpretation $[\![-]\!]$ in P. The proof is by induction on the derivation of ϕ $[\Gamma]$, which amounts to checking that all axiom schemata are satisfied and that all rules preserve satisfaction.

For the propositional fragment, beginning with rule RE, suppose $[\![\phi \supset\subset \psi]\!]$ is true in $P([\![\Gamma]\!])$. Expanding the abbreviation $\supset\subset$ and taking the interpretation of the connectives as in Definition 3, we have:

$$[\![\phi \supset \psi \wedge \psi \supset \phi]\!] = [\![\phi]\!] \supset [\![\psi]\!] \wedge [\![\psi]\!] \supset [\![\phi]\!].$$

It is a theorem in a Boolean algebra that the right-hand side implies $[\![\phi]\!] = [\![\psi]\!]$. Therefore, $\Box[\![\phi]\!] = \Box[\![\psi]\!]$, which is the interpretation of the formula $\Box\phi \supset\subset \Box\psi$ $[\Gamma]$, and so the rule RE preserves satisfaction. The rule MP may be checked in a similar way.

For the modal axiom schemata, satisfaction of schema E corresponds to the definition of the $\Diamond$ operator in a modal algebra, so $\Diamond[\![\phi]\!] = \neg\Box\neg[\![\phi]\!]$ in $P([\![\Gamma]\!])$. The interpretation of schema M is:

$$[\![\Box(\phi \wedge \psi) \supset (\Box\phi \wedge \Box\psi)]\!] = \Box([\![\phi]\!] \wedge [\![\psi]\!]) \supset (\Box[\![\phi]\!] \wedge \Box[\![\psi]\!]),$$

so M is satisfied in the interpretation if $\Box([\![\phi]\!] \wedge [\![\psi]\!]) \leq (\Box[\![\phi]\!] \wedge \Box[\![\psi]\!])$, by the equivalent condition for satisfaction of an implication established in 2. This corresponds clearly to condition M_A on the operator.

In a similar way, we can show that schema N corresponds to condition N_A and C corresponds to C_A. It is also clear that we may add more axiom schemata to $\mathbf{TFOL} + \mathbf{E}_X$ to get a system $\mathbf{TFOL} + \mathbf{S}$, and that these schemata are satisfied in the interpretation if we add corresponding conditions on the modal operator in the algebra. Satisfaction of the axiom schemata for the non-modal part of the proportional logic may be verified in the same way.

For the first-order fragment, the axiom schema $\forall$-*Elimination* is satisfied if and only if the interpretation $[\![(\forall x\phi)[x_1,\ldots,x_n] \supset \phi]\!]$ is true in $P([\![\sigma]\!] \times [\![\Gamma]\!])$. By 2, we can do this by showing

$$[\![(\forall x\phi)[x_1,\ldots,x_n]]\!] \leq [\![\phi]\!].$$

The logical expression on the left-hand side, $(\forall x\phi)[x_1,\ldots,x_n]$, is a formula in context $[x:\sigma,\Gamma]$, but which does not contain x, and so corresponds to weakening of the context. By the semantics of substitution, we have:

$$[\![(\forall x\phi)[x_1,\ldots,x_n]\ [x:\sigma,\Gamma]]\!] = P(\pi)([\![\forall x\phi\ [\Gamma]]\!]),$$

and by the interpretation of the universal quantifier,

$$P(\pi)([\![\forall x\phi\ [\Gamma]]\!]) = P(\pi)(\forall_\pi([\![\phi\ [x:\sigma,\Gamma]]\!])).$$

This turns the desired statement into another form of the adjointness condition for universal quantification, that is, the counit characterisation:

$$P(\pi)(\forall_\pi([\![\phi\ [x:\sigma,\Gamma]]\!])) \leq [\![\phi\ [x:\sigma,\Gamma]]\!].$$

To show that the $\forall$-*Introduction* rule preserves satisfaction, suppose

$$[\![\phi[x_1,\ldots,x_n] \supset \psi]\!]$$

is true in $P([\![\sigma]\!] \times [\![\Gamma]\!])$, or equivalently, $[\![\phi[x_1,\ldots,x_n]]\!] \leq [\![\psi]\!]$. Then we need to show that $[\![\phi \supset \forall x\psi]\!]$ is true in $P([\![\Gamma]\!])$, or equivalently, $[\![\phi]\!] \leq \forall_\sigma[\![\psi]\!]$. This logical rule directly translates to one direction of the adjointness correspondence when we observe that the formula $\phi[x_1,\ldots,x_n]\ [x:\sigma,\Gamma]$ is weakening of the formula $\phi[\Gamma]$. By the interpretation of substitution,

$$[\![\phi[x_1,\ldots,x_n]\ [x:\sigma,\Gamma]]\!] = P(\pi)([\![\phi\ [\Gamma]]\!]).$$

But if $P(\pi)([\![\phi]\!]) \leq [\![\psi]\!]$ holds, then by the adjointness condition for universal quantification, $[\![\phi]\!] \leq \forall_\sigma[\![\psi]\!]$ as required.

For the *Instantiation* rule, suppose $\top \leq [\![\phi]\!]$ in $P([\![\Gamma]\!])$. Applying the (order-preserving) modal algebra homomorphism

$$P(\langle[\![M_1:\sigma_1\ [\Gamma']]\!],\ldots,[\![M_n:\sigma_n\ [\Gamma']]\!]\rangle) : P([\![\Gamma]\!]) \to P([\![\Gamma']\!])$$

to both sides, we get:

$$\begin{aligned} &P(\langle[\![M_1:\sigma_1\ [\Gamma']]\!],\ldots,[\![M_n:\sigma_n\ [\Gamma']]\!]\rangle)(\top) \\ &\qquad\qquad \leq P(\langle[\![M_1:\sigma_1\ [\Gamma']]\!],\ldots,[\![M_n:\sigma_n\ [\Gamma']]\!]\rangle)([\![\phi\ [\Gamma]]\!]). \end{aligned}$$

Since modal algebra homomorphisms preserve $\top$, and by the semantics of substitution, we have $\top \leq [\![\phi[\vec{M}/\vec{x}]]\!]$ in $P([\![\Gamma']\!])$.

B Completeness of Modal Hyperdoctrine Semantics

Proof. Firstly, the base category **C** has finite products: for $\Gamma = \sigma_1, \ldots, \sigma_n$ and $\Gamma' = \tau_1, \ldots, \tau_m$, define $\Gamma \times \Gamma'$ as $\sigma_1, \ldots, \sigma_m, \tau_1, \ldots, \tau_n$. We then have, as an associated projection,

$$[y_1, \ldots, y_m] : \Gamma \times \Gamma' \to \Gamma',$$

where the y_i are variables $y_i : \tau_i\ [\Gamma, \Gamma']$. The other projection is defined similarly, and it is straighforward to show that this gives a categorical product in **C**.

Next, we check that the codomain of P is in fact the category of modal algebras and structure-preserving homomorphisms. For a context Γ in **C**, $P(\Gamma)$ forms a modal algebra with operations induced in the expected way by the logical connectives. Considering only the non-modal fragment of the logic, $P([t_1, \ldots, t_n])$ is a Boolean algebra homomorphism since substitution commutes with all the non-modal logical operations. To extend this to a modal algebra homomorphism, we require that $P([t_1, \ldots, t_n])$ preserves the modal operator $\Box$ and any extra conditions placed on $\Box$. This follows from the fact that $P([t_1, \ldots, t_n])$ performs substitution into a formula, and the syntax specifies that $\Box$ commutes with substitution.

Proceeding to the quantifier structure, universal quantification is given by a right adjoint to $P(\pi) : P(\Gamma') \to P(\Gamma \times \Gamma')$, where $\pi : \Gamma \times \Gamma' \to \Gamma'$ is the second projection in **C**. Let ψ be a formula in $P(\Gamma \times \Gamma')$; since the following arguments respect equivalence, we will identify ψ with the equivalence class to which it belongs. Define $\forall_\pi : P(\Gamma \times \Gamma') \to P(\Gamma')$ by

$$\forall_\pi(\psi) := \forall x_1 \ldots \forall x_n \psi,$$

with the formula on the right hand side denoting the corresponding equivalence class.

Suppose $\phi \in P(\Gamma')$; to show that $\forall_\pi$ is the right adjoint of $P(\pi)$ means showing $P(\pi)(\phi) \leq \psi$ in $P(\Gamma \times \Gamma')$ if and only if $\phi \leq \forall x_1 \ldots \forall x_n \psi$ in $P(\Gamma')$. For the first direction, assume $P(\pi)(\phi) \leq \psi$ in $P(\Gamma \times \Gamma')$. Since $P(\pi)(\phi)$ corresponds to weakening of the context of $\phi\ [\Gamma]$ to $\phi[y_1, \ldots, y_m]\ [\Gamma, \Gamma']$, we have $\phi[y_1, \ldots, y_m] \leq \psi$ in $P(\Gamma \times \Gamma')$. The partial order in $P(\Gamma \times \Gamma')$ is induced by its lattice structure, so the above ordering corresponds to the equation $\phi[y_1, \ldots, y_m] \wedge \psi = \phi[y_1, \ldots, y_m]$. By the definition of the syntactic hyperdoctrine, we can make the following derivability statement:

$$\vdash_{\mathbf{TFOL+S}} \phi[y_1, \ldots, y_m] \wedge \psi \supset\subset \phi[y_1, \ldots, y_m]\ [\Gamma, \Gamma']$$

from which it follows that

$$\vdash_{\mathbf{TFOL+S}} \phi[y_1, \ldots, y_m] \supset \psi\ [\Gamma, \Gamma'].$$

Repeated application of $\forall$-*Introduction* gives

$$\vdash_{\mathbf{TFOL+S}} \phi \supset \forall x_1 \ldots \forall x_n \psi \quad [\Gamma'],$$

from which it follows that

$$\vdash_{\mathbf{TFOL+S}} \phi \wedge \forall x_1 \ldots \forall x_n \psi \supset\subset \phi \quad [\Gamma'].$$

Translating back to the modal algebra, this means $\phi \wedge \forall x_1 \ldots \forall x_n \psi = \phi$ in $P(\Gamma')$, and so $\phi \leq \forall x_1 \ldots \forall x_n \psi$ in $P(\Gamma')$, as required.

For the other direction, assume $\phi \leq \forall x_1 \ldots \forall x_n \psi$ in $P(\Gamma')$. Using the same reasoning as before to translate from a statement in the modal algebra to one in the logic, we have

$$\vdash_{\mathbf{TFOL+S}} \phi \wedge \forall x_1 \ldots \forall x_n \psi \supset\subset \phi \quad [\Gamma'],$$

from which it follows:

$$\vdash_{\mathbf{TFOL+S}} \phi \supset \forall x_1 \ldots \forall x_n \psi \quad [\Gamma'].$$

Applying the *Instantiation* rule to weaken the context gives

$$\vdash_{\mathbf{TFOL+S}} (\phi \supset \forall x_1 \ldots \forall x_n \psi)[y_1, \ldots, y_m] \quad [x_1 : \sigma_1, \Gamma'],$$

where we substitute for the variables $y_i : \tau_i$ $[\Gamma']$ variables $y_i : \tau_i$ $[x_1 : \sigma_1, \Gamma']$. Since substitution commutes with $\supset$, we have:

$$\vdash_{\mathbf{TFOL+S}} \phi[y_1, \ldots, y_m] \supset (\forall x_1 \ldots \forall x_n \psi)[y_1, \ldots, y_m] \quad [x_1 : \sigma, \Gamma'] \tag{4}$$

We will prove $\phi[y_1, \ldots, y_m] \supset \forall x_2 \ldots \forall x_n \psi$ $[x_1 : \sigma_1, \Gamma']$ using the deduction theorem. Assume

$$\vdash_{\mathbf{TFOL+S}} \phi[y_1, \ldots, y_m] \; [x_1 : \sigma_1, \Gamma'], \tag{5}$$

then applying rule MP (modus ponens) to 5 and 4 gives:

$$\vdash_{\mathbf{TFOL+S}} (\forall x_1 \ldots \forall x_n \psi)[y_1, \ldots, y_m] \quad [x_1 : \sigma_1, \Gamma']. \tag{6}$$

The following is an instance of the $\forall$-*Elimination* schema:

$$\vdash_{\mathbf{TFOL+S}} (\forall x_1 \forall x_2 \ldots \forall x_n \psi)[y_1, \ldots, y_m] \supset \forall x_2 \ldots \forall x_n \psi \quad [x_1 : \sigma_1, \Gamma']. \tag{7}$$

Applying modus ponens to 6 and 7:

$$\vdash_{\mathbf{TFOL+S}} \forall x_2 \ldots \forall x_n \psi \; [x_1 : \sigma_1, \Gamma'].$$

Since this follows from the assumption that $\phi[y_1, \ldots, y_m]$ $[x_1 : \sigma_1, \Gamma']$ is derivable, we have

$$\vdash_{\mathbf{TFOL+S}} \phi[y_1, \ldots, y_m] \supset \forall x_2 \ldots \forall x_n \psi \; [x_1 : \sigma_1, \Gamma']$$

by the deduction theorem. Repeating this argument, we get

$$\vdash_{\mathbf{TFOL+S}} \phi[y_1, \ldots, y_m] \supset \psi \; [\Gamma, \Gamma'],$$

and translating this back into a statement in the modal algebra $P(\Gamma')$, we have $P(\pi)\phi \leq \psi$.

To show that the corresponding Beck-Chevalley condition is satisfied, let $\Gamma'' = v_1 : \mu_1, \ldots, v_l : \mu_l$ be a context up to α-equivalence. Then for every context morphism $[s_1, \ldots, s_m] : \Gamma'' \to \Gamma'$ with $s_i : \tau_i\ [\Gamma'']$ the following diagram must commute:

$$\begin{array}{ccc} P(\Gamma \times \Gamma') & \xrightarrow{\forall_\pi} & P(\Gamma') \\ {\scriptstyle P(\mathsf{id}_\Gamma \times [s_1,\ldots,s_m])}\downarrow & & \downarrow{\scriptstyle P([s_1,\ldots,s_m])} \\ P(\Gamma \times \Gamma'') & \xrightarrow[\forall_{\pi'}]{} & P(\Gamma'') \end{array}$$

where $\pi' : \Gamma \times \Gamma'' \to \Gamma''$ is a projection. Since we specified in the term calculus that the quantifiers commute with substitution, we can make the following argument, for $\psi \in P(\Gamma \times \Gamma')$:

$$\begin{aligned} P([s_1, \ldots, s_m]) \circ \forall_\pi(\psi) &= P([s_1, \ldots, s_m])(\forall x_1 \ldots \forall x_n \psi) \\ &= (\forall x_1 \ldots \forall x_n \psi)[s_1/y_1, \ldots, s_m/y_m] \\ &= \forall x_1 \ldots \forall x_n (\psi[s_1/y_1, \ldots, s_m/y_m]) \\ &= \forall_{\pi'}(\psi[s_1/y_1, \ldots, s_m/y_m]) \\ &= \forall_{\pi'} \circ P(1_\Gamma \times [s_1, \ldots, s_m])(\psi) \end{aligned}$$

References

1. Arló-Costa, H., Pacuit, E.: First-order classical modal logic. Studia Logica Int. J. Symb. Logic **84**(2), 171–210 (2006)
2. Awodey, S., Kishida, K., Kotzsch, H.C.: Topos semantics for higher-order modal logic. Logique et Anal. **57**(228), 591–636 (2014)
3. Braüner, T., Ghilardi, S.: First-order modal logic. Stud. Logic Pract. Reason. **3**, 549–620 (2007)
4. Cirstea, C., Kurz, A., Pattinson, D., Schröder, L., Venema, Y.: Stone coalgebras. Comput. J. **54**, 31–41 (2011)
5. Cresswell, M.J.: Incompleteness and the Barcan formula. J. Philos. Log. **24**(4), 379–403 (1995)
6. Dosen, K.: Duality between modal algebras and neighbourhood frames. Stud. Logica. **48**, 219–234 (1989)
7. Ghilardi, S.: Incompleteness results in Kripke semantics. J. Symb. Logic **56**(2), 517–538 (1991)
8. Ghilardi, S.: Substitution, quantifiers and identity in modal logic. In: Morscher, E., Hieke, A. (eds.) New Essays in Free Logic, pp. 87–115. Springer, Dordrecht (2001). https://doi.org/10.1007/978-94-015-9761-6_5
9. Ghilardi, S., Meloni, G.: Modal and tense predicate logic: models in presheaves and categorical conceptualization. In: Borceux, F. (ed.) Categorical Algebra and its Applications. Lecture Notes in Mathematics, vol. 1348, pp. 130–142. Springer (1988)

10. Ghilardi, S., Meloni, G.: Relational and topological semantics for temporal and modal predicative logic. In: Atti del congresso 'Nuovi problemi della logica e della scienza' Viareggio, vol. 2, pp. 59–77 (1990)
11. Ghilardi, S., Meloni, G.: Philosophical and mathematical investigations in first order modal logic. In: Usberti, G. (ed.) Problemi fondazionali in teoria del significato. Olsckhi (1991)
12. Jacobs, B.: Categorical Logic and Type Theory. Studies in Logic and the Foundations of Mathematics, vol. 141. Elsevier (1999)
13. Kotzsch, H.C.: Topos semantics for higher-order modal logic. Ph.D. thesis, Ludwig-Maximilians-Universität München (2016)
14. Kupke, C., Kurz, A., Venema, Y.: Stone coalgebras. Theoret. Comput. Sci. **327**, 591–636 (2004)
15. Lawvere, F.W.: Adjointness in foundations. Dialectica **23**, 281–296 (1969)
16. Lemmon, E.J.: Algebraic semantics for modal logics *I*. J. Symb. Logic **31**(1), 46–65 (1966)
17. Litak, T., Pattinson, D., Sano, K., Schröder, L.: Model theory and proof theory of coalgebraic predicate logic. Log. Methods Comput. Sci. **14**(1) (2018)
18. McKinsey, J.C.C., Tarski, A.: On closed elements in closure algebras. Ann. Math. **47**(1), 122–162 (1946)
19. Pitts, A.M.: Categorical logic. In: Abramsky, S., Gabbay, D.M., Maibaum, T.S.E. (eds.) Handbook of Logic in Computer Science, vol. VI. Oxford University Press, Oxford (1995)

Validity in Contexts
A Semantics for Indicatives and Epistemic Modals

Xuefeng Wen(✉)

Institute of Logic and Cognition, Department of Philosophy, Sun Yat-sen University, Guangzhou, China
wxflogic@gmail.com

Abstract. Inspired by McGee's semantics for conditionals, we define a language with contexts explicitly encoded in formulas to evaluate propositions under assumptions. We give a three-valued semantics for the language and define a ternary notion of validity, unifying two kinds of validity in the literature. By the new notion of validity, an inference is not just valid or invalid, but valid or invalid under a set of assumptions. Based on the three-valued semantics and ternary notion of validity, we give a unified solution to some typical puzzles concerning indicatives and epistemic modals.

Keywords: Validity · Modus Ponens · Conditional logic · Indicatives · Import-Export · Conditional Excluded Middle · Epistemic modality

1 Introduction

Compared to the logic of counterfactuals, the logic of indicatives are of more controversies. Some advocate that possible worlds semantics for counterfactuals is also suitable for indicatives, as long as some pragmatic components are supplemented (e.g. [20]). Others argue that material implication in classical logic is enough for indicatives, possibly with additional pragmatic analysis (e.g. [7]). Yet more are satisfied with neither approach, arguing that the classical approach validates too much whereas the Stalnakerian approach validates too little. In particular, they argue that the law of Import-Export, equating 'if A then if B then C' with 'if A and B then C', should be valid. One famous theory validating Import-Export is Kratzer's restrictor theory [10].

Validating Import-Export, however, is not without price. As Gibbard [6] noted, there is a tension between Import-Export and Modus Ponens. Together with some innocuous assumptions, validating both Modus Ponens and Import-Export leads to the collapse of conditionals: conditionals will be logically equivalent to material implication, which is unacceptable for those choosing the third approach. Noting that Modus Ponens does have counterexamples while Import-Export seems not, McGee [15] proposed a semantics based on Stalnaker's possible worlds semantics, while validating Import-Export but not Modus Ponens, as

G. Metcalfe et al. (Eds.): WoLLIC 2024, LNCS 14672, pp. 243–260, 2024.
https://doi.org/10.1007/978-3-031-62687-6_16

Krazter's theory. Since McGee's counterexamples to Modus Ponens, the validity of this fundament rule has been hotly debated. Different sides argue for or against Modus Ponens based on different senses of validity (cf. [9]).

This paper aims to shed some light on the debate, by incorporating both sides into one theory with a new notion of validity. Along resolving the debate on Modus Ponens and Import-Export, we also analyze some related puzzles involving indicatives and epistemic modals, including the (in)validity Or-to-If, Conditional Proof, and Conditional Excluded Middle (CEM). We'll discuss Moore sentences and the (in)felicity of some statements involving indicatives as well.

The basic idea is to take McGee's ternary notion of truth given in [15] seriously and define a ternary notion of validity. By the ternary validity, an inference is not just valid or invalid, but valid or invalid under a set of assumptions. So a complete inference is tripart: a set of (factual) premises, a conclusion, and a set of assumptions. Assumptions provide contexts for evaluating formulas. Like McGee's semantics, antecedents of conditionals are treated as making assumptions. We define a language with contexts explicitly encoded in formulas so that conditionals are evaluated in both global and local contexts, as advocated by Mandelkern [13]. We build the semantics in the framework of possible worlds semantics, using selection functions initiated by Stalnaker [19] and generalized by Lewis [11]. The new semantics with the new notion of validity may shed light on different senses of validity concerning the above principles, as well as different senses of consistency triggered by Moore sentences.

2 McGee's Semantics and Three Forms of Inferences

2.1 McGee's Semantics

One famous counterexample to Modus Ponens given by McGee [15] invites us to consider the 1980 US presidential election. Opinion polls showed that the republican Ronald Reagan was decisively ahead of the democrat Jimmy Carter, who was in turn decisively ahead of the other republican John Anderson. Then the premises (1a) and (1b) below ring true, while the conclusion (1c) does not.

(1) (a) If a republican wins the election, then if it's not Reagan who wins it will be Anderson.
(b) A republican will win the election.
(c) Therefore, if it's not Reagan who wins, it will be Anderson.

To validate Import-Export but not Modus Ponens, McGee [15] invented a ternary notion of truth to keep track of antecedents of conditionals. According to McGee, a formula is not true at a pointed model, but true at a pointed model under a set of assumptions, denoted $\mathfrak{M}, w \Vdash^{\Delta} A$, where Δ is the set of assumptions. Antecedents of conditionals are treated as making assumptions. When A is Boolean, the truth of A at $(\mathfrak{M}, w)$ under Δ is roughly treated as the truth of $\bigwedge \Delta > A$ in Stalnaker's semantics. To evaluate a conditional $B > C$ under Δ, the antecedent B is added to Δ and the consequent C is evaluated under the new set of assumptions. In formulation, $\mathfrak{M}, w \Vdash^{\Delta} B > C$ iff $\mathfrak{M}, w \Vdash^{\Delta \cup \{B\}} C$. Finally, McGee defined validity by truth preservation under the empty set of assumptions.

It can be easily seen that under McGee's semantics, $A > (B > C)$ and $A \wedge B > C$ have the same truth conditions and thus Import-Export is valid. The invalidity of Modus Ponens is also expected. I leave the details to the reader.

2.2 Three Forms of Inferences

One merit of McGee's semantics is that we can develop it to distinguish different forms of inferences in natural language, as listed below.

- **Standard Form**: A. Therefore, C. (Or, C, since A.)
- **Assumptive Form**: Suppose A. Then C.
- **Hybrid Form**: Suppose A. Then C, since B.

The difference between the standard form and the assumptive form is that the premise A in the former is a fact whereas it is an assumption in the latter. The assumptive form is usually followed by the conditional 'if A then C', cancelling the assumption, which is called *Conditional Proof.* In formal logic, the standard form and the assumptive form are usually not distinguished. Both are formalized by $A \vDash C$. Thus, the conditional proof is formalized by inferring $\vDash A > C$ from $A \vDash C$. For the same reason, neither are the two premises A and B distinguished in the hybrid form, which is formalized by $A, B \vDash C$.

In natural language reasoning, factual premises and assumptive ones are different. The logical effect of the former is only in the actual world, whereas the latter is in all epistemically possible worlds. In mathematical reasoning, the difference is unimportant, as a mathematical fact is a fact true in all epistemically possible worlds. This is why the three forms are not distinguished in standard formal logic. Nevertheless, if we want to characterize reasoning in natural language better, we should distinguish the three forms in formalization.

McGee's semantics, with a ternary notion of truth, provides a natural framework to distinguish the three forms. If we define validity using the ternary notion of truth, then we come up with a natural notion of validity as follows.

The inference from Γ to φ under the set of assumptions Δ is valid, denoted $\Gamma \vDash^{\Delta} \varphi$, if for all pointed models $(\mathfrak{M}, w)$, we have $\mathfrak{M}, w \Vdash^{\Delta} \varphi$ whenever $\mathfrak{M}, w \Vdash^{\Delta} \psi$ for all $\psi \in \Gamma$.

Armed with the ternary notion of validity, the three forms above can be formulated by $A \vDash^{\emptyset} C$, $\emptyset \vDash^{A} C$, and $B \vDash^{A} C$, respectively.

3 A New Language and Semantics

3.1 Problems of McGee's Semantics

McGee's semantics, however, has two problems. First, following standard conditional logics, it makes conditionals with impossible antecedents true, which is counterintuitive. It's odd to say 'if it is raining and it's not raining then...', whatever the consequent is. Such conditionals sound neither true nor false.

Second, conditionals are evaluated only in global contexts. But as Mandelkern [13] convincingly argued, they should also be evaluated in local contexts, which can be provided by other antecedents of a nested conditional. More precisely, when evaluating a nested conditional $A > (B > C)$, the nested antecedent B should not be evaluated only in the same context as that of $A > (B > C)$, namely the global context, but should be evaluated in the context of $A > (B > C)$ together with A, the local context of B. In McGee's semantics, when evaluating $A > (B > C)$, we just add both A and B into the global context. So A does not have any effect on B. But in natural language, B should be considered under the assumption A. When B is a Boolean statement, A does not have any effect on B. So we can ignore the local context provided by A. But if B itself is a conditional (or contains modalities), then it will be affected by A. This means that when B is a conditional, $A \wedge B > C$ means different from $A > (B > C)$, as B is evaluated independently of A in the former, whereas B is affected by the local context A in the latter. Thus, both Import and Export are invalid when B contains conditionals, as instantiated by Manderlkern [13] below, supposing we only know that Reagan is well ahead of Carter and Anderson.

(2) (a) If a Republican will win the election, and Anderson will win if Reagan doesn't win, then both Republicans are currently in a stronger position to win than Carter.
(b) If a Republican will win the election, then if Anderson will win if Reagan doesn't, then both Republicans are currently in a stronger position to win than Carter.

Intuitively, (2a) is true whereas (2b) is false. So we have $A \wedge B > C$ but not $A > (B > C)$.

(3) (a) If a Republican will win the election, then if Anderson will win if Reagan doesn't, then the polling data we've just received are correct.
(b) If a Republican will win the election, and Anderson will win if Reagan doesn't, then the polling data we've just received are correct.

Intuitively, (3a) is true whereas (3b) is false. So we have $A > (B > C)$ but not $A \wedge B > C$.

3.2 A New Language

In order to evaluate conditionals in both global contexts and local ones, we define a new language as follows, encoding contexts explicitly in formulas.

Definition 1. *Given a set At of atomic formulas, the* pure language $\mathcal{L}_0$ *and the* contextual language $\mathcal{L}$ *are given by the following BNF.*

$$\mathcal{L}_0 \ni A, B ::= \bot \mid p \mid \neg A \mid (A \wedge B) \mid (A \vee B) \mid (A > B) \mid \Box A$$
$$\mathcal{L} \ni \varphi, \psi ::= A \mid A^{\Delta}$$

where $\bot, p \in At$ *and* $\Delta \subseteq \mathcal{L}$. *We define* $\Diamond$ *to be the dual of* $\Box$, *namely,* $\Diamond A := \neg\Box\neg A$.

Pure language is just as usual, except that we include both conditionals and modals. A formula of the form A^Δ in the contextual language is to denote the formula A in the context Δ, which itself is a set of formulas in the contextual language. For brevity, we often omit the brackets of sets. The notation Δ, A is for $\Delta \cup \{A\}$ as usual. We use $A, B, C, \ldots$ for arbitrary formulas in $\mathcal{L}_0$ and $\varphi, \psi, \chi, \ldots$ for those in $\mathcal{L}$. We treat A and $A^\emptyset$ as the same formula. Pure formulas without $>$ and $\Box$ are called *Boolean.*

3.3 A New Semantics

We build our semantics based on selection models, which is adapted from Stalnaker's selection models. We make two modifications. First, we use a three-valued setting, allowing a formula to be neither true nor false. Second, pace Stalnaker and following Lewis, we allow the selection function to select a set of worlds rather than a single world.

Definition 2 (Selection models). *A (three-valued)* selection model *is a tuple* $\mathfrak{M} = (W, f, V^+, V^-)$, *where*

- $W \neq \emptyset$, *consists of possible worlds;*
- $f : W \times \wp(W) \to \wp(W)$ *is a selection function;*
- $V^+ : At \to \wp(W)$ *and* $V^- : At \to \wp(W)$ *are truth and falsity valuations, such that* $V^+(p) \cap V^-(p) = \emptyset$ *for all* $p \in At$ *and* $V^+(\bot) = \emptyset$, $V^-(\bot) = W$.

Given a selection model $\mathfrak{M}$ *and a world* w *in* $\mathfrak{M}$, *we call the pair* $(\mathfrak{M}, w)$ *a* pointed model.

Definition 3 (Normal models). *A selection model* $\mathfrak{M} = (W, f, V^+, V^-)$ *is* normal *if it satisfies the following conditions.*

(id)	$f(w, X) \subseteq X$
(cs)	$w \in X$ *implies* $f(w, X) = \{w\}$

Definition 4 (Truth and falsity conditions). *Given a selection model* $\mathfrak{M} = (W, f, V^+, V^-)$, *the* truth relation $\Vdash$ *and* falsity relation $\dashv\vert$ *between a pointed model and a contextual formula are defined as follows.*

- $\mathfrak{M}, w \Vdash p^\Delta$ *iff* $\emptyset \neq f(w, [\![\Delta]\!]^+_\mathfrak{M}) \subseteq V^+(p)$, *where*

$$[\![\Delta]\!]^+_\mathfrak{M} = \bigcap_{\delta \in \Delta} [\![\delta]\!]^+_\mathfrak{M} = \bigcap_{\delta \in \Delta} \{u \in W \mid \mathfrak{M}, u \Vdash \delta\}$$

- $\mathfrak{M}, w \dashv\vert\, p^\Delta$ *iff* $\emptyset \neq f(w, [\![\Delta]\!]^+_\mathfrak{M}) \subseteq V^-(p)$
- $\mathfrak{M}, w \Vdash (A \wedge B)^\Delta$ *iff* $\mathfrak{M}, w \Vdash A^\Delta$ *and* $\mathfrak{M}, w \Vdash B^\Delta$
- $\mathfrak{M}, w \dashv\vert\, (A \wedge B)^\Delta$ *iff* $\mathfrak{M}, w \dashv\vert\, A^\Delta$ *or* $\mathfrak{M}, w \dashv\vert\, B^\Delta$
- $\mathfrak{M}, w \Vdash (A \vee B)^\Delta$ *iff* $\mathfrak{M}, w \Vdash A^\Delta$ *or* $\mathfrak{M}, w \Vdash B^\Delta$

- $\mathfrak{M}, w \dashv\Vdash (A \vee B)^{\Delta}$ *iff* $\mathfrak{M}, w \dashv\Vdash A^{\Delta}$ *and* $\mathfrak{M}, w \dashv\Vdash B^{\Delta}$
- $\mathfrak{M}, w \Vdash \neg A^{\Delta}$ *iff* $\mathfrak{M}, w \dashv\Vdash A^{\Delta}$
- $\mathfrak{M}, w \dashv\Vdash \neg A^{\Delta}$ *iff* $\mathfrak{M}, w \Vdash A^{\Delta}$
- $\mathfrak{M}, w \Vdash (A > B)^{\Delta}$ *iff* $\mathfrak{M}, w \Vdash B^{\Delta, A^{\Delta}}$
- $\mathfrak{M}, w \dashv\Vdash (A > B)^{\Delta}$ *iff* $\mathfrak{M}, w \dashv\Vdash B^{\Delta, A^{\Delta}}$
- $\mathfrak{M}, w \Vdash \Box A^{\Delta}$ *iff* $\mathfrak{M}, u \Vdash A^{\Delta}$ *for all* $u \in W$
- $\mathfrak{M}, w \dashv\Vdash \Box A^{\Delta}$ *iff* $\mathfrak{M}, u \dashv\Vdash A^{\Delta}$ *for some* $u \in W$

We write $[\![\varphi]\!]^-_{\mathfrak{M}}$ for the set of worlds falsifying φ in $\mathfrak{M}$, i.e., $[\![\varphi]\!]^-_{\mathfrak{M}} = \{w \in W \mid \mathfrak{M}, w \dashv\Vdash \varphi\}$. We often omit the subscript $\mathfrak{M}$ if no confusion occurs.

We stipulate that $[\![\emptyset]\!]^+_{\mathfrak{M}} = W$, where W is the domain of $\mathfrak{M}$. If $\mathfrak{M}$ is normal, then by (cs), it follows that $\mathfrak{M}, w \Vdash p$ iff $\mathfrak{M}, w \Vdash p^{\emptyset}$ iff $w \in V^+(p)$, and $\mathfrak{M}, w \dashv\Vdash p$ iff $\mathfrak{M}, w \Vdash p^{\emptyset}$ iff $w \in V^-(p)$, as required.

Besides the three-valued setting, our semantics differs from McGee's semantics in four aspects. First, when f selects an empty set, we evaluate the corresponding conditional to be neither true nor false. Second, we take the truth and falsity conditions to be symmetry, so that the falsity of $A > p$ requires all closest A-worlds are $\neg p$-worlds rather than that some closest A-worlds are not p-worlds. This symmetric treatment is natural in a three-valued setting. Third, to reflect the effect of local contexts to conditionals, when evaluating $A > B$ under Δ, we add A^{Δ} instead of A to Δ to evaluate B. Finally, with contexts explicitly encoded in formulas, we do not need McGee's ternary notion of truth.

Equivalence of formulas in our framework can be defined in various ways.

Definition 5 (Equivalence). *We say that* φ *and* ψ *are*

1. positively (negatively) equivalent in $\mathfrak{M}$, *if* $[\![\varphi]\!]^+ = [\![\psi]\!]^+$ $([\![\varphi]\!]^- = [\![\psi]\!]^-)$ *;*
2. (contentually) equivalent in $\mathfrak{M}$, *denoted* $\varphi \equiv_{\mathfrak{M}} \psi$, *if both* $[\![\varphi]\!]^+ = [\![\psi]\!]^+$ *and* $[\![\varphi]\!]^- = [\![\psi]\!]^-$*;*
3. (contentually) equivalent, *denoted* $\varphi \equiv \psi$, *if* $\varphi \equiv_{\mathfrak{M}} \psi$ *for all normal* $\mathfrak{M}$*;*
4. contextually equivalent in $\mathfrak{M}$, *denoted* $\varphi \asymp_{\mathfrak{M}} \psi$, *if* $[\![\varphi^{\psi}]\!]^- = [\![\psi^{\varphi}]\!]^- = \emptyset$*;*
5. contextually equivalent, *denoted* $\varphi \asymp \psi$, *if* $\varphi \asymp_{\mathfrak{M}} \psi$ *for all normal* $\mathfrak{M}$.

Though we do not have a ternary notion of truth, we can still define a ternary notion of validity, with contexts playing the third part of an inference.

Definition 6 (Validity in contexts). *For all* $\Gamma \cup \{A\} \subseteq \mathcal{L}_0$ *and* $\Delta \subseteq \mathcal{L}$, *the inference from* Γ *to* A *in the context* Δ *is* valid, *denoted* $\Gamma \vDash^{\Delta} A$, *if there is no normal pointed model* $(\mathfrak{M}, w)$ *such that* $\mathfrak{M}, w \Vdash B^{\Delta}$ *for all* $B \in \Gamma$ *and* $\mathfrak{M}, w \dashv\Vdash A^{\Delta}$.

We often write $\Gamma \vDash A$ instead of $\Gamma \vDash^{\emptyset} A$, and $\vDash^{\Gamma} A$ instead of $\emptyset \vDash^{\Gamma} A$. Besides that it is ternary, another peculiarity of our notion of validity is that we adopt the *st*-validity proposed in Strict-Tolerant logic [4,17] rather than the standard notion of truth preservation. The *st*-validity can be regarded as a formalization of Strawson entailment [22, pp. 176–177], according to which the inference from A to B is valid if and only if B is true whenever A is true and all presuppositions involved are satisfied. If we assume that a statement is neither true nor false if its presuppositions are not satisfied, and a statement cannot be both true and false, then it turns out that Strawson entailment and *st*-validity coincide. One merit of *st*-validity as shown by Strict-Tolerant logic is that confined to Boolean formulas, the semantics above yields classical logic.

With the ternary notion of validity, we can distinguish three forms of the inference from Γ to A.

- **Standard Form** $\Gamma \models C$, which reads: Γ. Therefore A.
- **Assumptive Form** $\models^{\Gamma} C$, which reads: Suppose Γ. Then A.
- **Hybrid Form** $\Sigma \models^{\Delta} C$, with $\Sigma \cup \Delta = \Gamma$, which reads: Suppose Δ. Then A, since Σ.

The three forms are not always equivalent to each other. We will see in Sect. 4 that several puzzles concerning conditionals and epistemic modals can be resolved by distinguishing the three forms of inferences, together with two kinds of (in)consistency defined below.

Definition 7 (Inconsistency, Self-refuting). *Let* $\Gamma \cup \Delta \subseteq \mathcal{L}_0$.

1. Γ *is* inconsistent under Δ, *if* $\Gamma \models^{\Delta} \bot$; Γ *is* inconsistent, *if* $\Gamma \vdash \bot$.
2. Δ *is* self-refuting, *if there exists* $\varphi \in \Delta$ *such that* $\models^{\Delta} \neg\varphi$.

Clause 1 defines (in)consistency *under* assumptions, whereas Clause 2 defines (in)consistency *of* assumptions. A set can be consistent but self-refuting. A typical example is $\{\neg p, \Diamond p\}$. We will return to this topic in Sects. 4.4-4.6.

3.4 Semantic Properties

The following three lemmas can be easily verified by induction. The first says that a formula cannot be both true and false. The second says that Boolean formulas have the same truth and falsity conditions as atoms. The third says that formulas in positively equivalent contexts are equivalent.

Lemma 1. *For all selection models* $\mathfrak{M}$ *and* $\varphi \in \mathcal{L}$, *we have* $[\![\varphi]\!]^+_{\mathfrak{M}} \cap [\![\varphi]\!]^-_{\mathfrak{M}} = \emptyset$.

Lemma 2. *For all selection models* $\mathfrak{M} = (W, f, V^+, V^-)$ *and* $\Delta \subseteq \mathcal{L}$, *if* A *is Boolean, then*

1. $\mathfrak{M}, w \Vdash A^{\Delta}$ *iff* $\emptyset \neq f(w, [\![\Delta]\!]^+) \subseteq [\![A]\!]^+$;
2. $\mathfrak{M}, w \dashv\!\mid A^{\Delta}$ *iff* $\emptyset \neq f(w, [\![\Delta]\!]^+) \subseteq [\![A]\!]^-$.

Lemma 3. *For all selection models* $\mathfrak{M}$, *for all* $\Delta \cup \Delta' \subseteq \mathcal{L}$ *and* $A \in \mathcal{L}_0$, *if* $[\![\Delta]\!]^+ = [\![\Delta']\!]^+$, *then* $A^{\Delta} \equiv_{\mathfrak{M}} A^{\Delta'}$.

The following lemma says that a context together with a formula in that context is positively equivalent to the context together with the formula per se, provided that the formula is Boolean, which will be used to prove a restricted form of Import-Export, suggested by Mandelkern [13].

Lemma 4. *If $\mathfrak{M}$ is normal and A is Boolean then* $[\![\Delta, A^{\Delta}]\!]^{+}_{\mathfrak{M}} = [\![\Delta, A]\!]^{+}_{\mathfrak{M}}$.[1]

Proposition 1 (Restricted Import-Export). *Let $\mathfrak{M}$ be normal and B Boolean.*

1. $C^{A,B^A} \equiv_{\mathfrak{M}} C^{A,B}$;
2. $A > (B > C) \equiv_{\mathfrak{M}} A \wedge B > C$. *Hence,* $A > (B > C) \equiv A \wedge B > C$.

The following theorem says that confined to Boolean formulas, there is no difference between the four forms of the inference from $\{A, B\}$ to C, which are all equivalent to the inference in classical logic.

Theorem 1. *If A, B, C are Boolean then $A, B \vDash_c C$ iff $A, B \vDash C$ iff $\vDash^{A,B} C$ iff $A \vDash^{B} C$ iff $B \vDash^{A} C$, where $\vDash_c$ is the consequence relation of classical logic.*

4 Applications

4.1 Modus Ponens

Despite the differences given in Sect. 3.3, our semantics inherits most features of McGee's. Modus Ponens is still invalid in our semantics. With epistemic modals augmented, we can formulate more counterexamples. The following is one based on the same scenario of the 1980 election.

(4) (a) If a republican wins the election, then the winner must be Reagan.
(b) A republican will win the election.
(c) Therefore, the winner must be Reagan.

Both McGee's counterexample and this one are predicted in our semantics.

Proposition 2. *Modus ponens is invalid in the following forms.*

1. $p, p > (q > r) \nvDash q > r$
2. $p, p > \Box q \nvDash \Box q$

Nonetheless, giving up Modus Ponens completely takes too much price. Fortunately, we can keep some forms of Modus Ponens, as formulated below.

Proposition 3. *Modus ponens is valid in the following forms.*

1. **Standard Form:** $A, A > B \vDash B$, *where B is Boolean*
2. **Assumptive Form:** $\vDash^{A, A>B} B$, *where B is Boolean*
3. **Hybrid Form 1:** $A > B \vDash^{A} B$, *where A is Boolean*
4. **Hybrid Form 2:** $A \vDash^{A>B} B$, *where both A and B are Boolean*

[1] We put all proofs in the appendix. For lack of space, we omit some simple proofs.

The standard form restricted to Boolean formulas is inherited from McGee's semantics, while the other forms can only be formulated in our framework.

McGee's counterexamples to Modus Ponens had been objected by Over [16], among others. Over argued that if the premises of Modus Ponens have been certainly assumed, the conclusion cannot be false. This intuition is formulated by the assumptive form of Modus Ponens in our semantics. Though it is not generally valid, its restricted form for counterexamples above are valid.

Proposition 4. *For any* $p, q, r \in At$,

1. $\models^{p, p>(q>r)} q > r$
2. $\models^{p, p>\Box q} \Box q$

Now in the literature concerning the validity of Modus Ponens, often two notions of validity are distinguished. Mandelkern [12] categorized them as truth-preservation validity, which is the standard one, and informational validity, which was defended in [2]. The two notions of validity yield two forms of Modus Ponens. The truth-preservation form reads: if A and $A > B$ are true, then B is true. The informational form reads: if A and $A > B$ are fully accepted, then rationality requires B to be fully accepted. To better understand the four forms of Modus Ponens formulated in our framework, we can roughly equate the standard form with the truth-preservation form, the assumptive form with the informational form, and the hybrid form with a combination of them.

Bledin [3] argues that, though truth-preservation Modus Ponens may not be valid, informational Modus Ponens is still valid. Consider McGee's example again. If we fully accept that a republican will win, and that if a republican wins then if it is not Reagan who wins it will be Anderson, then we must accept that if Reagan does not win, then Anderson will win. The intuition is similar to Over's, which could also be formulated by the assumptive Modus Ponens.

But to dispel the counterexample does not require us to fully accept both premises. Fully accepting that a republican will win is enough, which is predicted by the validity of Hybrid Form 1 of Modus Ponens. Note that fully accepting the other premise only does not make the inference valid.

4.2 Or-to-If

The inference from $A \vee B$ to $\neg A > B$ is called Or-to-If (a.k.a., the Direct Argument). Note that it is different from Disjunctive Syllogism, which is inferring B from $A \vee B$ and $\neg A$. In Stalnaker-Lewisian conditional logics, Or-to-If is invalid. This has to be so, as their logics validate Modus Ponens, together with which, Or-to-If leads to the collapse: $A > B$ will be equivalent to $\neg A \vee B$. Or-to-If is not valid in our semantics either. Otherwise, the restricted Modus Ponens (which is valid in our semantics) also leads to the collapse.

Proposition 5. *Or-to-If is not valid in its standard form:* $p \vee q \not\models \neg p > q$.

Nevertheless, Or-to-If seems pervasive and innocuous in natural language reasoning. If there are only two cases, then ruling out one surely leads us to the other. To explain the plausibility of this inference, Stalnaker [20] distinguished reasonable inferences from valid ones. An inference is reasonable if in every context in which the premises could appropriately be asserted or supposed, it is impossible for anyone to accept the premises without accepting the conclusion. This idea is in line with informational validity mentioned in Sect. 4.1, which can be formulated in the assumptive form of Or-to-If. Moreover, it seems that we can not only infer $\neg A > B$ from $A \vee B$, but also $\neg A > \Box B$. The following is a common example.

(5) (a) Either the butler or the gardener did it.
(b) Therefore, if the butler didn't do it, it must be the gardener.

We call it modal Or-to-If. Besides, Or-to-If also has a conditional reading: If $A \vee B$, then if $\neg A$ then B. All the forms can be formulated in our framework.

Proposition 6. *Or-to-If is valid in the following forms.*

1. Assumptive form $\models^{A \vee B} \neg A > B$, *where A and B are Boolean.*
2. Assumptive modal form $\models^{A \vee B} \neg A > \Box B$, *where A and B are Boolean.*
3. Conditional form $\models (A \vee B) > (\neg A > B)$, *where A and B are Boolean.*

Clause 1 can be regarded as a formalization of Stalnaker's reasonable inference. Clause 2 predicts the inference from (5a) to (5b) above.[2]

With Proposition 6, we can easily prove the following theorem.

Theorem 2. *For all $A, B \in \mathcal{L}_0$, if A and B are Boolean, then $A > B \asymp \neg A \vee B$.*

The theorem may explain why some authors advocate that indicative implication is no more than material implication. According to our semantics, they are indeed 'equivalent', not in the sense that if one is *true* so is the other, but that if one is *assumed* then the other cannot be false. In our terminology, they are *contextually* equivalent rather than *contentually* equivalent.

4.3 Conditional Proof

Conditional Proof is also pervasively used in both mathematical and ordinary reasoning. But it is easily seen that standard forms of Conditional Proof and Modus Ponens lead to the collapse. In particular, by the standard form of Conditional Proof we will obtain the standard form of Or-to-If from Disjunctive Syllogism. Like Stalnaker-Lewisian conditionals logics and McGee's semantics, the standard form Conditional Proof is invalid in our semantics.

Proposition 7. *Conditional proof is not valid in the following forms, where $\Gamma \neq \emptyset$, even if A and B are Boolean.*

[2] The (in)validity of Antecedent Strengthening (inferring $A \wedge B > C$ from $A > C$), Contraposition (inferring $\neg B > \neg A$ from $A > B$), Hypothetical Syllogism (inferring $A > C$ from $A > B$ and $B > C$), and Simplification of Disjunctive Antecedents (inferring $(A > C) \wedge (B > C)$ from $A \vee B > C$) can be analyzed in the same way as that for Or-to-If. For lack of space, I omit the details.

1. $\Gamma, A \models B \not\Rightarrow \Gamma \models A > B$
2. $\Gamma \models^{A} B \not\Rightarrow \Gamma \models A > B$

But how do we explain our legitimate use of Conditional Proof? The following proposition gives an answer.

Proposition 8. *Conditional proof is valid in the following forms.*

1. $A \models B \Longrightarrow \models A > B$, *where* B *is Boolean*
2. $\models^{\Gamma, A} B \Longrightarrow \models^{\Gamma} A > B$, *where* A *is Boolean*
3. $\Gamma \models^{A} B \Longrightarrow \Gamma^{A} \models A > B$

Clause 1 says that if $A \wedge \neg B$ cannot be true then $A > B$ cannot be false. Clause 2 says that if B can be proved under the assumptions of Γ together with A, then $A > B$ can be proved under the assumptions of Γ, as long as A is Boolean. Clause 3 says that if B can be prove from Γ, assuming A, then $A > B$ can be prove from Γ^{A} (namely, Γ in the context of A). The moral is that the inferences involved in Conditional Proof should be represented by the assumptive form rather than the standard form. Indeed, in Conditional Proof we do not obtain $A > B$ by that B follows from A in the context of Γ, but by that B follows from *assuming* A in the context of Γ.

4.4 Moore Sentences

Moore sentences are of the form $\neg A \wedge \Diamond A$, where $\Diamond$ is an epistemic modal operator with an existential reading. They can also be formulated by $A \wedge \neg \Box A$, where $\Box$ often reads 'believe' or 'know', or epistemic 'must'. The puzzle about Moore sentences is that they can be true but cannot be consistently asserted, believed, or known, which received vast discussion ever since G. E. Moore's notice of it. If we have only one notion of (in)consistency, the puzzle can roughly be rephrased as: how can Moore sentences be both consistent and inconsistent. One more interesting fact, noted by Yalcin [25], is that Moore sentences with epistemic modality cannot be assumed or supposed either, as the following examples illustrate.[3]

(6) # If it is not raining and it might be raining, then...
(7) # Suppose it is not raining and possibly it is raining.

Both (6) and (7) sound infelicitous, though the statements prefixed by 'If' and 'Suppose' are innocuous. Armed with two notions of inconsistency, the puzzle can be resolved.

Proposition 9. *Let* $A = \neg p \wedge \Diamond p$. *Then*

1. $A \not\models \bot$

[3] Strictly speaking, Moore sentences only refer to $A \wedge \neg \Box A$ where $\Box$ reads 'believe' or 'know'. The sentence $A \wedge \neg \Box A$ where $\Box$ reads 'must' is sometimes called Wittgenstein sentence. A great difference noticed by Yalcin is that standard Moore sentences can be consistently assumed, whereas Wittgenstein sentence cannot.

2. $\models^{A} \neg A$

Clause 1 says that $\neg p \wedge \Diamond p$ is consistent, which explains why it can be true. Clause 2 says that $\neg p \wedge \Diamond p$ is self-refuting, which explains why it cannot be consistently assumed. Moreover, our semantics also predicts the order sensitivity in Moore sentences, which cannot be explained by Yalcin's semantics. As noted by Veltman [23], there are differences between the following two sequences of statements.

(8) (a) Someone is knocking at the door. Maybe it's Bill (and thus not Ann). It's Ann.
(b) # Someone is knocking at the door. It's Ann (and thus not Bill). Maybe it's Bill.

(8a) is felicitous, whereas (8b) sounds odd. The difference is predicted by the following result.

Proposition 10. *For any* $p \in At$,

1. $\neg p \not\models^{\Diamond p} \bot$
2. $\Diamond p \models^{\neg p} \bot$

Clause 1 says that $\neg p$ is consistent under $\Diamond p$. Assuming $\Diamond p$ does not rule out the possibility of $\neg p$, and thus $\neg p$ can be true. Clause 2 says that $\Diamond p$ is inconsistent under $\neg p$. Assuming $\neg p$ has ruled out the possibility of p, and thus $\Diamond p$ cannot be true.

4.5 Conditional Excluded Middle

The debate about CEM has been started ever since Stalnaker's work on conditional logic. Under Stalnaker's uniqueness assumption of closest worlds, CEM is valid, for the closest A-world is either B-world or $\neg B$-world. Lewis [11] famously rejected the uniqueness assumption and thus invalidated CEM in his conditional logics. He also gave an If-Might argument against CEM, which was further developed by Bennett [1]. The argument roughly goes as follows. First, there is strong intuition that $A > \neg B$ is inconsistent with $A > \Diamond B$, which can be formulated as follows.

If-Might Contradiction (IMC) $(A > \neg B) \wedge (A > \Diamond B) \models \bot$

From IMC, using reduction to absurdity, it follows that $A > \Diamond B \models \neg(A > \neg B)$. By CEM, using disjunctive syllogism, we have $\neg(A > \neg B) \models A > B$. Then by the transitivity of $\models$, it follows that $A > \Diamond B \models A > B$. Analogously, we obtain $A > B \models A > \Diamond B$. But it is absurd that $A > \Diamond B$ and $A > B$ are equivalent.

We argue that the If-Might argument against CEM is flawed. The problem of If-Might argument lies in the formulation of the If-Might contradiction. The inconsistency between $A > \neg B$ and $A > \Diamond B$ is not that they cannot both be true. It is that they cannot both be asserted or assumed, as the following examples shows.

(9) # If it rains, the match will not be held. But even if it rains, the match might be held.
(10) # Suppose that if it rains, the match will not be held, and that if it rains, the match might be held.

Analogous to the analysis of Moore sentences, in our terminology, $(A > \neg B) \wedge (A > \Diamond B)$ is consistent but self-refuting, which is expected, as it is equivalent to $(\neg B \wedge \Diamond B)^A$, namely, the Moore sentence $\neg B \wedge \Diamond B$ in the context of A.

Proposition 11. *Let* $A = (p > \neg q) \wedge (p > \Diamond q)$. *Then*

1. $A \not\models \bot$
2. $\models^A \neg A$

Since the correct If-Might contradiction should be formulated by Clause 2 rather than 1 above, the reasoning from IMC to the equivalence of $A > B$ and $A > \Diamond B$ is unjustified. In fact, more and more authors are defending CEM now (e.g., [8,18,21,24], among others). It is valid in our semantics, without the uniqueness assumption for selection functions, thanks to the *st*-validity we adopted.

Proposition 12. *For all* $A, B \in \mathcal{L}_0$, *we have* $\models (A > B) \vee (A > \neg B)$.

4.6 Infelicitous Statements Involving Conditionals

Mandelkern [14] noticed that some statements involving indicatives are infelicitous, though their logical forms seem felicitous. The following two indicatives sound odd.

(11) # If the die was thrown and landed four, then if it didn't land four, it landed two or six.
(12) # If the die was thrown and landed four and it didn't land four, it landed two or six.

The logical forms of (11) and (12) are $p > (\neg p > q)$ and $p \wedge \neg p > q$, respectively. The following proposition may explain why they are infelicitous.

Proposition 13. *If* $A = p > (\neg p > q)$ *or* $A = \neg p > (p > q)$ *or* $A = p \wedge \neg p > q$ *then* A *is neither true nor false in any normal selection model and hence* A *is both inconsistent and valid.*

The following supposition is also strange.

(13) # Suppose that Bob came to the party, and that if he didn't come he went to work.

The logical form of the statement prefixed by 'Suppose' in (13) is $p \wedge (\neg p > q)$. Though it consistent in our semantics, it is self-refuting, as shown by the following proposition.

Proposition 14. *If* $B = p \wedge (\neg p > q)$ *or* $B = \neg p \wedge (p > q)$ *then* $\models^B \neg B$.

The following conditional sounds weird too.

(14) # If Bob was at the party, but it's not the case that Bob was at the party if Sue was, then...

The logical form of the statement prefixed by 'If' in (14) is $q \wedge \neg(p > q)$. Though it is also consistent, it is self-refuting too, as shown by the following proposition.

Proposition 15. *If* $C = q \wedge \neg(p > q)$ *or* $C = \neg q \wedge (p > q)$ *then* $\vDash^C \neg C$.

5 Conclusion and Future Work

We define a new language and semantics for indicatives and epistemic modals, by tweaking McGee's semantics. The crucial contribution is a ternary notion of validity, by which an inference is not (in)valid per se, but (in)valid under a set of assumptions. Thus, an inference has three different forms: standard form (no premises are assumed), assumptive form (all premises are assumed), and hybrid form (some premises are assumed), which are not equivalent to each other. We also define two kinds of inconsistency: inconsistency under assumptions and inconsistency of assumptions (namely, self-refuting). Armed with these differentiations, we give a unified solution to several puzzles concerning indicatives and epistemic modals, by predicting linguistic data in natural language reasoning. This is a preliminary attempt to unify two kinds of validity proposed in the literature. Future work includes a full comparison to existing works, including Fitting's work on ternary consequence for modal logic [5]. Our logic also demands a proof theory suitable for its ternary notion of validity, so that the logic can be better understood and compared to other logics.

Acknowledgments. This work was supported by National Social Science Foundation of China (Grant No. 22BZX129). We thank the anonymous referees for their helpful comments.

Appendix

Proof of Lemma 4. We have $[\![\Delta, A^{\Delta}]\!]^+ = [\![\Delta]\!]^+ \cap [\![A^{\Delta}]\!]^+ = [\![\Delta]\!]^+ \cap \{w \in W \mid \emptyset \neq f(w, [\![\Delta]\!]^+) \subseteq [\![A]\!]^+\} = \{w \in [\![\Delta]\!]^+ \mid \emptyset \neq f(w, [\![\Delta]\!]^+ \subseteq [\![A]\!]^+\} = \{w \in [\![\Delta]\!]^+ \mid \{w\} \subseteq [\![A]\!]^+\} = [\![\Delta]\!]^+ \cap [\![A]\!]^+ = [\![\Delta, A]\!]^+$, where the fourth '=' is by (cs).

Proof of Proposition 1. Clause 1 is straightforward from Lemma 3 and Lemma 4. Clause 2 is a reformulation of 1.

Proof of Theorem 1. We prove that $A, B \vDash_c C \Longrightarrow A, B \vDash C \Longrightarrow \vDash^{A,B} C \Longrightarrow A \vDash^B C \Longrightarrow B \vDash^A C \Longrightarrow A, B \vDash_c C$.

For $A, B \vDash_c C \Longrightarrow A, B \vDash C$, suppose $A, B \nvDash C$. Then there is a normal selection model $\mathfrak{M} = (W, f, V^+, V^-)$ and $w \in W$ such that $\mathfrak{M}, w \Vdash A$, $\mathfrak{M}, w \Vdash B$ and $\mathfrak{M}, w \dashv\!\mid C$. Define $V : At \rightarrow \{0, 1\}$ such that for all $p \in At$, $V(p) = 1$ if $w \notin$

$V^-(p)$, $V(p) = 0$ if $w \in V^-(p)$. It can be verified by induction that $\mathfrak{M}, w \Vdash X$ iff $V(X) = 1$ and $\mathfrak{M}, w \dashv\!\vert\, X$ iff $V(X) = 0$. It follows that $V(A) = V(B) = 1$ and $V(C) = 0$. Hence, $A, B \nvDash_c C$.

For $A, B \vDash C \Longrightarrow\ \vDash^{A,B} C$, suppose $\nvDash^{A,B} C$. Then there is a normal selection model $\mathfrak{M} = (W, f, V^+, V^-)$ and $w \in W$ such that $\mathfrak{M}, w \dashv\!\vert\, C^{A,B}$. By Lemma 2, we have $\emptyset \neq f(w, [\![A, B]\!]^+) \subseteq [\![C]\!]^-$. By (id), $f(w, [\![A, B]\!]^+) \subseteq [\![A, B]\!]^+$. It follows that $[\![A, B]\!]^+ \cap [\![C]\!]^- \supseteq f(w, [\![A, B]\!]^+) \neq \emptyset$. Hence, $A, B \nvDash C$.

For $\vDash^{A,B} C \Longrightarrow A \vDash^B C$, suppose $A \nvDash^B C$. Then there is a normal selection model $\mathfrak{M} = (W, f, V^+, V^-)$ and $w \in W$ such that $\mathfrak{M}, w \Vdash A^B$ and $\mathfrak{M}, w \dashv\!\vert\, C^B$. By Lemma 2, from the former, we have $\emptyset \neq f(w, [\![B]\!]^+_{\mathfrak{M}}) \subseteq [\![A]\!]^+_{\mathfrak{M}}$; from the latter, we have $\emptyset \neq f(w, [\![B]\!]^+_{\mathfrak{M}}) \subseteq [\![C]\!]^-_{\mathfrak{M}}$. By (id), $f(w, [\![B]\!]^+_{\mathfrak{M}}) \subseteq [\![B]\!]^+_{\mathfrak{M}}$. Let $u \in f(w, [\![B]\!]^+_{\mathfrak{M}})$. Then $u \in [\![A]\!]^+_{\mathfrak{M}} \cap [\![B]\!]^+_{\mathfrak{M}} \cap [\![C]\!]^-_{\mathfrak{M}}$. Let $\mathfrak{N} = (\{u\}, g, U^+, U^-)$ such that $g(u, \{u\}) = \{u\}$, $u \in U^+(p)$ iff $u \in V^+(p)$, and $u \in U^-(p)$ iff $u \in V^-(p)$ for all $p \in At$. Since A, B, C are Boolean, it can be verified that $u \in [\![A]\!]^+_{\mathfrak{N}} \cap [\![B]\!]^+_{\mathfrak{N}} \cap [\![C]\!]^-_{\mathfrak{N}}$. Then we have $\mathfrak{N}, u \dashv\!\vert\, C^{A,B}$. Hence, $\nvDash^{A,B} C$.

For $A \vDash^B C \Longrightarrow\ B \vDash^A C$, suppose $B \nvDash^A C$. Then there is a normal selection model $\mathfrak{M} = (W, f, V^+, V^-)$ and $w \in W$ such that $\mathfrak{M}, w \Vdash B^A$ and $\mathfrak{M}, w \dashv\!\vert\, C^A$. By Lemma 2, from the former, we have $\emptyset \neq f(w, [\![A]\!]^+_{\mathfrak{M}}) \subseteq [\![B]\!]^+_{\mathfrak{M}}$; from the latter, we have $\emptyset \neq f(w, [\![A]\!]^+_{\mathfrak{M}}) \subseteq [\![C]\!]^-_{\mathfrak{M}}$. Let $u \in f(w, [\![A]\!]^+_{\mathfrak{M}})$. Then $u \in [\![A]\!]^+_{\mathfrak{M}} \cap [\![B]\!]^+_{\mathfrak{M}} \cap [\![C]\!]^-_{\mathfrak{M}}$. Let $\mathfrak{N} = (\{u\}, g, U^+, U^-)$ such that $g(u, \{u\}) = \{u\}$, $u \in U^+(p)$ iff $u \in V^+(p)$, and $u \in U^-(p)$ iff $u \in V^-(p)$ for all $p \in At$. Since A, B, C are Boolean, it can be verified that $u \in [\![A]\!]^+_{\mathfrak{N}} \cap [\![B]\!]^+_{\mathfrak{N}} \cap [\![C]\!]^-_{\mathfrak{N}}$. Then we have $\mathfrak{N}, u \Vdash A^B$ and $\mathfrak{N}, u \dashv\!\vert\, C^B$. Hence, $A \nvDash^B C$.

For $B \vDash^A C \Longrightarrow A, B \vDash_c C$, suppose $A, B \nvDash_c C$. Then there exists $V : At \to \{0, 1\}$ such that $V(A) = V(B) = 1$ and $V(C) = 0$. Let $\mathfrak{M} = (\{w\}, f, V^+, V^-)$ such that $f(w, \{w\}) = \{w\}$, $w \in V^+(p)$ iff $V(p) = 1$, $w \in V^-(p)$ iff $V(p) = 0$ for all $p \in At$. Since A, B, C are Boolean, it can be verified that $w \in [\![A]\!]^+_{\mathfrak{M}} \cap [\![B]\!]^+_{\mathfrak{M}} \cap [\![C]\!]^-_{\mathfrak{M}}$. It follows that $\mathfrak{M}, w \Vdash B^A$ and $\mathfrak{M}, w \dashv\!\vert\, C^A$. Hence, $B \nvDash^A C$.

Proof of Proposition 3. Let $\mathfrak{M} = (W, f, V^+, V^-)$ be any normal selection model and $w \in W$. For 1, suppose $\mathfrak{M}, w \Vdash A$ and $\mathfrak{M}, w \Vdash A > B$. We show that $\mathfrak{M}, w \Vdash B$. By $\mathfrak{M}, w \Vdash A > B$, we have $\mathfrak{M}, w \Vdash B^A$. Since B is Boolean, by Lemma 2, it follows that $\emptyset \neq f(w, [\![A]\!]^+) \subseteq [\![B]\!]^+$. By $\mathfrak{M}, w \Vdash A$ and (cs), we have $f(w, [\![A]\!]^+) = \{w\}$. Hence, $\mathfrak{M}, w \Vdash B$. By Lemma 1, we have $\mathfrak{M}, w \not\dashv\!\vert\, B$, as required.

For 2, by Lemma 2, if $f(w, [\![A, A > B]\!]^+) = \emptyset$ then $\mathfrak{M}, w \not\dashv\!\vert\, B$ and we are done. Otherwise, by Lemma 2 and Lemma 1, it suffices to show that $f(w, [\![A, A > B]\!]^+) \subseteq [\![B]\!]^+$. By (id), we have $f(w, [\![A, A > B]\!]^+) \subseteq [\![A]\!]^+$ and $f(w, [\![A, A > B]\!]^+) \subseteq [\![A > B]\!]^+$. Then by the proof of Clause 1 of this proposition, it follows that $f(w, [\![A, A > B]\!]^+) \subseteq [\![A]\!]^+ \cap [\![A, A > B]\!]^+ \subseteq [\![B]\!]^+$.

For 3, suppose $\mathfrak{M}, w \Vdash (A > B)^A$. Then $\mathfrak{M}, w \Vdash B^{A,A^A}$. By Proposition 1, we have $\mathfrak{M}, w \Vdash B^A$, and thus $\mathfrak{M}, w \not\dashv\!\vert\, B^A$ by Lemma 1.

For 4, suppose $\mathfrak{M}, w \Vdash A^{A>B}$. By Lemma 2, $f(w, [\![A > B]\!]^+) \subseteq [\![A]\!]^+$. By (id), $f(w, [\![A > B]\!]^+ \subseteq [\![A > B]\!]^+$. It follows that $f(w, [\![A > B]\!]^+) \subseteq [\![A]\!]^+ \cap [\![A > B]\!]^+ \subseteq [\![B]\!]^+$. Hence, $\mathfrak{M}, w \Vdash B^{A>B}$ and thus $\mathfrak{M}, w \not\dashv\!\vert\, B^{A>B}$ by Lemma 1.

Proof of Proposition 4. Let $\mathfrak{M} = (W, f, V^+, V^-)$ be any normal selection model and $w \in W$. For 1, note that $[\![p, p > (q > r), q^{p,p>(q>r)}]\!]^+ = [\![p \wedge (p > (q > r)) \wedge q^{p\wedge(p>(q>r))}]\!]^+ = [\![p \wedge (p > (q > r)) \wedge q]\!]^+ = [\![p \wedge (p \wedge q > r) \wedge q]\!]^+ = [\![(p \wedge q) \wedge r^{p\wedge q}]\!]^+ = [\![p \wedge q \wedge r]\!]$, where the second '=' and last '=' are by Lemma 4 and the third '=' is by Proposition 1. Hence, $[\![(q > r)^{p,p>(q>r)}]\!]^- = [\![r^{p,p>(q>r),q^{p,p>(q>r)}}]\!]^- = [\![r^{p\wedge q\wedge r}]\!]^- = \emptyset$, where the second '=' is by Lemma 3 and the last '=' is by (id).

For 2, we have $[\![p > \Box q]\!]^+ = [\![\Box q^p]\!]^+ = \begin{cases} W & \text{if } [\![q^p]\!]^+ = W \\ \emptyset & \text{otherwise} \end{cases}$. If $[\![p > \Box q]\!]^+ = W$, then $[\![q^{p,p>\Box q}]\!]^+ = [\![q^p]\!]^+ = W$ and thus $[\![\Box q^{p,p>\Box q}]\!]^+ = W$. If $[\![p > \Box q]\!]^+ = \emptyset$, then for any w, $f(w, [\![p, p > \Box q]\!]^+) = f(w, \emptyset) = \emptyset$ and thus $[\![q^{p,p>\Box q}]\!]^- = \emptyset$. In both cases, we have $[\![\Box q^{p,p>\Box q}]\!]^- = \emptyset$.

Proof of Proposition 6. For 1, we have $[\![(\neg A > B)^{A\vee B}]\!]^- = [\![B^{A\vee B,\neg A^{A\vee B}}]\!]^- = [\![B^{A\vee B,\neg A}]\!]^- = [\![B^{\neg A,B}]\!]^- = \emptyset$, where the second '=' is by Proposition 1, the third '=' is by Lemma 3 and the fact that $[\![A \vee B, \neg A]\!]^+ = [\![\neg A, B]\!]^+$, and the last '=' is by Lemma 2 and (id). Clause 2 is immediate from 1, and 3 is just a reformulation of 1.

Proof of Theorem 2. Let $\mathfrak{M} = (W, f, V^+, V^-)$ be any normal selection model. By Proposition 6, we have $[\![(\neg A \vee B) > (\neg\neg A > B)]\!]^-_{\mathfrak{M}} = \emptyset$. Since $A \equiv \neg\neg A$, it follows that $[\![(\neg A \vee B) > (A > B)]\!]^-_{\mathfrak{M}} = \emptyset$. For the other direction, suppose there exists $w \in W$ such that $\mathfrak{M}, w \dashv\!\!| (A > B) > (\neg A \vee B)$. Then $\mathfrak{M}, w \Vdash (A \wedge \neg B)^{A>B}$. By Lemma 2, we have $\emptyset \neq f(w, [\![A > B]\!]^+) \subseteq [\![A \wedge \neg B]\!]^+ \subseteq [\![A]\!]^+ \cap [\![B]\!]^-$. By (id), $f(w, [\![A > B]\!]^+) \subseteq [\![A > B]\!]^+$. It follows that $f(w, [\![A > B]\!]^+) \subseteq [\![A > B]\!]^+ \cap [\![A]\!]^+ \cap [\![B]\!]^- \subseteq [\![B]\!]^+ \cap [\![B]\!]^- = \emptyset$, contradiction, where the second '$\subseteq$' is by the proof Proposition 3.

Proof of Proposition 7. For 1, let $\Gamma = \{q\}$, $A = p$ and $B = q$. Then $\Gamma, p \Vdash q$. Consider $\mathfrak{M} = (W, f, V^+, V^-)$, where $W = \{w, u\}$, $f(w, \{u\}) = \{u\}$, $V^+(p) = \{u\}$, $V^+(q) = \{w\}$, $V^-(p) = \{w\}$, and $V^-(q) = \{u\}$. Then $\mathfrak{M}, w \Vdash q$. But $\mathfrak{M}, w \dashv\!\!| p > q$. Hence, $\Gamma \not\models p > q$.

For 2, let $\Gamma = \{q\}$, $A = p$ and $B = q$. Then it can be verified that $\Gamma \models^A B$, but $\Gamma \not\models A > B$ by Clause 1.

Proof of Proposition 8. We prove the contrapositive. For 1, suppose $\not\models A > B$. Then there is a normal pointed model $(\mathfrak{M}, w)$ such that $\mathfrak{M}, w \dashv\!\!| A > B$. By Lemma 2, we have $\emptyset \neq f(w, [\![A]\!]^+) \subseteq [\![B]\!]^-$. By (id), we have $f(w, [\![A]\!]^+) \subseteq [\![A]\!]^+$. It follows that $[\![A]\!]^+ \cap [\![B]\!]^- \supseteq f(w, [\![A]\!]^+) \neq \emptyset$. Hence, $A \not\models B$.

For 2, suppose $\not\models^\Gamma A > B$. Then there is a normal pointed model $(\mathfrak{M}, w)$ such that $\mathfrak{M}, w \dashv\!\!| (A > B)^\Gamma$. Thus, $\mathfrak{M}, w \dashv\!\!| B^{\Gamma, A^\Gamma}$. By Lemma 3 and Lemma 4, it follows that $\mathfrak{M}, w \dashv\!\!| B^{\Gamma, A}$, whence $\not\models^{\Gamma, A} B$.

For 3, suppose $\Gamma^A \not\models A > B$. Then there is a normal pointed model $(\mathfrak{M}, w)$ such that $\mathfrak{M}, w \Vdash \Gamma^A$ and $\mathfrak{M}, w \dashv\!\!| A > B$. From the latter, we have $\mathfrak{M}, w \dashv\!\!| B^A$. Hence, $\Gamma \not\models^A B$.

Proof of Proposition 9. For 1, consider any model with two worlds such that p is true at one and false at the other.

For 2, note that for any model $\mathfrak{M}$, $[\![\neg A^A]\!]^- = [\![A^A]\!]^+ = [\![\neg p^A]\!]^+ \cap [\![\Diamond p^A]\!]^+ \subseteq [\![\Diamond p^{\neg p \wedge \Diamond p}]\!]^+ = \emptyset$, since $[\![p^{\neg p \wedge \Diamond p}]\!]^+ = \emptyset$.

Proof of Proposition 10. For 1, consider $\mathfrak{M} = (W, f, V^+, V^-)$, where $W = \{w, u\}$, $f(w, W) = \{w\}$, $V^+(p) = \{u\}$, $V^-(p) = \{w\}$. Then $\mathfrak{M}, w \Vdash^{\Diamond p} \neg p$, since $f(w, [\![\Diamond p]\!]^+) = f(w, W) = \{u\} \subseteq [\![p]\!]^-$. And $\mathfrak{M}, w \dashV^{\Diamond p} \bot$. Hence, $\neg p \nvDash^{\Diamond p} \bot$.

For 2, suppose there exists $\mathfrak{M} = (W, f, V^+, V^-)$ and $w \in W$ such that $\mathfrak{M}, w \Vdash^{\neg p} \Diamond p$. Then $\mathfrak{M}, u \Vdash^{\neg p} p$ for some $u \in W$. Then $\emptyset \neq f(u, [\![\neg p]\!]^+) \subseteq [\![p]\!]^+$, which is impossible by (id) and Lemma 1.

Proof of Proposition 11. For 1, consider $\mathfrak{M} = (W, f, V^+, V^-)$, where $W = \{w, u\}$, $f(w, W) = \{w\}$, $f(u, W) = \{u\}$, $V^+(p) = W$, $V^+(q) = \{u\}$, $V^-(q) = \{w\}$. Then $\mathfrak{M}, w \Vdash p > \neg q$ and $\mathfrak{M}, u \Vdash p > q$ and hence $\mathfrak{M}, w \Vdash p > \Diamond q$.

For 2, $[\![\neg A^A]\!]^- = [\![A^A]\!]^+ = [\![(p > \neg q)^A]\!]^+ \cap [\![(p > \Diamond q)^A]\!]^+ \subseteq [\![(p > \Diamond q)^A]\!]^+ = [\![\Diamond q^{A, p^A}]\!]^+ = [\![\Diamond q^{A,p}]\!]^+ = [\![\Diamond q^{p > \neg q, p}]\!]^+ = \emptyset$, since $[\![q^{p > \neg q, p}]\!]^+ = \emptyset$.

Proof of Proposition 14. Let $\mathfrak{M}$ be any normal selection model. For $B = \neg p \wedge (p > q)$, we have $[\![\neg B^B]\!]^- = [\![B^B]\!]^+ = [\![p^B]\!]^+ \cap [\![q^{B, p^B}]\!]^+ \subseteq [\![q^{B, p^B}]\!]^+ = [\![q^{B \wedge p}]\!]^+ = [\![q^{p \wedge \neg p \wedge (p > q)}]\!]^+ = \emptyset$, where the third '=' is by Lemma 3 and Lemma 4, and the last '=' is by (id). For $B = p \wedge (\neg p > q)$, the prove is analogous.

Proof of Proposition 15. Let $\mathfrak{M}$ be any normal selection model. For $C = \neg q \wedge (p > q)$, we have $[\![\neg C^C]\!]^- = [\![C^C]\!]^+ = [\![\neg q^C]\!]^+ \cap [\![q^{C, p^C}]\!]^+ \subseteq [\![q^{C, p^C}]\!]^+ = [\![q^{C \wedge p}]\!]^+ = [\![q^{p \wedge \neg q \wedge (p > q)}]\!]^+ = \emptyset$, where the third '=' is by Lemma 3 and Lemma 4, and the last '=' is by (id). For $C = q \wedge \neg(p > q)$, similarly we have $[\![\neg C^C]\!]^- = [\![C^C]\!]^+ = [\![q^C]\!]^+ \cap [\![q^{C, p^C}]\!]^- \subseteq [\![q^{C, p^C}]\!]^- = [\![q^{C \wedge p}]\!]^- = [\![q^{p \wedge q \wedge \neg (p > q)}]\!]^- = \emptyset$.

References

1. Bennett, J.: A Philosophical Guide to Condtionals. Oxford University Press (2003)
2. Bledin, J.: Logic informed. Mind **123**(490), 277–316 (2014)
3. Bledin, J.: Modus ponens defended. J. Philos. **112**(2), 57–83 (2015)
4. Cobreros, P., Egré, P., Ripley, D., van Rooij, R.: Tolerant, classical, strict. J. Philos. Log. **41**(2), 347–385 (2012)
5. Fitting, M.: Proof Methods for Modal and Intuitionistic Logics. Springer Netherlands, Dordrecht (1983). https://doi.org/10.1007/978-94-017-2794-5
6. Gibbard, A.: Two recent theories of conditionals. In: Harper, W.L., Stalnaker, R., Pearce, G. (eds.) Ifs: Conditionals, Belief, Decision, Chance, and Time, pp. 211–248. Reidel, Dordrecht (1981)
7. Jackson, F.: On assertion and indicative conditionals. Philos. Rev. **88**(4), 565–589 (1979)
8. Klinedinst, N.: Quantified conditionals and conditional excluded middle. J. Semant. **28**(1), 149–170 (2011)
9. Kolodny, N., MacFarlane, J.: Ifs and Oughts. J. Philos. **107**(3), 115–143 (2010)
10. Kratzer, A.: The Notional Category of Modality. In: Eikmeyer, H.J., Rieser, H. (eds.) Words, Worlds, and Contexts: New Approaches to Word Semantics, pp. 38–74. de Gruyter. Reprinted in B. Partee and P. Portner (eds.), Formal Semantics: the Essential Readings. Blackwell (1981)

11. Lewis, D.: Counterfactuals. Harvard University Press (1973)
12. Mandelkern, M.: A counterexample to modus Ponenses. J. Philos. **117**(6), 315–331 (2020)
13. Mandelkern, M.: Import-export and 'And'. Res. **100**(1), 118–135 (2020)
14. Mandelkern, M.: If p, then p! J. Philos. **118**(12), 645–679 (2021)
15. McGee, V.: A counterexample to modus ponens. J. Philos. **82**(9), 462–471 (1985)
16. Over, D.: Assumptions and the supposed counterexamples to modus ponens. Analysis **47**(3), 142–146 (1987)
17. Ripley, D.: Conservatively extending classical logic with transparent truth. Rev. Symbol. Logic **5**(2), 354–378 (2012)
18. Santorio, P.: Path semantics for indicative conditionals. Mind **131**(521), 59–98 (2022)
19. Stalnaker, R.: A Theory of Conditionals. In: Rescher, N. (ed.) Studies in Logical Theory, pp. 98–112. Basil Blackwell Publishers (1968)
20. Stalnaker, R.: Indicative conditionals. Philosophia **5**(3), 269–286 (1975)
21. Stalnaker, R.C.: A defense of conditional excluded middle. In: Harper, W.L., Stalnaker, R., Pearce, G. (eds.) IFS: Conditionals, Belief, Decision, Chance and Time, pp. 87–104. The University of Western Ontario Series in Philosophy of Science, Springer, Netherlands, Dordrecht (1981)
22. Strawson, P.F.: Introduction to Logical Theory. Introduction to Logical Theory, Wiley, Oxford, England (1952)
23. Veltman, F.: Defaults in update semantics. J. Philos. Log. **25**(3), 221–261 (1996)
24. Williams, J.R.G.: Defending conditional excluded middle. Noûs **44**(4), 650–668 (2010)
25. Yalcin, S.: Epistemic modals. Mind **116**(464), 983–1026 (2007)

Logical Expressibility of Syntactic NL for Complementarity and Maximization

Tomoyuki Yamakami(✉)

Faculty of Engineering, University of Fukui, 3-9-1 Bunkyo, Fukui 910-8507, Japan
TomoyukiYamakami@gmail.com

Abstract. In a discussion on the computational complexity of "parameterized" NL (nondeterministic logarithmic-space complexity class), Syntactic NL or succinctly SNL was first introduced in 2017 as a "syntactically"-defined natural subclass of NL using a restricted form of second-order logic in close connection to the so-called linear space hypothesis. We further explore various properties of this complexity class SNL. In particular, we consider the expressibility of "complementary" problems of SNL problems. As a variant of SNL, we also study an optimization version of SNL, called MAXSNL, and its natural subclass, called MAXτSNL.

Keywords: second-order logic · NL · SNL · optimization problem · DSTCON · 2SAT · UK · MAX-CUT · linear space hypothesis

1 Background and Main Contributions

1.1 Motivational Discussion on Syntactic NL

Since its importance was first recognized in the 1970 s, the nondeterministic polynomial-time complexity class NP has been a centerfold of intensive research on the field of computer science for decades. Papadimitriou and Yannakakis [12] and Feder and Vardi [5,6] considered a subclass of NP, known as SNP, to capture a certain aspect of nondeterministic polynomial-time computation in terms of second-order logical sentences starting with a second-order existential quantifier followed by a first-order universal quantifier with no use of the first-order existential quantifiers. This complexity class SNP turns out to play an important role in promoting the better understanding of the logical expressibility of capturing nondeterministic polynomial-time computing. As Impagliazzo and Paturi [8] demonstrated, kSAT is complete for SNP under so-called *SERF reductions*, where kSAT is the collection of satisfiable Boolean formulas of *k-conjunctive normal form* (kCNF). This can be compared to the fact that kSAT is complete for NP under polynomial-time many-one reductions.

Space Bounded Computation is another important resource-bounded computation in theory and also in practice. In this work, our special attention goes to such space-bounded computation. In particular, we focus on the nondeterministic

G. Metcalfe et al. (Eds.): WoLLIC 2024, LNCS 14672, pp. 261–277, 2024.
https://doi.org/10.1007/978-3-031-62687-6_17

logarithmic space-bounded complexity class NL. Typical NL decision problems include the 2CNF formula satisfiability problem (2SAT) and the directed s-t connectivity problem (DSTCON). Interestingly, numerous properties that have been proven for NL seem quite different from those for NP. For instance, NL is closed under complementation [7,14] whereas NP is speculated not to be closed under the same set operation.

Analogous to SNP, in due course of a study on parameterized decision problems, a "syntactically"-defined natural subclass of NL dubbed as *Syntactic NL* (or succinctly, *SNL*) and its variant SNL_ω were introduced in [18] based on restricted forms of second-order sentences starting with second-order "functional" existential quantifiers. (For its detailed definition, refer to Sect. 2.2.) This parameterized complexity class SNL naturally contains a "parameterized" version of NL-complete problem, known as the directed s-t connectivity problem of degree at most 3 (3DSTCON), and SNL_ω contains a "parameterized" version of its variant, called exact3DSTCON, whose input graphs are restricted to vertices of degree exactly 3 [18]. Notice that $\mathrm{SNL}_\omega \subseteq \mathrm{SNL} \subseteq$ para-NL, where para-NL is the "parameterized" version of NL. See [18] for its precise definition. In particular, SNL_ω is closely related to a practical working hypothesis, known as the *linear space hypothesis* (LSH), which was introduced also in [18] and further developed in, e.g., [19,20]. This LSH is regarded as a log-space analogue of the exponential time hypothesis and the strong exponential time hypothesis of [8,9].

Up to now, little is known for the properties of SNL and SNL_ω. The primary purpose of this work is therefore to explore these properties of SNL and SNL_ω, particularly restricted to the framework of *non*-parameterized decision problems by setting $m_{\|}(x) = |x|$ as a size parameter for inputs x in order to make it easier to compare between the properties of SNL and those of SNP. For this purpose, we intend to redefine SNL as a non-parameterized complexity class and further study natural variants of SNL in a way similar to the study of SNP in the literature.

In the polynomial-time setting, nonetheless, an optimization version of SNP, called MAXSNP, was studied in 1991 by Papadimitriou and Yannakakis [12] in a discussion of the development of fast approximation algorithms. Notably, they showed that all optimization problems in MAXSNP can be approximated in polynomial time within a certain fixed approximation ratio. They also demonstrated that many of the typical NP optimization problems, including MAX-2SAT and MAX-CUT, are in fact complete for MAXSNP under polynomial-time linear reductions. Lately, Bringman, Cassis, Fisher, and Künnemann [2] studied a subclass of MAXSNP with respect to fine-grained complexity theory. By taking a similar approach, it is possible to study an optimization version of SNL, which we intend to call by MAXSNL. One may wonder what similarities and differences lay between MAXSNL and MAXSNP.

1.2 Major Contributions

We briefly describe two major contributions of this work on the complexity class SNL and its natural variants defined later in this work.

The first major result is concerning the structure of decision problems in SNL. To deal with decision problems in SNL, we use logarithmic-space many-one reductions (or L-m-reductions) and show that every decision problem in NL has an L-m-equivalent problem in SNL (Proposition 10), where two problems are said to be *L-m-equivalent* if one problem is reducible to another and vice visa under L-m-reductions. We will show that the 2COLOR (2-colorability problem) and its "complementary" problem belong to SNL (Proposition 11). In contrast, we will show that the "complementary" problem of DSTCON, called DSTNCON, is in a natural superclass of SNL (Theorem 12), which is called μSNL. This is proven by syntactically implementing a technique of *inductive counting* [7,14].

Secondly, we will consider the class MAXSNL of optimization problems. Instead of polynomial-time linear reductions of [12], we use logarithmic-space AP-reductions of [17, arXiv version]. The maximization problem MAX-CUT is then complete for MAXSNL under these reductions (Lemma 18). Regarding log-space approximation schemes [17], we construct them for a maximization version of the unary 0-1 knapsack problem (UK) [4], called MAX-UK (Proposition 19), and for a subclass of MAXSNL, called MAXτSNL (Theorem 20).

2 Basic Notions and Notation

2.1 Numbers, Machines, and Reducibility

Concerning numbers, we use three special notations $\mathbb{N}$, $\mathbb{Z}$, and $\mathbb{Q}$, which respectively consist of all *natural numbers* (including 0), of all *integers*, and all *rational numbers*. Moreover, we set $\mathbb{N}^+ = \mathbb{N} - \{0\}$ and $\mathbb{Q}^{>1} = \{r \in \mathbb{Q} \mid r > 1\}$. For two numbers $m, n \in \mathbb{Z}$ with $m \leq n$, the notation $[m, n]_\mathbb{Z}$ denotes the *integer interval* $\{m, m+1, m+2, \ldots, n\}$. Given $n \in \mathbb{N}^+$, $[n]$ is a shorthand for $[1, n]_\mathbb{Z}$.

We assume the reader's familiarity with *space-bounded deterministic Turing machines* (or DTMs, for short) with random-access mechanism, each of which is equipped with a read-only input tape, multiple work tapes, and an index tape to specify addresses of the input tape for an instant access to target input symbols. For any decision problem L, a DTM M is said to *solve* L if, for any instance x in L, M accepts it and, for any instance x in $\overline{L}$ ($= \Sigma^* - L$), M rejects it. A function f from Σ^* to Γ^* for two alphabets Σ and Γ is called *logarithmic-space (or log-space) computable* if there exists a DTM equipped with a write-once output tape that, on input $x \in \Sigma^*$, produces $f(x)$ on the output tape using $O(\log |x|)$ work space. We write FL to denote the class of all polynomial-time log-space computable functions.

Given two decision problems L_1 and L_2, we say that L_1 is L-*m-reducible to* L_2 (denoted $L_1 \leq_m^{\mathrm{L}} L_2$) if there is a function in FL such that, for all x, $x \in L_1$ holds exactly when $f(x) \in L_2$. Moreover, L_1 is said to be L-*m-equivalent to* L_2 (denoted $L_1 \equiv_m^{\mathrm{L}} L_2$) if $L_1 \leq_m^{\mathrm{L}} L_2$ and $L_2 \leq_m^{\mathrm{L}} L_1$ both hold.

2.2 Syntactic NL (or SNL)

Let us explain the fundamental terminology given in [18]. Although the original concepts were introduced in a discussion on the computational complexity of "parameterized" decision problems, in this work, we fix $m_{\|}(x) = |x|$ as our size parameter and modify these original concepts to fit in the setting of "standard" (i.e., non-parameterized) decision problems. When we need to refer to the original "parameterized" SNL, we distinguishingly write it as para-SNL for clarity.

As an introduction of the syntax of our logical system, we start with explaining *syntactic NL sentences* (or *SNL sentences*, for short).

Definition 1. *A* vocabulary *(an* input signature *or an* input relation*)* $\mathcal{T}$ *is a finite set composed of* (S_i, k_i), c_j, 0, n, *suc*, *pred for all* $i \in [d]$ *and* $j \in [d']$, *where* S_i *is a* predicate symbol *of arity* $k_i \geq 0$ *(or a* k_i*-arity predicate symbol), 0 and* n *are* constant symbols, c_j *is another specific symbol expressing an "input object" (such as a number, a vertex or an edge of a graph, and a size of columns or rows of a matrix) of a target computational problem, and pred and suc are two designated function symbols called respectively by the* successor function *and the* predecessor function.

The meanings of $suc(\cdot)$ and $pred(\cdot)$ are $suc(i) = i{+}1$ and $pred(i) = \max\{0, i-1\}$ for any $i \in \mathbb{N}$. We abbreviate $suc(suc(i))$ as $suc^2(i)$ and $suc(suc^2(i))$ as $suc^3(i)$, etc. We further write $i + e$ for $suc^e(i)$ when e is a constant in $\mathbb{N}^+$.

As in [18], two types of variables are used in this work. *First-order variables*, denoted by $i, j, \ldots, u, v, \ldots$, range over all natural numbers and input objects (such as vertices or edges of a graph and entries of a matrix) that describe a target computational problem. *Second-order variables*[1], denoted by $P, Q, \ldots$, in this work range over a specific form of *relations* whose first argument takes a natural number and the other arguments take multiple input objects. This restriction for second-order variables is necessary to "express" log-space computing. See [18] for more information.

An *atomic formula* has one of the following forms: $S_j(u_1, \ldots, u_{k_i})$, $P(i, v_1, v_2, \ldots, v_k)$, $u = v$, and $i \leq j$, where $i, j, u, v, u_1, \ldots, u_{k_i}, v_1, \ldots, v_k$ are *terms* composed of first-order variables, constant symbols, and function symbols, and P is a second-order variable. For clarity reason, we use i, j for number-related terms and $u, v, u_1, \ldots, u_{k_i}, v_1, \ldots, v_k$ for terms associated with other input objects. *Formulas* are built inductively from atomic formulas by connecting them with logical connectives ($\rightarrow$, $\neg$, $\vee$, $\wedge$) and first/second-order quantifiers ($\forall$, $\exists$).

In what follows, we concentrate on the specific case where second-order variables represent only "functions". It is therefore convenient to introduce a functional variant of the second-order quantifier. For this purpose, we use the special notation $\exists^f P[\psi(P)]$ with a formula ψ containing no second-order quantifiers as a shorthand for $\exists P[\psi(P) \wedge Func(P)]$, where $Func(P)$ is a unique sentence over a second-order variable P expressing that $P(\cdot,\cdot)$ works as a "function"; namely, $Func(P) \equiv Func_1(P) \wedge Func_2(P)$, where $Func_1(P) \equiv (\forall i)(\exists w_1, \ldots, w_k)[P(i, w_1, \ldots, w_k)]$ and $Func_2(P) \equiv$

[1] In [18], a second-order variable is limited to have only two argument places. Here, we further allow the second-order variable to have more than two argument places.

$(\forall i, u_1, \ldots, u_k, v_1, \ldots, v_k)[P(i, u_1, \ldots, u_k) \wedge P(i, v_1, \ldots, v_k) \rightarrow \bigwedge_{j=1}^{k}(u_i = v_i)]$. Here, the symbol "$\exists^f$" is called the *functional existential quantifier.*

Definition 2. *Let* $\mathcal{V} = \{(S_i, k_i), c_j, 0, n, suc, pred \mid i \in [d], j \in [d']\}$ *denote a vocabulary. A* syntactic NL sentence *(or an* SNL sentence*) over* $\mathcal{V}$ *is a second-order sentence* Φ *of the form:*

$$\Phi \equiv \exists^f P_1 \cdots \exists^f P_l \,\forall i_1 \cdots \forall i_r \,\forall y_1 \cdots \forall y_s$$
$$[\bigwedge_{j=1}^{t} \psi_j(P_1, \ldots, P_l, i_1, \ldots, i_r, y_1, \ldots, y_s, S_1, \ldots, S_d, c_1, \ldots, c_{d'})],$$

where $l, r, s, t \in \mathbb{N}$ *and each* ψ_j *(*$j \in [t]$*) is a quantifier-free second-order formula for which no two* ψ_j*'s share any common first-order variables. Here,* $P_1, \ldots, P_l$ *are second-order variables representing functions,* $i_1, \ldots, i_r$ *are first-order variables representing natural numbers, and* $y_1, \ldots, y_s$ *are also first-order variables representing all other input objects. Each* ψ_j *should satisfy the following two* second-order variable requirements*: (i) each* ψ_j *contains only second-order variables of the form* $P_k(i, \boldsymbol{v}_1), P_k(suc(i), \boldsymbol{v}_2), P_k(suc^2(i), \boldsymbol{v}_3), \ldots, P_k(suc^a(i), \boldsymbol{v}_{a+1})$ *for a fixed constant* $a \in \mathbb{N}^+$*, where each of* $\boldsymbol{v}_1, \ldots, \boldsymbol{v}_{a+1}$ *is a* k' *tuple for a fixed constant* $k' \in \mathbb{N}^+$*, and (ii)* ψ_j *can be rewritten in the logically equivalent form of finite disjunctions, each of which satisfies the following condition: there are only at most two disjuncts containing second-order variables and each of them must have the form* $(\bigwedge_{k,i,\boldsymbol{v}} P_k(i, \boldsymbol{v})) \wedge (\bigwedge_{k',i',\boldsymbol{v}'} \neg P_{k'}(i', \boldsymbol{v}')) \wedge R$*, where* R *is an appropriate subformula including no second-order variable.*

Next, we explain the semantics of SNL sentences.

Definition 3. *(1) Given a vocabulary* $\mathcal{V} = \{(S_i, k_i), c_j, 0, n, suc, pred \mid i \in [d], j \in [d']\}$*, a* relational structure $\mathcal{S}$ *over* $\mathcal{V}$ *is a set of tuples* (U_i, D_i, k_i) *and* $(\bar{c}_j, V_j)$ *with finite universes* U_i *and* V_j *of "input objects" (including natural numbers) and domains* D_i *associated with predicate symbols* S_i *in* $\mathcal{V}$ *satisfying* $D_i \subseteq U_i^{k_i}$*, and constants* $\bar{c}_j$ *in* V_j*. The constant symbols* c_j *are interpreted as* $\bar{c}_j$ *and the predicate symbols* S_i *are interpreted as* D_i *so that, if input objects* $\bar{s}_1, \bar{s}_2, \ldots, \bar{s}_{k_i}$ *in* U_i *are assigned respectively to variables* $x_1, x_2, \ldots, x_{k_i}$ *appearing in* S_i*,* $S_i(\bar{s}_1, \bar{s}_2, \ldots, \bar{s}_{k_i})$ *is true exactly when* $(\bar{s}_1, \bar{s}_2, \ldots, \bar{s}_{k_i}) \in D_i$*.*

(2) Let Φ *denote any SNL sentence of the form of Definition 2 with variables* $P_1, \ldots, P_l, i_1, \ldots, i_r, y_1, \ldots, y_s$*. A* domain structure $\mathcal{D}$ *for* Φ *is the union of three sets* $\{(P_j, [e_1] \times U'_{j_1} \times \cdots \times U'_{j_{k'}}, k'+1)\}_{j \in [l]}$*,* $\{(i_j, [e'_j])\}_{j \in [r]}$*, and* $\{(y_j, U''_j)\}_{j \in [s]}$*, which provide the scopes of variables of* Φ *in the following manner for fixed constants* $e_j, e'_j \in \mathbb{N}^+$*. Each second-order variable* P_j *(*$j \in [l]$*) ranges over all elements in* $[e_j] \times U'_{j_1} \times \cdots \times U'_{j_{k'}}$*, each first-order variable* i_j *(*$j \in [r]$*) ranges over all numbers in* $[e'_j]$*, and each variable* y_j *(*$j \in [s]$*) ranges over all elements in* U''_j*.*

A relational structure $\mathcal{S}$ over $\mathcal{V}$ is said to *describe* (or *represent*) an instance x of the target computational problem if every input object appearing in x has either its corresponding predicate symbol in $\mathcal{V}$ with its universe and domain in $\mathcal{S}$ or its corresponding constant symbol in $\mathcal{V}$ with its universe. Concrete examples will be given in Examples 6 and 7. It is important to remark that, when $\mathcal{S}$ describes x, since the universes U_i and V_i are specified inside x, their sizes $|U_i|$ and $|V_i|$ should be upper-bounded by $O(|x|)$.

When a relational structure $\mathcal{S}$ and a domain structure $\mathcal{D}$ are given for an SNL sentence Φ, it is possible to evaluate the *validity* of Φ by interpreting all predicate symbols S_i and all constant symbols c_j appearing in Φ as domains D_i and constants $\bar{c}_j$ in $\mathcal{S}$ and by assigning input objects in $\mathcal{S}$ and $\mathcal{D}$ to variables appropriately. This evaluation makes Φ either "true" or "false".

Definition 4. *Given a computational problem A and an* SNL *sentence Φ, we say that Φ* syntactically expresses *A if, for any instance x given to A, there are a relational structure $\mathcal{S}_x$ describing x and a domain structure $\mathcal{D}_x$ for Φ satisfying the following: $x \in A$ iff Φ is true on $\mathcal{S}_x$ and $\mathcal{D}_x$.*

Definition 5. *We denote by* SNL *the collection of all decision problems A such that there exist a vocabulary $\mathcal{V}$ and an SNL sentence Φ for which Φ syntactically expresses A.*

In [18], DSTCON was shown to be in SNL. As another quick example, we see how to construct an SNL sentence to express the decision problem 2COLOR, in which one asks whether a given undirected graph is colorable using only two colors. This is the same as checking that a given graph is bipartite. It is known that 2COLOR is in L (see [1] with the fact that SL = L).

Example 6. We wish to show that 2COLOR is in SNL by constructing an appropriate SNL sentence for 2COLOR. Given an undirected graph $G = (\hat{V}, \hat{E})$ as an instance x, we assume that $\hat{V} = \{v_1, v_2, \ldots, v_n\}$. We identify each vertex v_i with the integer i. Let E denote a predicate symbol associated with $\hat{E}$. We define $\mathcal{V} = \{(E, 2), 0, 1\}$ and $\mathcal{S}_x = \{(U_x, D_x, 2), (0, V_1), (1, V_2)\}$ with $U_x = [n]$, $D_x = \{(i, j) \mid (x_i, x_j) \in \hat{E}\}$, $V_1 = \{0\}$, and $V_2 = \{1\}$. Clearly, $\mathcal{S}_x$ describes x. Next, we define a sentence Φ to be $(\exists^f C)(\forall i, d, i', j', d', e')[\Phi_1(C, i, d) \wedge \Phi_2(C, E, i', j', d', e')]$, where i, j, i', d, d', e' are symbols expressing the first-order variables, $\Phi_1(C, i, d) \equiv C(i, d) \rightarrow 0 \leq d \leq 1$, and $\Phi_2(C, E, i', j', d', e') \equiv E(i', j') \wedge C(i', d') \wedge C(j', e') \rightarrow d' \neq e'$. By rewriting Φ_1 and Φ_2 in the disjunction form, we can show that Φ_1 and Φ_2 both satisfy the second-order variable requirements. We further define $\mathcal{D}_x = \{(C, [n] \times \{0, 1\}, 2)\} \cup \{(s, [n]) \mid s \in \{i, i', j'\}\} \cup \{(s', [2]) \mid s' \in \{d, d', e'\}\}$. It then follows that Φ is true on $\mathcal{S}_x$ and $\mathcal{D}_x$ iff $x \in$ 2COLOR.

Another example is the *unary 0-1 knapsack problem* (UK), which was discussed by Cook [4]. An instance of UK is a series $(1^b, 1^{a_1}, 1^{a_2}, \ldots, 1^{a_n})$ of unary strings with $b, a_1, a_2, \ldots, a_n \in \mathbb{N}^+$ and one asks to determine the existence of a subset S of $[n]$ satisfying $\sum_{i \in S} a_i = b$. It was shown in [21] that UK belongs to a subclass of NL, called 1t1NCA (see [21] for details).

Example 7. We claim that the decision problem UK is also in SNL. To see this, we prepare a predicate symbol I for which $I(i, c)$ means that c is the ith input value a_i. Let $ADD(c, a, b)$ mean $c = a + b$. We set $\Phi \equiv (\exists^f P)(\forall i, s, t)[P(0,0) \wedge P(n, b) \wedge (\psi_1(P, i, s, t) \rightarrow \psi_2(P, I, ADD, s, t))]$, where $\psi_1 \equiv i < n \wedge P(i, s) \wedge P(i + 1, t)$ and $\psi_2 \equiv (\forall z)[s = t \leq b \vee (s < t \leq b \wedge (ADD(t, s, z) \wedge z > 0 \rightarrow I(i+1, z)))]$. Notice that the formula $\psi_1 \rightarrow \psi_2$ satisfies the second-order variable requirements since $\psi_1 \rightarrow \psi_2$ can be rewritten as $\neg P(i, s) \vee \neg P(i + 1, t) \vee R$ for an appropriate formula R containing no second-order variables. Therefore, Φ is an SNL sentence.

3 Structural Properties of SNL

3.1 Basic Closure Properties and L-m-Reductions

In succession to the previous section, we intend to study the structural properties of SNL in depth.

Proposition 8. SNL *is closed under union and intersection.*

Given a decision problem A, the notation $\leq_m^{\mathrm{L}}(A)$ expresses the collection of all decision problems that are L-m-reducible to A. Furthermore, for a given complexity class $\mathcal{C}$, the notation $\leq_m^{\mathrm{L}}(\mathcal{C})$ denotes the union $\bigcup_{A \in \mathcal{C}} \leq_m^{\mathrm{L}}(A)$.

Proposition 9. NL $= \leq_m^{\mathrm{L}}$(SNL).

Proof. It is known in [18] that para-SNL $\subseteq$ para-NL. In the "non-parameterized" setting of this work, it is possible to rephrase this inclusion as SNL $\subseteq$ NL by restricting corresponding size parameters to $m_{||}$. Therefore, we obtain $\leq_m^{\mathrm{L}}$ (SNL) $\subseteq \leq_m^{\mathrm{L}}$ (NL). Since NL is closed under L-m-reductions, $\leq_m^{\mathrm{L}}$(NL) $=$ NL follows.

It is also shown in [18] that the decision problem exact3DSTCON is in SNL and that 3DSTCON is complete for NL under L-m-reductions. These results together imply that NL $\subseteq \leq_m^{\mathrm{L}}$(SNL). □

Actually, we can assert a stronger statement than Proposition 9. Here, we intend to claim that SNL occupies a "structurally" important portion of NL in the sense described in the following theorem.

Theorem 10. *For any decision problem in* NL, *there always exists an* L-*m-equivalent problem in* SNL.

3.2 Complementary Problems and μSNL

Recall that 2COLOR is equivalent to checking whether a given undirected graph is bipartite. Let us consider its "complementary" decision problem, known as the *non-bipartite graph problem* (NBG), in which one asks to determine whether a given undirected graph is not bipartite. We show that not only 2COLOR but also NBG are expressible by appropriate SNL sentences.

Proposition 11. 2COLOR *and its complementary problem* NBG *are both in* SNL.

Proof. Given an undirected graph $G = (\hat{V}, \hat{E})$, we prepare two predicate symbols, E and ODD, where E corresponds to $\hat{E}$ and $ODD(k)$ indicates that k is an odd number. We then define $\Phi \equiv (\exists^f P)(\forall i, k, l)(\forall u, v)[1 \leq i < n \wedge (\bigwedge_{m=1}^{5} \Phi_m)]$, where $\Phi_1 \equiv P(1, u, k) \rightarrow k = 1$, $\Phi_2 \equiv P(i, u, k) \wedge P(i+1, v, l) \rightarrow ((l = k \wedge u = v) \vee (l = k+1 \wedge u \neq v))$, $\Phi_3 \equiv P(i, u, k) \wedge P(i+1, v, k+1) \rightarrow E(u, v)$, $\Phi_4 \equiv P(1, u, k) \wedge P(n, v, l) \rightarrow u = v$, and $\Phi_5 \equiv P(n, u, k) \rightarrow ODD(k)$. □

We wonder if the situation like the above proposition always happens. Let us consider the decision problem DSTCON, which is in SNL [18], and its complementary decision problem, called DSTNCON, in which one asks to determine whether, given a directed graph G and two vertices s and t, no path exists in G from s to t. Since NL is closed under complementation [7,14], DSTNCON must fall in NL. Is it true that DSTNCON belongs to SNL as well? Although we know that there exists its L-m-equivalent problem in SNL by Theorem 10, it is not clear that DSTNCON itself falls in SNL.

Toward a partial solution to this question, nevertheless, we intend to expand the complexity class SNL by introducing the additional *μ-operator* applied to second-order variables quantified in SNL sentences. Recall that a second-order variable P indicates an arbitrary "function". Into our logical system, we add a new term (called a *μ-term*) of the form $\mu z.P(i, z)$ indicating the "minimal" object z satisfying $P(i, z)$ for a given number i, assuming a predetermined linear ordering on these objects. This new term allows us to write, e.g., $S(\mu z.P(i, z), \boldsymbol{j}, \boldsymbol{u})$ for a predicate symbol S in order to mean that $(\forall z)[P(i, z) \rightarrow S(z, \boldsymbol{j}, \boldsymbol{u})]$ as well as $(\exists z)[P(i, z) \wedge S(z, \boldsymbol{j}, \boldsymbol{u})]$ (because P indicates a function) by eliminating any use of quantifiers associated with z. However, we do not allow any nested application of the μ-operator, such as $\mu z.P(\mu y.Q(i, y), z)$. Moreover, each formula ψ_j in Definition 2 must contain at most one μ-term. We then expand the current form of SNL sentences by including such μ-terms. It is important to remark that μ-terms are exempt from the second-order variable requirements. The obtained sentences are succinctly called *μSNL sentences* and all decision problems syntactically expressed by those μSNL sentences form the class μSNL. Obviously, SNL $\subseteq$ μSNL follows.

Immerman [7] and Szelcepscényi [14] proved that NL is closed under complementation. Their proofs utilize an algorithmic technique known as *inductive counting*. We intend to adopt this useful technique to a logical setting and apply it to μSNL in order to demonstrate that DSTNCON belongs to μSNL.

Theorem 12. DSTNCON *is in* μSNL.

Proof Sketch. Let us consider any instance (G, s, t) given to DSTNCON with $G = (\hat{V}, \hat{E})$ and $s, t \in \hat{V}$. Recall that (G, s, t) is in DSTNCON iff there is no path from the vertex s to the vertex t in G. For simplicity, we assume that $\hat{V} = [0, n]_{\mathbb{Z}}$ with $s = 0$ and $t = n$ and that there is no self-loop (i.e., $(v, v) \notin \hat{E}$).

The predicate $E(u,w)$ expresses the existence of an edge (u,w) in G. To encode a pair (e,i) into one variable w, we use the formula $w = e(n+1)+i$ and we abbreviate this formula as $Enc_1(w,e,i)$. We introduce a second-order variable P and express the formula $0 \leq w < (n+1)^2 \wedge P(w,u) \wedge Enc_1(w,e,i)$ as $\tilde{P}(w,e,i,u)$.

The predicate $T^{(-)}(P,E,e,i)$ expresses that there is a path of length at most i in G from the vertex s to the vertex e. This predicate, abbreviated as $T^{(-)}(e,i)$ for brevity, can be expressed as $\Phi_1 \wedge \Phi_2 \wedge \Phi_3$. Three formulas Φ_1, Φ_2, Φ_3 are defined as $\Phi_1 \equiv (\forall w_1, u_1)[\tilde{P}(w_1,e,0,u_1) \rightarrow u_1 = 0]$, $\Phi_2 \equiv (\forall w_2, j, u_1, u_2)[\tilde{P}(w_2,e,j,u_1) \wedge \tilde{P}(w_2+1,e,j+1,u_2) \wedge u_1 \neq e \wedge u_1 \neq u_2 \rightarrow E(u_1,u_2)]$, and $\Phi_3 \equiv (\forall w_3, j, u_3)[\tilde{P}(w_3,e,j,e) \wedge \tilde{P}(w_3+1,e,j+1,u_3) \rightarrow u_3 = e]$.

Four second-order variables N, C_1, C_2, C_3 are further introduced. We intend to make $N(i,k)$ assert the existence of exactly k vertices in $\hat{V}$ reachable from s by at most i edges. We further make $C_1(e,h)$ express that there are h vertices in $[0,e]_{\mathbb{Z}}$ reachable from s. Given C_2, we set $\tilde{C}_2(w,e,i,h) \equiv 0 \leq w < (n+1)^2 \wedge C_2(w,h) \wedge Enc_1(w,e,i)$, which indicates that w encodes (e,i) and that h equals the total number of vertices in $[0,e]_{\mathbb{Z}}$ reachable from s through at most i edges. Similarly to $\tilde{C}_2$, we define $\tilde{C}_3(w,e,i,h)$ from C_3.

The desired sentence Φ is now set to be $(\exists^f P, N, C_1, C_2, C_3)[N(0,1) \wedge (\forall e,i)[\tilde{P}(w,e,i,e) \rightarrow T^{(-)}(e,i)] \wedge \Psi_1(N,\tilde{P},C_1) \wedge (\forall i)\Psi_2(N,\tilde{P},C_1,\tilde{C}_2,\tilde{C}_3,i)]$ with two specific formulas Ψ_1 and Ψ_2. The first formula Ψ_1 is defined as

$$\Psi_1 \equiv C_1(0,1) \wedge C_1(n-1, \mu z.N(n,z)) \wedge (\forall w,e,j)[0 \leq e < n \rightarrow \phi_1 \wedge \phi_2],$$

where $\phi_1 \equiv \tilde{P}(w,e,j,e) \rightarrow C_1(e+1, \mu z.C_1(e,z)+1)$ and $\phi_2 \equiv \neg T^{(-)}(e,n) \rightarrow C_1(e+1, \mu z.C_1(e,z))$. The second formula Ψ_2 is defined as $\Psi_2 \equiv 0 \leq i < n \rightarrow \Psi_{2,1} \wedge \Psi_{2,2} \wedge \Psi_{2,3}$, where

$$\begin{aligned} \Psi_{2,1} &\equiv (\forall w_0, k)[Enc_1(w_0,0,i) \rightarrow \tilde{C}_2(w_0,0,i,1)], \\ \Psi_{2,2} &\equiv (\forall w_1, k)[\tilde{C}_2(w_1,n,i+1,k) \rightarrow N(i+1,k)], \quad \text{and} \\ \Psi_{2,3} &\equiv (\forall w_2, e, j)[0 \leq e \leq n \wedge 0 \leq j \leq i \rightarrow \psi_1 \vee \psi_2]. \end{aligned}$$

Here, $\psi_1 \equiv \tilde{P}(w_2+1,e+1,j,e+1) \rightarrow \tilde{C}_2(w_2+1,e+1,i,\mu z.C_1(w_2,z)+1)$ and $\psi_2 \equiv [Enc_1(w_2,0,i) \rightarrow \tilde{C}_3(w_2,0,i,1)] \wedge (\forall w_3,k)[\tilde{C}_3(w_3,n,i,k) \rightarrow N(i,k)] \wedge (\forall w_4,d,j')[0 \leq d < n \rightarrow (\neg E(d,e) \rightarrow \xi_1 \vee \xi_2) \wedge (E(d,e) \rightarrow \xi_2)]$ with $\xi_1 \equiv \tilde{P}(w_4+1,d,j,d) \rightarrow \tilde{C}_3(w_4+1,e+1,i,\mu z.C_3(w_4,z)+1)$ and $\xi_2 \equiv \tilde{C}_3(w_4+1,e+1,i,\mu z.C_3(w_4,z))$. $\square$

4 Maximal SNL (or MAXSNL)

We expand the scope of our study of SNL by seeking out its direct application to other areas of computer science. In this regard, for SNP, Papadimitriou and Yannakakis [12] earlier studied the computational complexity of its optimization version, called MAXSNP. In a similar vein, we intend to study an optimization version of SNL in a hope of further promoting the better understandings of SNL.

Let us consider the maximization problem, known as MAX-2SAT, in which one asks to find the truth assignment of a given 2CNF Boolean formula that maximizes the number of satisfying clauses of the formula. Apart from the studies on polynomial-time optimization, there have been a few works on logarithmic-space optimization [15,17]. Along this line of studies, we further explore logarithmic-space optimization and approximation schemes based on SNL.

Definition 13. *Similarly to the definition of* MAXSNP, *we define* MAXSNL *to be composed of all maximization problems, each of which asks to find a solution* $(P_1, P_2, \ldots, P_l)$ *satisfying* $\bigwedge_{i=1}^{l} Func(P_i)$ *that maximizes the value of the objective function* $\Pi(P_1, P_2, \ldots, P_l)$ *defined to be* $|\{(\boldsymbol{i}, \boldsymbol{y}) \mid \bigwedge_{j=1}^{t} \psi_j(P_1, P_2, \ldots, P_l, \boldsymbol{i}, \boldsymbol{y}, \boldsymbol{S}, \boldsymbol{c})\}|$, *where* $P_1, \ldots, P_l, \psi_j, \boldsymbol{i}, \boldsymbol{y}, \boldsymbol{S}, \boldsymbol{c}$ *with* $\boldsymbol{i} = (i_1, \ldots, i_r)$, $\boldsymbol{y} = (y_1, \ldots, y_s)$, $\boldsymbol{S} = (S_1, \ldots, S_d)$, *and* $\boldsymbol{c} = (c_1, \ldots, c_{d'})$ *are the same as those in Definition 2. Notice that each* ψ_j *must satisfy the second-order variable requirements.*

It is shown in [18] that the parameterized decision problem $(2\mathrm{SAT}, m_{ver})$ is in para-SNL (a parameterized version of SNL) by constructing an appropriate SNL sentence for $(2\mathrm{SAT}, m_{ver})$, where $m_{ver}(\phi)$ denotes the total number of variables appearing in a formula ϕ. From this SNL sentence, by eliminating the presence of m_{ver}, we can conclude that MAX-2SAT belongs to MAXSNL. As another concrete example, we consider MAX-CUT, in which one is to find a set S of vertices of a given undirected graph $G = (V, E)$ for which the number of edges crossing between S and $V - S$ is maximized.

Example 14. As an instance of MAX-CUT, we take an arbitrary undirected graph $G = (V_G, E_G)$ with $V_G = [n]$ and $E_G \subseteq [n] \times [n]$ for a number $n \in \mathbb{N}^+$. We introduce a predicate symbol E for which $E(i,j)$ means that (i,j) is an edge in E_G. We use a second-order variable P for which $P(i,1)$ (resp, $P(i,0)$) indicates that vertex i belongs to the desired set S (resp., $V_G - S$). Consider the following SNL sentence expressing the existence of such a set S: $\Phi \equiv \exists^f P \forall i \forall j [\phi_1(P,i) \wedge \phi_1(P,j) \wedge (E(i,j) \rightarrow \phi_2(P,E,i,j))]$, where $\phi_1 \equiv (P(i,0) \vee P(i,1)) \wedge \neg(P(i,0) \wedge P(i,1))$ and $\phi_2 \equiv (P(i,1) \wedge P(j,0)) \vee (P(i,0) \wedge P(j,1))$. We can conclude that MAX-CUT belongs to MAXSNL.

We discuss another example, called MAX-UK, which is a maximization version of UK (discussed in Example 7) of the following specific form: one asks to find a subset $S \subseteq [n]$ that maximizes $\sum_{i \in S} a_i$ within the upper bound b for a given series $(1^b, 1^{a_1}, 1^{a_2}, \ldots, 1^{a_n})$ of unary strings with $b, a_1, a_2, \ldots, a_n \in \mathbb{N}^+$.

Example 15. We assert that MAX-UK is in MAXSNL. To prove this assertion, we recall the predicate symbols and the formulas ψ_1 and ψ_2 from Example 7. We introduce a second-order variable P and then define $\Pi(P)$ as $|\{(i,s,t,j) \mid 0 \leq i < n \wedge s \leq j \leq t \wedge P(0,0) \wedge P(i,s) \wedge P(i+1,t) \wedge (s = t \leq b \vee (s < t \leq b \wedge (\psi_1 \rightarrow \psi_2)))\}|$. If we choose P to represents the value $\sum_{i \in S} a_i$ for a subset S of $[n]$, then its objective function $\Pi(P)$ can compute $\sum_{i \in S} a_i + n$. Notice that $\sum_{i \in S} a_i$ is the maximum iff $\Pi(P)$ is the maximum.

A special reduction, called (polynomial-time) linear reduction, was introduced in [12] for optimization problems in MAXSNP. Concerning log-space computing, we instead use the notion of logarithmic-space AP-reducibility [17, arXiv version]. Given two optimization (i.e., either maximization or minimization) problems P_1 and P_2, we say that P_1 is *logarithmic-space (or log-space) AP-reducible to* P_2 if there are two constants $c_1, c_2 > 0$ and two functions f and g in FL such that, for any value $r \in \mathbb{Q}^{>1}$, (i) for any instance x of P_1, $f(x,r)$ is an instance of P_2 and (ii) for any solution s to the instance $f(x,r)$ of P_2, $g(x,s,r)$ is a solution to the instance x of P_1 satisfying $err(x, g(x,s,r)) \leq c_2 \cdot err(f(x,r), s)$. Here, $err(u,z)$ denotes the value $\max\{\frac{cost(opt(u))}{cost(z)}, \frac{cost(z)}{cost(opt(u))}\} - 1$ for stings u and z, assuming that these denominators are not zero, where $opt(u)$ means an optimal solution to instance u and $cost(z)$ means the value (or cost) of string z. To distinguish this reduction from (standard) log-space many-one reductions, we use the special notation of $\leq^{\mathrm{L}}_{AP}$ to express the log-space AP-reduction.

Lemma 16. *Let r denote any nondecreasing function from* $\mathbb{N}$ *to* $\mathbb{N}$. *Given two optimization problems Ξ_1 and Ξ_2, if $\Xi_1 \leq^{\mathrm{L}}_{AP} \Xi_2$ and Ξ_2 is log-space approximable within ratio $r(n)$, then Ξ_1 is also log-space approximable within ratio $O(r(n^t + t))$ for a certain fixed constant $t \geq 1$.*

It is important to note that every minimization problem can be log-space AP-reducible to its associated maximization problem. See [12] for a similar treatment. This fact helps us focus only on maximization problems in what follows.

Proposition 17. $\leq^{\mathrm{L}}_{AP}(\mathrm{MAXSNP}) = \leq^{\mathrm{L}}_{AP}(\mathrm{MAXSNL})$.

Papadimitriou and Yannakakis [12] demonstrated that every maximization problem in MAXSNP can be polynomial-time linear reducible to MAX-3SAT. Their reduction is actually carried out using only log space. Therefore, every maximization problem in MAXSNP is also log-space AP-reducible to MAX-3SAT. We thus conclude the following.

Lemma 18. MAX-CUT *is complete for* MAXSNL *under log-space AP-reductions.*

Proposition 17 instantly follows from Lemma 18 since MAX-CUT is in MAXSNL by Example 14.

It was shown in [12, Theoprem 1] that every optimization problem in MAXSNP is approximated in polynomial time within a certain fixed approximation ratio. In this work, we intend to discuss how to solve optimization problems approximately using log-space computation, which were studied earlier in [15,17]. Following [17], we define APXL to be the collection of NL optimization problems that can be approximated in polynomial time using log space with fixed constant approximation ratios.

Proposition 19. MAX-UK *is in* APXL.

Proof. Let $(1^b, 1^{a_1}, 1^{a_2}, \ldots, 1^{a_n})$ be any instance to MAX-UK. Consider the following procedure. Since we can enumerate unary-form integers $a_1, a_2, \ldots, a_n$ given as $(1^{a_1}, 1^{a_2}, \ldots, 1^{a_n})$ in descending order using log space (see, e.g., [21]), we assume that $a_1 \geq a_2 \geq \cdots \geq a_n$ in the rest of our argument. We inductively construct a subset S of $[n]$ starting with $S = \varnothing$. By incrementing i by one from $i = 0$, we inductively pick a_i and check if $\sum_{j \in S} a_j + a_i \leq b$. If so, then we add i to S; otherwise, we do nothing.

We show that this is an approximation scheme with approximation ratio of at most 2. Let $S = \{i_1, i_2, \ldots, i_k\}$ be the set constructed by the approximation scheme. If $\sum_{i=1}^{n} a_i \leq b$, then we obtain $S = [n]$, and thus the procedure correctly solves the given problem. Next, let us consider the other case of $\sum_{i=1}^{n} a_i > b$. We assume that $\sum_{j \in S} a_j < \frac{b}{2}$. It follows that $i_k < n$. Because of $\sum_{j \in S} a_j + a_{i_k+1} > b$, we obtain $a_{i_k+1} > \frac{b}{2}$. Since $a_{i_1} \geq a_{i_2} \geq \cdots \geq a_{i_k} \geq a_{i_k+1}$, it follows that $a_{i_j} > \frac{b}{2}$ for all indices $j \in [k]$. This is in contradiction with $\sum_{j \in S} a_j < \frac{b}{2}$. Thus, $\sum_{j \in S} a_j \geq \frac{b}{2}$ must hold. Since the optimal solution has a value of at most b, the approximation ratio cannot exceed 2. □

We wish to generalize Proposition 19 by introducing MAXτSNL as a subclass of MAXSNL whose underlying objective functions $\Pi(P_1, \ldots, P_l)$ given in Definition 13 compute the values $|\{(i, \boldsymbol{s}, \boldsymbol{u}_i, \boldsymbol{v}_i, \boldsymbol{w}) \mid \bigwedge_{j=1}^{t} \psi_j\}|$ with $\boldsymbol{s} = (\boldsymbol{s}_1, \ldots, \boldsymbol{s}_l)$, $\boldsymbol{u}_i = (\boldsymbol{u}_{i,1}, \ldots, \boldsymbol{u}_{i,l})$, and $\boldsymbol{v}_i = (\boldsymbol{v}_{i,1}, \ldots, \boldsymbol{v}_{i,l})$, where each ψ_j can be rewritten as $\bigwedge_{k=1}^{l}(0 \leq i < n \wedge P_k(0, \boldsymbol{s}_k) \wedge (i \geq 1 \wedge P_k(i-1, \boldsymbol{u}_{i-1,k})) \wedge P_k(i, \boldsymbol{v}_{i,k}) \wedge R_j(i, \boldsymbol{s}_k, \boldsymbol{u}_{i-1,k}, \boldsymbol{u}_{i,k}, \boldsymbol{w}))$. Note that R_j has no second-order variable. Notice that all variables in the tuple $(i, \boldsymbol{s}_k, \boldsymbol{u}_{i-1,k}, \boldsymbol{u}_{i,k}, \boldsymbol{w})$ range over only polynomially many input objects. Let $P\lceil_{i-1} = (\boldsymbol{P}(0), \ldots, \boldsymbol{P}(i-1))$ with $\boldsymbol{P}(0) = (P_1(0, \boldsymbol{s}_1), \ldots, P_l(0, \boldsymbol{s}_l))$ and $\boldsymbol{P}(r) = (P_1(r, \boldsymbol{u}_{r,1}), \ldots, P_l(r, \boldsymbol{u}_{r,l}))$ for any $r \in [i-1]$. It is also required that, if $\boldsymbol{s}$ and $\boldsymbol{u}_{i-1}$ satisfy $\bigwedge_{k=1}^{l}(P_k(0, \boldsymbol{s}_k) \wedge (i \geq 1 \wedge P_k(i-1, \boldsymbol{u}_{i-1,k})))$, then $|G[P\lceil_{i-1}(\boldsymbol{v})]| \leq c'$ holds for a fixed constant $c' \geq 1$, where $G[P\lceil_{i-1}](\boldsymbol{v}) = \{\boldsymbol{w} \mid \bigwedge_{j=1}^{t} R_j(i, \boldsymbol{s}_k, \boldsymbol{u}_{i-1,k}, \boldsymbol{v}, \boldsymbol{w})\}$. Let $g_{P,i}(\boldsymbol{v}) = |G[P\lceil_{i-1}](\boldsymbol{v})|$. We demand the following two conditions: (1) if $\Pi(P\lceil_{i-1}) + g_{P,i}(\boldsymbol{v}) \leq \Pi(P_{opt})$, then $(\exists \boldsymbol{w})[R(i, \boldsymbol{u}_{i-1}, \boldsymbol{v}, \boldsymbol{w})]$ is true, where P_{opt} denotes the "optimal" choice of P, and (2) for any index $i \in [0, n-1]_{\mathbb{Z}}$, $\max_{\boldsymbol{v}}\{g_{P,i}(\boldsymbol{v})\} \geq \max_{\boldsymbol{v}'}\{g_{P,i+1}(\boldsymbol{v}')\}$ holds as long as $g_{P,i}(\cdot)$ and $g_{P,i+1}(\cdot)$ exist. The symbol "τ" in MAXτSNL indicates the "transitive" nature of $P_k(\cdot)$ used in the above SNL sentences. It follows by definition that MAX-UK belongs to MAXτSNL.

Theorem 20. *Every maximization problem in* MAXτSNL *is in* APXL.

5 Brief Conclusion and Open Questions

In this work, we have studied the properties of *Syntactic NL* (or succinctly, *SNL*), which was introduced in [18] in direct association with a practical, working hypothesis, known as the linear space hypothesis (LSH). In particular, we have focused on two major issues: (1) the expressibility of complementary problems of SNL problems together with an introduction of μSNL, which is a variant of

SNL, and (2) the computational complexity of the optimization version of SNL (called MAXSNL) together with its variant MAXτSNL. Still unknown is any of the following equalities: MAXSNL = MAXSNP and MAXτSNL = MAXSNL. We still wonder if all complementary problems of SNL problems are in SNL.

Appendix

This appendix provides the omitted proofs to the assertions that have been stated with no proofs in the main text.

Proof of Proposition 8. Let $A, B \in$ SNL be any two decision problems and take two SNL-sentences Φ_A and Φ_B that syntactically express A and B, respectively. Assume that $\Phi_A \equiv \exists^f P_1 \cdots \exists^f P_l \forall \boldsymbol{i} \forall \boldsymbol{y} [\bigwedge_{j=1}^{t} \psi_j]$ and $\Phi_B \equiv \exists^f R_1 \cdots \exists^f R_{l'} \forall \boldsymbol{i'} \forall \boldsymbol{y'} [\bigwedge_{j=1}^{s} \xi_j]$ for two constants $s, t \in \mathbb{N}^+$, where ψ_j's and $\xi_{j'}$'s are all quantifier-free formulas and $\boldsymbol{i}, \boldsymbol{i'}, \boldsymbol{y}, \boldsymbol{y'}$ are variable tuples. Assume further that each ψ_j has the form $\bigvee_{k_j} \hat{\psi}_{k_j}$ and that each $\xi_{j'}$ has the form $\bigvee_{l_{j'}} \hat{\xi}_{l_{j'}}$. Moreover, Φ_A and Φ_B are assumed to satisfy the second-order variable requirements. For simplicity, we also assume that $(P_1, \ldots, P_l, \boldsymbol{i}, \boldsymbol{y})$ and $(R_1, \ldots, R_{l'}, \boldsymbol{i'}, \boldsymbol{y'})$ do not share any common variables.

For the desired intersection $C = A \cap B$, we define $\Phi \equiv \Phi_A \wedge \Phi_B$, which is logically equivalent to $\exists^f P_1 \cdots \exists^f P_l \exists R_1 \cdots \exists^f R_l \forall \boldsymbol{i} \forall \boldsymbol{i'} \forall \boldsymbol{y} \forall \boldsymbol{y'} [(\bigwedge_j \psi_j) \wedge (\bigwedge_{j'} \xi_{j'})]$. Since each ψ_j and $\xi_{j'}$ satisfy the second-order variable requirements, so does the formula $(\bigwedge_j \psi_j) \wedge (\bigwedge_{j'} \xi_{j'})$.

For the case of union $C = A \cup B$, on the contrary, we cannot simply define another sentence Φ' as $\Phi' \equiv \Phi_A \vee \Phi_B$. Instead, we define Φ' as follows. We first introduce a new variable k, which is assumed to take either 1 or 2. This k is intended to indicate which of Φ_A and Φ_B is true. Let $\Phi' \equiv \exists^f P_1 \cdots \exists^f P_l \exists^f R_1 \cdots \exists^f R_{l'} \forall \boldsymbol{i} \forall \boldsymbol{y} \forall \boldsymbol{i'} \forall \boldsymbol{y'} \forall k [1 \leq k \leq 2 \rightarrow \Xi_1 \wedge \Xi_2]$, where $\Xi_1 \equiv k = 1 \rightarrow \bigwedge_j \psi_j$ and $\Xi_2 \equiv k = 2 \rightarrow \bigwedge_{j'} \xi_{j'}$. Notice that Ξ is logically equivalent to the conjunction of $\bigwedge_j (\neg(1 \leq k \leq 2) \vee k \neq 1 \vee \psi_j)$ and $\bigwedge_{j'} (\neg(1 \leq k \leq 2) \vee k \neq 2 \vee \xi_{j'})$.

It is not difficult to check that the formula $1 \leq k \leq 2 \rightarrow \Xi_1 \wedge \Xi_2$ satisfies the second-order variable requirements. □

Proof of Theorem 10. It is known that all decision problems in NL are solvable in polynomial time by appropriate *4-counter two-way nondeterministic counter automata* (2ncta's). See, e.g., [21, Proposition 2.3] for the proof of this fact. Let L denote an arbitrary decision problem in NL and take a 4-counter 2ncta M of the form $(Q, \Sigma, \{1\}, \{\triangleright, \triangleleft\}, \delta, q_0, \bot, Q_{acc}, Q_{rej})$ that solves L in polynomial time. Note that δ maps $(Q - Q_{halt}) \times \check{\Sigma} \times \{1, \bot\}^4$ to $Q \times D \times (\{1\}^* \cup \{\varepsilon\})^4$, where $\check{\Sigma} = \Sigma \cup \{\triangleright, \triangleleft\}$, $D = \{-1, +1\}$ (tape head directions) and $Q_{ha,t} = Q_{acc} \cup Q_{rej}$. To ease the description of the following construction, M is assumed to halt exactly in n^k steps (for a constant $k \in \mathbb{N}^+$) with the counters empty (except for $\bot$). Moreover, we assume that $Q_{acc} = \{q_{acc}\}$ and that M takes exactly two nondeterministic choices at any step (i.e., $|\delta(q, l, \boldsymbol{a})| = 2$ for any $(q, l, \boldsymbol{a})$).

Let us consider the decision problem $HALT_M$, in which, for any given x, we must determine whether there exists an accepting computation path of M on the input x. In what follows, we wish to show that $HALT_M$ is in SNL.

Hereafter, we fix an instance x arbitrarily. We intend to express an accepting computation path of M on x. A *configuration* is of the form $(q, l, \boldsymbol{w})$ with $q \in Q$, $l \in [0, |x|+1]_{\mathbb{Z}}$, and $\boldsymbol{w} = (w_1, w_2, w_3, w_4) \in (\{1\}^*\bot)^4$. This means that M is in inner state q, scanning the lth tape cell with the ith counter holding w_i. For two configurations $(q, l, \boldsymbol{w})$ and $(p, m, \boldsymbol{v})$, we write $(q, l, \boldsymbol{w}) \vdash (p, m, \boldsymbol{v})$ if M changes $(q, l, \boldsymbol{w})$ to $(p, m, \boldsymbol{v})$ in a single step. We prepare three predicate symbols, Top, $Chan$, and $Delt$, whose intended meanings are given as follows. (i) $Top(l, \boldsymbol{w}, c, \boldsymbol{a})$ is true iff $c = x_{(l)}$ and $\boldsymbol{a}$ is top symbols of the counters, (ii) $Chan(\boldsymbol{w}, \boldsymbol{b}, \boldsymbol{v})$ is true iff $\boldsymbol{w}$ is changed to $\boldsymbol{v}$ by modifying the top symbols of $\boldsymbol{w}$ to $\boldsymbol{b}$ by applying δ, and (iii) $Delt(q, c, \boldsymbol{a}, p, d, \boldsymbol{b})$ is true iff $(p, d, \boldsymbol{b}) \in \delta(q, c, \boldsymbol{a})$.

We also prepare a second-order variable P such that $P(i, q, l, \boldsymbol{w})$ is true iff $(q, l, \boldsymbol{w})$ is a configuration at time i. We then define Φ to be $(\exists^f P)(\forall u, u', z, p, q, l, c, d, \boldsymbol{w}, \boldsymbol{a}, \boldsymbol{b})[\Phi_1 \wedge \Phi_2]$, where $\Phi_1 \equiv 0 \leq i < n^k \wedge P(i, q, l, \boldsymbol{w}) \wedge P(i+1, p, l+d, \boldsymbol{v}) \wedge Top(l, \boldsymbol{w}, c, \boldsymbol{a}) \rightarrow \bigvee_{(p,d,\boldsymbol{b}) \in \delta(q,l,\boldsymbol{a})} (Delt(q, c, \boldsymbol{a}, p, d, \boldsymbol{b}) \wedge Chan(\boldsymbol{w}, \boldsymbol{b}, \boldsymbol{v}))$ and $\Phi_2 \equiv P(n^k, q, l, \boldsymbol{w}) \rightarrow (q, l, \boldsymbol{w}) = (q_{acc}, n, \bot, \ldots, \bot)$. This Φ is clearly an SNL sentence. It then follows by definition that Φ is true iff M has an accepting computation path on x. □

Proof of Lemma 16. Take two constants $c_1, c_2 > 0$ and two functions $f, g \in$ FL that make Ξ_1 log-space AP-reducible to Ξ_2 via (f, g, c_1, c_2). Take another function h in FL such that, for any x, $h(x)$ is an approximate solution to the instance x of Ξ_2 within approximation ratio $r(|x|)$. In what follows, we intend to construct another function k that produces an approximate solution to each instance of Ξ_1.

Consider the composite function $k = g \circ h \circ f$. For any instance x, since $f(x)$ is an instance of Ξ_2, $h \circ f(x)$ is a solution to the instance $f(x)$. Thus, $k(x)$ is an approximate solution to the instance x of Ξ_1. It then follows that $cost(opt(x)) \leq c_1 \cdot cost(opt(f(x)))$ and $err(k(x), opt(x)) \leq c_2 \cdot err(h \circ f(x), opt(f(x)))$. Since the approximation ratio $r(|z|)$ for Ξ_2 equals $err(h(z), opt(z)) + 1$ for any instance z of Ξ_2, it follows that $err(h \circ f(x), opt(f(x)))$ equals $r(|f(x)|) - 1$. Thus, the value $err(k(x), opt(x)) + 1$ is upper-bounded by $c_2(r(|f(x)|) - 1) + 1$. Since $|f(x)| \leq |x|^t + t$ for a certain constant $t \in \mathbb{N}^+$, $err(k(x), opt(x)) + 1$ is at most $c_2 \cdot r(|x|^t + t) + 1$. This implies that Ξ_1 is approximable within ratio $c_2 r(|x|^t + t) + 1$. □

Proof of Lemma 18. Let us recall from Example 14 that MAX-CUT is in MAXSNL. Consider any maximization problem Ξ in MAXSNL with an associated SNL sentence Φ of the form $\exists^f P_1 \cdots \exists^f P_l \forall \boldsymbol{i} \forall \boldsymbol{y} [\bigwedge_{j=1}^t \phi_j(P_1, \ldots, P_l, \boldsymbol{i}, \boldsymbol{y})]$. We take three steps to construct a reduction from Ξ to MAX-CUT. Firstly, we reduce Ξ to MAX-2SAT and then reduce MAX-2SAT to MAX-WTDCUT. Here, MAX-WTDCUT is a "weighted" version of MAX-CUT, which is obtained by allowing each edge to hold a (positive integer) weight and maximizing the total weight of edges whose endpoints are assigned to two different sets S and $V - S$. Finally, we reduce MAX-WTDCUT to MAX-CUT.

When a domain structure $\mathcal{D}_x$ for Φ is given for an instance x, the variable tuples $(\boldsymbol{i}, \boldsymbol{y})$ take only polynomially many different values. We assign those values $(\bar{\boldsymbol{\imath}}, \bar{\boldsymbol{y}})$ to $(\boldsymbol{i}, \boldsymbol{y})$ one by one to generate polynomially many "formulas" $\phi_j(P_1, \ldots, P_l, \bar{\boldsymbol{\imath}}, \bar{\boldsymbol{y}})$. Notice that ϕ_j can be rewritten as a formula with variables of the form $P_k(\bar{\imath}, \bar{y})$ and the constants T(true) and F (false) because $S_r(\bar{\boldsymbol{\imath}}, \bar{\boldsymbol{y}})$'s are evaluated to be either T or F.

The reduction MAX-2SAT $\leq^{\mathrm{L}}_{AP}$ MAX-WTDCUT is given as follows. We loosely follow an argument of [12, Theorem 2]. Let ϕ be any 2CNF Boolean formula of the form $\bigwedge_{i=1}^{t} \phi_i$ with $\phi_i \equiv z_{i,1} \vee z_{i,2}$ for literals $z_{i,1}$ and $z_{i,2}$. We then construct a weighted undirected graph $G = (V, E)$. The vertices are variables as well as their negations together with a special vertex w. Sequentially, we choose a clause ϕ_i and then add three edges to form a triangle among three vertices $z_{i,1}, z_{i,2}, w$. Moreover, we add an edge between every variable x and its negation $\bar{x}$ with weight of $2k$, where k is the number of times that x or $\bar{x}$ appears in ϕ. The weight of any edge in each triangle $(z_{i,1}, z_{i,2}, w)$ is $2k$, where k is the number of clauses in which the pair $z_{i,1}, z_{i,2}$ appears simultaneously (ignoring their appearance order). This modification can be done in log space. As argued in [12], the objective value is twice as large as the sum of the numbers of literal occurrences and of satisfying clauses.

The third reduction MAX-WTDCUT $\leq^{\mathrm{L}}_{AP}$ MAX-CUT is done as follows. Notice that the weight of each edge is an even number. For each edge (v_1, v_2) with weight $2k$, we prepare k new vertices, say, $u_1, u_2, \ldots, u_k$ and add two edges (v_1, u_i) and (u_i, v_2) for each index $i \in [k]$. □

Proof of Theorem 20. Let D denote any maximization problem in MAXτSNL and take an objective function $\Pi(P_1, \ldots, P_l)$ associated with D in the definition of MAXτSNL. To simplify the subsequent argument, assuming $l = t = 1$, we write P_l as P and drop "k" and "j" from, e.g., $\boldsymbol{u}_{i,k}$, R_j, and ψ_j. Hence, the formula ψ used to define the objective function can be rewritten as $0 \leq i < n \wedge P(0, \boldsymbol{s}) \wedge (i \geq 1 \wedge P(i-1, \boldsymbol{u}_{i-1})) \wedge P(i, \boldsymbol{v}_i) \wedge R_j(i, \boldsymbol{s}, \boldsymbol{u}_{i-1}, \boldsymbol{v}_i, \boldsymbol{w})$. Note that variables and variable tuples $b, \boldsymbol{s}, \boldsymbol{u}_{i-1}, \boldsymbol{v}_i, \boldsymbol{w}$ are all evaluated as log-size objects.

The following approximation scheme is a generalization of the one given in the proof of Proposition 19. We consider the following recursive procedure on the value of i. Assume that $0 < i \leq n$. By induction hypothesis, we assume that $\boldsymbol{s}$ and $\boldsymbol{u}_{i-1}$ are already determined, and thus $P(0, \boldsymbol{s})$ and $P(i-1, \boldsymbol{u}_{i-1})$ are all true. At this moment, unknown is the value of $\boldsymbol{v}$ in $P(i, \boldsymbol{v})$. To determine this $\boldsymbol{v}$, we calculate $g_{P,i}(\boldsymbol{v})$ for all possible $\boldsymbol{v}$'s. If there is no such $\boldsymbol{v}$, then we terminate the procedure. Otherwise, we enumerate $\boldsymbol{v}$'s in a decreasing order according to the values of $|G[P\lceil_{i-1}](\boldsymbol{v})|$. We then choose the largest $\boldsymbol{v}$ making $R(i, \boldsymbol{s}, \boldsymbol{u}_{i-1}\boldsymbol{v}, \boldsymbol{w})$ true. We then make $P(i, \boldsymbol{v})$ true, output it, and move on to the next recursive step.

Take a maximal index $i_0 \in [n]$ satisfying $\Pi(P) = \Pi(P\lceil_{i_0})$. Since $\Pi(P\lceil_{i_0}) < \Pi(P_{opt})/2$, it follows that $g_{P,i_0}(\boldsymbol{v}_{i_0}) \leq \Pi(P\lceil_{i_0}) < \Pi(P_{opt})/2$. Let us consider $P(i_0 + 1, \cdot)$. If there exists an element $\boldsymbol{v}$ satisfying $g_{P,i_0+1}(\boldsymbol{v}) \leq \Pi(P_{opt})/2$, then we obtain $\Pi(P\lceil_{i_0}) + g_{P,i_0+1}(\boldsymbol{v}) \leq \Pi(P_{opt})$, which implies that $(\exists \boldsymbol{w})R(i_0 + 1, \boldsymbol{s}, \boldsymbol{u}_{i_0}, \boldsymbol{v}, \boldsymbol{w})$ is true. This means that the approximation scheme must have proceeded on $i_0 + 1$. Thus, we conclude that $g_{P,i_0+1}(\boldsymbol{v}) > \Pi(P_{opt})/2$ for any $\boldsymbol{v}$. This implies that $g_{P,i_0}(\boldsymbol{v}_{i_0}) < g_{P,i_0+1}(\boldsymbol{v})$. This is in contradiction with the definition of MAXτSNL. □

References

1. Àvarez, C., Greenlaw, R.: A compendium of problems complete for symmetric space. Comput. Complex. **9**, 123–145 (2000)
2. Bringman, K., Cassis, A., Fisher, N., Künnemann, M.: Fine-grained completeness for optimization in P. In: APPROX/RANDOM 2021, LIPIcs, vol. 207, pp. 9:1–9:22 (2021). An extended version is available at arXiv:2107.01721
3. Cook, S.A.: The complexity of theorem-proving procedures. In: STOC'71, pp. 151–158 (1971)
4. Cook, S.A.: A taxonomy of problems with fast parallel algorithms. Inform. Control **64**, 2–22 (1985)
5. Feder, T., Vardi, M.Y.: Monotone monadic SNP and constraint satisfaction. In: STOC'93, pp. 612–622 (1993)
6. Feder, T., Vardi, M.: The computational structure of monotone monadic SNP and constraint satsifaction: a study through Datalog and group theory. SIAM J. Comput. **28**, 57–104 (1999)
7. Immerman, N.: Nondeterministic space is closed under complement. SIAM J. Comput. **17**, 935–938 (1988)
8. Impagliazzo, R., Paturi, R.: On the complexity of k-SAT. J. Comput. System Sci. **62**, 367–375 (2001)
9. Impagliazzo, R., Paturi, R., Zane, F.: Which problems have strongly exponential complexity? J. Comput. System Sci. **63**, 512–530 (2001)
10. Jones, N.D.: Space-bounded reducibility among combinatorial problems. J. Comput. System Sci. **11**, 68–75 (1975)
11. Jones, N.D., Lien, Y.E., Laaser, W.T.: New problems complete for nondeterministic log space. Math. Systems Theory **10**, 1–17 (1976)
12. Papadimitriou, C.H., Yannakakis, M.: Optimization, approximation, and complexity classes. J. Comput. System Sci. **43**, 425–440 (1991)
13. Reingold, O.: Undirected connectivity in log-space. J. ACM **55**, article 17 (2008)
14. Szelepcsényi, R.: The method of forced enumeration for nondeterministic automata. Acta Inform. **26**, 279–284 (1988)
15. Tantau, T.: Logspace optimization problems and their approximation properties. Theory Comput. Syst. **41**, 327–350 (2007)
16. Williams, R.: Exact algorithms for maximum two-satisfiability. In: Encyclopedia of Algorithms, second edition (M-Y Kao, ed), pp. 683–688, Springer Reference (2016). https://doi.org/10.1007/978-1-4939-2864-4_227
17. Yamakami, T.: Uniform-circuit and logarithmic-space approximations of refined combinatorial optimization problems. In: COCOA 2013, LNCS, vol.8287, pp. 318–329 (2013). A complete and corrected version is available at arXiv:1601.01118
18. Yamakami, T.: The 2CNF Boolean formula satisfiability problem and the linear space hypothesis. J. Comput. System Sci. **136**, 88–112 (2023). A preliminary version appeared in the Proc. of MFCS 2017, LIPIcs, vol. 83, pp. 62:1–62:14 (2017)
19. Yamakami, T.: Parameterized graph connectivity and polynomail-time sub-linear-space short reductions (preliminary report). In: RP 2017, LNCS vol. 10506, pp. 176–191, Springer (2017). https://doi.org/10.1007/978-3-319-67089-8_13

20. Yamakami, T.: State complexity characterizations of parameterized degree-bounded graph connectivity, sub-linear space computation, and the linear space hypothesis. Theor. Comput. Sci. **798**, 2–22 (2019)
21. Yamakami, T.: When input integers are given in the unary numeral representation. In: ICTCS 2023, CEUR Workshop Proceedings (CEUR-WS.org), vol. 3587, pp. 268–282 (2023)

Polyadic Quantifiers on Dependent Types

Marek Zawadowski[1] and Justyna Grudzińska[2](✉)

[1] Faculty of Mathematics, Informatics and Mechanics, University of Warsaw, Warsaw, Poland
zawado@mimuw.edu.pl
[2] Faculty of Philosophy, University of Warsaw, Warsaw, Poland
j.grudzinska@uw.edu.pl

Abstract. An interaction between dependency relations and quantification underlies numerous phenomena in natural language. Dependencies are responsible for inverting scope, as illustrated by the example *a day of every month*. The *part-whole* relation, expressed by the preposition *of* in this example, introduces a dependency between wholes (months) and their respective parts (days). Quantifying over this dependency yields the inverse scope reading: for every month, there is a different day that belongs to it. Dependencies are also needed for tracking anaphoric reference to quantifier domains, as illustrated by the sentence *Every farmer who owns a donkey beats it*. By quantifying universally over the dependency between each of the farmers and the donkeys owned by them, we obtain the intended reading that every farmer beats every donkey he owns. In this paper, we show that polyadic quantifiers on dependent types are well-suited for modelling the interaction of dependency relations and quantification in these phenomena. Then we present, in a conceptual way, the mathematics behind the process of polyadic quantification over dependent types. The main new feature is the left strength on the cartesian monad over a basic fibration of a topos. It combines with what we call the right strength into an operation (pile'up) that turns tuples of quantifiers into polyadic ones.

Keywords: natural language quantification · polyadic quantifier · dependent type

1 Introduction

An interaction between dependency relations and quantification underlies numerous phenomena in natural language. Dependencies are responsible for inverting scope. Consider, for instance, the example in (1) that contains two scopally interacting quantified NPs (underlined below):

(1) A day of every month.

The research for this article is funded by the National Science Center, Poland (Grant No. DEC-2019/35/B/HS1/01541).

G. Metcalfe et al. (Eds.): WoLLIC 2024, LNCS 14672, pp. 278–291, 2024.
https://doi.org/10.1007/978-3-031-62687-6_18

Example (1) supports the inverse scope reading saying that there is a different day belonging to every month (*every month* > *a day*). The surface scope reading saying that there is some one day that belongs to every month (*a day* > *every month*) is strongly dispreferred in this example because it is contradicted by what we know about parts and wholes, namely that we can have many parts (days) belonging to the same whole (month), but a single part (day) cannot belong to more than one whole (month). The *part-whole* relation, expressed by the preposition *of* in (1), introduces a dependency between each whole (month) and its respective parts (days), and by quantifying over this dependency, we obtain the inverse scope reading for the example in question (see, e.g., [11,14]). Dependencies are also needed for tracking anaphoric reference to quantifier domains, as illustrated in example (2):

(2) Every farmer who owns a donkey beats it.

By quantifying universally over the dependency between each of the farmers and the donkeys owned by them, we obtain the intended reading for (2) that every farmer beats every donkey he owns (see, e.g., [4,6–8,29,30]). In the rest of this section, we show how polyadic quantifiers on dependent types can be used to model the interaction of dependency relations and quantification in these phenomena.

1.1 Dependent Types

The concept of dependent types is at the heart of a modern type-theoretical setting (see, e.g., [9,10,14,20,21,23–25,28]). Modern type-theoretical frameworks include many base types. Nominals (e.g. *month*) can be treated as types (e.g., type $Month$) and interpreted as sets of objects (e.g., set $|Month|$ of months). In a framework with many types, we can have dependent types, i.e., types can depend on the variables of other types. For instance, we know that parts (days) are dependent on wholes (months). Formally, the fact that the type of days depends on (the variables of) the type of months can be interpreted as a function (dependency): $\pi : |Day| \to |Month|$ (or, if one prefers, as an indexed family of sets). For any month $a \in |M|$, there is a corresponding set (fiber) $|D|_a = \pi^{-1}(a)$ of the days of that month (the inverse image of $\{a\}$ under π). If M is a type and D is a type depending on M, we can also form dependent sum types $\Sigma_{m:M} D(m)$ (whose interpretation consists of pairs $\langle a, b\rangle$ such that $a \in |M|$ and $b \in |D|(a)$), abbreviated as ΣD below, and dependent product types $\Pi_{m:M} D(m)$ (whose interpretation consists of functions which assign to each $a \in |M|$ an element of $|D|(a)$).

Furthermore, we can have contexts (lists of typed variables), i.e., databases that store (possibly nested) dependencies. Formally, context is (a linearization of) a partially ordered set of type declarations of the (individual) variables such that the declaration of a variable x of type X precedes the declaration of a variable y of type $Y(x)$:

$$\Gamma = x : X, y : Y(x), z : Z(x, y), u : U, \ldots$$

In the above example, type Y depends on the variable x of type X; type Z depends on the variables x and y of types X and Y, respectively; and types X and U are constant types (i.e., they do not depend on any variables). Dependencies given in the context determine the relative scoping of quantifiers, i.e., certain scopal configurations are compatible with the above context and certain scopal configurations are disallowed. For example, the interpretation of a construction with two quantifiers where $Q_{1\,x:X}$ outscopes $Q_{2\,y:Y(x)}$ ($Q_{1\,x:X} > Q_{2\,y:Y(x)}$) is available, whereas an interpretation where $Q_{2\,y:Y(x)}$ outscopes $Q_{1\,x:X}$ ($Q_{2\,y:Y(x)} > Q_{1\,x:X}$) is not available.

1.2 Polyadic Quantifiers

Quantified NPs (e.g., *every month*, *a day*, *most farmers*, etc.) are interpreted as generalized quantifiers (see, e.g., [1,3,15,27,32]). A generalized quantifier on a set X is an element of $\mathcal{C}(X)$, which is the value of the continuation monad $\mathcal{C}$ on X, i.e., for set X, $\mathcal{C}(X) = \mathcal{P}^2(X)$ where: $\mathcal{P}(X) = (X \to \mathbf{t})$, $\mathcal{C}(X) = (X \to \mathbf{t}) \to \mathbf{t}$, with $\mathbf{t} = \{\mathbf{true}, \mathbf{false}\}$. One major scope assignment strategy for multiply quantified constructions involves polyadic quantification (see, e.g., [17–19,26,33,34]). In this strategy, the scope relations for multi-quantifier constructions are derived by turning a sequence of quantifiers into a polyadic quantifier, using what we call left and right **pile′up**-operations (also known as iterations):

$$\mathbf{pile'up}^l, \mathbf{pile'up}^r : \mathcal{C}(X) \times \mathcal{C}(Y) \longrightarrow \mathcal{C}(X \times Y)$$

defined, for $\mathbf{M} : \mathcal{C}(X)$ and $\mathbf{N} : \mathcal{C}(Y)$, by lambda terms as:

$$\mathbf{pile'up}^l(\mathbf{M}, \mathbf{N}) = \lambda c_{:\mathcal{P}(X \times Y)}.\mathbf{M}(\lambda x_{:X}.\mathbf{N}(\lambda y_{:Y} c(x, y)))$$

and

$$\mathbf{pile'up}^r(\mathbf{M}, \mathbf{N}) = \lambda c_{:\mathcal{P}(X \times Y)}.\mathbf{N}(\lambda y_{:Y}.\mathbf{M}(\lambda x_{:X} c(x, y))).$$

The polyadic quantifier thus formed is then applied to the predicate. This scope assignment strategy can be straightforwardly extended to account for sentences involving three or more quantified NPs by allowing their permutations.

1.3 Polyadic Quantifiers on Dependent Types

Phenomena involving the interaction of dependency relations and quantification, as in (1) and (2), can be given an adequate analysis in terms of polyadic quantification over dependent types. For example, the *part-whole* relation, as expressed by the preposition *of* in (1), induces a dependency between wholes (months) and their respective parts (days):

$$m : Month, d : Day(m),$$

By quantifying over this dependency, we get the inverse ordering of the quantifiers involved:

$$\forall_{m:M} \exists_{d:D(m)}$$

In this case, only one dependent **pile′up**-operation can be derived. It has the following form:

$$\mathbf{dpile'up} : \Pi_{m:M}\mathcal{C}(D(m))\times\mathcal{C}(M) \longrightarrow \mathcal{C}(\Sigma D)$$

defined, for $\mathbf{M} : \Pi_{m:M}\mathcal{C}(D(m))$ and $\mathbf{N} : \mathcal{C}(M)$, by:

$$\mathbf{dpile'up}(\mathbf{M}, \mathbf{N}) = \lambda c_{:\mathcal{P}(\Sigma D)}\mathbf{N}(\lambda m_{:M}.\mathbf{M}(m)(\lambda d_{:D(m)}.c(m, d))).$$

1.4 Previous Work

In [12], it was shown that **pile′up**-operations combining quantifiers into polyadic ones can be derived from the strengths of the continuation monad. Here, we only recall the definitions of the continuation monad, strengths and derived **pile′up**-operations. For a more thorough understanding, readers are encouraged to consult [12,13].

Let us consider the category of sets *Set*, with sets as objects and functions between sets as morphisms. A monad on *Set* is a triple (T, η, μ), where $T : Set \longrightarrow Set$ is an endofunctor (the underlying functor of the monad), and $\eta : 1_{Set} \longrightarrow T$ and $\mu : T^2 \longrightarrow T$ are natural transformations. For the continuation monad, denoted $\mathcal{C}$, its functor part, at the level of objects, is a twice-iterated power-set construction, i.e., for set X, $\mathcal{C}(X) = \mathcal{P}^2(X)$. At the level of morphisms, it is an inverse image of an inverse image, i.e., function $f : X \longrightarrow Y$ induces an inverse image function between powersets:

$$\mathcal{P}(f) = f^{-1} : \mathcal{P}(Y) \longrightarrow \mathcal{P}(X).$$

Taking again an inverse image function, we have:

$$\mathcal{C}(f) = \mathcal{P}(f^{-1}) : \mathcal{C}(X) \longrightarrow \mathcal{C}(Y).$$

The **unit** lifts elements of X as $\mathcal{C}$-computations.

$$\eta_X : X \longrightarrow \mathcal{C}(X).$$

The **multiplication** flattens $\mathcal{C}$-computations on $\mathcal{C}$-computations to $\mathcal{C}$-computations.

$$\mu_X : \mathcal{C}^2(X) \longrightarrow \mathcal{C}(X).$$

Strengths, left and right, allow to lift pairs of $\mathcal{C}$-computations to $\mathcal{C}$-computations on products.

$$\mathbf{st}^l : \mathcal{C}(X) \times Y \longrightarrow \mathcal{C}(X \times Y)$$

$$\mathbf{st}^r : X \times \mathcal{C}(Y) \longrightarrow \mathcal{C}(X \times Y)$$

Using both strengths, we can derive two **pile′up**-operations, left and right.

– The **left pile up**

$$\mathbf{pile'up}^{l}{}_{X,Y} = \mu_{X\times Y} \circ \mathcal{C}(\mathbf{st}^{r}{}_{X,Y}) \circ \mathbf{st}^{l}{}_{X,\mathcal{C}(Y)} : \mathcal{C}(X)\times\mathcal{C}(Y) \longrightarrow \mathcal{C}(X\times Y)$$

defined from the diagram:

$$\begin{array}{ccc} \mathcal{C}(X)\times\mathcal{C}(Y) & \xrightarrow{\mathbf{pile'up}^{l}{}_{X,Y}} & \mathcal{C}(X\times Y) \\ {\scriptstyle \mathbf{st}^{l}{}_{X,\mathcal{C}(Y)}}\Big\downarrow & & \Big\uparrow{\scriptstyle \mu_{X\times Y}} \\ \mathcal{C}(X\times\mathcal{C}(Y)) & \xrightarrow[\mathcal{C}(\mathbf{st}^{r}{}_{X,Y})]{} & \mathcal{C}^2(X\times Y) \end{array}$$

– The **right pile up**

$$\mathbf{pile'up}^{r}{}_{X,Y} = \mu_{X\times Y} \circ \mathcal{C}(\mathbf{st}^{l}{}_{X,Y}) \circ \mathbf{st}^{r}{}_{\mathcal{C}(X),Y} : \mathcal{C}(X)\times\mathcal{C}(Y) \longrightarrow \mathcal{C}(X\times Y),$$

defined from the diagram:

$$\begin{array}{ccc} \mathcal{C}(X)\times\mathcal{C}(Y) & \xrightarrow{\mathbf{pile'up}^{r}{}_{X,Y}} & \mathcal{C}(X\times Y) \\ {\scriptstyle \mathbf{st}^{r}{}_{\mathcal{C}(X),Y}}\Big\downarrow & & \Big\uparrow{\scriptstyle \mu_{X\times Y}} \\ \mathcal{C}(\mathcal{C}(X)\times Y) & \xrightarrow[\mathcal{C}(\mathbf{st}^{l}{}_{X,Y})]{} & \mathcal{C}^2(X\times Y) \end{array}$$

In the first diagram, the operation $\mathbf{pile'up}^{l}{}_{X,Y}$ is defined as a composition of three operations: the first takes the $\mathcal{C}$-computation on X 'outside' to be a computation on $X \times \mathcal{C}(Y)$, the second takes the $\mathcal{C}$-computation on Y 'outside' to be a $\mathcal{C}$-computation on $X \times Y$. In this way, we have $\mathcal{C}$-computations coming from X on $\mathcal{C}$-computations coming from Y on $X \times Y$. Now the last morphism $\mu_{X\times Y}$ flattens these two levels to one, i.e., the $\mathcal{C}$-computation on $\mathcal{C}$-computations to $\mathcal{C}$-computations. In the second diagram, the operation $\mathbf{pile'up}^{r}{}_{X,Y}$ takes the $\mathcal{C}$-computations in reverse order and so they pile up in the opposite way.

In the rest of this paper, we describe the mathematical aspects of polyadic quantification lifted to dependent types. In the context of quantification over simple types the strengths are used to combine (possibly generalized) quantifiers into polyadic quantifiers on the product of types. To explain the semantics of generalized quantifiers over dependent types in an analogous way, we use the basic fibration over *Set* or any other elementary topos $\mathcal{S}$. Moreover, we need a cartesian monad $\mathbf{T}$ over basic fibration $\mathcal{S}^{\rightarrow} \rightarrow \mathcal{S}$ with suitably generalized notions of strengths, left and right. As we will see, the left strength is more problematic and, as a result, we can pile up terms/quantifiers only one way. This is an explanation of why the order of quantification over dependent types is fixed.

2 Fibrations

In this section we describe the mathematical/logical/categorical notions needed to describe the semantic operation used to combine quantifiers into polyadic ones in the context of dependent types.

2.1 Basic Fibration of a Topos

Let $\mathcal{S}$ be an elementary topos. In the following applications, $\mathcal{S}$ will be *Set*, the category of sets and functions. We will illustrate the notions introduced in this section in *Set*, but the considerations are of a more general nature and can be used in a more demanding constructive and/or intensional context. This is why it is natural to keep it at this level of generality. For unexplained notions concerning category theory, categorical logic, fibration, the reader can consult [2,5,16,22,31].

The fundamental fibration $\pi : \mathcal{S}^{\rightarrow} \rightarrow \mathcal{S}$ is a functor from the arrow category $\mathcal{S}^{\rightarrow}$ to $\mathcal{S}$, sending a map $a : A \rightarrow X$ to X. The fiber of π over object X is denoted $\mathcal{S}_X$, and it is the category of objects and morphisms of $\mathcal{S}^{\rightarrow}$ that are sent by π to X and id_X, respectively. $\mathcal{S}_X$ can be thought of as a category of families in $\mathcal{S}$ indexed by a fixed object X. For any morphism $f : Y \rightarrow X$ in $\mathcal{S}$, there is a reindexing/pullback functor $f^* : \mathcal{S}_X \longrightarrow \mathcal{S}_Y$ that has both adjoints $\Sigma_f \dashv f^* \dashv \Pi_f$. For $a : A \rightarrow Y$, $\Sigma_f(A, a) = (A, f \circ a)$ is a dependent sum and $\Pi_f(A, a)$ is a dependent product. The cartesian morphism $ca_{f,(A,a)}$ over $f : Y \rightarrow X$ with codomain $a : A \rightarrow X$ in $\mathcal{S}_X$ is given by the pullback:

$$\begin{array}{ccc} f^*(A) & \xrightarrow{ca_{f,(A,a)}} & A \\ \downarrow & & \downarrow a \\ Y & \xrightarrow[f]{} & X \end{array}$$

The cocartesian morphism $cc_{f,(B,b)}$ over $f : Y \rightarrow X$ with domain $a : B \rightarrow Y$ in $\mathcal{S}_Y$ is given by the square:

$$\begin{array}{ccc} B & \xrightarrow{cc_{f,(B,b)} = 1_B} & B \\ b \downarrow & & \downarrow f \circ b \\ Y & \xrightarrow[f]{} & X \end{array}$$

We write $\Sigma_f(B, b) = (B, f \circ b)$.

In *Set*, if $a : A \rightarrow Y$ is a function, i.e. an object of Set_Y, we write A_y for the fiber of a over $y \in Y$, i.e., the set $a^{-1}(y) = \{a \in A | f(a) = y\}$. The dependent product of (A, a) along $f : Y \rightarrow X$ is given by the formula:

$$\Pi_f(A, a) = (\coprod_{x \in X} \prod_{y \in Y_x} A_y, a_f).$$

Thus an element of $\Pi_f(A, a)$ in the fiber over x is a local section of a defined on the fiber of f over x, i.e., it is a pair $\langle x, s : Y_x \to A \rangle$ such that $a(s(y)) = y$, for $y \in Y_x$. We have $a_f(x, s) = x$.

2.2 Cartesian Monads over a Topos

Cartesian monad $\mathbf{T}$ on the fundamental fibration of topos $\mathcal{S}$ in a 2-category of fibrations over $\mathcal{S}$ is an endofunctor:

$$\begin{array}{ccc} \mathcal{S}^{\to} & \xrightarrow{\ \mathbf{T}\ } & \mathcal{S}^{\to} \\ & {\scriptstyle \pi}\searrow \quad \swarrow{\scriptstyle \pi} & \\ & \mathcal{S} & \end{array}$$

commuting over the base $\mathcal{S}$ and preserving cartesian morphism, together with vertical natural transformations $\eta : 1_{\mathcal{S}^{\to}} \to \mathbf{T}$, $\mu : \mathbf{T}^2 \to \mathbf{T}$ satisfying $\mu\mathbf{T}(\eta) = 1_{\mathbf{T}} = \mu\eta_{\mathbf{T}}$ and $\mu\mu_{\mathbf{T}} = \mu\mathbf{T}(\mu)$. Intuitively, monad $\mathbf{T}$ applies to fibers of the indexed families.

Such a monad $\mathbf{T}$ restricts to monads on fibers $\mathbf{T}_X : \mathcal{S}_X \to \mathcal{S}_X$. In the following, we list some morphisms between such monads. For a morphism $f : Y \to X$ in $\mathcal{S}$, we have a natural isomorphism $\iota : \mathbf{T}_Y \circ f^* \to f^* \circ \mathbf{T}_X : Set_X \to Set_Y$ which is a part of a (strong) morphism of monads $(f^*, \iota) : \mathbf{T}_Y \to \mathbf{T}_X$.

Examples. The main example (for us) of a cartesian monad is the continuation monad. The object $(\Omega_X, \omega_X) = (\Omega \times X, \pi_2)$ is the subobject classifier in the topos $\mathcal{S}_X$. The functor part of the continuation monad $\mathcal{C}$ is given, for an object (A, a) in $\mathcal{S}_X$, by

$$\mathcal{C}_X(A, a) = (\Omega_X, \omega_X)^{(\Omega_X, \omega_X)^{(A,a)}}.$$

This functor can be thought of as the composition with itself of the contravariant powerset functor $\mathcal{P}$ (from the dual of the fundamental fibration of $\mathcal{S}$) given, for an object (A, a) in $\mathcal{S}_X$, by

$$\mathcal{P}_X(A, a) = (\Omega_X, \omega_X)^{(A,a)}.$$

One can easily check that, for $f : Y \to X$ in $\mathcal{S}$, we have a natural isomorphism $\Pi_f \circ \mathcal{P}_Y \to \mathcal{P}_X \circ \Sigma_f : \mathcal{E}_Y \longrightarrow \mathcal{E}_X$.

In fundamental fibration over set Set the continuation monad $\mathcal{C}$, applied to an object $a : A \to X$ in Set_X, is a family $\{\mathcal{P}\mathcal{P}(A_x)\}_{x \in X}$ with the obvious projection.

3 Strengths on a Cartesian Monad

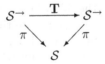

The strength $\mathbf{st}^{\mathbf{T}}_{X,Y} : X \times T(Y) \to \mathbf{T}(X \times Y)$ on a monad $\mathbf{T}$ on a category with finite products lifts 'terms' from object Y to the 'terms' on product with another object, say X. In Set this map can be defined via some sections of the projection $\pi_2 : X \times Y \to Y$. Note that any element $x \in X$ gives rise to a section $s_x : Y \to X \times Y$, so that $s_x(y) = \langle x, y\rangle$. Then $\mathbf{st}^{\mathbf{T}}_{X,Y}(x,t) = \mathbf{T}(s_x)(t)$, for $x \in X$ and $t \in \mathbf{T}(Y)$. Since the product is symmetric, we have another strength $\mathbf{st'}^{\mathbf{T}}_{X,Y} : T(X) \times Y \to \mathbf{T}(X \times Y)$, induced by the symmetry.

If we think about an object $a : A \to X$ of $\mathcal{S}_X$ as a 'product of X with a varying fiber $\{A_x\}_{x \in X}$', then we can generalize the notion of strength in two ways. The right strength lifts 'terms' on the fibers of a to the 'terms' on the whole A, and the left strength lifts 'terms' from X, the codomain of a, to the 'terms' on the whole A.

3.1 Strength

A strong monad (T, η, μ) on a category with product $\mathcal{S}$ is a monad equipped with a natural transformation (strength) $\mathbf{st}^T$ between functors from $\mathcal{S} \times \mathcal{S}$ to $\mathcal{S}$ such that, for X, Y in $\mathcal{S}$, we have maps $\mathbf{st}^T_{X,Y} : X \times T(Y) \to T(X \times Y)$. Moreover, for X, Y, Z in $\mathcal{S}$, the following diagrams commute:

$$\begin{array}{ccc} 1 \times T(X) & \xrightarrow{\mathbf{st}^T_{1,X}} & T(1 \times X) \\ & {\scriptstyle \pi_2} \searrow \quad \swarrow {\scriptstyle T(\pi_2)} & \\ & T(X) & \end{array}$$

and

$$\begin{array}{ccc} X \times Y \times T(Z) & \xrightarrow{1 \times \mathbf{st}^T_{Y,Z}} & X \times T(Y \times Z) \\ & {\scriptstyle \mathbf{st}^T_{X \times Y,Z}} \searrow \quad \swarrow {\scriptstyle \mathbf{st}^T_{X,Y \times Z}} & \\ & T(X \times Y \times Z) & \end{array}$$

The strength increases the computational power of monads. Reinterpreting 'terms' of a monad T from an object to the product with another object is even more useful when the monad is defined on a cartesian closed category. For example, a strong monad T on a cartesian closed category $\mathcal{S}$ gives rise to the following 'evaluation' maps:

$$\mathbf{ev}^T_{X,Y} : T(X) \times Y^X \longrightarrow T(Y),$$

i.e., the composition of the strength and the usual evaluation map:

$$T(X) \times Y^X \xrightarrow{\mathbf{st}^{r,T}_{X,Y^X}} T(X \times Y^X) \xrightarrow{T(\mathbf{ev}_{X,Y})} T(Y)$$

3.2 Right Strength

As we said, the right strength lifts 'terms' on the fibers of $a : A \to Z$ to the 'terms' on the whole A. The terms on the fiber A_z are the elements of the fiber of $\mathbf{T}_Z(A, a) \to Z$ over x. In *Set*, they can be naturally interpreted as term on $A \supseteq A_z$.

All the restrictions $\mathbf{T}_Z$ of the cartesian monad $\mathbf{T}$ are strong, for Z in $\mathcal{S}$. Let $g : Z \to Y$ be a map in $\mathcal{S}$. We have (unique) maps

$$\mathbf{st}^{r,\mathbf{T}}_{g,(A,a)} : \Sigma_g(\mathbf{T}_Z(A, a)) \longrightarrow \mathbf{T}_Y(\Sigma_g(A, a)),$$

making the following triangles commute:

$$\begin{array}{ccc} & \Sigma_g(\mathbf{T}_Z(A,a)) & \\ {\scriptstyle cc_{g,\mathbf{T}_Z(A,a)}} \nearrow & & \searrow {\scriptstyle \mathbf{st}^{r,T}_{g,(A,a)}} \\ \mathbf{T}_Z(A,a) & \xrightarrow[\mathbf{T}(cc_{g,(A,a)})]{} & \mathbf{T}_Y(\Sigma_g(A,a)) \end{array}$$

Together they form a natural transformation:

$$\mathcal{E}_Z \; \underset{T_Y \circ \Sigma_g}{\overset{\Sigma_g \circ T_Z}{\rightrightarrows}} \; \mathcal{E}_Y \qquad \Downarrow \mathbf{st}^{r,\mathbf{T}}_g$$

so that $(\Sigma_g, \mathbf{st}^{r,\mathbf{T}}) : \mathbf{T}_Z \longrightarrow \mathbf{T}_Y$ is an oplax morphism of monads. If (A, a) is $(D \times Z, \pi_2)$ and g is $Z \to 1$, then we get the usual strength on $\mathbf{T}_1$.

Moreover, these maps satisfy the following axioms. For $g : Z \to Y$, $f : Y \to X$ in $\mathcal{S}$ and any object (A, a) in $\mathcal{S}_Z$, the following triangles commute:

Unit.

$$\begin{array}{ccc} & \Sigma_{id_Z}(T_Z(A,a)) & \\ {\scriptstyle cc_{id_Z}} \nearrow & & \searrow {\scriptstyle \mathbf{st}^{r,T}_{f,\Sigma_{id_Z}(A,a)}} \\ T_Z(A,a) & \xrightarrow[T_Z(cc_{id_Z})]{} & T_Z \Sigma_{id_Z}(A,a) \end{array}$$

Associativity.

$$\begin{array}{ccc} & \Sigma_f T_Y \Sigma_g(A,a) & \\ {\scriptstyle \Sigma_f(\mathbf{st}^{r,T}_{g,(A,a)})} \nearrow & & \searrow {\scriptstyle \mathbf{st}^{r,T}_{f,\Sigma_g(A,a)}} \\ \Sigma_{fg}(T_Z(A,a)) & \xrightarrow[\mathbf{st}^{r,T}_{fg,(A,a)}]{} & T_X \Sigma_{fg}(A,a) \end{array}$$

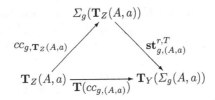

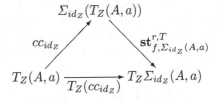

Remark. Note that, for morphism $f : Y \to X$ in $\mathcal{S}$ and any cartesian monad $\mathbf{T}$ of the fundamental fibration of $\mathcal{S}$, the right strength gives rise to the oplax morphism of monads $(\Sigma_f, st_f^{r,\mathbf{T}}) : T_Y \to T_X$, i.e., we have a natural transformation:

$$\mathbf{st}_f^{r,\mathbf{T}} : \Sigma_f \circ T_Y \to T_X \circ \Sigma_f,$$

satisfying the suitable axioms.

3.3   Left Strength

The left strength lifts 'terms' from Z, the codomain of a, to the 'terms' on the whole A. In order to 'lift terms', we need to have a section of a. In fact, any section[1] $s : Z \to A$ such that $a \circ s = id_Z$ can transfer the 'terms' from Z to A, as in the case of the usual strength in *Set*. This is why, for $(A, a : A \to Z)$ in $\mathcal{S}_Z$ and $f : Z \to Y$ a map in the base $\mathcal{S}$, the left strength is defined as the map:

$$T_Y(Z, g) \times_Y \Pi_g(A, a) \xrightarrow{\mathbf{st}_g^{l,\mathbf{T}}(A, a)} T_Y(\Sigma_g(A, a)).$$

To define this map, we first define the map $\phi_{(A,a)}$ as follows:

$$
\frac{
\frac{
\frac{g^*(\Pi_g(A, a)) \xrightarrow{\varepsilon_{(A,a)}} (A, a)}{\Sigma_g(g^*(\Pi_g(A, a))) \xrightarrow{\Sigma_g(\varepsilon_{(A,a)})} \Sigma_g(A, a)} \; \Sigma_g(-)
}{(Z, g) \times_Y \Pi_g(A, a) \xrightarrow{\Sigma_g(\varepsilon_{(A,a)})} \Sigma_g(A, a)} \; \Sigma_g \dashv g^*
}{\Pi_g(A, a) \xrightarrow{\phi_{(A,a)}} \Sigma_g(A, a)^{(Z,g)}}
$$

Then we define the left strength as the following composition:

$$
\begin{array}{ccc}
T_Y(Z, g) \times_Y \Pi_g(A, a) & \xrightarrow{\quad \mathbf{st}_{g,(A,a)}^{l,T} \quad} & T_Y(\Sigma_g(A, a)) \\
{\scriptstyle 1 \times \phi_{(A,a)}} \searrow & & \nearrow {\scriptstyle \mathbf{ev}_{(Z,g),\Sigma_g(A,a)}^{T_Y}} \\
& T_Y(Z, g) \times_Y (\Sigma_g(A, a))^{(Z,g)} &
\end{array}
$$

Thus, for a fixed $g : Z \to Y$ in $\mathcal{S}$, such maps give rise to a natural transformation:

$$
\begin{array}{ccc}
 & \xrightarrow{\; T_Y(Z, g) \times_Y \Pi_g \;} & \\
\mathcal{E}_Z & \Downarrow \mathbf{st}_g^{l,\mathbf{T}} & \mathcal{E}_Y \\
 & \xrightarrow[\; T_Y \circ \Sigma_g \;]{} &
\end{array}
$$

---

[1] Any morphism $Z \to A$ would do.

The axioms for the left strength are analogous to the axioms for the strength and the right strength (they talk about identities and compositions).

Before we state the axioms, we need to define the composition map. To phrase the associativity, we need to define, for (A, a) in $\mathcal{S}_X$, the composition map:

$$\gamma^{f,g}_{(A,a)} : \Pi_f(Z, g) \times_X \Pi_{fg}(A, a) \longrightarrow \Pi_f(\Sigma_g(A, a))$$

that composes sections, where $f : Y \to X$ is another map in $\mathcal{S}$.

Unit. The map

$$\mathbf{T}_Y(Z, g) \times_Y \Pi_g(Z, id_Z) \xrightarrow{\mathbf{st}^{l,\mathbf{T}}_{g,(Z,g)}} \mathbf{T}_Y(Z, g)$$

is the first projection.

Associativity. The following diagram expressing the fact that the left strength is associative

$$\begin{array}{ccc}
\mathbf{T}_X(Y,f) \times_X \Pi_f(Z,g) \times_X \Pi_{fg}(A,a) & \xrightarrow{\mathbf{st}^{l,\mathbf{T}}_{f,(Z,g)} \times 1} & \mathbf{T}_X(\Sigma_f(Z,g)) \times_X \Pi_{fg}(A,a) \\
\downarrow{\scriptstyle 1 \times \gamma^{f,g}_{(A,a)}} & & \downarrow{\scriptstyle \mathbf{st}^{l,\mathbf{T}}_{fg,(A,a)}} \\
\mathbf{T}_X(Y,f) \times_X \Pi_f(\Sigma_g(A,a)) & \xrightarrow{\mathbf{st}^{l,\mathbf{T}}_{f,\Sigma_g(A,a)}} & \mathbf{T}_X(\Sigma_{fg}(A,a)
\end{array}$$

commutes.

3.4 Pile'up

Even if the strengths on dependent types are not symmetric, they can still be combined together giving rise to a (left) pile'up. However, in this case we have only one way to combine them as we have to apply the left strength first.

For an object $(A, a : A \to Z)$ in $\mathcal{S}_Z$ and a morphism $f : Z \to Y$, we define the (left, dependent) pile'up $\mathbf{dpile'up}^{\mathbf{T}}_{g,(A,a)}$ as the composition of the following three maps:

$$\begin{array}{ccc}
T_Y(Z,g) \times_Y \Pi_g(T_Z(A,a)) & & \\
\Big\downarrow \mathbf{st}^{l,\mathbf{T}}_{g,T_Z(A,a)} & \searrow^{\mathbf{dpile'up}^{\mathbf{T}}_{g,(A,a)}} & \\
 & & T_Y(\Sigma_g(A,a)) \\
T_Y(\Sigma_g(T_Z(A,a))) & & \Big\uparrow (\mu_Y)_{\Sigma_g(A,a)}) \\
 & \searrow_{T_Y(\mathbf{st}^{r,\mathbf{T}}_{g,(A,a)})} & \\
 & & T^2_Y(\Sigma_g(A,a))
\end{array}$$

These maps taken together form the following natural transformation:

$$\mathcal{E}_Z \quad \begin{array}{c} T_Y(Z,g) \times_Y \Pi_g \circ T_Z(-) \\ \longrightarrow \\ \Downarrow \mathbf{dpile'up}^{\mathbf{T}}_g \\ \longrightarrow \\ T_X \circ \Sigma_g(-) \end{array} \quad \mathcal{E}_Y$$

defined for any map $g : Z \to Y$ in the base $\mathcal{S}$.

3.5 Case Study: Continuation Monad on the Fundamental Fibration of *Set*

We show below how the above definitions work when applied to the continuation monad on the basic fibration over the category *Set*. The pile'up on dependent types does not do anything unexpected, it combines a quantifier in the base with quantifiers in the fibers into one polyadic quantifier on the whole 'set'.

Let $a : A \to Z$ and $g : Z \to Y$ be two functions. The pile'up function:

$$\mathcal{C}_Y(Z,g) \times_Y \Pi_g(\mathcal{C}_Z(A,a)) \xrightarrow{\mathbf{dpile'up}^{\mathcal{C}}_{g,(A,a)}} \mathcal{C}_Y(\Sigma_g(A,a))$$

for $y \in Y$, a quantifier $Q \in \mathcal{C}_Y(Z,g)_y = \mathcal{C}(Z_y)$ and a function $Q' : Z_y \to \mathcal{C}_Z(A,a) \in \Pi_g(\mathcal{C}_Z(A,a))_y$ so that $Q'(z) \in \mathcal{C}(A_y)$, is given by:

$$\mathbf{dpile'up}^{\mathcal{C}}_{g,(A,a)}(Q,Q') =$$

$$\{U \subseteq A_y : \{z \in Z_y : U \cap A_z \in Q'(z)\} \in Q\}\}.$$

In the above formula $A_y = \{x \in A : g \circ a(x) = y\}$ and $A_z = \{x \in A : a(x) = z\}$, for $y \in Y$ and $z \in Z$.

Thus it is indeed the polyadic quantifier on set A combining the quantifier on the base with the quantifiers on the fibers.

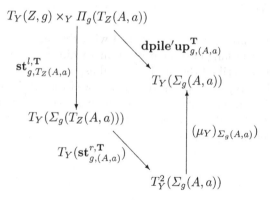

4 Conclusion

In this paper, we showed how we can deal with the interaction of dependency relations and natural language quantification within a modern type-theoretical setting, and then described the mathematical aspects of polyadic quantification lifted to dependent types. In particular, we showed that the dependent **pile′up**-operation (combining quantifiers into polyadic ones) can be derived from the strength of the continuation monad on the basic fibration over the category *Set* (or any other elementary topos).

References

1. Barker, C., Shan, C.C.: Continuations and Natural Language, vol. 53. Oxford Studies in Theoretical Linguistics (2014)
2. Barr, M., Wells, C.: Toposes, Triples and Theories, vol. 278. Springer-Verlag, New York (1985)
3. Barwise, J., Cooper, R.: Generalized quantifiers and natural language. In: Philosophy, Language, and Artificial Intelligence, pp. 241–301. Springer (1981). https://doi.org/10.1007/BF00350139
4. van den Berg, M.: Some Aspects of the Internal Structure of Discourse. Ph.D. thesis, University of Amsterdam (1996)
5. Borceux, F.: Handbook of Categorical Algebra: Volume 2, Categories and Structures, vol. 50. Cambridge University Press, Cambridge (1994)
6. Brasoveanu, A.: Structured Nominal and Modal Reference. Ph.D. thesis, Rutgers University (2007)
7. Brasoveanu, A.: Decomposing modal quantification. J. Semant. **27**(4), 437–527 (2010)
8. Brasoveanu, A., Farkas, D.F.: How indefinites choose their scope. Linguist. Philos. **34**, 1–55 (2011)
9. Chatzikyriakidis, S., Luo, Z. (eds.): Modern Perspectives in Type-Theoretical Semantics. SLP, vol. 98. Springer, Cham (2017). https://doi.org/10.1007/978-3-319-50422-3
10. Chatzikyriakidis, S., Luo, Z.: Formal Semantics in Modern Type Theories. John Wiley & Sons (2020)
11. Grudzińska, J., Zawadowski, M.: Inverse Linking: taking scope with dependent types. In: Proceedings of the 21st Amsterdam Colloquium, pp. 285–294 (2017)
12. Grudzińska, J., Zawadowski, M.: Scope ambiguities, monads and strengths. J. Lang. Model. **5**(2), 179–227 (2017)
13. Grudzińska, J., Zawadowski, M.: Continuation semantics for multi-quantifier sentences: operation-based approaches. Fund. Inform. **164**(4), 327–344 (2019)
14. Grudzińska, J., Zawadowski, M.: Inverse linking, possessive weak definites and haddock descriptions: a unified dependent type account. J. Logic Lang. Inform. **28**(2), 239–260 (2019)
15. Hendriks, H.: Studied Flexibility: Categories and Types in Syntax and Semantics. Institute for Logic, Language and Computation (1993)
16. Johnstone, P.T.: Sketches of an Elephant: A Topos Theory Compendium, vol. 2. Oxford University Press, Oxford (2002)

17. Keenan, E.L.: Unreducible N-Ary quantifiers in natural language. In: Generalized Quantifiers, pp. 109–150. Springer (1987). https://doi.org/10.1007/978-94-009-3381-1_5
18. Keenan, E.L.: Beyond the Frege boundary. Linguist. Philos. **15**(2), 199–221 (1992)
19. Lindström, P.: First order predicate logic with generalized quantifiers. Theoria **32**(3), 186–195 (1966)
20. Luo, Z.: Formal semantics in modern type theories with coercive subtyping. Linguist. Philos. **35**(6), 491–513 (2012)
21. Luo, Z., Soloviev, S.: Dependent event types. In: Proceedings of the International Workshop on Logic, Language, Information, and Computation, pp. 216–228 (2017)
22. Mac Lane, S.: Categories for the Working Mathematician. GTM, vol. 5. Springer, New York (1978). https://doi.org/10.1007/978-1-4757-4721-8
23. Makkai, M.: First order logic with dependent sorts, with applications to category theory. Preprint: http://wwwmath.mcgill.ca/makkai(1995)
24. Martin-Löf, P.: An intuitionistic theory of types: predicative part. Stud. Logic Found. Math. **80**, 73–118 (1975)
25. Martin-Löf, P., Sambin, G.: Intuitionistic Type Theory, vol. 9. Bibliopolis Napoli (1984)
26. May, R.: Logical Form: Its Structure and Derivation, vol. 12. MIT press (1985)
27. Mostowski, A.: On generalization of quantifiers. Fundam. Math. **44**, 12–36 (1957)
28. Ranta, A.: Type-Theoretical Grammar. Oxford University Press, Oxford (1994)
29. Schlenker, P.: Scopal independence: a note on branching and wide scope readings of indefinites and disjunctionss. J. Semant. **23**(3), 281–314 (2006)
30. Steedman, M.: Taking Scope: The Natural Semantics of Quantifiers. MIT Press (2012)
31. Streicher, T.: Fibred categories a la Jean Benabou. arXiv preprint arXiv:1801.02927 (2018)
32. Szabolcsi, A.: Quantification. Cambridge University Press, Cambridge (2010)
33. Van Benthem, J.: Polyadic quantifiers. Linguist. Philos. **12**(4), 437–464 (1989)
34. Zawadowski, M.: Formalization of the feature system in terms of pre-orders. Bellert, Feature System for Quantification Structures in Natural Language. Foris Dordrecht, pp. 155–172 (1989)

Author Index

G. Metcalfe et al. (Eds.): WoLLIC 2024, LNCS 14672, p. 293, 2024.
https://doi.org/10.1007/978-3-031-62687-6

Printed in the United States
by Baker & Taylor Publisher Services